THE HIDDEN PREJUDICE

The LAW AND PUBLIC POLICY: PSYCHOLOGY AND THE SOCIAL SCIENCES series includes books in three domains:

Legal Studies—writings by legal scholars about issues of relevance to psychology and the other social sciences, or that employ social science information to advance the legal analysis;

Social Science Studies—writings by scientists from psychology and the other social sciences about issues of relevance to law and public policy; and

Forensic Studies—writings by psychologists and other mental health scientists and professionals about issues relevant to forensic mental health science and practice.

The series is guided by its editor, Bruce D. Sales, PhD, JD, University of Arizona; and coeditors, Stephen J. Ceci, PhD, Cornell University; Norman J. Finkel, PhD, Georgetown University; and Bruce J. Winick, JD, University of Miami.

***

THE HIDDEN PREJUDICE

Mental Disability on Trial

Michael L. Perlin

AMERICAN PSYCHOLOGICAL ASSOCIATION

WASHINGTON DC

Published by
American Psychological Association
750 First Street, NE
Washington, DC 20002

Copies may be ordered from
APA Order Department
P.O. Box 92984
Washington, DC 20090-2984

In the UK, Europe, Africa, and the Middle East, copies may be ordered from
American Psychological Association
3 Henrietta Street
Covent Garden, London
WC2E 8LU England

Typeset in Times Roman by GGS Information Services, York, PA

Printer: Automated Graphic Systems, White Plains, MD
Cover Designer: Berg Design, Albany, NY
Technical/Production Editor: Allison L. Risko and Rachael J. Stryker

The opinions and statements published are the responsibility of the authors, and such opinions and statements do not necessarily represent the policies of the APA.

Library of Congress Cataloging-in-Publication Data
Perlin, Michael L., 1946-
    The hidden prejudice : mental disability on trial / Michael L. Perlin. — 1st ed.
        p.   cm.
    Includes bibliographical references and index.
    ISBN 1-55798-616-9 (alk. paper)
    1. Insanity—Jurisprudence—United States. 2. Mental health laws—United States. I. Title.
KF480.P474   1999
345.73'04—dc21   99-20607
                                                              CIP

British Library Cataloguing-in-Publication Data

A CIP record is available from the British Library

Printed in the United States of America
First Edition

CONTENTS

PREFACE

The ideas that led to the writing of this book came to me at two different points in time, both in the 1970s. When I was a rookie public defender in Trenton, New Jersey, I often filed motions to suppress evidence on behalf of my clients in criminal cases, arguing that the police behavior in seizing contraband (usually small amounts of street drugs) violated the Fourth Amendment's ban on "unreasonable searches and seizures". In almost all of these cases, the arresting officer's testimony was basically the same: The officer would testify that when my client saw him coming, my client would make a "furtive gesture," and then reach into his pocket, take out a glassine envelope (filled with the illegal drug), and throw it on the ground, blurting out, "That's heroin [or whatever], and it's mine." My client—not surprisingly—told a different story: That the police officer approached him, stuck his hands into my client's pockets, pulled out the glassine envelope, and then placed my client under arrest.

I had no doubt that my client was telling the truth. And I suspected that the judge and the prosecutor had the same intuition. Yet in such cases—they are called "dropsy" cases to all familiar with the reality of criminal procedure—the judge invariably found the police officer to be more credible, and would thus rule that the search came within the "plain-view" exception of search and seizure law, upholding the search. It was no surprise to me years later when I read Myron Orfeld's article (studying "dropsy" cases in Chicago), which reported that 86% of judges, public defenders, and prosecutors questioned (including 77% of judges) believed that police officers fabricate evidence in case reports at least "some of the time" and that a staggering 92% (including 91% of judges) believe that police officers lie in court to avoid suppression of evidence at least "some of the time."[1]

Although I did not know it at the time, this was my first introduction to pretextuality in law.[2]

My second introduction followed soon after and involved questions of mental disability law. Again as a rookie public defender, I was assigned to represent individuals at the Vroom Building, New Jersey's maximum security facility for the "criminally insane," on their applications for writs of *habeas corpus*. The cases were—to be charitable—charades. The

---

[1]Myron W. Orfield, *Deterrence, Perjury, and the Heater Factor: An Exclusionary Rule in the Chicago Criminal Courts,* 63 U. COLO. L. REV. 75, 100–07 (1992). *See infra* Chapter 3.

[2]By this I mean simply that fact finders accept (either implicitly or explicitly) testimonial dishonesty and engage similarly in dishonest (frequently meretricious) decision making, specifically where witnesses, especially *expert* witnesses, show a "high propensity to purposely distort their testimony in order to achieve desired ends." Michael L. Perlin, *Morality and Pretextuality, Psychiatry and Law: Of "Ordinary Common Sense," Heuristic Reasoning, and Cognitive Dissonance,* 19 BULL. AM. ACAD. PSYCHIATRY & L. 131, 133 (1991); *see generally infra* Chapter 3.

attorney general asked the hospital doctor two questions: Was the patient mentally ill and did he or she need treatment? The answer was always "yes," and the writs were denied.[3]

Some years later, after I became director of New Jersey's Division of Mental Health Advocacy, I read a story in the *New York Times* Magazine that summarized for me many of the frustrations of my job. The article dealt with an ex-patient, Gerald Kerrigan, who wandered the streets of the Upper West Side of Manhattan. Kerrigan never threatened or harmed anybody, but he was described as "different," "off," and "not right somehow." It made other residents of that neighborhood, which is traditionally home to one of the nation's most liberal voting blocs, nervous to have him in the vicinity, and the story focused on the response of a community association to his presence. The story darkly hinted that the social "experimentation" of deinstitutionalization was somehow the villain. Soon after that, I read an excerpt from Elizabeth Ashley's autobiography in *New York* (a magazine read by many of those same Upper West Siders). Ashley, a prominent and strikingly attractive actress, told of her institutionalization in one of New York City's most esteemed private psychiatric hospitals and of her subsequent release from that hospital to live with George Peppard and to co-star with Robert Redford in Broadway's *Barefoot in the Park.*

Although Ashley was praised for her courage, Kerrigan was presented as being emblematic of a major "social problem." Both were persons who had been diagnosed with mental illness, both of their mental illnesses were serious enough to require hospitalization, and both were subsequently released. Yet their stories were presented and read in entirely different ways.

Gerald Kerrigan's story reflected the failures of "deinstitutionalization" and demonstrated why the application of civil libertarian concepts to the involuntary civil commitment process was a failure. Elizabeth Ashley's story reflected the fortitude of a talented and gritty woman who had the courage to expose and share her battle with mental illness. No one discussed Gerald Kerrigan's autonomy values (or the quality of life in the institution from which he was released). No one (in discussing Ashley's case) characterized George Peppard's condo as a "deinstitutionalization facility" or labeled Ashley's starring in a Broadway smash as participation in an "aftercare program."

Ashley was beautiful, talented, and wealthy. Thus, she was different. Kerrigan was "different," but in a troubling and different way (albeit not in the same vivid way that Billie Boggs and Larry Hogue—two high-visibility ex-patients whose cases came to dominate mental disability law policy discussions in New York City in the 1980s and 1990s—were.) But the connection between Kerrigan and Ashley was never made.[4]

---

[3]This changed radically (in New Jersey, at least) after the U.S. Supreme Court's decision in Jackson v. Indiana, 406 U.S. 715 (1972) (applying substantive and procedural due process protections to incompetency-to-stand-trial process; *see generally* 3 MICHAEL L. PERLIN, MENTAL DISABILITY LAW: CIVIL AND CRIMINAL § 14.15 (1989), at 248–50). *See, e.g.,* Dixon v. Cahill, Docket No. L. 30977-71 P.W. (N.J. Super. Ct., Law Div. 1973) (consent order implementing *Jackson*), *reprinted in* 3 PERLIN, *supra,* § 14.17, at 256–59. *But see* Grant Morris & J. Reid Meloy, *Out of Mind? Out of Sight: The Uncivil Commitment of Permanently Incompetent Criminal Defendants,* 27 U.C. DAVIS L. REV. (1993) (more than half the states never implemented *Jackson*).

[4]I discuss Kerrigan and Ashley's cases in Michael L. Perlin, *The Deinstitutionalization Myths: Old Wine in New Bottles, in* CONFERENCE REPORT: THE SECOND NATIONAL CONFERENCE ON THE LEGAL RIGHTS OF THE MENTALLY DISABLED 20 (Karl Menninger & Heather Watts eds. 1979). *Cf.* Boggs v. NYC Health & Hosp. Corp., 525 N.Y.S.2d 796 (1988), *and* Seltzer v. Hogue, 594 N.Y.S.2d 781 (App. Div. 1993).

Around the same time, I read a short article by Morton Birnbaum[5] in which he discussed the concept of "sanism."[6] Specifically, he urged that sanism—like racism, sexism, and other stereotyping "isms,"—had become a part of our social "pathology of oppression"[7]—He also argued that sanism controlled mental disability law policy.

I remember (this was 20 years ago) the moment I read Birnbaum's essay, and how something immediately clicked for me. At that point in time, I had already spent several years providing individual and class-action representation to institutionalized persons with mental disabilities, and I had grown accustomed to asides, snickers, and comments from judges; to eye rolling from my adversaries; and to running monologues by bailiffs and court clerks (about my clients' "oddness"), but I had never before consciously identified what Birnbaum had been writing about: That this was sanist behavior on the part of the other participants in the mental disability law system.

From that moment on, I began to think about mental disability law in different ways. I'd already tried to come to grips with its pretexts (the charade of the Vroom Building hearings in the era before *Jackson v. Indiana*), but this explanation began to flesh out the picture in ways that finally enabled me to make sense of what was going on.

In 1984, I became a full-time professor, and for the past 15 years I have taught a variety of mental disability law courses. I also speak about a full range of mental disability law topics at conferences and workshops on both a national and local basis. My audience is sometimes filled with lawyers, sometimes judges, sometimes psychiatrists and psychologists, sometimes hospital staffs, sometimes ex-patients and their families. No matter who is in the audience, I cannot escape the sanist and pretextual bases of mental disability law.

Several years ago, I wrote a mental disability law treatise that I update yearly. As part of that update, I have read virtually every reported case involving mental disability law that has been published in the past decade. Again, I cannot escape the sanist and pretextual bases of mental disability law.

I write frequently for a variety of professional publications—sometimes for those read by lawyers, sometimes for others read by mental health professionals, and sometimes for crossover journals (read in equal measure by both). For the past several years, I have focused on the sanist and pretextual bases of mental disability law. I wrote this book to develop these themes on a slightly larger scale and to set out an overarching theory of mental disability law—a theory that applies whether the subject is an involuntary civil commitment case, a right to refuse treatment hearing, an interpretation of the Americans With Disabilities Act's ban on discrimination against persons with mental disabilities, the competence of a criminal defendant to waive counsel, or the aftermath of a "successful" insanity defense. Again that theme, that theory, is the reality of the sanist and pretextual bases of mental disability law.

---

[5]*See* Morton Birnbaum, *The Right to Treatment: Some Comments on Its Development, in* MEDICAL, MORAL AND LEGAL ISSUES IN HEALTH CARE 97, 106–07 (Frank Ayd ed. 1974) [hereinafter Birnbaum, *Comments*]. Dr. Birnbaum is universally regarded as having first developed and articulated the constitutional basis of the right to treatment doctrine for institutionalized mental patients. *See* Morton Birnbaum, *The Right to Treatment,* 46 A.B.A. J. 499 (1960), *discussed in* 2 PERLIN, *supra* note 3, § 3A-2.1, at 8–12 (2d ed. 1999).

[6]Simply put, sanism is an irrational prejudice of the same quality and character of other irrational prejudices that cause (and are reflected in) prevailing social attitudes of racism, sexism, homophobia, and ethnic bigotry. It infects both our jurisprudence and our lawyering practices. Sanism is largely invisible and largely socially acceptable. It is based predominantly on stereotype, myth, superstition and deindividualization, and is sustained and perpetuated by our use of alleged "ordinary common sense" and heuristic reasoning in an unconscious response to events both in everyday life and in the legal process. *See infra* chapters 1 and 2.

[7]Birnbaum, *Comments, supra* note 5, at 107 (quoting civil rights leader Florynce Kennedy).

ACKNOWLEDGMENTS

I have many loved ones, friends, colleagues, and students, to thank, including Keri Gould and Debbie Dorfman (my collaborators on several of the articles on which I draw in this book and the two people who have always been my best "reality check" and sounding board for the thoughts and ideas that I am expressing here). Bob Sadoff, Joel Dvoskin, Richard Sherwin, Doug Mossman, David Wexler, and Bruce Winick (my frequent draft readers whose critiques and advice have been so helpful over the years); Pam Cohen and Susan Stefan (who were especially helpful with sections on the Americans With Disabilities Act); Jen Burgess and Chris Morton (my student assistants who have done a Herculean job in making sure that this manuscript was finished in a timely manner); and all of the other student research assistants over the years who have helped me so much on the articles and chapters on which I draw. In addition Dawn Fasano was especially helpful with her editing suggestions. Kate McLeod and Camilla Broussard of the New York Law School Library provided invaluable help in all phases of this project. I am also deeply grateful to New York Law School Dean Harry Wellington (and former Dean Jim Simon) for their confidence in me and for the generous support of the New York Law School Summer Research Grant Fund. And a very special thank you to Roberta Tasley for her continued support and assistance in the production of this manuscript.

Finally, and most important, I want to thank my family. They are my strength and my inspiration. My daughter Julie organized, sorted, and stored hundreds of source materials for me, making my job so much easier. My son Alex went through the entire manuscript and read each of the nearly 4,000 footnotes, "flagging" where I had marked reminders to make my last round of changes. My mother, Sophie Perlin, has continued to mail me newspaper clippings about all aspects of mental disability law, and one of those clippings provided the structure for my concluding chapters.

My final thanks are to my wife Linda. It is a truism to say, "I couldn't have done this without her," but it is also totally accurate. As always, I draw on Bob Dylan for my inspiration in my thank you to her:

> And every one of [her] words rang true
> And glowed like burning coal
> Pourin' off of every page
> Like it was written in my soul.
> From me to you. . . .[8]

To my family, to my late father, Jacob W. Perlin, to my late father-in-law, Nat J. Mason, and to my mother-in-law, Vivian Mason, I dedicate this book.

Michael L. Perlin
November 19, 1999

SOURCES

Much of this book is new, but I have also incorporated much of my previous writings. Chapter 1 draws primarily on THE JURISPRUDENCE OF THE INSANITY DEFENSE (Carolina Academic Press 1994) (INSANITY DEFENSE) and *Psychodynamics and the Insanity Defense: "Ordinary Common Sense" and Heuristic Reasoning,* 69 NEB. L. REV. 3 (1990) *(OCS)*; Chapters 2 and 3 on *Pretexts and Mental Disability Law: The Case of Competency,* 47 U. MIAMI L. REV. 625 (1993) *(Pretexts); Sanism, Social Science, and the Development of Mental Disability Law Jurisprudence,* 11 BEHAV. SCI. & L. 47 (1993) (with Deborah A. Dorfman) *(Sanism and Social Science); Morality and Pretextuality, Psychiatry and Law: Of "Ordinary Common Sense," Heuristic Reasoning, and Cognitive Dissonance,* 19 BULL. AM. ACAD. PSYCHIATRY & L. 131 (1991) *(Morality and Pretextuality); On "Sanism,"* 46 SMU L. REV. 373 (1992); and *The Sanist Lives of Jurors in Death Penalty Cases: The Puzzling Role of "Mitigating" Mental Disability Evidence,* 8 NOTRE DAME J.L., ETHICS & PUB. POL'Y 239 (1994) *(Sanist Lives).* Chapter 4 relies on portions of LAW AND MENTAL DISABILITY (Michie Co. 1994) (L&MD); *Competency, Deinstitutionalization, and Homelessness: A Story of Marginalization,* 28 HOUS. L. REV. 63 (1991) *(Homelessness); Morality and Pretextuality; and Therapeutic Jurisprudence and the Civil Rights of Institutionalized Mentally Disabled Persons: Hopeless Oxymoron or Path to Redemption?* 1 PSYCHOL., PUB. POL'Y & L. 80 (1995) (with Keri K. Gould and Deborah A. Dorfman) *(Oxymoron).* Chapter 5 draws mostly on *Oxymoron,* and Chapter 6 on *Is It More Than "Dodging Lions and Wastin' Time"? Adequacy of Counsel, Questions of Competence, and the Judicial Process in Individual Right to Refuse Treatment Cases,* 2 PSYCHOL., PUB. POL'Y & L. 114 (1996) (with Deborah A. Dorfman); *Decoding Right to Refuse Treatment Law,* 16 INT'L J.L. & PSYCHIATRY 151 (1993); *Sanism and Social Science; Oxymoron;* L&MD; and *Are Courts Competent to Decide Questions of Competency? Stripping the Facade From* United States v. Charters, 38 U. KAN. L. REV. 957 (1990). Chapter 7 draws on *Hospitalized Patients and the Right to Sexual Interaction: Beyond the Last Frontier?* 20 NYU REV. L. & SOC'L CHANGE 302 (1993–94). Chapter 8 relies on *The ADA and Persons With Mental Disabilities: Can Sanist Attitudes Be Undone?* 8 J.L. & HEALTH 15 (1993–94) and on *"Make Promises by the Hour": Sex, Drugs, the ADA, and Psychiatric Hospitalization,* 46 DEPAUL L. REV. 947 (1997).

Chapter 9 draws on *"Dignity Was the First To Leave":* Godinez v. Moran, *Colin Ferguson, and the Trial of Mentally Disabled Criminal Defendants,* 14 BEHAV. SCI. & L. 61 (1996). Chapter 10 incorporates portions of INSANITY DEFENSE; *The Insanity Defense: Deconstructing the Myths and Reconstructing the Jurisprudence* (from LAW, MENTAL HEALTH AND MENTAL DISORDER 341 (Bruce Sales & Daniel Shuman eds. 1996)); *Myths, Realities, and the Political World: The Anthropology of Insanity Defense Attitudes,* 24 BULL. AM. ACAD. PSYCHIATRY & L. 5 (1996); and *"The Borderline Which Separated You From Me": The Insanity Defense, the Authoritarian Spirit, the Fear of Faking, and the Culture of Punishment,* 82 IOWA L. REV. 1375 (1997). And much of Chapter 11 is from *Rashomon and the Criminal Law: Mental Disability and the Federal Sentencing Guidelines,* 22 AM. J. CRIM. L. 431 (1995) (with Keri K. Gould). Finally, the material in Chapters 12–13 comes primarily from *Therapeutic Jurisprudence: Understanding the Sanist and Pretextual*

Bases of Mental Disability Law, 20 N. ENG. J. CRIM. & CIV. CONFINEMENT 369 (1994) and *What Is Therapeutic Jurisprudence?* 10 N.Y.L. SCH. J. HUM. RTS. 623 (1993); other sections draw on many of the other articles cited here.

Finally, the introduction and conclusion chapters form the core of *"Half-Wracked Prejudice Leaped Forth": How and Why Mental Disability Law Developed As It Did,* 10 J. CONTEMP. LEGAL ISSUES 3 (1999).

In addition, I discuss many of these same topics in depth in 1–3 MICHAEL L. PERLIN, MENTAL DISABILITY LAW: CIVIL AND CRIMINAL (Michie Co. 1989) (updated yearly), and 1 MICHAEL L. PERLIN, MENTAL DISABILITY LAW: CIVIL AND CRIMINAL (Lexis Law Publishing, 2d ed. 1998), and 2 *id.* (2d ed. 1999).

INTRODUCTION

> The States have traditionally exercised broad power to commit persons found to be mentally ill. The substantive limitations on the exercise of this power and the procedures for invoking it vary drastically among the States. The particular fashion in which the power is exercised . . . reflects different combinations of distinct bases for commitment sought to be vindicated. The bases that have been articulated include dangerousness to self, dangerousness to others, and the need for care or treatment or training. *Considering the number of persons affected, it is perhaps remarkable that the substantive constitutional limitations on this power have not been more frequently litigated.*[1]

So wrote Justice Harry Blackmun more than a quarter of a century ago in *Jackson v. Indiana,* the U.S. Supreme Court opinion that first applied due process principles to a case involving a litigant with a mental disability.[2] *Jackson,* a case nominally about the constitutional limitations on indefinite involuntary commitment following a finding of incompetency to stand trial, was truly revolutionary. It opened the courthouse doors to persons with mental disabilities; for the first time, the Supreme Court acknowledged that the ''nature and duration'' of a court-ordered commitment was constitutionally bounded, and that issues involving personal freedom and liberty of mentally disabled persons subject to institutionalization were appropriate ones for court determination.[3]

The principles established in *Jackson* (and in *Lessard v. Schmidt,*[4] a contemporary federal district court case challenging the constitutionality of a state commitment code) quickly caught hold, and the next several years saw an explosion of litigation questioning all aspects of the processes by which persons with mental disabilities were committed to psychiatric institutions, kept and treated in such institutions, and released from institutional confinement. A cadre of public interest lawyers listened to Justice Blackmun's observation in *Jackson,* and a dizzying proliferation of cases followed, eventually leading to the articulation of a constitutional right to treatment, the more controversial right to refuse treatment (mostly in cases dealing with the unwanted imposition of psychotropic or antipsychotic medications), and a series of cases sketching out the substantive and procedural constitutional limitations on the involuntary civil commitment power.[5]

This is not to say that trial judges hearing individual cases were necessarily enthusiastic about these developments. As I will discuss subsequently, decisions such as *Jackson, Lessard,* and *O'Connor v. Donaldson*[6] (setting out a constitutional right to liberty) were never popular with trial judges or with court administrators for a variety of instrumental,

---

[1]Jackson v. Indiana, 406 U.S. 715, 737–38 (1972) (footnotes omitted; emphasis added).

[2]*See id.* at 727–31. *See generally* 1 MICHAEL L. PERLIN, MENTAL DISABILITY LAW: CIVIL AND CRIMINAL §§ 2A-4.4, at 122–25 (2d ed. 1998).

[3]*Jackson,* 406 U.S. at 738.

[4]349 F. Supp. 1078 (E.D. Wis. 1971) (subsequent citations omitted); *see generally* 1 PERLIN, *supra* note 2, §§ 2A-4.4a, 4.4c, at 126–33, 139–42.

[5]*See generally* 1 PERLIN, *supra* note 2, chap. 2A & 2C; MICHAEL L. PERLIN, LAW AND MENTAL DISABILITY, chap. 1 (1994).

[6]422 U.S. 563 (1975).

functional, normative, and philosophical reasons.[7] Nonetheless, the U.S. Supreme Court, the highest courts in state systems,[8] and certain other federal courts[9] appeared to be taking seriously—for the first time—''how [institutionalized mental patients] are treated as human beings.''[10]

At the same time that these cases were unfolding, the relationship between mental disability and the criminal law was undergoing a rapid recalibration, but under very different circumstances and in very different ways.

John Hinckley's attempted assassination of President Ronald Reagan dramatically ended years of quiet and thoughtful study of the future of the insanity defense, and led to strident political posturing, eventually resulting in the passage of the Insanity Defense Reform Act.[11] That legislation returned the federal courts to a more restrictive version of the English *M'Naghten* standard (the so-called right-from-wrong test), a formulation that had been seen as outmoded from the time of its first articulation in 1843.[12] Hinckley also placed the entire question of how mentally disabled defendants are dealt with in the criminal trial process under the legislative and judicial microscope. Like a moth to a flame, the U.S. Supreme Court became fascinated—perhaps preoccupied—with the full range of questions involving this population, deciding, in the past 15 years, a stream of cases dealing with such questions as competency to stand trial, competency to waive counsel and/or plead guilty, the relationship between mental disability and the death penalty, impact of mental disability on confessions law, the application of the right to refuse treatment in the prison and pretrial setting, and the constitutional boundaries of the commitment and retention procedures that follow a successful insanity defense. And this stream shows no sign of drying up.[13]

Private civil law has changed as well. In 1976 the California Supreme Court held, in *Tarasoff v. Board of Regents of University of California,* that a mental health professional who has reason to believe that her client presents a serious danger of violence to another incurs an obligation to use reasonable care to protect the intended victim against such danger.[14] *Tarasoff* led to a firestorm of mostly intensely critical commentary, followed by a flurry of follow-up litigation in other states.[15] By the 1990s *Tarasoff* had become seen as the national tort standard of behavior, notwithstanding the fact that many states had either distinguished or limited it in a variety of fact settings.[16] There was a concomitant explosion in other tort litigation, ranging from questions of premature release of violent patients to

---

[7]For eight years I was director of the Division of Mental Health Advocacy in the New Jersey Department of the Public Advocate and a member of that state's Supreme Court Committee on Civil Commitments. This position was expressed to me on literally dozens of occasions by both judges and administrative personnel.

[8]*E.g.,* State v. Krol, 344 A.2d 289 (N.J. 1975) (application of procedural due process to retention hearings following insanity acquittals); Rivers v. Katz, 504 N.Y.S.2d 74 (1986) (state constitutional right to refuse treatment).

[9]*E.g.,* Wyatt v. Aderholt, 503 F.2d 1305 (5th Cir. 1974) (prior and subsequent citations omitted) (constitutional right to treatment); Rennie v. Klein, 720 F.2d 266 (3d Cir. 1983) (prior citations omitted) (constitutional right to refuse treatment).

[10]Falter v. Veterans Admin., 502 F. Supp. 1178, 1184 (D.N.J. 1980).

[11]*See generally* MICHAEL L. PERLIN, THE JURISPRUDENCE OF THE INSANITY DEFENSE (1994); 18 U.S.C. 617.

[12]3 PERLIN, *supra* note 2, § 15.04, at 286–94.

[13]*See generally* Michael L. Perlin, *''No Direction Home'': The Law and Criminal Defendants With Mental Disabilities,* 20 MENT. & PHYS. DIS. L. REP. 605 (1996).

[14]131 CAL. RPTR. 14 (1976).

[15]3 PERLIN, *supra* note 2, §§ 13.09–13.21, at 151–84, and *id.,* §§ 13.09–13.21A, at 373–88 (1998 Cum. Supp.).

[16]*Id.,* §§ 13.13–13.17, at 164–70.

sexual misconduct by therapists to the improper use of the involuntary civil commitment process.[17]

Finally, Congress was not dormant. After the enactment of a flurry of mostly hortatory laws,[18] it enacted the Americans With Disabilities Act (ADA),[19] legislation characterized— perhaps a bit ambitiously—as "the Emancipation Proclamation for those with disabilities."[20] The ADA, which on its face bars disability-based discrimination in virtually every aspect of private and public life,[21] appears to offer great promise to persons with mental disabilities. However, the case law has been spotty,[22] and not withstanding the Supreme Court's 1999 decision in *Olmstead v. L.C.*, it is not at all clear that this promise will be fulfilled.[23]

It is impossible, however, to understand mental disability law simply by reading the Supreme Court's cases, studying the courts' holdings and analyzing the doctrine, and by taking federal legislation at face value. For these cases—and other "great" cases that are subject to intense scrutiny and academic deconstruction and practitioner commentary[24] and

---

[17]*See, e.g.,* 3 *id.,* §§ 12.08–12.25, at 27–72.

I have limited the substantive scope of this book to certain discrete questions of *public* mental disability law (commitment, institutionalization, civil rights of patients, application of the Americans With Disabilities Act), and the relationship of mental disability to specific aspects of the criminal trial process (competence to waive counsel and/or plead guilty; the insanity defense; application of the federal sentencing guidelines). The reader should not conclude that the concepts that are at the core of this work—sanism and pretextuality—do not also affect other aspects of public mental health law (e.g., right to aftercare, the relationship between deinstitutionalization and homelessness, implications of counsel assignment systems, other questions of criminal competencies, the relationship between mental disability and the death penalty), and *private* mental disability law as well. I have written about these topics in, *inter alia,* Michael L. Perlin, *The Voluntary Delivery of Mental Health Services in the Community, in* LAW, MENTAL HEALTH AND MENTAL DISORDER 150 (B. Sales & D. Shuman eds. 1996); Michael L. Perlin, *Fatal Assumption: A Critical Evaluation of the Role of Counsel in Mental Disability Cases,* 16 LAW & HUM. BEHAV. 39 (1992) [hereinafter Perlin, *Fatal*]; Michael L. Perlin, *Pretexts and Mental Disability Law: The Case of Competency,* 47 U. MIAMI L. REV. 625 (1993) [hereinafter Perlin, *Pretexts*]; Michael L. Perlin, *"The Executioner's Face Is Always Well-Hidden": The Role of Counsel and the Courts in Determining Who Dies,* 41 N.Y.L. SCH. L. REV. 201 (1996) [hereinafter Perlin, *Executioner's Face*]; Michael L. Perlin, *Competency, Deinstitutionalization, and Homelessness: A Story of Marginalization,* 28 HOUS. L. REV. 63 (1991) [hereinafter Perlin, *Marginalization*].

[18]*See, e.g.,* Mental Health Systems Act (MHSA), 42 U.S.C. §§ 9511 *et seq.;* Developmentally Disabled Bill of Rights Act (DD Bill of Rights Act), 42 U.S.C. § 6009; Protection and Advocacy for the Mentally Ill Act (PAMI), 42 U.S.C. §§ 10801 *et seq.* Case law construing the substantive portions of both the MHSA and the PAMI has been paltry. *See, e.g.,* PERLIN, *supra* note 2, § 6.44, at 136 (1998 Cum. Supp). The Supreme Court has held that sections of the DD Bill of Rights Act do not create substantive, privately enforceable rights. *See* Pennhurst State Sch. & Hosp. v. Halderman, 451 U.S. 1, 8 (1981). I discuss the dilemma raised by hortatory language in disability rights statutes in Michael L. Perlin, *"Make Promises by the Hour": Sex, Drugs, the ADA, and Psychiatric Hospitalization,* 46 DEPAUL L. REV. 947 (1997).

[19]42 U.S.C. §§ 12101 *et seq.*

[20]Kimberly A. Ackourey, *Insuring Americans with Disabilities: How Far Can Congress Go to Protect Traditional Practices?* 40 EMORY L.J. 1183, 1183 n.2 (1991) (quoting statement by bill's sponsors).

[21]The accompanying congressional report is clear: the purpose of the ADA is to "provide a clear and comprehensive national mandate to end discrimination against individuals with disabilities and to bring those individuals into the economic and social mainstream of American life." HOUSE COMM. ON THE JUDICIARY, AMERICANS WITH DISABILITIES ACT OF 1990, H.R. REP. No. 485 (III), 101st Cong., 2d Sess., at 23 (1990).

[22]*See generally* PERLIN, *supra* note 2, § 6.44A, at 169–98 (1998 Cum. Supp.), and *id.* at nn.473.43–473.43z72 (citing cases).

[23]*See* Olmstead v. L.C., 119 S.Ct. 2176 (1999); *see infra* Chapter 8.

[24]*E.g.,* Wyatt v Aderholt, 503 F.2d 1305 (5th Cir. 1974) (prior and subsequent citations omitted) (constitutional right to treatment). For a sampling of the literature on *Wyatt, see, e.g.,* 2 PERLIN, *supra* note 2, § 3A– 3.2c, at 54–55 (2d ed. 1999).

hortatory federal statutes[25]—tell us virtually nothing about the related questions that are, in many ways, of far greater importance: *How* is mental disability law applied in "unknown" cases, and *why* is it applied that way?

I have spent nearly my entire career representing persons with mental disabilities, teaching mental disability law, writing about mental disability law, and thinking about the ways that the public has constructed "mental disability" and the ways that courts treat cases involving litigants with mental disabilities. I have done this on nearly every level that a lawyer can work: from representing inmates of New Jersey's Vroom Building (the so-called Maximum Security Hospital for the Criminally Insane) in individual *habeas corpus* hearings, and indigent criminal defendants in individual incompetency-to-stand-trial hearings and insanity defense trials,[26] to representing classes of civilly committed mental patients in class action test cases seeking to vindicate their basic constitutional and civil rights,[27] to filing briefs in the U.S. Supreme Court on a wide range of issues affecting mental disability law in civil and criminal contexts.[28] I have taught mental disability law for 15 years from a variety of pedagogic perspectives: constitutional law, criminal procedure, therapeutic jurisprudence, and "lawyering skills." And I have consulted with, trained, or presented workshops or continuing education programs to state mental health officials, attorneys general, public defenders, legal aid lawyers, and clinical, administrative, and forensic psychiatrists and psychologists.

In the more than a quarter of a century that I have worked, taught, thought, and written about this area, two overarching issues dominate and overwhelm the subject matter: Mental disability law is *Sanist*,[29] and mental disability law is *pretextual*.[30] I am further convinced that it is impossible to truly understand anything about mental disability law—the doctrine, the debate, the discourse, the decisions, the dissents—without first coming to grips with this reality. I am equally convinced that the apparent contradictions, internal inconsistencies, and cognitive dissonances of mental disability law cannot be understood without understanding the power and pervasiveness of these concepts. Because of sanism and pretextuality, mental disability law proceeds at the edge of a hidden prejudice. This prejudice, then, has led to the corruption of mental disability law.

Simply put, *sanism* is an irrational prejudice of the same quality and character of other irrational prejudices that cause (and are reflected in) prevailing social attitudes of racism,

---

[25]Perlin, *supra* note 18, at 958–60.

[26]*See, e.g.,* Dixon v. Cahill, Docket No. L30977–71 P.W. (N.J. Super. Ct., Law. Div., Mercer Cty. 1973) (consent order in class action implementing Jackson v. Indiana, 406 U.S. 715 (1972), *see supra* text accompanying notes 1–3), *reprinted in* 3 PERLIN, *supra* note 2, § 14.17, at 256–58.

[27]*See, e.g.,* Rennie v. Klein, 720 F.2d 266 (3d Cir. 1983) (right to refuse treatment).

[28]*E.g.,* Ake v. Oklahoma, 470 U.S. 68 (1985) (right of indigent defendant to access to expert psychiatric assistance in death penalty case); Colorado v. Connelly, 479 U.S. 156 (1986) (impact of mental disability on admissibility of criminal confession), and Jones v. United States, 463 U.S. 354 (1983) (application of procedural due process principles to retention hearing following not-guilty-by-reason-of-insanity verdict).

[29]*See, e.g.,* Michael L. Perlin, On *"Sanism,"* 46 SMU L. REV. 373 (1992); Michael L. Perlin & Deborah A. Dorfman, *Sanism, Social Science, and the Development of Mental Disability Law Jurisprudence,* 11 BEHAV. SCI. & L. 47 (1993); Michael L. Perlin, *The Sanist Lives of Jurors in Death Penalty Cases: The Puzzling Role of "Mitigating" Mental Disability Evidence,* 8 NOTRE DAME J.L., ETHICS & PUB. POL. 239 (1994) [hereinafter Perlin, *Sanist Lives*]; Michael L. Perlin, *The ADA and Persons With Mental Disabilities: Can Sanist Attitudes Be Undone?* 8 J.L. & HEALTH 15 (1993–94).

[30]*See, e.g.,* Michael L. Perlin, *Morality and Pretextuality, Psychiatry and Law: Of "Ordinary Common Sense," Heuristic Reasoning, and Cognitive Dissonance,* 19 BULL. AM. ACAD. PSYCHIATRY & L. 131 (1991) [hereinafter Perlin, *Morality and Pretextuality*]; Perlin, *Pretexts, supra* note 17; Michael L. Perlin, *Therapeutic Jurisprudence: Understanding the Sanist and Pretextual Bases of Mental Disability Law,* 20 N. ENG. J. CRIM. & CIV. CONFINEMENT 369 (1994).

sexism, homophobia, and ethnic bigotry.[31] It infects both our jurisprudence and our lawyering practices.[32] Sanism is largely invisible and largely socially acceptable. It is based predominantly on stereotype, myth, superstition, and deindividualization, and is sustained and perpetuated by our use of alleged "ordinary common sense" (OCS) and heuristic reasoning in an unconscious response to events both in everyday life and in the legal process.[33]

Pretextuality means that courts accept (either implicitly or explicitly) testimonial dishonesty and engage similarly in dishonest (frequently meretricious) decision making, specifically where witnesses, especially *expert* witnesses, show a "high propensity to purposely distort their testimony in order to achieve desired ends."[34] This pretextuality is poisonous; it infects all participants in the judicial system, breeds cynicism and disrespect for the law, demeans participants, and reinforces shoddy lawyering, blasé judging, and, at times, perjurious and/or corrupt testifying.

As I will demonstrate throughout the course of this book, these two concepts have controlled—and *continue* to control—modern mental disability law. Just as important (perhaps more important), they *continue* to exert this control invisibly. This invisibility means that the most important aspects of mental disability law—not just the law "in the books," but the law in action and practice—remains hidden from the public discussions about mental disability law.

We must also ponder another reality: Mental disability law is a giant *trompe l'oeil*. From one perspective it is a topic of great interest to the Supreme Court and other appellate courts, and its "cutting-edge" issues sound very much like the cutting-edge issues of other areas of constitutional law: allocations of burdens of proof,[35] scope of the liberty clause,[36] categorizations for "heightened scrutiny" purposes,[37] and so on.

From another perspective, however, it is a topic dealt with on a daily basis by trial courts across the country in a series of unknown cases involving unknown litigants, where justice is often administered in assembly-line fashion. Sophisticated legal arguments are rarely made,

---

[31]The classic treatment is GORDON ALLPORT, THE NATURE OF PREJUDICE (1955). For an important new, and different, perspective, see ELISABETH YOUNG-BRUEHL, THE ANATOMY OF PREJUDICES (1996).

[32] The term *sanism* was, to the best of my knowledge, coined by Morton Birnbaum. *See* Morton Birnbaum, *The Right to Treatment: Some Comments on Its Development, in* MEDICAL, MORAL AND LEGAL ISSUES IN HEALTH CARE 97, 106–07 (F. Ayd ed. 1974); Koe v. Califano, 573 F. 2d 761, 764 (2d Cir. 1978); *see* Perlin, *Marginalization, supra* note 17 at 92–93 (discussing Birnbaum's insights). Birnbaum is universally regarded as having first developed and articulated the constitutional basis of the right to treatment doctrine for institutionalized mental patients. *See* Morton Birnbaum, *The Right to Treatment,* 46 A.B.A. J. 499 (1960), discussed in 2 PERLIN, *supra* note 2, § 3A–2.1, at 8–12 (2d ed. 1999).

[33]*See, e.g.,* Perlin, *supra* note 11. *See generally infra* Chapter 2.

[34]PERLIN, *Morality and Pretextuality, supra* note 30, at 133; Charles Sevilla, *The Exclusionary Rule and Police Perjury,* 11 SAN DIEGO L. REV. 839, 840 (1974). *See generally infra,* Chapter 3.

[35]*See, e.g.,* Medina v. California, 505 U.S. 437 (1992) (imposing burden of proof by preponderance of evidence on defendant claiming incompetence to stand trial not violative of due process clause); Cooper v. Oklahoma, 517 U.S. 348 (1996) (imposing burden of proof by clear and convincing evidence on defendant claiming incompetence to stand trial violative of due process clause).

[36]*See, e.g.,* Washington v. Harper, 494 U.S. 210 (1990) (right of prisoners to refuse antipsychotic medical).

[37]*See, e.g.,* City of Cleburne v. Cleburne Living Ctr., Inc., 473 U.S. 432 (1985) (mental retardation neither suspect class nor quasisuspect class for equal protections purposes); Heller v. Doe, 509 U.S. 312 (1993) (no equal protection violation where state statute allows commitment of persons with mental retardation on a lesser standard of proof than persons with mental illness).

expert witnesses are infrequently called on to testify, and lawyers all too often provide barely perfunctory representation.[38]

From this perspective, mental disability law is often invisible, both to the general public and to the academy. Consider these remarks of the eminent criminal law scholar George Fletcher, speaking at a teaching conference on criminal law and criminal procedure sponsored by the Association of American Law Schools:

> The elite schools in the east are still dominated by two schools of criminal law that I would call Dead School #1 [emphasizing the Model Penal Code] and Dead School #2. . . . Dead School #2 is most clearly reflected at Yale, and that is the school of social science and the criminal law, and I think my attitude toward Dead School #2 is one more of regret than of sarcasm. I wish it were the case that the social sciences had something to offer us in the study of criminal law, but frankly I haven't seen anything come out in this school for a long time. . . . [M]aybe some of you will . . . [know of] an important article that's been published suggesting, clarifying, social science, psychoanalytic, or sociological perspectives on the criminal law. I have not seen anything in a long time, and yet the old insights of times gone by still prevail in significant quarters of the field.[39]

There is more. Although Supreme Court doctrine and "high theory" give us needed building blocks, they do not—cannot—tell us what really happens in involuntary civil commitment cases, in competency-to-stand-trial determinations, in recommitment hearings for insanity acquittees, in individual challenges to the imposition of unwanted antipsychotic medication. For us to truly understand what mental disability law is all about, it is vital that we think about these questions.

There is a wide gap between law on the books and law in action. There is probably such a gap in every area of the law. But the omnipresence of sanism and pretextuality make the gap even more problematic in mental disability law.

Mental disability law suffers from both over- and underattention. A handful of sensational criminal cases—those involving Hinckley, Colin Ferguson, John DuPont, Theodore Kaczynski—are, by nature of the facts of the underlying crime or identity of the victim, subject to intense analysis and scrutiny. The mental disability law issues raised in these cases—the insanity defense, competence to stand trial, competence to waive counsel—are reported on as if they typify (a) other cases involving the same issue, and (b) cases

---

[38]See, e.g., JAMES A. HOLSTEIN, COURT-ORDERED INSANITY: INTERPRETIVE PRACTICE AND INVOLUNTARY COMMITMENT (1993) [hereinafter Holstein, Insanity]; James A. Holstein, Court Ordered Incompetence: Conversational Organization in Involuntary Commitment Hearings, 35 SOCIAL PROBS. 459 (1988) [hereinafter Holstein, Incompetence].

[39]David Wexler, Therapeutic Jurisprudence and the Criminal Courts, 35 WM. & MARY L. REV. 279, 279 (1993), quoting George Fletcher, "A Critical Appraisal of Criminal Law and Procedure," Address at the Teaching Conference on Criminal Law and Criminal Procedure sponsored by the Association of American Law Schools (May 16–21, 1987).

I believe that Fletcher was dead wrong when he spoke in 1987. Even then, scholars were beginning to explore the deeper textures of mental disability law. See, e.g., THERAPEUTIC JURISPRUDENCE: THE LAW AS A THERAPEUTIC AGENT (David Wexler ed. 1990) (collection of mental disability law essays dating to the mid–1970s). Over the past decade since Fletcher spoke, there have been many important new scholarly and intellectual developments, especially (but not exclusively; in the field of "therapeutic jurisprudence," see, e.g., Susan Stefan, Leaving Civil Rights to the "Experts": From Deference to Abdication Under the Professional Judgment Standard, 102 YALE L.J. 639 (1992)). See, e.g., LAW IN A THERAPEUTIC KEY: DEVELOPMENTS IN THERAPEUTIC JURISPRUDENCE (David Wexler & Bruce Winick eds. 1996) (collection of more recent essays); see generally, 1 PERLIN, supra note 2, § 2D–3, at 534–41 (2d ed. 1998) (discussing recent developments). But what is equally important is the perception: that mental disability law develops in the dark without the sunshine that often floods the decision-making process in other areas of constitutional law, criminal procedure, civil rights law, and tort law.

involving other aspects of mental disability law.[40] Civil cases are rarely the focus of so much interest, but court decisions in a handful of cases involving potential professional liability—*Tarasoff* is, by far, the most famous—are disseminated widely to professional audiences, and their holdings (and significance for practitioners) are regularly exaggerated and distorted.[41]

On the other hand, the overwhelming number of cases involving mental disability law issues are ''litigated'' in pitch darkness. Involuntary civil commitment are routinely disposed of in minutes in closed courtrooms.[42] Right-to-refuse treatment hearings often honor the letter and spirit of decisions such as *Rivers v. Katz*[43] with little more than lip service.[44] Nearly 90% of all insanity defense cases are ''walk-throughs'' (i.e., stipulated on the papers).[45] The complex textures of mental disability law are rarely raised in the garden variety tort case brought by a mentally disabled plaintiff.[46]

Often constitutional doctrines articulated by the Supreme Court in mental disability law cases are regularly ignored. The Court has held—on more than one occasion—that the right to refuse treatment is protected, at least in part, by the liberty clause of the Fourteenth Amendment.[47] Yet in case after case, a patient's apparent desire to enforce or vindicate this constitutional right is relied on as evidence in support of the patient's involuntary civil commitment.[48] The Supreme Court has held—on several occasions—that the possibility of side effects resulting from antipsychotic medications (especially irreversible neurological side effects such as tardive dyskinesia) is a factor to be considered in determining whether the Fourteenth Amendment has been violated in an individual case.[49] Yet an examination of the universe of reported individual right-to-refuse-treatment cases shows that side effects are rarely, if ever, mentioned.[50]

---

[40]*See generally* PERLIN, *supra* note 11; Michael L. Perlin, *Myths, Realities, and the Political World: The Anthropology of Insanity Defense Attitudes,* 24 BULL. AM. ACAD. PSYCHIATRY & L. 5 (1996) [hereinafter Perlin, *Political World*]; Michael L. Perlin, *''The Borderline Which Separated You From Me'': The Insanity Defense, the Authoritarian Spirit, the Fear of Faking, and the Culture of Punishment,* 82 IOWA L. REV. 1375 (1997) [hereinafter Perlin, *''The Borderline''*].

[41]For example, more than three quarters of the clinicians surveyed reported that issuing warning was the sole acceptable means of protecting potential victims and avoiding *Tarasoff* liability. David J. Givelber et al., Tarasoff, *Myth and Reality: An Empirical Study of Private Law in Action,* WIS. L. REV. 443, 465 (1984), *discussed in* Michael L. Perlin, Tarasoff *and the Dilemma of the Dangerous Patient: New Directions for the 1990's,* 16 LAW & PSYCHOL. REV. 29, 54 (1992).

[42]*See, e.g.,* HOLSTEIN, INSANITY, *supra* note 38. The Supreme Court has noted that the average time for involuntary civil commitment hearings is 9.2 minutes. *See* Parham v. J. R., 442 U.S. 584, 609 n.17 (1979).

[43]504 N.Y.S.2d 74 (1986) (state constitutional right to refuse treatment); *see, generally, infra* Chapter 6.

[44]*See, e.g.,* cases discussed in 2 PERLIN, *supra* note 2, § 3B-7.2b, at 265–76 (2d ed. 1999).

[45]On the average, there is examiner agreement in 88% of all insanity cases. Richard Rogers et al., *Insanity Defense: Contested or Conceded?* 141 AM. J. PSYCHIATRY 885, 885 (1984); Kenneth Fukunaga et al., *Insanity Plea: Interexaminer Agreement in Concordance of Psychiatric Opinion and Court Verdict,* 5 LAW & HUM. BEHAV. 325, 326 (1981). *See* Perlin, *Political World, supra* note 40, at 12.

[46]For exceptions, *see, e.g.,* Moore v. Wyoming Med. Ctr., 825 F. Supp. 1531 (D. Wyo. 1993) (improper involuntary civil commitment case); Fair Oaks Hosp. v. Pocrass, 628 A.2d 829 (N.J. Law Div. 1993) (same).

[47]*See, e.g.,* Mills v. Rogers, 457 U.S. 291, 299 (1982); Washington v. Harper, 494 U.S. 210, 221 (1990).

[48]*See, e.g.,* Michael L. Perlin & Deborah A. Dorfman, *Is It More Than ''Dodging Lions and Wastin' Time''? Adequacy of Counsel, Questions of Competence, and the Judicial Process in Individual Right to Refuse Treatment Cases,* 2 PSYCHOL., PUB. POL'Y & L. 114, 133–34 (1996), and sources cited *id.* at n.181; Michael L. Perlin, *Reading the Supreme Court's Tea Leaves: Predicting Judicial Behavior in Civil and Criminal Right to Refuse Treatment Cases,* 12 AM. J. FORENS. PSYCHIATRY 37, 52–59 (1991).

[49]Riggins v. Nevada, 504 U.S. 127, 133–35 (1992); *Harper,* 494 U.S. at 229–30.

[50]*See, e.g.,* 1 PERLIN, *supra* note 2, §§ 3B-7.2c and 3B-7.2e, at 276–84, 288–90, (2d ed. 1999) (citing cases).

State legislatures craft elaborate commitment codes, often mandating the need for an "overt act" as a predicate to commitment.[51] Yet the expression of wishes, desires, or the recitation of fantasies has been relied on as a basis for commitment in individual cases.[52] The right to counsel is provided for in virtually every state commitment statute.[53] That right is often honored only in the breach; lawyers representing patients—and, just as important, those representing mentally disabled criminal defendants—often reflect Judge Bazelon's worst nightmare of "walking violations of the Sixth Amendment."[54]

State legislatures pass broad-based "patients' bills of rights," purporting to provide inpatients with the same bundle of civil and constitutional rights mandated in a series of federal class action–law reform cases litigated in the early 1970s (all flowing from the decisions in the *Wyatt v. Stickney* litigation).[55] Yet there has been virtually no follow-up litigation seeking to give life to, implement, or construe these laws.[56] Moreover, trial courts regularly refuse to consider right-to-treatment issues in the context of individual commitment cases.[57] And as I have already pointed out, Congress has passed the Americans With Disabilities Act, and, in doing so, buttressed the substantive antidiscrimination provisions of the act with findings that appear to provide—at the least—equal protection safeguards for covered individuals.[58] Yet there have been literally only a handful of cases brought by institutionalized (or formerly institutionalized) persons with mental disabilities to effect these provisions and even fewer that have granted relief.[59]

Supreme Court cases are also routinely ignored, sometimes for decades. In 1990, in *Zinermon v. Burch*,[60] the Court ruled that there must be some sort of a due process hearing (albeit a modest one) before a patient's voluntary application for hospitalization could be accepted. Yet only a few states have amended their court rules or voluntary admission statutes to comply with *Zinermon's* mandate and, again, there has been virtually no follow-up litigation.[61] Even more astonishing, in 1972 the Court ruled in *Jackson v. Indiana*[62] that an incompetent-to-strand-trial criminal defendant could not be housed indefinitely in a maximum-security forensic facility because of that status unless it appeared likely that he

---

[51]*See id.*, § 2A-4.5, at 152–57 (2d ed. 1998) (citing cases).

[52]*See, e.g.*, People v. Stevens, 761 P.2d 768, 775 n.12 (Colo. 1988) (relying on presumed sexually inappropriate dress and manner—"posing provocatively in front of a mirror in a hospital day room in a tight-fitting leotard"—as sufficient evidence of a patient's danger to self to support his order of commitment); State v. Hass, 566 A.2d 1181, 1185 (N.J. Super. Ct. Law Div. 1988) (holding that a patient's sexual fantasies can serve as confirmatory evidence supporting his need for treatment under state Sexual Offenders Act).

[53]*See* ROBERT LEVY & LEONARD RUBENSTEIN, THE RIGHTS OF PERSONS WITH MENTAL DISABILITIES 74 (1996); *see generally* 1 PERLIN, *supra* note 2, § 2B–3.1, at 197–201 (citing cases).

[54]David Bazelon, *The Defective Assistance of Counsel*, 42 U. CIN. L. REV. 2 (1973). For recent cases in the death penalty context, *see* Perlin, *Executioner's Face, supra* note 17, at 204–07.

[55]*See generally* Michael L. Perlin, Keri K. Gould, & Deborah A. Dorfman, *Therapeutic Jurisprudence and the Civil Rights of Institutionalized Mentally Disabled Persons: Hopeless Oxymoron or Path to Redemption?* 1 PSYCHOL., PUB. POL'Y & L. 80 (1995); *see* 2 PERLIN, *supra* note 2, § 3A-14.2, at 128–131 (2d ed. 1999) (citing statutes).

[56]Note the paucity of subsequent developments in 2 PERLIN, *supra* note 2, § 3A-14.5a, at 141–47 (2d ed. 1999).

[57]*See id.*, § 2C–8.1, at 507–09 (2d ed. 1998) (citing cases).

[58]Perlin, *supra* note 18, at 948–49.

[59] This may change as a result of the Supreme Court's recent decision in Olmstead v. L.C., 119 S.Ct. 2176 (1999); *see infra*, Chapter 8.

[60]494 U.S. 113 (1990). 119 S. Ct. 2176 (1999).

[61]*See* 1 PERLIN, *supra* note 2, § 2C–7.2a, at 490–91 nn.1373–75 (2d ed. 1998) (citing cases).

[62]406 U.S. 715 (1972).

would regain his competence to stand trial within the "foreseeable future."[63] Yet more than 25 years later, nearly half the states had still not implemented *Jackson*.[64]

Criminal court prosecutors compound the problems. "Find this man not guilty by reason of insanity," they warn jurors, "and he will walk away a free man after a few weeks of 'country club' treatment."[65] The reality, of course, is far different. Studies from the mid-1990s reveal that insanity acquittees spend almost double the amount of time in maximum-security forensic settings that defendants convicted of like charges serve in prison;[66] in one study California defendants found not guilty by reason of insanity (NGRI) in cases involving nonviolent offenses were confined for periods *nine* times as long as individuals found guilty of similar offenses.[67] The Supreme Court decision in *Shannon v. United States*[68]—holding that, as a matter of federal criminal procedure, the defendant had no right to have the jury informed about the possible consequences of an NGRI verdict—will only increase the amount of pretextuality in decision making in this areas of the law.[69] And insanity defense matters are but a small fraction of criminal cases in which sanism and pretextuality flourish.[70]

This area of the law is further infected by an excess of finger pointing and blame attributing. Some clinicians and hospital administrators are quick to point at "the law" to explain many of the failures of institutional mental health care. Doctors such as E. Fuller Torrey regularly unleash jeremiads at patients' rights lawyers as the true culprits in the drama, painting this lurid picture:

> Nurtured by radical psychiatrists (such as Thomas Szasz and R.D. Laing), spurred on by politically-activist organizations pushing egalitarian social agendas (such as the ACLU), a cadre of brilliant but diabolical patients' rights lawyers dazzled sympathetic and out-of-touch judges with their legal *legerdemain*—abetted by wooly-headed social theories, inapposite constitutional arguments, some oh-my-god worst-case anecdotes about institutional conditions, and a smattering of "heartwarming, successful [deinstitutionalization] case [studies]"—as a result of which courts entered orders "emptying out the mental institutions" so that patients could "die with their rights on." When cynical bureaucrats read the judicial handwriting on the hospital walls, they then joined the stampede, and the hospitals were thus emptied. Ergo deinstitutionalization. Ergo homelessness. Endgame.[71]

---

[63]*Id.* at 738.

[64]*See* Perlin, *Fatal, supra* note 17, at 47–49, citing, *inter alia,* Bruce Winick, *Restructuring Competency to Stand Trial,* 32 UCLA L. REV. 921, 940 (1985); *see also* Grant Morris & J. Reid Meloy, *Out of Mind? Out of Sight: The Uncivil Commitment of Permanently Incompetent Criminal Defendants,* 27 U.C. DAVIS L. REV. 1 (1993).

[65]*See, e.g.,* Perlin, *"The Borderline," supra* note 40, at 1406, discussing, *inter alia,* People v. Aliwoli, 606 N.E.2d 347, 352 (Ill. App. 1992).

[66]PERLIN, *supra* note 11, at 110, citing, *inter alia,* Joseph Rodriguez, Laura LeWinn, & Michael L. Perlin, *The Insanity Defense Under Siege: Legislative Assaults and Legal Rejoinders,* 14 RUTGERS L.J. 397, 403–04 (1983).

[67]PERLIN, *supra* note 11, at 110–11, citing HENRY STEADMAN ET AL., REFORMING THE INSANITY DEFENSE: AN ANALYSIS OF PRE- AND POST-HINCKLEY REFORMS 58–61 (1993).

[68]512 U.S. 573 (1994).

[69]For recent cases, *see* PERLIN, *supra* note 2, § 15.16A, at 510 n.372.42 (1998 Cum. Supp.).

[70]*See, e.g.,* Michael L. Perlin: Keri K. Gould, Rashomon and the Law. *Mental Disability and the Federal Sentencing Guidelines* 22 AM. J. CRIM. L. 431, 451 (1995). ("in each [reported federal sentencing guidelines case in which mental disability was an issue], without exception, the U.S. Attorney's Office opposed the use of mental disability as a mitigating factor"). On the ways that jurors process social science evidence (and mitigating mental disability evidence) in death penalty cases, *see* Perlin, *supra* note 17, at 216–21; Perlin, *Sanist Lives, supra* note 29, at 260–65.

[71]Quoted in Michael L. Perlin, *Book Review,* 8 N.Y.L. SCH. J. HUM. RTS. 557, 559–60 (1991) (reviewing ANN BRADEN JOHNSTON, OUT OF BEDLAM: THE TRUTH ABOUT DEINSTITUTIONALIZATION (1990)).

Staff at major inpatient psychiatric hospitals tell the press that their "hands are tied" and that they are unduly frustrated by laws that are overly protective of patients' civil liberties but that ignore (or are counterproductive to) their clinical and medical needs. These allegations have become the script of much contemporary mental disability law policy. Yet in addition to being inflammatory and confrontational, they are also largely baseless. Several years ago I received a telephone call from the editorial desk of a major metropolitan newspaper, asking about a local cause célèbre—an apparently randomly violent, former mental patient who was allegedly victimizing a block of a New York City neighborhood well-known for its traditional adherence to liberal social causes.[72] My caller told me that, in answer to his question about why this individual was not committable in a state psychiatric hospital, he had been told by hospital staff that such commitment required proof of a "recent overt act."

I told him that that was the standard in several jurisdictions but it was emphatically not a prerequisite for commitment in his state (and, in fact, that test had been specifically rejected by the state's appellate courts).[73] Indeed, the New York courts had made it crystal clear that a recent overt act is not required, and a challenge to that standard had failed in the federal appellate courts more than a decade earlier.[74] My caller was quite reasonably perplexed about why he had been given this misinformation.[75]

So what explanation is there for all of this? There is, in short, often a huge gap—a chasm, virtually—between what mental disability law appears to be and what it actually is. This gap is widened further by the reality that we—lawyers, professors, psychologists, psychiatrists, expert witnesses, clinicians, jurors, the press, the public—know very little about what *really* happens in most mental disability law cases.

Mental disability is incoherent, because it is based on deep and corrosive prejudices that are both socially acceptable and often hidden from view. Although the database of case law is huge (and constantly growing), although the Supreme Court returns to mental disability law questions again and again, and although scholars have patiently studied and scrutinized most of the "high ticket" issues, the notion of a coherent body of mental disability law jurisprudence is an illusion. The jurisprudence's incoherence flows, in large part, from the nihilistic impact of *sanism* and *pretextuality*. I have written this book to expose the pernicious power of sanism and pretextuality; the ways in which these two factors infect judicial decisions, legislative enactments, administrative directives, jury behavior, and public attitudes; the ways that these factors undercut any efforts at creating a unified body of mental disability law jurisprudence; the ways that these factors contaminate scholarly discourse and lawyering practices alike; and the ways that the prejudice that lies at the roots of these attitudes has truly corrupted the fabric of mental disability law. I have written it to argue that, unless and until we come to grips with these concepts—and their stranglehold on

---

[72]*See* Seltzer v. Hogue, 594 N.Y.S.2d 781 (A.D. 1993).

[73]*See, e.g., In re* Scopes, 398 N.Y.S.2d 911, 913 (1977).

[74]   [W]e are of the opinion that such a requirement [of an overt act] is too restrictive and not necessitated by substantive due process. The lack of any evidence of a recent overt act, attempt or threat, especially in cases where the individual has been kept continuously on certain medications, does not necessarily diminish the likelihood that the individual poses a threat of substantial harm to himself or others.

Id. at 913. *See also* Project Release v. Prevost, 722 F.2d 960, 973 (2d Cir. 1983).

[75]I discuss the implications of this interchange extensively in Michael L. Perlin, *Back to the Past: Why Mental Disability Law "Reforms" Don't Reform* (Book Review of JOHN Q. LA FOND & MARY DURHAM, BACK TO THE ASYLUM: THE FUTURE OF MENTAL HEALTH LAW AND POLICY IN THE UNITED STATES (1992)), 4 CRIM. L. FORUM 403, 403–05 (1993).

mental disability law development—any efforts at truly understanding this area of the law, or at understanding the relationship between law and psychology, are doomed to failure.

Organization of the Book

In Section 1, I will discuss what I call the ''forerunner'' concepts of *heuristics* and *ordinary common sense* and will demonstrate how society's reliance on these cognitive devices that simplify the way we process information helps to set the stage for all future jurisprudential developments in this area, and I then explain the roots of sanism and the roots of pretextuality, how both sanism and pretextuality developed (inside and outside of the legal system), and how an understanding of these factors can illuminate why mental disability law jurisprudence has developed the way it has.

In section 2, I will consider relevant substantive areas of mental disability law (focusing primarily, but not exclusively, on involuntary civil commitment, on institutional and civil rights issues, on the ADA, and on selected criminal procedure issues) in an effort to illuminate the ways that sanism and pretextuality explain the otherwise often incoherent jurisprudence that has developed in these areas. In section 3, I will consider the application of therapeutic jurisprudence to some of these substantive areas and show how its careful and creative use can expose the pretextual and sanist roots of mental disability law. Finally, I will conclude with a consideration of the implications of these developments and offer some suggestions about how mental disability law can be rid of these distortive factors. I hope that I provide a blueprint by which the prejudices that permeate mental disability law can be exposed. I also hope that we can place mental disability law—and the way the legal system treats persons with mental disabilities—on trial, and that we can begin to deal with the intellectual and moral corruption that has always engulfed it.

PART I:

SANISM AND PRETEXTUALITY

Chapter 1
SETTING THE STAGE:
Why Mental Disability Is on Trial

Any study of any area of mental disability law—commitment law, institutional rights law, psychiatric malpractice law, community rights law, criminal procedure law—leads to the conclusion that *something* goes on in the mental disability law process that cannot be explained by the usual modes of legal analysis that are typically used in doctrinal studies of, for example, tort law, contracts law, or securities regulation law. Something happens in mental disability law that distorts the litigation, the fact finding, and the appellate process. This "something" negatively affects *all* participants: litigants, lawyers, lay and expert witnesses, trial and appellate judges, jurors, scholars, legislators, the media, and the public.

I teach civil procedure to first-semester, first-year law students. I have never begun the introductory discussion of subject matter and personal jurisdiction (the starting point for most introductory procedure courses) only to have a student raise her hand and say, "Professor, I really think the 'stream of commerce' rule in the *Asahi* case is silly."[1] None of my colleagues who teach introductory contracts law has ever related a story of a student walking in on the first day, saying, "Gee, Professor, what do you think about the Uniform Commercial Code?"[2] Yet on the first day of class, before I get past "Hi, I'm Professor Perlin, and welcome to mental health law," hands shoot up, and I'm peppered with questions such as:

> "Professor, I saw this crazy guy on the subway today on my way to class and he scared the hell out of me. Is he one of the ones the ACLU got out of the hospital?"
> "Professor, can we talk about how everyone seems to be pleading insanity in criminal cases these days—and they're all getting off?"
> "Professor, is it really true that mental patients can't ever be made to take their medication?"
> "Professor, is it so that if you go to a therapist and tell him what's on your mind, he's gotta go to the cops if you say anything scary?"

I've come to expect this in late August and early January, and am rarely surprised. I also expect that I'll be hearing this (with slight variants, depending on what the current hot case is on "Hard Copy" or "Ricki Lake") as long as I continue to teach.[3] To a significant degree, it was questions such as these that helped crystalize my thinking on the roles of sanism and pretextuality in the incoherent development of mental disability law jurisprudence. But as these thoughts jelled, I realized that there were other concepts—concepts describing the ways by which human beings process information, simplify our thinking, and, self-referentially, extrapolate our own narrow vision of the world to explain all behavior—that

---

[1] In Asahi Metal Indus. Co. v. Superior Ct. of California, 480 U.S. 102, 109–12 (1987), the U.S. Supreme Court articulated the "stream of commerce" test for determining the limits of *in personam* jurisdiction.

[2] The Uniform Commercial Code—a model statute governing sales, contracts, and commercial instruments— is the law in all American Jurisdictions. *See* Delaware v. New York, 507 U.S. 490, 504 (1992).

[3] Three weeks after I wrote the first draft of this chapter, on the evening of the first mental health law class of the fall semester, a student raised her hand and asked, "Professor, I heard this story on TV the other day—about some guy who was driving his neighbors crazy, and whose family wanted to send him to the hospital, but the police were saying their 'hands were tied' because he 'hadn't hurt anyone yet'—is that really true?"

must be considered and weighed before we can begin a meaningful discussion of the two constructs to which most of this book will be devoted.

Thus in this chapter I will focus on *heuristics* (a cognitive psychology construct that refers to the ways people simplify complex, information-processing tasks, how that simplification leads to distorted and systematically erroneous decisions, and how it causes decision makers to "ignore or misuse items of rationally useful information")[4] and on *ordinary common sense* (OCS) (a prereflective mode of reasoning exemplified by the attitude of "what I know is 'self-evident'; it is 'what everybody knows'")[5] as jurisprudential forerunners of sanism and pretextuality. I do not believe that the full depths of these distortive devices can be measured without a full understanding of these concepts.

This is not to say that these are the *only* additional concepts that must be understood if we are to truly grasp how and why mental disability law jurisprudence has developed as it has. I believe, for instance, that structural anthropology offers us many insights into these developments.[6] And I believe that once an understanding of sanism and pretextuality is in place we must turn to therapeutic jurisprudence as a means of understanding how this area can best be restructured.[7] But I also believe that, without an understanding of why heuristics and OCS dominate our decision-making processes, we can never make sense of the problems before us.

Heuristics

Behavioral scientists are aware of the power of what David Rosenhan has characterized as the "distortions of vivid information."[8] As part of this phenomenon, "concrete and vivid information" about a specific case "overwhelms the abstract data on which rational choices are often made."[9] Thus "the more vivid and concrete is better remembered, over recitals of

---

[4]*See* Michael L. Perlin, *Are Courts Competent to Decide Questions of Competency? Stripping the Facade From* United States v. Charters, 38 U. KAN. L. REV. 957, 966 n.46 (1990), quoting, in part, John Carroll & John Payne, *The Psychology of the Parole Decision Process: A Joint Application of Attribution Theory and Information-Processing Psychology, in* COGNITION AND SOCIAL BEHAVIOR 13, 21 (John Carroll & John Payne eds. 1976) (COGNITION)

[5]Richard Sherwin, *Dialects and Dominance: A Story of Rhetorical Fields in the Law of Confessions,* 136 U. PA. L. REV. 729, 737 (1988) [hereinafter Sherwin, *Dialects*]; *See also* Sherwin, *A Matter of Voice and Plot: Belief and Suspicion in Legal Story Telling,* 87 MICH. L. REV. 543, 595 (1988) [hereinafter Sherwin, *Plot*] ("Common sense probably would not surrender concrete evidentiary truth to abstract constitutional principle...."). *See generally* Michael L. Perlin, *Psychodynamics and the Insanity Defense: "Ordinary Common Sense" and Heuristic Reasoning,* 69 NEB. L. REV. 3 (1990).

[6]I explore these concepts more fully in Michael L. Perlin, *Myths, Realities, and the Political World: The Anthropology of Insanity Defense Attitudes,* 24 BULL. AM. ACAD. PSYCHIATRY & L. 5 (1996) [hereinafter Perlin, *Political World*], and Michael L. Perlin, *"The Borderline Which Separated You From Me": The Insanity Defense, the Authoritarian Spirit, the Fear of Faking, and the Culture of Punishment,* 82 IOWA L. REV. 1375 (1997).

[7]*See generally infra* section 3; *see* Michael L. Perlin, *Therapeutic Jurisprudence: Understanding the Sanist and Pretextual Bases of Mental Disability Law,* 20 N. ENG. J. ON CRIM. & CIV. CONFINEMENT 369 (1994). The most important writings in this area are collected in THERAPEUTIC JURISPRUDENCE: THE LAW AS A THERAPEUTIC AGENT (David Wexler ed. 1990) (TJ); ESSAYS IN THERAPEUTIC JURISPRUDENCE (David Wexler & Bruce Winick eds. 1991) (ESSAYS); LAW IN A THERAPEUTIC KEY: RECENT DEVELOPMENTS IN THERAPEUTIC JURISPRUDENCE (David Wexler & Bruce Winick eds. 1996) (KEY); and THERAPEUTIC JURISPRUDENCE APPLIED: ESSAYS ON MENTAL HEALTH LAW (Bruce Winick ed. 1998).

[8]For a comprehensive one-volume survey of the issues discussed in this section, see JUDGMENT UNDER UNCERTAINTY: HEURISTICS AND BIASES (Daniel Kahneman et al. eds. 1982); *see generally* 1 MICHAEL L. PERLIN, MENTAL DISABILITY LAW: CIVIL AND CRIMINAL, § 2D-2, at 523–28 (2d ed. 1998). For a recent helpful and thorough overview, see *Behavioral Theories of Judgment and Decision Making in Legal Scholarship: A Literature Review,* 51 VAND. L. REV. 1499 (1998).

[9]David Rosenhan, *Psychological Realities and Judicial Policies,* 10 STAN. LAW. 10, 13, 14 (1984).

fact and logic.''[10] Studies have shown further that the "vividness" effect is actively present in judicial proceedings[11] and in perceptions of judicial proceedings.[12]

This distortion results in "trial by heuristics,"[13] the use of problem-solving methods to keep "the information-processing demands of a task within the bounds of [individuals'] limited cognitive capacity."[14] Through the use of social-cognitive research and behavior-decision theory,[15] I will examine how the use of such principles that *appear* to guide the simplification of complex, information-processing tasks—"simplifying heuristics"— actually lead to distorted and systematically erroneous decisions[16] and lead decision makers "to ignore or misuse items of rationally useful information."[17]

These principles include the following:

Representativeness: We erroneously view a random sample drawn from a population as highly representative of that population—in other words, similar in all essential characteristics.[18] Thus the high rate of false positives (the consistent overprediction of dangerousness by psychiatrists and clinical psychologists) is, in part a result of inappropriate reliance on the representative heuristic in which a person facing involuntary civil commitment is compared to the stereotype of a dangerous person.[19] Because the rare false negative receives such extensive negative publicity, we overattribute representativeness to that category.[20]

---

[10]Marilyn Chandler Ford, *The Role of Extralegal Factors in Jury Verdicts,* 11 JUST. SYS. J. 16, 23 (1986); *see also* Steven C. Bank & Norman G. Poythress, *The Elements of Persuasion in Expert Testimony,* 10 J. PSYCHIATRY & L. 173 (1982).

[11]*See, e.g.,* Brad E. Bell & Elizabeth F. Loftus, *Vivid Persuasion in the Courtroom,* 49 J. PERSONALITY ASSESSMENT 659, 663 (1985) (vivid information at trial may "garner more attention, recruit more attention from memory, cause people to spend more time in thought, be more available in memory, be perceived as having a more credible source, and have a greater affective impact"); Ruth Hamill et al., *Insensitivity to Sample Bias: Generalizing From Atypical Cases,* 39 J. PERSONAL. & SOC. PSYCHOL. 578 (1980) (research participants presented with information about one welfare recipient generalized data to all recipients even when told the particular exemplar was "highly atypical of the population at large"). On the impact that vivid events have on police policies dealing with mentally disabled persons, see Peter Finn & Monique Sullivan, *Police Handling of the Mentally Ill: Sharing Responsibility With the Mental Health System,* 17 J. CRIM. JUST. 1, 4 (1989).

[12]*See, e.g.,* Shari Seidman Diamond & Loretta J. Stalans, *The Myth of Judicial Leniency on Sentencing,* 7 BEHAV. SCI. & L. 73, 87–88 (1989) (vividness of media stories about particularly violent criminal offenses has a "disproportionate impact" on public perceptions about crime); Albert W. Alschuler, *"Close Enough for Government Work": The Exclusionary Rule After* Leon, 1984 SUP. CT. REV. 309, 347–48 (fear that application of exclusionary rule might potentially free "next year's Son of Sam" will overwhelm empirically based arguments in support of rule); Stephan Slovic et al., *Facts Versus Fears: Understanding Perceived Risk, in id.* at 463, 468 (impact of biased newspaper coverage on perceived risks in cases of various disaster scenarios); Loretta J. Stalans & Arthur J. Lurigio, *Law and Professionals' Beliefs About Crime and Criminal Sentences: A Need for Theory, Perhaps Schema Theory,* 17 CRIM. JUST. & BEHAV. 333 (1990) (lay persons rely disproportionately on unrepresentative impressions in forming beliefs about punishment and crime).

[13]Michael J. Saks & Robert F. Kidd, *Human Information Processing and Adjudication: Trial by Heuristics,* 15 LAW & SOC'Y REV. 123 (1980–81).

[14]Carroll & Payne, *supra* note 4, at 21.

[15]Saks & Kidd, *supra* note 13, at 125. For a full elaboration, *see, e.g.,* David Kahneman & Amos Tversky, *On the Psychology of Prediction,* 80 PSYCHOL. REV. 237 (1973).

[16]Saks & Kidd, *supra* note 13, at 132. *See also* Ward Edwards & Detlof von Winterfeldt, *Cognitive Illusions and Their Implications for the Law,* 59 S. CAL. L. REV. 225, 227 (1986) (discussing elements of cognitive illusions).

[17]Carroll & Payne, *supra* note 4, at 21.

[18]*See generally* Michael L. Perlin, *Unpacking the Myths: The Symbolism Mythology of Insanity Defense Jurisprudence,* 40 CASE W. RES. L. REV. 599 (1989–90); *see generally* Donald N. Bersoff, *Judicial Deference to Nonlegal Decisionmakers: Imposing Simplistic Solutions on Problems of Cognitive Complexity in Mental Disability Law,* 46 SMU L. REV. 329 (1992).

[19]*See* Saks & Kidd, *supra* note 13, at 133, discussing Daniel Kahneman & Amos Tversky, *Subjective Probability: A Judgment of Representativeness,* 3 COGNITIVE PSYCHOL. 430 (1972).

[20]*See* Edwards & von Winterfeldt, *supra* note 16, at 237.

Insensitivity to sample size: We "intuitively" reject the statistical reality that larger samples are more likely to approximate the characteristics of the population from which it is drawn.[21] As Amos Tversky and David Kahneman have noted, "This fundamental notion of statistics is evidently not part of people's repertoire of intuitions."[22]

The illusion of validity: Individuals tend to make intuitive predictions by selecting an outcome most similar to a preexisting stereotype, and express extreme confidence in such predictions, even when they are given scanty, outdated, or unreliable information about an unknown. Moreover, we frequently fill in the gaps in our evidence base with information consistent with our "preconceived notions of what evidence should support our belief," a phenomenon also known as "filling."[23]

Availability: People are likely to judge the probability or frequency of an event based on the ease with which they can recall instances or occurrences of the event.[24] Thus extensive publicity about "some atrocious crime . . . greatly enhances lay assessment of how probable the event is."[25] However, because the most salient experiences are the ones that are the most bizarre and extreme, they are precisely the "poorest instances on which to construct decision making policies."[26]

An example of the availability heuristic in a collateral area should be illustrative: When asked about whether a sentencing judge was too lenient in an individual case, 80% of all respondents who had read a newspaper account of the case said yes, yet only 14.8% of those who had read the court transcript came to the same conclusion.[27] As a correlate of this phenomenon, Michael Saks and Robert Kidd also pointed out that studies confirming that experts reporting scientific or statistical data are likely to have less impact on fact finders than a person who reports a case study and relates a compelling personal experience or offers anecdotal evidence. Such anecdotal evidence is viewed as "more concrete, vivid and emotion-arousing" and thus more accessible to fact finders.[28] According to David Van Zandt, "Anecdotal evidence plays a major role in people's understanding of their society. The most obvious examples are the use of oral stories, tales, and myths. Individuals routinely accept as highly probative evidence that would constitute hearsay."[29]

On a CNN call-in broadcast of "Sonya Live," for example, in response to a discussion of the Jeffrey Dahmer case, a caller from North Carolina told the national audience that his father had been murdered by a defendant who pled the insanity defense and was hospitalized

---

Although there has been some recent modest improvement in making such predictions—*see* John Monahan, *The Scientific Status of Research on Clinical and Actuarial Predictions of Violence, in* MODERN SCIENTIFIC EVIDENCE: THE LAW AND SCIENCE OF EXPERT TESTIMONY §§ 7-2.0 to 7-2.4 (D. Faigman ed. 1997)—there is no evidence that the use of these heuristics in individual clinical decision making has diminished.

[21]*See* Edwards and von Winterfeldt, *supra* note 16, at 235.

[22]Saks & Kidd, *supra* note 13, at 134, quoting Kahneman & Tversky, *supra* note 19.

[23]Saks & Kidd, *supra* note 13, at 135; Bersoff, *supra* note 18, at 345–48.

[24]Saks & Kidd, *supra* note 13, at 137.

[25]Edwards and von Winterfeldt, *supra* note 16 at 248.

[26]Saks & Kidd, *supra* note 13 at 139.

[27]Diamond & Stalans, *supra* note 12, at 88, citing Anthony Doob & Julian Roberts, *Social Psychology, Social Attitudes, and Attitudes Toward Sentencing,* 16 CANAD. J. BEHAV. SCI. 269 (1984).

For more recent confirmatory empirical evidence (on public views of juvenile crime and the juvenile justice system), see, for example, in Jane Sprott, *Understanding Public Views of Youth Crime and the Youth Justice System,* 38 CANAD. J. CRIMINOL. 271 (1996).

[28]Saks & Kidd, *supra* note 13, at 137, citing Richard E. Nisbett, *Is There an "External" Cognitive Style?* 33 J. PERSONALITY & SOC. PSYCHOL. 36 (1976).

[29]David E. Van Zandt, *Common Sense Reasoning, Social Change and the Law,* 81 Nw. U. L. REV. 894, 917 n.120 (1987) (citation omitted).

for less than a year.[30] Assuming that this was so, the case disposition was clearly anomalous;[31] yet using the availability heuristic will make this accessible personal story the dominant image retained by listeners.

Illusory correlation: We erroneously report correlations between two classes of events that, in reality, are not correlated, are correlated to a lesser extent than is reported, or are correlated in an opposite direction.[32]

Adjustment and anchoring: Our adjustments or revisions of initial estimates frequently depend heavily on initial values. Even where new information is introduced, initial decisions are often not subsequently corrected or altered in light of the additional data.[33]

Overconfidence in judgments: Fact finders tend to overestimate how much they already know and underestimate how much they have recently learned.[34] Lawyers, by way of example, are found to be significantly overconfident in predicting their chances of winning a hypothetical case, and very difficult judgments produce the most overconfidence.[35]

Underincorporation of statistical information: Contrary to the common belief that statistical reliance results in the production of "unduly persuasive" data, individuals do not process probabilistic information well, and, as a result, unduly ignore statistical information.[36]

The myth of particularistic proofs: We misassume that case-specific, anecdotal information is qualitatively different from base-rate, statistical information.[37]

When acknowledged, considered, and understood, these heuristic reasoning devices can shed new light on the hidden issues underlying mental disability law decision making. For example, the simplifying heuristic of attribution theory[38] teaches that once a stereotype is adopted, a wide variety of evidence can be read to support that stereotype, including events

---

[30]"Sonya Live," *CNN News* (March 9, 1992), transcript no. 6-2, at 3 (full text available on NEXIS).

[31]*See* Perlin, *Political World, supra* note 6, at 12: "NGRI acquittees spend almost *double* the amount of time that defendants convicted of similar charges spend in prison settings, and often face a lifetime of post-release judicial oversight. In California, those found NGRI of non-violent crimes were confined for periods over *nine* times as long."

[32]Saks & Kidd, *supra* note 13, at 139, citing, *inter alia,* Charles Chapman et al., *The Genesis of Popular but Erroneous Psychodiagnostic Signs,* 74 J. ABNORMAL PSYCHOL. 193 (1967).

[33]Bersoff, *supra* note 18, at 348, discussing Charles Turk et al., *Psychotherapy: An Information-Processing Perspective, in* REASONING, INFERENCE AND JUDGMENT IN CLINICAL PSYCHOLOGY 1, 9 (Charles Turk & Peter Salovey eds. 1988) (TURK & SALOVEY).

[34]Saks & Kidd, *supra* note 13, at 143. Accordingly, jurors rank expert witnesses' firmness of conclusion as more important in assessing believability than either the expert's educational credentials or reputation. Anthony Champagne et al., *Expert Witnesses in the Courts: An Empirical Examination,* 76 JUDICATURE 5, 8 (1992); *see also* Ruth McGaffey, *The Expert Witness and Source Credibility—The Communication Perspective,* 2 AM. J. TRIAL ADVOC. 57, 68–69 (1978) ("strength of witness" was significant determination of extent to which jurors found testimony believable); Daniel Shuman et al., *Assessing the Believability of Expert Witnesses: Science in the Jurybox,* 37 JURIMETRICS J.L. SCI. & TECH. 23 (1996); Daniel Shuman, *The Use of Empathy in Forensic Examinations,* 3 ETHICS & BEHAV. 289 (1993); *see generally* Daniel Shuman, Anthony Champagne, & Elizabeth Whitaker, *Juror Assessment of the Believability of Expert Witnesses: A Literature Review,* 36 JURIMETRICS J.L. SCI. & TECH. 371 (1996).

[35]*See* Elizabeth F. Loftus & Willem A. Wagenaar, *Lawyers' Predictions of Success,* 28 JURIMETRICS J.L. SCI. & TECH. 437 (1988).

[36]Saks & Kidd, *supra* note 13, at 149; *see also, e.g.,* Jane Goodman, *Jurors' Comprehension and Assessment of Probabilistic Evidence,* 16 AM. J. TRIAL ADVOC. 361 (1992).

[37]Saks & Kidd, *supra* note 13, at 151; *see also* Laurens Walker & John Monahan, *Social Frameworks: A New Use of Social Science in Law,* 73 VA. L. REV. 559, 576 (1987) ("It appears that aggregate 'statistical' information is likely to be highly *undervalued* by lay decisionmakers") (emphasis in original).

[38]*See, e.g.,* Harold H. Kelley, *The Process of Causal Attribution,* 28 AM. PSYCHOLOGIST 107 (1973); Nisbet & Temoshok, *Is There an "External" Cognitive Style?,* 33 J. PERSONALITY & SOC. PSYCHOL. 36 (1976).

that could equally support the opposite interpretation.[39] This process is sometimes characterized as "dispositional consistency."[40] There is also a "well-documented tendency for people to seek information which confirms rather than disconfirms their beliefs."[41]

A stereotype, in short, functions as a self-fulfilling prophecy; once formed, beliefs about the self, others, or relationships can even survive and persevere in light of "the total discrediting of the evidence that first gave rise to such beliefs."[42] Thus the biased assimilation processes "may include a propensity to remember the strengths of confirming evidence, but not the weaknesses of disconfirming evidence, to judge confirming evidence as relevant and reliable but disconfirming evidence as irrelevant and unreliable, and to accept confirming evidence at face value while scrutinizing disconfirming evidence hypercritically."[43] Stereotypes drive the sanist thought processes and judicial opinions that are at the root of virtually all mental disability law jurisprudence.[44]

Data relevant to a belief are not processed impartially,[45] and people who hold strong opinions on complex social issues are likely to examine relevant empirical evidence in a biased manner.[46] As a corollary, individuals will irrationally exaggerate a person's causal responsibility for an event while underestimating other causal factors that are logically involved in the event's occurrence.[47] Our reasoning is also distorted by the "hindsight illusion" through which we "consistently exaggerate what could have been anticipated in foresight," a phenomenon characterized as "a probabilistic version of 'I told you so.'"[48]

Public perceptions of a legal order and judicial system "burdened by citizen demands and assailed by unprecedented efforts to use courts as a vehicle for social engineering" have been found to be based on "a handful of 'worst' case studies" or "an anecdotal parade of horribles."[49] We thus respond to social policies "in terms of the symbols or metaphors they evoke, or in conformity with views expressed by opinion leaders we like or respect." The "evidence" brought to bear in the formulation of such policies is apt to be "incomplete,

---

[39]Mark Snyder, Elizabeth Tanke, & Ellen Berscheid, *Social Perception and Interpersonal Behavior: On the Self- Fulfilling Nature of Social Stereotypes,* 35 J. Personality & Soc. Psychol. 656, 657 (1977).

[40]Susan T. Fiske, *Attention and Weight in Person Perception: The Impact of Negative and Extreme Behaviors,* 38 J. Personality & Soc. Psychol. 889 (1980).

[41]Doob & Roberts, *supra* note 27, at 279, citing Mark Snyder & William B. Swann, *Hypothesis-Testing Processes in Social Interaction,* 36 J. Personality & Soc. Psychol. 1202 (1978).

[42]Charles Y. Lord et al., *Biased Assimilation and Attitude Polarization: The Effects of Prior Theories on Subsequently Considered Evidence,* 37 J. Personality & Soc. Psychol. 2098, 2108 (1979).

[43]Lord et al., *supra* note 42, at 2099.

[44]*See generally infra* section 2.

[45]Lord et al., *supra* note 42, at 2099; *see also* Edwards & von Winterfeldt, *supra* note 16, at 23, quoting Maya Bar-Hillel, *The Base Rate Fallacy in Probability Judgments,* 44 Acta Psychologica 211, 230 (1980): "People integrate two items of information only if both seem to them equally relevant. Otherwise, high relevance information renders low information irrelevant. One item of information is more relevant than another if it somehow pertains to it more specifically."

[46]Laurence T. White, *Juror Decision Making in the Capital Penalty Trial: An Analysis of Crimes and Defense Strategies,* 11 Law & Hum. Behav. 113, 127 (1987).

[47]David Landy & Elliot Aronson, *The Influence of the Character of the Criminal and His Victim on the Decisions of Simulated Jurors,* 5 J. Experimental Soc. Psychol. 141 (1969).

[48]Edwards and von Winterfeldt, *supra* note 16, at 243, quoting, in part, Baruch Fischhoff, *For Those Condemned to Study the Past: Reflections on Historical Judgments, in* New Directions for Methodology of Social and Behavioral Science: Fallible Judgment in Behavioral Research (R. Schweder & D. Fiske eds. 1980), *reprinted in modified form in* Kahneman, *supra* note 8, at 325. *See also* James Schutte & Mark Howell, *Coping With Juror Hindsight Bias,* 20 Trial Diplomacy J. 73 (1997).

[49]Ralph Cavanagh & Austin Sarat, *Thinking About Courts: Toward and Beyond a Jurisprudence of Judicial Competence,* 14 Law & Soc'y Rev. 371, 373, citing Donald L. Horowitz, The Courts and Social Policy (1977), and *id.,* at 396.

biased, and of marginal probative value—typically, no more than a couple of vivid, concrete, but dubiously representative instances or cases."[50] The fact that such a significant segment of the American public thought that the O. J. Simpson trial was somehow typical of murder trials (or even more startlingly, of *all* criminal trials) speaks eloquently to this point.[51]

In the same vein, individuals tend to generalize from specific cases to the population from which such cases were drawn, and tend to remember and recall negative and extreme behaviors more easily than positive, more moderate behaviors.[52] Thus (a) individuals who are statistically rare, rare in context, or "visually highlighted . . . all have been shown to attract [disproportionate] attention"; (b) impressions are most influenced "by their extreme terms"; and (c) individuals read negative cues as more important than positive ones, in part, because they "stand out by virtue of being rare."[53] Also, when multiple forces contribute to an unfortunate outcome, people select the most blameworthy as the predominant causal factor.[54]

Neither scholars nor those who work directly in the administration of criminal justice are immune to the use of heuristics. Henry Steadman and his colleagues report that, when they described their data collection process to court clerks, those clerks tended to remember only successful insanity pleas even though those examples are only a minor percentage (25%) of total pleas.[55]

Scholars do not fare much better:

> The similarity of the political reactions to the M'Naghten and Hinckley cases is understandable. . . . Less understandable, however, is the similarity of scholarly reactions to the two trials. In each instance, opponents of the insanity defense have cited the controversial case, and often grossly distorted its facts, as evidence that exculpation by insanity fosters lawlessness, frees the guilty, and undermines public confidence in the criminal justice system. . . .[56]

Heuristics and Mental Disability Law

In this section I will briefly show how heuristics affects two important substantive areas of mental disability law, the judicial decision-making process and the decision-making processes of expert witnesses and clinicians. The substantive examples—involuntary civil

---

[50]Lord et al., *supra* note 42, at 2098.

[51]*See, e.g.,* Christo Lassiter, *The O.J. Simpson Verdict: A Lesson in Black and White,* 1 MICH. J. RACE & L. 69 (1996); Craig Bradley & Joseph Hoffman, People v. Simpson: *Justice and the "Search for Truth" in Criminal Cases,* 69 S. CAL. L. REV. 1267 (1996); Larry Hammond & Osborn Maledon, *Rich Man, Poor Men.* 32 ARIZ. ATT'Y 13 (Jan. 1996).

[52]Diamond & Stalans, *supra* note 12, at 87, citing SUSAN T. FISKE & STEVEN TAYLOR, SOCIAL COGNITION (1984), and Fiske, *supra* note 40; *see also* Eric Roberts & Paul White, *Public Estimates of Recidivism Rates,* 28 CANAD. J. CRIMINOL. 229 (1986).

[53]Fiske, *supra* note 40, at 890–91, 904, citing, *inter alia,* Steven Taylor & Susan T. Fiske, *Salience, Attention and Attribution: Top of the Head Phenomena, in* 11 ADVANCES IN EXPERIMENTAL SOCIAL PSYCHOLOGY (L. Berkowitz ed. 1978); Peter Warr & Paul Jackson, *The Importance of Extremity,* 32 J. PERSONALITY & SOC. PSYCHOL. 278 (1975); Kenneth Kanouse et al., *Negativity in Evaluations, in* ATTRIBUTION: PERCEIVING THE CAUSES OF BEHAVIOR (Edward E. Jones et al., eds. 1972).

[54]Mark D. Alicke, *Culpable Causation,* 63 J. PERSONALITY & SOC. PSYCHOL. 368 (1992).

[55]HENRY J. STEADMAN et al., BEFORE AND AFTER HINCKLEY: EVALUATING INSANITY DEFENSE REFORM 58 (1993); *see generally supra* Chapter 10.

[56]Ira Mickenberg, *A Pleasant Surprise: The Guilty but Mentally Ill Verdict Has Both Succeeded in Its Own Right and Successfully Preserved the Traditional Role of the Insanity Defense,* 55 U. CIN. L. REV. 943, 948 (1987). *See also id.* (discussing heuristic response of defense's supporters).

commitment and incompetency to stand trial—are merely representative. Similar conclusions could be drawn about any of the other major strands of this jurisprudence.

Heuristic thinking dominates the mental disability law process.[57] The vividness effect distorts perceptions of civil commitment candidates, the relationship between civil commitment and the criminal process, and civil commitment outcomes.[58] In these instances "the drama of a few cases caused their retelling while the mundane cases faded from memory."[59] Publicly salient events have dramatic impacts on involuntary civil commitment rates, especially in cases in which (a) the vivid event is a homicide of a stranger, (b) the actor has prior contact with the mental health system, and (c) the mental health system either discharges the patient as "cured" or declines to admit him or her. Furthermore, the empirical effect of a single instance such as this is independent of any legislative change that might follow such an event.[60]

Experts often use the typification heuristic in cases that involve the improper prescription of medication.[61] In such cases the treating doctor "'slots' his patient into certain categories and prescribes a similar regimen for all."[62] Also, clinicians significantly overestimate their diagnostic and predictive accuracy and ignore supplemental means of interpretation that might enhance their accuracy.[63] Through use of the attribution heuristic,

---

[57]See generally infra Chapters 2 and 3.

[58]On the role of heuristic decision making in involuntary civil commitment law (following the commission of a criminal act by an individual whose application for civil hospitalization had been denied), see Michael L. Perlin, Morality and Pretextuality, Psychiatry and Law: Of "Ordinary Common Sense," Heuristic Reasoning, and Cognitive Dissonance, 19 BULL. AM. ACAD. PSYCHIATRY & L. 131 (1991) (Perlin, Morality); R. Michael Bagby & Leslie Atkinson, The Effects of Legislative Reform on Civil Commitment Admission Rates: A Critical Analysis, 6 BEHAV. SCI. & L. (1988) ("publicly salient events such as a heinous murder of an innocent victim at the hands of a discharged mental patient, or community intolerance of deviance, may have the effect of increasing the rate of commitment").

See Virginia A. Hiday & Lynn N. Smith, Effects of the Dangerousness Standard in Civil Commitment, 15 J. PSYCHIATRY & L. 433, 449 (1987) (aberrant behavior by a small number of patients in sample distorted outcome perceptions; mental health professionals significantly overstate percentage of involuntary civil commitment cases that begin as police referrals and that jeopardized staff safety); see also Henry J. Steadman et al., Psychiatric Evaluations of Police Referrals in a General Hospital Emergency Room, 8 INT'L J.L. & PSYCHIATRY 39 (1986).

[59]Hiday & Smith, supra note 58, at 449.

[60]Bagby & Atkinson, supra note 58, at 46. William H. Fisher et al., How Flexible Are Our Civil Commitment Statutes?, 39 HOSP. & COMMUNITY PSYCHIATRY 711 (1988). For an explanation of how one salient case can lead to the restructuring of an entire body of jurisprudence, see James R. P. Ogloff, The Juvenile Death Penalty: A Frustrated Society's Attempt for Control, 5 BEHAV. SCI. & L. 447 (1987) (discussing the scenario preceding Vermont's elimination of a minimum age for prosecuting children as adults in murder cases); see also People v. Seefeld, 290 N.W.2d 123, 124 (Mich. Ct. App. 1980) (discussing the impetus for adopting the "guilty but mentally ill" verdict).

[61]See Hale v. Portsmouth Receiving Hosp., 338 N.E.2d 371 (Ohio Ct. Cl. 1975) (doctor failed to change prescription following his observation of side effects and self-destructive behavior by patient); Rosenfeld v. Coleman, 19 Pa. D. & C.2d 635 (C.P. Northampton County 1959) (doctor prescribed addictive drugs to help patient see nature of his addictive personality); Perlin, Power, infra note 62, at 125 (discussing Watkins v. United States, 589 F.2d 214 (5th Cir. 1979) (doctors prescribed 50-day supply of Valium without taking medical history or checking patient's medical records).

[62]Michael L. Perlin, Power Imbalances in Therapeutic and Forensic Relationships, 9 BEHAV. SCI. & L. 111, 125 n.112 (1991) (citing sources discussing "slotting" practices); see also, e.g., People v. Feagley, 535 P.2d 373, 397 n.31 (Cal. 1975) (state hospital report on treatability of convicted sex offender was "mimeographed" and "very minimum-grade form letter").

[63]David Faust, Data Integration in Legal Evaluations: Can Clinicians Deliver on Their Promises? 7 BEHAV. SCI. & L. 469, 480 (1989) (discussing results found in Robyn M. Dawes et al., Clinical Versus Actuarial Judgment, 243 SCIENCE 1668 (1989)).

these data are ignored in the mental disability law process.[64] The fact that some expert witnesses, referred to as "imperial experts" by Michael Saks, "display a willingness . . . to disregard what knowledge has been developed by the field from which they claim to derive their expertise, and to substitute for that their own guesses" is also ignored.[65]

The issue is clearly drawn on the wisdom of broadening the criteria for involuntary civil commitment as a strategy for "correcting" deinstitutionalization errors and thus reducing the number of homeless mentally ill individuals.[66] Whether or not we accept the premise that civil-libertarian-based statutes "went too far" and that it has become time for "the pendulum to be reversed,"[67] we must confront an important reality: Legislative activity in this area is driven by heuristic reasoning. The vivid, "outrageous" case that shows the public what happens when "someone falls through the cracks" animates legislative reform designed to ensure that such errors are not replicated.[68]

---

[64]*See* Hal R. Arkes, *Principles in Judgment/Decisionmaking Research Pertinent to Legal Proceedings,* 7 BEHAV. SCI. & L. 429, 430–31 (1989).

[65]Saks & Kidd, *supra* note 13, at 294; *see also* James Wyda & Bert Black, *Psychiatric Predictions and the Death Penalty: An Unconstitutional Sword for the Prosecution but a Constitutional Shield for the Defense,* 7 BEHAV. SCI. & L. 505, 513 (1989) (clinicians overvalue evidence that supports their conclusions and deny counterevidence).

[66]*Cf.* Mary Durham & John LaFond, *A Search for the Missing Premise of Involuntary Therapeutic Commitment: Effective Treatment for the Mentally Ill,* 40 RUTGERS L. REV. 303, 357–62 (1988) (arguing that involuntary commitment for nondangerous mentally ill patients does more harm than good), Mary Durham & John LaFond, *"Thank You Dr. Stone:" A Response to Dr. Alan Stone and Some Further Thoughts in the Wisdom of Broadening the Criteria for Involuntary Therapeutic Commitment of the Mentally Ill,* 40 RUTGERS L. REV. 865, 886–88 (1988) [hereinafter Durham & LaFond, *Further Thoughts*] (asserting that coercive commitment is ineffective in treating persons with mental illness and that scarce resources should be concentrated on providing care on a voluntary basis), and Mary Durham & John LaFond, *The Empirical Consequences and Policy Implications of Broadening the Statutory Criteria for Civil Commitment,* 3 YALE L. & POL'Y REV. 395, 444 (1985) [hereinafter Durham & LaFond, *Empirical Consequences*] (concluding through empirical research that expanding involuntary commitment results in overcrowding in state institutions, chronic use of state psychiatric hospitals, and lack of available treatment for voluntary patients), *with* Alan A. Stone, *Broadening the Statutory Criteria for Civil Commitment: A Reply to Durham & LaFond,* 5 YALE L. & POL'Y REV. 412, 422–27 (1987) (attacking Durham and LaFond's research, and asserting that "therapeutically oriented criteria" for commitment protects the patient's rights and limits inappropriate confinements).

[67]On the pendulum theory, see 1 PERLIN, *supra* note 8, § 1-2.3, at 32 n.201 (2d ed. 1998) (discussing Durham & LaFond, *Empirical Consequences, supra* note 66, at 398) (restrictiveness and inflexibility of statutes based on dangerousness have led several states to broaden commitment requirements); John Myers, *Involuntary Civil Commitment of the Mentally Ill: A System in Need of Change,* 29 VILL. L. REV. 367, 379 (1983–84) (some mental health professionals who initially applauded the changes in involuntary commitment laws eventually criticized them as "antitherapeutic" and even harmful); Daniel Shuman, *Innovative Statutory Approaches to Civil Commitment: An Overview and Critique,* 13 L. MED. & HEALTH CARE 284, 286 (1985) (trend away from the dangerousness standard precipitated by the apparently inappropriate exclusion of people from hospitals, thus forming the "mental patient ghettos" in the larger cities); David Wexler, *Grave Disability and Family Therapy: The Therapeutic Potential of Civil Libertarian Commitment Codes,* 9 INT'L J.L. & PSYCHIATRY 39, 39 (1986) (asserting that statutory broadening of commitment criteria results from public opinion that "the pendulum has swung too far in favoring 'rights' over 'therapy'").

[68]*See, e.g.,* Bagby & Atkinson, *supra* note 58 at 45, 46 ("publicly salient events such as a heinous murder of an innocent victim at the hands of a discharged mentally ill patient, or community intolerance of deviance, may have the effect of increasing the rate of commitments"); Durham & LaFond, *Empirical Consequences, supra* note 66, at 416–18 (increase in commitments before the effective date of Washington's new broadened statutory-commitment criteria may have been attributable to a well-publicized murder by a person denied voluntary admission to a state hospital); Fisher et al., *supra* note 60, at 712 (reporting that after an individual was denied admission to a Washington state hospital and murdered two elderly neighbors commitments from that vicinage rose by nearly 100% even prior to legislative reform); Dody Tsiantar, *New York State Seeks to Reduce Psychiatric*

Scholars who have studied this process carefully have reached two divergent conclusions. First, when new, broader criteria are actually adhered to, the results raise troubling issues relating to social control, allocation of resources, and the role of the public hospital in the mental health system.[69] Second, and perhaps even more important for our purposes, in cases of jurisdictions in which commitment standards are more narrow, little evidence suggests that mental health professionals adhere to the legislative guidelines.[70] R. Michael Bagby and Leslie Atkinson have speculated that such professionals exhibit "psychological reactance"[71] in resisting legislative attempts to reduce their prerogative.[72] Because of this resistance—grounded in what some professionals see as their "moral obligation"[73]— restrictive laws are ignored and some psychiatrists continue to commit those "whom they believe should be committed."[74]

Beds; City Officials Fear Results Will Be an Increase in Mentally Ill Homeless People, WASH. POST, Sept. 19, 1986, at F5 (discussing impact on deinstitutionalization debate of highly publicized murder of 11 people on the Staten Island Ferry committed by expatient). Durham and LaFond respond to the major psychiatric critique of their earlier work—*see* Stone, *supra* note 66—by accusing Stone of relying on "anecdotal accounts, armchair speculation, and two idiosyncratic prospective studies." Durham & LaFond, *Further Thoughts, supra* note 66, at 886; *see also* Richard H. Lamb, *Involuntary Treatment for the Homeless Mentally Ill,* 4 NOTRE DAME J.L. ETHICS & PUB. POL'Y 269, 277 (1989) (criticizing the use of improperly narrow involuntary civil commitment criteria, but without citing to a single court decision demonstrating a tendency to apply such criteria too "literally").

[69]Under amended criteria in Washington, the number of involuntarily committed patients increased significantly, including many first-time commitments. The Washington guidelines also extended the lengths of stay for new patients, thus raising the number of chronic users of inpatient mental health services. The extreme overcrowding caused by implementing these guidelines virtually excluded voluntary admissions from all state hospital facilities. *See* Durham & LaFond, *Empirical Consequences, supra* note 66, at 401. Conversely, when legislatures have attempted to tighten civil commitment criteria, the number of involuntary admissions has not been significantly reduced. *See* Bagby & Atkinson, *supra* note 58, at 57–59; *see also* Michael Bagby, *The Effects of Legislative Reform on Admission Rates to Psychiatric Units of General Hospitals,* 10 INT'L J.L. & PSYCHIATRY 383, 385–86 (1987) (analyzing the impact of legislative revision on involuntary admission rates).

[70]*Cf.* Bagby & Atkinson, *supra* note 58, at 57 (reaction of mental health professionals who perceive legislation as an unnecessary constraint on the treatment of the mentally ill); Stewart Page, *New Civil Commitment Legislation: The Relevance of Commitment Criteria,* 25 CANAD. J. PSYCHIATRY 646, 646 (1980) (Canadian Civil Liberties Union concluded that about 70% of civil commitment criteria did not meet the requirements of the mental health act); T. S. Page, *Civil Commitment: Operational Definition of New Criterion,* 26 CANAD. J. PSYCHIATRY 419, 420 (1981) (because of low compliance the Canadian mental health act was modified); Stewart Page & John Firth, *Civil Commitment Practices in 1977: Troubled Semantics and/or Troubled Psychiatry,* 24 CANAD. J. PSYCHIATRY 329, 330–31 (1979) (exploring why civil commitment practices are not followed); T. S. Page, et al., *Civil Commitment and the Danger Mandate,* 18 CANAD. PSYCHIATRIC ASS'N 267, 268–70 (1973) (examination of Ontario's new mental health act as contrasted with the narrow criteria of the Canadian mental health act).

[71]SHARON S. BREHM & JACK W. BREHM, PSYCHOLOGICAL REACTANCE: A THEORY OF FREEDOM AND CONTROL, 357–72 (1981); Perlin, *supra* note 5, at 12 n.46; Perlin, *Morality, supra* note 58.

[72]Bagby & Atkinson, *supra* note 58, at 58; *See generally* Michael L. Perlin, *Pretexts Within the Forensic System: Why Are We Really Doing This This Way?* (Paper presented at Grand Rounds, Clarke Institute of Psychiatry, Toronto, Ontario, Canada, June 1990).

[73]*See infra* Chapter 3.

[74]*See generally* R. Michael Bagby et al., *Effects of Mental Health Legislative Reform in Ontario,* 28 CANAD. PSYCHOLOGIST 21, 27–28 (1987) (raising serious questions about the ability of lawmakers to legislate the practices of mental health professionals); *Cf.* Randolph Martin & Shu Cheung, *Civil Commitment Trends in Ontario: The Effect of Legislation on Clinical Practice,* 30 CANAD. J. PSYCHIATRY 259, 259 (1985) (mental health legislation had little effect on local commitment practice). Although Peters and his colleagues have reported significant changes in Florida's admissions and census following legislative change, *see* Roger Peters et al., *The Effects of Statutory Change on the Civil Commitment of the Mentally Ill,* 11 L. & HUM. BEHAV. 73, 77 (1987), Bagby and Atkinson have suggested that such initial postreform changes are not predictive of subsequent commitment rates. Bagby & Atkinson, *supra* note 58, at 56–57.

Heuristics and "Ordinary Common Sense" (OCS)

There appears to be some connection between heuristic fallacies and reliance on "ordinary common sense" (OCS),[75] to be discussed later.[76] In his dissent from a Fifth Circuit decision in an insanity defense case abandoning the control component of the Model Penal Code's substantive test,[77] Judge Alvin Rubin focused astutely and presciently on one aspect of the majority's (likely unconscious) decision-making process:

> Judges are not, and should not be, immune to popular outrage over this nation's crime rate. Like everyone else, judges watch television, read newspapers and magazines, listen to gossip. and are sometimes themselves victims. They receive the message trenchantly described in a recent book criticizing the insanity defense: "Perhaps the bottom line of all these complaints is that *guilty people go free*—guilty people who do not have to accept judgment or responsibility for what they have done and are not held accountable for their actions. . . . These are not cases in which the defendant is *alleged* to have committed a crime. *Everyone knows he did it.*" Although understandable as an expression of uninformed public opinion, such a viewpoint ought not to serve as the basis for judicial decisionmaking; for it misapprehends the very meaning of guilt. . . .[78]

The Justice Department's position on post-*Hinckley* insanity defense reform illuminated the issue:

> What [the IDRA Act] is really saying [is], how do we get a hook into this person, so that he isn't going to go out and do this again to me, to any of my family, or to my brothers and sisters. . . . If you are so disturbed mentally that it manifests itself in . . . assassinations . . . society has a right to put a hook into you . . . until I think it's demonstrated beyond a shadow of a doubt that you are no longer that type of danger to the community. . . . The people really don't care if he couldn't help himself. They want to know what do you do to protect me.[79]

This type of decision making mimics what is characterized as implicit personality theory: "an untested, unconfirmed collection of ideas that people rely on to explain or predict others."[80] Thus if OCS is a prereflective attitude exemplified by the attitude of "what I know is 'self-evident'; it is 'what everybody knows,'"[81] then the use of the heuristic bias

---

[75]*See generally* Sherwin, *Dialects, supra* note 5.

[76]*See infra* Chapter 1, at text accompanying notes 103–31.

[77]United States v. Lyons, 731 F.2d 243 (5th Cir. 1984). *Lyons* preceded the adoption of the Insanity Defense Reform Act of 1984 (IDRA). *See* 18 U.S.C. § 20 (1988); *see generally* section 3.

[78]*Lyons*, 739 F.2d 994, 999–1000 (5th Cir. 1984) (Rubin, J., dissenting) (footnote omitted), quoting, in part, WILLIAM J. WINSLADE & JUDITH WILSON ROSS, THE INSANITY PLEA 2–3 (1983) (emphasis added in opinion).

[79]*Proceedings of the Forty-Sixth Judicial Conference of the District of Columbia Circuit*, 111 F.R.D. 91, 227 (1985) (remarks of Assistant U.S. Attorney General Stephen Trott). *See generally* Richard E. Nisbett et al., *Popular Induction: Information Is Not Necessarily Informative, in* COGNITION, *supra* note 4, at 113, 128 (in assessing impact of "sheer number of instances" as against "instances of some emotional interest," researchers have found that "emotional instance *in every case* carried the day") (emphasis added).

[80]Saks & Kidd, *supra* note 13, at 135 n.15, citing Gordon W. Allport, *The Perception of People, in* 2 HANDBOOK OF SOCIAL PSYCHOLOGY (Gardner Lindzey ed. 1954).

[81]Sherwin, *Dialects, supra* note 5, at 737; *see also* Sherwin, *Plot, supra* note 5, at 595.

For a paradigmatic judicial characterization in a collateral area, *see* State v. Vaughan, 232 S.E.2d 328, 331 (S.C. 1977) ("The effect of drunkenness on the mind and on men's actions . . . is a fact known to everyone"), quoting 22 C.J.S., CRIMINAL LAW § 66 (1961).

becomes even more pernicious in insanity defense decision making.[82] In the case of *State v. Van Horn*,[83] for instance, the court reversed an insanity verdict based on evidence of lay persons (police personnel) who were able to testify as to their "perceptions of [defendant's] normalcy" formed on the defendant's arrest and her subsequent incarceration.[84]

The Heuristic Life of Expert Witnesses and Clinicians

The problem before us is exacerbated by the reality of an impressive universe of evidence that demonstrates persuasively that mental health professionals are just as susceptible to heuristic biases as are lay persons.[85] These biases affect clinical judgment and psychiatric decision making in much the same way that they affect decisions made by individuals without mental health backgrounds.[86]

Mental health professionals—even experienced mental health professionals[87]—have been found to be susceptible to the availability heuristic, the representative heuristic, and the illusion of validity heuristic.[88] So if a clinician has been repeatedly exposed to a certain type of disorder, that diagnostic category may show a relatively permanent increase in availability.[89] The representativeness bias can cause "scripted thinking," which leads clinicians to make erroneous predictions of violence in involuntary civil commitment settings.[90] Finally, the illusion of validity causes clinicians to place an inappropriately high level of confidence

---

[82]The public's view that the use of the insanity defense exculpates the factually guilty makes this even more problematic. *See, e.g.,* Sherwin, *Plot, supra* note 5, at 595: "Can common sense make sense of interpretive principles, deriving, say, from a constitutional text, which trump our 'natural' inclination to blame the factually guilty?"

[83]528 So.2d 529 (Fla. App. 1988).

[84]*Id.* at 530.

[85]*See generally* Bersoff, *supra* note 18, at 351–62; *see also* Margaret Windsor Jackson, *Psychiatric Decision-Making for the Courts: Judges, Psychiatrists, Lay People?* 9 INT'L J.L. & PSYCHIATRY 507 (1986) (psychiatric decision makers may be as susceptible to heuristic bias as lay persons); R. Michael Bagby, *The Indigenous Paraprofessional and Involuntary Civil Commitment: A Return to Community Values,* 25 CANAD. PSYCHOL. 167, 172 (1984) (psychiatric judgment is often "inextricably woven with social class bias").

[86]*See* Jackson, *supra* note 85, at 519 ("in clinical practice, a knowledge of how heuristics and biases work to affect judgment may be every bit as important as clinical acumen *per se*"); Margaret Windsor Jackson, *The Clinical Assessment and Prediction of Violent Behavior: Toward a Scientific Analysis,* 16 CRIM. JUST. & BEHAV. 114, 115–18 (1989) (same); CHRISTOPHER WEBSTER ET AL., CLINICAL ASSESSMENTS BEFORE TRIAL 121 (1982) ("the rules of psychiatric decision-making are not substantially divergent from the canons and heuristics of everyday life"). On lawyers' susceptibility to heuristic thinking, see Steven Bundy, *The Policy in Favor of Settlement in an Adversary System,* 44 HASTINGS L.J. 1, 19 (1992).

[87]*See* Bersoff, *supra* note 18, at 360; Gregory Garb, *Clinical Judgment, Clinical Training, and Professional Experience,* 105 PSYCHOL. BULL. 387 (1989). *Cf.* Dorothy Mack & Laura Weinland, *Not Guilty by Reason of Insanity Evaluations: A Study of Defendants and Examiners,* 17 J. CRIM. JUST. 39 (1989) (insanity assessments varied with examiner's length of professional experience).

[88]*See supra* text accompanying notes 18–37.

[89]Mark Snyder & Cynthia Thomsen, *Interactions Between Therapists and Clients: Hypothesis Testing and Behavioral Confirmation,* in TURK & SALOVEY, *supra* note 33; Tory Higgins, Gillian King, & Gregory H. Marvin, *Individual Construct Accessibility and Subjective Impressions and Recall,* 43 J. PERSONALITY & SOC. PSYCHOL. 35 (1982). On the ethical implications of clinicians' "slotting" their patients, *see* Perlin, *supra* note 62.

The same heuristic affects nonclinical staff. *See* "Sonya Live," *supra* note 30, at 4: "I work at Koskoney Jail in Chicago in the psych unit. And I find my experience with a lot of people is that the malingerers . . . if they are going to trial and pleading the insanity plea, they go off to a mental hospital, they come back. A lot of times they fool the psychiatrist. . . ." (comments of "Pamela in Illinois," a telephone caller).

[90]Daniel Kahneman & Amos Tversky, *Subjective Probability: A Judgment of Representativeness,* 3 COGNITIVE PSYCHOL. 430 (1972); Saks & Kidd, *supra* note 13; Jordan et al., *Attributional Biases in Clinical Decisionmaking, in* TURK & SALOVEY, *supra* note 33.

in judgments that are based on data that actually decrease diagnostic accuracy and to be resistant to change from their initial clinical impressions.[91]

The use of such heuristic devices may also explain why clinicians frequently rely on a wide array of nonclinical factors—including sociodemographic and legal variables—in making treatment recommendations. One retrospective study, for example, revealed that marital status, personality characteristics, and prior criminal history were the strongest discriminants, and clinical variables such as prior treatment response, psychometric data, and diagnosis were relied on minimally.[92] Another investigation showed that the only variable that distinguished those determined to be dangerous from those determined not to be was the alleged crime: The more serious the crime, the more likely that the examiner would find dangerousness.[93] Further, there was a discrepancy between the criteria actually used by the examiners (the crime's seriousness) and the criteria that the examiners reported actually animated their decisions (presence of impaired or delusional thinking).[94]

In reviewing the literature, Bersoff has thus concluded,

> These incorrect intuitive judgments result from the use of simplifying heuristic strategies in all situations where decisionmakers' cognitive capacities cannot otherwise efficiently process information. As the research illustrates, judgmental errors are not limited to lay decisionmakers but have been observed in the work of mental health professionals arriving at diagnoses, formulating treatment regiments, and predicting behavior.[95]

These heuristic errors infect clinician decision making in incompetency-to-stand-trial decisions, in predictions of violence, and in malingering assessments,[96] as well as in insanity-defense evaluations.[97] One study found that experts' preexisting attitudes about the insanity defense substantially and significantly affected their evaluations of marginal test

---

[91]Snyder & Thomsen, *supra* note 89; Arthur Houts & Mercedes Galante, *The Impact of Evaluative Disposition and Subsequent Information on Clinical Impressions,* 3 J. SOC. & CLINICAL PSYCHOL. 201 (1985); Robyn Dawes et al., *Clinical Versus Actuarial Judgment,* 243 SCIENCE 1668, 1672 (1989); RICHARD NISBETT & LEE ROSS, HUMAN INFERENCE: STRATEGIES AND SHORTCOMINGS OF SOCIAL JUDGMENT (1980).

[92]Jose B. Ashford, *Factors Used in Treatment Discriminations Used in Ohio Drug Legislation,* 6 BEHAV. SCI. & L. 139 (1988); *see also* Richard Rogers, *Ethical Dilemmas in Forensic Evaluations,* 5 BEHAV. SCI. & L. 149, 152 (1987) (mental health professionals unduly influenced by "extraneous sociodemographic variables" such as status, race, and sex); Robert J. Menzies et al., *Dimensions of Dangerousness: Evaluating the Accuracy of Psychometric Predictions of Violence Among Forensic Patients,* 9 LAW & HUM. BEHAV. 49 (1985) (same). *See generally infra* Chapter 3.

[93]Joseph J. Cocozza & Henry J. Steadman, *The Failure of Psychiatric Predictions of Dangerousness: Clear and Convincing Evidence,* 29 RUTGERS L. REV. 1084, 1096 (1976); *see also* Vernak Quinsey & Rudolf Ambtman, *Variables Affecting Psychiatrists' and Teachers' Assessments of the Dangerousness of Mentally Ill Offenders,* 47 J. CLINICAL & CONSULTING PSYCHOL. 353 (1978).

[94]Cocozza & Steadman, *supra* note 93, at 1096.

[95]Bersoff, *supra* note 18, at 350.

[96]*See id.* at 354–60, discussing research reported in, *inter alia,* Menzies et al., *The Nature and Consequences of Forensic Psychiatric Decision-Making,* 27 CANAD. J. PSYCHIATRY 463 (1982) (incompetency to stand trial); Roger Klassen et al., *A Prospective Study of Predictors of Violence in Adult Male Mental Health Admissions,* 12 LAW & HUM. BEHAV. 143 (1988) (violence predictions); James R. P. Ogloff, *The Admissibility of Expert Testimony Regarding Malingering and Deception,* 8 BEHAV. SCI. & L. 27 (1990) (malingering).

[97]Another collateral question asks the extent to which clinicians actually know what the insanity standard is. Research by Richard Rogers and his colleagues reveals that an astounding 88% of experienced forensic mental health professionals surveyed did not know the operative insanity standard in their jurisdiction. Richard Rogers et al., *Forensic Psychiatrists' and Psychologists' Understanding of Insanity: Misguided Expertise?* 33 CANAD. J. PSYCHIATRY 691 (1988); *see also* Richard Rogers & Bruce Turner, *Understanding Insanity: A National Survey of Forensic Psychiatrists and Psychologists,* 7 HEALTH L. IN CANAD. 71 (1987).

cases.[98] In another test, clinical psychology graduate students who believed they had been appointed to evaluate a defendant by the defense were significantly more likely to find the defendant insane than were those who believed that they had been appointed by the prosecution.[99]

Bersoff has summed this research up in this manner:

> Despite attempts to educate clinicians about heuristics, behavior decision theory, information processing, and the availability of actuarial or mechanical methods that have been shown for decades to produce markedly more accurate and less biased clinical decisions,[100] the vast majority of clinicians persist, either in ignorance or with misplaced confidence, in using instruments of questionable validity and ignore relevant factors that contribute to more accurate decisionmaking.[101]

In reviewing some of these studies, Michael Bagby concluded that they revealed that intuitive or implicit beliefs rather than expert knowledge often guided examiners' decisions.[102] We ignore these findings, though, and continue to assume that true expertise drives the forensic assessment process. The social significance of this error is dramatically magnified when it is next weighed in the context of the power of OCS.

"Ordinary Common Sense"

The positions frequently taken by Chief Justice Rehnquist and Justice Thomas in criminal procedure cases best highlight the power of "ordinary common sense" (OCS) as an unconscious animator of legal decision making.[103] Such positions frequently demonstrate a total lack of awareness of the underlying psychological issues and focus on such superficial issues as whether a putatively mentally disabled criminal defendant bears a "normal appearance."[104]

---

[98]Robert J. Homant & Daniel B. Kennedy, *Judgment of Legal Insanity as a Function of Attitude Toward the Insanity Defense,* 8 INT'L J.L. & PSYCHIATRY 67 (1986).The correlation between attitude and a determination of whether a hypothetical defendant was insane was so high that, according to the authors, it would occur less than 1 time in 1000 by chance. *Id.* at 442.

[99]Randy K. Otto, *Bias and Expert Testimony of Mental Health Professionals,* 7 BEHAV. SCI. & L. 267 (1989).

[100]*See, e.g.,* Robyn Dawes, *Experience and Validity of Clinical Judgment,* 7 BEHAV. SCI. & L. 457 (1989).

[101]Bersoff, *supra* note 18, at 360.

[102]*See* Bagby, *supra* note 85, at 170–71; R. Michael Bagby, *The Deprofessionalization of Civil Commitment,* 29 CANAD. PSYCHOL. 234 (1988).

[103]*See, e.g.,* Grigsby v. Mabry, 569 F. Supp. 1273, 1332 (E.D. Ark. 1983), *aff'd,* 758 F.2d 226 (8th Cir. 1985), *rev'd sub. nom.,* Lockhart v. McCree, 476 U.S. 162 (1986), relying on, *inter alia,* Robert M. Berry, *Death-Qualification and the "Fireside Induction,"* 5 U. ARK. LITTLE ROCK L. REV. 1 (1982), to define "fireside induction" as "those common sense, empirical generalizations about human behavior which derive from introspection, anecdotal evidence, and culturally transmitted beliefs").

[104]Michael L. Perlin, *The Supreme Court, the Mentally Disabled Criminal Defendant and Symbolic Values: Random Decisions, Hidden Rationales, or "Doctrinal Abyss?"* 29 ARIZ. L. REV. 1, 83 n.811 (1987).

Chief Justice Rehnquist's opinions reflect the "meta-myths" of "fear of feigning"—*see* Ake v. Oklahoma, 470 U.S. 68, 87, 91 (1985) (Rehnquist, J., dissenting); Ford v. Wainwright, 477 U.S. 399, 435 (1986) (Rehnquist, J., dissenting); of stereotypical visions of mental disability informed primarily by surface views of defendants' external appearance, see Wainwright v. Greenfield, 474 U.S. 284, 297–98 (1986) (Rehnquist, J., concurring); and of mental illness as an improperly exculpatory excuse, see Colorado v. Connelly, 479 U.S. 157, 163–69 (1987).

Justice Thomas's majority opinions in *Godinez v. Moran*[105] and his dissents in *Riggins v. Nevada*[106] and *Foucha v. Louisiana*[107] reflect the most banal sort of OCS.[108] As I will discuss subsequently, Thomas's opinions are "cynical and meretricious,"[109] parrot sanist and pretextual fears and worries,[110] and reflect "the fewest insights" of any member of the Court into the bases of mental disability and mental disability law.[111]

The Chief Justice and Justice Thomas are certainly not the first jurists to exhibit this sort of close-mindedness.[112] Trial judges will typically say, "he [the defendant] doesn't look sick to me," or, even more revealingly, "he is as healthy as you or me."[113] In short, where defendants do not conform to "popular images of 'craziness,'"[114] the notion of a handicapping mental disability condition is flatly, and unthinkingly, rejected. Similarly, the

---

In a revealing speech, the Chief Justice discussed the impact of public opinion on judicial decision making:

> Somewhere "out there"—beyond the walls of the courthouse—run currents and tides of public opinion which lap at the courthouse door. . . . If these tides of public opinion are sufficiently great and sufficiently sustained, they will very likely have an effect upon the decision of some of the cases decided within the courthouse. This is not a case of judges "knuckling under" to public opinion, and cravenly abandoning their oaths of office. Judges, so long as they are relatively normal human beings, can no more escape being influenced by public opinion in the long run than can people working at other jobs.

William Rehnquist, *Constitutional Law and Public Opinion*, 20 SUFFOLK U. L. REV. 751, 768 (1986).

The degree to which Rehnquist's views mirror public consensus on "craziness," the appearance of normality, and criminal nonresponsibility as an exculpating condition is probably not coincidental.

[105]509 U.S. 389 (1993) (standard for competency to plead guilty or waive counsel no more stringent than for competency to stand trial); *see* Michael L. Perlin, *"Dignity Was the First to Leave": Godinez v. Moran, Colin Ferguson, and the Trial of Mentally Disabled Criminal Defendants*, 14 BEHAV. SCI. & L. 61 (1996); *see generally infra* Chapter 9.

[106]504 U.S. 127 (1992); *see generally* Michael L. Perlin, *Decoding Right to Refuse Treatment Law*, 16 INT'L J.L. & PSYCHIATRY 151 (1993); *see infra* Chapter 6.

[107]504 U.S. 71 (1992); *see generally* Michael L. Perlin, *"No Direction Home": The Law and Criminal Defendants With Mental Disabilities*, 20 MENT. & PHYS. DIS. L. REP. 605 (1996).

[108]Although beyond the scope of this book, Justice Thomas's majority opinion in Kansas v. Hendricks, 521 U.S. 346 (1997) (upholding Kansas's Sexually Violent Predator Act), *see* 1 PERLIN, *supra* note 8, § 2A-3.3, at 75–92 (2d ed. 1998), reflects precisely the same sort of stunted and pretextual OCS. *See generally* Michael L. Perlin, *"There's No Success Like Failure/and Failure's No Success at All": Exposing the Pretextuality of* Kansas v. Hendricks, 92 Nw. U. L. REV. 1247 (1998).

[109]Perlin, *supra* note 105, at 81.

[110]Perlin, *supra* note 107, at 607.

[111]Michael L. Perlin, *What Is Therapeutic Jurisprudence?* 10 N.Y.L. SCH. J. HUM. RTS. 623, 635 (1993), see *infra* Chapters 6, 9, and 10.

[112]*See also* Craig Haney, *Psychology and Legal Change: On the Limits of a Factual Jurisprudence*, 4 LAW & HUM. BEHAV. 147, 154 (1980) ("Courts regularly and routinely make assumptions about how and why people behave in certain ways"). For a rare example of a judicial opinion "unpacking" the mythology that serves as the building blocks of OCS, see United States v. Lyons, 739 F.2d 994, 999–1000 (5th Cir. 1984) (Rubin, J., dissenting), discussed *supra* text accompanying note 78.

[113]Michael L. Perlin, *Psychiatric Testimony in a Criminal Setting*, 3 BULL. AM. ACAD. PSYCHIATRY & L. 143, 147 (1975).

[114]Harold D. Lasswell, *Foreword*, to RICHARD ARENS, THE INSANITY DEFENSE xi (1974). For an empirical evaluation of how defendants who do so conform are differentially treated by prosecutors and by courts, see Henrik Hochstedler, *Twice-Cursed? The Mentally Disordered Criminal Defendant*, 14 CRIM. JUST. & BEHAV. 251, 260 (1987) (mentally disabled defendants were prosecuted in "significant[ly]" different ways from the general population; courts commonly subjected mentally disabled defendants to court-ordered treatment and were reluctant to release on their own recognizance previously hospitalized defendants; prosecutors showed "selective leniency," issuing charges less frequently to the formerly hospitalized but more frequently to defendants with histories of chronic health problems). On the ways that correctional officials perceive mentally ill inmates less favorably than other inmates, see R. Randall Kropp et al., *The Perceptions of Correctional Officers Toward Mentally Disordered Offenders*, 12 INT'L J.L. & PSYCHIATRY 181 (1989).

"slippery slope" conflation of mental illness and dangerousness is blindly accepted.[115] Views such as these[116] reflect a false kind of "ordinary common sense,"[117] a falseness that is made even more pernicious by the fact that we "believe most easily what [we] most fear and most desire."[118] In criminal procedure, OCS presupposes two "self-evident" truths: "First, everyone knows how to assess an individual's behavior. Second, everyone knows when to blame someone for doing wrong."[119]

One example should suffice. Empirical investigations similarly corroborate the inappropriate application of OCS to insanity-defense decision making.[120] Judges "unconsciously express public feelings . . . reflect[ing] community attitudes and biases because they are 'close' to the community."[121] Virtually no members of the public can actually articulate what the substantive insanity defense test is.[122] The public is seriously misinformed about both the "extensiveness and consequences" of an insanity defense plea.[123]

---

[115]Jones v. United States, 463 U.S. 354, 365 n.14 (1983), quoting Overholser v. O'Beirne, 302 F.2d 852, 861 (D.C. Cir. 1961) (Burger, J.) ("To describe the theft of watches and jewelry as 'nondangerous' is to confuse danger with violence. Larceny is usually less violent than murder or assault, but in terms of public policy the purpose of the [postinsanity acquittal commitment] statute is the same as to both").

[116]*See also, e.g.,* Anthony Amsterdam, *The Supreme Court and the Rights of Suspects in Criminal Cases,* 45 N.Y.U. L. REV. 785, 805–09 (1980) (discussing Supreme Court's implicit use of OCS in deciding the lead confession–coercion case of Brown v. Mississippi, 297 U.S. 278 (1936)).

[117]Sherwin, *Dialects, supra* note 5, at 737. One important example of such thinking is reflected in courts' persistent adherence to patterns of jury instructions in spite of overwhelming social science evidence as to the instructions' confusion. Professors Steele and Thornburg thus articulate the OCS position: "Since [judges and lawyers] understand the instructions, they believe that jurors understand them as well." Walter W. Steele & Elizabeth G. Thornburg, *Jury Instructions: A Persistent Failure to Communicate,* 67 N.C. L. REV. 77, 99 (1988).

On how jurors' verdicts in criminal cases reflect "common sense justice," see NORMAN FINKEL, COMMONSENSE JUSTICE: JURORS' NOTION OF THE LAW (1995); *see also, e.g.,* Norman Finkel & Christopher Slobogin, *Insanity, Justification, and Culpability: Toward a Unifying Scheme,* 19 LAW & HUM. BEHAV. 447 (1995); Norman Finkel, *Culpability and Commonsense Justice: Lessons Learned Betwixt Murder and Madness,* 10 NOTRE DAME J.L., ETHICS & PUB. POL'Y 11 (1996).

[118]Thomas Barton, *Violence and the Collapse of the Imagination,* 81 IOWA L. REV. 1249, 1249 (1996) (book review of WENDY KAMINER, IT'S ALL THE RAGE: CRIME AND CULTURE (1995)).

[119]Sherwin, *Dialects, supra* note 5, at 738; *see also* Doob & Roberts, *supra* note 27, at 275 (public "appears simply to accept the information they have as adequate" in assessing perceived leniency of criminal sentences); Loretta J. Stalans & Shari Seidman Diamond, *Formation and Change in Lay Evaluations of Criminal Sentencing: Misperception and Discontent,* 14 LAW & HUM. BEHAV. 199 (1990).

[120]*See, e.g.,* Norman J. Finkel et al., *Insanity Defenses: From the Jurors' Perspectives,* 9 LAW & PSYCHOL. REV. 77, 92 (1985) (characterizing the layman's perspective toward the insanity defense as reflecting "intuitive, common sense"). *Cf.* State v. Van Horn, 528 So.2d 529, 530 (Fla. Dist. App. 1988) (rebuttal lay witness provided jury with "probative perceptions of *normalcy*") (emphasis added), discussed *supra* text accompanying note 81.

[121]Richard Arens & Jackwell Susman, *Judges, Jury Charges, and Insanity,* 13 HOW. L.J. 1, 34 n.43 (1966). The case law reflects each of these traps. *See, e.g.,* Regina v. Turner, 1 Q.B. 834, 841 (1975) ("Jurors do not need psychiatrists to tell them how ordinary folk who are not suffering from any mental illness are likely to react to the stresses and strains of life"). Finkel's research suggests that expert witnesses reinforce this sense of conventional morality as well. N. FINKEL, INSANITY ON TRIAL 349 (1985).

[122]Of 434 Delaware residents surveyed, only one gave a "reasonably good approximation" of the insanity test then operative in that jurisdiction. Valerie P. Hans & Dan Slater, *"Plain Crazy": Lay Definitions of Legal Insanity,* 7 INT'L J.L. & PSYCHIATRY 105–06 (1984). *See also* Rogers et al., *supra* note 97 (88% of experienced forensic witnesses did not know the correct substantive insanity standard in their jurisdiction).

[123]Valerie P. Hans, *An Analysis of Public Attitudes Toward the Insanity Defense,* 24 CRIMINOL. 393, 411 (1986).

And the public explicitly and consistently rejects any such defense substantively broader than the "wild beast" test.[124]

These realities may lead into yet one more trap. Although judges and attorneys are accustomed to weighing and interpreting several factors at once, conflict arises "from the attorney's fear that a jury will reject, or will be less impressed by, explanations that require complex analysis and a lengthy rationale."[125] Yet other research shows that mock jurors often use their own schemas when deciding the outcome of an insanity defense trial, and that variables such as the burden or standard of proof may not have a significant effect on their deliberations.[126] And the truth claims to which OCS gives rise are "complex and conflicting and revelatory perhaps of diverse situational factors, such as geography, class, education, familial background, religion, and current events. . . ."[127]

Contemporary psychologists and researchers are no strangers to these issues. In a study of the beliefs of 100 psychologists about depression and antidepressive behavior, consensus about the truth of certain assertions ranged from total to near complete disagreement. This prompted the study's director to conclude that a far greater study was needed in exploring "the paradoxically unknown territory of 'what everybody knows' about depression."[128]

In the same vein, the terrain of "what everybody knows" about insanity is perilously unchartered.[129] Yet courts and legislatures regularly base decisions on perceptions (or, more likely, misperceptions) about OCS and mental illness. In a related context, for instance, recent research demonstrates that all segments of the public lacked substantial knowledge about battered woman's syndrome, but subsamples of police officers and individuals eligible to be jurors knew the least.[130]

---

[124]Caton F. Roberts et al., *Implicit Theories of Criminal Responsibility Decision Making and the Insanity Defense*, 11 LAW & HUM. BEHAV. 207, 226 (1987). *Cf.* Washington v. United States, 390 F.2d 444, 445 (D.C. Cir. 1967) ("Presumably, [the 18th-century] jury and the witnesses knew a wild beast when they saw one").

[125]Patricia Anderten et al., *On Being Ethical in Legal Places*, 11 PROF. PSYCHOL. 764, 769 (1980). ("Thus, the psychologist might be led into this more simplistic manner of reasoning that scientifically and ethically misrepresents the complexity of most psychological conclusions and potentially distorts the results.)"

[126]James R. P. Ogloff, *A Comparison on Insanity Defense Standards on Juror Decision Making*, 15 LAW & HUM. BEHAV. 509, 524 (1991); *see also* Laurence J. Severance & Elizabeth F. Loftus, *Improving the Ability of Jurors to Comprehend and Apply Criminal Jury Instructions*, 17 LAW & SOC'Y REV. 153 (1992).

[127]Sherwin, *Dialects, supra* note 5, at 829. On the way different ethnic and socioeconomic groups perceive and define deviance, *see* Bruce Dohrenwend & Edwin Chin-Song, *Social Status and Attitudes Toward Psychological Disorder: The Problem of Tolerance of Deviance*, 32 AM. SOC. REV. 417 (1967); *see also, e.g.,* Joseph R. Gusfield, *On Legislating Morals: The Symbolic Process of Designating Deviance*, 56 CALIF. L. REV. 54, 55–56 (1968) ("To assume a common culture or a normative consensus in American society, as in most modern societies, is to ignore the deep and divisive role of class, ethnic, religious, status, and regional culture conflicts which often produce widely opposing definitions of goodness, truth, and moral virtue"). *Cf.* Martha A. Myers, *Social Background and the Sentencing Behavior of Judges*, 26 CRIMINOL. 649, 669 (1988) (older judges found to be more lenient to the "selected, advantaged offenders, in particular, those who were white and older"), to Cecil L. Willis & Richard L. Wells, *The Police and Child Abuse: An Analysis of Police Decisions to Report Illegal Behavior*, 26 CRIMINOL. 695, 711 (1988) (police more likely to report white families for child physical and sexual abuse, perhaps reflecting "negative stereotyping of [B]lack life-style and behavior"). *See also, e.g.,* Randall Gordon et al., *Majority Group Perceptions of Criminal Behavior: The Accuracy of Race-Related Crime Stereotypes*, 26 J. APPLIED SOC. PSYCHOL. 148 (1996) (role of racial stereotypes in perceptions of criminal behaviors).

[128]Vicky Rippere, *Commonsense Beliefs About Depression and Antidepressive Behaviour: A Study of Social Consensus*, 15 BEHAV. RES. & THERAPY 465, 467 (1977); *see also, e.g.,* Vicky Rippere, *"What's the Thing to Do When You're Feeling Depressed?"—A Pilot Study*, 15 BEHAV. RES. & THERAPY 185 (1977).

[129]*See* Richard Rogers et al., *Forensic Psychiatrists and Psychologists' Understanding of Insanity: Misguided Expertise?*, 33 CANAD. J. PSYCHIATRY 671 (1988) (on high level of misinformation on part of experienced forensic psychiatrists as to proper legal standard).

[130]Debra Kronsky & Brian Cutler, *The Battered Woman Syndrome: A Matter of Common Sense?* 2 FORENS. REPS. 173 (1989).

Just as OCS cannot be used as the tool by which confessions or confrontation clause law developments can be charted, neither is it applicable to insanity defense law jurisprudence, where human behavior is very often opposite to what OCS would suggest. The reliance on such propositions by legal decision makers is risky, at best, and probably reflective of a refusal to acknowledge the bases and applicability of psychodynamic principles to the questions at hand.[131]

Conclusion

Human beings seek to simplify our information-processing tasks by engaging in heuristic thinking and by taking refuge in a false OCS. Both of these limiting and narrowing devices cut us adrift from critical thinking and both offer overly pat solutions for complex behavior. Through the typification and vividness heuristics, we highlight the ''worst-case'' anecdote and make that a template for all behavior (and all expected outcomes). Our use of the attribution heuristic reifies preexisting stereotypes and allows us to wilfully blind ourselves to the gray areas of human behavior. OCS is the ultimate form of self-referentiality, and its use stops us from looking at issues from external or alternative points of view. Most important, both the use of heuristics and OCS help create an environment in which sanism and pretextuality can fester. It is to these concepts that I now turn.

---

[131]*See, e.g.,* GROUP FOR THE ADVANCEMENT OF PSYCHIATRY, CRIMINAL RESPONSIBILITY AND PSYCHIATRIC TESTIMONY, Report #26 (May, 1954), at 1 (''It is abundantly clear that not all individuals are accountable—even the *M'Naghten* rules accept this—and that the problem involves more than 'common sense''').

Chapter 2
ON SANISM

Imagine the uproar if a published appellate court decision in 1974 referred to an adult person of color as a "boy." Imagine the fallout if the *New York Times* stated in 1964 that *Plessy v. Ferguson* was the lead case on the question of "separate but equal" accommodations. Imagine if, 10 years after *Roe v. Wade,* a member of Congress had been complimented for his "thoughtful" remarks when he stated that not only was it still legal to criminalize first-trimester abortions but that a state could also lawfully bar all women from using contraception. Imagine if left-liberal candidates in one of the most progressive legislative districts in the country ran for office on a platform of excluding racial minorities from living in that district.

These acts would quickly—and correctly—be labeled either as racist, sexist, or bizarre, and would be decried by well-meaning citizens on virtually all points on the political spectrum. Yet when we substitute "person with mental disability" for "person of color," "racial minority" or "woman," we let such acts pass without notice or comment.[1] In fact, when a sitting state trial court judge endorsed Judge Oliver Wendell Holmes' infamous *dictum* from *Buck v. Bell*—that "three generations of imbeciles are enough"—his endorsement was greeted with total silence.[2]

These examples are not exceptional. They reflect, rather, an irrational prejudice (an "ism") not unlike other irrational prejudices that cause (and are reflected in) prevailing social attitudes of racism, sexism, homophobia, and ethnic bigotry[3] and that have similarly been reflected both in the U.S. legal system and in the ways that lawyers represent clients. This prejudice, which I call "sanism," infects both our jurisprudence and our lawyering

---

[1]*See, e.g.,* State v. Johnston, 527 P.2d 1310, 1312 (Wash. 1974) (defendant was a 30-year-old college graduate; defense counsel asserted to trial court that he was a "highly intelligent boy"); Ira Mickenberg, *A Pleasant Surprise: The Guilty but Mentally Ill Verdict Has Succeeded in Its Own Right and Successfully Preserved the Insanity Defense,* 55 U. CIN. L. REV. 943, 946–47 n.14 (1987), quoting Steven Roberts, *High U.S. Officials Express Outrage, Asking for New Law on Insanity Plea,* N.Y. TIMES, June 23, 1982, at B6, col. 3 (asserting that Durham v. United States, 214 F.2d 862 (D.C. Cir. 1954), *overruled,* United States v. Brawner, 471 U.S. 2d 969, 981 (D.C. Cir. 1972), was the operative insanity test at the time of the *Hinckley* acquittal); *Insanity Defense in Federal Courts: Hearings Before the Subcomm. on Criminal Justice of the House Comm. on the Judiciary,* 97th Cong., 2d Sess., at 151, 153 (1982) (statement of Rep. Lagomarsino; response of Rep. Conyers) (same assertion as to operative test; also asserting that, under the *Durham* test, the insanity defense was expanded to include "heartburn and itching"); Michael L. Perlin, *Competency, Deinstitutionalization, and Homelessness: A Story of Marginalization,* 28 HOUS. L. REV. 63, 93 n.173 (1991) (citing examples of demands for residential exclusion).

[2]274 U.S. 200 (1927); Kenneth Robertson, *Letter to the Editor,* 11 DEVELOPMENTS IN MENTAL HEALTH LAW 4 (Jan.–June 1991).

[3]The classic study is GORDON W. ALLPORT, THE NATURE OF PREJUDICE (1955). *But see* ELISABETH YOUNG-BRUEHL, THE ANATOMY OF PREJUDICES (1996), discussed *infra* text accompanying notes 53–56.

practices.[4] It reflects what civil rights lawyer Florynce Kennedy has characterized as "the pathology of oppression."[5]

Sanism is as insidious as other "isms" and is, in some ways, more troubling, because it is (a) largely invisible, (b) largely socially acceptable, and (c) frequently practiced (consciously and unconsciously) by individuals who regularly take "liberal" or "progressive" positions decrying similar biases and prejudices that involve sex, race, ethnicity, or sexual orientation.[6] It is a form of bigotry that "respectable people can express in public."[7] Like other "isms," sanism is based largely on stereotype, myth, superstition, and deindividualization. To sustain and perpetuate it, we use prereflective "ordinary common sense" (OCS) and other cognitive-simplifying devices such as heuristic reasoning[8] in an unconscious response to events both in everyday life and in the legal process. The way that some members of the Senate Judiciary Committee obsessively focused on Anita Hill's alleged psychiatric disorders in an effort to discredit her testimony charging Judge Clarence Thomas with sexual harassment reflected this stereotyping at its most insidious.[9]

---

[4]The term *sanism* was, to the best of my knowledge, coined by Morton Birnbaum. *See* Morton Birnbaum, *The Right to Treatment: Some Comments on Its Development, in* MEDICAL MORAL AND LEGAL ISSUES IN HEALTH CARE 97, 106–07 (Frank Ayd ed. 1974); Koe v. Califano, 573 F.2d 761, 764 n.12 (2d Cir. 1978). I discuss this insight of Birnbaum's in Perlin, *supra* note 1, at 92–93. Birnbaum is universally regarded as having first developed and articulated the constitutional basis of the right-to-treatment doctrine for institutionalized mental patients. *See* Morton Birnbaum, *The Right to Treatment,* 46 A.B.A. J. 499 (1960), *discussed in* 2 MICHAEL L. PERLIN, MENTAL DISABILITY LAW: CIVIL AND CRIMINAL § 3A-2.1, at 8–12 (2d ed. 1999).

I recognize that the use of the word *sanism* (based on the root "sane" or "sanity") is troubling from another perspective: The notion of "sanity" or "insanity" is a legal construct that has been rejected by psychiatrists, psychologists, and other behavioralists for more than 150 years. I nevertheless use it here, in part to reflect the way that inaccurate, outdated, and distorted language has confounded the underlying political and social issues and in part to demonstrate how ignorance continues to contribute to this bias.

[5]Birnbaum, *supra* note 4, at 107 (quoting Kennedy). *See also id.* at 106 ("It should be understood that sanists are bigots").

[6]*See, e.g.,* DAVID ROTHMAN & SHEILA ROTHMAN, THE WILLOWBROOK WARS 188–89 (1984) (discussing role of paradigmatically liberal Rep. Elizabeth Holtzman in attempting to block group homes for mentally retarded individuals from opening in her district).

It is also demonstrated by those attempting to illuminate how "political correctness" can inappropriately stereotype other groups. Thus in the course of Douglas Laycock's criticism of Wendy Brown's purportedly biased depictions of beer-drinking, men's-magazine-reading, hunting-club members (*see* Wendy Brown, *Guns, Cowboys, Philadelphia Mayors, and Civic Republicanism: On Sanford Levinson's The Embarrassing Second Amendment,* 99 YALE L.J. 661, 666–67 (1989)), Laycock implicitly exempts "psychopaths" from his proscription: "There are indeed people in our society who have no more respect for humans than for animals. We call them psychopaths and when they act on their impulses and we catch them, we lock them up." Douglas Laycock, *Vicious Stereotypes,* 8 CONST. COMMENTARY 395, 399 (1991).

[7]*Cf.* J. Michael Bailey & Richard Pillard, *Are Some People Born Gay?* N.Y. TIMES, Dec. 17, 1991, at A21 (arguing that *homophobia* is the only form of bigotry that can be expressed).

[8]I explain how these approaches have distorted U.S. insanity defense policies in Michael L. Perlin, *Unpacking the Myths: The Symbolism Mythology of Insanity Defense Jurisprudence,* 40 CASE W. RES. L. REV. 599 (1989–90) [hereinafter Perlin. *Myths*], and Michael L. Perlin, *Psychodynamics and the Insanity Defense: "Ordinary Common Sense" and Heuristic Reasoning,* 69 NEB. L. REV. 3 (1990) [hereinafter Perlin, *OCS*]; *see generally* MICHAEL L. PERLIN, THE JURISPRUDENCE OF THE INSANITY DEFENSE (1994); *see infra* Chapter 10.

[9]*See, e.g.,* Allesandra Stanley, *Erotomania: A Rare Disorder Runs Riot—In Men's Minds,* N.Y. TIMES, Nov. 10, 1991, § 4, at 2; Steve Wick, *Psychoanalysis Via TV: She's Not Crazy,* NEWSDAY, Oct. 16, 1991, at 21; Rupert Cornwell, *Out of the West: Mysteries of Sex Too Much for America,* THE INDEPENDENT, Oct. 6, 1991, at 11; *To The Witness,* N.Y. TIMES, Oct. 17, 1991 § A, at 26 (editorial); Stanley Greenspan & Nancy Greenspan, *Lies, Delusions and Truths: The Abuse of Psychiatry in the Thomas Hearings,* WASH. POST, Oct. 29, 1991, at 6; Peter Breggin, *Abuse of Privilege,* 7 TIKKUN 17 (Jan.–Feb. 1992). The Thomas hearings is not the only recent example. *See, e.g., Psychologists Cleared in Remarks on Dukakis,* WASH. TIMES, Dec. 11, 1989, at A6; Anthony Flint, *Board Ends Inquiry of Psychologists,* BOSTON GLOBE, Dec. 9, 1989, at 29 (on Kitty Dukakis); Goldwater v. Ginsberg, 414 F.2d 324, 328–30 (2d Cir. 1969), *cert. denied,* 396 U.S. 1049 (1970) (on Barry Goldwater).

The practicing bar, courts, legislatures, professional psychiatric and psychological associations, and the scholarly academy are all largely silent about sanism. A few practitioners, lawmakers, scholars, and judges have raised lonely voices,[10] but the topic is simply off the agenda for most members of these groups. As a result, individuals with mental disabilities—"the voiceless, those persons traditionally isolated from the majoritarian democratic political system"—are frequently marginalized to an even greater extent than are others who fit within the *Carolene Products* definition of "discrete and insular minorities."[11] The Americans With Disabilities Act[12] cites this very language in its findings section; at this time, however, it is not at all clear whether this statement will be viewed merely as aspirational or as a congressional command for authentic behavioral and societal change.[13]

At its base, sanism is irrational. Any investigation of the roots or sources of mental disability jurisprudence must factor in society's irrational mechanisms that govern our dealings with mentally disabled individuals.[14] The entire legal system makes assumptions about persons with mental disabilities—who they are, how they got that way, what makes them different, what there is about them that lets us treat them differently, and whether their conditions are immutable.[15] These assumptions reflect our fears and apprehensions about mental disability, persons with mental disability, and the possibility that *we* may become mentally disabled.[16] The most important question of all—why do we feel the way we do about these people?—is rarely asked.[17]

---

[10]*See, e.g.,* Martha Minow, *When Difference Has Its Home: Group Homes for the Mentally Retarded, Equal Protection and Legal Treatment of Difference,* 22 HARV. C.R.-C.L. L. REV. 22 (1987); David Bazelon, *Institutionalization, Deinstitutionalization, and the Adversary Process,* 75 COLUM. L. REV. 897 (1975); City of Cleburne v. Cleburne Living Ctr., 473 U.S. 432, 454 (1985) (Stevens, J., concurring) (mentally retarded individuals subjected to "history of unfair and often grotesque mistreatment"), quoting 726 F.2d 191, 197 (5th Cir. 1974) (decision below), *and id.,* at 461 (Marshall, J., concurring in part and dissenting in part) ("virulence and bigotry" of state-mandated segregation of the institutionalized mentally retarded "rivaled, and indeed paralleled, the worst excesses of Jim Crow").

For recent scholarly considerations of sanism, *see, e.g.,* PETER BLANCK, THE AMERICANS WITH DISABILITIES ACT AND THE EMERGING WORKFORCE: EMPLOYMENT OF PEOPLE WITH MENTAL RETARDATION 59–60 (1998); Grant Morris, *Defining Dangerousness: Risking a Dangerous Definition,* 10 J. CONTEMP. LEGAL ISSUES 61 (1999); Bruce Winick, *Therapeutic Jurisprudence and the Civil Commitment Hearing,* 10 J. CONTEMP. LEGAL ISSUES 37 (1999).

[11]I discuss United States v. Carolene Prods. Co., 304 U.S. 144, 152 n.4 (1938), more broadly in this context in Michael L. Perlin, *State Constitutions and Statutes as Sources of Rights for the Mentally Disabled: The Last Frontier?* 20 LOY. L.A. L. REV. 1249, 1250–51 (1987).

[12]42 U.S.C. § 12101(a)(7).

[13]*See* Michael L. Perlin, *"Make Promises by the Hour": Sex, Drugs, the ADA, and Psychiatric Hospitalization,* 46 DEPAUL L. REV. 947, 958–60 (1997). *See* Olmstead v. L.C., 119 S. Ct. 2176 (1999), discussed extensively *infra* chapter 8.

[14]*See generally* Perlin, *Myths, supra* note 8.

[15]*See generally* MARTHA MINOW, MAKING ALL THE DIFFERENCE: INCLUSION, EXCLUSION AND AMERICAN LAW (1990); SANDER GILMAN, DIFFERENCE AND PATHOLOGY: STEREOTYPES OF SEXUALITY, RACE AND MADNESS (1985).

[16]*See, e.g.,* Joseph Goldstein & Jay Katz, *Abolish the "Insanity Defense"—Why Not?* 72 YALE L.J. 853, 868–69 (1963); Perlin, *supra* note 1, at 108 (on society's fears of persons with mental disabilities), and *id.,* at 93 n.174 ("While race and sex are immutable, we all *can* become mentally ill, homeless, or both. Perhaps this illuminates the level of virulence we experience here") (emphasis in original). On the way that public fears about the purported link between mental illness and dangerousness "drive the formal laws and policies governing mental disability jurisprudence," see John Monahan, *Mental Disorder and Violent Behavior: Perceptions and Evidence,* 47 AM. PSYCHOLOGIST 511, 511 (1992).

[17]*See* Perlin OCS, *supra* note 8, at 6–7 (asking this question). *Cf.* Carmel Rogers, *Proceedings Under the Mental Health Act 1992: The Legalisation of Psychiatry,* 1994 N.Z. L.J. 404, 408 ("Because the preserve of psychiatry is populated by 'the mad' and 'the loonies,' we do not really want to look at it too closely—it is too frightening and maybe contaminated").

These conflicts compel an inquiry about the extent to which social science data does (or should) inform the development of mental disability law jurisprudence. After all, if we agree that mentally disabled individuals can be treated differently (because of their mental disability or because of behavioral characteristics that flow from that disability),[18] it would appear logical that this difference in legal treatment is—or should be—founded on some sort of empirical database that confirms both the *existence* and the *causal role* of such difference. Yet we tend to ignore, subordinate, or trivialize behavioral research in this area, especially when acknowledging that such research would be cognitively dissonant with intuitive (albeit empirically flawed) views.[19] And the steady stream of publication of new, comprehensive research does not promise any change in society's attitudes.[20]

These ends are sanist. Sanist attitudes also lead to pretextual decisions. As I will demonstrate, the legal system regularly accepts (either implicitly or explicitly) dishonest testimony in mental disability cases and countenances liberty deprivations in disingenuous ways that bear little or no relationship to case law or to statutes.[21] This pretextuality—along with sanism—drives the mental disability law system.

In this chapter I will first discuss stereotypes and stereotyping behavior, then consider some other "isms" that have been the focus of far greater academic and public attention as well as the way the legal system has responded (or has failed to respond). I will then consider the specific roots of sanism, the public attitudes that reify and perpetuate sanism, and the myths of sanism. Finally, I will examine how the legal system is a sanist system.

The Development of Other "Isms": On Stereotyping

Stereotypes are the "attribution of general psychological characteristics to large human groups."[22] The first step of forming stereotypes is categorization: For us to be able to single out, perceive, and treat members of a social group in a discriminatory way, we must be able to attribute some identifiable features to classify them as group members.[23] We frequently behave more generously toward members of a group to which we see ourselves as belonging, and we perceive such individuals in a more favorable light on a variety of personal and social characteristics.[24]

According to the social psychologist Gordon Allport, stereotypes are attitudes that result in "gross oversimplification of experience and in prejudgments."[25] The separation of

---

[18]On the Supreme Court's confusion over the meaning of "mental disorder," see 1 PERLIN, *supra* note 4, § 2A-3.3, at 75–92 (2d ed. 1998), discussing Kansas v. Hendricks, 521 U.S. 346 (1997), (upholding Kansas's Sexually Violent Predator Act). KAN. STAT. ANN. §§ 59–29a01 et seq.

[19]*See generally* J. Alexander Tanford, *The Limits of a Scientific Jurisprudence: The Supreme Court and Psychology,* 66 IND. L.J. 137 (1990).

[20]For the most comprehensive research on predictions of violence, e.g., see John Monahan, *Clinical and Actuarial Predictions of Violence, in* MODERN SCIENTIFIC EVIDENCE: THE LAW AND SCIENCE OF EXPERT TESTIMONY, §§ 7-2.0 to 7-2.4, at 300 (David Faigman et al., eds. 1997).

[21]*See generally infra* Chapter 3.

[22]Henri Tajfel, *Cognitive Aspects of Prejudice,* 25 J. SOC. ISSUES 79, 81–82 (1969). *See generally* Larry Alexander, *What Makes Wrongful Discrimination Wrong? Biases, Preferences, Stereotypes, and Proxies,* 141 U. PA. L. REV. 149 (1992).

[23]David L. Hamilton, *Cognitive Biases in the Perception of Social Groups, in* COGNITION AND SOCIAL BEHAVIOR 81, 83 (John S. Carroll & John W. Payne eds. 1976).

[24]*Id.* at 84; *see, e.g.,* Michael Billig & Henri Tajfel, *Social Categorization and Similarity in Intergroup Behavior,* 3 EUR. J. SOC. PSYCHOLOGY 27 (1973); Willem Doise & Anne Sinclair, *The Categorisation Process in Intergroup Relations,* 3 EUR. J. SOC. PSYCHOLOGY 145 (1973).

[25]Gordon W. Allport, *Attitudes, in* HANDBOOK OF SOCIAL PSYCHOLOGY 809 (Carl Murchison ed. 1935). Although I am stressing the social–psychological view of stereotyping, that is by no means the only helpful theoretical construct of prejudice. Authoritarianism and the authoritarian personality are discussed in this context in Richard Delgado et al., *Fairness and Formality: Minimizing the Risk of Prejudice in Alternative Dispute*

others into categorized groups is enough to trigger the psychological processes leading to intergroup prejudice,[26] which Adorno has defined as "an antipathy based upon a faulty and inflexible generalization."[27] This act of separation is frequently at the basis of what can be called "ismic" behavior.[28]

Operating as "relatively rigid and oversimplified or biased perception[s] . . . of an aspect of reality," stereotypes efficiently, but mostly inaccurately, generalize in ways that have little basis in individual fact or practical experience, that are based on preconceived and misinformed opinions about the nature of difference, that make little reference to actual information, and that imply cause-and-effect relationships that do not exist.[29] They operate in the same way as do other fundamental cognitive errors—heuristics—that frequently lead to distorted and systematically erroneous decisions through ignoring or misusing rationally useful information.[30] They do this through the use of exaggeration, emotionally toned intergroup labels, dichotomization, and overgeneralization.[31] We stereotype those we fear (or those who make us anxious) because of their differences.[32]

It is ironic that stereotypes help us restructure and impose order on the world in a way that reduces anxiety, and lend an appearance of legitimacy and "self-evident truth to what we have invented":[33] "Our internal, mental representations of the world become the world. We act as if this world were real, external to ourselves. . . ."[34]

Labels accompany stereotypes. These labels stigmatize, assign negative associations to an outsider, "complicate any effort to resist the designation implied by difference,"[35] and allow the labeler to fail to imagine the perspective of the outsider.[36] Labels are especially

---

Resolution, 1985 WIS. L. REV. 1359, 1375–77; Delgado, *Campus Antiracism Rules: Constitutional Narratives in Collision,* 85 NW. U. L. REV. 343, 372 (1991); *see generally* THEODOR W. ADORNO ET AL., THE AUTHORITARIAN PERSONALITY (1969); Michael L. Perlin, *"The Borderline Which Separated You From Me": The Insanity Defense, the Authoritarian Spirit, the Fear of Faking, and the Culture of Punishment,* 82 IOWA L. REV. 1375 (1997) [hereinafter Perlin, *Borderline*]; PERLIN, JURISPRUDENCE, *supra* note 8, at 331–75.

[26]ALLPORT, *supra* note 3, at 20. On the significance of categorization in this context, see MINOW, *supra* note 15, at 21.

[27]ALLPORT, *supra* note 3, at 9.

[28]*See generally* Anne E. Freedman, *Feminist Legal Method in Action: Challenging Racism, Sexism and Homophobia in Law School,* 24 GA. L. REV. 849 (1990).

[29]Arthur G. Miller, *Historical and Contemporary Perspectives on Stereotyping, in* IN THE EYE OF THE BEHOLDER 1, 4 (A. Miller ed. 1982); Gary Minda, *The Jurisprudential Movements of the 1980s,* 50 OHIO ST. L.J. 599, 602 n.12 (1988); Anita Cava, *The Judicial Notice of Sexual Stereotyping,* 43 ARK. L. REV. 27, 32 (1990); Joshua A. Fishman, *A Examination of the Process and Function of Social Stereotyping,* 43 J. SOC. PSYCHOLOGY 27, 31 (1956).

[30]*See* Perlin, *OCS, supra* note 8, at 12–22; Michael J. Saks & Robert F. Kidd, *Human Information Processing and Adjudication: Trial by Heuristics,* 15 LAW & SOC'Y REV. 123 (1980–81). For further discussion on involuntary civil commitment; *see generally supra* section 1.

[31]ALLPORT, *supra* note 3, at 178, 191, 400–08.

[32]Helen Hershkoff & Adam S. Cohen, *Begging to Differ: The First Amendment and the Right to Beg,* 104 HARV. L. REV. 896, 913–14 (1991). On the ways that social images of Black welfare mothers differ from those of White welfare mothers (and its impact of welfare policy "reform"), see Martin Gilens, *"Race Coding" and White Opposition to Welfare,* 90 AM. POL. SCI. REV. 593 (1996).

[33]MINOW, *supra* note 15, at 179.

[34]GILMAN, *supra* note 15, at 240. On the role of the unconscious in the creation of stereotypes, see, e.g., Sheri Lynn Johnson, *Unconscious Racism and the Criminal Law,* 73 CORNELL L. REV. 1016, 1027–29 (1988); *see generally* Charles Lawrence, *The Id, the Ego, and Equal Protection: Reckoning With Unconscious Racism,* 39 STAN. L. REV. 317 (1986). On the role of the unconscious in the development of the criminal law, see, e.g., Perlin, *Myths, supra* note 8; PERLIN, JURISPRUDENCE, *supra* note 8, at 37–71.

[35]Martha Minow, *Forward: Justice Engendered,* 101 HARV. L. REV. 10, 38 (1987); GILMAN, *supra* note 15, at 12, 18–35.

[36]MINOW, *supra* note 15, at 51 n.201. *See generally* N.Y. State Office of Mental Health, *Final Report: Task Force on Stigma and Discrimination* (March 6, 1990), at 1–2 ("Stigma Task Force").

pernicious, because they frequently lead labeled individuals to internalize negative expectations and social practices that majoritarian society identifies as characteristically endemic to the labeled group.[37] From these labels, "categorizations assume a life of their own."[38] In turn, any act that fails to follow standards set by a dominant group becomes a deviation.[39]

Through the use of stereotypes and labels, we structure polarized and dichotomized categories: If a positive image is of an industrious, intelligent, knowledgable, law-abiding, and responsible self, the correlative negative image is of a lazy, unintelligent, immoral, ignorant, criminal, shiftless other.[40] Historically, society has negatively stereotyped Blacks, women, Asians, Jews, Catholics, gays, Native Americans, physically disabled persons, physically unattractive persons, and others. These stereotypes have often been premised on political, scientific, religious, and cultural theories that, in turn, relied on other distorted stereotypes and characterizations.[41]

Structural anthropology may offer some help in explaining how we construct these polarizations.[42] Structuralists agree that all culture consists of sets of concepts that are in psychological tension with each other—we cannot, for example, make sense of *black* without realizing that it contrasts with *white;* we cannot understand *citizenship* without understanding that it contrasts with *alienage.*[43] Richard Merelman has characterized the phenomena in this way: "Such narratives appear in myths, rituals, popular culture, ceremonies or even institutionalized behavior in which exemplary persons (heroes, villains, etc.) . . . depict components of the sets themselves. In effect, such persons 'act out,' 'display,' or 'exercise' the culture."[44] And, as forensic psychiatrist Douglas Mossman, in an article looking at the way we construct the category of "mentally ill homeless persons," has explained,

---

[37]Note, *Teaching Inequality: The Problem of Public School Tracking,* 102 HARV. L. REV. 1318, 1333 (1989); *see generally* Louis A. Weithorn, *Mental Hospitalization of Troublesome Youth: An Analysis of Skyrocketing Admission Rates,* 40 STAN. L. REV. 773, 805–07, 820–26 (1988); Robert W. Sweet, *Deinstitutionalization of Status Offenders: In Perspective,* 18 PEPP. L. REV. 389 (1991).

[38]Richard Delgado et al., *Fairness and Formality: Minimizing the Risk of Prejudice in Alternative Dispute Resolution,* 1985 WIS. L. REV. 1359, 1381 (1985) at 1381: ("What enables people to reject members of other races is the supportive (unconscious and automatic) bias elicited by categorization.") Knuds Larsen, *Social Categorization and Attitude Change,* 111 J. SOC. PSYCHOL. 113, 114 (1980). On labeling and the development of welfare policies, see Larry Cata Becker, *By Hook or By Crook: Conformity, Assimilation and Liberal and Conservative Poor Relief Theory,* 7 HASTINGS WOMEN'S L.J. 391 (1996).

[39]C. Ronald Chester, *Perceived Relative Deprivation as a Cause of Property Crime,* 22 CRIME & DELINQ. 17, 22 (1976), *as quoted in* Christine L. Wilson, *Urban Homesteading: A Compromise Between Squatters and the Law,* 35 N.Y.L. SCH. L. REV. 709, 714–15 n.38 (1990).

[40]Kimberlé W. Crenshaw, *Race, Reform and Retrenchment: Transformation and Legitimation in Antidiscrimination Law,* 101 HARV. L. REV. 1331, 1372 (1988); *see also* Peggy C. Davis, *Law as Microaggression,* 98 YALE L.J. 1559, 1561 (1989); Sheri Lynn Johnson, *Black Innocence and the White Jury,* 83 MICH. L. REV. 1611, 1645 (1985).

[41]*See generally* STEPHEN J. GOULD, THE MISMEASURE OF MAN 20–145 (1981); *see also, e.g.,* Herbert Hovencamp, *Social Science and Segregation Before Brown,* 1985 DUKE L.J. 624; Steven Hartwell, *Understanding and Dealing With Deception in Legal Negotiation,* 6 OHIO ST. J. DISPUTE RES. 171, 175 n.15 (1991); Nicole H. Rafter, *The Social Construction of Crime and Crime Control,* 27 J. RES. CRIME & DELINQ. 376, 379 (1990).

[42]*See, e.g.,* Michael L. Perlin, *Myths, Realities, and the Political World: The Anthropology of Insanity Defense Attitudes,* 24 BULL. AM. ACAD. PSYCHIATRY & L. 5 (1996); Perlin, *Borderline, supra* note 25.

[43]Richard Merelman, *On Culture and Politics in America: A Perspective From Structural Anthropology,* 19 BRIT. J. POL. SCI. 465, 473 (1989). For other helpful perspectives, *see, e.g.,* Horacio Fabrega, *The Concept of Somatization as a Cultural and Historical Product of Western Medicine,* 52 PSYCHOSOMATIC MED. 653 (1990); Lloyd Rogler, *Culturally Sensitizing Psychiatric Diagnosis: A Framework for Research,* 181 J. NERVOUS & MENTAL DIS. 401 (1993).

[44]Merelman, *supra* note 43, at 477.

This . . . helps us appreciate how mentally ill persons . . . are ambiguous, perplexing, figures in the context of present day American political culture. American legal institutions ascribe to persons a high level of autonomy, personal responsibility and rationality. These qualities mirror the attributes—independence and the capacity for conscientious choice—through which mythologized individuals express their natural goodness amidst corrupting social influences. [Because of changes in involuntary civil commitment laws and state hospital funding, m]entally ill homeless persons are now free to reject society's norms, [and] to make unwise decisions about their life styles. . . . [S]uch behavior . . . reflects unconventional and therefore troubling choices. Mentally ill homeless persons thus represent a set of culturally contextual contradictions, because their behavior violates the set of structural oppositions that Americans use to organize their social perceptions.[45]

Until recently, most scholars who have studied prejudice and stereotyping have treated outgroups as "virtually interchangeable," attributing—as Allport did—all prejudice to "one nature and one root."[46] This singular nature approach has recently been criticized vigorously by Elisabeth Young-Bruehl, who has argued that prejudices such as anti-Semitism, racism, sexism, and homophobia—prejudices that she calls "ideologies of desire"[47]—differ from each other in their inner "logic" and structure and fulfill different unconscious needs on the part of the prejudiced person.[48] Young-Bruehl did not discuss prejudice toward persons with mental disabilities, and it is not clear how she would classify sanist behavior.[49] Nonetheless, sanism appears to share the dominant and overarching principle shared by all "isms": an ideological rationalization or justification for stigmatizing and marginalizing the other.

Eventually stereotypes—often brought together in a "web"[50]—come to serve as the basis of a legitimating ideology that perpetuates the mythology and rationalizes racial, sexual, or religious oppression.[51] These stereotypes lead to yet others: The separated and stigmatized others are seen as "different, deviant and morally weak" or as individuals "without hope or dignity."[52] We thus think of the stereotyped as "'them' and not 'us'[;] we are [thus] less likely to share in their pain and humiliation."[53]

---

[45]Douglas Mossman, *Deinstitutionalization, Homelessness, and the Myth of Psychiatric Abandonment: A Structural Anthropology Perspective*, 44 Soc. Sci. & Med. 71, 76 (1997).

[46]*See* YOUNG-BRUEHL, *supra* note 3, at 16–17.

[47]*Id.* at 184–88.

[48]*Id.* at 28–35.

[49]"It is probably worth pointing out that, while race and sex are immutable, we all can become mentally ill, homeless, or both. Perhaps this illuminates the level of virulence we experience here." Perlin, *supra* note 1, at 93 n.174. Also, the way that we simultaneously demonize and infantilize persons with mental disabilities in matters of sexuality, *see* Michael L. Perlin, *Hospitalized Patients and the Right to Sexual Interaction: Beyond the Last Frontier?* 20 N.Y.U. REV. L. & Soc. CHANGE 517, 537 (1993–94), appears to parallel at least some racist views of Black sexuality; *see* YOUNG-BRUEHL, *supra* note 3, at 431–32.

[50]GILMAN, *supra* note 15, at 240. This "web" leads individuals to conflate negative stereotypes of different others in a way that further perpetuates exclusion discrimination. *See, e.g.*, Note, *Facial Discrimination: Extending Handicap Law to Employment Discrimination on the Basis of Physical Appearance*, 100 HARV. L. REV. 2035, 2051–52 (1987).

[51]Crenshaw, *supra* note 40, at 1370–71, and sources cited at nn.147–51; Johnson, *supra* note 40, at 1637 ("bias against black defendants is based upon subconscious stereotypes").

[52]Thomas Ross, *The Rhetoric of Poverty: Their Immorality, Our Helplessness*, 79 GEO. L.J. 1499, 1503, 1507 (1991); *see also* Perlin, *supra* note 1, at 72 (discussing popular images of homeless persons as "lazy, degenerate bums," or "crazy, possibly dangerous people who ought to be put away").

[53]Ross, *supra* note 52, at 1542. *See also* MINOW, *supra* note 10, at 3–4:

Sometimes, classifications express and implement prejudice, . . . intolerance for difference. When we respond to persons' traits rather than their conduct, we may treat a given trait as a justification for excluding someone we think is "different." We feel no need for further justification; we attribute the consequences to the differences we see.

Judges have consistently used these assumptions about stereotyped others. The Supreme Court's decision in *City of New York v. Miln*[54]—upholding a statute requiring shipmasters to report their passengers' occupations—specifically equated the potential "moral pestilence of paupers" with the potential "physical pestilence" that could arise from "infectious articles" or crew members "laboring under an infectious disease."[55] As I will discuss in the specific context of persons with mental disabilities, these stereotypes have led also to widespread feelings of both social and judicial helplessness—that the social problems we face are somehow beyond remediation.[56]

The use of stereotypes precludes empathic behavior. Lynne Henderson has defined empathy as encompassing three interrelated phenomena: "(1) feeling the emotion of another; (2) understanding the experience or situation of another, both affectively and cognitively, often achieved by imagining oneself to be in the position of the other; and (3) action brought about by experiencing the distress of another (hence the confusion of empathy with sympathy and compassion)."[57]

We are more likely to emphasize (in an unreflective way)[58] with people like ourselves; yet because empathic understanding involves the "recognition of and regard for the other,"[59] empathy operates to blunt stereotyped thinking that fails to imagine another's alternative perspectives.[60]

None of us is immune from the use of stereotypes, least of all lawyers. According to Stanley Brodsky and his colleagues:

> Trial lawyers recognize that jury selection in both civil and criminal actions is typically based on long-standing stereotypes, assumed to identify pre-existing attitudes and biases. Women are said to be empathic; men are not. Accountants, engineers, and military officers are thought of as punitive and not people-oriented. Social workers, teachers, liberal Protestants, and most Jews are described as good jurors for the defense in criminal case and for the plaintiffs in civil cases. Catholics, fundamental Christians, and Orthodox Jews are not. . . . Trial lawyers who represent the state in criminal cases, and the defense in civil cases, should pick jurors with the "six *R*s"; religious, racist, rigid, righteous, Republican, and repressed.[61]

The law's treatment of minority groups—giving that phrase its broadest possible *Carolene Products* "Footnote 4" reading[62]—has frequently been based on the most

---

[54]36 U.S. (11 Pet.) 102 (1837).

[55]*Id.* at 142.

[56]Ross, *supra* note 52, at 1509–13.

[57]Lynne E. Henderson, *Legality and Empathy,* 85 MICH. L. REV. 1574, 1579 (1987); *see also id.* at 1580 n.29. *See also* Susan Bandes, *Empathy, Narrative, and Victim Impact Statements,* 63 U. CHI. L. REV. 361, 412 (1996).

[58]Henderson, *supra* note 57, at 1581 n.59, 1584. On the way that much "common sensical" thinking is prereflective and self-referential, see Richard K. Sherwin, *Dialects and Dominance: A Study of Rhetorical Fields in the Law of Confessions,* 136 U. PA. L. REV. 729, 737 (1988); Perlin, *OCS, supra* note 8, at 22–38.

[59]Henderson, *supra* note 57, at 1586.

[60]Minow, *supra* note 10, at 51 n.201. On our faulty and unstated assumptions about difference, see MINOW, *supra* note 15, at 50–74 (difference is intrinsic, not a comparison; the norm need not be stated; the observer can see without a perspective; other perspectives are irrelevant; the status quo is natural, uncoerced, and good).

On the role of empathy in the psychiatric assessment process, see Janet Eppard & Judith Anderson, *Emergency Psychiatric Assessment: The Nurse, Psychiatrist, and Counselor Roles During the Process,* 10 J. OF PSYCHOSOCIAL NURSING & MENT. HEALTH SERVS. 17 (1995).

[61]Stanley L. Brodsky et al., *Jury Selection in Malpractice Suits: An Investigation of Community Attitudes Toward Malpractice and Physicians,* 14 INT'L J.L. & PSYCHIATRY 215, 215 (1991).

[62]For important contemporary perspectives on *Carolene Products, see, e.g.,* Bruce R. Ackerman, *Beyond Carolene Products,* 98 HARV. L. REV. 713 (1985); Robert M. Cover, *The Origins of Judicial Activism in the Protection of Minorities,* 91 YALE L.J. 1287 (1982); Louis Lusky, *Footnote Redux: A Carolene Products Reminiscence,* 82 COLUM. L. REV. 1093 (1982); J. M. Balkin, *The Footnote,* 83 NW. U. L. REV. 275 (1989); Daniel

inflexible generalizations and the most polarized categories. As I will discuss, inappropriate stereotypes and categorizations have led to discriminatory legislation, judicial decisions, and lawyering practices.[63] Although the "isms" reflected in these practices—among them racism, sexism, and anti-Semitism—have since been significantly *officially* repudiated, the distorted cognitive processes still frequently dominate our thought processes and decision making. As Johnson has argued, either prejudice or discrimination may be present without the other, and official discrimination may be inhibited *despite* virulent prejudice: "Where discrimination is not legally or socially approved, social scientists predict it will be practiced only when it is possible to do so covertly and indirectly. On the other hand, discrimination may be engaged in without the presence of prejudiced attitudes when it will lead to social approval."[64] Such distorted thought processes and socially approved prejudice still dominate our discourse when the subject is persons with mental disabilities.

On Specific "Isms"

American legal history reflects a persistent and unrelenting pattern of statutes and court decisions that are based on racial, gender, sexual preference, and ethnic stereotypes. In this part of the chapter I will speak briefly of questions of race and then simply allude to biases faced by other stereotyped and marginalized groups. The common thread is the way that "ismic" behavior regularly pervades the law.

Race

All components of the legal system, especially the courts, "must bear a heavy share of the burden of American racism." To an "outrageous and humiliating extent," American lawyers, judges, and legislators "created, perpetuated, and defended racist American institutions."[65] Racist laws historically enforced segregation in the community in education, accommodations, transportation, and social organizations,[66] and enforced two-tier citizen-

---

A. Farber & Philip P. Frickey, *Is* Carolene Products *Dead? Reflections on Affirmative Action and the Dynamics of Civil Rights Legislation,* 79 CALIF. L. REV. 686 (1991); Bradley P. Hogin, *Equal Protection, Democratic Theory, and the Case of the Poor,* 21 RUTGERS L.J. 1 (1989).

I discuss the significance of this footnote to interpretations of the Americans With Disabilities Act in Perlin, *supra* note 13, at 948–50; *see generally infra* Chapter 8.

[63]*See* MINOW, *supra* note 15, at 9 ("The law has failed to resolve the meaning of equality for people defined as different by the society").

[64]Johnson, *supra* note 40, at 1650.

[65]Hovencamp, *supra* note 41, at 624.

[66]*Id.* at 624–25; *see also* sources cited *id.* n.1; *see also* Henderson, *supra* note 57, at 1593–1609; Harold H. Horowitz, *Fourteenth Amendment Aspects of Racial Discrimination in "Private" Housing,* 52 CALIF. L. REV. 1 (1964); *see generally* GEORGE M. FREDERICKSON, THE BLACK IMAGE AND THE WHITE MIND: THE DEBATE ON AFRO-AMERICAN CHARACTER AND DESTINY, 1817–1914 (1971); GILBERT T. STEPHENSON, RACE DISTINCTIONS IN AMERICAN LAW (1910).

ship in the courts in such areas as testimonial exclusion,[67] jury selection,[68] bar membership,[69] and intermarriage.[70] Remnants of this two-tier system remain today in such areas as
selective prosecution of crime[71] and susceptibility to the death penalty,[72] as well as in other
aspects of the criminal justice system.[73]

Supporters of segregationist and racist laws drew regularly on "scientific" theories to
buttress their arguments.[74] Narrow and distorted stereotypes regularly grounded both the
legal arguments and the underlying explanatory "theories" offered in support of such
laws.[75] In all cases, the "ismic" behavior—frequently operative on an unconscious
level[76]—legitimated the ideology that perpetuated the mythology that rationalized the
oppression.[77]

Although civil rights reforms have eliminated much of the formal and symbolic
subordination to which Blacks were previously subjected, much of the material subordina-

---

[67]J. A. C. Grant, *Testimonial Exclusion Because of Race: A Chapter in the History of Intolerance in
California,* 17 UCLA L. REV. 192 (1969).

[68]S. W. Tucker, *Racial Selection in Jury Selection in Virginia,* 52 VA. L. REV. 736 (1966).

[69]Michael Rustad & Thomas Koenig, *The Impact of History on Contemporary Prestige Images of Boston's
Law Schools,* 24 SUFFOLK U. L. REV. 621, 634–35 (1990).

[70]Paul A. Lombardo, *Miscegenation, Eugenics, and Racism: Historical Footnotes to* Loving v. Virginia, 21
U.C. DAVIS L. REV. 421 (1988).

[71]Tonya I. Hernandez, *Bias Crimes: Unconscious Racism in the Prosecution of "Racially Motivated
Violence,"* 99 YALE L.J. 845 (1990); Johnson, *supra* note 40; Samuel Cameron, *Race and Prosecution
Expenditures,* REV. BLACK POL. ECON. 79 (Summer 1990). *See generally* McCleskey v. Kemp, 418 U.S. 279 (1987);
Anthony Amsterdam, *Race and the Death Penalty,* 7 CRIM. JUST. ETHICS 2 (1988).

[72]Michael G. Radelet & Glenn L. Pierce, *Choosing Those Who Will Die: Race and the Death Penalty in
Florida,* 43 FLA. L. REV. 1 (1991).

[73]*See, e.g.,* Ronald L. Poulson, *Mock Juror Attribution of Criminal Responsibility: Effects of Race and the
Guilty But Mentally Ill (GBMI) Verdict Option,* 20 J. APPLIED SOC. PSYCHOL. 1596 (1990); Patricia Van Voorhis et
al., *The Impact of Race and Gender on Criminal Officers' Orientation to the Integrated Environment,* 28 J. RES.
CRIME & DELINQ. 472 (1991).

[74]*See generally* GILMAN, *supra* note 15; GOULD, *supra* note 41, at 30–72, 174–234. *See also* Lawrence, *supra*
note 34, at 374, discussing, *inter alia,* JEFFREY BLUM, PSEUDOSCIENCE AND MENTAL ABILITY 30–72, 99–103 (1978);
THOMAS GOSSETT, RACE: THE HISTORY OF AN IDEA IN AMERICA 5, 62–63 (1963); RICHARD KLUGER, SIMPLE JUSTICE
84–86 (1976).

[75]*See* Henderson, *supra* note 57, at 1607, partially quoting KLUGER, *supra* note 74, at 595, discussing response
of Supreme Court Justice Reed to District of Columbia v. John R. Thompson Co., 346 U.S. 100 (1953) (holding
segregation of restaurants in the District of Columbia unlawful): "[Mr. Justice Reed] had had difficulty with [the
John R. Thompson case] because he did not like the notion that "a nigra (*sic*) can walk into the restaurant at the
Mayflower Hotel and sit down . . . right next to Mrs. Reed."

On the specific roots of the linkage between sexual stereotypes and racial stereotypes, see GILMAN, *supra* note
15, at 109–27; Elizabeth Iglesias, *Race, Rape, and Representation: The Power of Discourse, Discourses of Power,
and the Reconstruction of Heterosexuality,* 49 VAND. L. REV. 869 (1996). On the prejudice associated with another
odious stereotype (that non-Whites possess an "offensive odor") and its place in the justification of segregationist
practices, see Stevens v. Dobs, Inc., 483 F.2d 82, 83–84 (4th Cir. 1973) (minority individual seeking to rent
apartment turned down purportedly because of "peculiar odor").

[76]*See* Johnson, *supra* note 34, at 1017.

[77]Crenshaw, *supra* note 40, at 1370–71.

tion remains.[78] Today's ongoing debate on affirmative action, race consciousness, and quotas thus makes it impossible to ignore race, for the debate underscores the incontrovertible fact that many Whites refuse to see Blacks as "full members and equal partners in society."[79] President George Bush's cynical and vicious manipulation of the Willie Horton image in the 1988 presidential campaign, Klan member David Duke's strong showing in the 1991 gubernatorial election in Louisiana, and Pat Buchanan's comments about the specter of one million immigrant "Zulus" suggest that these stereotypes remain dangerously near the surface today.[80]

Other "Isms"

Our legal history similarly reveals patterns of court decisions, statutes, and lawyering practices that reflect sexist,[81] anti-Semitic,[82] anti-Catholic,[83] anti-Asian,[84] anti-Native

---

[78]*Id.* at 1377; *see also, e.g.,* Robert J. Cottrol, *A Tale of Two Cultures: On Making the Proper Connections Between Law, Social History and the Political Economy of Despair,* 25 SAN DIEGO L. REV. 989 (1988). On the related question of racial discrimination as an animator of juror bias, see for example, Johnson, *supra* note 40, at 1637. On the way that visibility can "lock" racial minorities to stereotypes, see Otey v. Common Council of City of Milwaukee, 281 F. Supp. 264, 270 n.8 (E.D. Wis. 1968).

[79]T. Alexander Aleinikoff, *A Case for Race-Consciousness,* 91 COLUM. L. REV. 1061, 1125 (1991).

[80]For recent research on the relationship between race and fear of crime, see Ted Chiricos et al., *Racial Composition of Neighborhood and Fear of Crime,* 35 CRIMINOLOGY 107 (1997) (perception that one is a racial minority elevates fear levels for Whites but not for Blacks); Arthur Garrison, *Disproportionate Minority Arrest: A Note on What Has Been Said and How It Fits Together,* 23 NEW ENG. J. ON CRIM. & CIV. CONFINEMENT 29 (1997) (concluding that race and racism play a disproportionate role in minority arrest rates).

The politics of fear continues. *See* Sam Howe Verhovek, *Gov. Bush Denies Pardon in Rape Case, Despite DNA,* N.Y. TIMES, Sept. 14. 1997, § 1, at 23 ("He doesn't want to take any risk that [the defendant] could become his Willie Horton") (quoting defense counsel).

[81]*See, e.g.,* CATHERINE A. MACKINNON, FEMINISM UNMODIFIED (1987); GENDER DIFFERENCES: THEIR IMPACT ON PUBLIC POLICY (Mary Lou Kendrigan ed. 1991); DEBORAH RHODE, JUSTICE AND GENDER: SEX DISCRIMINATION AND THE LAW (1989); Susan Okin, *Justice and Gender,* 16 PHILOS. & PUB. AFF. 42 (1987); Elizabeth M. Schneider, *The Dialectic of Rights and Politics: Perspectives From the Women's Movement,* 61 N.Y.U. L. REV. 589 (1986); Judith Resnik, *On the Bias: Feminist Reconsiderations of the Aspirations for Our Judges,* 61 S. CAL. L. REV. 1877 (1988).

[82]Rustad & Koenig, *supra* note 69, at 635; JEROLD S. AUERBACH, UNEQUAL JUSTICE 99–100 (1976); First, *Competition in the Legal Education Industry,* 53 N.Y.U. L. REV. 36 (1978). For case law examples, see State v. Millstein, 513 A.2d 1253, 1256–58 (Conn. 1986), *cert. denied,* 518 A.2d 72 (Conn. 1986) (defendant not deprived of fair trial when prosecutor referred to arson as "Jewish lightning"); State v. Levitt, 176 A.2d 465, 466–67 (N.J. 1961) (anti-Semitic comments by jurors); United States v. Lane. 883 F.2d 1484, 1499–1500 (10th Cir. 1989), *cert. denied,* 493 U.S. 1059 (1990) (anti-Semitic comments by codefendant).

[83]Barbara Perry, *The Life and Death of the "Catholic Seat" on the United States Supreme Court,* 6 J.L. & POL. 55 (1989); Dale E. Carpenter, *Free Exercise and Dress Codes: Toward a More Consistent Protection of a Fundamental Right,* 63 IND. L.J. 601, 617, n.112 (1988) (discussing Pierce v. Society of Sisters, 286 U.S. 510 (1925)).

[84]*See, e.g.,* Richard Delgado & Jean Stefancic, *Norms and Narratives: Can Judges Avoid Serious Moral Error?* 69 TEX. L. REV. 1929, 1943–47 (1991) (discussing Chinese exclusion cases and Japanese internment cases); Charles McClain, *Of Medicine, Race, and American Law: The Bubonic Plague Outbreak of 1900,* 13 LAW & SOC. INQ. 447 (1988); Arneja v. Gildar, 541 A.2d 621, 622 (D.C. 1988) (anti-Asian comments by lawyer to adversary); Doriane Coleman, *Individualizing Justice Through Multiculturalism: The Liberals' Dilemma,* 96 COLUM. L. REV. 1093 (1996).

American,[85] homophobic,[86] disability-based,[87] and "ageist"[88] attitudes.[89] In each example, reliance on "science," culture, and stereotypes reifies the ultimate subordination of the other.[90] In some cases, the subordinating practices are aimed at those subject to multiple stereotypes,[91] and, in many of these, social classism[92] further contaminates the process.[93]

---

[85]Jeanette Wolfley, *Jim Crow, Indian Style: The Disenfranchisement of Native Americans*, 1 AM. INDIAN L. REV. 167 (1990); Yasuhide Kawashima, *Forced Conformity: Puritan Criminal Justice and Indians*, 25 U. KAN. L. REV. 361 (1977); Avian Soifer, *The Paradox of Paternalism and Laissez-Faire Capitalism: United States Supreme Court, 1888–1921*, 5 LAW & HIST. REV. 249 (1987); Jill Norgren, *Protection of What Rights They Have: Original Principles of Federal Indian Law*, 64 N.D. L. REV. 73 (1988); Robert Miller & Maril Hazlitt, *The "Drunken Indian": Myth Distilled Into Reality Through Federal Indian Alcohol Policy*, 28 ARIZ. ST. L.J. 223 (1996.)

[86]Arthur Leonard, *From Law: Homophobia, Heterosexism and Judicial Decision Making*, 1 J. GAY & LESBIAN PSYCHOTHERAPY 65 (1991); Anne B. Goldstein, *History, Homosexuality, and Political Values: Searching for the Hidden Determinants of* Bowers v. Hardwick, 97 YALE L.J. 1073 (1988); Toni Massaro, *Gay Rights: Thick and Thin*, 49 STAN. L. REV. 45 (1996); Katheryn Katz, *Majoritarian Morality and Parental Rights*, 52 ALB. L. REV. 405 (1988); Larry Cata Becker, *Constructing a "Homosexual" for Constitutional Theory: Sodomy Narrative, Jurisprudence, and Antipathy in United States and British Courts*, 71 TUL. L. REV. 529 (1996); John E. Boswell, *Jews, Bicycle Riders, and Gay People: The Determination of Social Consensus and Its Impact on Minorities*, 1 YALE J.L. & HUMAN. 205 (1989); David Bernstein, *From Pesthouses to AIDS Hospices: Neighbors' Irrational Fears of Treatment Facilities for Contagious Diseases*, 22 COLUM. HUM. RTS. L. REV. 1 (1990).

[87]Martha T. McCluskey, *Rethinking Equality and Difference: Disability Discrimination in Public Transportation*, 97 YALE L.J. 863 (1988); David M. Engel & Alfred S. Konefsky, *Law Students With Disabilities*, 38 BUFF. L. REV. 551 (1990); Michelle Fine & Adrienne Asch, *Disability Beyond Stigma: Social Interaction, Discrimination, and Activism*, 44 J. SOC. ISS. 3 (1988); *see also, e.g.*, Chiari v. City of League City, 920 F.2d 311, 313 (5th Cir., 1991) (employee with Parkinson's disease).

[88]Charles R. Tremper, *Respect for the Human Dignity of Minors: What the Constitution Requires*, 39 SYRACUSE L. REV. 1293 (1988); William S. Geimer, *Juvenileness: A Single-Edged Constitutional Sword*, 22 GA. L. REV. 949 (1988); Weithorn, *supra* note 37; Howard B. Gelt, *Psychological Considerations in Representing the Aged Client*, 17 ARIZ. L. REV. 293 (1975); Jessica D. Silver, *From Baby Doe to Grandpa Doe: The Impact of the Federal Age Discrimination Act on the "Hidden" Rationing of Medical Care*, 37 CATH. U. L. REV. 993 (1988); *cf.* Suzanne Meeks, *Age Bias in the Decision-Making Behavior of Clinicians*, 21 PROF. PSYCHOL.: RES. & PRAC. 279 (1990); Sidney Hollar, *The Never-Never Land of Mental Health Law: A Review of the Legal Rights of Youth Committed by Their Parents to Psychiatric Facilities in California*, 4 BERKELEY WOMEN'S L.J. 300 (1989); Teresa Davis et al., *Predictors of Sentencing Decisions: The Beliefs, Personality Variables, and Demographic Factors of Juvenile Justice Personnel*, 23 J. APPLIED SOC. PSYCHOL. 451 (1993).

[89]For examples of other "ismic" behavior targeting other groups, see for example, Soifer, *supra* note 85, at 255, 264–65 (sailors); Welsh v. Boy Scouts of America, 742 F. Supp. 1413, 1416 n.1 (N.D. Ill. 1990) (nonbelievers in Supreme Being); Jane Korn, *Fat*, 77 B.U. L. REV. 25 (1997) (obesity); Frazier v. Heebe, 788 F.2d 1049 (5th Cir. 1986), *rev'd*, 482 U.S. 641 (1987) (out-of-state attorneys); Johnson, *supra* note 27, at 1638; Ellen C. Wertleib, *Individuals With Disabilities in the Criminal Justice System: A Review of the Literature*, 18 CRIM. JUST. & BEHAV. 332, 333 (1991); Leslie A. Zebrowitz & Susan M. McDonald, *The Impact of Litigants' Baby-Facedness and Attractiveness on Adjudications in Small Claims Court*, 15 LAW & HUM. BEHAV. 603 (1991) (all dealing with physical unattractiveness); on the relationship between mental disability and irrational self-perceptions of physical unattractiveness, see Alison Bass, *When the Mirror Reflects a Distorted Self-Image*, BOSTON GLOBE, Oct. 21, 1991, at 27. *See generally* LAURENCE FUCHS, THE AMERICAN KALEIDOSCOPE: RACE, ETHNICITY, AND THE CIVIC CULTURE (1990).

[90]*See generally* GILMAN, *supra* note 15; *see, e.g.*, Lawrence, *supra* note 34, at 374.

[91]*But see* Judy Scales-Trent, *Black Women and the Constitution: Finding Our Place, Asserting Our Rights*, 24 HARV. C.R.-C.L. L. REV. 9, 42 (1989) (characterizing Black movement and women's movement as "two distinct and often warring social movements"). *Cf.* Martha Minow, *Breaking the Law: Lawyers and Clients in Struggles for Social Change*, 52 U. PITT. L. REV. 723, 731 (1991) (discussing Scales-Trent's insight):

> Part of the problem, I believe, stems from the ways that the women's movement and the movement for racial justice have each framed goals of equal treatment in terms set by the very legal system that excludes them. The movement for racial justice looks to the treatment of white people and the women's movement looks to the treatment of men. This approach lends large significance to the categories already prevailing in legal rules, and makes departures from those categories seem problematic.

[92]On how the ways that we look to poverty to help shape our stereotypes, see generally Ross, *supra* note 52.

[93]*See, e.g.*, Frances L. Ansley, *Stirring the Ashes: Race, Class and the Future of Civil Rights Scholarship*, 74 CORNELL L. REV. 993 (1989); Regina Austin, *Sapphire Bound*, 1989 WIS. L. REV. 539; Dorothy E. Roberts, *Punishing Drug Addicts Who Have Babies: Women of Color, Equality and the Right of Privacy*, 104 HARV. L. REV. 1419 (1991); Tauyna L. Banks, *Women and AIDS—Racism, Sexism, and Classism*, 17 N.Y.U. REV. L. & SOC. CHANGE 351 (1989–90) (all race, class, and gender); Gary A. Debele, *The Due Process Revolution and the Juvenile*

Although more recent legislation and court decisions have, to some extent, blunted the symbolic weight of some of these patterns, evidence of material subordination remains. As with race, stereotypes dominate both the legal and political discourses.[94]

On the Response of the Legal System

After a time, all components of the legal system respond (slowly) to "isms" and stereotypes. Frequently jolted by a cataclysmic "shock the conscience" event,[95] and often prodded by both analytic scholarship and moving, personal stories,[96] legislation may be passed to ameliorate some of the most wretched excesses of the underlying behavior.[97] Courts may then respond in "activist" ways (if they self-perceive themselves as minoritarian) or in "conservative" ways (if they view themselves as majoritarian).[98] Some lawyers may pay no attention to such responses; others may change their behavior either directly (by articulating codes and standards prohibiting "ismic" behavior),[99] or indirectly (by adopting more empthatic modes of interpersonal connections and by attempting to "put themselves in the shoes" of the stereotyped other).[100] The Supreme Court now concedes that private bias may be "outside the reach of the law," but warns that "the law cannot directly or indirectly give [such bias] effect."[101]

These belated responses do not—cannot—serve to extinguish the residue of "ismic" behavior on the parts of the various actors in the legal system: legislators who write statutes, judges who try cases and hear appeals, and lawyers who represent clients. Such judges reflect

---

Court: The Matter of Race in the Historical Evolution of a Doctrine, 5 LAW & INEQUAL. 513 (1987) (race, age, and class); Ann E. Freedman, *Feminist Legal Method in Action: Challenging Racism, Sexism and Homophobic in Law School,* 24 GA. L. REV. 849 (1990) (race, gender, and sexual preference); Lesley Slavin, *The Social World and Political Community of Head-Injured People: Difference by Gender and Family Life Cycle, in* GENDER DIFFERENCES: THEIR IMPACT ON PUBLIC POLICY 889 (MaryLou Kendrigan ed. 1991) (physical disability and gender).

[94]For a particularly vivid example of the use of gay stereotypes in the judicial decision-making process, see Bowers v. Hardwick, 478 U.S. 186 (1986) (statute prohibiting consensual sodomy found not unconstitutional); *cf.* Steffan v. Cheney, 41 F.3d 677 (D.C. Cir. 1994) (rational basis exists to sustain policy excluding gays from armed services). *See generally* Bailey & Pillard, *supra* note 7 ("respectable people" can publicly express their homophobia).

[95]*See* Perlin, *supra* note 1, at 66.

[96]*See generally* David Luban, *Difference Made Legal: The Court and Dr. King,* 87 MICH. L. REV. 2152, 2156 (1989), considering impact of MARTIN LUTHER KING, WHY WE CAN'T WAIT 76, 79 (1964).

[97]*See, e.g.,* CHARLES W. WHALEN & BARBARA WHALEN, THE LONGEST DEBATE: A LEGISLATIVE HISTORY OF THE 1964 CIVIL RIGHTS ACT (1985).

[98]*See* Perlin, *supra* note 11, at 1256–59; Perlin, *Are Courts Competent to Decide Competency Questions? Stripping the Facade from* United States v. Charters, 38 U. KAN. L. REV. 957, 998–99 (1990); David Rudenstine, *Judicially Ordered Social Reform: Neofederalism and Neonationalism and the Debate Over Political Structure,* 59 S. CAL. L. REV. 451 (1986); Suzanna Sherry, *Issue Manipulation by the Burger Court: Saving the Community From Itself,* 70 MINN. L. REV. 611 (1986).

[99]*See, e.g.,* LINDSAY G. ARTHUR ET AL., INVOLUNTARY CIVIL COMMITMENT: A MANUAL FOR LAWYERS AND JUDGES 9–11 (1988).

[100]*See generally* Henderson, *supra* note 57, at 1605–06. On the role of empathy in lawyers' interpersonal contacts with clients, *see, e.g.,* DAVID A. BINDER & SUSAN C. PRICE, LEGAL INTERVIEWING AND COUNSELING: A CLIENT-CENTERED APPROACH (1977).

[101]Palmore v. Sidoti, 466 U.S. 429, 433 (1984). I argue that this ban has not been read to include persons who have been deinstitutionalized or are homeless in Perlin, *supra* note 1, at 138–42. *See also* Wilson, *Reconstructing Section Five of the Fourteenth Amendment to Assist Impoverished Children,* 38 CLEV. ST. L. REV. 391, 438 (1990) (courts have a duty "to root out unconstitutional prejudices").

"dominant, conventional morality";[102] their preexisting social values and views can "taint their perceptions" in their consideration of cases involving "ismic" biases.[103]

Judges most frequently come from the middle- and upper-classes.[104] They are disproportionately male, White, Protestant, middle-aged, and well-educated.[105] This privileged background has been looked on as one of the reasons that such judges are more likely to believe police officers rather than criminal defendants,[106] are slow to take seriously discrimination claims by a variety of ethnic groups,[107] are less likely to show empathy in cases involving sexual minorities,[108] ignore a range of voices and narratives of "subordinated groups,"[109] fail to acknowledge the significance of their own perspective,[110] and readily accept a model of an economically efficient, rational human.[111] They also respond carefully to public opinion when they are appointed, rather than elected.[112] Reported cases

---

[102]Wojciech Sadurski, *Conventional Morality and Judicial Standards,* 73 Va. L. Rev. 339, 341 (1987); Perlin, *Myths, supra* note 8, at 704–06; Perlin, *OCS, supra* note 8, at 31–36.

[103]Ann Woolhandler, *Rethinking the Judicial Reception of Legislative Facts,* 41 Vand. L. Rev. 111, 118–20 (1988); Perlin, *OCS, supra* note 8, at 59.

[104]On judicial bias in criminal cases in general, see Judge Hugh W. Silverman, *Judicial Bias,* 33 Crim. L.Q. 486 (1990).

[105]*See* Peter J. Hammer, *Free Speech and the "Acid Bath": An Evaluation and Critique of Judge Richard Posner's Economic Interpretation of the First Amendment,* 87 Mich. L. Rev. 499, 505 (1988); *see also* Charles A. Johnson, *The Salience of Judicial Candidates and Elections,* 89 Soc. Sci. Q. 371 (1978); Joel B. Grossman, *Social Backgrounds and Judicial Decisions: Notes for a Theory,* 29 J. Pol. 334 (1968). On the way judges are "deliberately removed from society," and thus more likely to be out of touch with practical concerns, see David A. Strauss, *Tradition, Precedent, and Justice Scalia,* 12 Cardozo L. Rev. 1699, 1707 (1991).

[106]Anthony Amsterdam, *The Supreme Court and the Rights of Suspects in Criminal Cases,* 45 N.Y.U. L. Rev. 785, 792 (1980) ("Trial judges . . . are functionally and psychologically allied with the police, their co-workers in the unending and scarifying work of bringing criminals to book"); *see also* Tracey Maclin, *Constructing Fourth Amendment Principles From the Government Perspective: Whose Amendment Is It, Anyway?* 25 Amer. Crim. L. Rev. 669 (1988). On how Amsterdam's insights go to explain a significant amount of courts' pretextuality, *see infra* Chapter 3.

[107]Christopher E. Smith, *The Supreme Court and Ethnicity,* 69 Or. L. Rev. 797 (1990).

[108]Henderson, *supra* note 57, at 1638–50 (discussing *Bowers*), and especially at 1638 ("[*Bowers*] bristles with emotion, to be sure, but it is the emotion of hate, not that of empathy"); *see also* Katheryn D. Katz, *Majoritarian Morality and Parental Rights,* 52 Alb. L. Rev. 405, 465 (1988) (judges "rely on their own views of what is or should be the prevailing morality"), discussing *L. v. D.,* 630 S.W.2d 240, 244 (Mo. Ct. App. 1982) (denying lesbian mother custody).

[109]Delgado & Stefancic, *supra* note 84, at 1929–34.

[110]Minow, *supra* note 10, at 60–70, *See, e.g.,* United States v. Kras, 409 U.S. 434, 460 (1973) (Marshall, J., dissenting): "It is perfectly proper for judges to disagree about what the Constitution requires. But it is disgraceful for an interpretation of the Constitution to be premised upon unfounded assumptions about how people live."

In at least one important subject matter area, judges' personal views were found to be the most important determinant in case dispositions. *See* Janet Ford et al., *Case Outcomes in Domestic Violence Court: Influence of Judges,* 77 Psychol. Rev. 587 (1995).

[111]Peter A. Bell, *Analyzing Tort Law: The Flawed Promise of Neocontract,* 74 Minn. L. Rev. 1177, 1212 (1990); Mark M. Hager, *The Emperor's Clothes Are Not Efficient: Posner's Jurisprudence of Class,* 41 Am. U. L. Rev. 7 (1991); Gary B. Melton, *Law, Science, and Humanity: The Normative Foundation of Social Science in Law,* 14 Law & Hum. Behav. 315 (1990).

[112]*See, e.g.,* David Bowers & Jerold Waltman, *Are Elected Judges More in Tune With Public Opinion? A Look at Sentences for Rape,* 18 Int'l J. Compar. & Applied Crim. Just. 113 (1994) (finding that appointed judges adopt public preferences in rape cases). On similarities and dissimilarities between elected and appointed judges in general, see Burt Neuborne, *The Myth of Parity,* 90 Harv. L. Rev. 1105 (1977).

offer countless examples of racial, sexual, and religious bias,[113] and Patricia Cain has questioned the "cost to public confidence" if we would be "willing to be honest about the possible racial biases of our judges."[114]

This is not to say that there are no constraints on "ismic" behavior in the legal system. Some appellate judges have "struck out against the inhumanities of existing law"[115] in ways that have led to systemic law reform;[116] other judges (trial and appellate) have sensitively dismantled some of the older and more pernicious stereotypes and limited the impact of "ismic" behavior in individual cases;[117] scholars are now turning to narrative as a means of highlighting prejudice and bias and of analyzing experience and culture through individual stories.[118]

In short, in many areas of the law in which stereotypes, prejudice, and "ismic" behavior have long dominated legal discourse there is now a substantial counterweight. This counterweight, though, is largely missing in the area of sanism,[119] and the pathology of oppression still dominates legal discourse involving persons with mental disabilities.

---

[113]For an exhaustive analysis of race bias, see Judge A. Leon Higginbotham, *Racism in American and South African Courts: Similarities and Differences,* 65 N.Y.U. L. REV. 479 (1990); *see also, e.g.,* Matter of Pearson, 386 S.E.2d 249 (S.C. 1989) (judge called individual a "nigger lover"); *In re* Stevens, 183 Cal. Rptr. 48 (1982) (judge used phrases "nigger," "coon," and "jungle bunny"); Peek v. State, 488 So.2d 52 (Fla. 1986) (judge in capital punishment case called Black defendant's family "niggers"). The implications of *Peek* (and the state Supreme Court's tepid response) are discussed in Radelet & Pierce, *supra* note 72, at 32.

[114]Patricia A. Cain, *Good and Bad Bias: A Comment on Feminist Theory and Judging,* 61 S. CAL. L. REV. 1945, 1953 (1988); *see generally* Lawrence, *supra* note 34, On the role of racial bias in judicial qualification matters, see John Leubsdorf, *Theories of Judging and Judicial Disqualification,* 62 N.Y.U. L. REV. 237, 259–60 (1987).

[115]Patricia M. Wald, *Disembodied Voices—An Appellate Judge's Response,* 66 TEX. L. REV. 623, 627 (1988).

[116]*See, e.g.,* 1 PERLIN, *supra* note 4, § 1-2.1, at 6–20 (2d ed. 1998), and Perlin, *supra* note 11, at 1249–54, discussing how civil rights cases led to first judicial reform of mental disability law system.

[117]*See, e.g.,* Sheppard v. Sheppard, 655 P.2d 895 (Idaho 1982) (anti-Indian prejudice); United States v. Lavallie, 666 F.2d 1217 (8th Cir. 1981) (same); High Tech Gays v. Defense Indus. Sec. Clearance Office, 668 F. Supp. 1361 (N.D. Cal. 1987), *rev'd in part, vacated in part,* 895 F.2d 563 (9th Cir. 1990), *reh'g denied,* 909 F.2d 375 (9th Cir. 1990); Jantz v. Muci, 759 F. Supp. 1543 (homophobia); United States v. Weiss, 930 F.2d 185, 200 (2d Cir. 1991), *cert. denied,* 502 U.S. 842 (1991) (Restani, J., dissenting) (anti-Semitism).

[118]Kathryn Abrams, *Hearing the Call of Stories,* 79 CALIF. L. REV. 971 (1991), and *see id.* at 973–75 nn.6–10, and sources cited; Jody Armour, *Stereotypes and Prejudice: Helping Legal Decisionmakers Break the Prejudice Habit,* 83 CALIF. L. REV. 733 (1995).

[119]Institutionalized mentally disabled individuals remain largely invisible to the rest of society. They have little or no political leverage, and rarely have powerful political allies or interest groups to take up their cause. *See, e.g.,* Anthony Lewis, *Enforcing Our Rights,* 50 GEO. WASH. L. REV. 414, 420 (1982).

On rights as empowerment for both the institutionalized mentally disabled and oppressed racial minorities, see Patricia J. Williams, *Alchemical Notes: Restructuring Ideals From Deconstructed Rights,* 22 HARV. C.R.-C.L. L. REV. 401, 416 (1987):

> For slaves, sharecroppers and mental patients . . . the experience of poverty and need is fraught with the realization that they are dependent "on the uncertain and fitful protection of a world conscience." . . . For the historically disempowered, the conferring of rights is symbolic of all the denied aspects of humanity: rights imply a respect which places them within the referential range of self and others, which elevates one's status from human body to social being. . . .

See generally Sheri Lynn Johnson, *Confessions, Criminals and Community,* 26 HARV. C.R.-C.L. L. REV. 328, 357–58 (1991) (discussing Williams's insights).

The Roots of Sanism[120]

The roots of sanism are deep. Mental illness has always been inextricably linked to sin, to evil, to God's punishment, to crime, and to demons.[121] Evil spirits were commonly relied on as an explanation for abnormal behavior.[122] The "face of madness . . . haunts our imagination."[123] The mentally ill were considered beasts; a person who lost his or her capacity to reason was also seen as having lost the claim "to be treated as a human being."[124]

Mental illness is a dominant model of pathology. According to Sander Gilman,

> The most elementally frightening possibility is the loss of control over the self, and loss of control is associated with loss of language and thought perhaps even more than with physical illness. Often associated with violence (including aggressive sexual acts), the mad are perceived as the antithesis to the control and reason that define the self. Again, what is perceived is in large part a projection; for within everyone's fantasy life there exists . . . an incipient madness that we control with more or less success.[125]

Such profound images allow us to see the mentally ill individual as the other. They animate our "keen . . . desire to separate 'us' and 'them'";[126] they allow us to use the label of "sickness" as reassurance that the other—seen as "both ill and infectious, both damaged and damaging"[127]—is not like us.[128]

We respond to these images by perpetuating reductionist symbolic stereotypes of mental illness that reify social, cultural, medical, behavioral, and political myths.[129] These stereotypes color and shape the way we treat mentally ill individuals and the ways we think

---

[120]*See generally* PERLIN, JURISPRUDENCE, *supra* note 8, at 37–41.

[121]*See, e.g.,* MICHAEL MOORE, LAW AND PSYCHIATRY: RETHINKING THE RELATIONSHIP 64–65 (1984); JOHN BIGGS, THE GUILTY MIND 26 (1955); JUDITH NEAMAN, SUGGESTION OF THE DEVIL: THE ORIGINS OF MADNESS 31, 50, 144 (1975); WALTER BROMBERG, FROM SHAMAN TO PSYCHOTHERAPIST: A HISTORY OF THE TREATMENT OF MENTAL ILLNESS 63–64 (1975 ed.). On the similar ways that mental retardation has been seen as God's means of punishing sin or as a manifestation of evil, see WOLF WOLFENSBERGER, NORMALIZATION: THE PRINCIPLE OF NORMALIZATION IN HUMAN SERVICES 12–25 (1972); Marie Appelby, *The Mentally Retarded: The Need for Intermediate Scrutiny,* 7 B.C. THIRD WORLD L.J. 109, 115 (1987).

On the significance of the perceived relationship between sin and sickness in contemporary mental disability law policy, see Bernard Weiner, *On Sin Versus Sickness: A Theory of Perceived Responsibility and Social Motivation,* 48 AM. PSYCHOLOGIST 957 (1993).

[122]GEORGE ROSEN, MADNESS IN SOCIETY: CHAPTERS IN THE HISTORICAL SOCIOLOGY OF MENTAL ILLNESS 12, 33 (1969 ed.).

[123]MICHAEL FOUCAULT, MADNESS AND CIVILIZATION 15 (1965).

[124]*Id.* at 76; Andrew T. Scull, *Moral Treatment Reconsidered: Some Sociological Comments on an Episode in the History of British Psychiatry, in* MADHOUSES, MAD-DOCTORS, AND MADMEN: THE SOCIAL HISTORY OF PSYCHIATRY IN THE VICTORIAN ERA 105 108–09 (A. Scull ed. 1981). For a historical perspective see also, for example, Samuel Kottek, *The Image of the Insane in Ancient Jewish Lore,* 11 MED. & L. 653 (1992).

[125]GILMAN, *supra* note 15, at 23–24.

[126]CHRISTOPHER HARDING & RICHARD W. IRELAND, PUNISHMENT: RHETORIC, RULE, AND PRACTICE 105 (1989).

[127]GILMAN, *supra* note 15, at 130.

[128]*See* PERLIN, JURISPRUDENCE, *supra* note 8, at 389 n.113–16 (citing sources). On the way that our perceptions of individuals as members of outsider groups affects criminal justice policies, see Jonathon Kelley & Joan Braithwhite, *Public Opinion and the Death Penalty in Australia,* 7 JUST. Q. 529 (1990).

[129]On symbolism in general, see 11 STUDIES IN SYMBOLIC INTERACTION: A RESEARCH ANNUAL (Norman Denzin ed. 1990). On its role in mental disability law policy making, see PERLIN, *supra* note 8, at 30–37.

about mental illness.[130] These stereotypes are further encouraged by media distortions[131] and exacerbated by our reliance on cognitive heuristics and OCS.[132] We cannot empathize with such people.[133]

Stereotypes of mental illness are frequently conflated with stereotypes of race,[134]

---

[130]Perlin, *supra* note 1, at 111–12; Perlin, *Myths, supra* note 8, at 618–23, 706–31; *see generally* "Stigma Task Force," *supra* note 43. On the way that "insanity has served as a metaphor for our nation's fears of its own craziness," see Herbert A. Eastman, *Metaphor and Madness, Law and Liberty,* 40 DePaul L. Rev. 281, 283 (1991). *Cf.* Stephen Morse, *Treating Crazy People Less Specially,* 90 W. Va. L. Rev. 353 (1987)

[131]The small- to medium-town press is especially notorious. *See, e.g, Jailed Psycho Kills Self With Pen Through Eye,* The Trentonian (Jan. 3, 1992), at 4. On media distortions in this context in general, see, for example, Mark A. Kaufman, *"Crazy" Until Proven Innocent: Civil Commitment of the Mentally Ill Homeless,* 19 Colum. Hum. Rts. L. Rev. 333, 363 (1988); David A. Snow et al., *The Myth of Pervasive Mental Illness Among the Homeless,* 33 Soc. Probs. 407, 407–08 (1986); *see generally* Henry Steadman & Joseph Cocozza, *Selective Reporting and the Public's Misconception of the Criminally Insane,* 41 Pub. Opinion Q. 523, 531 (1977–78). On the role of the media in the perpetuation of these stereotypes, *see e.g.,* Catherine Cobb, *Challenging a States Bias Mental Health Inquires Leader, The ADA,* 32 Hous. L. Rev. 1383, 1394 n.70 (1996).

See, e.g., Sawsan Reda, *Public Perceptions of Former Psychiatric Patients in England,* 47 Psychiatric Serv. 1253 (1997) (neighborhood resident revealed "extremely negative" attitudes toward persons with mental illness; these attitudes were largely formed by media depictions); *See generally* Fred Berlin & Martin Malin, *Media Distortion of the Public's Perceptions of Recidivism and Psychiatric Rehabilitation,* 148 Am. J. Psychiatry 1572 (1991). On the portrayal of persons with mental disabilities in the movies, see Steven Hyler, Glen Gabbard, & Irving Schneider, *Homicidal Maniacs and Narcissistic Parasites: Stigmatization of Mentally Ill Persons in the Movies,* 46 Hosp. & Community Psychiatry 1044 (1991). On media coverage of cases involving mentally disabled criminal defendants, see Richard Bonnie, *Excusing and Punishing in Criminal Adjudication: A Reality Check,* 5 Cornell J.L. & Pub. Pol'y 1 (1995); Thomas Grisso, *Forensic Evaluations and the Fourth Estate,* 3 Forens. Rep. 427 (1990). *See generally* Perlin, Jurisprudence, *supra* note 8, at 172–73, 338–39; John Monahan, *Mental Disorder and Violent Behavior,* 47 Am. Psychologist 511 (1992).

[132]*See supra* section 1; *see* Perlin, *OCS, supra* note 8, at 12–28; Saks & Kidd, *supra* note 30; Sherwin, *supra* note 65, at 737–39; Donald N. Bersoff, *Judicial Deference to Non Legal Decisionmakers: Imposing Simplistic Solutions on Problems of Cognitive Complexity in Mental Disability Law,* 46 SMU L. Rev. 329 (1992).

Parallels are found in all aspects of the treatment of persons with mental retardation. *See, e.g.,* Minow, *supra* note 15, at 110–39; James W. Ellis, *Mental Retardation at the Close of the 20th Century: A New Realism,* 28 Mental Retardation 263 (1990); Note, *Community Housing Rights for the Mentally Retarded,* 3 Det. C.L. Rev. 869, 872–74 (1987); Robert Hayman, *Presumptions of Justice: Law, Politics, and the Mentally Retarded Parent,* 103 Harv. L. Rev. 1201 (1990).

[133]On empathy in general, see Henderson, *supra* note 57; *see also* Susan Bandes, *Empathy, Narrative, and Victim Impact Statements,* 63 U. Chi. L. Rev. 361 (1996). On how empathy is the "enemy of . . . stereotypes" in the context of the jury system, see Douglas Linder, *Juror Empathy and Race,* 63 Tenn. L. Rev. 887, 916 (1996).

[134]On the relationship between race and mental illness's stigma, see Mary Lou Siantz, *The Stigma of Mental Illness in Children of Color,* 6 J. Clin. Ped. Nursing. 10 (Oct.–Dec. 1993). On the relationship between race and mental health diagnosis, admission and length of stay in hospitals, see John Crowley & Susan Simmons, *Mental Health, Race, and Ethnicity: A Retrospective Study of the Care of Ethnic Minorities and Whites in a Psychiatric Unit,* 17 J. Adv. Nursing 1078 (1992) (finding significant differences in the treatment of Whites and persons of Afro-Caribbean ancestry); Lonnie R. Snowden & Freda K. Cheung, *Use of Inpatient Mental Health Services by Members of Ethnic Minority Groups,* 45 Am. Psychologist 347 (1990) (African Americans more likely to be hospitalized and committed); H. Neighbors et al., *The Influence of Racial Factors on Psychiatric Diagnosis: A Review and Suggestion for Research,* 25 Community Ment. Health J. 301 (1989) (African Americans overrepresented among patients diagnosed with schizophrenia); Jay Wade, *Institutional Racism: An Analysis of the Mental Health System,* 63 Am. J. Orthopsychiatry 536 (1993) (alleging that institutional racism helps explain wide racial disparities in diagnosis, treatment, and use of mental health services); Sarah Rosenfeld, *Race Differences in Involuntary Hospitalization: Psychiatric vs. Labeling Perspectives,* 25 J. Health & Soc. Behav. 14 (1984) [hereinafter, Rosenfield, *Race*] (more coercive conditions under which non-Whites enter treatment accounts for greater involuntary hospitalization rate); Sarah Rosenfeld, *Sex Roles and Societal Reactions to Mental Illness: The Labeling of "Deviant" Deviance,* 23 J. Health & Soc. Behav. 18 (1982) [hereinafter, Rosenfeld, *Sex Roles*] (in commitment context, both men and women treated more harshly when their deviant behavior is inconsistent with traditional gender-role norms).

gender,[135] ethnicity,[136] economic class,[137] and culture.[138] Research demonstrates, for instance, that African Americans are significantly overrepresented in state inpatient psychiatric hospitals,[139] that psychopathology is overestimated in Black defendants,[140] and that race is significantly related to referral of adolescents from juvenile courts to psychiatric hospitals.[141]

Pathology—disorder and the loss of control—is associated with deviant sexuality and with outsider groups such as racial and religious minorities.[142] Gilman thus located the "structural relationship between madness and blackness"—"the Union of two abstractions of the Other"—in "antiquity,"[143] and traced the historical roots of the belief that Jews, like women, "possessed a basic biological predisposition to specific forms of mental illness."[144]

---

[135]On the impact of sexist attitudes on the operations of mental disability law, see Mary Finn & Loretta Stalans, *The Influence of Gender and Marital State on Police Decisions in Domestic Assault Cases*, 24 CRIM. JUST. & BEHAV. 157 (1997) (mentally ill female assailants more likely than male assailants to be referred for involuntary civil commitment; gender influenced arrest decisions through officers' assessments of credibility and responsibility in hypothetical domestic assault cases); Anthony Scott, Alan Shiell, & Madeleine King, *Is General Practitioner Decision Making Associated With Patient Socio-Economic Status?* 42 SOC. SCI. & MED. 35 (1996) (women more likely than men to receive medical prescriptions). *See generally* Susan Stefan, *Silencing the Different Voice: Competence, Feminist Theory and Law*, 47 U. MIAMI L. REV. 763 (1993); SHERRY GLIED & SHARON KOFMAN, WOMEN'S MENTAL HEALTH: ISSUES FOR HEALTH REFORM (1995).

[136]*See, e.g.,* Lauren Kim & Chu-Ah Chun, *Ethnic Differences in Psychiatric Diagnosis Among Asian American Adolescents*, 181 J. NERVOUS & MENT. DIS. 612 (1993) (Asians received significantly more nonpsychiatric diagnoses than did Caucasians).

[137]*See, e.g.,* Scott et al., *supra* note 135 (patients of higher socioeconomic status more likely to receive prescriptions than those of lower socioeconomic status); Martha L. Bruce et al., *Poverty and Psychiatric Status*, 48 ARCHIVES GEN. PSYCHIATRY 470 (1991) (on the relationship between psychiatric disorder and social class). For an excellent overview, *see generally* Carl Cohen, *Poverty and the Course of Schizophrenia: Implications for Research and Policy*, 44 HOSP. & COMMUNITY PSYCHIATRY 951 (1993).

[138]*See, e.g.,* Peter Gregware, *Courts, Criminal Process, and AIDS: The Institutionalization of Culture in Legal Decision Making*, 16 LAW & POL'Y 341 (1993) (discussing role of cultural bias in creating AIDS policies).

For an excellent overview of related issues, see Susan Stefan, *Issues Relating to Women and Ethnic Minorities in Mental Health Treatment and Law, in* LAW, MENTAL HEALTH, AND MENTAL DISORDER 140 (Bruce Sales & Daniel Shuman eds. 1996).

[139]William Lawson et al., *Race as a Factor in Inpatient and Outpatient Admissions and Diagnosis*, 45 HOSP. & COMMUNITY PSYCHIATRY 72 (1994).

[140]Gerald Cooke et al., *A Comparison of Blacks and Whites Committed for Evaluation of Competency to Stand Trial on Criminal Charges*, 2 J. PSYCHIATRY & L. 319, 319 (1974).

[141]W. John Thomas & Dorothy Stubbe, *A Comparison of Correctional and Mental Health Referrals in Juvenile Court*, 24 J. PSYCHIATRY & L. 379 (1996).

[142]GILMAN, *supra* note 15, at 24–25. On the ways that we impute mental illness to those who challenge sexual stereotypes, see *supra* sources cited at note 9; Kent Streseman, *Headshrinkers, Manmunchers, Moneygrubbers, Nuts & Sluts: Reexamining Compelled Mental Examinations in Sexual Harassment Actions Under the Civil Rights Act of 1991*, 80 CORNELL L. REV. 1268 (1995).

[143]GILMAN, *supra* note 15, at 142, 148. On the traditionally perceived link between mental retardation and miscegenation, see James Ellis & Ruth Luckasson, *Mentally Retarded Criminal Defendants*, 53 GEO. WASH. L. REV. 414, 419 n.23 (1985).

[144]GILMAN, *supra* note 15, at 162. On the important question of cultural variance in diagnosing and treating mental illness, see, for example, George S. Howard, *Culture Tales: A Narrative Approach to Thinking, Cross-Cultural Psychology, and Psychotherapy*, 46 AM. PSYCHOLOGIST 187, 194–95 (1991); Horacio Fabrega, *An Ethno-Medical Perspective of Anglo-American Psychiatry*, 146 AM. J. PSYCHIATRY 588 (1989); Lloyd H. Rogler, *The Meaning of Culturally Sensitive Research in Mental Health*, 146 AM. J. PSYCHIATRY 296 (1989). On the relationship between cultural bias and mistreatment of persons with mental disabilities, see Robert Hayman Jr., *Presumptions of Justice: Law, Politics and the Mentally Retarded Parent*, 103 HARV. L. REV. 1201, 1228 (1990).

Sanist, racist, and sexist stereotypes remain frequently grounded in similar sorts of eugenic and cultural pseudoscience in ways that reflect broader sets of public attitudes.[145] In one example, Black students historically have been more readily assigned to classes for the "educable mentally retarded" than have White students;[146] in another, *all* postnatal women were seen as mentally impaired.[147] Yet other studies show that decisions to hospitalize are positively related to behavioral stereotypes of race and sex.[148] These conflations suggest the power of the underlying stereotypes, and force us to reconsider mental disability law developments in their context.

Public Attitudes

Society fears, victimizes, and brutalizes persons with mental illness.[149] Such individuals have been subject to "a regime of state-mandated segregation and degradation . . . that in its violence and bigotry rivaled, and indeed paralleled, the worst excesses of Jim Crow."[150] Persons labeled as mentally ill or mentally retarded face prejudice and discrimination; the stigmatic label of "expatient" makes the obtaining of housing and employment significantly more difficult.[151] The public is now convinced—despite an impressive array of evidence to the contrary—that homelessness is largely a problem of mental illness, and that, if mental patients had never been granted their modest amount of civil rights, homelessness

---

[145]*See, e.g.,* Lawrence, *supra* note 34, at 373–74. On the explicit link between governmentally sanctioned racial and disability-based segregation, see Timothy M. Cook, *The Americans With Disabilities Act: The Move to Integration,* 64 TEMP. L. REV. 393, 399–407 (1991).

See, e.g., Robert Weinstock et al., *Psychiatric Patients and AIDS: The Forensic Clinician Perspective,* 35 J. FORENS. SCI. 644 (1990) (on the question of whether psychiatric hospitals should be allowed to refuse admissions to persons with AIDS); Kirk Heilbrun et al., *Comparing Females Acquitted by Reason of Insanity, Convicted, and Civilly Committed in Florida, 1977–1984,* 12 LAW & HUM. BEHAV. 295 (1988) (on relationship between gender, age, and race and insanity defense success); Martha Livingston Bruce et al., *Poverty and Psychiatric Status,* 48 ARCHIVES GEN. PSYCHIATRY 470 (1991) (on the relationship between psychiatric disorder and social class).

[146]Debra P. v. Turlington, 730 F.2d 1405, 1414 (11th Cir. 1984).

[147]Kimberly Waldron, *Postpartum Psychosis as an Insanity Defense,* 21 RUTGERS L.J. 669, 680–81 (1990). On the relationship between stereotypes of the "mad" and the "bad" infanticidal woman, see Anih Wilczynski, *Images of Women Who Kill Their Infants: The Mad and the Bad,* 2 WOMEN & CRIM. JUST. 71 (1991). *See generally* Michele Oberman, *Mothers Who Kill: Coming to Terms With Modern American Infanticide,* 34 CRIM. L. REV. 1 (1996).

[148]Rosenfeld, *Sex Roles, supra* note 134, at 18 (in commitment context, both men and women receive more severe societal reaction when their deviation is inconsistent with traditional gender-role norms); Rosenfeld, *Race supra,* note 134, at 14. (more coercive conditions under which non-Whites enter treatment accounts for greater involuntary hospitalization rate). On the relationship between institutionalization and women's social and political status, see Hendrick Hartog, *Mrs. Packard on Dependency,* 1 YALE J.L. & HUMAN. 92 (1988).

[149]On the significance of the legal definition of "mental illness," see Bruce Winick, *Ambiguities on the Legal Meaning and Significance of Mental Illness,* 1 PSYCHOL., PUB. POL'Y & L. 534 (1995). *Cf.* Kansas v. Hendricks, 521 U.S. 346, 359 (1997) (pedophilia qualifies as "mental disorder" for purposes of commitment under Kansas's Sexually Violent Predators Act); *see* 1 PERLIN, *supra* note 4, § 2A-3.3 (2d ed. 1998).

[150]City of Cleburne v. Cleburne Living Ctr., 473 U.S. 432, 462 (1985) (Marshall, J., concurring in part and dissenting in part).

[151]Gary B. Melton & Ellen G. Garrison, *Fear, Prejudice and Neglect: Discrimination Against Mentally Disabled Persons,* 42 AM. PSYCHOLOGIST 1007, 1007 (1987); Stewart Page, *Psychiatric Stigma: Two Studies of Behaviour When the Chips Are Down,* 2 CANAD. J. COMMUNITY MENTAL HEALTH 13 (1983); Cynthia Okolo & Samuel Guskin, *Community Attitudes Toward Community Placement of Mentally Retarded Persons, in* 12 INT'L REV. RES. IN MENTAL RETARDATION 26 (Norman R. Ellis & N. W. Bray eds. 1984). *See also generally* Michelle Fine & Adrienne Asch, *Disability Beyond Stigma: Social Interaction, Discrimination and Activism,* 44 J. SOC. ISSUES 3 (1988).

would largely disappear as a social phenomenon.[152] Persons with mental disabilities are seen as individuals with "immutable differences that set them apart from the rest of society, and thus warrant different legal treatment."[153] And police attitudes—reflected in decision making about apprehension, arrest, and level of charges filed—also demonstrate the negative power of sanist stereotyping,[154] notwithstanding empirical studies that show that not even severe mental disorder predicts the commission of violent crime after release from jail.[155]

Thus we are sanist because we fear the unknown, and we fear the possibility that *we* may become mentally ill. To make the world less indeterminate, we simplify via stereotypes that simultaneously demonize and infantilize. And we continue to irrationally conflate mental illness with dangerousness.

In a comprehensive review of the available research literature, the MacArthur Research Network on Mental Health and Law[156] (along with the National Stigma Clearinghouse) recently stressed the following:

> The expertise of people with psychiatric conditions and of their family members paints a picture dramatically different from the stereotype. The results of several recent large-scale research projects conclude that only a weak association between mental disorders and violence exists in the community. Serious violence by people with major mental disorders appears concentrated in a small fraction of the total number, and especially in those who use alcohol and other drugs. Mental disorders—in sharp contrast to alcohol and drug abuse—account for a minuscule portion of the violence that afflicts American society.[157]

John Monahan, the director of the MacArthur Network, concluded, "Clearly, mental health status makes at best a *trivial* contribution to the overall level of violence in society."[158] Ninety percent of persons with mental disabilities are *not* violent.[159] Monahan added, "*None* of the data give *any* support to the sensationalized caricature of the mentally disordered served up by the media, the shunning of former patients by employers and neighbors in the community, or 'lock 'em all up' laws proposed by politicians pandering to public fears."[160] Yet sanist stereotyping continues virtually unabated.

People with mental disabilities have largely been invisible and without political power.[161] Hidden for decades in large, remote institutions, their "stories" have never been

---

[152]*See generally* Perlin, *supra* note 1 (addressing the misconception that all homeless persons were deinstitutionalized from mental hospitals); *Special Issue: Homelessness*, 46 AM. PSYCHOL. 1108–1252 (1991) (collection of articles addressing the social problem of homelessness).

[153]MINOW, *supra* note 15, at 107.

[154]Linda Teplin & Nancy Pruett, *Police as Streetcorner Psychiatrist: Managing the Mentally Ill*, 15 INT'L J.L. & PSYCHIATRY 139, 154 (1992) ("extrapsychiatric variables" rather than rules of law or degree of psychiatric symptomatology determine whether police choose to hospitalize, arrest, or "manage" a mentally ill citizen).

[155]*See, e.g.*, Linda Teplin, Karen Abram, & Gary McClelland, *Does Psychiatric Disorder Predict Violent Crime Among Released Jail Detainees? A Six-Year Longitudinal Study*, 49 AM. PSYCHOLOGIST 335 (1994).

[156]*See generally*, Leonard Rubenstein, *Ending Discrimination Against Mental Health Treatment in Publicly Financed Health Care*, 40 ST. LOUIS V.L.J. 315, 349 (1996).

[157]MONAHAN, *SUPRA* NOTE 20, § 7-2.2.1, AT 316; *SEE GENERALLY* JOHN MONAHAN & JEAN ARNOLD, *VIOLENCE BY PEOPLE WITH MENTAL ILLNESS: A CONSENSUS STATEMENT BY ADVOCATES AND RESEARCHERS*, 19 PSYCHIATRIC REHABILITATION J. 67 (1996).

[158]Monahan, *supra* note 20, at 315.

[159]Jeffrey Swanson et al., *Violence and Psychiatric Disorder in the Community: Evidence From the Epidemiologic Catchment Area Surveys*, 41 HOSP. & COMMUNITY PSYCHIATRY 761 (1990).

[160]Monahan, *supra* note 20, at 315.

[161]*See* Robert A. Burt, *Constitutional Law and the Teaching of the Parables*, 93 YALE L.J. 455, 462 (1984) (cases such as Youngberg v. Romeo, 457 U.S. 307 (1982) and Pennhurst State Sch. & Hosp. v. Halderman, 451 U.S. 1 (1981) raise issue as to whether we "are inescapably obliged to regard retarded people as members of our community").

incorporated into our social fabric or consciousness.[162] Although there are now "Black seats" in Congress (and a "gay seat" in the New York City council), the idea of an "ex-patient's seat" in any generally elected public body is beyond comprehension to most of us.[163]

Patients—and ex-patients—are often invisible to those who treat them. Few mentally ill patients are ever consulted about their treatment program or informed of their rights.[164] The potential of a consumer voice is often "neglect[ed] or even discouraged."[165] Drug researchers fail to consider the quality of life of patients with schizophrenia.[166] And therapists' ubiquitous undervaluation of the nonbiological aspects of treatment, such as social support, is a significant cause of patient dissatisfaction.[167]

Although mental health researchers are beginning—finally—to study questions of treatment from the perspective of the person being treated,[168] of the relationships between

---

[162]There is now a significant body of literature by expatients, see, for example, JUDI CHAMBERLIN, ON OUR OWN: PATIENT-CONTROLLED ALTERNATIVES TO THE MENTAL HEALTH SYSTEM (1979), as well as some modest recognition of the role of expatients' groups in law-reform litigation and political reform activity; see Neal Milner, *The Right to Refuse Treatment: Four Case Studies of Legal Mobilization*, 21 LAW & SOC'Y REV. 447 (1987) (Milner I) ; Milner, *The Dilemmas of Legal Mobilization: Ideologies and Strategies of Mental Patient Liberation Groups*, 8 LAW & POL'Y 105 (1986) (Milner II). Yet it does not appear that these stories have had a major impact on the consciousness of the general public. On the other hand, the passage of the Americans With Disabilities Act, 42 U.S.C. §§ 12101 *et seq.* (1990), may lead to greater public awareness of the stories of physically disabled individuals. *See, e.g.,* A. Birnbaum, *No Voice for the Disabled,* VILLAGE VOICE, Nov. 5, 1991, at 5 (letter to the editor): "The *Voice,* while standing firm behind most minorities and oppressed groups, seems to ignore the political, social, and civil issues concerning persons with disabilities."

[163]On the importance of congressional "Black seats," see Julius L. Crockett, *Special Report: What Color Is the Constitution? The Summer of '64, When Young American Men and Women Fought and Smiled, Struggled and Died, and Won, in America,* 15 HUM. RTS. 14, 15 (1988). In New York City, an openly homosexual man was elected in 1991 in a city council election. The gay council member, Tom Duane, represented Manhattan's Third District, which includes portions of the Greenwich Village, Chelsea, and Soho neighborhoods. *See* Michael Spencer, *Gay Candidates Face Off in Single-Issue N.Y. Race,* WASH. POST, Sept. 11, 1991; on the increase in openly gay candidates in state and local political elections, see generally Lisa Leff, *Gay Cause Is Gaining Attention,* WASH. POST (Aug. 26, 1986). Also *see generally,* David Rosenblum, *Geographically Sexual?: Advancing Lesbian and Gay Interests Through Proportional Representation,* 31 HARV. C.R.-C.L. L. REV. 119 (1996); William Kysella, *Gerrymandering Against Gays?* 4 LAW & SEX 249 (1994).

[164]*See, e.g.,* Baukje Miedma, *Control or Treatment? Experiences of People Who Have Been Psychiatrically Hospitalized in New Brunswick,* 13 CANAD. J. COMMUNITY MENT. HEALTH 111 (1994)

[165]Marc Rodwin, *Patient Accountability and Quality of Care: Lessons From Medical Consumerism and the Patients' Rights, Women's Health, and Disability Rights Movement,* 20 AM. J.L. & MED. 147 (1994)

[166]A. George Awad, *Quality of Life of Schizophrenic Patients on Medications and Implications for New Drug Trials,* 43 HOSP. & COMMUNITY PSYCHIATRY 262 (1992).

[167]Michael Perreault, *Patients' Requests and Satisfaction With Services in an Outpatient Psychiatric Setting,* 47 PSYCHIATRIC SERV. 287 (1996).

[168]On patients' attitudes toward being civilly committed, see Gail Edelsohn & Virginia Hiday, *Civil Commitment: A Range of Patient Attitudes,* 18 BULL. AM. ACAD. PSYCHIATRY & L. 65 (1990) (majority of patients reported positive views but a substantial minority expressed negative reactions). On the issue of patients' right to refuse medication, see William Greenberg, Lanna Moore-Duncan & Rachel Herron, *Patients' Attitudes Toward Having Been Forcibly Medicated,* 24 BULL. AM. ACAD. PSYCHIATRY & L. 513 (1996) (significant minorities of involuntarily medicated patients reported feeling angry, helpless, fearful, or embarrassed); *cf.* Rennie v. Klein, 476 F. Supp. 1294, 1306 (D.N.J. 1978) ("schizophrenics have been asked every question except, 'How does the medication agree with you?' Their response is worth listening to"), citing Van Putten & Ray, *Subjective Response as a Predictor of Outcome in Pharmacotherapy,* 35 ARCHIVES GEN. PSYCHIATRY 477, 478–80 (1978). On patients' attitudes toward the use of physical restraints, see Yvette Sheline & Teresa Nelson, *Patient Choice: Deciding Between Psychotropic Medication and Physical Restraints in an Emergency,* 21 BULL. AM. ACAD. PSYCHIATRY & L. 321 (1993) (nearly two-thirds of patient polled preferred medication; slightly more than one-third preferred restraints).

patients and expatients and their families,[169] and of the attitudes of family members toward their relatives' mental illness,[170] the results of these studies rarely—if ever—are incorporated into legislation or judicial opinions.[171] Frequently deprived of the vote[172] or the right to be parents,[173] removed from political discourse,[174] and often invisible to their own attorneys,[175] persons with mental disabilities remain a largely hidden,[176] fragmented,[177] and disencranchised minority. When they are depicted in the news or entertainment media, it is usually in a negative or distorted way.[178]

---

[169]On the impact that such relationships have on recidivism rates, see, for example, W. Kim Halford, Robert Schweitzer, & Frank Varghese, *Effects of Family Environment on Negative Symptoms and Quality of Life of Psychotic Patients,* 42 HOSP. & COMMUNITY PSYCHIATRY 1241 (1991) (patients who live after hospital discharge with families with higher levels of emotional expressiveness exhibit fewer negative symptoms and enjoy a better quality of postdischarge life).

[170]*See, e.g.,* Marcio Pinheiro, *The Selling of Clinical Psychiatry in America,* 43 HOSP. & COMMUNITY PSYCHIATRY 102 (1992) (critiquing organized psychiatry's alliance with family groups that seek an exclusively biological explanation of mental illness).

[171]On the important—but rarely asked—question of whether disability rights legislation may have the unwanted side result of *perpetuating* certain disabilities, see Martha Minow, *Not Only for Myself: Identity, Politics, and Law,* 75 OR. L. REV. 647, 677 (1996), discussing KRISTIN BUMILLER, THE CIVIL RIGHTS SOCIETY (1988) (questioning whether civil rights laws require individuals to claim the status of victims in ways that "recapitulate their group-based exclusion").

[172]*See* 2 PERLIN, *supra* note 4, § 7.21, at 655 n.514. More than 30 years ago, researchers had discovered that mental patients were no more "illogical, inconsistent, or unprepared" to vote than a similar sample of individuals who had never been institutionalized. *See* Marguerite Hertz et al., *Mental Patients and Civil Rights: A Study of Opinions of Mental Patients on Social and Political Issues,* 2 J. HEALTH & HUM. BEHAV. 251, 258 (1961).

[173]*See generally* Hayman, *supra* note 144, and *cf. id.* at 1221 (no reason to believe that mentally retarded parents are unable to meet the emotional needs of their children).

[174]*See, e.g.,* Roy P. van den Brink-Budgen, *Liberal Dialogue, Citizenship and Mentally Handicapped Persons,* 34 POL. STUD. 374 (1980); Martha T. McCluskey, *supra* note 87, at 863. For comprehensive surveys of the history of legislation that has excluded persons with mental disabilities from the political process, see BRUCE D. SALES ET AL., DISABLED PERSONS AND THE LAW (1982) (SALES), and SAMUEL J. BRAKEL ET AL., MENTAL DISABILITY AND THE LAW (3d ed. 1985) (BRAKEL).

[175]*See generally* Michael L. Perlin & Robert Sadoff, *Ethical Issues in the Representation of Individuals in the Commitment Process,* 45 LAW & CONTEMP. PROBS. 161 (1982); Michael L. Perlin, *Fatal Assumption: A Critical Evaluation of the Role of Counsel in Mental Disability Cases,* 16 LAW & HUM. BEHAV. 39 (1992); *see also, e.g.,* N. Pinsley, *A Wild Week at Bellevue Murder Trial,* MANHATTAN LAWYER, Oct. 31–Nov. 6, 1989, at 1 (criminal defense lawyer did not know if his client had been medicated for a court appearance; "I don't talk to [the defendant] the lawyer said. "We got enough psychotics in this courtroom").

[176]Of course, other mentally disabled individuals—persons with mental illness who have been deinstitutionalized and are homeless—are all too visible to many citizens. *See* Perlin, *supra* note 1, at 106–08.

[177]Within the advocacy community, it is well-known that certain disabled groups wish to distance themselves from others (i.e., groups advocating for individuals with developmental disabilities emphasize that their clients are not mentally ill—thus avoiding the dangerousness stereotype; those advocating for persons with mental illness often focus on their clients' intellectual capacities and potential—thus separating themselves from individuals with mental retardation). One of the most troubling moments of my career as a public interest litigator came when I suggested to a representative of an advocacy group seeking to ameliorate conditions of institutionalized autistic children that he seek out a certain state senator to introduce legislation on behalf of his clientele. "Not Senator X," he quickly replied, "He's the *captive of the retardates!* (*sic*)." *Cf.* Seide v. Prevost, 536 F. Supp. 1121 (S.D.N.Y. 1982) (action by Board of Visitors of children's psychiatric hospital to enjoin opening of homeless shelter).

[178]*See generally* Douglas Biklen, *The Culture of Policy: Disability Images and Their Analogues in Public Policy,* 15 POL. STUD. J. 515 (1987); *see, e.g.,* Stephen E. Hyler et al., *Homicidal Maniacs and Narcissistic Parasites: Stigmatization of Mentally Ill Persons in the Movies,* 42 HOSP. & COMMUNITY PSYCHIATRY 1044 (1991);

This marginalization has served as a petri dish for sanist social attitudes. These attitudes—rooted in prejudice—have led to a sanist environment, sanist myths, and sanist behavior.[179] As with other myths based on stereotypes, they are the result of rigid categorization and overgeneralization, created to "localize our anxiety, to prove to ourselves that what we fear does not lie within."[180] Sanist myths are unlike other myths, though, in a critical way: Whereas most other myths deal with populations that possess fairly immutable qualities (e.g., race, sex), any of us *could* become mentally ill (or at least, on an unconscious level, *fear* becoming mentally ill). This, as much as any other reason, may account for the level of public virulence. The following are just a few of the sanist myths that dominate our social discourse.

1. Mentally ill individuals are "different," and perhaps less than human.[181] They are erratic, deviant, morally weak, unattractive, sexually uncontrollable, emotionally unstable, lazy, superstitious, ignorant, and demonstrate a primitive morality.[182]

Fred S. Berlin & Martin H. Malin, *Media Distortion of the Public's Perception of Recidivism and Psychiatric Rehabilitation,* 148 AM. J. PSYCHIATRY 1572 (1991). *See also* Gregory Leong et al., *Dangerous Mentally Disordered Criminals: Unresolvable Societal Fear?* 36 J. FORENS. SCI. 210, 210 (1991) (caricature of "psychotic criminal . . . strikes terror in the mind of the common person").

[179]*Cf.* Doe v. Colautti, 592 F.2d 704, 711 (3d Cir. 1979) ("Although the mentally ill have been the victims of stereotypes, the disabilities imposed on them have often reflected that many of the mentally ill do have reduced ability for personal relations, for economic activity, and for political choice"). On the fallacy of using the "abnormal persons" approach in this context, see MINOW, *supra* note 15, at 105–07 (discussing majority opinion in *City of Cleburne*), and *id.* at 130 (finding a "striking connection between current conceptions of abnormal persons and remnants or re-creations of a feudal hierarchical order").

[180]GILMAN, *supra* note 15, at 240. *See* "Stigma Task Force," *supra* note 36, at 1: "Individuals experience stigma and discrimination after they have been labeled "mentally ill" by society or by the mental health system. . . . Once people are labeled mentally ill, regardless of the precipitating cause, they are categorized and treated as members of a single group who are assumed implicitly to be more alike than different. . . ." The stereotyping and the subsequent response to people with mental illness or psychiatric disabilities are based on unexamined assumptions. These assumptions are negative and affect our social response.

[181]*See* Perlin, *Myths, supra* note 8, at 721–24; *see also* Bruce Winick, *Competency to Consent to Voluntary Hospitalization: A Therapeutic Jurisprudence Analysis of* Zinermon v. Burch, 14 INT'L J.L. & PSYCHIATRY 169 (1991), *reprinted in* ESSAYS IN THERAPEUTIC JURISPRUDENCE 83, 102 (David Wexler & Bruce J. Winick eds. 1991) (ESSAYS) ("The difference between 'crazy' and normal people is not as great as commonly is supposed"). For a stark example of difference in the way persons with mental disabilities are treated, even after death, see, for example, Joan Gallen, *Mental Patients Finally Put to Rest With Dignity,* NEWS TRIBUNE (Woodbridge, N.J.), Oct. 10, 1991, (nearly 1000 patients buried on New Jersey state hospital grounds in unmarked graves); David Corcoran, *Graves Without Names for the Forgotten Mentally Retarded,* N.Y. TIMES, Dec. 9, 1991, at B6 (850 residents of New York state school for mentally retarded similarly buried).

[182]*See generally* GILMAN, *supra* note 15. This description is borrowed, almost verbatim, from Peggy Davis' quotation of Gordon Allport's (*see supra* note 3, at 196–98) description of *Black* stereotypes; *see* Davis, *supra* note 47, at 1561, and from Thomas Ross' characterization of public attitudes toward the *poor; see* Ross, *supra* note 52, at 1503, 1507, and 1516: "The Justices of the contemporary Court have resurrected the rhetorical theme of the moral weakness of the poor. They have relied on the initial step of separating the poor from us and labeling them as deviant. And the plea of judicial helplessness has also returned to prominence."

On the way that "positive" images of persons with mental retardation (such as amiability) are consistent with stereotypic perceptions of ethnic minorities and women, see Robert F. Williams, *Perceptions of Mentally Retarded Persons,* 21 EDUC. & TRAINING OF THE MENTALLY RETARDED 13, 18 (1986); *cf.* McCluskey, *supra* note 87, at 870 (discussing how seemingly positive images may express harmful stereotypes in context of disabled children and telethon broadcasts); *see also* Elizabeth OuYang, *Women With Disabilities in the Work Force: Outlook for the 1990's,* 13 HARV. WOMEN'S L.J. 13, 18 (1990).

They lack the capacity to show love or affection.[183] They smell different from "normal" individuals,[184] and are somehow worth less.[185]

2. Most mentally ill individuals are dangerous and frightening.[186] At worst, they are invariably more dangerous than nonmentally ill persons.[187] Experts can accurately identify such dangerousness.[188] At best, mentally disabled individuals are simple and contented, like children.[189]

---

[183]Susan Stefan, *Whose Egg Is It Anyway? Reproductive Rights of Incarcerated, Institutionalized, and Incompetent Women,* 13 NOVA L. REV. 405, 448–49 (1989), discussing *In re* MacDonald, 201 N.W.2d 447, 450 (Iowa 1972); *see generally* Hayman, *supra* note 144. *Expression* of emotions affect our perceptions of others. The riskiness of a mental illness defense must be considered in the context of yet other evidence that a significant percentage of actual jurors saw certain aspects of a defendant's demeanor—whether he or she looked passive, unremorseful, or emotionless—as a critical operative factor in determining whether or not to return a death sentence. *See* William Geimer & Jonathan Amsterdam, *Why Jurors Vote Life or Death: Operative Factors in Ten Florida Death Penalty Cases,* 15 AM. J. CRIM. L. 1, 40–41, 51–52 (1987). Other studies reveal that a defendant's attractiveness is a significant trial variable (with jurors treating attractive defendants more leniently than unattractive defendants). Marybeth Zientek, Riggins v. Nevada: *Medicated Defendants and Courtroom Demeanor From the Jury's Perspective,* 30 AM. CRIM. L. REV. 215, 227 (1992), reporting on research in Wayne Weiten & Shari Diamond, *A Critical Review of the Jury Simulation Paradigm: The Case of Defendant Characteristics,* 3 LAW & HUM. BEHAV. 71, 74 (1979).

[184]*See* Stevens v. Dobs, Inc., 483 F.2d 82 (4th Cir. 1973), discussed *supra* note 75. *Cf.* G. PETIEVICH, PARAMOUR 260 (1991) (describing St. Elizabeth's Hospital in Washington, DC):

> Inside, Powers was met by the strong warm odor of mental illness. Though there was no way to quantify or determine whether such a smell actually existed, among themselves all Secret Service Agents acknowledged it. Over the years, when investigating persons making threats against the life of the President, Powers had searched hundreds of . . . rooms . . . looking for . . . evidence. Though some places were more pungent than others, each had at least a hint of the scent . . . best described . . . as a combination of nervous perspiration and dead human skin: the odor of schizophrenia.

[185]Steven Schwartz, *Damage Actions as a Strategy for Enhancing the Quality of Care of Persons With Mental Disabilities,* 17 N.Y.U. REV. L. & SOC. CHANGE 651, 681 (1989–90).

> Mental patients are not inherently more incompetent than nonmentally ill medical patients. *See* Michael L. Perlin & Deborah Dorfman, *Is It More Than "Dodging Lions and Wastin' Time"? Adequacy of Counsel, Questions of Competence, and the Judicial Process in Individual Right to Refuse Treatment Cases,* 2 PSYCHOL., PUB. POL'Y & L. 114, 120 (1996), citing Thomas Grisso & Paul Appelbaum, *The MacArthur Treatment Competence Study. III: Abilities of Patients to Consent to Psychiatric and Medical Treatments,* 19 LAW & HUM. BEHAV. 149 (1995).

[186]*See* Perlin, *Myths, supra* note 8, at 693–96; Stephen Rachlin, *The Limits of* Parens Patriae, *in* FOR THEIR OWN GOOD? ESSAYS ON COERCIVE KINDNESS 1, 5 (Aaron Rosenblatt ed. 1988); Eric Doherty, *Misconceptions About Mentally Ill Patients,* 146 AM. J. PSYCHIATRY 131 (1989) (letter to editor) (discussing the perception of dangerousness of persons with mental disabilities); Hayman, *supra* note 144, at 1220 (research shows no correlation between mental retardation and violence); Matter of M. M. B., 431 N.W.2d 329 (Wis. App. Ct. 1988) ("It is difficult to separate evidence of mental illness from evidence of dangerousness, because all persons have their own concepts of the effects of mental illness."); Linda Teplin, *The Criminality of the Mentally Ill: A Dangerous Misconception,* 142 AM. J. PSYCHIATRY 593, 597–98 (1982) ("The stereotype of the mentally ill as dangerous is not substantiated by our data.").

[187]*Cf.* Perlin, *Myths, supra* note 8, at 693–96; Bruce Ennis & Thomas Litwack, *Psychiatry and the Presumption of Expertise: Flipping Coins in the Courtroom,* 62 CALIF. L. REV. 693 (1974).

[188]*Cf.* JOHN MONAHAN, THE CLINICAL PREDICTION OF VIOLENT BEHAVIOR 60 (1981) (psychiatrists wrong two out of three times), *to* Monahan, *supra* note 20, at 317 (most contemporary research suggests that clinicians are able to distinguish violent from nonviolent patients with a modest, better-than-chance level of accuracy), citing Douglas Mossman, *Assessing Predictions of Violence: Being Accurate About Accuracy,* 62 J. CONSULTING & CLINICAL PSYCHOL. 783, 790 (1994), and Douglas Mossman, *Further Comments on Portraying the Accuracy of Violence Predictions,* 18 LAW & HUM. BEHAV. 587 (1994).

[189]Early insanity tests established a mental age of seven years as the baseline for criminal responsibility. *See* 6 & 7 Edw. II 109 (Selden Society 1313–14); *see also* Janet Ainsworth, *Re-Imaging Childhood and Reconstructing the Legal Order: The Case for Abolishing Juvenile Court,* 69 N.C. L. REV. 1083, 1098 n.95 (1991). *But cf.* David Faigman, *To Have and Have Not: Assessing the Value of Social Science to the Law as Science and Policy,* 38 EMORY

3. Mentally ill individuals are presumptively incompetent to participate in "normal" activities, to make autonomous decisions about their lives (especially in areas involving medical care), and to participate in the political arena.[190]

4. If a person in treatment for mental disability declines to take prescribed antipsychotic medication, that decision is an excellent predictor of (a) future dangerousness and (b) the need for involuntary institutionalization.[191]

5. Mental illness can easily be identified by lay persons and matches up closely to popular media depictions. It comports with our "common sense" notion of "crazy behavior."[192]

6. It is—and should be—socially acceptable to use pejorative labels to describe and single out mentally ill individuals; this singling out is not problematic in the way that the use of other pejorative labels to describe women, Blacks, Jews, or gay men and lesbians might be.[193]

L.J. 1005, 1034 (1989) (children as young as 15 may be competent to decide whether or not to seek commitment to mental hospitals), discussing studies reported in Lois A. Weithorn & Susan B. Campbell, *The Competency of Children and Adolescents to Make Informed Treatment Decisions*, 53 CHILD DEV. 1589, 1596 (1982).

[190]As a matter of law, incompetency cannot be presumed as a result of either mental illness or institutionalization. Bruce J. Winick, *Competency to Consent to Treatment: The Distinction Between Assent and Objection*, 28 HOUS. L. REV. 15 (1991), *reprinted in* ESSAYS, at 41, 46–50, n.181; *see generally* Bruce Winick, *On Autonomy: Legal and Psychological Perspectives*, 37 VILL. L. REV. 1705 (1992); Perlin, *supra* note 1, at 113–14; *In re* LaBelle, 107 Wash.2d 196, 728 P.2d 138, 146 (1986), and there is "no necessary relationship between mental illness and incompetency which renders [mentally ill persons] unable to provide informed consent to medical treatment." Davis v. Hubbard, 506 F. Supp. 915, 935 (N.D. Ohio 1980). The word "competency" encompasses many judicial statuses; a finding of incompetency (or competency) for one does not necessarily imply a similar finding for any other. *See* Perlin, *supra* note 98, at 967. *Cf.* Thomas Grisso & Paul Appelbaum, *Mentally Ill and Non-Mentally Ill Patients' Abilities to Understand Informed Consent Disclosures for Medication*, 15 LAW & HUM. BEHAV. 377, 385–86 (1991) (test results do not support generalized presumptions about capacities of mentally ill patients to understand informed consent); *see also* Campbell v. Talladega City Bd. of Educ., 518 F. Supp. 47, 55 (N.D. Ala. 1981) (school's failure to offer student full range of appropriate tests may have stemmed from "widely held social stereotypes concerning the abilities of retarded citizens").

[191]Michael L. Perlin, *Reading the Supreme Court's Tea Leaves: Predicting Judicial Behavior in Civil and Criminal Right to Refuse Treatment Cases*, 12 AM. J. FORENS. PSYCHIATRY 37, 49–52 (1991) [hereinafter, Perlin, *Tea Leaves*]; 1 PERLIN, *supra* note 4, § 2C-5.2, at 414–16 (2d ed. 1998); Theresa Scheid-Cook, *Commitment of the Mentally Ill to Outpatient Treatment*, 23 COMMUNITY MENT. HEALTH J. 173, 180–81 (1987).

[192]Perlin, *Myths, supra* note 8, at 727, n.608 (discussing Battalino v. People, 199 P.2d 897, 901 (Colo. 1948) (defendant not insane where there was no evidence of a "burst of passion with paleness, wild eyes and trembling"); Walter Bromberg & Henry M. Cleckley, *The Medico–Legal Dilemma: A Suggested Solution*, 42 J. CRIM. L. & CRIMINOL. 729, 738 (1952) (contrasting lay perceptions of "insanity" with actual attributes of schizophrenia); State v. Van Horn, 528 So.2d 529, 530 (Fla. App. 1988) (discussing probativeness of lay witnesses' "perception of [defendant's] normality").

On the role of demeanor in arrest decision making, see, for example, David Klinger, *Demeanor or Crime: Why "Hostile" Citizens Are More Likely to Be Arrested*, 32 CRIMINOL. 475 (1994); David Klinger, *More on Demeanor and Arrest in Dade County*, 34 CRIMINOL. 61 (1996).

[193]On the ways that negative characterization of mental illness and persons with mental illness are used by prosecutors in criminal trial summations, *see* Annotation, 88 A.L.R. 4th 8 (1991); Randy V. Cargill, *"Hard Blows" Versus "Foul Ones": Restrictions on Trial Counsel's Closing Argument*, ARMY LAWYER (Jan. 1991), at 20, 26. On the descriptions used by members of Congress to describe mentally disabled individuals ("the demented," "the deranged," "lunatics," "madmen," "idiots and morons," "psychopaths and nincompoops"), see U.S. Dep't of Treasury v. Galioto, No. 84-1904 (1986), Motion for Leave to File and Brief of Amicus New Jersey Department of the Public Advocate and ACLU (quoting legislative debate on 1968 gun control legislation).

For a fascinating counterpoint, compare *Paramount Denies Wrongdoing in 'Crazy People' Campaign*, PSYCHIATRIC NEWS (May 18, 1990), at 9 (mental health and patient advocacy groups claim credit for persuading Hollywood studio to "kill" offensive ad campaign), *to* Judi Chamberlin, *Warning: This Article Is Intended to Be Provocative*, NAPS NEWS (Spring 1990), at 6 (expatient activist argues that groups' antistigma efforts are "misdirected"; use of phrase "crazy" not "a slur").

7. Mentally ill individuals should be segregated in large, distant institutions; their presence threatens the economic and social stability of residential communities.[194]

8. The mentally disabled person charged with crime is presumptively the most dangerous potential offender, as well as the most "morally repugnant" one.[195] The insanity defense is used frequently and improperly as a way for such individuals to "beat the rap";[196] insanity tests are so lenient that virtually any mentally ill offender gets a "free ticket" through which to evade criminal and personal responsibility.[197] The insanity defense should be considered only when the mentally ill person demonstrates "objective" evidence of mental illness.[198]

9. Mentally disabled individuals simply don't try hard enough. They give in too easily to their basest instincts, and do not exercise appropriate self-restraint.[199]

10. If do-gooder, activist attorneys had not meddled in the lives of persons with mental disabilities, such individuals would be where they belong (in institutions), and all of

---

[194]*See, e.g.,* N.Y. State Ass'n for Retarded Children, Inc. v. Carey, 551 F. Supp. 1165, 1185 (E.D.N.Y. 1982):

The larger the facility the less likely it is that residents will become part of the community and will be accepted by their neighbors. Larger community facilities exacerbate community opposition to and fear of the retarded. This is because neighbors have more difficulty adjusting to a large group of individuals who happen to be different, and have more difficulty breaking down stereotypes in order to see these residents as individuals who happen to be retarded.

[195]Richard Rogers, *APA's Position on the Insanity Defense: Empiricism Versus Emotionalism,* 42 AM. PSYCHOLOGIST 840, 845 (1987). On the way that insanity acquittees have been viewed as "the most despised and feared group in society," see Deborah C. Scott et al., *Monitoring Insanity Acquittees: Connecticut's Psychiatric Security Review Board,* 41 HOSP. & COMMUN. PSYCHIATRY 980, 982 (1990). On the specific stereotypes applied to forensic patients, see Robert Menzies et al., *The Nature and Consequences of Forensic Decision-Making,* 27 CANAD. J. PSYCHIATRY 463 (1982). I believe that sex offenders have now supplanted insanity acquittees as the "most despised" group. *See* Michael L. Perlin, *"There's No Success Like Failure/and Failure's No Success at All": Exposing the Pretextuality of* Kansas v. Hendricks, 92 NW. U. L. REV. 1247 (1998).

[196]*See generally* HENRY J. STEADMAN, BEATING A RAP? DEFENDANTS FOUND INCOMPETENT TO STAND TRIAL (1979); Perlin, *Myths, supra* note 8, at 727–30; *cf., e.g.,* Moore v. State, 525 So.2d 870, 871 (Fla. 1988) (juror who rejected insanity defense as basis for exculpatory criminal defense not excused for cause) (reversing conviction), *to* Boblett v. Commonwealth, 396 S.E.2d 131, 135 (Va. Ct. App. 1990) (no abuse of discretion where trial court refused to excuse for cause juror who indicated he might have difficulty voting for an not guilty by reason of insanity verdict). On the extent to which the public is misinformed about the insanity defense, see Valerie P. Hans, *An Analysis of Public Attitudes Toward the Insanity Defense,* 24 CRIMINOL. 393 (1986) [hereinafter Hans, *Analysis of Public Attitudes*]; Valerie P. Hans & Dan Slater, *"Plain Crazy": Lay Definitions of Legal Insanity,* 7 INT'L J.L. & PSYCHIATRY 105, 111 (1984).

[197]*See, e.g.,* Richard Jeffrey & Richard A. Pasewark, *Altering Opinions About the Insanity Plea,* 11 J. PSYCHIATRY & L. 29 (1983); Richard A. Pasewark & Deborah Seidenzahl, *Opinions Concerning the Insanity Plea and Criminality Among Mental Patients,* 7 BULL. AM. ACAD. PSYCHIATRY & L. 199 (1979); Hans, *Analysis of Public Attitudes, supra* note 196.

[198]PERLIN, JURISPRUDENCE, *supra* note 8, at 123–28.; Lawrence T. White, *The Mental Illness Defense in the Capital Penalty Hearing,* 5 BEHAV. SCI. & L. 411, 417 (1987).

[199]*See, e.g.,* J. M. Balkin, *The Rhetoric of Responsibility,* 76 VA. L. REV. 197, 238 (1990) (Hinckley prosecutor suggested to jurors if Hinckley had emotional problems, they were largely his own fault); State v. Duckworth, 496 So.2d 624, 635 (La. App. 1986) (juror who felt defendant would be responsible for action as long as he "wanted to do them" not excused for cause) (no error); K. Gould, I. Keilitz, & J. Martin, "Criminal Defendants With Trial Disabilities: The Theory and Practice of Competency Assistance" (unpublished manuscript, 1995) (on file with the author), at 68 (trial judge responding to National Center for State Courts' survey indicated that, in his mind, defendants who were incompetent to stand trial *could have* communicated with and understood their attorneys "if they [had] only wanted"); *see also* Charles Krauthammer, *Nature Made Me Do It,* WASH. POST, May 11, 1990, at A27 (decrying use of "medical alibis"). *Cf.* MINOW, *supra* note 15, at 47 (discussing the oversignificance that we attribute to traits "that are largely or entirely beyond the control of the individuals who are identified by them"). On the role of perceptions of effort in positive and negative behavior attributions, see Weiner, *supra* note 121.

us would be better off.[200] In fact, there's no reason for courts to involve themselves at all in mental disability cases.[201]

Although I have described these as *public* attitudes, it is clear that they pervade all components of the *legal* system as well. Judges "are embedded in the cultural presuppositions that engulf us all."[202] Their discomfort with social science[203] (or any other system that may appear to challenge law's hegemony over society) makes them skeptical of new thinking and allows them to take deeper refuge in heuristic thinking and flawed, non-reflective OCS, both of which reflect the myths and stereotypes of sanism.[204] Legislators respond—pander, some say—to constituent outcry.[205] Lawyers and jurors, clearly, *are* the public, and their views are often identical with those expressed in the myths.[206] Neither expert witnesses—forensic psychiatrists and psychologists—nor treating mental health professionals are immune from the myths' powers and sway.[207]

When we are informed that our views are biased and based on myths not grounded in empiricism, science, or philosophy, we simply demur and say, in effect, "It doesn't matter. This is *still* the way I feel."[208] It is no wonder that these sanist attitudes pervade statutes, court decisions, and lawyering practices and thus infect all aspects of mental disability law.

---

[200]Perlin, *supra* note 1, at 98–108; Perlin, Michael L. *Book Review,* 8 N.Y. L. SCH. J. HUM. RTS. 557, 559–60 (1991) (review of ANNE BRADEN JOHNSON, OUT OF BEDLAM: THE TRUTH ABOUT DEINSTITUTIONALIZATION (1990)). *Cf.* S. M. Saccomando Burke, *Deinstitutionalization Has Failed—Miserably,* WASH. POST, Apr. 11, 1989, at A26 (letter to editor); James P. McGrath, *A Hoax Called "Deinstitutionalization,"* WASH. POST, Oct. 19, 1989, at A26 (letter to editor) (blaming patients' rights lawyers for deinstitutionalization failures).

[201]This myth owes a great debt to the Supreme Court's decision in Parham v. J. R., 442 U.S. 584, 605–06 (1979) (characterizing civil commitment hearings for juveniles as "time-consuming procedural minuets"); *cf.* Michael L. Perlin, *An Invitation to the Dance: An Empirical Response to Chief Justice Warren Burger's "Time-Consuming Procedural Minuets" Theory in* Parham v. J.R., 9 BULL. AM. ACAD. PSYCHIATRY & L. 149 (1981).

[202]Anthony D'Amato, *Harmful Speech and the Culture of Indeterminacy,* 32 WM. & MARY L. REV. 329, 332 (1991).

[203]Perlin, *OCS, supra* note 8, at 59–61; Perlin, Michael L. *Morality and Pretextuality, Psychiatry and Law: Of "Ordinary Common Sense," Heuristic Reasoning, and Cognitive Dissonance,* 19 BULL. AM. ACAD. PSYCHIATRY & L. 131, 133–37 (1991) [hereinafter Perlin, *Morality*]; *See infra* note 251, discussing McMullen v. State, 660 So.2d 340, 342–43 (Fla. Dist. App. 1995), *reh'g denied,* (1995).

[204]Perlin, *OCS, supra* note 8, at 61–69; Perlin, *Myths, supra* note 8, at 718–30.

[205]On the way that legislative reform may be nothing more than "an intellectual charade played for the benefit of an uninformed public," see Richard Rogers, *Assessment of Criminal Responsibility: Empirical Advances and Unanswered Questions,* 15 J. PSYCHIATRY & L. 73, 78 (1987) (insanity defense reform); *see generally* Jodie English, *The Light Between Twilight and Dusk: Federal Criminal Law and the Volitional Insanity Defense,* 40 HASTINGS L.J. 1 (1988) (same).

[206]On juror use of heuristic reasoning in decision making, see Perlin, *OCS, supra* note 8, at 39–53; Morrison Torrey, *When Will We Be Believed? Rape Myths and the Idea of a Fair Trial in Rape Prosecutions,* 24 U.C. DAVIS L. REV. 1013, 1050 (1991); Juliane Eule, *The Presumption of Sanity: Bursting the Bubble,* 25 UCLA. L. REV. 637, 661 (1978); *see also* Caton F. Roberts & Stephen L. Golding, *The Social Construction of Criminal Responsibility and Insanity,* 15 LAW & HUM. BEHAV. 349, 372 (1991) (jurors' preexisting attitudes toward insanity defense strongest predictor of individual verdicts).

[207]*See, e.g.,* Perlin, *Tea Leaves, supra* note 191 at 135–36; Michael L. Perlin, *Power Imbalances in Therapeutic and Forensic Relationships,* 9 BEHAV. SCI. & L. 111, 118–19 (1991); Stephen L. Deitschman et al., *Self-Selection Factors in the Participation of Mental Health Professionals in Competency for Execution Evaluations,* 15 LAW & HUM. BEHAV. 287, 299–300 (1991); Rogers, *supra* note 195, at 844; Jack Zusman & Robert Simon, *Differences in Repeated Psychiatric Examinations of Litigants to a Lawsuit,* 140 AM. J. PSYCHIATRY 1300 (1983); Jean C. Beckham et al., *Decision Making and Examiner Bias in Forensic Expert Recommendations for Not Guilty by Reason of Insanity,* 13 LAW & HUM. BEHAV. 79 (1989); Robert Homant & Daniel B. Kennedy, *Judgment of Legal Insanity as a Function of Attitudes Toward the Insanity Defense,* 8 INT'L J.L. & PSYCHIATRY 67 (1985).

[208]*See* Perlin, *Myths, supra* note 8, at 640–46.

The Sanist Legal System

Sanism pervades the legal system. It infects the judiciary, the legislature, the bar, and the legal academy. Its presence is particularly pernicious in the processing of mental disability law cases.

Sanist Legislators

Legislators traditionally have responded to socially expressed fears by enacting laws focusing on the perceived different-ness of persons with mental disabilities in almost all aspects of social intercourse. These laws respond to sanist attitudes and sanist myths.[209]

In the community, persons with mental disabilities have traditionally been treated differently in matters of political participation (voting, serving on juries, running for office),[210] interpersonal relationships (parenting, marriage, control of reproductive autonomy),[211] economic freedom (capacity to contract, capacity to bequeath money),[212] and other civil rights (access to housing, automobile licensure, welfare entitlements).[213] In the institutionalization process, individuals with mental disabilities were regularly denied counsel, hearings, and the full panoply of due process rights that accompany other processes through which liberty could be lost, and were subject to commitment on a variety of paternalistic bases.[214]

Historically, once individuals with mental disabilities were institutionalized, they were regularly deprived of virtually all civil rights,[215] most notably their right to autonomy in medication decision making.[216] In the criminal justice system, the mentally disabled were doubly cursed as "mad" and "bad,"[217] and regularly consigned to lifetime commitments in maximum-security facilities[218] (generally the worst available institutions in the state).[219]

This discussion is mostly past tense. After the civil rights revolution of the 1950s and 1960s reached persons with mental illness in the 1970s, lawmakers began—belatedly—to recognize the "grotesque" conditions to which such persons were subjected in institutional settings. Following decisions such as *Wyatt v. Stickney,*[220] *O'Connor v. Donaldson,*[221] and

---

[209]*Cf.* J. M. Balkin, *The Constitution of Status,* 106 Yale L.J. 2313, 2357 (1997) (explaining why the government cannot "create or sanction Pariah or outcast groups").

[210]*See generally* John Parry, *Decision Making Rights Over Persons and Property, in* Brakel et al., *supra* note 174 at 435–47; Sales et al., *supra* note 174 at 99–112; 2 Perlin, *supra* note 4, § 7.21, at 655.

[211]*See generally* Samuel Jan Brakel, *Family Laws, in* Brakel et al., *supra* note 210, at 507, 508–10, 515–20; Sales et al., *supra* note 210, at 10–38, 62–76, 85–87; Hayman, *supra* note 144.

[212]*See generally* Parry, *supra* note 210, at 438–41; Sales et al., *supra* note 210, at 54–61.

[213]*See generally* Parry, *supra* note 210, at 441–44; Sales et al., *supra* note 210, at 113–29; 2 Perlin, *supra* note 4, § 7.21, at 654–57.

[214]1 Perlin, *supra* note 4, § 2A-2.1c, at 59–61 (2d ed. 1998).

[215]*Id.,* §§ 3A-2 to 3A-2.2, at 4–15 (2d. ed. 1999).

[216]*Id.,* § 3B-3, at 168.70 (2d ed. 1999).

[217]*See, e.g.,* Ellen Hochstedler, *Twice-Cursed? The Mentally Disordered Criminal Defendant,* 14 Crim. Just. & Behav. 251 (1987).

[218]*See, e.g.,* N.J. Stat. Ann. § 2A:163-3 (1975), declared unconstitutional in State v. Krol, 344 A.2d 289 (N.J. 1975); *see generally* 1 Perlin, *supra* note 4, § 2A-4.4b, at 133–39 (2d ed. 1998).

[219]*See, e.g.,* Scott v. Plante, 532 F.2d 939 (3d Cir. 1976).

[220]325 F. Supp. 781 (M.D. Ala. 1971) (subsequent citations omitted); *see generally* 2 Perlin, *supra* note 4, §§ 3A-3.1 to 3A-3.3, at 24–60 (2d ed. 1999). On the specific impact of *Wyatt* in this context, see *The* Wyatt *Standards: An Influential Force in State and Federal Rights,* 28 Hosp. & Community Psychiatry 374 (1977).

[221]422 U.S. 563 (1975); *see generally* 1 Perlin, *supra* note 4, § 2A-4.4d, at 142–52 (2d ed. 1998).

Jackson v. Indiana,[222] most states narrowed civil commitment standards[223] and enacted patients' bills of rights to provide some level of civil rights to those still institutionalized.[224] Federal legislation mandated a modest level of access to counsel for those institutionalized,[225] and more recently the Americans With Disabilities Act (ADA) forbids discrimination against the mentally disabled in a wide variety of employment, educational, civic, medical, and social settings.[226]

Yet I believe that sanism still pervades the legislative process. Debates on charged issues such as a former mental patient's right to purchase a firearm or the appropriate substantive and procedural standards for the insanity defense are sanist texts; all the myths that I referred to earlier are repeated, reified, and relegitimated. Soon after states revised their civil commitment laws to comport with constitutional requirements, legislators indicated that the "pendulum had swung too far,"[227] and new "reform" laws, once again widening the commitment net, were passed.[228] When it appeared that expert witnesses openly subverted stricter laws (testifying in light of their own self-referential concepts of "morality"),[229] the legislatures were largely silent.

Reports of the substandard level of counsel that was made available to patients facing hospitalization were met with thundering silence.[230] When patients were deinstitutionalized without access to community mental health services, legislators failed to rewrite funding statutes to ensure that these individuals had access to such services.[231]

In the months after John Hinckley's insanity acquittal, Congress returned the federal insanity defense to a more restrictive version of the *M'Naghten* right-and-wrong test, one that was seen as outdated at the time of its original promulgation in 1843.[232] At the same

---

[222]406 U.S. 715 (1972); *see generally* 1 PERLIN, *supra* note 4, § 2A-4.4, at 121–25 (2d ed. 1998).

[223]1 PERLIN, *supra* note 4, § 2A-5, at 176–83 (2d ed. 1998).

[224]*Id.,* § 11.03, at 953–58. For a comprehensive overview, *see generally* Martha A. Lyon, Martin L. Levine, & Jack Zusman, *Patients' Bills of Rights: A Survey of State Statutes,* 6 MENT. DIS. L. RPTR. 178 (1982).

[225]*See, e.g.,* 42 U.S.C. §§ 6021 *et seq.* (Developmental Disabilities Assistance and Bill of Rights Act), discussed in 2 PERLIN, *supra* note 4, § 8.13, at 788–91, and 42 U.S.C. §§ 10801 *et seq.* (Protection and Advocacy for the Mentally Ill Act), discussed in 2 PERLIN, *supra* note 4, § 8.16, at 797–99.

[226]42 U.S.C. §§ 12101 *et seq.; see generally* PERLIN, *supra* note 4, § 6.44A, at 137–98 (1998 Cum. Supp.); Nancy Lee Jones, *Overview and Essential Requirements of the Americans With Disabilities Act,* 64 TEMP. L. REV. 471 (1991); Thomas M. Cook, *The Americans With Disabilities Act: The Move to Integration,* 64 TEMP. L. REV. 393 (1991).

[227]*See* Michael L. Perlin, *Fatal Assumption: A Critical Evaluation of the Role of Counsel in Mental Disability Cases,* 16 LAW & HUM. BEHAV. 39, 56 n.105 (1992), discussing, *inter alia,* Daniel Shuman, *Innovative Statutory Approaches to Civil Commitment: An Overview and Critique,* 13 LAW, MED. & HEALTH CARE 284, 286 (1985); Mary Durham & John LaFond, *The Empirical Consequences and Policy Implications of Broadening the Statutory Criteria for Civil Commitment,* 3 YALE LAW & POL'Y REV. 395, 398 (1985).

[228]*See, e.g.,* R. Michael Bagby & Leslie Atkinson, *The Effects of Legislative Reform on Civil Commitment Admission Rates,* 6 BEHAV. SCI. & L. 45 (1988); R. Michael Bagby, *The Effects of Legislative Reform on Admissions Rates to Psychiatric Units of General Hospitals,* 10 INT'L J.L. & PSYCHIATRY 383 (1987).

[229]*See* Perlin, *Morality, supra* note 203, at 135–36; Perlin, *Power, supra* note 207, at 119–20, discussing, *inter alia,* Paul Chodoff, *The Case for Involuntary Hospitalization of the Mentally Ill,* 133 AM. J. PSYCHIATRY 496 (1976).

[230]*See* Michael L. Perlin & Robert Sadoff, *Ethical Issues in Representation of Individuals in the Commitment Process,* 45 LAW & CONTEMP. PROBS. 161, 164 (1982); Virginia Hiday, *The Attorney's Role in Involuntary Civil Commitment,* 60 N.C. L. REV. 1027 (1982).

[231]*See* Perlin, *supra* note 1, at 106, n.253, discussing, *inter alia,* K. C. v. State, 771 P.2d 774 (Wyo. 1989), and Board of Supervisors v. Superior Court, 207 Cal. App. 3d 552, 254 Cal. Rptr. 905 (1989).

[232]Perlin, *Myths, supra* note 8, at 637–39, and *id.* at 638 n.173 (citing sources).

time, states endorsed the guilty-but-mentally-ill verdict, despite nearly unanimous criticism that the defense was little more than a meretricious sham.[233]

In short, just as Kimberlé Crenshaw found in her study of race, laws, and stereotypes,[234] although much of the formal and symbolic subordination to which the mentally disabled have been subjected has been eliminated, the material subordination largely remains. The legislature serves as a mirror for the public, and, in doing so, perpetuates myth and stereotypes[235] and fosters the perpetuation of prejudice.

Sanist Courts

As I have already argued, judges reflect and project the conventional morality of the community. Like the rest of society, judges take refuge in flawed OCS, heuristic reasoning, and biased stereotypes to justify their sanist decisions.[236] Although Justice Holmes' infamous and florid language in *Buck v. Bell*[237] is rarely repeated,[238] judicial decisions in all areas of mental disability law continue to reflect and perpetuate sanist stereotypes[239] as well as a lack of understanding of mental illness.[240]

---

[233]*See, e.g.,* Christopher Slobogin, *The Guilty But Mentally Ill Verdict: An Idea Whose Time Should Not Have Come,* 53 GEO. WASH. L. REV. 494 (1985); Linda Fentiman, *"Guilty But Mentally Ill": The Real Verdict Is Guilty,* 26 B.C. L. REV. 601 (1985); *but see* Ira Mickenberg, *A Pleasant Surprise: The Guilty But Mentally Ill Verdict Has Both Succeeded in Its Own Right and Successfully Preserved The Traditional Role of the Insanity Defense,* 55 U. CIN. L. REV. 943 (1987).

[234]*See* Crenshaw, *supra* note 40, at 1370–77.

[235]On the ways that stereotyping and labeling have poisoned the mental disability law system, see H. Archibald Kaiser, *Book Review* of JULIO ARBOLEDA-FLOREZ & MARGARET COPITHORNE, MENTAL HEALTH LAW AND PRACTICE: A GUIDE TO THE ALBERTA MENTAL HEALTH ACT AND RELATED CANADIAN LEGISLATION, 16 HEALTH L. IN CAN. 51 (Nov. 1995). On how such stereotypes contaminate the entire criminal justice system, see Emilio Viano, *Stereotyping and Prejudice: Crime Victims and the Criminal Justice System,* 5 STUDIES ON CRIME & CRIME PREVENTION 182 (1996).

[236]The problem is compounded by other historical, political and economic factors beyond the scope of this book. Institutional biases—about housing, about health care, about community systems—affect judges and serve as an additional brake on judicial creativity and on efforts to dismantle sanist legal systems. But I believe that until sanism is confronted, addressed and ameliorated, these other biases will never be reached.

[237]"Three generations of imbeciles are enough." 274 U.S. 200, 207 (1927). For contemporary evaluations of this opinion, the factual record in *Buck,* and Justice Holmes' personal view, *see, e.g.,* Stephen Jay Gould, *Carrie Buck's Daughter,* 2 CONST. COMMENTARY 331 (1985); Paul Lombardo, *"Three Generations, No Imbeciles" New Light on Buck v. Bell,* 60 N.Y.U. L. REV. 31 (1985); Mary Dudziak, *Oliver Wendell Holmes as a Eugenic Reformer: Rhetoric in the Writing of Constitutional Law,* 71 IOWA L. REV. 833 (1986); Comment, *We Have Met the Imbeciles and They Are Us: The Courts and Citizens With Mental Retardation,* 65 NEB. L. REV. 768 (1986).

[238]*But see supra* text accompanying note 2, discussing Robertson (sitting trial judge's endorsement of Holmes's *dictum*).

[239]None is perhaps as chilling as the following story. Sometime after the federal district court's decision in Rennie v. Klein, 462 F. Supp. 1131 (D.N.J. 1978) (granting involuntarily committed mental patients a limited right to refuse medication), I had occasion to speak to a state court trial judge about *Rennie.* He asked me, "Michael, do you know what I would have done had you brought *Rennie* before me [the *Rennie* case was litigated by counsel in the New Jersey division of Mental Health Advocacy; I was director of the division at that time]?" I replied, "No," and he then answered, "I'd've taken the son-of-a-bitch behind the courthouse and had him shot."

[240]*See, e.g.,* Kansas v. Hendricks, 521 U.S. 346 (1997) (upholding constitutionality of Kansas's Sexually Violent Predator Act), discussed in 1 PERLIN, *supra* note 4 § 2-3.3 (2d ed. 1998). On the Supreme Court's reading of mental illness in general, see Bruce Winick, *Ambiguities in the Legal Meaning and Significance of Mental Illness,* 1 PSYCHOL., PUB. POL'Y & L. 534 (1995), critiquing the decision in Foucha v. Louisiana, 504 U.S. 71 (1992); *see* PERLIN, *supra* note 4, § 15.25A, at 532–38 (1998 Cum. Supp.).

These stereotypes have tainted mental health professionals as well.[241] Forensic psychiatrists testifying in criminal cases were viewed "as attempting to cloud our moral standards and to ignore the limits of community tolerance."[242] From their first involvement in court proceedings, "'alienists . . . have been perceived as a threat to public security and a fancy means for 'getting criminals off.'"[243] Expert opinions were seen as "especially entitled to little or no weight" when based on a "feigned state of mind."[244] The myths are cherished by trial judges, appellate judges, and Supreme Court justices alike.

Judges, especially, are not immune from sanism. "Embedded in the cultural presuppositions that engulf us all,"[245] they express discomfort with social science[246] (or any other system that may appear to challenge law's hegemony over society) and skepticism about new thinking; this discomfort and skepticism allows them to take deeper refuge in heuristic thinking and flawed, nonreflective OCS, both of which perpetuate the myths and stereotypes of sanism.[247]

Sanism and the Court Process in Mental Disability Law Cases

Judges reflect and project the conventional morality of the community, and judicial decisions in all areas of civil and criminal mental disability law continue to reflect and perpetuate sanist stereotypes. Their language demonstrates bias against mentally disabled individuals[248] and contempt for the mental health professions.[249] Courts often appear impatient with mentally disabled litigants, ascribing their problems in the legal process to weak character or poor resolve.

---

[241]*See, e.g.,* United States v. Hall, 93 F.3d 1337, 1343 (7th Cir. 1996) ("Because the fields of psychology and psychiatry deal with human behavior and mental disorders, it may be more difficult at times to distinguish between testimony that reflects genuine expertise—a reliable body of genuine specialized knowledge—and something that is nothing more than fancy phrases for common sense").

[242]William Weitzel, *Public Skepticism: Forensic Psychiatry's Albatross,* 5 BULL. AM. ACAD. PSYCHIATRY & L. 456, 459 (1977).

[243]Andrew Watson, *On the Preparation and Use of Psychiatric Expert Testimony: Some Suggestions in an Ongoing Controversy,* 6 BULL. AM. ACAD. PSYCHIATRY & L. 226, 226 (1978).

[244]Commonwealth v. Patskin, 100 A.2d 472, 475 (Pa. 1953).

[245]Anthony D'Amato, *Harmful Speech and the Culture of Indeterminacy,* 32 WM. & MARY L. REV. 329, 332 (1991).

[246]Perlin, *OCS, supra* note 8, at 59–61; Perlin, *Morality, supra* note 203, at 133–37. The discomfort that many judges feel in having to decide mental disability law cases is often palpable. *See, e.g.,* Perlin, *supra* note 98, at 991, discussing United States v. Charters, 863 F.2d 302, 310 (4th Cir 1988) *(en banc), cert. denied,* 494 U.S. 1016 (1990).

[247]Perlin, *OCS, supra* note 8, at 61–69; Perlin, *Myths, supra* note 8, at 618–30.

[248]*See, e.g.,* Corn v. Zant, 708 F.2d 549, 569 (11th Cir. 1983), *reh'g denied,* 714 F.2d 159 (11th Cir. 1983), *cert. denied,* 467 U.S. 1220 (1984) (defendant referred to as a "lunatic"); Sinclair v. Wainwright, 814 F.2d 1516, 1522 (11th Cir., 1987), quoting Shuler v. Wainwright, 491 F.2d 213 (5th Cir. 1974) (using "lunatic"). Judges also regularly and readily ignore evidence that jurors may share these same biases. *Cf., e.g.,* Moore v. State, 525 So.2d 870, 871 (Fla. 1988) (juror who rejected insanity defense as potential basis for exculpatory criminal defense not excused for cause) (reversing conviction); Noe v. State, 586 So.2d 371, 375–78 (Fla. Dist. App. 1991), *reh'g denied* (1991) (same), *to* Boblett v. Commonwealth, 396 S.E.2d 131, 135 (Va. App. 1990) (no abuse of discretion where trial court refused to excuse for cause juror who indicated he might have difficulty voting for an insanity acquittal).

[249]*See, e.g.,* Commonwealth v. Musolino, 467 A.2d 605 (Pa. Super. 1983) (reversible error for trial judge to refer to expert witnesses as "headshrinkers"); *cf.* State v. Percy, 507 A.2d 955, 956 (Vt. 1986), *appeal after remand,* 595 A.2d 248 (Vt. 1990), *cert. denied,* 502 U.S. 927 (1991) (conviction reversed where prosecutor referred to expert testimony as "psycho-babble"), *to* Commonwealth v. Cosme, 575 N.E.2d 726, 731 (Mass. 1991) (not error where prosecutor referred to defendant's expert witnesses as "a little head specialist" and a "wizard").

Rarely, if ever, is behavioral or scientific authority cited to support sanist opinions.[250] It is not coincidental that this sort of sanist judicial behavior ignores available social science research. Through sanist thinking, judges allow themselves to avoid difficult choices in mental disability law cases; their refuge in alleged OCS contributes further to the pretextuality that underlies much of this area of the law. In a remarkably candid opinion—concurring in a decision affirming a conviction on the grounds that expert testimony about psychological factors that affect reliability of eyewitness identifications was properly excluded—Florida District Court of Appeal Judge Farmer noted,

> Indeed, I should admit to a certain quarrel with the social "sciences" in general and psychology in particular. They are, it seems to me, founded on an almost indefensible premise: that one can fairly deduce some truths about an individual by what classes of human beings do in the aggregate. That seems to me so at odds with the human free will that any conclusions founded on the premise are intrinsically unreliable. By such methodology one might stumble into the truth about as often as 60 computers typing randomly for infinity might turn out all of the great literary works of western civilization.[251]

Individuals incompetent for one purpose are presumed incompetent for all other purposes, and judges sometimes question whether it is even possible to distinguish between different kinds of incompetencies.[252] If a person subject to civil commitment refuses to take medication—a constitutional right in most jurisdictions—that refusal is often seen as a presumptive indicator of dangerousness and need for institutionalization.[253] Adherence to involuntary civil commitment statutory criteria is subverted because of fears that strict construction of those laws would lead inexorably to homelessness.[254] The minimalist "substantial professional judgment" test[255] is endorsed in a wide variety of institutional cases so that only the most arbitrary and baseless decision making can be successfully challenged.[256] Even when nonsanist court decisions reject sanist myths and stereotypes, the enforcement of such decisions is frequently only sporadic.[257]

---

[250]See, e.g., People v. LaLone, 437 N.W.2d 611, 613 (Mich. 1989), reh'g denied, (1989) (without citation to an authority, court found that it is less likely that medical patients will "fabricate descriptions of their complaints" than will "psychological patients"); In re Melton, 597 A.2d 892, 898 (D.C. 1991) (psychiatric predictivity of future dangerousness likened to predictions made by an oncologist as to consequences of an untreated and metastasized malignancy); Braley v. State, 741 P.2d 1061, 1064–65 (Wyo. 1987) (expert testimony on a homicide defendant's reactions to fear and stress rejected on grounds that such emotions are "experienced by all mankind" and thus not related to any body of scientific knowledge).

[251]McMullen v. State, 660 So.2d 340, 342–43 (Fla. Dist. App. 1995) (Farmer, J., concurring), reh'g denied (1995).

[252]See, e.g., United States v. Charters, 863 F.2d 302, 310 (4th Cir. 1988) (en banc), cert. denied, 494 U.S. 1016 (1990); Perlin, supra note 98, at 987–88; David Wexler, Grave Disability and Family Therapy: The Therapeutic Potential of Civil Libertarian Commitment Codes, reprinted in THERAPEUTIC JURISPRUDENCE: THE LAW AS A THERAPEUTIC AGENT 165, 170 (D. Wexler ed. 1990) (THERAPEUTIC JURISPRUDENCE) (discussing courts' historic improper equation of serious mental illness with "incompetence, grave disability and committability").

[253]In re Melas, 371 N.W.2d 653, 655 (Minn. Ct. App. 1985); Matter of J. B., 705 P.2d 598, 602 (Mont. 1985); Perlin, supra note 198, at 49–50; 1 PERLIN, supra note 4, § 2C-5.2, at 414–16 (2d ed. 1998). Cf. Mary Durham & John La Fond, A Search for the Missing Premise of Involuntary Therapeutic Commitment: Effective Treatment of the Mentally Ill, 40 RUTGERS L. REV. 303 (1988), reprinted in THERAPEUTIC JURISPRUDENCE, supra note 252, at 133, 154 (literature review suggests that anywhere from 21 to 79% of patients studied who were treated with drugs may do no better than those given placebos).

[254]See Perlin, supra note 1, at 116–17, n.308, discussing In re Melton, 565 A.2d 635, 649 (D.C. 1989) (Schwelb, J., dissenting), hearing granted & opinion vacated, 581 A.2d 788 (D.C. 1990), superseded on reh'g, 597 A.2d 892 (D.C. 1991).

[255]See Youngberg v. Romeo, 457 U.S. 307, 323 (1982).

[256]See Charters, 863 F.2d at 313, critiqued sharply in Perlin, supra note 98, at 935.

[257]See, e.g., Perlin, supra note 227, at 47–48 (discussing lack of implementation of Jackson v. Indiana, 406 U.S. 715 (1972)) (applying due process clause to postincompetency to stand trial commitment proceedings); see

Criminal trial process case law is riddled with sanist stereotypes and myths. Examples include the following:

- Reliance on a fixed vision of popular, concrete, visual images of "craziness";[258]
- Obsessive fear of feigned mental states;[259]
- Presumed absolute linkage between mental illness and dangerousness;[260]
- Sanctioning of the death penalty in the case of mentally retarded defendants, some defendants who are "substantially mentally impaired," or defendants who have been found guilty but mentally ill (GBMI);[261]
- Incessant confusion and conflation of substantive mental status tests[262] and of legal and medical terminology;[263]
- Determination that an insanity acquittee's need for medication renders him or her not "fully recovered" so as to be eligible for outpatient care or conditional release;[264]
- Appropriateness of continuing an insanity acquittee's mental hospital confinement when he or she is no longer mentally ill but remains dangerous to others;[265]
- Use of language such as "lunatic" in published opinions;[266]
- Use of a unitary standard to assess all levels of criminal incompetency;[267]
- Refusal in insanity cases of providing jury instructions that NGRI defendants face long-term postacquittal commitment;[268] and

---

also Bruce Winick, *Restructuring Competency to Stand Trial,* 32 UCLA L. REV. 921, 940–41 (1985); Wertleib, *supra* note 96, at 336.

[258]*See, e.g.,* Wainwright v. Greenfield, 474 U.S. 284, 297 (1986) (Rehnquist, J., concurring); State v. Clayton, 656 S.W.2d 344, 350–51 (Tenn. 1983); Perlin, *OCS, supra* note 8, at 66–67. Similar standards are employed in civil cases. *See, e.g.,* St. Louis S.W. Ry. Co. v. Penington, 553 S.W.2d 436, 448 (Ark. 1977) (recovery for mental anguish of adult survivors of wrongful death victims allowed where survivors demonstrated they suffered "more than the normal grief").

[259]*See, e.g.,* Lynch v. Overholser, 369 U.S. 705, 715 (1962); United States v. Brown, 478 F.2d 606, 611 (D.C. Cir. 1973), as discussed in Peter Margulies, *The "Pandemonium Between the Mad and the Bad:" Procedures for the Commitment and Release of Insanity Acquittees After* Jones v. United States, 36 RUTGERS L. REV. 793, 806–07 n.85 (1984).

[260]*See, e.g.,* Jones v. United States, 463 U.S. 354, 365 (1983); Overholser v. O'Beirne, 302 F.2d 852, 861 (D.C. Cir. 1961).

[261]Penry v. Lynaugh, 492 U.S. 302 (1989) (mental retardation); Commonwealth v. Faulkner, 595 A.2d 28, 38 (Pa. 1991) (substantial mental impairment); Harris v. State, 499 N.E.2d 723 (Ind. 1986) (GBMI); *see also* People v. Crews, 522 N.E.2d 1167 (Ill. 1988) (permissible to sentence GBMI defendant to postlife expectancy term). *Cf.* Ford v. Wainwright, 477 U.S. 399 (1986) (barring execution of the currently insane). On the question of whether mentally retarded individuals' lessened capacity for moral development prohibits their execution, see *Penry,* 492 U.S. at 345 (Brennan, J., concurring in part and dissenting in part).

[262]*See, e.g.,* Buttrum v. Black, 721 F. Supp. 1268, 1295 (N.D. Ga. 1989), *aff'd,* 908 F.2d 695 (11th Cir. 1990). *See generally* R. ROESCH & S. GOLDING, COMPETENCY TO STAND TRIAL 15–17 (1980).

[263]Kansas v. Hendricks, 117 S. Ct. 2075 (1997), criticized in 1 PERLIN, *supra* note 4, § 2-3.3 at 75–92 (2d ed. 1998).

[264]People v. DeAnda, 114 Cal. App. 3d 480, 170 Cal. Rptr. 830, 832–33 (1980), *discussed in* David Wexler, *Inappropriate Patient Confinement and Appropriate State Advocacy,* 45 LAW & CONTEMP. PROBS. 193 (Spring 1982), *reprinted in* THERAPEUTIC JURISPRUDENCE, *supra* note 252, at 347, 350–51.

[265]State v. Foucha, 563 So.2d 1138, 1141 (La. 1990), *rev'd,* 504 U.S. 71 (1992), *discussed in this context in* Michael L. Perlin, Tarasoff *and the Dilemma of the Dangerous Patient: New Directions for the 1990's,* 16 LAW & PSYCHOL. REV. 29 (1992).

[266]Sinclair v. Wainwright, 814 F.2d 1516, 1522 (11th Cir. 1987), quoting Shuler v. Wainwright, 491 F.2d 213 (5th Cir. 1974); Blair v. Equifax Check Services, Inc., 1999 WL 116225 (N.D. Del. 1999), at 3, quoting Rand v. Monsanto Co., 926 F.2d 596, 599 (7th Cir. 1991); King v. Beavers, 148 F.3d 1031, 1035 (8th Cir. 1998).

[267]Godinez v. Moran, 509 U.S. 389 (1993); *see infra* Chapter 9.

[268]Shannon v. United States, 512 U.S. 573 (1994).

- Characterization of the allocation of treatment resources for GBMI defendants as "not . . . helpful" or a "waste."[269]

Perhaps as troubling is judicial ignorance about laws that affect persons with mental disabilities. A Louisiana commitment order was reversed when a trial court judge did not even know that a state mental health advocacy service was available to provide representation to indigent individuals facing involuntary civil commitment;[270] a Texas study revealed that a significant number of judges were not even aware of a state statutory patient–psychotherapist privilege.[271] Other courts have, with little public attention, regularly entered commitment orders without any precedent statutory authority.[272] And empirical research demonstrates that, as the length of a patient's hospitalization increases, the hearings become shorter and less adversarial.[273]

To be sure, not all judges write in this voice. Some nonsanist opinions such as Judge Johnson's *Wyatt v. Stickney*[274] decisions are firmly rooted in a rights–empowerment model;[275] others like Justice Blackmun's dissent in *Barefoot v. Estelle,*[276] Justice Stevens' partial dissent in *Washington v. Harper,*[277] or the New Jersey Supreme Court's opinion in *State v. Krol*[278] specifically rebut sanist myths.[279] Others such as Justice Stevens' dissent in *Pennhurst II,*[280] Justices Stevens' and Marshall's separate opinions in *Cleburne,*[281] and Judge Kaufman's use of a "Gulag archipelago" metaphor in a second circuit case involving a mentally disabled prisoner[282] express eloquent outrage at institutional conditions that flow inevitably from a sanist society; yet others—see Judge Brotman's class-action opinion in *Rennie v. Klein*[283]—express true empathy and understanding about the plight of the institutionalized persons with mental disabilities. A handful of judges—David Bazelon is a fine example—has spent careers rooting out sanist myths and stereotypes and raising the

---

[269]Robinson v. Solem, 432 N.W.2d 246, 249 (S.D. 1988).

[270]*In re C. P. K.,* 516 So.2d 1323, 1325 (La. Ct. App. 1987).

[271]Daniel Shuman & Myron Weiner, *The Privilege Study: An Empirical Examination of the Psychotherapist–Patient Privilege,* 60 N.C. L. REV. 893 (1982), *reprinted in* THERAPEUTIC JURISPRUDENCE, *supra* note 252, at 75, 103.

[272]Wexler, *supra* note 252, *reprinted in* THERAPEUTIC JURISPRUDENCE, *supra* note 252, at 348.

[273]Charles Parry & Eric Turkheimer, *Length of Hospitalization and Outcome of Commitment and Recommitment Hearings,* 43 HOSP. & COMMUNITY PSYCHIATRY 65 (1992).

[274]325 F. Supp. 781 (M.D. Ala. 1971), 334 F. Supp. 1341 (M.D. Ala. 1972), 344 F. Supp. 373 (M.D. Ala. 1972), 344 F. Supp. 387 (M.D. Ala. 1972) (subsequent citations omitted).

[275]*See generally* M. MINOW, *supra* note 15, at 131–45; *see also* Johnson, *supra* note 119, at 357–58.

[276]463 U.S. 880, 916 (1983). *See,* 3 Perlin, *supra* note 4, § 17.13, at 529–36.

[277]494 U.S. 210, 239–40 (1990). *See,* 2 Perlin, *supra* note 4, § 3B-8.2, at 313–22 (2d. ed. 1999).

[278]344 A.2d 289 (N.J. 1975). *See,* 1 Perlin, *supra* note 4, § 2A-4.4b, at 139–42 (2d. ed. 1998).

[279]*See also, e.g.,* Riggins v. Nevada, 504 U.S. 127 (1992) (trial court's failure to determine need for continued administration of antipsychotic medications to insanity-pleading defendant or to make inquiry about reasonable alternatives violated defendant's liberty interest in freedom from such drugs; conviction reversed); Foucha v. Louisiana, 504 U.S. 71 (1992) (statute that permits continued hospitalization of insanity acquittee found to be no longer mentally ill violates due process).

[280]Pennhurst State Sch. & Hosp. v. Halderman, 465 U.S. 89, 126 (1984). *See,* 2 Perlin, *supra* note 2, § 7.15, at 627-36.

[281]City of Cleburne v. Cleburne Living Ctr., 473 U.S. 432, 452 (1985) (Stevens, J., concurring), and *id.* at 455 (Marshall, J., concurring in part and dissenting in part). *See,* 2 Perlin, *supra* note 2, § 7.22, at 657–71.

[282]United States *ex rel.* Schuster v. Vincent, 524 F.2d 153, 154 (2d Cir. 1975).

[283]476 F. Supp. 1294, 1309 (D.N.J. 1979): "Medicine has not yet found a cure for the terrible pain of mental illness. The law cannot assist in this endeavor. But the Constitution can and does prevent those who have suffered so much at the hands of nature from being subjected to further suffering at the hands of man."

legal system's consciousness about sanism's impact on all of society;[284] other judges in lesser known cases have also shown real sensitivity to the underlying issues.[285]

These examples, however, are clearly the minority. Sanism regularly and relentlessly infects the courts in the same ways that it infects the public discourse.

Sanist Lawyers

Writing with Robert L. Sadoff some 17 years ago surveying the role of counsel in cases involving individuals with mental disabilities, I observed,

> Traditional, sporadically-appointed counsel . . . were unwilling to pursue necessary investigations, lacked . . . expertise in mental health problems, and suffered from "rolelessness," stemming from near total capitulation to experts, hazily defined concepts of success/failure, inability to generate professional or personal interest in the patient's dilemma, and lack of a clear definition of the proper advocacy function. As a result, counsel . . . functioned "as no more that a clerk, ratifying the events that transpired, rather than influencing them."[286]

Commitment hearings were meaningless rituals, serving only to provide a facade of respectability to illegitimate proceedings;[287] in one famous survey, lawyers were so bad that patients had a better chance to be released at commitment hearings if they appeared *pro se*.[288] Merely educating lawyers about psychiatric techniques and psychological nomenclature did not materially improve lawyers' performance, because lawyers' attitudes were not changed.[289] Counsel was especially substandard in cases involving mentally disabled criminal defendants.[290]

In recent years the myth has developed that organized, specialized, and aggressive counsel is now available to mentally disabled individuals in commitment, institutionalization, and release matters. The availability of such counsel is largely illusory, however; in

---

[284]*See* Wald, *supra* note 115, at 627 (Bazelon one of the "greatest appellate judges"); Heathcoate Wales, *The Rise, the Fall, and the Resurrection of the Medical Model*, 63 GEO. L.J. 87 (1974) (Judge Bazelon "invited the world of mental health professionals and criminologists into his courtroom" to "extend his courtroom back to the world"). *See generally, e.g.,* David L. Bazelon, *Institutionalization, Deinstitutionalization, and the Adversary Process,* 75 COLUM. L. REV. 897 (1975); David Bazelon, *Veils, Values and Social Responsibility,* 37 AM. PSYCHOLOGIST 115 (1982).

[285]*See, e.g.,* S. H. v. Edwards, 860 F.2d 1045, 1053 (11th Cir. 1989) (Clark, J., dissenting), *cert. denied,* 491 U.S. 905 (1989), *vacated,* 880 F.2d 1203 (11th Cir. 1989), *on reh'g,* 886 F.2d 1292 (11th Cir. 1989).

And the enormity of the stigma *is* finally becoming clear to at least a handful of judges. Concurring in a case holding that an appeal from an involuntary civil commitment order was not mooted solely by the individual's release from hospitalization, Florida Supreme Court Judge Gerald Kogan revealed his understanding of the role of sanism in mental disability law: "The law itself is beginning a process of rooting out acts of irrational prejudice based on mental disability, just as the law in the 1960's began eliminating the irrational bigotry posed by racism." Godwin v. State, 593 So.2d 211, 215 (Fla. 1992) (Kogan, J., concurring in part & dissenting in part).

[286]Perlin & Sadoff, *supra* note 230, at 164 (footnotes omitted).

[287]Hiday, *supra* note 230, at 1030.

[288]Elliot Andalman & David Chambers, *Effective Counsel for Persons Facing Civil Commitment: A Survey, a Polemic, and a Proposal,* 45 MISS. L.J. 43, 72 (1974).

[289]Norman Poythress, *Psychiatric Expertise in Civil Commitment: Training Attorneys to Cope With Expert Testimony,* 2 LAW & HUM. BEHAV. 1, 15 (1978).

[290]*See* Perlin, *Myths, supra* note 8, at 654; DAVID BAZELON, QUESTIONING AUTHORITY: JUSTICE AND CRIMINAL LAW 49 (1988). A survey conducted by Harvard Medical School revealed that the "great majority" of defense counsel interviewed were unaware of the operative competency-to-stand-trial criteria. 3 PERLIN, *supra* note 4, § 14.10, at 239 (citing study). For a particularly shocking example of poor counsel in a death penalty case involving a mentally disabled criminal defendant, see Alvord v. Wainwright, 469 U.S. 956 (1984) (Marshall, J., dissenting from denial of grant of *certiorari*).

many jurisdictions, the level of such representation remains almost uniformly substandard,[291] and even within the same jurisdictions the provision of counsel can be "wildly inconsistent."[292] Without the presence of effective counsel, substantive mental disability law reform recommendations may turn into "an empty shell."[293] Representation of individuals with mental disabilities falls far short of even the most minimal model of "client-centered counseling."[294] What is worse, few courts even seem to notice.[295]

Counsel's failure is inevitable, given the bar's abject disregard of both consumer groups (made up predominantly of former recipients, both voluntary and involuntary, of mental disability services) and mentally disabled individuals, many of whom have written carefully, thoughtfully, and sensitively about these issues.[296] This inadequacy further reflects sanist practices on the parts of the lawyers representing persons with mental disabilities, as well as the political entities vested with the authority to hire such counsel. Although a handful of articulate scholars are beginning to take this question seriously, these questions do not appear to be a priority agenda item for litigators or for most academics writing in this area.[297]

Sanist Scholars

The legal academy is not immune from sanist criticisms.[298] Although scholars writing from a wide variety of perspectives have begun to look at "stories" and "narratives" told by women, racial and sexual minorities, and other disenfranchised individuals, the stories of individuals with mental disabilities are rarely told in the pages of law reviews. Traditional

---

[291]See Perlin, supra note 227, at 49–52.

[292]Perlin & Dorfman, Dodging Lions, supra note 185 at 114, 122.

[293]Id. at 121.

[294]The standard text is DAVID BINDER & SUSAN PRICE, LEGAL INTERVIEWING AND COUNSELING: A CLIENT-CENTERED APPROACH (1977).

[295]See, e.g., In re C. P. K., 516 So.2d 1323, 1325 (La. Ct. App. 1987), discussed supra text accompanying note 276; but cf. State ex rel. Memmel v. Mundy, 75 Wis.2d 276, 249 N.W.2d 573 (1977), setting out duties of adversary counsel in involuntary civil commitment cases.

There is now some empirical data suggesting that patients represented by public defender organizations generally obtain significantly more favorable outcomes in contested involuntary civil commitment cases than do patients represented by private counsel hired on short-term contracts. Mary Durham & John LaFond, The Impact of Expanding a State's Therapeutic Commitment Authority, in THERAPEUTIC JURISPRUDENCE, supra note 252, at 121, 122; Mary Durham & John LaFond, The Empirical and Policy Implications of Broadening the Statutory Criteria for Civil Commitment, 3 YALE L. & POL'Y REV. 395 (1985).

[296]On the involvement of consumer groups in important patients' rights litigation, see 1 PERLIN, supra note 4, § 1-2.1, at 10 n.43 (2d ed. 1998); Milner I, supra note 162; Milner II, supra note 162; see generally Symposium Challenging the Therapeutic State: Critical Perspectives on Psychiatry and the Mental Health System, 11 J. MIND & BEHAV. 1–328 (1990).

[297]See, e.g., Stanley Herr, Representation of Clients With Disabilities: Issues of Ethics and Control, 17 N.Y.U. REV. L. & SOC. CHANGE 609 (1991); Stanley Herr, The Future of Advocacy for Persons With Mental Disabilities, 39 RUTGERS L. REV. 443 (1987); Peter Margulies, "Who Are You To Tell Me That?" Attorney–Client Deliberation Regarding Nonlegal Issues and the Interests of Nonclients, 68 N.C. L. REV. 213 (1990); Paul Tremblay, On Persuasion and Paternalism: Lawyer Decisionmaking and the Questionably Competent Client, 1987 UTAH L. REV. 515; Steven Schwartz, Damage Actions as a Strategy for Enhancing the Quality of Care of Persons With Mental Disabilities, 17 N.W.U. REV. L. & SOC. CHANGE 657 (1989–90).

See also Perlin, Myths, supra note 8, at 58–59.

[298]On the "objective, neutral, impersonal, authoritative, judgmental and certain . . . disembodied voice" that has traditionally been the hallmark of legal scholarship, see Gerald Wetlaufer, Rhetoric and Its Denial in Legal Discourse, 76 VA. L. REV. 1545, 1568 (1990).

constitutional law courses normally do not include the study of cases involving the constitutional rights of individuals with mental disabilities.[299]

Articles discussing the "continuing revolution in . . . the structure of the curriculum" at American law schools do not even mention mental disability law.[300] Tenure-track professors know that articles about mental disability law topics do not augur a fast path to tenure; most law reviews are mildly interested in, but far from eager to solicit and publish, mental disability law scholarship.[301] In short, the study and teaching of mental disability law are marginalized in ways that are structurally like the ways that mentally disabled individuals are themselves marginalized.[302] The news is not that the academy is sanist (for why would professors be immune from the pernicious impact of bias and stereotypes), but that, with some major and important exceptions,[303] so little attention is being paid to this fact.

One story should illustrate. Several years ago, I was the keynote speaker at the annual Society of American Law Teachers (SALT) conference. SALT draws from the ranks of politically progressive law professors, including many who articulate their commitment to social justice as one of the reasons they joined the academy. It has been a constant voice in the fight to ensure diversity in the classroom and the curriculum.[304] My keynote presentation was titled, "Mental Disability, Sanism, Pretextuality, Therapeutic Jurisprudence, and Teaching Law," and basically outlined much of the material in this volume. The next issue of the *SALT Equalizer,* the group's house organ, contained a review by Rogelio Lasso, finding it "particularly disturbing that 'Sanism' merited a plenary presentation but the disgraceful lack of diversity of law school faculties did not."[305]

---

[299]*Cf.* Fred Schauer, *Easy Cases,* 58 S. CAL. L. REV. 399–400 n.2 (1985) ("To generalize about constitutional law from certain particular topics within a course somewhat artificially named 'Constitutional Law' runs a serious risk of distortion").

[300]*See, e.g.,* David Barnhizer, *The Revolution in American Law Schools,* 37 CLEV. ST. L. REV. 227 (1989).

[301]*See* Thomas Hafemeister, *Comparing Law Reviews for Their Amenability to Articles Addressing Mental Health Issues: How to Disseminate Law Related Social Science Research,* 16 LAW & HUM. BEHAV. 219 (1992).

[302]*See* Allen Macurdy, *Disability Ideology and the Law School Curriculum,* 4 B.U. PUB. INT. L.J. 443 (1995).

[303]I do not want to overstate the case. Martha Minow's application of the social relations approach to cases involving persons with mental disabilities, *see* MINOW, *supra* note 15, at 114–20, David Wexler and Bruce Winick's groundbreaking work on "therapeutic jurisprudence," in THERAPEUTIC JURISPRUDENCE: THE LAW AS A THERAPEUTIC AGENT 165 (David Wexler ed., 1990), and the work of Gary Melton, Michael Saks, Dan Shuman, Stephen Morse, and others in developing a psychology of jurisprudence are important exceptions.

The concept of sanism is now being considered by important scholars writing in this area of the law. *See, e.g,* PETER BLANCK, THE AMERICANS WITH DISABILITIES ACT AND THE EMERGING WORKFORCE: EMPLOYMENT OF PEOPLE WITH MENTAL RETARDATION 59–60 (1998); Peter Blanck, *Civil Rights, Learning Disability, and Academic Standards,* 2 J. GENDER, RACE & JUST. 33, 53–54 (1998); Grant Morris, *Defining Dangerousness: Risking a Dangerous Definition,* 10 J. CONTEMP. LEGAL ISSUES 61 (1999); Leonard Rubenstein, *Ending Discrimination Against Mental Health Treatment in Publicly Financed Health Care,* 40 ST. LOUIS U. L.J. 315, 350 (1996); Bruce Winick, *Forward: A Summary of the MacArthur Treatment Competence Study and an Introduction to the Special Theme,* 2 PSYCHOL., PUB. POL'Y & L. 3, 15–16 (1996); Christopher Slobogin, *"Appreciation" as a Measure of Competency: Some Thoughts About the MacArthur Group's Approach,* 2 PSYCHOL., PUB. POL'Y & L. 18, 23 (1996); Trudi Kirk & Donald Bersoff, *How Many Procedural Safeguards Does It Take to Leave the Lightbulb Unchanged? A Due Process Analysis of the MacArthur Treatment Competence Study,* 2 PSYCHOL., PUB. POL'Y & L. 45, 64 (1996); Bruce Winick, *The MacArthur Treatment Competence Study: Legal and Therapeutic Implications,* 2 PSYCHOL., PUB. POL'Y & L. 137, 164–65 (1996).

[304]*9:00 A.M. Opening Plenary,* 75 WASH. U.L.Q. 1586, 1653 (1997) ("The Society of American Law Teachers, for example, is an organization of progressive law professors who have annual or sometimes twice-annual teaching conferences, many of which are directed at how our teaching can reflect our social values and how we can effectively raise these issues in the classroom").

[305]Rogelio Lasso, *Conference Review,* SALT EQUALIZER 18–19 (Dec. 1994). I discuss the implications of this reaction in Keri K. Gould & Michael L. Perlin, "'Johnny's in the Basement/Mixing Up His Medicine': Therapeutic Jurisprudence and Clinical Teaching" (unpublished manuscript, 1998), at 21 n.90 (on file with author).

Conclusion

Sanism is as prevalent as racism or sexism—perhaps even more so—yet it is almost completely ignored. Fifty years ago, before *Brown v. Board of Education,* before the Civil Rights Acts of the 1960's, before the awakening of the civil rights movement and the feminist movement, it was unfathomable to many White Americans that Black children might have a right to attend an integrated public school or that any Black person could sit where he or she wished on a local bus, just as it was unfathomable to many males that a female could compete in the job market or demand equal pay. A half-century of civil rights activism has created a new society in which these views are condemned by a broad majority of our citizens. Yet, sanism continues to dominate our legal system and our social interactions—ironically, very often sanist thoughts and acts flow from those who have reflected progressive and compassionate positions on questions of sex and race. Sanism is often invisible, and remains socially acceptable. And there have been no attempts, so far, to answer the question that has bedeviled civil rights activists since the 1950s: how to capture "the hearts and minds"[306] of the American public so as to best insure that statutorily and judicially articulated rights are incorporated—freely and willingly—into the day-to-day fabric and psyche of society.[307]

Unfounded assumptions about individuals with mental disabilities are often considered fact, and the pretexts under which lawmakers and law enforcers mete out the law to persons with mental disabilities are often based on sanist ideas. In the next chapter, I discuss this other corrupt root of mental disability law: pretextuality.

---

[306]The phrase was first used in Chief Justice Warren's opinion in Brown v. Bd. of Educ. of Topeka, 347 U.S. 483, 494 (1954).

[307]Michael L. Perlin, *The ADA and Persons with Mental Disabilities: Can Sanist Attitudes Be Undone?* 8 J.L. & HEALTH 15, 22 (1993–94).

Chapter 3
ON PRETEXTUALITY

In the preface of this book I mentioned the most widespread example of pretextuality. It bears repeating: An undercover officer swears that on a certain date he was on narcotics surveillance duty on the corner of two streets in a "well-known high-crime area." At that time (generally late at night), he observed John Jones (now the defendant), standing under a dimly illuminated streetlight on the other side of the block. Recognizing Jones as a "long-time drug user and seller," the officer crossed the street to confront Jones. When Jones saw the plain-clothed officer, he responded by "making furtive gestures" and dropping a handful of small glassine packets (packets that the officer quickly recognized as potentially containing heroin). Before the officer could either properly identify himself as a police officer, or place the defendant under arrest and administer the *Miranda* warnings, the defendant spontaneously blurted out an uncoerced confession: "That's heroin, and it's mine."

Predictably, the police officer's testimony proves unimpeachable on cross-examination. Basically, all the defense counsel can ask is, "Officer, you're lying aren't you?" The witness then replies, "No I'm not, counselor." The defendant's motion to suppress is shortly denied. Soon thereafter, the defendant pleads guilty to a drug offense.

This is the famous "dropsy" scenario that transpires regularly in urban courthouses throughout the country. Did these events really transpire this way? Of course not.

This entire scenario is pretextual.[1] The defendant never dropped the packets voluntarily, and never "spontaneously" blurted out, "It's my heroin." Everybody knows that—the police officer, the prosecutor, the defense counsel, the defendant, the judge, and ultimately the appellate court that will eventually uphold the suppression denial and subsequent conviction (in the rare case of an appeal).[2] Yet the legal system condones, and perhaps encourages, this entire web of deceit and pretextuality.

---

[1] For examples of confirmatory descriptions, *see* Albert W. Alschuler, *"Close Enough for Government Work": The Exclusionary Rule After* Leon, 1984 SUP. CT. REV. 309, 347–49; Tom Barker, *An Empirical Study of Police Deviance Other Than Corruption,* 6 J. POL. SCI. & ADMIN. 264 (1978); Tom Barker & David Carter, *"Fluffing Up the Evidence and Covering Your Ass": Some Conceptual Notes on Police Lying,* 11 DEVIANT BEHAV. 61 (1990); Charles M. Sevilla, *The Exclusionary Rule and Police Perjury,* 11 SAN DIEGO L. REV. 839, 839–40 (1974); Stanley Z. Fisher, *"Just the Facts, Ma'am: Lying and the Omission of Exculpatory Evidence in Police Reports,* 28 N. ENG. L. REV. 1 (1993). *See generally* Christopher Slobogin, *The World Without a Fourth Amendment,* 39 UCLA L. REV. 1, 11–12 nn. 27–28 (1991). On the empirical impact of such behavior, *see, e.g.,* William C. Heffernan & Richard W. Lovely, *Evaluating the Fourth Amendment Exclusionary Rule: The Problem of Police Compliance With the Law,* 24 U. MICH. J. L. REF. 311 (1991); Peter F. Nardulli, *The Societal Cost of the Exclusionary Rule: An Empirical Assessment,* 1983 AM. B. FOUND. RES. J. 585. Courts have suppressed such evidence in a handful of cases. *See, e.g.,* State v. Brunori, 578 A.2d 139, 142 n.6 (Conn. App. Ct. 1990); People v. Acosta, N.Y. L.J., June 25, 1991, at 23 (N.Y. Sup. Ct. 1991); People v. Roberts, N.Y. L.J., Dec. 31, 1990, at 30 (N.Y. Sup. Ct. 1990); *cf.* People v. Berrios, 270 N.E.2d 709 (N.Y. 1971) (Fuld, J., dissenting); *see also* People v. McMurty, 314 N.Y.S.2d 194, 196–98 (N.Y. Crim. Ct. 1970) (denying suppression motion but warning about the need for "especial caution" in dropsy cases).

[2] For an important empirical study confirming this view, *see* Myron W. Orfield, *Deterrence, Perjury, and the Heater Factor: An Exclusionary Rule in the Chicago Criminal Courts,* 63 U. COLO. L. REV. 75, 100–07 (1992) (86% of judges, public defenders, and prosecutors questioned, including 77% of judges, believe that police officers fabricate evidence in case reports at least "some of the time"; 92% (including 91% of judges) believe that police officers lie in court to avoid suppression of evidence at least "some of the time").

What does this have to do with competency and mental disability law? Plenty. The entire relationship between the legal process and mentally disabled litigants is often pretextual. By pretextuality, I mean simply that courts accept (either implicitly or explicitly) testimonial dishonesty and engage similarly in dishonest (frequently meretricious) decision making.[3] This pretextuality infects all players, breeds cynicism and disrespect for the law, demeans participants, reinforces shoddy lawyering, invites blasé judging, and, at times, promotes perjurious and corrupt testifying. The reality is well-known to frequent consumers of judicial services in this area: to mental health advocates and other public defender/legal aid/legal service lawyers assigned to represent patients and mentally disabled criminal defendants, to prosecutors and state attorneys assigned to represent hospitals, to judges who regularly hear such cases, to expert and lay witnesses, and, most important, to the person with mental disabilities who is involved in the litigation in question.

Pretextuality, in combination with the impact of sanism on expert testimony and judicial decisions,[4] often helps create a system that (a) accepts dishonest testimony unthinkingly; (b) regularly subverts statutory and case law standards; and (c) raises insurmountable barriers that ensure the allegedly "therapeutically correct" social outcome and avoidance of the worst-case-disaster-fantasy, the false negative. In short, the mental disability law system often deprives individuals of liberty disingenuously and for reasons that have no relationship to case law or to statutes.

This aspect of the mental disability law system is astonishingly underconsidered by advocates,[5] scholars, and professional associations alike. Examining the way that "moral" experts testify in sanist courts promotes better understanding of the extent of the prevailing pretexts. This understanding will encourage new strategies for confronting the underlying biases, creating a new structure, and developing a new research agenda by which these issues can be examined openly.

How did pretextuality come to infect the legal system? Americans pride ourselves on the fairness and inherent sense of rationality of the U.S. justice system.[6] The legal trial process presupposes an ascertainable "truth" as a basis for testimony,[7] and severe sanctions are imposed for committing perjury.[8] Psychiatry and psychology, in turn, reject notions of a unitary concept of "reason," pointing out that the range of human behavior is infinite and

---

[3]*See* Michael Perlin, *Morality and Pretextuality, Psychiatry and Law: of "Ordinary Common Sense," Heuristic Reasoning, and Cognitive Dissonance,* 19 BULL. AM. ACAD. PSYCHIATRY & L. 131, at 133. This is apparent specifically where witnesses, especially expert witnesses, show a "high propensity to purposely distort their testimony in order to achieve desired ends." Sevilla, *supra* note 1, at 840; *cf.* Edwin J. Butterfoss, *Solving the Pretext Puzzle: The Importance of Ulterior Motives and Fabrications in the Supreme Court's Fourth Amendment Pretext Doctrine,* 79 KY. L. J. 1, n.1 (1990–91) (defining "pretexts" to include situations in which "the government offers a justification for activity that, if the motivation of the [police] officer is not considered, would be a legally sufficient justification for the activity" as well as for those activities for which the preferred justification is "legally insufficient").

[4]*See supra* Chapter 2.

[5]On counsel's role in general, *see* Michael L. Perlin, *Fatal Assumptions: A Critical Evaluation of the Role of Counsel in Mental Disability Cases,* 16 LAW & BEHAV. 39 (1992).

[6]*See, e.g.,* RONALD DWORKIN, LAW'S EMPIRE 243, 405–07 (1986); Ernest Weinrib, *Legal Formalism: On the Immanent Rationality of Law,* 97 YALE L.J. 949, 954 n.14 (1988), *citing* Thomas Aquinas, *Treatise on Law,* in SUMMA THEOLOGICA I–II QQ 90–105, *reprinted in* ON LAW, MORALITY, AND POLITICS 11–83 (W. Baumgarth & R. Regan eds. 1988).

[7]*See, e.g.,* State v. Stevens, 558 A.2d 833, 840 (N.J. 1989), and Pena v. State, 780 P.2d 316, 334 (Wyo. 1989), *both citing* Note, *Other Crimes Evidence at Trial,* 70 YALE L.J. 763, 770–71 (1961); State *ex rel.* Okla. Bar Ass'n v. Lloyd, 787 P.2d 855, 859 (Okla. 1990); Slaughter v. Commonwealth, 744 S.W.2d 407, 414 (Ky. 1987), *reh'g denied* (1988).

[8]*See, e.g.,* N.Y. PENAL L. §§ 210.15 and 70.00(2)(d) (up to seven years); N.J. STAT. ANN. § 2C:28–1 (three to five years); FLA. STAT. ANN. §§ 837.02 & 775.082 (up to five years and $5000 fine).

that unconscious variables and processes, conflicts, anxieties and defenses—the *irrational*—are frequently the primary causes of behavior.[9] The mental health professions also counsel practitioners not to impose their sense of ''morality'' on patients or clients,[10] or to use their authority as a defense in dealing with such clients.[11]

At the point that these two systems intersect, something strange happens. Perhaps because of the ''substantial gulf between scientific and legal discourse,''[12] perhaps because of the different training received by mental health professionals and lawyers,[13] perhaps because of the public's radically differing perceptions of the substance of law and the mental health professions,[14] those who are involved in both professional arenas must consider the way that these internal and inherent differences create tensions that have a measurable effect on what happens when these cultures collide, especially in the forensic mental disability system.

This collision can be viewed from several vantage points that, to the best of my knowledge, have not been seriously explored: from the perspectives of the way that law—the system extolling ''truth'' as a highest virtue—adopts pretextuality as a means of dealing with information or situations that it finds troubling or dissonant, and the way that the mental health professions—the systems that counsel against attributions of ''morality'' in interpersonal dealings—impose a self-referential concept of morality in dealing with legal interactions. I believe that if we are to understand *why* the historic relationship[15] between the law and the mental health professions is seen as a rocky one, characterized variously as an uneasy *détente,* a shotgun marriage, or a marriage of convenience,[16] it is necessary to consider the question through these two filters of pretextuality and morality.

---

[9]*See generally* OTTO A. WILL, PROCESS, PSYCHOTHERAPY AND SCHIZOPHRENIA (1961), *reprinted in* JAY KATZ, JOSEPH GOLDSTEIN, & ALAN DERSHOWITZ, PSYCHOANALYSIS, PSYCHIATRY AND LAW 680–84 (1967); *see also* MICHAEL MOORE, LAW AND PSYCHIATRY: RETHINKING THE RELATIONSHIP 142 (1984).

[10]*See, e.g.,* ALFRED BENJAMIN, THE HELPING INTERVIEW 140–43 (1969); 2 ROBERT LANGS, THE TECHNIQUES OF PSYCHOANALYTIC PSYCHOTHERAPY 294–97 (2d ed. 1976); CARL R. ROGERS, COUNSELING AND PSYCHOTHERAPY: NEWER CONCEPTS IN PRACTICE 327 (1942); 2 FREDERICK PERLS, RALPH F. HEFFERLINE, & PAUL GOODMAN, GESTALT THERAPY 510–11 (2d ed. 1973); ROSEMARY BALSAM & ALAN BALSAM, THE BOOK OF FAMILY THERAPY: BECOMING A PSYCHOTHERAPIST: A CLINICAL PRIMER 108–11 (1974).

[11]BENJAMIN, *supra* note 10, at 92–95.

[12]Harold Green, *The Law–Science Interface in Public Policy Decision Making,* 51 OHIO ST. L.J. 375, 405 (1990).

[13]Some psychiatrists see this difference as critical in explaining what they perceive as differences in the perspectives of the two professions. *See, e.g.,* H. Richard Lamb, Involuntary Treatment for the Homeless Mentally Ill, 4 NOTRE DAME J.L. ETHICS. & PUB. POL'Y 169, 276 (1989) (discussing Szasz, Goffman, and Laing as intellectually animating sources for ''many attorneys''); MICHAEL PESZKE, INVOLUNTARY TREATMENT OF THE MENTALLY ILL 133–36 (1975) (law students' interest in law and psychiatry comes from students' desires ''to learn how to punch holes and to show the psychiatrist up in court'').

[14]*See, e.g.,* S. B. Cohen, *The Evolutionary Relationship Between Psychiatry and Law,* in AMNON CARMI, STANLEY SCHNEIDER & ALBERT HEFEZ, PSYCHIATRY, LAW AND ETHICS 69 (1986); Bentley, *The Infant and the Dream: Psychology and the Law,* in PSYCHOLOGY, LAW AND LEGAL PROBLEMS 35 (David Farrington, Keith Hawkins, & Sally Lloyd-Bostock eds. 1979).

[15]*See* JUDITH NEAMEN, SUGGESTION OF THE DEVIL: THE ORIGINS OF MADNESS 67–110 (1975) (relationship dates back to Roman law and Justinian codes).

[16]*See* JONAS ROBITSCHER, PURSUIT OF AGREEMENT: PSYCHIATRY AND THE LAW 12 (1966), citing F. WHITLOCK, CRIMINAL RESPONSIBILITY AND MENTAL ILLNESS (1963). *See generally* 1 MICHAEL L. PERLIN, MENTAL DISAIBLITY LAW: CIVIL AND CRIMINAL § 1–1, at 3 n.6 (2nd ed. 1998). *cf.* Michael L. Perlin & Robert L. Sadoff, *The Adversary System,* in Seymour Kutash et al., VIOLENCE: PERSPECTIVES ON MURDER AND AGGRESSION 394 (1978) (''the intersection of law and mental health stands at a significant focal point in the development of human behavior, at a point where motives, intents, and drives can and must be examined in the contexts of rights, obligations, duties and the social order'').

Much of what lawyers say about forensic testimony is pretextual.[17] Much of what forensic mental health professionals who frequently wear the hat of expert witness say about individual cases is similarly pretextual, ostensibly for reasons of "morality." And much of the way judges interpret forensic testimony is teleological.[18] That is, the legal system selectively, telelogically, either accepts or rejects social science evidence depending on whether the use of that data meets the system's *a priori* needs. In cases where fact-finders are hostile to social science teachings, such data often meets with tremendous judicial resistance, evidenced by the courts' expression of their skepticism about, suspicions of, and hostilities toward such evidence.[19] I believe that these interpretive clues help explain much of the confusion in mental disability law.

The relationship between the mutually symbiotic systems of law and forensic mental health is an increasingly more fragile one, and, as the Hinckley acquittal demonstrated, one vivid, outrageous case can wipe out the results of years of study, collection of empirical data and reflective inquiry into any aspect of the mental health system.[20] Finally, most of what is written—in both law and the mental health professions—utterly ignores both of the premises of this book as well as these two propositions. I hope that this book leads both lawyers and mental health professionals to come to recognize that, even if the pursuit of agreement[21] appears to be beyond us, we can at least acknowledge that there are bridges to be built.

In this chapter, I will explain the roots of pretextuality,[22] the specific ways it infects decision making in mental disability law cases,[23] the singular relationship between pretextuality and the role of "morality" in expert testimony,[24] and the ways that the legal system's teleological use of social science data further perpetuates pretextuality as a constant undercurrent in this entire area of law.[25]

---

[17]*See generally,* Perlin, *supra* note 3.

[18]*See generally id.*

[19]Michael L. Perlin, *"The Borderline Which Separated You From Me": The Insanity Defense, the Authoritarian Spirit, the Fear of Faking, and the Culture of Punishment,* 82 IOWA L. REV. 1375, 1419 (1997). *See also e.g.,* Paul S. Appelbaum, *The Empirical Jurisprudence of the United States Supreme Court,* 13 AM. J.L. & MED. 335, 341 (1987) (discussing Barefoot v. Estelle, 463 U.S. 880 (1983)); David L. Faigman, *"Normative Constitutional Fact-Finding": Exploring the Empirical Component of Constitutional Interpretation,* 139 U. PA. L. REV. 541, 581 (1991); J. Alexander Tanford, *The Limits of a Scientific Jurisprudence: The Supreme Court and Psychology,* 66 IND. L.J. 137, 144–50 (1990).

[20]*See generally* Michael L. Perlin, *Unpacking the Myths: The Symbolism Mythology of Insanity Defense Jurisprudence,* 40 CASE W. RES. L. REV. 599 (1989–90); *cf.* Jonas Rappeport, *Editorial: Is Forensic Psychiatry Ethical,* 12 BULL. AM. ACAD. PSYCHIATRY & L. 205 (1984) (society's response to the Hinckley acquittal "placed the blame on the insanity plea and the psychiatrists"). It is necessary to acknowledge that there are at least two universes worthy of consideration in this context: the case such as Hinckley's that captures the attention of the whole nation and the vivid case that may be unknown nationally but in which local interest is so heavy that its disposition may overwhelm a statewide legal system. *See, e.g.,* William H. Fischer, Glenn L. Pierce, & Paul S. Appelbaum, *How Flexible Are Our Civil Commitment Statutes?* 39 HOSP. & COMMUNITY PSYCHIATRY 711 (1978) (commitment rates in one Washington county increased 100% following murder by mentally disabled individual who had been denied voluntary admission to psychiatric hospital).

[21]*See generally* JONAS B. ROBITSCHER, PURSUIT OF AGREEMENT: PSYCHIATRY AND THE LAW 12 (1966).

[22]*See infra* text accompanying notes 26–61.

[23]*See infra* text accompanying notes 62–85.

[24]*See infra* text accompanying notes 85–106.

[25]*See infra* text accompanying notes 107–28.

Pretexts in the Legal System

It may sound presumptuous or nihilistic to say that the U.S. legal system condones or encourages (or even demands) pretextuality; I do not mean to be either. The fact that the phrase "mere pretext" appears in 4228 reported state and federal cases[26] suggests that, at the least, pretexts are a matter with which the legal system has more than a passing familiarity.

Pretextuality is two-sided. There are areas in which courts willingly accept dishonesty on the part of participants in the legal and legislative process. On the other side of the coin, there are areas in which courts erect insurmountable barriers to guard against what is perceived of as malingering, feigning, or otherwise misusing the legal system.[27] Both types of pretexts infect all areas of the legal system, but their pernicious impact is especially problematic in the trial of mental disability cases.

As I already suggested, the pretextuality paradigm testimony in "dropsy" cases fulfills a defined police purpose and is condoned as an acceptable "necessary evil" required to solve "the basic problems of police work."[28] Because the goal is perceived as both legitimate (putting criminals in jail and preventing future crime) and necessary (as a means of mediating against "improper" liberal rules of law imposed by the U.S. Supreme Court),[29] courts condone "deviant lies." There also is often a moral justification offered for these actions. Because of their unique experiences with criminals, police officers feel that they "know" the factual guilt or innocence of arrestees and can therefore appropriately shape their testimony to serve a greater social good.[30] The courts are compliant partners in crime.[31] An empirical study suggests that judges refuse to follow the law and suppress evidence because of their "personal sense of 'justice.'" As one state's attorney pointed out, "When judges apply the exclusionary rule, they feel they are doing something wrong."[32] According

---

[26]As of a WESTLAW search conducted on November 19, 1999.

[27]Perlin, *supra* note 5, at 57 n.113; Michael L. Perlin, *Morality and Pretextuality, Psychiatry and Law: of "Ordering Common Sense," Heuristic Reasoning, and Cognitive Dissonance,* 19 BULL. AM. ACAD. PSYCHIATRY & L. 131, 133–35 (1991) [hereinafter Perlin, *Morality*].

[28]*See* Barker & Carter, *supra* note 1, at 62–66.

[29]*See* Irving Younger, *The Perjury Routine,* THE NATION, May 8, 1967, at 596 (quoted in People v. McMurty, 314 N.Y.S.2d 194, 196 (Sup. Ct. 1970)). *See also, e.g.,* Stephen Saltzburg, *Criminal Procedure in the 1960s: A Reality Check,* 42 DRAKE L. REV. 179, 202 (1993) ("To the extent that there was a revolution in the criminal justice jurisprudence of the 1960's, it had to do with the [Supreme] Court's unwillingness to blink at the realities of crime, investigations, and prosecutions.")

[30]Peter K. Manning, *Lying, Secrecy and Social Control, in* POLICING: A VIEW FROM THE STREET 238 (Peter K. Manning & John Van Maaness eds., 1978). For an analysis of police misconceptions about basic criminal procedure principles, see Kevin Corr, *Debunking the Myths: A Compendium of Law Enforcement Misconceptions,* 23 AM. J. CRIM. L. 121 (1995) (author is chief division counsel to the Federal Bureau of Investigation).

[31]Anthony Amsterdam offers a psychodynamically grounded explanation for this behavior:

> Only a few appellate judges can throw off the fetters of their middle-class backgrounds—the dimly remembered, friendly face of the school crossing guard, their fear of a crowd of "toughs," their attitudes engendered as lawyers before their elevation to the bench, by years of service as prosecutors or as private lawyers for honest, respectable business clients—and identify with the criminal suspect instead of with the policeman or with the putative victim of the suspect's theft, mugging, rape, or murder. Trial judges still more, and magistrates beyond belief, are functionally and psychologically allied with the police, their co-workers in the unending and scarifying work of bringing criminals to book.

Anthony Amsterdam, *The Supreme Court and the Rights of Suspects in Criminal Cases,* 45 N.Y.U. L. REV. 785, 792 (1970).

[32]Orfield, *supra* note 2 at 121 (emphasis added) [hereinafter Orfield, *Exclusionary*]; *see also* Myron Orfield, *The Exclusionary Rule and Deterrence: An Empirical Study of Chicago Narcotics Officers,* 54 U. CHI. L. REV. 1016, 1018 (1987) ("in-court police perjury clearly exists in Chicago").

On the interplay between racism and the selective enforcement of other search and seizure doctrines, see Adrina Schwartz, *"Just Take Away Their Guns": The Racism of* Terry v. Ohio, 23 FORDHAM URB. L.J. 317 (1996).

to Christopher Slobogin, ''To the extent judges ignore obvious perjury, it is probably for the same reasons attributable to the prosecutor—sympathy for the police officer's ultimate goal, and as Professor Morgan Cloud put it, 'tact'— the fact that '[j]udges simply do not like to call other government officials liars—especially those who appear regularly in court.'''[33]

Pretextuality extends far beyond the question of police lies.[34] Pretextuality results from the condoning of legal fictions. Legal fictions ''propounded with a complete or partial consciousness of [their] falsity'' or ''false statement[s] recognized as having utility''[35] are centuries-old devices courts use as a means to sidestep legislation deemed, in Blackstone's words, ''so intolerably mischievous [but which] the legislature would not then consent to repeal.''[36]

Courts use these fictions to falsely interpret the true meaning of legislation through alleged legislative intent,[37] or to read imaginary unarticulated legislative assumptions into statutes in efforts to sustain such laws by a ''rationality'' standard.[38] Such fictions remain sanctioned by the Supreme Court in a wide variety of subject matters.[39]

The acceptance of legal fictions creates ambivalence toward concepts of law and justice. Toleration of ''sleight of hand'' in the law's theoretical bases breeds cynicism and fosters an

---

[33]Christopher Slobogin, *Testilying: Police Perjury and What to Do About It,* 67 U. COLO. L. REV. 1037, 1060 (1996), *relying on* Orfield, *supra* note 2, at 113, and quoting Morgan Cloud, *The Dirty Little Secret,* 43 EMORY L.J. 1311, 1323–24 (1994).

[34]For an excellent analysis of why we lie and why some lies are condoned, see Dan Subotnik, ''*Sue Me, Sue Me, What Can You Do Me? I Love You'': A Disquisition on Love, Sex, and Talk,* 47 FLA. L. REV. 311 (1995) (in the context of a ''sex fraud'' (misrepresentations designed to get sexual benefits) tort action). On the role of pretextuality in the dispositions of cases involving sex offenders, see Eric Janus, *Sex Offender Commitments: Debunking the Official Narrative and Revealing the Rules-in-Use,* 8 STAN. L. & POL'Y REV. 71, 72 n.18 (1997).

[35]LON FULLER, LEGAL FICTIONS 9 (1967).

[36]M. B. W. Sinclair, *The Use of Evolution Theory in Law,* 64 U. DET. L. REV. 451, 475 n.142 (1987) (quoting 2 W. BLACKSTONE, COMMENTARIES ON THE LAWS OF ENGLAND 117 [facsimile edition, published by Garland Publishing, New York and London, 1978]; *see id.* at 475 (quoting Oliver R. Mitchell, *The Fictions of the Law: Have They Proved Useful or Detrimental to Its Growth,* 7 HARV. L. REV. 863, 870 (1930)).

[37]*See, e.g.,* Max Radin, *Statutory Interpretation,* 43 HARV. L. REV. 863, 870 (1930) (discussing legislative intent as a ''transparent and absurd fiction''); *cf.* Green v. Bock Laundry Mach. Co., 490 U.S. 504, 509–10 (1989) (assuming a common understanding on the part of each Congressional representative as to meaning of legislation is a ''benign fiction.'' *See generally* George A. Costello, *Average Voting Members and Other ''Benign Fictions'': The Relative Reliability of Committee Reports, Floor Debates, and Other Sources of Legislative History,* 1990 DUKE L.J. 39.

[38]*See* John Monahan & Laurens Walker, *Empirical Questions Without Empirical Answers,* 1991 WIS. L. REV. 569, 583 (discussing McGowan v. Maryland, 366 U.S. 420 (1961), upholding Sunday ''blue law'' retail store closings).

[39]For recent examples, *see, e.g,* Marquez v. Screen Actors Guild, 119 S. Ct. 292, 304 (1998) (Kennedy, J., concurring) (terms of collective bargaining agreement); United States v. Ursery, 518 U.S. 267, 267 (1996) (forfeiture); Board. of Educ. of Kiryas Joel Village Sch. Dist. v. Board of Educ. of Monroe-Woodbury Cent. Sch. Dist., 512 U.S. 687, 701 (1994) (private school district serving handicapped children); United States v. Irvine, 511 U.S. 224, 240 (1994) (disclaimer of testamentary gift); Cruzan v. Director, Mo. Dep't of Health, 497 U.S. 2611 (1990) (right to die); United States v. Dalm, 494 U.S. 596, 622 (1990) (Stevens, J., dissenting) (gift tax refund recoupment process); Carden v. Arkoma Assocs., 494 U.S. 185, 202–03 (1990) (O'Connor, J., dissenting) (determining partnership residency in diversity cases); Caplin & Drysdale, Chartered v. United States, 491 U.S. 617, 644 (1989) (Blackmun, J., dissenting) (applying property-forfeiture statute in narcotics-enterprise case).

The Supreme Court's decision in Lee v. Weisman, 505 U.S. 577 (1992) (establishment clause case) is criticized as an example of the Court's ''duplicity'' in Donald Bersoff, *Autonomy for Vulnerable Populations: The Supreme Court's Reckless Disregard for Self-Determination and Social Science,* 37 VILL. L. REV. 1569, 1603 (1992). *See also* Saltzburg, *supra* note 29, at 202, criticizing INS v. Delgado, 466 U.S. 210 (1984) (immigration search case): ''The notion that people in a factory would not feel they were detained when immigration agents armed with weapons and walkie-talkies enter a plant and station themselves at exits is difficult to fathom.''

atmosphere of systemic manipulation by litigants, legislators, litigators, and courts.[40] Now we are blind to their "evident strangeness," having become inured to the use of such fictions.[41] Such fictions, traditionally used in cases involving substantive questions of property and commercial law and procedural questions of personal jurisdiction,[42] are no longer limited to such private-law questions.

Two public-law examples are illustrative. The legal fiction of "substituted judgment" is at the heart of the Supreme Court's decision in the *Cruzan* case and in all courts' "right to die" decision making.[43] It also pervades the law of mental patients' right to refuse antipsychotic drug treatment.[44] In an entirely different area of the law, the legal fiction of "territorial exclusion" drives the law that governs the detention of aliens lacking proper entry documentation.[45] One example is that of an excludable alien, who is incarcerated in an American prison yet who is fictively deemed not to actually be within the territorial jurisdiction of the United States.[46]

Legal fictions are seductive and dangerous.[47] They foster an environment in which pretextual testimony, pretextual legislative activity, and pretextual court decisions "no longer strike the eye" as strange.[48] In addition to the paradigm dropsy case (one of many aspects of constitutional criminal procedure so infected by pretextuality),[49] damaging pretexts contaminate legal decision making in a variety of civil rights, civil liberties, and other constitutionally grounded cases.

When a state legislator stated that his introduction of a "moment of silence" bill had nothing to do with school prayer but merely would insure that students had time for "private contemplation and inspection," his statement was clearly pretextual.[50] A state prejudgment replevin statute was pretextual when it provided a discovery mechanism not invoked by a single defendant in a 442-case sample.[51] When the Supreme Court treated administrative rulings written after the enactment of the welfare rule whose constitutionality is before the court as "history" and "long-standing precedent," that decision was pretextual.[52]

---

[40]Stephen Wizner, *What Is a Law School?*, 38 EMORY L.J. 701, 705 (1989).

[41]Eben Moglen, Fictional Reasoning in the Common Law Tradition: Prospects for Historical Investigation (paper presented at New York Law School Faculty Development Seminar, Oct. 18, 1988), at 25.

[42]*See generally* Moglen, *supra* note 41; Sinclair, *supra* note 36.

[43]*See* Cruzan v. Director, Mo. Dep't of Health, 497 U.S 261 (1990). *See generally* Louise Harmon, *Falling off the Vine: Legal Fictions and the Doctrine of Substituted Judgment*, 100 YALE L.J. 1 (1990).

[44]*See, e.g.,* Michael L. Perlin, *Are Courts Competent to Decide Questions of Competency? Stripping the Facade* United States v. Charters, 38 U. Kan. L. Rev. 957 (1990).

[45]*See* Mark D. Kemple, Note, *Legal Fictions Mask Human Suffering: The Detention of the Mariel Cubans Constitutional, Statutory, International Law, and Human Considerations*, 62 S. CAL. L. REV. 1733, 1743 (1989) (discussing Garcia-Mir v. Meese, 788 F.2d 1446 (11th Cir. 1986) and Palma v. Verdeyen, 676 F.2d 100 (4th Cir. 1982)).

[46]*See* United States v. Verdugo-Urquidez, 494 U.S. 259 (1990).

[47]*See* Harmon, *supra* note 43, at 15–16, 69–70.

[48]Moglen, *supra* note 41, at 25.

[49]For discussions concerning the relationship between pretextuality and the availability of *Gideon*-mandated counsel, *see* Michael B. Mushlin, *Foreword to Conference, Gideon v. Wainwright Revisited: What Does the Right to Counsel Guarantee Today?* 10 PACE L. REV. 327, 341 (1990) (Burt Neuborne explains that the legal system functions as if *Gideon* "had never been decided"); Alissa P. Worden & Robert E. Worden, *Local Politics and the Provision of Indigent Defense Counsel*, 11 LAW & POL'Y REV. 401 (1989); *see also* James J. Tomkovicz, *The Truth About Massiah*, 23 U. MICH. J.L. REF. 641 (1990). *See generally,* Gideon v. Wainwright, 372 U.S. 335 (1963) (right to counsel applies to all felony prosecutors).

[50]May v. Cooperman, 780 F.2d 240, 243 (3d Cir. 1985), *appeal dissmissed sub nom.*, Karcher v. May, 484 U.S. 721 (1987).

[51]Fuentes v. Shevin, 407 U.S. 67, 85 n.14 (1972).

[52]Lukhard v. Reed, 481 U.S. 368 (1987).

When courts sanction "curative" jury instructions knowing full well that the jurors have cognitively processed the damaging testimony in question, that sanctioning is pretextual.[53] A court's reading of testimony that depicts sexual coercion as reflecting the victim's willing participation was pretextual.[54] When a court excluded testimony concerning the existence of a code of silence among police officers deterring them from testifying in cases in which other officers are charged with using excessive force in resisting arrest cases, that exclusion is pretextual.[55] The Supreme Court's expansion of clear limiting language of the Eleventh Amendment to bar certain federal cases brought by citizens against their own states was pretextual.[56] And when courts failed to acknowledge that unconscious racism influences prosecutorial and juror decision making, that failure was pretextual.[57]

The most glaring example is *McCleskey v. Kemp,*[58] in which the Court rejected statistical evidence proffered by the defendant to demonstrate systemic racial discrimination in prosecutors' decisions to seek the death penalty and in jurors' decisions to impose capital punishment.[59] After *McCleskey,* a prevailing defendant must show that the decision makers "in his case acted with discriminatory purpose." We can expect that intelligent state prosecutors can evade the proscription of this nearly impossible-to-fail test.[60]

Courts are also plagued by empirical pretextuality. Courts appear willing to accept popular myths about such alleged phenomenon as the "litigation explosion," the frequent use of exaggerated testimony in personal injury and medical malpractice cases, the insubstantiality of most *pro se* prisoner writs, and the "flood" of constitutional tort litigation, notwithstanding the fact that empirical reality discredits each of these myths.[61]

---

[53]*See, e.g.,* Robert R. Calo, *Joint Trials, Spillover Prejudice, and the Ineffectiveness of a Bare Limiting Instruction,* 9 AM. J. TRIAL ADV. 21, 25–26 (1985). Some studies suggest that curative charges actually increase prejudice. *See* SAUL M. KASSIN & LAWRENCE S. WRIGHTSMAN, THE AMERICAN JURY ON TRIAL: PSYCHOLOGICAL PERSPECTIVES 108–09 (1988); Abraham R. Ordover, *Balancing the Presumptions of Guilt and Innocence: Rules 404(b), 608(b), and 609(a),* 38 EMORY L.J. 135, 175 (1989).

[54]Michael M. v. Superior Court, 450 U.S. 464, 484–85 (1981) (Blackmun, J., concurring); *see also* Kim L. Schepple, *The Re-Vision of Rape Law,* 54 U. CHI. L. REV. 1095 (1987). For discussion on courts' pretextual misstatement of facts in general, see Anthony D'Amato, *The Ultimate Injustice: When a Court Misstates the Facts,* 11 CARDOZO L. REV. 1313 (1990).

[55]Maynard v. Sayles, 817 F.2d 50, 52 (8th Cir. 1987), *vacated,* 831 F.2d 173 (8th Cir. 1987).

[56]Hans v. Louisiana, 134 U.S. 1, 18–20 (1890); *see also* Ann Althouse, *When to Believe a Legal Fiction: Federal Interests and the Eleventh Amendment,* 40 HASTINGS L.J. 1123 (1989); George D. Brown, *Has the Supreme Court Confessed Error on the Eleventh Amendment? Revisionist Scholarship and State Immunity,* 68 N.C. L. REV. 867 (1990); Erwin Chemerinsky, *Congress, the Supreme Court, and the Eleventh Amendment: A Comment on the Decisions During the 1988–89 Term,* 39 DEPAUL L. REV. 321 (1990). For more recent developments, see Seminole Tribe of Fla. v. Florida, 517 U.S. 44 (1996); *see generally* Erwin Chemerinsky, *Formalism and Functionalism in Federalism Analysis,* 13 GA. ST. U. L. REV. 959 (1997).

[57]*See, e.g.,* Sheri L. Johnson, *Unconscious Racism and the Criminal Law,* 73 CORNELL L. REV. 1016 (1985); *see also* McCleskey v. Kemp, 481 U.S. 279 (1987) (racial discrimination in death penalty decision making); Batson v. Kentucky, 476 U.S. 79 (1986) (racial discrimination in prosecutor's use of peremptory challenges); Turner v. Murray, 476 U.S. 28 (1986) (racial discrimination in jury selection in death penalty cases).

[58]481 U.S. 279 (1987).

[59]*Id.* at 313.

[60]*Id.* at 292. For discussion on the teleology of courts in dealing with such social science evidence in general, *see* Perlin, *Morality, supra* note 27, at 136–37. For discussion on its role in mental disability cases, *see generally* Michael L. Perlin & Deborah Dorfman, *Is It More Than "Dodging Lions and Wastin' Time"? Adequacy of Counsel, Questions of Competence, and the Judicial Process in Individual Right to Refuse Treatment Cases,* 2 PSYCHOL., PUB. POL'Y & L. 114, 120 (1996).

[61]For case law concerning the "litigation explosion," see Swidryk v. St. Michael's Med. Ctr., 493 A.2d 641, 645 (N.J. Super. Law Div. 1985) (educational malpractice case); *see also* Cunningham v. George Hyman Constr. Co., 603 A.2d 446, 450 n.10 (D.C. 1992) (time limits on workers' compensation suits); Whittington v. Ohio River Co., 115 F.R.D. 201, 204 (E.D. Ky. 1987); Inlet Assocs. v. Harrison Inn Inlet, Inc., 596 A.2d 1049, 1068 (Md. 1991)

Pretexts and Mental Disability Cases

The relationship between empirical pretextuality and the trial of mental disability cases is an important and profound one. Pretextual devices, such as condoning perjured testimony, distorting readings of trial testimony, subordinating statistically significant social science data, and enacting prophylactic civil rights laws that have absolutely no real-world impact similarly dominate the mental disability law landscape. These devices usually flow from the same motives that inspire similar behavior by courts and legislatures in other cases.

A few examples illustrate this point. Although the District of Columbia Code contains a provision that patients can seek either periodic review of their commitment or an independent psychiatric evaluation, in the first 22 years following the law's passage, not a single patient exercised her right to statutory review.[62] Although Attorney General William French Smith told Congress that the insanity defense "allows so many persons to commit crimes of violence," one of his top aides candidly told a federal judicial conference that the number of insanity defense cases was, statistically, "probably insignificant."[63] When a state enacts a new statutory scheme to "treat" sex offenders but fails to hire any professionals experienced in providing such treatment, that new statute is pretextual.[64]

In a case that turned on the question of whether a defendant had the requisite specific intent to attempt a bank robbery, a federal district court judge refused to allow a county jail psychiatrist to testify that he prescribed antipsychotic medications for the defendant for a particular purpose and a particular length of time. The judge reasoned that such testimony "might be interfering with the treatment of [other] prisoners in jails because [they] might ask for more drugs to create the impression they need more drugs."[65] The Ninth Circuit affirmed this decision as "not manifestly erroneous," even though there was no evidence anywhere in the case that spoke to this issue.[66] Finally, and more globally, courts and commentators regularly assume that vigorous, independent, advocacy-focused counsel is now available to all mentally disabled litigants, in spite of an empirical reality that, in almost every jurisdiction, it is totally to the contrary.[67]

(Bell, J., dissenting) (third-party action based on attorney–client advice). *Cf.* John H. Barton, *Behind the Legal Explosion,* 27 STAN. L. REV. 567 (1975) and Bayless Manning, *Hyperlexis: Our National Disease,* 71 NW. U. L. REV. 767 (1977) (setting out myths) with William L. F. Feltstiner et al., *The Emergence and Transformation of Disputes: Naming, Blaming, Claiming . . . ,* 15 LAW & SOC'Y REV. 631 (1981); Marc Galanter, *Reading the Landscape of Disputes: What We Know (and Think We Know) About Our Allegedly Contentious and Litigious Society,* 31 UCLA L. REV. 4, 38–39 (1983), Marc Galanter, *News From Nowhere: The Debased Debate on Civil Justice,* 71 DENVER U. L. REV. 78 (1993); Randy M. Mastro, *The Myth of the Litigation Explosion,* 60 FORDHAM L. REV. 199 (1991); and Henry J. Reske, *Was There a Liability Crisis?* 75 ABA J. 46 (1989) (setting out reality).

[62]Streicher v. Prescott, 663 F. Supp. 335, 343 (D.D.C. 1987); *cf.* In Interest of C. W., 453 N.W.2d 806, 809 (N.D. 1990) (rejecting patient's argument that discharge hearings were "rare occurrence[s]").

[63]Perlin, *Morality, supra* note 27, at 134 (quoting Ira Mickenberg, *A Pleasant Surprise: The Guilty But Mentally Ill Verdict Has Both Succeeded in Its Own Right and Successfully Preserved the Traditional Role of the Insanity Defense,* 55 U. CIN. L. REV. 943, at 980 (1987), and Proceedings of the Forty-Sixth Judicial Conference of the District of Columbia Circuit, 111 F.R.D. 91, 225 (1985)).

[64]*See* Michael L. Perlin, *"There's No Success Like Failure and Failure's No Success at All": Exposing the Pretextuality of* Kansas v. Hendricks, 92 NW. U. L. REV. 1247 (1998), critiquing Supreme Court decision in Kansas v. Hendricks, 521 U.S. 346 (1997) (upholding constitutionality of Kansas's sexually violent predator act); *see generally* 1 PERLIN, *supra* note 16, § 2A-3.3, at 75–92 (2d ed. 1998) (discussing *Hendricks*).

[65]United States v. Still, 857 F.2d 671, 672 (9th Cir. 1988), *cert. denied,* 489 U.S. 1060 (1989).

[66]*Id.* In another case, a testifying doctor conceded that he may have "hedged" in earlier testimony (as to whether an insanity acquittee could be released) "because he did not want to be criticized should [the defendant] be released and then commit a criminal act." Francois v. Henderson, 850 F.2d 231, 234 (5th Cir. 1988).

[67]*See* Perlin, *supra* note 5, at 40, 49, 54.

Police officers perjure themselves in dropsy cases "to ensure that criminals do not get off on 'technicalities,'"[68] and trial judges condone such behavior to "mediate the draconian effect of imposed-from-above constitutional decisions,"[69] such as *Mapp v. Ohio.*[70] In the same way, expert witnesses in civil commitment cases often impose their own self-referential concept of "morality" to ensure that patients who "really need treatment" remain institutionalized.[71] Judges accept this testimony in light of their own "instrumental, functional, normative and philosophical" dissatisfaction[72] with decisions such as *O'Connor v. Donaldson,*[73] *Jackson v. Indiana,*[74] and *Lessard v. Schmidt.*[75] Just as judges, including former Chief Justice Burger, express doubt that police testimony in dropsy cases requires special scrutiny,[76] many also express astonishment at the assertion that expert testimony in involuntary civil commitment cases may be factually inaccurate.[77]

In addition, courts fantasize about feared pretextuality in cases in which anecdotal myths prevail or in which unconscious values predominate.[78] For instance, the North Carolina Supreme Court deemed a sheriff's lay opinion that a potentially incompetent-to-stand-trial defendant learned how to feign mental illness after speaking to (presumably sophisticated) state prisoners during his pretrial incarceration more persuasive than the uncontradicted clinical testimony that the defendant was schizophrenic, mentally retarded, and suffering from acute pathological intoxication.[79] The fear that defendants will "fake" the insanity defense to escape punishment continues to paralyze the legal system in spite of

---

[68]Barker & Carter, *supra* note 1, at 69.

[69]Perlin, *Morality, supra* note 27, at 134; *see also* Orfield, *Deterrance, supra* note 2 at 121 (judges refuse to suppress evidence because of: (a) their personal "sense of justice"; (b) the fear of adverse publicity; and (c) the fear that such a decision might lead to reelection difficulties). For a rare candid judicial articulation of this position, see Rogers v. State, 332 So.2d 165, 167 (Ala. Crim. App. 1976) (quoting trial judge, "In Alabama we had sensible [criminal procedure] rules until the damn Supreme Court went crazy."), *cert. denied,* 332 So.2d 168 (Ala. 1976).

[70]367 U.S. 643 (1961).

[71]*See* William O. McCormick, *Involuntary Commitment in Ontario: Some Barriers to the Provision of Proper Care,* 124 Can. Med. Ass'n. J. 715, 717 (1981).

[72]Perlin, *Morality, supra* note 27, at 134.

[73]422 U.S. 563 (1975) (right to liberty).

[74]406 U.S. 715 (1972) (application of due process clause to commitments following incompetency-to-stand trial findings).

[75]349 F. Supp. 1078 (E.D. Wis. 1972) (application of substantive and procedural due process clauses to involuntary civil commitment process).

[76]Bush v. United States, 375 F.2d 602, 604 (D.C. Cir. 1967) ("It would be a dismal reflection on society to say that when the guardians of its security are called to testify in court under oath, their testimony must be viewed with suspicion."). *But see* People v. McMurty, 314 N.Y.S.2d 194, 197 (N.Y. Crim. Ct. 1970) (Younger, J.) (disagreeing with Justice Burger's point of view); Orfield, *supra* note 2. *McMurty* is discussed in Comment, *Police Perjury in Narcotics "Dropsy" Cases: A New Credibility Gap,* 60 Geo. L.J. 507 (1971).

[77]Opinion testimony by psychiatrists is "routinely and unquestioningly accepted" at involuntary civil commitment hearings. Marilyn Hammond, *Predictions of Dangerousness in Texas: Psychotherapists' Conflicting Duties, Their Potential Liability, and Possible Solutions,* 12 St. Mary's L.J. 141, 150 n.71 (1980); *see also In re* Melton, 597 A.2d 892, 902–03 (D.C. 1991) (asking, "Where else would the doctor go for such information?" in response to a patient's argument that it was violation of the hearsay rules for witness to base his medical conclusion on factual information given him by the patient's relatives). For discussion on applying the hearsay rules to the involuntary civil commitment process in general, *see* 1 Perlin, *supra* note 16, § 2C-4.13a, at 377–82 (2d ed. 1998); *see also* United States v. Charters, 863 F.2d 302, 310 (4th Cir. 1988) *(en banc), cert. denied,* 494 U.S. 1016 (1990). Appellate courts rarely consider whether mental disability law proceedings elicit or suppress "the truth." For thoughtful and conflicting visions, compare the majority opinion in *In re* Commitment of Edward S., 570 A.2d 917 (N.J. 1990), to *id* at 936 (Judge Handler's concurrence) (statutory mandate requiring that involuntary civil commitment hearings be held *in camera* deemed inapplicable to cases involving insanity acquittees).

[78]*See* Perlin, *Morality, supra* note 27, at 134.

[79]*See* State v. Willard, 234 S.E.2d 587, 591–93 (N.C. 1977).

an impressive array of empirical evidence revealing (a) the minuscule number of such cases; (b) the ease with which trained clinicians are usually able to "catch" malingering in such cases; (c) the inverse greater likelihood that defendants, even at grave peril to their life, will more likely try to convince examiners that they are "not crazy"; (d) the high risk in pleading the insanity defense (leading to statistically significant greater prison terms meted out to unsuccessful insanity pleaders); and (e) the fact that most of the small number of insanity pleaders who are successful remain in maximum security facilities for a longer period than they would have if convicted of the underlying criminal indictment.[80]

Consider the more recent New Jersey state case of *State v. Inglis*,[81] in which the court— citing to no authority—simply stated, "The insanity defense has a high potential of serving as an instrument of pretext."[82] None of the easily accessible, empirically grounded evidence[83] had an impact on the trial judge in *Inglis*, nor does it generally have such an impact on decision makers in other such cases. It is no wonder that, in writing about the U.S. Supreme Court's decision in *Parham v. J.R.*,[84] Stephen Morse noted, "As is so often true in mental health cases, the Court based its opinion on a number of factual assumptions that are simply insupportable."[85]

In short, mental disability law is replete with textbook examples of both conscious and unconscious pretextuality in the law. This pretextuality is reflected both consciously (in the receiving and privileging of "moral" testimony that flaunts legislative criteria) and unconsciously (in using heuristic devices in decision making and in applying sanist attitudes toward such decisions).

"Morality" of Mental Health Professionals

It is now necessary to consider the specific reading of "morality" engaged in by certain forensic mental health professionals.[86] We should begin by reflecting on Bernard Diamond's concern that, because of a witness' unconscious identification with one "side" of a legal battle or more conscious identification with his or her own value system or ideological leanings, his or her "secret hope for victory for his [or her] own opinion [may lead to]

---

[80]Perlin, *supra* note 20, at 648–55, 713–21.

[81]698 A.2d 1296 (N.J. Super. Law Div. 1997).

[82]*Id.* at 1298. And *see also id.* ("the insanity defense has a high potential for pretext").

[83]*See* HENRY STEADMAN ET AL., BEFORE AND AFTER HINCKLEY: EVALUATING INSANITY DEFENSE REFORM (1993).

[84]442 U.S. 584 (1979) (limiting procedural due process rights of juveniles facing involuntary civil commitment); *see generally* 1 PERLIN, *supra* note 16, § 2C-7.1a at 467-76 (2d ed. 1998); see *infra* Chapter 4.

[85]Stephen Morse, *Treating Crazy People Less Specially*, 90 W. VA. L. REV. 353, 382 n.64 (1987); *see generally* Gail Perry & Gary Melton, *Precedential Value of Judicial Notice of Social Facts:* Parham *as an Example*, 22 J. FAM. L. 633 (1984) (sharply criticizing *Parham* decision); Michael L. Perlin, *An Invitation to the Dance: An Empirical Response to Chief Justice Warren Burger's "Time-Consuming Procedural Minuets" Theory* in Parham v. J. R., 9 BULL. AM. ACAD. PSYCHIATRY & L. 149 (1981) (same).

[86]On the many hats worn by the testifying mental health professional expert witness, see Steven R. Smith, *Mental Health Expert Witnesses: Of Science and Crystal Balls*, 7 BEHAV. SCI. & L. 145, 151–57 (1989) (teacher, priest, wizard, magician, decision maker, scapegoat, advocate, adviser, and smokescreen); *see also* Orest E.Wasyliw, James L. Cavanaugh, & Richard Rogers, *Beyond the Scientific Limits of Expert Testimony*, 13 BULL. AM. ACAD. PSYCHIATRY & L. 147, 153–56 (1985); Douglas Mossman & Marshall Kapp, *"Courtroom Whores?"— Or Why Do Attorneys Call Us?: Findings From a Survey on Attorneys' Use of Mental Health Experts*, 26 J. AM. ACAD. PSYCHIATRY & L. 27 (1998).

innumerable subtle distortions and biases in his [or her] testimony that spring from this wish to triumph.''[87]

Research by Robert Homant and Daniel Kennedy similarly seems to show that experts' opinions of insanity defense claims are positively correlated with the witness' underlying political ideology.[88] Ben Bursten has argued further that *any* decision about whether behavior is a product of mental illness is not a matter of scientific expertise ''but a matter of social policy.''[89] Teresa Scheid has demonstrated persuasively the ''obvious[ness]'' of the proposition that ''treatment ideologies impinge upon the medical care provided to [mental health] clients.''[90] We cannot blind ourselves to the possibility that, in a whole variety of fact settings, social bias frequently ''infects and hides behind scientific judgments.''[91] Other studies seem to confirm the influence of ideology on evaluators' assessments of civil psychic trauma cases.[92]

These positions and findings must be weighed against the backdrop of other research that demonstrates that an overwhelming percentage of all experienced forensic mental health professionals have significantly mistaken beliefs about the substantive insanity defense standard actually used in the jurisdictions in which they practice and testify.[93] This becomes yet more problematic when witnesses testify about conclusions of law, either in defining the appropriate legal standard for forensic cases or in concluding whether a patient meets that legal standard.[94]

Other evidence suggests that variables such as race, sex, culture, sexual orientation, physical attractiveness, and economic status significantly affect expert testimony.[95] Some other research suggests that less secure mental health professionals are preoccupied with

---

[87]Bernard Diamond, *The Fallacy of the Impartial Expert,* 3 ARCHIVES CRIM. PSYCHODYNAMICS 221, 222 (1959), *as quoted in* Sonja Goldstein, *Hiring the Hired Guns: Lawyers and Their Psychiatric Experts,* 11 LEG. STUD. FORUM 41 (1987). On the potential role of psychiatric bias in the penalty phase of capital punishment trials, see Smith v. Estelle, 602 F.2d 694, 708 (5th Cir. 1979), *aff'd,* 451 U.S. 454, 471 (1981).

[88]*See, e.g.,* Robert J. Homant & Daniel B. Kennedy, *Judgment of Legal Insanity as a Function of Attitude Toward the Insanity Defense,* 8 INT'L J.L. & PSYCHIATRY 67 (1986); Robert J. Homant & Daniel B. Kennedy, *Subjective Factors in the Judgment of Insanity,* 14 CRIM. JUST. & BEHAV. 38 (1987); Robert J. Homant & Daniel B. Kennedy, *Definitions of Mental Illness as a Factor in Expert Witnesses: Judgments of Insanity,* 31 CORRECTIVE & SOC. PSYCHOL. J. BEHAVIOR TECH. METHODS & THERAPY 125 (1985).

[89]BEN BURSTEN, BEYOND PSYCHIATRIC EXPERTISE 167 (1984).

[90]Teresa Scheid, *An Explication of Treatment Ideology Among Mental Health Care Providers,* 16 SOC. OF HEALTH & ILLNESS 668, 689 (1994).

[91]Peggy Davis, *Law, Science and History: Reflections Upon ''In The Best Interests of the Child,''* 86 MICH. L. REV. 1096, 1107(1988), citing STEPHEN J. GOULD, THE MISMEASURE OF MAN 21–22 (1981) (book review of JOSEPH GOLDSTEIN, ALBERT J. SOLNIT, & SONJA GOLDSTEIN, IN THE BEST INTERESTS OF THE CHILD (1986)).

[92]Jack Zusman & Jesse Simon, *Differences in Repeated Psychiatric Examinations of Litigants to a Lawsuit,* 140 AM. J. PSYCHIATRY 1300, 1302–04 (1983) (interview setting, training, orientation, and identification with one side all helped shape forensic evaluations). On the influence of such variables as ''physical attractiveness, interpersonal adeptness, and social likeability'' on the related question of degree of punitiveness exhibited toward defendants in sentencing decisions, see Richard Rogers, *Ethical Dilemmas in Forensic Evaluations,* 5 BEHAV. SCI. & L. 149, 152 (1987), *discussing findings reported in* MICHAEL J. SAKS & REID HASTIE, SOCIAL PSYCHOLOGY IN COURT (1978).

[93]Richard Rogers et al., *Forensic Psychiatrists' and Psychologists' Understanding of Insanity: Misguided Expertise,* 33 CAN. J. PSYCHIATRY 691 (1988).

[94]*See* People v. Anderson, 421 N.W.2d 200, 205–06 (Mich. Ct. App. 1988) (diminished capacity); People v. Doan, 366 N.W.2d 593 (Mich. Ct. App. 1985) (incompetency to stand trial); People v. Matulonis, 320 N.W.2d 238, 240 (Mich. Ct. App. 1982) (same); People v. Drossart, 297 N.W.2d 863, 869 (Mich. Ct. App. 1980) (insanity defense) (defining standard); State v. Bennett, 345 So.2d 1129, 1138 (La. 1977) (Dennis, J., on rehearing) (competency to plead guilty) (legal conclusion). *But cf.* State v. Widenhouse, 582 So.2d 1374, 1385–86 (La. Ct. App. 1991) (not error to allow state's witness to inform jury of legal insanity standard), *cert. denied,* 503 U.S. 910 (1992).

[95]*See supra* Chapter 2, text accompanying notes 134–138.

eliciting pathology as a demonstration of their own expertise. Their competence as examiners may rest on their ability to demonstrate incompetency on the part of the defendant.[96] Also, professionals with different education and training rely on different sets of data in doing forensic evaluations.[97] Finally, forensic witnesses concede that they distort their testimony ''because [they] did not want to be criticized should [an insanity acquittee] be released and then commit a criminal act.''[98]

In short, both social ideology and misinformed, inaccurate information about the substantive tests against which defendants' behavior must be measured often drive experts' conclusions. Most important, this tableau seemingly has arisen with little or no awareness on the part of the forensic experts themselves. Thus when Michael Saks charged that such witnesses act like ''imperial experts'' who install themselves as ''temporary monarch[s]'' by replacing a ''social preference expressed through the law and legal process with [their] own preferences,''[99] the expert community did not offer heated denials.[100] Rather, the implications of this tacit reliance on self-referential ''morality'' remain virtually unnoticed. This, of course, contrasts sharply with the way that scholars[101] and judges regularly scrutinize and weigh morality–value choices in a wide variety of other legal contexts and determine whether the decision making processes in those cases are pretextual.[102]

---

[96]A. Louis McGarry, *Demonstration and Research in Competency for Trial and Mental Illness: Review and Preview,* 49 B.U.L. REV. 46, 52–53 (1969); *see also* Saleem A. Shah, *Dangerousness: A Paradigm for Exploring Some Issues in Law and Psychology,* 33 AM. PSYCHOLOGIST 224 (1978) (standard rule of medical decisions is, ''When in doubt, suspect illness'').

[97]Jean C. Beckham et al., *Decision Making and Examiner Bias in Forensic Expert Recommendations for Not Guilty by Reason of Insanity,* 13 LAW & HUM. BEHAV. 79 (1989).

[98]Francois v. Henderson, 850 F.2d 231, 234 (5th Cir. 1988).

[99]Michael J. Saks, *Expert Witnesses, Nonexpert Witnesses, and Nonwitness Experts,* 14 LAW & HUM. BEHAV. 291, 294 (1990); *see also, e.g.,* Stephen J. Morse, *Crazy Behavior, Morals, and Science: An Analysis of Mental Health Law,* 51 S. CAL. L. REV. 527, 619 (1978) (experts should not ''propound commonsense factual or moral judgments as scientific ones'').

[100]On the scripting of forensic testimony in mental health cases, see Derek Chadwick, *Psychiatric Testimony in Britain: Remembering Your Lines and Keeping to the Script,* 15 INT'L J.L. & PSYCHIATRY 177 (1992).

[101]Other scholars and practitioners have begun to consider the role of pretextuality in mental disability law. *See, e.g.,* Hava Villaverde, *Racism in the Insanity Defense,* 50 U. MIAMI L. REV. 209, 236–27 (1995); Christopher Slobogin, *Therapeutic Jurisprudence: Five Dilemmas to Ponder,* 1 PSYCHOL., PUB. POL'Y & L. 193, 199 n.35 (1995); Henry Dlugacz, *Riggins v. Nevada: Towards a Unified Standard for a Prisoner's Right to Refuse Medication,* 17 LAW & PSYCHOL. REV. 41, 42 (1993); Deborah A. Dorfman, *Through a Therapeutic Jurisprudence Filter: Fear and Pretextuality in Mental Disability Law,* 10 N.Y.L. SCH. J. HUM. RTS. 805 (1993).

[102]*See* Regina Austin, *Sapphire Bound!,* 1989 WIS. L. REV. 539, 550–51 (discussing Chambers v. Omaha Girls Club, 629 F. Supp. 925 (D. Neb. 1986), *aff'd,* 834 F.2d 697 (8th Cir. 1987) (no violation of discrimination law for Girls Club to fire unmarried pregnant employee under club's ''negative role model'' policy); Martha Chamallas & Linda K. Kerber, *Women, Mothers, and the Law of Fright: A History,* 88 MICH. L. REV. 814, 818 (1990) (critiquing pretextual nature of case law that incorporates double standard of sexual morality in dealing with ''the tortious consequences of adultery''); Nancy S. Ehrenreich, *Pluralist Myths and Powerless Men: The Ideology of Reasonableness in Sexual Harassment Law,* 99 YALE L.J. 1177, 1209 (1990) (critiquing the pretextual nature of sexual harrassment decisions for reinforcing a ''boys will be boys'' ideology); Lawrence M. Friedman, *Two Faces of Law,* 1984 WIS. L. REV. 13, 21–23 (critiquing pretextual nature of prostitution-control law); Thomas B. Griffen, Note, *Zoning Away the Evil of Alcohol,* 61 S. CAL. L. REV. 1373, 1405 (1988) (criticizing zoning laws as ''pretext[s]'' for suppressing adult entertainment); David L. Neal, *Women as a Social Group: Recognizing Sex-Based Persecution as Grounds for Asylum,* 20 COLUM. HUM. RTS. L. REV. 203, 217 (1988) (''Laws regulating morality are manifestly designed to subjugate women.''); Wojciech Sadurski, *Conventional Morality and Judicial Standards,* 73 VA. L. REV. 339, 364 (1987) (criticizing Justice Marshall's death penalty jurisprudence as ''pretextual'' and as ''disguise for his own substantive morality''); Laura E. Santilli & Michael C. Roberts, *Custody Decisions in Alabama Before and After the Abolition of the Tender Years Doctrine,* 14 LAW & HUM. BEHAV. 123 (1990) (critiquing pretextual nature of child custody laws); *see also* Cumpiano v. Banco Santander Puerto Rico, 902 F.2d 148 (1st Cir. 1990) (finding stated reasons for discharging bank employee for violating company rule requiring ''public morality'' a pretextual ''cover'' for discriminatory treatment of female employee).

I teach a course titled "Mental Disability Litigation Seminar and Workshop." As part of the course, students are placed "in the field" a day a week, either with a service provider or a mental health advocacy office. Recently, one of my students reported on an encounter she had had with a psychiatrist (in one of New York's most prominent teaching hospitals): "I was on the elevator, going up to the wards, and all of a sudden, Dr. [X] started screaming at me. 'It's all your fault,' he yelled. 'You fill the patients' heads with these ridiculous ideas about them having rights, and you ruin everything. It's *your* fault!'"[103] Fortunately, the student was mature and with sufficient aplomb to be able to withstand this barrage. But there is no doubt in my mind that the doctor's anger reflected precisely the sort of alleged "morality" to which I have referred.

This sort of behavior is not limited to American jurisdictions. Elaine Murphy has written in the context of the promulgation of the United Kingdom's Mental Health Commission's guidelines:

> The main point to take issue with is that these "safeguards" or rules are imposed on a profession that has not evolved and agreed [to] them from within its own ranks. . . . it is possible that a "responsible body of skilled and experienced doctors" might not agree that *slavish attention* to the Commission's safeguards was necessary for the proper discharge of one's duty of care. Rules of good practice must evolve from within the profession, in consultation with others, and should not be imposed by *some external body.*[104]

Such an attitude reflects the "considerable pain and offence occasioned by a perceived invasion of the law into the *ex cathedra* judgment of psychiatrists," concluded Carmel Rogers in his analysis of relatively recent New Zealand legislation regulating the relationship between law and psychiatry.[105] And such "pain and offense" is found in the responses of much of organized psychiatry in the United States to similar regulation.[106]

Teleology

The legal system selectively—teleologically—either accepts or rejects social science evidence depending on whether or not the use of that data meets the *a priori* needs of the legal system.[107] In cases in which fact-finders are hostile to social science teachings, such data thus often meets with tremendous judicial resistance, and the courts express their skepticism about, suspicions of, and hostilities toward such evidence.[108] Specifically, the skepticism toward statistical data and evidence about the behavioral sciences appears to stem directly from the belief that such data are not "empirical" in the same way that "true" sciences are

---

[103]Classroom comment by Deborah Meyer (Sept. 25, 1997).

[104]Elaine Murphy, *Psychiatric Implications, in* CONSENT AND THE INCOMPETENT PATIENT: ETHICS, LAW AND MEDICINE 65, 68 (Steven Hirsh & John Harris eds. 1988) (emphasis added).

[105]Carmel Rogers, *Proceedings Under the Mental Health Act 1992: The Legalisation of Psychiatry,* 1994 N.Z. L.J. 404, 406.

[106]*See also, e.g.,* William Bernet, *Running Scared: Therapists' Excessive Concerns About Following Rules,* 23 BULL. AM. ACAD. PSYCHIATRY & L. 367 (1995).

[107]*See, e.g.,* Paul Appelbaum, *The Empirical Jurisprudence of the United States Supreme Court,* 13 AM. J.L. & MED. 335, 341–42 (1987). On how social science can be used positively in a related area, see Christopher Slobogin, *Is Justice Just Us? Using Social Science to Inform Substantive Criminal Law,* 87 J. CRIM. L. & CRIMINOL. 315 (1996) (book review of PAUL ROBINSON & JOHN DARLEY, JUSTICE, LIABILITY, AND BLAME: COMMUNITY VIEWS AND THE CRIMINAL LAW (1995)).

[108]Perlin, *Morality, supra* note 27, at 136–37.

and therefore are not trustworthy.[109] Social science data are seen as overly subjective and as falsifiable, and as being subject to researcher bias.[110]

Courts are often threatened by the use of such data. Social science's "complexities [may] shake the judge's confidence in imposed solutions."[111] In addition, judges may be especially threatened by social science when it is presented to a jury, as such presentation may appear to undermine "judicial control" of trial proceedings.[112]

Judges' general dislike of social science is reflected in the self-articulated claim that judges are unable to understand the data and are thus unable to apply them properly to a particular case.[113] Judges do tend to be shamefully poor in the application of such data;[114] their track record has been "dreadful."[115] It is not at all clear, though, why judges have such difficulty when they regularly decide complex cases in a wide array of social and scientific contexts.[116]

This dislike and distrust of social science data has led courts to be teleological in their use of this evidence. Social science literature and studies that enable courts to meet predetermined sanist ends are often privileged, whereas data that would require judges to question such ends are frequently rejected.[117] Judges often select certain proferred data that adhere to their preexisting social and political attitudes, and use heuristic reasoning in

---

[109]See, e.g., David Faigman, *To Have and Have Not: Assessing the Value of Social Science to the Law as Science and Policy*, 38 EMORY L.J. 1005, 1010 (1989); Note, *Social Science Statistics in the Courtroom: The Debate Resurfaces in* McCleskey v. Kemp, 62 NOTRE DAME L. REV. 688, 705–08 (1987) (on possible roots of courts' hostility toward statistical evidence).

[110]Faigman, *supra* note 109, at 1016, 1026.

[111]Perlin, *Morality, supra* note 27, at 136, citing Ann Woolhandler, *Rethinking the Judicial Reception of Legislative Facts*, 41 VAND. L. REV. 111, 125 n.84 (1988), quoting DAVID HOROWITZ, THE COURTS AND SOCIAL POLICY 284 (1977); *see generally* Donald N. Bersoff, *Judicial Deference to Nonlegal Decisionmakers: Imposing Simplistic Solutions on Problems of Cognitive Complexity in Mental Health Disability Law*, 46 SMU L. REV. 329 (1992).

[112]Constance Lindman, *Sources of Judicial Distrust of Social Science Evidence: A Comparison of Social Science Jurisprudence*, 64 IND. L.J. 755, 755 (1989); Elizabeth Loftus & John Monahan, *Trial by Data: Psychological Research as Legal Evidence*, 35 AM. PSYCHOLOGIST 270, 270–71 (1980).

[113]See, e.g., Perlin, *supra* note 44, at 986–93, discussing decision in United States v. Charters, 863 F.2d 302 (4th Cir. 1988) (*en banc*), *cert. denied*, 496 U.S. 1016 (1990) (limiting right of pretrial detainees to refuse medication). The Charters court rejected as incredulous the possibility that a court could make a meaningful distinction between competency to stand trial and competency to engage in medication decision making: "[Such a distinction] must certainly be of such subtlety and complexity as to tax perception by the most skilled medical or psychiatric professionals. . . . To suppose that it is a distinction that can be fairly discerned and applied even by the most skilled judge on the basis of an adversarial fact-finding proceeding taxes credulity." *Charters*, 863 F.2d at 310. *And see* McMullen v. State, 660 So.2d 340, 342–43 (Fla. Dist. App. 1995) (Farmer, J., concurring), *reh'g denied* (1995), discussed *supra* Chapter 2 text accompanying note 251.

[114]Gary Melton, *Bringing Psychology to the Legal System: Opportunities, Obstacles, and Efficacy*, 42 AM. PSYCHOLOGIST 488 (1987).

[115]Peter Sperlich, *Trial by Jury: It May Have a Future, in* SUPREME COURT REVIEW 191, 208 (P. Kurland & G. Casper eds. 1979); Bernard Grofman, *The Slippery Slope: Jury Size and Jury Verdict Requirements—Legal and Social Science Approaches*, 2 LAW & POL'Y Q. 285, 300 (1980). *See also* David Suggs, *The Use of Psychological Research by the Judiciary*, 3 LAW & HUM. BEHAV. 135, 147 (1979) (courts have failed to develop methods to ensure validity of research used in opinions).

[116]See, e.g., John Monahan & Laurens Walker, *Social Authority: Obtaining, Evaluating, and Establishing Social Science in Law*, 134 U. PA. L. REV. 477, 511 n.119 (1986) ("Anyone who can comprehend the Federal Tort Claims Act can learn what standard deviation and statistical significance mean").

[117]Perlin, *Morality, supra* note 27, at 136–37; Michael L. Perlin, *The Supreme Court, the Mentally Disabled Criminal Defendant and Symbolic Values: Random Decisions, Hidden Rationales, or "Doctrinal Abyss?"* 29 Ariz. L. Rev. 1, 71 (1987); J. Alexander Tanford, *The Limits of a Scientific Jurisprudence: The Supreme Court and Psychology*, 66 IND. L.J. 137, 144–50 (1990); David Faigman, *"Normative Constitutional Fact-Finding": Exploring the Empirical Component of Constitutional Interpretation*, 139 U. PA. L. REV. 541, 581 (1991).

rationalizing such decisions.[118] Social science data are used pretextually in such cases and are ignored in other cases (especially death penalty cases)[119] to rationalize otherwise baseless judicial decisions.[120]

Judges thus will take the literature out of context,[121] misconstrue the data or evidence being offered,[122] or read such data selectively,[123] or inconsistently.[124] Other times judges choose to flatly reject this data or ignore its existence.[125] In other circumstances, judges simply "rewrite" factual records to avoid having to deal with social science data that one cognitively dissonant with their OCS.[126] In other cases, they ignore readily available legal precedent from their own jurisdiction and reach out to case law from other states to find support for a position that limits the rights of persons with disabilities.[127] Even when judges

---

[118]On the courts' heuristic use of social science data, *see* Michael L. Perlin, *Pretext and Mental Disability Law: The Case of Competency,* 47 U. Miami L. Rev. 625, 664–68 (1993).

[119]James Acker, *A Different Agenda: The Supreme Court, Empirical Research Evidence, and Capital Punishment Decisions, 1986–1989,* 27 Law & Soc'y Rev. 65, 180–81 (1993) ("The prevailing opinions in the Court's recent major capital punishment decisions have increasingly displayed an unwillingness to incorporate the results of relevant social science findings"); Phoebe Ellsworth, *Unpleasant Facts: The Supreme Court's Response to Empirical Research on Capital Punishment, in* Challenging Capital Punishment: Legal and Social Science Approaches 177, 208 (K. Haas & J. Inciardi eds. 1988) ("The parsimonious explanation for the failure of social science data to influence the Court in death penalty cases seems to be that the outcome of these cases is frequently a foregone conclusion").

[120]*See* Perlin, *supra* note 118, at 668–69, discussing decisions in Barefoot v. Estelle, 463 U.S. 880 (1983) (testimony as to future dangerousness admissible at penalty phase in capital punishment case), McCleskey v. Kemp, 481 U.S. 279 (1987) (rejecting statistical evidence offered to show racial discrimination in death penalty prosecutions), and United States v. Charters, 863 F 2d 302 (4th Cir. 1988) (en blanc) (curtailing rights of criminal defendant awaiting trial to refuse antipsychotic medication).

[121]Faigman, *supra* note 117, at 577.

[122]*Id.* at 581.

[123]Katheryn Katz, *Majoritarian Morality and Parental Rights.* 52 Alb. L. Rev. 405, 461 (1988) (on courts' reading of impact of parents' homosexuality in child custody decisions); Tanford, *supra* note 117, at 153–54; *see, e.g.,* Holbrook v. Flynn, 475 U.S. 560, 571 n.4 (1986) (defendant's right to fair trial not denied where uniformed state troopers sat in front of spectator section in courtroom; court rejected contrary empirical study and based decision on its own "experience and common sense").

[124]*See, e.g.,* Thomas Hafemeister & Gary Melton, *The Impact of Social Science Research on the Judiciary, in* Reforming the Law: Impact of Child Development Research 27 (G. Melton ed. 1987) Peter Sperlich, *The Evidence on Evidence: Science and Law in Conflict and Cooperation, in* The Psychology of Evidence and Trial Procedure 325 (S. Kassin & C. Wrightsman eds. 1985); Craig Haney, *Data and Decisions: Judicial Reform and the Use of Social Science, in* The Analysis of Judicial Reform 43 (P. Du Bois ed. 1982).

[125]*See, e.g.,* Barefoot v. Estelle, 463 U.S. 880, 897–902 (1983); Faigman, *supra* note 117, at 581, discussing Parham v. J. R., 442 U.S. 584 (1979); *see also, e.g.,* Watkins v. Sanders, 449 U.S. 341 (1981) (refusal of courts to acknowledge social science research on ways that jurors evaluate and misevaluate eyewitness testimony).

[126]The classic example is Chief Justice Burger's opinion for the court in *Parham,* 442 U.S. at 605–10 (approving more relaxed involuntary civil commitment procedures for juveniles than for adults). *See, e.g.,* Gail Perry & Gary Melton, *Precedential Value of Judicial Notice of Social Facts:* Parham *as an Example,* 22 J. Fam. L. 633, 645 (1984):

> The *Parham* case is an example of the Supreme Court's taking advantage of the free rein on social facts to promulgate a dozen or so of its own by employing one tentacle of the judicial notice doctrine. The Court's opinion is filled with social facts of questionable veracity, accompanied by the authority to propel these facts into subsequent case law and, therefore, a spiral of less than rational legal policy making.

[127]*See* Josh Bernstein, *The Efforts of Texas Courts to Disable Disability Law,* 2 Tex. Forum on Civ. Lib. & Civ. Rts. 43, 46 (1995) (discussing court's reliance in Chevron Corp. v. Redmon, 745 S.W.2d 314 (Tex. 1987) (limiting definition of "handicapped" under state civil rights law) on Chicago, Milwaukee, St. Paul & Pac. R.R. Co. v. Department of Indus., Labor & Human Relations, 215 N.W.2d 443 (Wis. 1974).

do acknowledge the existence and possible validity of studies that take a contrary position from their decisions, this acknowledgement is frequently little more than mere lip service.[128]

Conclusion

I believe that sanism and pretextuality drive and dominate mental disability law jurisprudence. An understanding of sanism and pretextuality, therefore, is the only way we can decipher mental disability law jurisprudence.

Sanism and pretextuality are insidious. They permeate the discourse and corrupt our fact-finding processes. They contaminate judges, lawyers, legislators, and expert witnesses. Their corrosive influence is rarely acknowledged, and they remain invisible to the public and to most participants in the mental disability law system.

In the next section of this book, I will demonstrate how sanism and pretextuality affect and alter each major area of public mental disability law.

---

[128]*See, e.g.,* Washington v. Harper, 494 U.S. 210, 229–30 (1990) (prisoners retain limited liberty interest in right to refuse forcible administration of antipsychotic medications), in which the majority acknowledges, and emphasizes in response to the dissent, the harmful, and perhaps fatal, side effects of the drugs. The court also stressed the ''deference that is owed to medical professionals . . . who possess . . . the requisite knowledge and expertise to determine whether the drugs should be used.'' *Id.* at 230 n.12. *Cf. id.* at 247–49 (Stevens, J., concurring in part and dissenting in part) (suggesting that the majority's side effects acknowledgement is largely illusory). *But cf.* Riggins v. Nevada, 504 U.S. 127(1992), discussed *infra,* Chapter 6.

PART II:

THE SANIST AND PRETEXTUAL ROOTS OF MENTAL DISABILITY LAW

Chapter 4
INVOLUNTARY CIVIL COMMITMENT LAW

The law of civil commitment[1] has always reflected dual policy bases: commitment based on the power of the state to protect itself against breaches of the peace (police power commitments) and commitments based on the power of the state to act on behalf of persons with mental illness who are incapable of providing for their own welfare (*parens patriae* commitments).[2] As recently as 1961, however, only five states looked to dangerousness as a predicate base for such commitments; at least seven based commitment solely on a patient's need for care and treatment.[3]

A series of decisions in the early 1970s called all such laws into question.[4] As a result of these cases, there can no longer be any doubt that some finding of "mental illness" is a prerequisite to an application for involuntary civil commitment.[5] In holding in *Jackson v. Indiana* that the due process clause applied to commitment procedures,[6] the Supreme Court simply noted that the states "have traditionally exercised broad power to commit persons found to be mentally ill."[7] In analyzing the substantive due process limitations on the duration of commitment for treatment, a commentator has even noted that the need for a threshold finding of mental illness was so "sufficiently obvious as to not be a matter of discussion."[8] Similarly, in declaring a "right to liberty" in *O'Connor v. Donaldson,*[9] the

---

[1]*See generally* MICHAEL L. PERLIN, LAW AND MENTAL DISABILITY §§ 1.01–1.05 (1994), at 4–38.

[2]*E.g.,* John LaFond, *An Examination of the Purposes of Involuntary Civil Commitment,* 30 BUFF. L. REV. 499, 500–05 (1981); *see generally* 1 MICHAEL L. PERLIN, MENTAL DISABILITY LAW: CIVIL AND CRIMINAL §§ 2A-1 to 2A-7.2 (2d ed. 1998), at 44–188. For a helpful overview, see Paul Appelbaum, *Civil Mental Health Law: Its History and Its Future,* 20 MENT. & PHYS. DIS. L. REP. 599 (1996).

[3]*E.g.,* CARL LINDMAN & FRANK MCINTYRE, THE MENTALLY DISABLED AND THE LAW 17 (1961).

[4]David Wexler has clearly and concisely set out the impact of the civil rights revolution on involuntary civil commitment law:

> In the very late 1960s, a revolution began in civil commitment legislation. From then until the mid or late 1970, nearly every state revised its mental health code. . . . The revolution, motivated by civil libertarian concerns, prompted a rethinking of such questions as who should be forcibly committed, on what grounds, for how long, and with what sort of procedural safeguards. The result was a setting of durational limits on the length of commitment, a massive increase in procedural protections and, substantively, stricter and more explicit commitment criteria.

David Wexler, *Grave Disability and Family Therapy: The Therapeutic Potential of Civil Libertarian Commitment Codes, in* THERAPEUTIC JURISPRUDENCE: THE LAW AS A THERAPEUTIC AGENT 165 (David Wexler ed. 1990). For a recent thoughtful analysis, see PAUL APPELBAUM, ALMOST A REVOLUTION: MENTAL HEALTH LAW AND THE LIMITS OF CHANGE (1994); *see also* Paul Appelbaum, *Almost a Revolution: An International Perspective on the Law of Involuntary Commitment,* 25 J. AM. ACAD. PSYCHIATRY & L. 135 (1997).

[5]*E.g., Developments in the Law—Civil Commitment,* 87 HARV. L. REV. 1190, 1202 (1974). *Cf.* Kansas v. Hendricks, 521 U.S. 346 (1997), upholding Kansas' Sexually Violent Predator Act, discussed in 1 PERLIN, *supra* note 2, § 2-3.3, at 75–92 (pedophilia, a "mental abnormality," was a sufficient basis for commitment under state law).

[6]Jackson v. Indiana, 406 U.S. 715, 738 (1972).

[7]*Id.* at 736.

[8]Note, *Substantive Due Process Limits on the Duration of Civil Commitment for the Treatment of Mental Illness,* 16 HARV. C.R.-C.L. L. REV. 205, 223 n.84 (1981).

[9]422 U.S. 573, 576 (1975); *see generally* 1 PERLIN, *supra* note 2, § 2A-4.4d, at 142–52 (2d ed. 1998).

same Court found a "constitutional right not to be physically confined by the State when [one's] freedom will pose a danger neither to himself nor to others."[10]

For the first time, psychiatrists were subjected to rigorous cross-examination[11] and were required to substantiate their medical opinions rather than merely make medical conclusions. At the same time, psychiatric diagnostic and predictive skills were more closely scrutinized.[12] Lawyers were often successful in convincing courts of the inaccuracy of psychiatric diagnosis and predictions of dangerousness.[13] At the same time, the meaning of "dangerousness" became an important area of litigation.[14] Critics charged that the concept was vague and amorphous, and its elasticity has made it "one of the most problematic and elusive concepts in mental health law."[15]

"Dangerousness" and Commitment Law

No question in the area of involuntary civil commitment law has proved to be more perplexing than the definition of the word "dangerousness" or the related issue of whether it is a legal concept, a medical concept, or simply a "socially defined condition."[16] Few other concepts in this area of the law are as elusive or inspire the same "I-know-it-when-I-see-it" attitude.

In perhaps the most comprehensive and thorough attempt at defining "dangerousness" ever offered by an appellate court, the New Jersey Supreme Court emphasized,

> Dangerous conduct involves not merely violation of social norms enforced by criminal sanctions, but significant physical or psychological injury to persons or substantial destruction of property. Persons are not to be indefinitely incarcerated because they present a risk of future conduct which is merely socially undesirable. Personal liberty and autonomy are of too great value to be sacrificed to protect society against the possibility of future behavior which some may find odd, disagreeable, or offensive, or even against the possibility of future nondangerous acts which would be ground for criminal prosecution if actually committed. Unlike inanimate objects, people cannot be suppressed simply because they may become public nuisances.[17]

---

[10]422 U.S. at 573 n.8.

[11]This of course assumes a fact never in evidence: that the lawyers assigned to represent mentally disabled individuals were able (or cared) to do a competent job of such cross-examination. *See generally* Michael L. Perlin, *Fatal Assumption: A Critical Evaluation of the Role of Counsel in Mental Disability Cases,* 16 LAW & HUM. BEHAV. 39 (1992). *Cf.* Matter of Lindsey C., 473 S.E.2d 110 (W. Va. 1995) (appointment of guardian *ad litem* required in child neglect case for mother who was involuntarily civil committed at time of hearing), to *id.* at 126 (W. Va. 1996) (Workman, J., dissenting) (decrying majority for creating "meaningless procedural hoops").

[12]Joseph Cocozza & Henry Steadman, *The Failure of Psychiatric Predications of Dangerousness: Clear and Convincing Evidence,* 29 RUTGERS L. REV. 1084 (1976); Alan Dershowitz, *The Law of Dangerousness: Some Fiction About Predictions,* 23 J. LEGAL EDUC. 24 (1970); Bruce Ennis & Thomas Litwack, *Psychiatry and the Presumption of Expertise: Flipping Coins in the Courtroom,* 62 CAL. L. REV. 693 (1974). This battle has continued to rage. *Cf.* Richard Rogers et al., *Can Ziskin Withstand His Own Criticisms? Problems With His Model of Cross-Examination,* 11 BEHAV. SCI. & L. 223 (1993), *to* Jay Ziskin, *Ziskin Can Withstand His Own Criticisms: A Response to Rogers, Bagby and Perera,* 15 AM. J. FORENS. PSYCHIATRY 41 (1994).

[13]*E.g.,* People v. Murtishaw 175 Cal. Rptr. 738 (1981).

[14]1 PERLIN, *supra* note 2, §§ 2A-4 to 2A-4.3d, at 92–121 (2d. ed. 1998).

[15]*Id.* at 97 (citing sources), and at 103 (cmt. following § 2A-4.2).

[16]*See* PERLIN, *supra* note 1, § 1-2.1, at 12–13 (2d. ed. 1998); *see generally* Donald Herrmann, *Preventive Detention, a Scientific View of Man, and State Power,* 1973 U. ILL. L. F. 673, 685.

[17]State v. Krol, 344 A.2d 289, 301–02 (N.J. 1975).

It continued by noting that commitment required there be "a substantial risk of dangerous conduct within the reasonably foreseeable future."[18] Evaluation of the magnitude of the risk involved considering both the likelihood of dangerous conduct and the seriousness of the harm that may ensue if such conduct takes place: "It is not sufficient that the state establish a possibility that defendant might commit some dangerous acts at some time in the indefinite future. The risk of danger, a product of the likelihood of such conduct and the degree of harm which may ensue, must be substantial within the reasonably foreseeable future. On the other hand, certainty of prediction is not required and cannot reasonably be expected."[19]

A defendant may be dangerous in only certain types of situations or in connection with relationships with certain individuals, the court continued, and any evaluation of dangerousness in such cases "must take into account the likelihood that the patient will be exposed to such situations or come into contact with such individuals."[20] Dangerousness determinations involve predicting defendant's future conduct rather than mere characterization of past conduct, the court added, pointing out that "past conduct is important evidence as to [a patient's] probable future conduct."[21]

Finally, on this point, the court stressed,

> While courts in determining dangerousness should take full advantage of expert testimony presented by the State and by defendant, the decision is not one that can be left wholly to the technical expertise of the psychiatrists and psychologists. The determination of dangerousness involves a delicate balancing of society's interest in protection from harmful conduct against the individual's interest in personal liberty and autonomy. This decision, while requiring the court to make use of the assistance which medical testimony may provide, is ultimately a legal one, not a medical one.[22]

Scholars have sought to deconstruct the term by breaking "dangerousness" into component elements (magnitude, probability, frequency, and imminence),[23] and into dimensions of potentially dangerous behavior (type, frequency, recency, severity, and object).[24] Nonetheless, "dangerousness" remains an "amorphous"[25] and "vague"[26] concept, typically misunderstood by mental health professionals, lawyers for patients, courts, legislators, and the public at large.[27]

---

[18]*Id.* at 302.

[19]*Id.*

[20]*Id.*

[21]*Id.*

[22]*Id.*

[23]ALEXANDER BROOKS, LAW, PSYCHIATRY AND THE MENTAL HEALTH SYSTEM 680–82 (1974).

[24]Virginia Aldigé Hiday, *Court Discretion: Application of the Dangerousness Standard in Civil Commitment,* 5 LAW & HUM. BEHAV. 275, 278 (1981).

[25]Note, *Involuntary Civil Commitment: The Dangerousness Standard and Its Problems,* 63 N.C. L. REV. 241, 246 (1984).

[26]Hiday, *supra* note 24, at 276. This vagueness, of course, may not be totally unwelcome by committing agencies (that may find that the lack of precision in drafting gives this category an elasticity that aids in committing individuals who might not meet the criteria of more precisely drafted statutes).

[27]*See* PERLIN, *supra* note 1, § 1.03, at 19 nn.24–28 (citing sources). For recent research, *see, for example,* Robert Zeiss et al., *Dangerousness Commitments: Indices of Future Violence Potential?* 24 BULL. AM. ACAD. PSYCHIATRY & L. 247 (1996); Robert Schopp, *Communicating Risk Assessments: Accuracy, Efficacy, and Responsibility,* 51 AM. PSYCHOLOGIST 939 (1996); Randy Borum, *Improving the Clinical Practice of Violence Risk Assessment: Technology, Guidelines, and Training,* 51 AM. PSYCHOLOGIST 945 (1996); Jan Volovka et al., *Characteristics of State Hospital Patients Arrested for Offenses Committed During Hospitalization,* 46 PSYCHIATRIC SERVICES 796 (1995); Charles Golden et al., *Neuropsychological Correlates of Violence and Aggression: A Review of the Clinical Literature,* 1 AGGRESSION & VIOLENT BEHAV. 3 (1996).

Researchers have made tremendous gains in recent years in their understanding of the relationship between dangerousness and mental illness, and the implications of these new findings. More conceptual light has been shed on this murky area of the law by the recent publication of research by the MacArthur Foundation's Network on Mental Health and the Law (the Network). For the past several years, the Network has conducted an extensive study of three areas that are essential to an informed understanding of mental disability law: competence, coercion, and risk.[28] The competence aspect of the research has been published[29] as well as reports on the researchers' attempts to develop a reliable and valid information base on which to address clinical and policy questions about mentally disabled persons' ability to provide informed consent to treatment.[30]

On the question of the relationship between mental illness and dangerousness, John Monahan, the director of the MacArthur Network and a leading thinker in this field of study,[31] recently concluded that although there appeared to be a "greater-than-chance relationship between mental disorder and violent behavior,"[32] mental health makes "at best a trivial contribution to the overall level of violence in society."[33]

The Split in Commitment Law

Courts are not in accord on all aspects of involuntary civil commitment law. There is, for example, a significant split in the law on the question of the necessity that there be evidence of an "overt act" prior to commitment. Although state and federal courts have unanimously found dangerousness to be a predicate to a constitutionally valid commitment, they have split sharply as to whether, for example, there needs to be proof of an overt act as a precondition to such a finding. In the lead case of *Lessard v. Schmidt,*[34] the court found that proof of "a recent overt act, attempt, or threat to do substantial harm to oneself or another"

---

[28]Bruce J. Winick, *Foreword: A Summary of the MacArthur Treatment Competence Study and an Introduction to the Special Theme,* 2 PSYCHOL., PUB. POL'Y & L. 3, 3 (1996); *The MacArthur Violence Risk Assessment Study,* 16 AM. PSYCHOL.-L. SOC. NEWSL. 3 (Fall 1996), at 1. *See also, e.g.,* Thomas Grisso & Alan Tomkins, *Communicating Violence Risk Assessments,* 51 AM. PSYCHOLOGIST 928 (1996).

[29]*See, e.g.,* Paul S. Appelbaum & Thomas Grisso, *The MacArthur Treatment Competence Study. I: Mental Illness and Competence to Consent to Treatment,* 19 LAW & HUM. BEHAV. 105 (1995) [hereinafter Appelbaum & Grisso, *Study I*]; Thomas Grisso et al., *The MacArthur Treatment Competence Study. II: Measures of Abilities Related to Competence to Consent to Treatment,* 19 LAW & HUM. BEHAV. 127 (1995) [hereinafter Grisso, *Study II*]; Thomas Grisso & Paul S. Appelbaum, *The MacArthur Treatment Competence Study. III: Abilities of Patients to Consent to Psychiatric and Medical Treatments,* 19 LAW & HUM. BEHAV. 149 (1995) [hereinafter Grisso & Appelbaum, *Study III*]. *See generally* THOMAS GRISSO & PAUL APPELBAUM, ASSESSING COMPETENCE TO CONSENT TO TREATMENT (1998).

[30]Winick, *supra* note 28, at 3.

[31]Monahan has been characterized as "the leading thinker on this issue" in Barefoot v. Estelle, 463 U.S. 880, 901 (1983), and in *id.* at 920 (Blackmun, J., dissenting).

[32]John Monahan, *Clinical and Actuarial Predictions of Violence, in* 1 MODERN SCIENTIFIC EVIDENCE: THE LAW AND SCIENCE OF EXPERT TESTIMONY § 7-2.2.1, at 314 (David Faigman et al. eds. 1997). Clinicians were found to be no better than chance when it came to predicting violence among female patients. Monahan, J. *Mental Illness and Violent Crime,* NAT'L INST. OF JUST. RES. PREVIEW (Oct. 1996), at 1, 2.

[33]Monahan, *supra* note 32, at 315. *See also* Jeffrey Swanson et al., *Psychotic Symptoms and Disorders and the Risk of Violent Behaviour in the Community,* 6 CRIM. BEHAV. & MENT. HEALTH 309, 210 (1996) (mental disorder a "modest risk factor" for the occurrence of interpersonal violent behavior). Of course, when there is a vivid, criminal case involving an expatient, this research is totally ignored. *See, e.g., The Cruelty of Deinstitutionalization,* N.Y. POST, Jan. 6, 1999, at 30 (discussing murder allegedly committed by expatient) ("We have already seen enough evidence to suggest that deinstitutionalization was a mistake. Let Kendra Webdale's fate be further proof of the need for change.")

[34]349 F. Supp. 1078 (E.D. Wis. 1972).

was a predicate for a dangerousness finding.[35] Courts in other jurisdictions, however, rejected this as a constitutional requirement, as it would place an "unnecessarily heavy burden on the State,"[36] and more recent statutory enactments have generally abandoned this requirement as a prerequisite as well.[37]

These splits reflect, to some extent, the policy pendulum swings that have dominated mental disability law developments for more than two decades. Commitment schemes are thus often criticized from two diametrically opposed perspectives.[38] The pro-treatment proponents argue that the standards for involuntary psychiatric commitment give too much protection to individual rights at the expense of providing necessary treatment and care to those persons with mental illness. The pro-rights proponents argue that the standards provide too little protection to individuals who find themselves at the mercy of the civil commitment process.[39]

Multiple social and political forces drive involuntary civil commitment law developments. The day has long passed when commitment abolitionists appeared to be amassing support for their efforts.[40] The ubiquitous "pendulum swing"[41] has resulted in a call for expanded commitment powers in many jurisdictions;[42] the perceived linkages between involuntary civil commitment requirements and homelessness make it likely that the time of the abolition movement has come and gone.[43] The public is indignant when it appears—in a few idiosyncratic, yet widely publicized cases—that a "clearly crazy" person is to be released from a psychiatric hospital because of some technical deficiency in the court papers or because judges unthinkingly accept abstract civil libertarian arguments from young, naive lawyers.[44] And when public officials such as former New York City Mayor Ed Koch characterize the constitution as "dumb" (after learning that nondangerous mentally ill persons cannot be institutionalized against their will),[45] the level of indignation is increased further.

---

[35]*Id.* at 1093.

[36]State v. Robb, 484 A.2d 1130, 1134 (N.H. 1984).

[37]Mary Durham & John LaFond, *The Empirical Consequences and Policy Implications for Broadening the Statutory Criteria for Civil Commitment,* 3 YALE L. & POL'Y REV. 395, 398 (1985).

[38]William Pincus, *Civil Commitment and the "Great Confinement" Revisited: Straightjacketing Individual Rights, Stifling Culture,* 36 WM. & MARY L. REV. 1769, 1775–85 (1995).

[39]*Id.* at 1775–76.

[40]1 PERLIN, *supra* note 2, § 2.24. In 1978 President Jimmy Carter's Commission on Mental Health's Task Force Panel on Legal and Ethical Issues recommended a "modified abolition" position. *See id.,* § 2.26, at 172–75.

[41]*See, e.g.,* Michael L. Perlin, *"Make Promises by the Hour": Sex, Drugs, the ADA, and Psychiatric Hospitalization,* 46 DEPAUL L. REV. 947, 953 (1997), *and id.* n.48, citing Durham & LaFond, *supra* note 37, at 398; Daniel W. Shuman, *Innovative Statutory Approaches to Civil Commitment: An Overview and Critique,* 13 LAW, MED. & HEALTH CARE 284, 286 (1985).

[42]*See, e.g.,* 1 PERLIN, *supra* note 2, § 2A-7.2, at 188 (2d ed. 1998).

[43]H. Richard Lamb has, in fact, called for a moratorium on future deinstitutionalization programs. *See* H. Richard Lamb, *Is It Time for a Moratorium on Deinstitutionalization?* 43 HOSP. & COMMUNITY PSYCHIATRY 669 (1992); *cf.* Douglas Mossman & Michael L. Perlin, *Psychiatry and the Homeless Mentally Ill: A Reply to Dr. Lamb,* 149 AM. J. PSYCHIATRY 951 (1992).

[44]*See, e.g.,* E. FULLER TORREY, NOWHERE TO GO: THE TRAGIC ODYSSEY OF THE HOMELESS MENTALLY ILL 156–59 (1988); *see also The Cruelty of Deinstitutionalization, supra* note 33.

[45]*See, e.g.,* Molly Ivins, *Koch Seeks Law for Roundups to Aid the Homeless,* N.Y. TIMES, March 27, 1981, at B3; *In From the Cold,* N.Y. TIMES, Jan. 24, 1985, at A24 (editorial); *Forced Shelter,* N.Y. TIMES, Feb. 19, 1982, at A30 (editorial).

"Morality" of Mental Health Professionals

Involuntary civil commitment cases depend heavily on the quality of expert testimony in individual cases.[46] Even if clinicians are capable of predicting dangerousness at a "better-than-chance" rate, the issue of predictivity is confounded further by issues of bias that infect these predictions. We know, for instance, that issues such as race and gender influence civil commitment decision making.[47] Research shows that Blacks are diagnosed with schizophrenia almost twice as often as are Whites, that they receive higher dosages of psychotropic medication than do Whites, and that they are involuntarily civilly committed at a statistically significant higher level than are Whites.[48] The potential for pretext is self-evident.

Just as important is a consideration of the specific reading of "morality" engaged in by certain forensic mental health professionals. As I have already noted, there is a robust body of evidence showing that expert decision making is positively correlated with the witness' underlying political ideology,[49] that a witness' unconscious identification with one "side" of a legal battle may distort his or her testimony,[50] and that much expert testimony is *not* a matter of scientific expertise "but a matter of social policy."[51]

We cannot ignore the possibility that, in a whole variety of fact settings, social bias frequently "infects and hides behind scientific judgments."[52] Research teaches us that interview setting, training, orientation, and identification with one side all helps to shape the content of forensic evaluations.[53] As discussed previously, variables such as "physical attractiveness, interpersonal adeptness, and social likeability" affect the degree of punitiveness exhibited toward defendants in sentencing decisions.[54] These positions and findings must be weighed against the backdrop of other research that demonstrates that an overwhelming percentage of all experienced forensic mental health professionals (MHPs) have

---

[46]*See, e.g.,* Robert Schopp & Michael Quattrocchi, *Predicting the Present: Expert Testimony and Civil Commitment,* 13 BEHAV. SCI. & L. 159 (1995).

[47]*See generally* Susan Stefan, *Race, Competence Testing, and Disability Law: A Review of the MacArthur Competence Research,* 2 PSYCHOL. PUB. POL'Y & L. 31 (1996); *see also, e.g.,* Mary Lou Siantz, *The Stigma of Mental Illness on Children of Color,* 6 J. CLIN. PEDIATRIC NURSING 10 (Oct.–Dec. 1993); Jay Wade, *Institutional Racism: An Analysis of the Mental Health System,* 63 AM. J. ORTHOPSYCHIATRY 536 (1993); William Lawson et al., *Race as a Factor in Inpatient and Outpatient Admissions and Diagnosis,* 45 HOSP. & COMMUNITY PSYCHIATRY 72 (1994).

[48]Stefan, *supra* note 47, at 33 (citing, *inter alia,* Grisso & Appelbaum, *supra* note 29, at 172); *id.* at 37 (citing, *inter alia,* William Glazer et al., *Race and Tardive Dyskinesia Among Outpatients at a CMHC,* 45 HOSP. & COMMUNITY PSYCHIATRY 38, 39–40 (1994); Lawson et al., *supra* note 47.

[49]*See, e.g.,* Robert J. Homant & Daniel B. Kennedy, *Judgment of Legal Insanity as a Function of Attitude Toward the Insanity Defense,* 8 INT'L J.L. & PSYCHIATRY 67 (1986); Homant & Kennedy, *Subjective Factors in the Judgment of Insanity,* 14 CRIM. JUST. & BEHAV. 38 (1987); Homant & Kennedy, *Definitions of Mental Illness as a Factor in Expert Witnesses: Judgments of Insanity,* 31 CORRECTIVE & SOC. PSYCH. J. BEHAVIOR TECH. METHODS & THER. 125 (1985).

[50]Bernard Diamond, *The Fallacy of the Impartial Expert,* 3 ARCHIVES CRIM. PSYCHODYNAMICS 221, 222 (1959), *as quoted in* Robert Lloyd Goldstein, *Hiring the Hired Guns: Lawyers and Their Psychiatric Experts,* 11 LEG. STUD. FORUM 41 (1987).

[51]BEN BURSTEN, BEYOND PSYCHIATRIC EXPERTISE 167 (1984).

[52]Peggy C. Davis, *Law, Science and History: Reflections Upon "In The Best Interests of the Child,"* 86 MICH. L. REV. 1096, 1107(1988), citing STEPHEN JAY GOULD, THE MISMEASURE OF MAN 21–22 (1981) (book review of JOSEPH GOLDSTEIN ET AL., IN THE BEST INTERESTS OF THE CHILD (1986)).

[53]Jack Zusman & Jesse Simon, *Differences in Repeated Psychiatric Examinations of Litigants to a Lawsuit,* 140 AM. J. PSYCHIATRY 1300, 1302–04 (1983).

[54]*See* Richard Rogers, *Ethical Dilemmas in Forensic Evaluations,* 5 BEHAV. SCI. & L. 149, 152 (1987), discussing findings reported in MICHAEL J. SAKS & REID HASTIE, SOCIAL PSYCHOLOGY IN COURT (1978).

significantly mistaken beliefs about the substantive insanity defense standard actually used in their jurisdictions.[55]

Thus when involuntary civil commitment criteria were significantly tightened in the 1970s,[56] it should not be surprising that some—but not all[57]—mental health professionals responded fairly negatively to these developments, frequently seen as "turf invasions."[58] In a series of papers, Paul Chodoff, a prominent psychiatrist, suggested that experts go along with legal standards "as long as they are . . . not tyrannical,"[59] that they neither "acced[e] too readily to current trends" nor "succumb to prevailing fashion when they are convinced that it is not always in the best interests of [their] patients,"[60] and that, in spite of legislative or judicial standards mandating a dangerousness finding as the *sine qua non* of involuntary hospitalization, a "wise and benevolent paternalism" will lead to the "moral judgment" that they are obligated to seek such hospitalization for a patient "incapable of voluntarily accepting help."[61] And H. Richard Lamb—organized psychiatry's most visible critic of deinstitutionalization—has assailed courts for interpreting civil commitment laws too "literally."[62]

Similarly, William McCormick has quoted an anonymous (but allegedly knowledgeable) medical colleague who reported, following the 1978 amendments to the Ontario Mental Health Act, "Doctors will continue to certify those *whom they really believe* should be certified. They will merely learn a new language."[63] Although there has been some empirical work responding to these philosophical positions and examples of anecdotal evidence,[64] it can in no way diminish the arguments' power. And the subsequent empirical data partially suggests that this prediction came true.[65] Other studies similarly confirm that

---

[55]Richard Rogers et al., *Forensic Psychiatrists' and Psychologists' Understanding of Insanity: Misguided Expertise*, 33 CAN. J. PSYCHIATRY 691 (1988).

[56]*See* 1 PERLIN, *supra* note 2, §§ 2A-4.4–4.4c (2d. ed. 1998).

[57]One carefully controlled study, clinicians *did* conform to the controlling involuntary civil commitment law. *See* Charles W. Lidz et al., *The Consistency of Clinicians and the Use of Legal Standards*, 146 AM. J. PSYCHIATRY 176 (1989).

[58]*See* Philip Reich, *Psychiatric Diagnosis as an Ethical Problem*, in PSYCHIATRIC ETHICS 72 (Sidney Bloch & Paul Chodoff eds. 1981) (Bloch & Chodoff).

[59]Paul Chodoff, *The Case for Involuntary Hospitalization of the Mentally Ill*, 133 AM. J. PSYCHIATRY 496, 501 (1976).

[60]McGarry & Paul Chodoff, *The Ethics of Involuntary Hospitalization*, in Bloch & Chodoff, *supra* note 58, at 203, 211, 212.

[61]Paul Chodoff, *Involuntary Hospitalization of the Mentally Ill as a Moral Issue*, 141 AM. J. PSYCHIATRY 384, 388 (1984).

[62]Lamb, *supra* note 43, at 277.

[63]William McCormick, *Involuntary Commitment in Ontario: Some Barriers to the Provision of Proper Care*, 124 CAN. MED. ASS'N J. 715, 717 (1981).

[64]*See* Lynn R. Kahle, et al., *On Unicorns Blocking Commitment Law Reform*, 6 J. PSYCHIATRY & L. 89 (1978), *as cited in* Virginia Aldigé Hiday, *Sociology of Mental Health Law*, 67 SOCIAL & SOC'Y RES. 111, 120–21 (1983).

[65]Studies of the impact of Ontario's reform laws concluded that mental health legislation had "little effect" on commitment practices. B. A. Martin & K. D. Cheung, *Civil Commitment Trends in Ontario: The Effect of Legislation on Clinical Practice*, 30 CAN. J. PSYCHIATRY 259 (1985). For a discussion concerning clinician adherence to the legislatively abandoned criteria, see Stewart Page, *Civil Commitment: Operational Definition of New Criteria*, 26 CAN. J. PSYCHIATRY 419 (1981). In some jurisdictions, the involuntary civil commitment rate actually increased following the supposed tightening of criteria. *See, e.g.*, R. Michael Bagby et al., *Effects of Mental Health Legislative Reform in Ontario*, 28 CAN. PSYCHOL. 21 (1987). Studies elsewhere report similar results. *See, e.g.*, William H. Fisher et al., *How Flexible Are Our Civil Commitment Statutes?* 39 HOSP. & COMMUNITY PSYCHIATRY 711, 712 (1988) (when legislation sought to expand bases of commitment, commitment rates increased in certain vicinages by nearly 100% before the date that the new act was to have gone into effect); Mark Munetz et al., *Modernization of a Mental Health Act: I. Commitment Patters*, 8 BULL AM ACAD PSYCHIATRY BL. 83, 92 (1980); Glenn L. Pierce et al., *The Impact of Public Policy and Publicity on Admissions to Health Hospitals*, 11 J. HEALTH, POL. POL'Y & L. 41 (1986).

involuntary civil commitment decision making simply "may not rest on statutory grounds."[66] A more recent study by Harold Bursztajn and his colleagues show the extent to which extrajudicial concepts—"patients' competence, predictability and reliability," concepts that are not "reducible to the . . . core concepts that define the black letter of the law"[67]—drive involuntary civil commitment decision making.

This notion that there is a higher morality to which forensic MHPs owe some sort of duty[68] is, empirically, an extraordinarily important one, and one that requires far greater attention on the part of all those concerned about the underlying issues.[69] Although some researchers and scholars have taken seriously the importance of this call in their reading of the effects of "legislative reform" on psychiatric hospital admissions rates,[70] the whole question is strangely underdiscussed.

Michael Saks' reference to such witnesses as "imperial experts" who install themselves as "temporary monarch[s]" by replacing a "societal preference" expressed through the law and legal process with [their] own preferences"[71] should encourage us to confront more seriously the dimensions of this issue. Although the sort of arrogation to which he

---

[66]Judith S. Thompson & Joel W. Ager, *An Experimental Analysis of the Civil Commitment Recommendations of Psychologists and Psychiatrists,* 6 BEHAV. SCI. & L. 119, 120 (1988) (discussing considerations such as available bed space and potential liabilities); *see also* Virginia Aldigé Hiday, *Dangerousness of Civil Commitment Candidates: A Six-Month Follow-Up,* 14 LAW & HUM. BEHAV. 551, 551 (1990) [hereinafter Hiday, *Six-Month*] (little dangerousness found on part of involuntary civil commitment candidates in six months following hospital release); Virginia Aldigé Hiday, *Reformed Commitment Procedures: An Empirical Study in the Courtroom,* 11 LAW & SOC'Y REV. 651 (1977) (only 24% of sample of committed patients met statutory criteria); Virginia Aldigé Hiday & Lynn N. Smith, *Effects of the Dangerousness Standard in Civil Commitment,* 15 J. PSYCHIATRY & L. 433, 441 (1987) (no allegations of dangerous behavior listed on affidavits in support of one third of all applications for admission supposedly filed under dangerousness standard); Stewart Page & John L. Firth, *Civil Commitment Practices in 1977: Troubled Semantics and/or Troubled Psychiatry,* 24 CAN. J. PSYCHIATRY 329, 330 (1979) (80–90% of filed commitment forms failed to meet legal criteria); R. A. Richert & A. H. Moyes, *Reasons for Involuntary Commitment in Manitoba and Ontario,* 28 CAN J. PSYCHIATRY 358, 358 (1983) (reporting similar 80–90% failure rates); R. Michael Bagby et al., *Decision Making in Psychiatric Civil Commitment: An Experimental Analysis,* 148 AM. J. PSYCHIATRY 28, 32 (1991) (psychiatrists failed to recommend commitment for 26% of a mock sample study that met the applicable legal criteria, and recommended commitment for 20% of the sample that did not meet the criteria).

[67]Harold Bursztajn, Robert Hamm, & Thomas Gutheil, *Beyond the Black Letter of the Law: An Empirical Study of an Individual Judge's Decision Process for Civil Commitment Hearings,* 25 J. AM. ACAD. PSYCHIATRY & L. 79, 85 (1997).

[67]Harold Bursztajn, Robert Hamm, & Thomas Gutheil, *Beyond the Black Letter of the Law: An Empirical Study of an Individual Judge's Decision Process for Civil Commitment Hearings,* 25 J. AM. ACAD. PSYCHIATRY & L. 79, 85 (1997).

[68]It would appear as if this position almost attempts to suggest the appropriateness of a duress or necessity doctrine to be employed in such cases. In standard tort law, such a defense typically applies when one commits what would otherwise be tortious behavior to save another's life in the face of a violent storm or other "act of God." *See, e.g.,* Ploof v. Putnam, 71 A. 188 (Vt. 1908); Vincent v. Lake Erie Transp., 124 N.W. 221 (Minn. 1910). This situation is fairly far removed from the more parallel use of the necessity defense in criminal cases where one acts to avoid a perceived political or social harm. *See, e.g.,* State v. Warshow, 410 A.2d 1000 (Vt. 1979) (protest at nuclear power plant); Sigma Reproductive Health Ctr. v. State, 467 A.2d 483 (Md. 1983) (abortion clinic trespass case). Perhaps a closer tort law analogy can be found in the false imprisonment, religious deprogramming cases. *See, e.g.,* Peterson v. Sorlien, 299 N.W.2d 123 (Minn. 1980).

[69]On the role of therapeutic jurisprudence as a tool for exploring such issues, see *infra* section 3.

[70]*See, e.g.,* R. Michael Bagby, *The Effects of Legislative Reform on Admission Rates to Psychiatric Units of General Hospitals,* 10 INT'L J.L. & PSYCHIATRY 383 (1987). As to what Richard Rogers and his associates refer to as an "arrogation of power," see Rogers et al., *supra* note 55, at 694.

[71]Michael Saks, *Expert Witnesses, Nonexpert Witnesses, and Nonwitness Experts,* 14 LAW & HUM. BEHAV. 291, 294 (1990), and *id.* n.2. *See supra* Chapters 1, 3.

refers is certainly not limited to forensic witnesses,[72] and although it is clear that such an attitude would not flourish if it were not tacitly endorsed by both jurors and litigators,[73] it is a problem—a pretextual problem—that forensic mental health professionals (and lawyers working with such forensic experts) must carefully confront.

Civil-commitment decision making may not rest on clinically coherent grounds either. Doctors recommend hospitalization "whenever they are in doubt about a patient's potential for suicide 'since it is always better to err on the side of safety,'"[74] notwithstanding empirical research concluding that it is not possible to predict suicide, even among high-risk groups of inpatients.[75] This type of decision making blocks access to any inquiry about whether the patient has social support in the community, a factor that is frequently associated with positive mental health outcomes.[76]

There is a flip side to this arrogation of morality. Using the rankest form of passive–aggressive behavior,[77] some mental health professionals have advised families to put their mentally ill relatives out on the streets where they will either find life so difficult that they will accept treatment or will deteriorate to the point at which there will no longer be any question as to their eligibility for involuntary civil commitment.[78] To suggest that this stands both medical ethics and the legal system on their heads belabors the obvious.

What does this mean? Do the leaders of the forensic profession ask forensic witnesses to lie, just as police officers frequently do in dropsy cases, for a greater social value? That social interest purportedly involves ensuring that patients who "really" need "help" receive it in spite of statutes and court decisions that require proof of dangerous behavior as a prerequisite

---

[72]*Cf.* Matter of Eaton, 740 P.2d 907, 911–12 (Wash. App. 1987) (rejecting argument of state social service department that only it, and not the court, is in the best position to make juvenile institutional placement decisions).

[73]*See* Saks, *supra* note 71, at 299 (reporting on an interview with a state prosecutor who said that he preferred using local forensic science experts rather than experts from the FBI's crime laboratory, because "it was harder to get the FBI experts to say what you want them to").

[74]Norman G. Poythress, *Mental Health Expert Testimony: Current Problems*, J. PSYCHIATRY & L. 201, 207 (1977) (quoting Itamar Salamon, *Evaluation of Suicidal Patients*, 24 N.Y. ST. J. MED. 65 (1974)).

[75]Rise B. Goldstein et al., *The Prediction of Suicide: Sensitivity, Specificity, and Predictive Value of a Multivariate Model Applied to Suicide Among 1906 Patients With Affective Disorders*, 48 ARCHIVES GEN. PSYCHIATRY 418 (1991).

[76]Hiday *supra* note 66, at 564 (citing findings reported in Virginia Aldigé Hiday & Theresa Scheid-Cook, *The North Carolina Experience With Outpatient Commitment: A Critical Appraisal*, 10 INT'L J.L. & PSYCHIATRY 215–32 (1987)).

[77]*See, e.g.,* Julie M. Zito et al., *One Year Under* Rivers: *Drug Refusal in a New York State Psychiatric Facility*, 12 INT'L J.L. & PSYCHIATRY 295 (1989); Philip Leaf, Wyatt v. Stickney: *Assessing the Impact in Alabama*, 28 HOSP. & COMMUNITY PSYCHIATRY 351, 354 (1977). *See generally* William Bernet, *Running Scared: Therapists' Excessive Concerns About Following Rules*, 23 BULL. AM. ACAD. PSYCHIATRY & L. 367, 367 (1995) ("Sometimes therapists make up rules and regulations that do not actually exist; sometimes they extend the meaning or exaggerate the intent of a rule to a degree that does not make any sense").

[78]David Wexler, *Grave Disability and Family Therapy: The Therapeutic Potential of Civil Libertarian Commitment Codes*, in THERAPEUTIC JURISPRUDENCE: THE LAW AS A THERAPEUTIC AGENT 165, 182 n.100 (David Wexler ed. 1990); *see also* John J. Ensminger & Thomas D. Liguori, *The Therapeutic Significance of the Civil Commitment Hearing: An Unexplained Potential*, in THERAPEUTIC JURISPRUDENCE, *supra* note 4, at 250 (discussing decision by doctors to remove patients from medication prior to involuntary civil commitment hearings "so that overt symptomatology will reappear"); *cf. In re* Burton, 464 N.E.2d 530, 537–38 (Ohio 1984) (error for court to order defendant withdrawn from all psychotropic medication during incompetency to stand trial evaluation period).

See also Samuel Malcolmson, *Are Mental Health Laws a Barrier to Treatment?* 9 HEALTH L. IN CAN. 14, 14 (1988) ("Patients who need treatment are not receiving it. Some psychiatrists use the new legislation as a rationalization to avoid helping ill people. In-patient psychiatry is becoming less attractive to the psychiatric profession").

to involuntary institutionalization?[79] This is happening both explicitly and implicitly. And again, it happens pretextually.

It seems that this arrogation of morality works in other directions as well. Susan Reed and Dan Lewis's study of voluntary hospital admission patterns at several Chicago community mental health centers reveals that staff workers will deviate from their routine behavior and select certain patients for special attention (in the admission and treatment processes) if the workers feel that the specific patients in question are "worth it."[80]

This research is troubling for two overlapping reasons. First, the assessment of who is "worth it" is easily distorted by prejudices and overgeneralizations about race, sex, sexual preference, ethnicity, and social class.[81] Although it might optimally reflect an expert evaluation of which patient is most likely to live a productive life on the outside free from further behavioral episodes that might require reinstitutionalization, there is no reason to expect that this is the type of normative decision making that informs the meaning of "worth." We know, for instance, that pathology is frequently overestimated in samples in which individuals do not comport with publicly acceptable gender role behavior, and can only speculate as to the extent to which this sort of attitude spills over to evaluations of patient worth.[82]

Second, the gatekeepers in the Chicago study were not all trained mental health professionals. Although a few had advanced degrees in psychology, and some were social workers or were trained in "something like 'rehab counseling,'" others had no apparent specialized mental health–behavioral training.[83] Similarly, street police officers—in many cases, the true institutional gatekeepers—use purportedly common sensical concepts of

---

[79]Casia Spohn & Julie Horney, *"The Law Is the Law But Fair Is Fair:" Rape Shield Laws and Official's Assessments of Sexual History Evidence,* 29 CRIMINOLOGY 132, 139 (1991) ("A reform that contradicts deeply held beliefs may result either in open defiance of the law or in a surreptitious attempt to modify the law" (citing ROBERT T. NAKAMURA & FRANK SMALWOOD, THE POLITICS OF POLICY IMPLEMENTATION (1980)). On the relevance of "dropsy" cases, see *supra* Chapter 2.

[80]Susan C. Reed & Dan A. Lewis, *The Negotiation of Voluntary Admission in Chicago's State Mental Hospitals,* 18 J. PSYCHIATRY & L. 137, 139 (1990); *see also* Michael J. Churgin, *An Essay on Commitment and the Emergency Room: Implications for the Delivery of Mental Health Services,* 13 LAW. MED. & HEALTH CARE 297, 301 (1985) (emergency certification process not used in cases where "the individual [was] a very 'interesting' patient").

[81]*See, e.g.,* Jay Wade, *Institutional Racism: An Analysis of the Mental Health System,* 63 AM. J. ORTHOPSYCHIATRY 536 (1993).

[82]*See* Sarah Rosenfeld, *Sex Roles and Societal Reactions to Mental Illness: The Labeling of "Deviant" Deviance,* 23 J. HEALTH & SOC. BEHAV. 18 (1982). For a parallel example of how "worth" is measured in other populations, see Charles H. Baron, *Medical Paternalism and the Rule of Law: A Reply to Dr. Relman,* 4 AM. J.L. & MED. 337, 350 (1979) (patient's intelligence, personality, and socioeconomic status all taken into account in determining degree of care given to patient on arrival in emergency room where death is a possibility); Laura Ryan, Note, *Washington State Prison Procedure for the Forcible Administration of Antipsychotic Medication to Prison Inmates Does Not Violate Due Process,* 59 U. CIN. L. REV. 1373, 1407–08 n.225 (1991) (suggesting that Baron's findings also apply to situations involving delegating medical decision making power to prison officials, thus creating the possibility that similar illegitimate criteria will be used; discussing Washington v. Harper, 494 U.S. 210 (1990), limiting right of convicted prisoners to refuse antipsychotic medication and vested broad discretion in prison officials in medication decision making); *see also* Ira Sommers & Deborah R. Baskin, *The Prescription of Psychiatric Medications in Prison: Psychiatric Versus Labeling Perspectives,* 7 JUST. Q. 739 (1990) (decision to medicate mildly impaired prisoners influenced by social factors, including sex and age).

[83]Reed & Lewis, *supra* note 80, at 142. On the impact that other "gatekeepers"—that is, state hospital admissions officers—have on commitment rates, see Glenn L. Pierce et al., *The Impact of Public Policy and Publicity on Admissions to State Mental Hospitals,* 11 J. HEALTH POL. POL'Y & L. 41, 52 (1986) (noting that the impact of publicity surrounding the vivid case significantly affected behavior of county admissions personnel, leading to disproportionately higher civil commitment rates in that county but not in other like counties).

mental illness (manifested as the display of "disrespect, recalcitrance and moral defect") and reshape their police reports to "magnify the subjective madness [sic] and dangerousness of their subjects" to ensure their admission into forensic hospitals.[84] The fusion of mental illness with "moral defect" is sanism at its most pernicious.

Line-treatment staff often view hospitalized patients who attempt to assert their constitutional and statutory rights as "trouble makers," and thus privilege quietly compliant patients and subordinate "difficult" patients (who are considered less "worth it").[85] This becomes even more important (and troubling) when considering the power that hospital staff frequently have over patients' access to their counsel. If an institutionalized patient wants to contact counsel, she or he frequently must ask ward line-staff personnel to place the necessary telephone call. If, for whatever reason, the staff member determines that this is "inappropriate"—for example, if the patient is labeled a "trouble maker"[86]—the promise of counsel becomes little more than a hoax.

This alleged, presumptuous, and oppressive "morality" of nonprofessional gatekeepers thus contributes to, and in some cases controls, frequently pretextual involuntary civil commitment decision making.[87] Expert attempts at making self-referentially "moral" decisions as to worth (to ensure access to treatment)[88] and either exaggerating[89] or downplaying[90] certain behavioral characteristics either to ensure or deprive patients of treatment further accentuates the pretextual nature of the commitment system. This also forces the concession that the doctrinal differences in substantive commitment standards that frequently are the focus of appellate test-case litigation as well as scholarly articles—for example, is an overt act a necessary predicate for a dangerousness finding? Can one be

---

[84]Michael L. Perlin, *Morality and Pretextuality, Psychiatry and Law: of "Ordinary Common Sense," Heuristic Reasoning, and Cognitive Dissonance,* 19 BULL. AM. ACAD. PSYCHIATRY & LAW 131, 140 (1991) (quoting Robert A. Menzies, *Psychiatrists in Blue: Police Apprehension of Mental Disorder and Dangerousness,* 25 CRIMINOLOGY 429, 446 (1987)); *see also* BURSTEN, *supra* note 51, at 95 (arresting officer has far more impact on whether mentally disabled criminal suspect is treated as "mad" or "bad" than does the entire insanity defense system); John Petrila, *The Insanity Defense and Other Mental Health Dispositions in Missouri,* 5 INT'L J.L. & PSYCHIATRY 81, 91 n.36 (1982) (reporting on attitudes of forensic staff toward patients and staff's use of OCS to *deny* presence of mental disability in patients); *cf.* Thomas L. Kuhlman, *Unavoidable Tragedies in Madison, Wisconsin: A Third View,* 43 HOSP. & COMMUNITY PSYCHIATRY 72, 73 (1992) (police officers "have seen many of their efforts at emergency detention circumvented by mental health professionals or commitment courts").

[85]*See* SUSAN SHEEHAN, IS THERE NO PLACE ON EARTH FOR ME (1982). Other examples are more malignant. *See, e.g.,* Rennie v. Klein, 720 F.2d 266, 268 (3d Cir. 1983) (attendants beat a psychotic patient while he was restrained to his bed after patient filed right to refuse treatment lawsuit).

[86]Interview with Keri Gould, former senior attorney for the Mental Hygiene Legal Service, New York City (March 3, 1992) (currently professor of law at St. John's University School of Law). Staff have similar power over voluntary patients seeking to exercise their right to leave the hospital, something that may not be done in many jurisdictions unless a 72-hour notice is given to the hospital (to give administrators the option of converting the patient to voluntary status). *See* 1 PERLIN, *supra* note 2, § 2C-7.2, at 481–82.

[87]This does not mean that the testimonial process should exclude nonprofessionals. In many instances, nonprofessionally trained hospital staff line workers will have the most day-to-day knowledge of a patient's behavior and can offer true insights into the questions typically before courts. *Cf. In re* Miller, 362 N.Y.S.2d 628, 633 (N.Y. App. Div. 1974) (suggesting that at "not guilty by reason of insanity" (NGRI) release hearing, witnesses should include "hospital employees such as nurses, orderlies, housekeepers and other who have had daily or frequent contact with petitioner") with People v. Bolden, 266 Cal. Rptr. 724, 727 (Cal. App. 1990) (conflicting testimony between medical doctor and psychologist, who stated NGRI acquittee would stop taking medication in outpatient program and then become violent, and recreational therapist and nursing assistant, who stated that acquittee understood value of medication and would continue to take medication in outpatient setting).

[88]*See* Reed & Lewis, *supra* note 80, at 146.

[89]*See* Menzies, *supra* note 84.

[90]*See* Petrila, *supra* note 84.

"gravely disabled" without being dangerous to one's self under a *parens patriae* standard?—appear even less empirically significant in this context.[91]

H. Richard Lamb's attack on courts for interpreting involuntary civil commitment laws too "literally"[92] suggests further that there is nothing transparent or *sub rosa* about the entire "morality" attack on the legal process. It is a blatant attempt to aggregate power, to subvert the law, and to privilege expertise over all competing social values. In short, it suggests that the entire involuntary civil commitment process may be pretextual.[93] It also suggests that the courts' prereflective OCS on this question—that it can be "safely assume[d]" that hospitals and their medical professionals are disinterested decision makers who certainly "have no bias against the patient or against release"[94]—is no more accurate than the U.S. Supreme Court's OCS in *United States v. Leon* that there is "no evidence" to suggest that judges ignore or subvert the Fourth Amendment or to suggest that they have any stake in the outcomes of criminal prosecutions.[95]

This assumes yet another fact-not-in-evidence: That judges actually interpret involuntary civil commitment laws "strictly," by imposing by-the-book burdens on hospital and state lawyers, by zealously protecting patients' procedural rights, and by regularly dismissing, on so-called legal technicalities, "worthy" involuntary civil commitment petitions.[96] This, of course, happens rarely (if ever). Cases are frequently decided in an expedited

---

[91]*See, e.g.,* Michael L. Perlin, *Psychodynamics and the Insanity Defense: "Ordinary Common Sense" and Heuristic Reasoning,* 69 NEB. L. REV. 3 (1990); Michael L. Perlin, *Unpacking the Myths: The Symbolism Mythology of Insanity Defense Jurisprudence,* 40 CASE W. RES. L. REV. 599 (1989–90) (questioning whether difference in various substantive insanity defense standards makes a "real world" difference in the way the public views the insanity defense or in the way courts treat insanity pleaders).

[92]H. Richard Lamb, *Involuntary Treatment for the Homeless Mentally Ill,* 4 NOTRE DAME J.L. ETHICS & PUB. POL'Y 269, 277 (1989).

[93]*Cf.* Lamb's acceptance of pretextual testimony with other scholarly inquiries focusing on the ways that other false testimony may taint the legal process. *See, e.g.,* MICHAEL AVERY & DAVID RUDOVSKY, POLICE MISCONDUCT, LAW AND LITIGATION 8-5 (2d ed. 1987); J. Martin Kaplan, *Children Don't Always Tell the Truth,* 35 J. FORENS. SCI. 661 (1990).

[94]Stitt v. State Dep't of Mental Health & Mental Retardation, 562 So.2d 259, 262 (Ala. Civ. App. 1990) (quoting Williams v. Wallis, 734 F.2d 1434, 1438 (11th Cir. 1984)). Another field of inquiry involves economically oriented bias in the way that the commitment process may be abused by for-profit hospitals. *See, e.g.,* Michael L. Perlin, *Power Imbalances in Therapeutic and Forensic Relationships,* 9 BEHAV. SCI. & L. 111, 119 (1991) (increase in for-profit psychiatric hospitals increases the number of children admitted at a time when some "physicians are pressured . . . to maintain a maximal census and thus increase profits" (discussing results reported in Richard Dalton & Marc A. Foreman, *Conflicts of Interest Associated With the Psychiatric Hospitalization of Children,* 57 AM. J. ORTHOPSYCHIATRY 12, 13 (1987)). These pressures have not abated with time. *See, e.g.,* Herbert Sacks, *Who's on First, What's on Second, I Don't Know's on Third (For-Profit Psychiatric Hospitals and the Games They Play),* PSYCHIATRIC NEWS (Sept. 5, 1997), at 3 (discussing indictments of officials at National Medical Enterprises for bribing doctors for patient referrals).

[95]468 U.S. 897, 916–17 (1984). *See generally supra* Chapter 3, and *see especially* Myron W. Orfield, *Deterrence, Perjury, and the Heater Factor: An Exclusionary Rule in the Chicago Criminal Courts,* 63 U. COLO. L. REV. 75, 100–07 (1992) (86% of judges, public defenders, and prosecutors questioned, including 77% of judges, believe that police officers fabricate evidence in case reports at least "some of the time"; 92% (including 91% of judges) believe that police officers lie to avoid suppression of evidence at least "some of the time").

[96]*See* Perlin, *supra* note 11, at 44 n.33 ("Experienced lawyers confirm that attempts at vigorous cross-examination and at the development of novel defenses are frequently rebuffed angrily by trial judges assigned to civil commitment dockets").

manner,[97] counsel for patients are usually passive,[98] and, in some states, trial court commitment decisions are virtually never appealed.[99]

The available evidence paints a gloomy picture. As length of proposed hospitalization increases, hearings become shorter in length and less adversarial.[100] At patients' initial hearings, fewer than one third of judges told the patients of their right to counsel, fewer than one fourth of judges told them of their right to seek voluntary commitment status, and only about two fifths of judges told them of their right to appeal. These percentages dropped precipitously by the time of the patient's second review hearing.[101] The District of Columbia Code contains a provision that patients can invoke seeking either periodic review of their commitment or an independent psychiatric evaluation, but not a single patient exercised the right to statutory review in the first 22 years following the law's passage.[102] It is assumed that vigorous, independent, advocacy-focused counsel is now made available to all mentally disabled litigants, but in almost every jurisdiction, the empirical reality is totally to the contrary.[103]

In addition, judges' attitudes closely mimic those of Chodoff's "moral expert." Michael Saks quoted from a Massachusetts trial judge, speaking to mental health law students and their professors who had observed a commitment docket: "I guess you noticed that some of these people were not fit subjects for commitment under the statute. But, after all, I am a human being. I care about what is best for these people, and I have to do what I think is right."[104] As Saks concluded, "This judge in effect abolished the state's commitment laws, substituted his own, and produced the result he wanted notwithstanding the democratic and legal processes that existed to control these decisions."[105]

It is important to consider how closely this sort of "morality" comports with the "moral" message sent by Lamb, Chodoff, and others to their psychiatric colleagues. Such expert witnesses could not freely testify in ways that subvert statutes and case law if the legal system did not tacitly approve.[106]

It is probably not coincidental that Lamb is among those urging courts not to take commitment standards too literally. According to Lamb, there is a link between deinstitutionalization and homelessness that has been exacerbated by activist and exces-

---

[97]See, e.g., Parham v. J. R., 442 U.S. 584, 609 n.17 (1979) (statistical studies reveal that average commitment hearing lasted from 3.8 to 9.2 minutes); Leslie Scallet, *The Realities of Mental Health Advocacy:* State ex rel. Memmel v. Mundy, in MENTAL HEALTH ADVOCACY: AN EMERGING FORCE IN CONSUMERS' RIGHTS 79, 81 (L. Kopolow & H. Bloom eds. 1977) (former system of representation in place in Milwaukee County operated as a "greased runway to the county mental health center").

[98]Perlin, *supra* note 11, at 43.

[99]*Id.* at 50. (In Virginia, from 1976 to 1986, only two reported appellate civil cases dealt with questions of mental hospitalization.)

[100]Charles D. Parry & Eric Turkheimer, *Length of Hospitalization and Outcome of Commitment and Recommitment Hearings,* 43 HOSP. & COMMUNITY PSYCHIATRY 65 (1992).

[101]*Id.* at 66.

[102]Streicher v. Prescott, 663 F. Supp. 335, 343 (D.D.C. 1987) discussed *supra* Chapter 3, text accompanying note 62.

[103]Perlin, *supra* note 11.

[104]Saks, *supra* note 71, at 293.

[105]*Id.; see also* Ensminger & Liguori, *supra* note 78, at 252 ("The judge may tell the patient that he is [being committed] because it is the benevolent thing to do, when he will admit privately that he would not want the patient walking around in the neighborhood he lives in.").

[106]*Cf.* Uri Aviram, *Care or 'Convenience? On the Medical–Bureaucratic Model of the Commitment of the Mentally Ill,* 13 INT'L J.L. & PSYCHIATRY 163 (1990) (discussing collusive behavior between courts and doctors in Israel's commitment system).

sively civil libertarian courts.[107] If medication noncompliance in the community leads to deterioration and decompensation, and this then "causes" homelessness, psychiatrists can exert moral suasion in the forensic setting by making predictions about such deterioration at the involuntary civil commitment hearing. Whether or not psychiatrists have expertise to predict noncompliance—a power that is presumably a necessary predicate to this testimony—is neatly forgotten.[108]

Finally, tort remedies are generally not available to persons aggrieved by misuse of the involuntary civil commitment process.[109] Many reasons are offered: the fact that the psychiatrist in the commitment process allegedly acts in a position not unlike that of a judicial officer; the lack of psychiatrists willing to testify at such hearings; the privileging of public safety values over personal autonomy values; the need for psychiatrists to be able to act without fear of liability; the availability of other remedies (e.g., criminal statutes) in cases of patently false testimony.[110] Although recently courts have appeared more sympathetic to tort plaintiffs in such cases,[111] individuals victimized by pretextuality are mostly left without recourse.

Sanism, Pretextuality, and Civil Commitment Law

A full understanding of the involuntary civil commitment process requires a consideration of the substantive and procedural limitations on the commitment power.[112] It is necessary to consider further the relationship between commitment and competency and how sanist testimony can subvert legal standards in this specific context, especially in the context of what appears to be the most important issue being litigated in the involuntary civil commitment process in recent reported appellate decisions: whether a patient is "competent" to make the "right choice" and self-medicate in the community if commitment is not ordered.[113]

---

[107]See Michael L. Perlin, *Competency, Deinstitutionalization, and Homelessness: A Story of Marginalization,* 28 HOUS. L. REV. 63, 86–97 (1991) [hereinafter Perlin, *Marginalization*] (discussing Lamb's critique). My colleague and I respond directly to this critique in Mossman & Perlin, *supra* note 43, at, 952

[108]See generally *infra* Chapter 6.

[109]See 3 PERLIN, *supra* note 2, § 12.25 at 438; *see also* Laurence Tancredi, *Psychiatric Malpractice, in* 3 PSYCHIATRY, ch. 29 (J. Cavenar ed. 1986), at 1, 7.

[110]Note, *The Liability of Psychiatrists for Malpractice,* 36 U. PITT. L. REV. 108, 112 (1974); *see also* Samuel Knapp & Leon VandeCreek, *A Review of Tort Liability in Involuntary Civil Commitment,* 38 HOSP. & COMMUNITY PSYCHIATRY 648 (1987).

[111]See cases cited in 3 PERLIN, *supra* note 2, § 12.15, at 328 n.438.1 (1998 Cum. Supp.). *See, e.g.,* Demarco v. Sadiker, 952 F. Supp. 134 (E.D.N.Y. 1996) (denying defendants' motion to dismiss where plaintiff alleged doctor never examined him as part of commitment application process).

[112]See, e.g., John Petrila, *Redefining Mental Health Law: Thoughts on a New Agenda,* 16 LAW & HUM. BEHAV. 89, 100–01 (1992) ("discussions of the commitment process that ignore . . . political realities run the risk of being largely academic").

[113]See generally Perlin, *Marginalization, supra* note 107, at 116–17 nn.306–08; Michael L. Perlin, *Reading the Supreme Court's Tea Leaves: Predicting Judicial Behavior in Civil and Criminal Right to Refuse Treatment Cases,* 12 AM. J. FORENSIC PSYCHIATRY 37, 50–51 (1991) (Perlin, *Tea Leaves*); Michael L. Perlin, *Decoding Right to Refuse Treatment Law,* 16 INT'L J.L. & PSYCHIATRY 151 (1993) (Perlin, *Decoding*).

This issue is discussed in Donald A. Treffert, *The Obviously Ill Patient in Need of Treatment: A Fourth Standard for Civil Commitment,* 36 HOSP. & COMMUNITY PSYCHIATRY 259, 260 (1985) (arguing that, as a result of the legislative tightening of commitment criteria, a patient "with an obvious and severe mental illness that was formerly well controlled on antipsychotic medication [would] become unable to make an informed decision about treatment and slowly deteriorate until he or she would "qualify" for detention or commitment under harsh, realistic commitment criteria").

This inquiry begins with three basic principles. First, individuals are presumed to be competent, and this presumption generally may not be overcome except by a judicial determination.[114] This articulation of a competency presumption dates from 1972, when a Wisconsin federal district court struck down a state statute that had presumed the inverse: that a civilly committed individual was presumed to be incompetent, although that presumption was rebuttable.[115] However, the medical profession's record of complying with this mandate of presumed competency has been significantly spotty.[116] Recent evidence reported by the MacArthur Network—that 50% of patients diagnosed with schizophrenia score in the nonimpaired range (when measuring for competency)[117]—has had no effect whatsoever on either hospital or judicial practices.

Second, competency is not a "fixed state." A person may be competent for some legal purposes and incompetent for others at the same time. Incompetency and mental illness are not identical states.[118] As the Supreme Court of Washington has noted, "The mere fact that an individual is mentally ill does not mean that the person is incapable of making a rational choice with respect to his or her need for treatment."[119] Even if a person is found incompetent to stand trial, that does not mean that she or he is incompetent to function in society.[120]

Third, assessments of competency are also muddled by the lack of a unitary-competency standard. The observation by Loren Roth and his colleagues more than 20 years ago that the search for a single test was akin to a "search for the Holy Grail"[121] resonates today. Although scholars such as Paul Appelbaum and Thomas Grisso have carefully conceptualized competency standards in four categories (ability to communicate choices, to understand relevant information, to appreciate a situation and its consequences, and to manipulate information rationally),[122] the response of the *en banc* court in *United States v. Charters*[123]—suggesting that *no one* could possibly distinguish between competency to

---

[114]*See, e.g.,* William M. Brooks, *A Comparison of a Mentally Ill Individual's Right to Refuse Medication Under the United States and New York State Constitutions,* 8 Touro L. Rev. 1, 36 (1991); Rogers v. Commissioner, 390 Mass. 489, 459 N.E.2d 308, 314–315 (1983). *Cf.* A. E. v. Mitchell, 724 F.2d 864, 867 (10th Cir. 1983) (incompetent prerequisite for involuntary civil commitment under Utah statute).

[115]Lessard v. Schmidt, 349 F. Supp. 1078, 1088 (E.D. Wis. 1972).

[116]Paul R. Tremblay, *On Persuasion and Paternalism: Lawyer Decisionmaking and the Questionably Competent Client,* 1987 Utah L. Rev. 515, 538–39 n.97.

[117]Elyn Saks & Stephen Behnke, *Competency to Decide on Treatment and Research: MacArthur and Beyond,* 10 J. Contemp. Leg. Iss. 103, 110 (1999), reporting on research reported *in* Thomas Grisso & Paul Appelbaum, MacArthur Competence Assessment Tool–Treatment (MacCAT–T) 17 (1995). For a recent empirical investigation, concluding that "adult voluntary psychiatric inpatients . . . score almost as competent as general hospital patients," see Stephen Billick, Peter Della Bella, & Woodward Burgert, *Competency to Consent to Hospitalization in the Medical Patient,* 25 J. Am. Acad. Psychiatry & L. 191, 196 (1997).

[118]*See* Bruce J. Winick, *Competency to Consent to Voluntary Hospitalization: A Therapeutic Jurisprudence Analysis of* Zinermon v. Burch, *in* Essays in Therapeutic Jurisprudence 83, 102–05 (D. Wexler & B. Winick, eds. 1991), citing sources; *see also* David Wexler, *The Structure of Civil Commitment: Patterns, Pressures, and Interactions in Mental Health Legislation,* 7 Law & Hum. Behav. 1, 8–9 (1983).

[119]*In re* LaBelle, 728 P.2d 138, 146 (Wash. 1986).

[120]Linda C. Fentiman, *Whose Right Is It Anyway? Rethinking Competency to Stand Trial in Light of Synthetically Sane Insanity Defendants,* 40 U. Miami L. Rev. 1109, 1166 (1986).

[121]Loren Roth et al., *Tests of Competency to Consent to Treatment,* 134 Am. J. Psychiatry 279, 283 (1977).

[122]Paul Appelbaum & Thomas Grisso, *Assessing Patients' Capabilities to Consent to Treatment,* 319 New Eng. J. Med. 1635, 1635–36 (1988).

[123]863 F.2d 302 (4th Cir. 1988) *(en banc), cert. denied,* 494 U.S. 1016 (1990).

stand trial and competency to refuse antipsychotic medication[124]—is not an atypical response of appellate courts faced with this problem.[125]

How do courts construe expert testimony on the relationship between competency, treatment refusal, and the involuntary civil commitment process? There is an initial paradox. Only a handful of reported involuntary civil commitment cases have frontally considered right-to-refuse treatment claims in the civil commitment context;[126] most courts dismiss such claims as not justiciable in the involuntary civil commitment context.[127]

Yet courts regularly and routinely weigh experts' predictions of a patient's potential refusal to take antipsychotic medication in a community setting[128] as the most probative evidence on the question of whether involuntary civil commitment should be ordered. Although David Wexler noted this link more than 15 years ago,[129] the academic journals have been strangely silent about the implications of the reality that the perceived linkage between drug refusal and need for involuntary commitment has become the absolutely dominant issues in dispute in such commitment cases.

Most of the reported cases rely on psychiatric expert predictions as the dispositive evidence.[130] Although there is widespread belief that refusal to take such medication will make some patients more dangerous,[131] there is no evidence that psychiatrists have any special ability to predict compliance to take medication in the community.[132] There is also a body of evidence that suggests that this population is made up of poor or uneducated people that many community mental health centers do not want to treat.[133]

Yet involuntary civil commitment is regularly ordered where testifying experts find it "doubtful" that the patient would self-medicate in the community.[134] Thus where the

---

[124]*Id.* at 310 (any distinction between two competency states "must certainly be one of such subtlety and complexity as to tax perception by the most skilled medical or psychiatric professionals"); *cf.* Michael L. Perlin, *Are Courts Competent to Decide Competency Questions? Stripping the Facade From* United States v. Charters, 38 U. KAN. L. REV. 957, 988 (1990) (characterizing this aspect of the court's opinion as reflecting "passive–aggressive behavior").

[125]*But cf.* United States v. Hoskie, 950 F.2d 1388, 1390 n.2 (9th Cir. 1991) (differentiating between incompetency to stand trial and competency to plead guilty); for other jurisdictions in accord, see 3 PERLIN, *supra* note 2, § 14.20 (listing cases).

[126]*See, e.g.,* Matter of Commitment of J. L. J., 509 A.2d 184, 186 (N.J. App. Div. 1985).

[127]*See, e.g., In re* Harhut, 367 N.W.2d 628, 632 (Minn. App. 1985). *See generally* 1 PERLIN, *supra* note 2, § 2C-5.2, at 414–16 (2d ed. 1998).

[128]The empirical validity of this assumption is questioned in *In re* Richardson, 481 A.2d 473, 479 n.5 (D.C. 1984) ("Not every instance of the outpatient's failure to take prescribed medication or attend therapy sessions justifies the conclusion that he is not cooperating with the treatment program," citing Virginia Aldigé Hiday & Rodney R. Goodman, *The Least Restrictive Alternative to Involuntary Hospitalization, Outpatient Commitment: Its Use and Effectiveness,* 10 J. PSYCHIATRY & L. 81, 89 (1982)).

[129]David Wexler, *The Structure of Civil Commitment: Patterns, Pressures, and Interactions in Mental Health Legislation,* 7 LAW & HUM. BEHAV. 1, 9 (1983).

[130]For an example of a court rejecting this line of thinking, see *In re* J. S. C., 812 S.W.2d 92, 95–96 (Tex. App. 1991) (testimony that patient will deteriorate if he fails to take medication insufficient basis on which to sustain involuntary civil commitment determination).

[131]Teresa Scheid-Cook, *Commitment of the Mentally Ill to Outpatient Treatment,* 23 COMMUNITY MENT. HEALTH J. 173, 180 (1987).

[132]The literature reveals no studies on this question. A recent reconsideration of dangerousness studies lists more than 40 factors to be considered by experts in assessing probabilities of an individual's future violence; community medication compliance is not included. George B. Palermo et al., *On the Predictability of Violent Behavior: Considerations and Guidelines,* 36 J. FORENS. SCI. 1435, 1440 (1991), and *see id.* at 1439 ("One should not deduce the possibility for future dangerousness from an isolated individual trait").

[133]*See, e.g.,* Scheid-Cook, *supra* note 131, at 181–82.

[134]*E.g., In Interest of* L. B., 452 N.W.2d 75, 77 (N.D. 1990).

operative state statute included a presumption that the subject of the commitment petition did not require treatment,[135] and where civil commitment required clear and convincing evidence of a "serious risk of harm,"[136] a commitment order was affirmed where the experts testified that the patient would "benefit" from medication and that the "only way" such medication could be provided in a supervised basis was in a "structured residential type of placement" and that "if she was discharged from the hospital, she would quit taking her medication."[137] In another case brought under a statute requiring proof that the respondent would be "likely to physically harm others unless the commitment is continued,"[138] testimony that the individual was in need of long-term medication to help control his mental illness, and that he was "unlikely" to take the medication absent extended hospitalization was a sufficient basis on which to order commitment.[139]

Similarly, other courts rely regularly on like testimony in recommitment hearings following insanity acquittals. If such an individual "would not likely take his medication regularly as an outpatient" (even where the potential danger would not be "imminent"), or if there were a "high likelihood that without adequate supervision [the patient] would stop taking his medication," the commitments are continued.[140]

This entire inquiry takes on new meaning when we consider recent empirical studies that demonstrate how little information is given to released patients about their medication regimens or how poorly such information is processed. More than half the patients discharged from short-stay treatment programs (including one conducted at an Ivy League medical school's teaching hospital) did not know the name or the appropriate dosage of the antipsychotic medications prescribed for them or why they were being asked to take these medications.[141]

Finally, consider the different ways in which courts weigh expert testimony by state psychiatrists in commitment cases and by defense experts in insanity defense cases. Judges value psychiatric expertise when it contributes to the social control functions of law and disparage it when it does not. In the criminal justice system, psychiatrists are viewed skeptically as accomplices of defense lawyers who get criminals "off the hook" of responsibility. But in the commitment system, they are more confidently seen as therapeutic helpers who get patients *on* the hook of treatment and control.[142] In short, sanism and pretextuality permeate the involuntary civil commitment process. If we do not acknowledge their presence and their power, our attempts at understanding what really happens in this process can never succeed.

Other pretexts infect other cases. In *Addington v. Texas,*[143] in the course of its opinion establishing at least "clear and convincing evidence" as the burden of proof in a

---

[135]N.D.C.C. § 25-03.1-19 (1992); *In re* Kupperion, 331 N.W.2d 22, 26 (N. Dak. 1985).

[136]Defined as a "substantial deterioration in mental health which would predictably result in dangerousness to that person, others, or property, based upon acts, threats, or patterns in the person's treatment, current condition, and other relevant factors." N.D.C.C. § 25-03.1-02(10)(d) (1992).

[137]*In Interest of* R. N., 453 N.W.2d 819, 822 (N.D. 1990).

[138]MINN. STAT. § 253B.12, subd. 4 (1993).

[139]*Matter of* Thornblad, 1991 WL 271491, at 2 (Minn. App. 1991).

[140]*See, e.g.,* Lawrence v. State, 410 S.E.2d 136, 137 (Ga. 1991); People v. Bolden, 266 Cal. Rptr. 724, 727 (Cal. App. 1990), *rev'd denied* (1990).

[141]Steven Clary et al., *Psychiatric Inpatients' Knowledge of Medication at Hospital Discharge,* 43 HOSP. & COMMUNITY PSYCHIATRY 140 (1992).

[142]I discuss the implications of this discontinuity in Michael L. Perlin, *Back to the Past: Why Mental Disability Law "Reforms" Don't Reform,* 4 CRIM. L.F. 403, 410 (1993) (reviewing JOHN Q. LAFOND AND MARY L. DURHAM, BACK TO THE ASYLUM: THE FUTURE OF MENTAL HEALTH LAW AND POLICY IN THE UNITED STATES (1992)).

[143]441 U.S. 418 (1979).

commitment hearing, the Supreme Court contrasted commitment hearings to criminal trials, and rejected the argument made there that the risk of error to the individual must be minimized ''even at the risk that some who are guilty might go free.''[144] The analogy failed, the Court reasoned, for two separate reasons. First, because concerned friends and families generally will ''provide continuous opportunities for an erroneous commitment to be corrected,''[145] a rationale premised on the assumption that most individuals subject to commitment have such friends and families standing by and ready to intervene on their behalf (an argument for which there appears no supporting evidence either in the opinion or in the behavioral literature). Second, because the Court felt, ''it is not true that the release of a *genuinely mentally ill* person is no worse for the individual than the failure to convict the guilty.''[146] Here the Court makes two pretextual assumptions: that *all* persons subject to the civil commitment process are ''genuinely'' mentally ill, and that hospitalization cannot help but ameliorate such a person's condition. Whether these statements are simply naive or meretricious, they are, in either case, pretextual.

Other commitment cases presume that treatment is available to patients after commitment.[147] In upholding a North Carolina commitment law, a three-judge district court sanctioned deprivations of individuals' liberty because ''the state is providing treatment to those individuals who may not otherwise have the wisdom or wherewithal to seek it themselves.''[148] Subsequent ongoing litigation in another federal court in North Carolina has made it crystal clear that such treatment was *not* made available to all persons institutionalized because of mental disability.[149] And certainly, at the time the three-judge court had convened, the abysmal lack of adequate treatment in many of this nation's public mental hospitals was well-known, and well-documented in reported federal litigation.[150] Again, the court's decision rested on a pretextual basis.[151]

Finally, consider the Supreme Court's decision in *Heller v. Doe.*[152] In *Heller,* the Court ruled that a Kentucky commitment statute—allowing for the commitment of persons with mental retardation based on a standard of clear and convincing evidence but requiring proof beyond a reasonable doubt in cases of persons with mental illness—did not run afoul of the Equal Protection clause.[153] The Court accepted the state's argument that the distinction was rational, because (a) mental retardation was easier to diagnose, (b) the ''permanen[cy]'' of mental retardation allowed predictions of dangerousness to be made with more accuracy, and (c) mentally retarded persons were subject to ''much less invasive'' means of treatment following institutionalization than were mentally ill persons.[154]

---

[144]*Id.* at 428, citing Patterson v. New York, 432 U.S. 197, 208 (1977).

[145]*Id.* at 429.

[146]*Id.* (emphasis added).

[147]*See generally infra* Chapter 5.

[148]French v. Blackburn, 428 F. Supp. 1351, 1354 (M.D.N.C. 1977).

[149]*See, e.g.,* Thomas S. by Brooks v. Morrow, 601 F. Supp. 1055 (W.D.N.C. 1984).

[150]Michael L. Perlin, Keri K. Gould, & Deborah Dorfman, *Therapeutic Jurisprudence and the Civil Rights of Institutionalized Mentally Disabled Persons: Hopeless Oxymoron or Path to Redemption?* 1 PSYCHOL., PUB. POL'Y & L. 80 (1995); *see generally* 2 PERLIN, *supra* note 2, Chap. 3A (2d. ed. 1999).

[151]Even the paradigmatically nonsanist and nonpretextual case of Lessard v. Schmidt, 349 F. Supp. 1078 (E.D. Wis. 1971), may have fallen into the same trap. *See id.* at 1100 (justifying limits on a patient's privilege against self-incrimination at an involuntary civil commitment hearing because of the prospect that it was ''ludicrous'' to countenance a situation in which counsel's advice to remain silent could lead to ''the prospect of a seriously ill individual being prevented from obtaining needed treatment.''

[152]509 U.S. 312 (1993).

[153]*Id.* at 318–30.

[154]*Id.* at 322–25.

In his dissent, Justice Souter exposed the pretextual nature of the majority opinion:

> The question whether a lower burden of proof is rationally justified, then, turns not only on whether ease of diagnosis and proof of dangerousness differ as between cases of illness and retardation, but also on whether there are differences in the respective interests of the public and the subjects of the commitment proceedings, such that the two groups subject to commitment can rationally be treated differently by imposing a lower standard of proof for commitment of the retarded. The answer is clearly that they can not. . . . We do not lower burdens of proof merely because it is easy to prove the proposition at issue, nor do we raise them merely because it is difficult. . . . Both the ill and the retarded may be dangerous, each may require care, and the State's interest is seemingly of equal strength in each category of cases. No one has or would argue that the value of liberty varies somehow depending on whether one is alleged to be ill or retarded, and a mentally retarded person has as much to lose by civil commitment to an institution as a mentally ill counterpart, including loss of liberty to "choos[e] his own friends and companions, selec[t] daily activities, decid[e] what to eat, and retai[n] a level of personal privacy," among other things. Brief for American Association on Mental Retardation (AAMR) et al. as Amici Curiae 12 (AAMR Br.). We do not presume that a curtailment of the liberty of those who are disabled is, because of their disability, less severe than the same loss to those who are ill. . . . Even assuming, then, that the assertion of different degrees of difficulty of proof both of mental illness and mental retardation and of the dangerousness inherent in each condition is true (an assertion for which there is no support in the record), it lends not a shred of rational support to the decision to discriminate against the retarded in allocating the risk of erroneous curtailment of liberty.[155]

Also, Justice Souter looked to social science to expose the pretextual basis of the "less invasive" argument. The most contemporaneous research revealed that anywhere between 30 and 76% of residents for facilities for mentally retarded persons receive psychotropic medications, that these drugs are frequently misused in such facilities, and that residents have been "seriously endangered and injured" by such misuse.[156] Other social science evidence showed that mentally retarded persons in institutions were also often subject to behavior modification therapy, including "aversive conditioning," and that such treatment has been used "inappropriately" in institutional contexts. He thus concluded that both drugs and invasive therapies are "routinely administered to the retarded as well as the mentally ill, and there are "no apparent differences of therapeutic regimes that would plausibly explain less rigorous commitment standards for those alleged to be mentally retarded than for those alleged to be mentally ill."[157]

It may be that pretexts will be harder to justify in the coming years because of the "rush" of new and important behavioral research. The MacArthur Network's study on the "pervasive role"[158] of coercion in the involuntary civil commitment process[159] is a powerful indictment of commitment practice in "real life." This research reveals that patients were able to give coherent accounts of their experiences and coercion and that these

---

[155]*Id.* at 341.

[156]*Id.* at 343.

[157]*Id.* at 345.

[158]William Gardner, *Two Scales for Measuring Patients' Perceptions for Coercion During Mental Hospital Admission,* 11 BEHAV. SCI. & L. 307, 307 (1993).

[159]For a preliminary explanation of the research (and the finding that, until this point in time, reliable and valid methods of quantifying perceptions of coercion had not been developed), see Steven K. Hoge et al., *Patient, Family, and Staff Perceptions of Coercion in Mental Hospital Admission: An Exploratory Study,* 11 BEHAV. SCI. & L. 281 (1993).

responses were "highly internally consistent."[160] Other research demonstrated that patients who felt they had "little voice" and against whom threats and force were used in the hospitalization process experienced high levels of coercion as well.[161] Again, contemporary research tells us that half of patients with schizophrenia—the group usually seen as the most impaired—score within the "nonimpaired" range on the MacArthur Network's research instruments.[162]

Researchers and clinicians have begun to draft research instruments assessing whether individual patients are truly capable of consenting to treatment.[163] Recent research concludes that policy makers and advocates "must look beyond formal status" in their studies of coercion in the commitment process," concluding that the use of admission legal status as the "sole criterion for coercion is flawed."[164] Yet another study further illuminates pretexts in the voluntary commitment system, revealing that patients employ "heavily moralized theories of coercion."[165] According to Nancy Bennett and her colleagues:

> Patients believe that they should be included as much as they wish in the process of determining whether they will be admitted to the hospital. They believe that those involved in the admission process should be motivated by an appropriate degree of concern for their well-being, and they evaluate the legitimacy of involved persons' actions in light of the motivations they attribute to them. Finally, patients believe that others should act toward them in good faith. The others should be personally or professionally qualified to participate in the admission process, should act without deceit, and should treat the patient with equality and respect.[166]

However, this research—and other MacArthur Network data—has fallen on deaf judicial ears.[167] A sanist and pretextual commitment system cannot—will not—treat the patient with "equality and respect." It is this presence of sanism and pretextuality that inevitably corrupts the civil commitment process and thwarts any beneficent goal that system ostensibly might have.

Nonsanist and Nonpretextual Cases

Not all decisions, of course, are pretextual or sanist. Some relatively recent individual cases have carefully read records in involuntary civil commitment hearings to determine

---

[160]Gardner, *supra* note 158, at 318.

[161]Charles Lidz et al., *Perceived Coercion in Mental Hospital Admission: Pressure and Process*, 52 ARCHIVES GEN. PSYCHIATRY 1034 (1995); Subsequent researchers have confirmed these findings. *See, e.g.,* Virginia Aldigé Hiday, *Patient Perceptions of Coercion in Mental Hospital Admission*, 20 INT'L J.L. & PSYCHIATRY 227 (1997); *see generally* John Monahan et al., *Coercion and Commitment: Understanding Involuntary Mental Hospital Admission*, 18 INT'L J.L. & PSYCHIATRY 249 (1995).

[162]*See* Saks & Behnke, *supra* note 117, at 110–11.

[163]Stephen Billick et al., *A Clinical Study of Competency in Psychiatric Inpatients*, 24 BULL. AM. ACAD. PSYCHIATRY & L. 505 (1996); Norman Poythress, Michele Cascardi, & Lee Ritterband, *Searching for a Satisfactory Zinermon Screen*, 24 BULL. AM. ACAD. PSYCHIATRY & L. 439 (1996). *See generally* GRISSO & APPELBAUM, *supra* note 117.

[164]Steven K. Hoge et al., *Perceptions of Coercion in the Admission of Voluntary and Involuntary Psychiatric Patients*, 20 INT'L J.L. & PSYCHIATRY 167 (1997).

[165]Nancy Bennett et al., *Inclusion, Motivation, and Good Faith: The Morality of Coercion in Mental Hospital Admission*, 11 BEHAV. SCI. & L. 295, 305 (1993).

[166]*Id.* at 305; *see also* Nancy Bennett et al., *Inclusion, Motivation and Good Faith: The Morality of Coercion in Mental Hospital Admission*, 13 DEVS. IN MENT. HEALTH L. 25 (1993).

[167]As of November 14, 1999, there have been *no* cites to the MacArthur literature in the case law.

whether the state adequately proved the "necessary causal nexus" between a patient's mental disorder and her inability to provide for her own needs or her status as a danger to herself,[168] or whether it so proved that another patient was "unable to care for her basic needs."[169] And the New Jersey Supreme Court—long a pioneer in this area[170]—struck down a court rule allowing for the involuntary civil commitment of minors based solely on need for "intensive institutional psychiatric therapy"[171] with these words:

> The State assuredly has a deep and abiding interest in insuring the mental health and well-being of its children. That interest clearly authorizes the State to provide treatment and care for children who suffer from mental illness, and who may benefit from such care. However, that interest, while significant, is not sufficiently compelling to justify the curtailment of a child's liberty interests by involuntary commitment to a psychiatric hospital. . . . "[I]n the specific context of involuntary commitment to a mental hospital where the deprivation of liberty is very great, and the possibility of stigmatization is very real, the mere possibility of benefit is not enough to justify such official paternalism[.]". . . . cf. Lois A. Weithorn, Mental Hospitalization of Troublesome Youth: An Analysis of Skyrocketing Admission Rates, 40 Stan. L. Rev. 773, 797 (1988) (noting inappropriate hospitalization can have serious adverse psychological consequences that must be considered when weighing compelling interests at stake in authorizing involuntary commitment).
>
> There has been some recognition that in the case of minors a need-for-treatment standard does not express a State interest sufficiently compelling to warrant a child's loss of liberty through involuntary civil commitment. See Johnson v. Solomon, 484 F. Supp. 278, 284 (D. Md. 1979) (ruling that need-of-care standard did not satisfy due process "in light of the serious nature of the child's loss of liberty," citing Colyar v. Third Judicial District Court, 469 F. Supp. 424, 429 (D. Utah 1979) (ruling in adult commitment case that only compelling state interest sufficient to offset loss of individual liberties at stake in commitment process would be state's interest in protecting citizens who posed danger to themselves). We, therefore, determine that a standard based only on the "need of intensive [institutional] psychiatric therapy" as the condition for the involuntary commitment of a minor does not vindicate a compelling state interest, and is insufficient to protect the individual liberty interests of such a minor. We hold that the involuntary commitment of a minor who is mentally ill and found to be in need of intensive institutional psychiatric therapy may not be undertaken without a finding based on clear and convincing evidence that the minor without such care is a danger to others or self.[172]

But these cases are the rarities. Their *lack* of sanism and pretextuality stands out in stark contrast to the vast majority of reported decisions in this area of the law.

"Other" Populations

Any study of the role of sanism and pretextuality in the involuntary civil commitment process must also consider the case law and literature that has developed around the question of "other populations" subject to the process. Are there significant differences in the way we construct the "standard" involuntary civil commitment case and the way we construct a

---

[168]State v. Gjerde, 935 P.2d 1224 (Or. App. 1997).

[169]State v. Headings, 914 P.2d 1129 (Or. App. 1996).

[170]*See, e.g.* State v. Krol, 344 A.2d 289 (N.J. 1975) (defining dangerousness); State v. Fields, 390 A.2d 574 (N.J. 1978) (extending periodic review rights to insanity acquittees); *In re* S. L., 462 A.2d 1252 (N.J. 1983) (establishing category of "discharged pending placement").

[171]*Matter of* Commitment of N. N., 679 A.2d 1174 (N.J. 1996).

[172]*Id.* at 1183–84.

case involving, for example, a juvenile patient or an outpatient?[173] In the next section, I will briefly review the law as it applies to these populations and then consider the role of sanism and pretextuality in the development of this area of jurisprudence.

Juvenile Commitments[174]

Traditionally, in virtually all states, parents could commit their children to mental institutions without any sort of due process hearing or other form of judicial scrutiny.[175] The child, in the words of James Ellis, was denied access to "virtually all procedural protections—notice, hearing, appellate review, and *habeas corpus*—rights afforded all other patients institutionalized against their will."[176] Although it had traditionally been argued that it was countertherapeutic and psychologically damaging for children to be subject to a judicial hearing at which their parents would testify for their need for commitment,[177] other commentators noted that nearly unfettered parental discretion in the hospital admission process was subject to abuse on a variety of conscious and unconscious levels,[178] a problem especially exacerbated in families of low socioeconomic status.[179] Further, it was also suggested that—given the peculiar double bind in which a psychiatrist is placed when a parent seeks to have a child committed—psychiatrists often could not adequately perform their screening function in the case of juvenile hospital admissions.[180]

The Supreme Court faced the question of juvenile commitments in *Parham v. J. R.*[181] In upholding state's procedures as passing constitutional muster,[182] the Court ruled that (a) the risk of error inherent in parental decision making on the question of institutionalizing a child was sufficiently great to mandate an independent inquiry by a "neutral fact finder" to determine whether statutory admission requirements were met;[183] (b) although the hearing need not be formal or conducted by a judicial officer,[184] the inquiry must "carefully probe the child's background using all available services, including, but not limited to, parents, schools and other social agencies";[185] (c) the decision maker has the authority to refuse to admit a child who does not meet the medical standards for admission; and (d) the need for continued commitment must be reviewed periodically by a similarly independent procedure.[186]

---

[173]There are other "other populations" as well. *See, e.g.,* 1 PERLIN, *supra* note 2, § 2C-7.2–7.2a (2d ed. 1998) (voluntary patients); § 2C-7.5 (2d ed. 1998) (temporary commitments); § 2C-7.4 (2d ed. 1998) (emergency commitments); § 2C-7.7 (2d ed. 1998) ("criminal commitments"). On the question of persons subject to commitment based on their drug dependency, see Thomas Hafemeister & Ari Amirshahi, *Civil Commitment for Drug Dependency: The Judicial Response,* 26 LOY. L.A. L. REV. 39 (1992). On the question of persons so subject based on a diagnosis of tuberculosis, see Carlos Ball & Mark Barnes, *Public Health and Individual Rights: Tuberculosis Control and Detention Procedures in New York City,* 12 YALE L. POL'Y REV. 38 (1994).

[174]This section is generally adapted from PERLIN, *supra* note 1, § 1.35.

[175]James Ellis, *Volunteering Children: Parental Commitment of Minors to Mental Institutions,* 62 CALIF. L. REV. 840, 840 (1974). *See* statutes collected *id.* at n.1.

[176]Ellis, *supra* note 175, at 841.

[177]*Id.* at 843. *See generally* Parham v. J. R., 442 U.S. 584, 602–12 (1979).

[178]*See* Ellis, *supra* note 175, at 850–63.

[179]*Id.* at 851–52.

[180]*Id.* at 863–64.

[181]442 U.S. 584 (1979). The Supreme Court also decided, in tandem, the case of Institutionalized Juveniles v. Secretary of Pub. Welfare, 442 U.S. 640 (1979). *See* 1 PERLIN, *supra* note 2, § 2C-7.1a, at 470–71 (2d ed. 1998).

[182]*Parham,* 442 U.S. at 620–21.

[183]*Id.* at 606.

[184]*Id.* at 607.

[185]*Id.* at 606–07.

[186]*Id.* at 607.

In the course of his opinion for the Court, Chief Justice Burger set out a specific vision of the application of the commitment process to juveniles. First, he discussed the state's interest "in not imposing procedural obstacles that may discourage the mentally ill or their families from seeking needed psychiatric assistance."[187] Next, he focused on the "embarrassing" potential of the contested, interfamilial juvenile commitment process:

> The *parens patriae* interest in helping parents care for the mental health of their children cannot be fulfilled if the parents are unwilling to take advantage of the opportunities because the admission process is too onerous, too embarrassing or too contentious. It is surely not idle to speculate as to how many parents who believe they are acting in good faith would forego state-provided hospital care if such care is contingent on participation in an adversary proceeding designed to probe their motives and other private family matters in seeking the voluntary admission.

> The state also has a genuine interest in allocating priority to the diagnosis and treatment of patients as soon as they are admitted to a hospital rather than to time-consuming procedural minuets before the admission. One factor that must be considered is the utilization of the time of psychiatrists, psychologists and other behavioral specialists in preparing for and participating in hearings rather than performing the task for which their special training has fitted them. Behavioral experts in courtrooms and hearings are of little help to patients.[188]

There is no explanation offered about *how* the admission process is "too onerous, too embarrassing or too contentious," nor is there any basis suggested for the speculation that a significant percentage of parents would forego state-provided hospital care if it is "contingent on participation in an adversary proceeding."[189] Similarly, neither data nor theory is offered about *why* such hearings would be "time-consuming procedural minuets."[190]

The Chief Justice in *Parham* characterized the questions in juvenile admission matters as being "essentially medical in character,"[191] and although he acknowledged the "fallibility of medical and psychiatric diagnosis"—citing to his own concurring opinion in *O'Connor v. Donaldson*[192]—he added that he did not "accept the notion that the shortcomings of specialists can always be avoided by shifting the decision from a trained specialist using the traditional tools of medical science to an untrained judge or administrative hearing officer after a judicial-type hearing."[193]

Finally, the opinion stated its major philosophical premise: that hearings would intrude into the parent–child relationship:

> Another problem with requiring a formalized, factfinding hearing lies in the danger it poses for significant intrusion into the parent–child relationship. Pitting the parents and child as adversaries often will be at odds with the presumption that parents act in the best interests of their child. It is one thing to require a neutral physician to make a careful review of the parents'

---

[187]*Id.* at 605.

[188]*Id.* at 605–06 (footnote omitted).

[189]Michael L. Perlin, *An Invitation to the Dance: An Empirical Response to Chief Justice Warren Burger's "Time-Consuming Procedural Minuets" Theory in Parham v. J. R.,* 9 BULL. AM. ACAD. PSYCHIATRY AND L. 149, 151 (1981). *See generally Brief of Amicus* N.J. Dep't of the Pub. Advocate, Parham v. J. R., 442 U.S. 584 (1979), at 29–51 (evidence "persuasive" that procedural due process safeguards are beneficial to "all parties" in juvenile commitment matters).

[190]Perlin, *supra* note 189, at 152.

[191]*Parham*, 442 U.S. at 609.

[192]422 U.S. 563, 584 (1975) (Burger, C. J., concurring).

[193]*Parham*, 442 U.S. at 609.

decision in order to make sure it is proper from a medical standpoint; it is a wholly different matter to employ an adversary contest to ascertain whether the parents' motivation is consistent with the child's interests.[194]

This opinion was sharply criticized by Justice Brennan in a three-justice opinion, concurring in part and dissenting in part.[195] This opinion charged that the majority "ignore[d] reality [when it] assume[d] blindly that parents act in their children's best interests when making commitment decisions."[196] Although the minority agreed that *pre*admission adversarial hearings "might traumatize both parent and child and make the child's eventual return to his family more difficult,"[197] it recommended the institution of *post*admission commitment hearings: "The interest in avoiding family discord would be less significant at this stage, since the family autonomy already will have been fractured by the institutionalization of the child. In any event, post-admission hearings are unlikely to disrupt family relationships."[198]

No modern U.S. Supreme Court civil case dealing with the rights of the mentally handicapped has been criticized as consistently or as thoroughly as have been *Parham* and *Institutionalized Juveniles.*[199] The decisions have been criticized for helping create "a greased runway leading to the incarceration of handicapped children in institutions,"[200] for their "confusing and inaccurate" interpretations of the lower court decisions,[201] for "misstatements" of the factual record of the cases,[202] and for "accord[ing] little weight to the juveniles' interest in self respect."[203] As Stephen Morse noted, "As is so often true in mental health cases, the Court based its opinion on a number of factual assumptions that are simply unsupportable."[204]

Gail Perry and Gary Melton similarly argued that the opinion improperly relied on the technique of judicial notice "to carve rather elaborate, if one-sided, images of the

---

[194]*Id.* at 610 (footnote omitted).

[195]*Id.* at 625 (Brennan, J., concurring in part and dissenting in part).

[196]*Id.* at 625, 632 (Brennan, J., concurring in part and dissenting in part).

[197]*Id.* at 633 (Brennan, J., concurring in part and dissenting in part).

[198]*Id.* at 635 (Brennan, J., concurring in part and dissenting in part).

[199]*See, e.g.,* 1 PERLIN, *supra* note 2, § 2C-7.1a, at 471–72 n.1239 (2d ed. 1998) (citing articles).

[200]Allen Edward Schoenberger, *"Voluntary" Commitment of Mentally Ill or Retarded Children: Child Abuse by the Supreme Court,* 7 U. DAYTON L. REV. 1, 30–31 (1981).

[201]Schoenberger, *supra* note 200, at 4.

[202]*See id.* at 4–7.

[203]*Id.* at 30. In one of the most sharply worded critiques, the counsel for plaintiffs in *Institutionalized Juveniles* has written,

> The decisions by the Supreme Court in *Institutionalized Juveniles* and *Parham* ignore the facts, distort the law and condemn children to second-class citizenship. The physical conditions, isolation and dangers of day-to-day life in institutions are ignored. Inevitable bias and conflict of interest of institutional professional staff are dangerously and incorrectly underplayed. Also overlooked and underdiscussed is the critical necessity of a hearing and a children's advocate to assure noninstitutional care whenever possible. Those children most in need of protection, the youngest and most disabled, are denied any protection at all. Children who are already under the State's control and without the limited protection parents can provide are denied hearings as well.

David Ferleger, *Special Problems in the Commitment of Children, in* 1 LEGAL RIGHTS OF MENTALLY DISABLED PERSONS 255 (Practicing Law Institute, Paul Friedman ed. 1979).

[204]Stephen Morse, *Treating Crazy People Less Specially,* 90 W. VA. L. REV. 353, 382 n.64 (1987); *see generally* Gail Perry & Gary Melton, *Precedential Value of Judicial Notice of Social Facts:* Parham *as an Example,* 22 J. FAM. L. 633 (1984) (sharply criticizing *Parham* decision); Perlin *supra* note 189.

functioning of American families, mental hospitals and judicial proceedings,"[205] charging that, without supporting evidence, the Chief Justice "made no fewer than fifteen empirical assumptions, many of them directly contrary to existing social-science research, about the psychology and sociology of [juvenile mental] institutions."[206] They concluded, "The *Parham* case is an example of the Supreme Court's taking advantage of the free rein on social facts to promulgate a dozen or so of its own by employing one tentacle of the judicial notice doctrine. The Court's opinion is filled with social facts of questionable veracity, accompanied by the authority to propel these facts into subsequent case law and, therefore, a spiral of less than rational legal policy making.[207] In an earlier article, I agreed "in summary, in spite of the Chief Justice's assertions, the credible—and uncontroverted—evidence before the Court could only lead to the inescapable conclusion that counseled due process hearings for juveniles are necessary, effective and ameliorative; the suggestion that they are merely 'time-consuming procedural minuets' distorts the fact, the law and reality."[208]

Parham may be the Supreme Court's most sanist *and* most pretextual civil mental health law case. The Court's utter failure to offer empirical support for any of its social science speculations is legal pretextuality at its most insidious. Its refusal to take seriously the possibility of institutional bias and conflict of interests, its disregard of the interest of the juveniles who are the subject of the commitment orders, and its lack of concern about institutional realities all demonstrate equally insidious sanism.

Outpatient Commitments

Cases such as *O'Connor v. Donaldson*[209] and *Addington v. Texas*[210] made it clear that patients cannot be forced to stay in institutions once they are no longer dangerous to themselves or others.[211] State court decisions such as *State v. Fields*[212] and *Fasulo v. Arafeh*[213] extended procedural due process commitment protections to periodic review

---

[205]Perry & Melton, *supra* note 204, at 634. *See also* Gary B. Melton, *Family and Mental Hospitals as Myths: Civil Commitment of Minors, in* CHILDREN, MENTAL HEALTH AND THE LAW 151, 155 (N. Dickon Reppucci et al. eds. 1984); Gary B. Melton, *The Significance of Law in the Everyday Lives of Children and Families,* 22 GA. L. REV. 851 (1988).

[206]Perry & Melton, *supra* note 204, at 635.

[207]*Id.* at 645. *See also, e.g.,* Winsor C. Schmidt Jr., *Considerations of Social Science in a Reconsideration of* Parham v. J. R. *and the Commitment of Children to Public Mental Institutions,* 13 J. PSYCHIATRY & L. 339 (1985) (court used behavioral science in an "unsophisticated and non-comprehensive manner for support of specific value positions"); Perlin, *supra* note 189, at 161–62.

[208]Perlin, *supra* note 189, at 161–62. For a more recent empirical inquiry into the actual capacities of juvenile inpatients to consent to hospitalization, see Kenneth C. Casimir & Stephen Billick, *Competency in Adolescent Inpatients,* 22 BULL. AM. ACAD. PSYCHIATRY & L. 19 (1994) (only 22% of adolescents studied met both legal and clinical criteria for competency).

[209]422 U.S. 563, 576 (1975) (a state cannot confine, without more, a nondangerous individual who is capable of surviving safely in freedom by him- or herself or with the help of family or friends merely because he or she is mentally ill).

[210]441 U.S. 418, 431–33 (1979) (clear and convincing proof is needed to sustain involuntary civil commitment).

[211]This section is generally adapted from PERLIN, *supra* note 1, § 1.37.

[212]390 A.2d 574, 583 (N.J. 1978) (the state must renew its authority to continue to deprive a committed individual of his or her liberty at each periodic review hearing).

[213]378 A.2d 553, 556 (Conn. 1977) (the due process clause of the Connecticut constitution mandates that involuntarily confined civilly committed individuals be granted periodic judicial reviews of the propriety of their continued confinement).

hearings.[214] Questions of competency are not generally cognizable at such hearings where the question is the patient's present dangerousness.[215]

Yet the public's perception of deinstitutionalization as being fueled by "inappropriate" civil liberties decisions such as *O'Connor* or *Lessard v. Schmidt*[216] attributes homelessness, in an important way, to the inevitable outcome of such decisions:[217] Some patients, although perhaps not "technically"[218] dangerous to others (especially where they have committed no "overt act")[219] inevitably become dangerous and thus, more likely commitable after release because, in the vernacular sense of the phrase, they are not competent to make life decisions.[220]

In partial response, attention has turned to the option of outpatient commitment (OPC) as a solution to the perceived problems. The American Psychiatric Association has recommended that legislatures revise involuntary civil commitment laws to allow for this option and that existing OPC laws be "more widely used."[221] Building on the development and expansion of the concept of the least restrictive alternative in involuntary civil commitment procedures,[222] most states permit some form of outpatient commitment.[223]

---

[214]*See generally* 1 PERLIN, *supra* note 1, § 2C-6.5c (2d ed. 1998) (discussing the right of involuntarily confined civilly committed individuals to periodic judicial review).

[215]*Cf.* Diana Brahams & Malcolm Weller, *Crime and Homelessness Among the Mentally Ill,* 54 MEDICO–LEGAL J. 42, 47–48 (1986) (in England, "no decision" as to whether a mentally ill patient can form the necessary intent to "voluntarily" discharge him- or herself from a psychiatric hospital). *But see In re* S. L., 462 A.2d 1252, 1258–59 (N.J. 1983) (ordering placement review hearings for patients no longer dangerous but unable to survive independently in the community).

[216]349 F. Supp. 1078 (E.D. Wis. 1972) (applying procedural and substantive due process to involuntary civil commitment decision making).

[217]*Cf.* E. FULLER TORREY, NOWHERE TO GO: THE TRAGIC ODYSSEY OF THE HOMELESS MENTALLY ILL 37, 156–60 (1988), with Hendrick Wagenaar & Dan A. Lewis, *Ironies of Inclusion: Social Class and Deinstitutionalization,* 14 J. HEALTH POL., POL'Y & L. 503, 506 (1989) (extension of civil rights to persons with mental disabilities has "irrevocably altered" their relationships with their therapists). On the therapeutic potential of the legal process for mentally ill individuals, see generally David Wexler, *Grave Disability and Family Therapy: The Therapeutic Potential of Civil Libertarian Commitment Codes,* 9 INT'L J.L. & PSYCHIATRY 39, 54 (1986) (the very process of gathering evidence of a person's commitability under a libertarian law may operate therapeutically to render commitment unnecessary). *See generally* Wexler, *supra* (discussing the therapeutic aspects of civil commitment hearings, voluntary confinement compared to forced hospitalizations, and the roles of judges and lawyers in the process); Ensminger & Liguori, *supra* note 78 (the civil commitment process contains considerable potential for therapeutic effects on the involuntarily committed patient); Perlin, *supra* note 124, at 981–82 (discussing Supreme Court's failure to consider therapeutic outcomes in juvenile commitment cases).

[218]On the question of the way "moral" psychiatrists may consciously subvert the legislative commitment standards to ensure commitment of individuals who may not "technically" meet such standards, *see* Michael Bagby & Leslie Atkinson, *The Effects of Legislative Reform on Civil Commitment Admission Rates: A Critical Analysis,* 6 BEHAV. SCI. & L. 45, 58–59 (1988); Michael L. Perlin, *Morality and Pretextuality, Psychiatry and Law: Of "Ordinary Common Sense," Heuristic Reasoning and Cognitive Dissonance,* 19 BULL. AM. ACAD. PSYCHIATRY & L. 131 (1991).

[219]*See* 1 PERLIN, *supra* note 2, § 2A-4.5, at 152–56 (2d ed. 1998).

[220]*See, e.g.,* Pamela J. Fischer & William R. Breakey, *Homelessness and Mental Health: An Overview,* 14 INT'L J. MENTAL HEALTH 6, 27–32 (1986); Virginia Aldigé Hiday & Theresa Scheid-Cook, *The North Carolina Experience With Outpatient Commitment: A Critical Appraisal,* 10 INT'L J.L. & PSYCHIATRY 215, 215–16 (1987).

[221]*See* Robert D. Miller, *Commitment to Outpatient Treatment: A National Survey,* 36 HOSP. & COMMUNITY PSYCHIATRY 265, 267 (1985) (although OPC can be effective for those who will not obtain treatment voluntarily, states must seek input from clinicians to properly develop OPC procedures).

[222]On the relationship between the "least restrictive alternative" doctrine and civil commitment law, see 1 PERLIN, *supra* note 2, §§ 2C-5.3 to -5.3e, at 417–34 (2d ed. 1998).

[223]Ingo Keilitz & Terry Hall, *State Statutes Governing Involuntary Outpatient Civil Commitment,* 9 MENT. & PHYS. DIS. L. REP. 378 (1985). *See id.* at 379 n.3 & *id.* at 380–97. The authors define "outpatient commitment" as "the dispositional options (lying between inpatient hospitalization and outright release) available to a civil court after an adjudication' of involuntary civil commitment." *Id.* at 378.

Supporters of OPC argue that such statutes are necessary to prevent a discrete group of the mentally ill from "slip[ping] through [the law's] cracks[:] [t]he chronic mentally ill who failed to obtain treatment on their own, who then decompensated and exhibited bizarre behavior, [but who] could not be civilly committed until they did something dangerous even though they had a history of becoming dangerous in the later stages of decompensation following the bizarre behavior."[224]

Such statutes would ensure that these individuals—a group that appears to include many of those persons with mental illness who have been deinstitutionalized who are most susceptible to homelessness—have enhanced access to what proponents have characterized as protective liberty through broad-based treatment mechanisms in an atmosphere that would overcome "rehabilitative inertia."[225] Its opponents respond that outpatient commitment means little more than disguised "benevolent coercion" accompanied by excessive state intervention; where implemented, it will subvert the dangerousness standard, lead to significant quality control problems, defeat the right to refuse treatment, and "undermin[e] therapeutic relationships."[226]

In North Carolina, a state usually viewed as a trailblazer in this regard,[227] the outpatient civil commitment law[228] allows an examining mental health professional to recommend outpatient commitment in the case of a mentally ill patient[229] "capable of surviving safely in the community with available supervision from family, friends, or others,"[230] where the individual is "in need of treatment in order to prevent further disability or deterioration which would predictably result in dangerousness,"[231] and where the patient is unable to make an informed decision "to seek voluntary treatment or comply with recommended

---

[224]Hiday & Scheid-Cook, *supra* note 220, at 215.

[225]*See* Edward Mulvey et al., *The Promise and Peril of Involuntary Outpatient Commitment*, 42 Am. Psychologist 571, 577–79 (1987) ("involuntary outpatient commitment rests on the state's obligation to provide positive liberty rather than simple noninterference, the likelihood of more efficacious treatment through broad-based intervention, and the possibility of initiating a positive cycle of community involvement"). For a recent perspective urging the adoption of OPC laws, *see* Sally Satel, *Real Help for the Mentally Ill*, N.Y. Times, Jan. 7, 1999, at A31.

[226]*See* Mulvey et al., *supra* note 225, at 575–77 (setting forth opposing arguments to OPC that the costs to individual rights and professional relationships are too great).

[227]Keilitz & Hall, *supra* note 223, at 378, quoting *Four States Enact New Mental Health Statutes in 1984*, 2 Ment. Health Rep. 3 (Jan. 1985).

[228]N.C. Gen. Stat. §§ 122C-263 to 122C-275 (1997)

[229]N.C. Gen. Stat. § 122C-263(d)(1)(a) (1997).

[230]N.C. Gen. Stat. § 122C-263(d)(1)(b) (1997).

[231]N.C. Gen. Stat. § 122C-263(d)(1)(c) (1997).

See, e.g., Matter of Mental Condition of W.R.B., 411 N.W.2d 142, 143 (Wis. App. 1987), *rev. den.,* 416 N.W.2d 297 (Wis. 1987).

> The clear intent of the legislature . . . was to avoid the "revolving door" phenomenon whereby there must be proof of a recent overt act to extend the commitment but because the patient was still under treatment, no overt acts occurred and the patient was released only to commit a dangerous act and be recommitted. The result was a vicious circle of treatment, release, overt act, recommitment.

Statutes typically look at medication compliance as one of the criteria for invoking OPC, *see, e.g.,* Wis. Stat. Ann. § 51.20(dm) (1998) (OPC permissible if court finds dangerousness of patient "is likely to be controlled with appropriate medication administered on an outpatient basis"); Tenn. Code Ann. § 33-6-201(b)(2) (1997) (allowing OPC where patient is subject to the "obligation to participate in any medically appropriate outpatient treatment, including . . . medication . . ."), and case law seems to explicitly endorse this use of OPC, see, for example, *In re* Anderson, 140 Cal. Rptr. 546, 550 (Cal. 1977) (medication an appropriate condition of outpatient treatment). *Cf., In re* Richardson, 481 A.2d 473, 479 n.5 (D.C. 1984) ("Not every instance of the outpatient's failure to take prescribed medication or attend therapy sessions justifies the conclusion that he is not cooperating with the treatment program").

treatment."[232] Such patients are then given the name and address of the outpatient treatment center to which they are to report.[233] If they fail to appear, they may be taken into custody and then taken to the center for evaluation pending a judicial hearing.[234]

If the hearing judge finds that such patients meet the criteria considered initially by the examining mental health professional, he or she shall order an outpatient commitment, showing on the face of the commitment order the name of the treatment center or physician "responsible for the management and supervision of the [patient's] outpatient commitment."[235] If the court finds that patients are mentally ill and a danger to themselves or others, however, it may order inpatient commitment or "a combination of inpatient and outpatient commitment" for a 90-day period.[236] Prior to ordering outpatient commitment, however, the court shall make findings of fact as to such treatment is available.[237]

Empirical reviews have been mixed. In one study, researchers who examined all court-ordered outpatient commitments in one court for a two-year period found a high success rate for the patients involved;[238] fewer than 13% of patients involved were rehospitalized during the time frame,[239] leading the researchers to conclude that such commitment "has been effective in providing treatment and control of dangerousness while enabling respondents to maintain their roles and networks in familiar surroundings," and was "not only more rational in terms of human costs, but also . . . more rational in terms of financial costs to the taxpayer."[240] Another North Carolina survey conducted by other researchers, however, reported that the new statute "did not seem to have made a significant difference in the use of outpatient commitment,"[241] reporting that, although the number of cases in which hospital staff recommended outpatient treatment significantly increased after the effective date of statutory change,[242] the *percentage* of cases studied in which outpatient commitment was ordered actually decreased slightly.[243]

The second group of researchers concluded that what they perceived as outpatient commitment's lack of success is attributable to a combination of factors: (a) court reluctance to use outpatient commitment when "dangerousness" is a commitment criteria; (b) reluctance of community facility staff to treat unwilling patients; (c) lack of interest by community facility staff in outpatient commitment; and (d) lack of knowledge about the procedures involved.[244]

---

[232]N.C. GEN. STAT. § 122C-263(d)(1)(d) (1997).

[233]N.C. GEN. STAT. § 122C-263(f) (1997).

[234]N.C. GEN. STAT. § 122C-265(a) (1997).

[235]N.C. GEN. STAT. § 122C-267(h) (1997). *See also* N.C. GEN. STAT. § 122C-271(b)(1) (1997).

[236]N.C. GEN. STAT. § 122C-271(b)(2) (1997).

[237]N.C. GEN. STAT. § 122C-271(b)(4) (1997). *Cf.* 1 PERLIN, *supra* note 2, § 2D-5.3d (2d ed. 1998).

[238]Virginia Aldigé Hiday & Rodney R. Goodman, *The Least Restrictive Alternative to Involuntary Hospitalization, Outpatient Commitment: Its Use and Effectiveness,* 10 J. PSYCHIATRY & L. 81, 88 (1982).

[239]*Id.* at 81.

[240]*Id.* at 91.

[241]Robert D. Miller & Paul B. Fiddleman, *Involuntary Civil Commitment in North Carolina: The Result of the 1979 Statutory Changes,* 60 N.C. L. REV. 985, 1013 (1982).

[242]*Id.* at 1010 (staff recommended outpatient commitment for 44% of committed patients who were committed to outpatient treatment prior to the laws effective date and 77% of those committed afterward).

[243]*Id.* (percentage dropped from 4.7% to 3.1%). The authors reported further that, of the 35 outpatient commitment cases studied, only 1 satisfied all the requisite statutory provisions. *Id.* at 1013, and *see id.* at n.118.

[244]Robert D. Miller & Paul B. Fiddleman, *Outpatient Commitment: Treatment in the Least Restrictive Environment,* 35 HOSP. & COMMUNITY PSYCHIATRY 147, 149–51 (1984). *See also* Hiday & Scheid-Cook, *supra* note 220, at 230 (empirical study suggests that extent of community mental health center "dedication to making [outpatient commitment] work" important variable in success of outpatient commitment status).

Subsequent empirical investigations have been more optimistic, finding that patients committed to outpatient treatment were "significantly more likely" than either released patients or involuntarily hospitalized patients to use aftercare services and continue in treatment,[245] than, of those outpatient committees who participated in treatment, the outpatient status "works in terms of keeping patients in treatment and on medication, increasing compliance, permitting residence outside an institution and social interaction outside the home, and maintaining patients in the community with few dangerous episodes,"[246] and that outpatient commitment induces compliance and leads to treatment maintenance even among "revolving-door" patients.[247]

Another recent analysis concluded that although outpatient commitment succeeds in terms of keeping patients on medication, thus extending their maintenance in the community,[248] its ultimate success may depend on the dedication of community mental health centers "to making [it] work."[249] Where centers pay only "lip service" to outpatient commitment, the law becomes undermined.[250] This is especially troubling in light of E. Fuller Torrey's broad indictment of community mental health centers (CMHCs): They have never provided aftercare for expatients and have exhibited attitudes toward public hospitals ranging from "difficult" to "adversarial."[251] In their desire to treat the "worried well"— patients with inter- and intrapersonal problems amenable to counseling and psychotherapy—CMHCs have historically rejected precisely the population that OPC was designed to serve.[252] Members of the Oregon Task Force on Civil Commitment have reported, for instance, that commitment investigators involved in that state's commitment program expressed concern about the lack of community resources inhibiting the diversion of clients from the inpatient involuntary civil commitment system.[253]

In a powerful critique from a civil libertarian perspective, Steven Schwartz and Cathy Costanzo focused on outpatient commitment as "an expression of the much enlarged authority which developed over the past century to promote the health or interests of persons considered to be mentally infirm."[254] Schwartz and Costanzo characterized outpatient

---

[245]See Virginia Aldigé Hiday & Theresa Scheid-Cook, A Follow-Up of Chronic Patients Committed to Outpatient Treatment, 40 HOSP. & COMMUNITY PSYCHIATRY 52 (1989).

[246]Hiday & Scheid-Cook, supra note 220, at 229.

[247]Virginia Aldigé Hiday & Theresa Scheid-Cook, Outpatient Commitment for "Revolving Door" Patients, 179 J. NERVOUS & MENT. DIS. 83 (1991).

[248]See Hiday & Scheid-Cook, supra note 220, at 229.

[249]Id. at 230; see also Note, 1986 Amendments to Georgia's Mental Health Statutes: The Latest Attempt to Provide a Solution to the Problem of the Chronically Mentally Ill, 36 EMORY L.J. 1313, 1344 n.183 (1987), quoting Gail S. Perry, The Status of Mental Health Partial Hospitalization Services in the Atlanta Region, in 2 EXPLORING MENTAL HEALTH PARAMETERS 66 (1976) (concluding that "even if clinicians support community treatment in theory, the attitudes, prejudices, and non-coordination of support staff in a program of [community] treatment can be quite debilitating in lowering the quality of an existing program and in preventing an increase in the scale of the program'").

[250]See Hiday & Scheid-Cook, supra note 220, at 230–31; see also id. at 230: Some centers paid lip service to OPC, treating a respondent ordered to them as another deinstitutionalized chronic patient who soon would have to be readmitted to the hospital or as another problem patient with whom no one could do anything. They showed little understanding of the intent or provisions of the law. Some primary clinicians at these centers did not know that OPC was not for alcoholics, that the sheriff could be called to bring in a respondent, or that the OPC could be extended.

[251]E. FULLER TORREY, supra note 217, at 142–51.

[252]Id.; see also Steven Schwartz & Cathy Costanzo, Compelling Treatment in the Community: Distorted Doctrine and Violated Values, 20 LOY. L.A. L. REV. 1329, 1386–89 (1987).

[253]Benton McFarland et al., Investigators' and Judges' Opinions About Civil Commitment, 17 BULL. AM. ACAD. PSYCHIATRY & L. 15 (1989).

[254]Schwartz & Costanzo, supra note 252, at 1346.

commitment as a "significant distortion of the historical purpose and benign motivation of the parens patriae principle"[255] and, primarily, as a "guise for substantially modifying the criteria for state-imposed psychiatric intervention."[256] In addition, Susan Stefan has unpacked outpatient commitment to differentiate "traditional" OPCs (premised on least restrictive alternative constructs and conditional release schemata) from the postdeinstitutionalization model that she has characterized as "preventative commitment."[257] According to Stefan, by focusing on the specter of deterioration, an implied presumption of incompetency, and an assumed availability of treatment,[258] preventative commitment "broadens the class of people subject to commitment, and expands the conditions under which the state can intervene in a person's life."[259] Although this is clearly a laudable goal to critics such as Torrey and Lamb, this expansion inadequately considers the additional procedural and substantive due process dilemmas regarding the right to treatment, the right to refuse treatment, and rights of economic sovereignty that are raised by the possibility of a greatly expanded use of this commitment status.[260] In short, this attempt to solve the perceived deinstitutionalization–homelessness link through focusing on a patient's competency may not prove to be a panacea at all.[261]

Stefan, Schwartz, and Costanzo focus sharp criticism on precisely the issue that is frequently seen as the lynch pin of OPC's efficiency value: its use as a tool to compel medication compliance in the community.[262] Stefan characterized forced medication as the "core of OPC";[263] Schwartz and Costanzo speculated that OPC "already has or will become synonymous with forced medications."[264] Although the OPC statutes rarely address this issue squarely,[265] they raise serious constitutional, philosophical, and operational concerns that must be addressed.[266] This is especially true when we remind ourselves that, as is the case with all other involuntary commitment mechanisms, it is the socially marginalized, indigent patient—precisely the one in whom CMHCs traditionally have been

---

[255]*Id.* at 1348.

[256]*Id.* at 1404.

[257]Susan Stefan, *Preventive Commitment: The Concept and Its Pitfalls,* 11 MENT. & PHYS. DIS. L. REP. 288, 288 (1987). *See generally* 1 PERLIN, *supra* note 2, §§ 2C-5.3 to -6.1b, at 417–44 (2d ed. 1998) (discussing "least restrictive alternative" and "conditional release" models).

[258]Stefan, *supra* note 257, at 288–91.

[259]*Id.* at 296.

[260]*Id.* at 291–95.

[261]*Id.* at 289; *see also* Schwartz & Costanzo, *supra* note 252, at 1379–80 (arguing that states will not be likely to provide the necessary funds to adequately assist those who will not seek help voluntarily).

[262]*See* Schwartz & Costanzo, *supra* note 252, at 1380–85. *See generally* Bruce Winick, *Competency to Consent to Treatment: The Distinction Between Assent and Objection,* 28 HOUS. L. REV. 15 (1990). *But see* Robert D. Miller & Paul B. Fiddleman, *Outpatient Commitment: Treatment in the Least Restrictive Environment?,* 35 HOSP. & COMMUNITY PSYCHIATRY 147, 149 (1984) (presenting clinicians' arguments that patient's history of psychotic behavior when medication is stopped justifies coercion and continued court supervision).

[263]Stefan, *supra* note 257, at 294; *see also* John LaFond, The Homeless Mentally Ill: Is Coercive Psychiatry the Answer? (Paper presented at annual meeting of American Association of Law Schools, San Francisco, January 1990: tape available through AALS) (in outpatient settings, "drugs—with all their risks—will undoubtedly be the treatment of choice").

[264]Schwartz & Costanzo, *supra* note 252, at 1368.

[265]*See id.* (reporting that as of 1987, "only seven states explicitly authorize[d] [forced] medication as a form of community treatment," although no OPC statutes precluded it).

[266]*See id.* at 1382; *see also* Mulvey et al., *supra* note 225, at 580–81. *See also* Elizabeth Furlong, *Coercion in the Community: The Application of* Rogers *Guardianship to Outpatient Commitment,* 21 N. ENG. J. CRIM. & CIV. CONFINEMENT 485 (1995).

disinterested—who likely will be disproportionately represented in any outpatient commitment caseload.[267]

Researchers are beginning to confront the extent to which OPC can be pretextual. A recent systemic analysis thus concluded,

> Coercion and paternalism are increasing areas of concern for community-based mental health treatment systems. Coercion refers not just to court-ordered treatment, but to all ways that staff controls a client's behavior. Clinicians in comprehensive community treatment systems can often control the client's money, influence access to housing, or use contact with family or probation officers to increase adherence to treatment regimens. The same qualities of being tenacious and involved in other areas of the client's life that allows assertive community treatment . . . to be effective, also allow them to be coercive.[268]

Other researchers have warned of another pretext. A British study concluded, "If patients are to be obliged to be subject to compulsory orders in the community as well as in hospital, to suffer further loss of rights, of privacy or to refuse to consent to treatment, then they are entitled to expect at least a reasonable standard of care. This places an obligation on authorities to provide that care."[269] If this standard is not met, then OPC commitment is pretextual.

In at least two Indiana cases, by way of example, outpatients were held by trial courts to be in *criminal* contempt for failing to adhere to medication regimens. In one, the appellate court found that the trial court erred in so doing without determining whether the patient's conduct was "willful [or] a manifestation of mental illness;"[270] in the other, after an intermediate appellate court affirmed the lower court's finding where patient's counsel expressly stated that the refusal was "willful and voluntary,"[271] the state supreme court reversed, holding that the trial court had no authority either to order the patient to take medication as an outpatient or to hold him in contempt for refusing to do so.[272]

Pretexts in OPC decision making are also reflected in the recent Michigan appellate case of *In re K. B.*[273] K. B. had been institutionalized on at least five occasions over a 10-year period.[274] On November 18, 1993, she was discharged from the hospital and enrolled in an outpatient treatment program.[275] Less than three weeks later, program officials notified the

---

[267]*See* Note, *supra* note 249, at 1323–24, 1341.

[268]Ronald Diamond, *Coercion in the Community: Issues for Mature Treatment Systems*, 66 NEW DIRECTIONS FOR MENT. HEALTH SERVICES 3, 16 (Summer 1995). *Cf.* Francis Boudreau & Philip Lambert, *Compulsory Community Treatment? II. The Collision of Views and Complexities Involved: Is It "The Best Possible Alternative"?* 12 CANAD. J. COMMUNITY MENTAL HEALTH 79, 90 (1993) ("Appropriate housing, jobs and skills training, educational programs, recreation, child care, home visits: isn't it likely that these are the determining factor of 'success' and not the compulsory nature of the 'treatment'?"); *see also generally* Francis Boudreau & Philip Lambert, *Compulsory Community Treatment? I: Ontario Stakeholders' Responses to "Helping Those Who Won't Help Themselves,"* 12 CANAD. J. COMMUNITY MENT. HEALTH 57 (1993).

[269]Tim Exworthy, *Compulsory Care in the Community: A Review of the Proposals for Compulsory Supervision and Treatment of the Mentally Ill in the Community,* 5 CRIM. BEHAV. & MENT. HEALTH 218, 237–38 (1995).

[270]*Matter of* Utley, 565 N.E.2d 1152, 1156–57 (Ind. App. 1991) (affirming judgment because patient did not attack underlying commitment order).

[271]*Matter of* Tarpley, 566 N.E.2d 71, 77 (Ind. App. 1991), *cf. id.* at 77, 78 (Sullivan, J., dissenting) (counsel's concession does not "exclude the very real possibility, if not probability, that the refusal was induced by Tarpley's severe delusions and withdrawal from reality").

[272]*Matter of* Tarpley, 581 N.E.2d 1251, 1252 (1991), *reh'g denied* (1992).

[273]562 N.W.2d 208 (Mich. App. 1997).

[274]*Id.* at 209.

[275]*Id.*

probate court that she was refusing to take her medication because she feared it would ''harm her unborn child.'' Two days later, the probate court met with her treatment case manager and ordered her rehospitalized.[276] She then appealed this order, arguing that rehospitalization without a hearing violated her due process rights. This appeal was denied by the probate court, and that order was affirmed by the circuit court. She then appealed to the state court of appeals.

The Michigan statute central to the case provides for an involuntary civil commitment hearing before a judge or jury prior to a person's commitment.[277] At such a hearing, the individual is entitled to a ''full court hearing'' that includes the right to be present at the hearing, to legal representation, to a jury trial, and to an independent medical evaluation.[278] After a person is found to meet the criteria for treatment, the probate court may order hospitalization, alternative treatment that does not include hospitalization, or combined hospitalization and alternative treatment.[279]

The court of appeals affirmed the decision. Although the court conceded that it was ''settled that the revocation of a conditional release from hospitalization involves a liberty interest that should be afforded due process protection,''[280] it rejected the patient's argument that the lack of a hearing brought with it an unacceptable risk of an erroneous hospitalization:

> This risk is significantly reduced because the statute provides many protections to the individual in the original proceedings and because of the limited time frame that the court orders may encompass. The court's rehospitalization order must be entered less than ninety days from the original treatment determination. Moreover, the more distant the rehospitalization determination is from the original order, the less significant the duration of the deprivation of liberty would be because the treatment is capped at a total of ninety days from the original order.[281]

The court also characterized the probable value of such a hearing as ''minimal,'' relying on the case of *In re Richardson*[282] for the position that ''the question is peculiarly medical in nature and more properly left to medical professionals as opposed to the judiciary.''[283] Finally, the court found that the government's interests in protecting the individual and the general public to be ''significant.''[284] ''In this case, respondent, who was pregnant, had shown a history of suicidal behavior and was refusing to take prescribed medications. The delays attendant with requiring a prior hearing before rehospitalization may have proved detrimental to respondent and her fetus.''[285]

Consider also in this context the Oregon case of *State v. Vonahlefeld*.[286] The appellate court relied on the skimpiest legislative history (an unexplained modification of a bill's final draft that had been characterized as ''minor'' at the legislative hearing) to find that a person

---

[276]*Id.* at 209–210. *K. B.*, 562 N.W.2d at 210.

[277]MICH. COMP. L. ANN § 330.1469(9)(b) (since repealed).

[278]*K. B.*, 562 N.W. at 210.

[279]*Id.*

[280]*Id.* at 211, citing Lewis v. Donahue, 437 F. Supp. 112, 114 (W.D. Okla., 1977), *In re* True, 645 P.2d 891 (Idaho 1982); *In re* Anderson, 140 Cal. Rptr. 546 (Cal. App. 1977).

[281]*K. B.* 562 N.W. at 211.

[282]481 A.2d 473, 483 (D.C. 1984).

[283]*K. B.*, 562 N.W.2d at 211.

[284]*Id.*

[285]*Id.*

[286]914 P.2d 1104 (Or. App. 1996).

had no right to an explanation of his procedural rights at a hearing to determine whether his trial visitor status should be revoked.[287]

K. B. and *Vonahlefeld* are indefensible decisions. A fair hearing is the touchstone of procedural due process.[288] To characterize its probable value as "minimal" is to ignore virtually all that we have learned about the meaning of "voice"[289] and the significance of "procedural justice"[290] in the involuntary civil commitment system. To find that it is constitutionally permissible to hold such a hearing without informing a patient of his or her procedural rights is to cruelly mock the entire legal process.[291]

The *K. B.* case is especially striking because of the medication subtext.[292] Recommitment was sought in *K. B.* because the patient refused to take her medication. Her rationale for that refusal was—on its surface, at least—an entirely "rational" one (her fear that the medications would harm her unborn child).[293] The dangers of side effects are not ephemeral;[294] such dangers are, no doubt, one of the main reasons why the Supreme Court has specifically found the potential presence of such side effects to be an element to be appropriately considered in the formulation of a due process calculus.[295] Here, K. B.'s assertion of that right became the rationale by which she was stripped of due process at her recommitment hearing. The language relied on by the court—that these are essentially "medical" questions—ignores the full panoply of procedural protections built into state statutes and found to be constitutionally required. It is *precisely* questions of the sort raised by K. B. that can be—and should be—considered at contested due process hearings. *K. B.* is both sanist and pretextual in its holding, its reasoning, and its likely real-life outcome.[296]

The crabbed reading of the *Vonahlefeld* case also demonstrates both sanism and pretextuality. It is sanist because of its cynicism (that it really doesn't *matter* if a patient is told of his or her rights at a "due process hearing"). It is pretextual because of its minimalistic reading of the underlying state statute and its reliance on mere crumbs of ambiguous legislative history.

---

[287]*Id.* at 1105–06.

[288]*See, e.g.,* Smith v. Phillips, 455 U.S. 209, 219 (1982); Gagnon v. Scarpelli, 411 U.S. 778, 790 (1972).

[289]*See, e.g.,* Bennett et al., *supra* note 165, at 305 ("patients expect staff to recognize them, in a morally fundamental way, as being people *just like them,* albeit people in need of help") (emphasis in original).

[290]*See, e.g.,* Tom Tyler, *The Psychological Consequences of Judicial Procedures: Implications for Civil Commitment Hearings,* 46 SMU L. REV. 433, 443 (1992).

[291]For a recent empirical consideration, see Alexander Greer, Mary O'Regan, & Amy Traverso, *Therapeutic Jurisprudence and Patients' Perceptions of Procedural Due Process of Civil Commitment Hearings, in* LAW IN A THERAPEUTIC KEY: DEVELOPMENTS IN THERAPEUTIC JURISPRUDENCE 923 (David Wexler & Bruce Winick eds. 1996).

[292]*K. B.* also ignores the recent literature on clinical approaches to "revolving door patients" who are noncompliant with medications. *See, e.g.,* Jeffrey Geller, *Treating Revolving Door Patients Who Have "Hospitaliphilia": Compassion, Coercion, and Common Sense,* 44 HOSP. & COMMUNITY PSYCHIATRY 141 (1993).

[293]*K. B.,* 562 N.W. 2d at 209.

[294]*See, e.g.,* T. Howard Stone, *Therapeutic Implications of Incarceration for Persons With Severe Mental Disorders: Searching for Rational Health Policy,* 24 AM. J. CRIM. L. 283, 307 (1997) (discussing potential fetal or neonate harms); *see generally* Anne Ryan, *True Protection for Persons With Severe Mental Disabilities, Such as Schizophrenia, Involved as Subjects in Research? A Look and Consideration of the "Protection of Human Subjects,"* 9 J.L. & HEALTH 349 (1994–95). *Cf.* Grant Morris, *Judging Judgment: Assessing the Competence of Mental Patients to Refuse Treatment,* 32 SAN DIEGO L. REV. 343, 423 (1995) (reporting on case of patient who sought to refuse medication because of fear of fetal damage; conclusive medical proof introduced that patient was not pregnant).

[295]*See* Washington v. Harper, 494 U.S. 210, 229 (1990); *see also,* Reggins v. Nevada, 540 U.S. 127, 138–39 (1992) (Kennedy, J., concurring).

[296]For a nonsanist and nonpretextual approach to the same issues, see Geller, *supra* note 292.

Conclusion

The involuntary civil commitment process is the core of the relationship between the law and mental disability. Commitment hearings affect tens of thousands of individuals,[297] are short,[298] are closed, and are invisible to the public.[299] The individual disposition of such hearings rarely is a topic for the public discourse, except for the rare, vivid case that becomes a heuristic symbol for public policy debates.[300]

The early leading cases governing aspects of procedural and substantive commitment law—*Lessard v. Schmidt, Jackson v. Indiana,* and *O'Connor v. Donaldson*—were neither sanist nor pretextual. Rather, they took seriously the underlying issues, and thoughtfully and maturely sought to apply constitutional law concepts to questions of institutionalization on ways that ensured patients' civil rights and liberties in ways that would optimally maximize the opportunity for the patient to receive adequate and ameliorative treatment.

But the history of involuntary civil commitment litigation has *not* been the history of robust interpretations of these cases. It has, rather, been one of sanism and pretextuality. It is this history, as much as that of any aspect of mental disability law, that has led to the incoherence—and corruption—of contemporary mental disability law jurisprudence.

---

[297]*See* STATISTICAL ABSTRACT OF THE UNITED STATES, 1996 (1996), at 137 (in 1992, the average daily inpatient census in mental health facilities was 216,900).

[298]The average hearing lasts 9.2 minutes; Parham v. J. R., 442 U.S. 584, 609 n.17 (1979).

[299]*See, e.g., Matter of* Belk, 420 S.E.2d 682 (N.C. App. 1992); *Matter of* Commitment of Edward S., 570 A.2d 917 (N.J. 1990).

[300]*See generally supra* Chapter 1.

Chapter 5
THE RIGHT TO TREATMENT

The right-to-treatment movement grew out of dissatisfaction in the 1950s and 1960s with the non- and antitherapeutic condition of large public state institutions for mentally disabled persons.[1] The earliest cases—especially *Wyatt v. Stickney*[2]—made the overt link between therapeutic "rights" and constitutional rights. Early cases that flowed from *Wyatt*—both right to treatment cases and "other institutional rights" cases—often relied specifically on therapeutic justifications for constitutional holdings. These decisions are nonsanist and nonpretextual. Had their spirit been followed for the subsequent quarter-century, mental disability law would have taken a markedly different path. It is a tragedy—for persons with mental disabilities and the mental disability law system—that that has not happened.

As has been well-documented,[3] the path of right-to-treatment litigation changed significantly following the Supreme Court's 1982 decision in *Youngberg v. Romeo*.[4] Although the Court acknowledged that institutionalized persons retained certain constitutional rights—to food, shelter, clothing, and medical care[5]—it stopped short of finding a constitutional right to treatment.[6] Post-*Youngberg* cases have split sharply in their readings of the case's ultimate scope, some building on Justice Blackmun's concurrence[7] and others simply adopting a far narrower interpretation.[8] Although *Youngberg* provided some building blocks for later nonsanist opinions and nonpretextual developments, at heart it is a profoundly pretextual case that in many ways created the template for pretextuality in all institutional mental disability law.

In this section I will first trace the background of the *Wyatt* case, demonstrate how therapeutic ends were consciously and overtly in the minds both of counsel and the courts in *Wyatt* and its progeny, then show how the Supreme Court's decision in *Youngberg* largely halted that movement. Finally, I will demonstrate how the standard charges leveled against the mental disability law "movement" (and the lawyers largely responsible for its early development) are simply incorrect.

Wyatt and Its Progeny

By 1960 social reformers had become a major voice in the call to reinvent state public mental hospitals. The president of the American Psychiatric Association called the facilities

---

[1] *See* 2 Michael L. Perlin, Mental Disability Law: Civil and Criminal § 3A-2.2, at 13 (2d ed. 1999).
[2] 325 F. Supp. 781 (M.D. Ala. 1971), 334 F. Supp. 1341 (M.D. Ala. 1972), 344 F. Supp. 373 (M.D. Ala. 1972), 344 F. Supp. 387 (M.D. Ala. 1972), *aff'd sub. nom.*, Wyatt v. Aderholt, 503 F.2d 1305 (5th Cir. 1974).
[3] *See* 2 Perlin, *supra* note 1, §§ 3A-12 to 3A-12.3, at 111-23 (2d. ed 1999).
[4] 457 U.S. 307 (1982).
[5] *Id.* at 315.
[6] *See generally id.* at 316–17.
[7] *Id.* at 327–31; *see generally* 2 Perlin, *supra* note 1, § 3A-9.9, at 106–108 (2d. ed. 1999).
[8] *See* 2 Perlin, *supra* note 1, § 3A-12.2, at 118-21 (2d. ed. 1999).

"bankrupt beyond remedy";[9] the social critic Albert Deutsch testified before Congress as to his earlier investigations of state hospitals with these chilling words:

> Some physicians I interviewed frankly admitted that the animals of nearby piggeries were better housed, fed and treated than many of the patients on their wards. I saw hundreds of sick people shackled, strapped, straitjacketed, and bound to their beds. I saw mental patients forced to eat meals with their hands because there were not enough spoons and other tableware to go around—not because they couldn't be trusted to eat like humans. . . . I found evidence of physical brutality, but that paled into insignificance when compared with the excruciating suffering stemming from prolonged, enforced, idleness, herdlike crowding, lack of privacy, depersonalization, and the overall atmosphere of neglect. The fault lay . . . with the general community that not only tolerated but enforced these subhuman conditions through financial penury, ignorance, fear and indifference.[10]

At about the same time, Morton Birnbaum published his seminal article in the *American Bar Association Journal* calling for a declaration of "the recognition and enforcement of the legal right of a mentally ill inmate of a public mental institution to adequate medical treatment for his mental illness,"[11] and for courts to openly consider the question of whether "the institutionalized mentally ill person receives adequate medical treatment so that he may regain his health, and therefore his liberty, as soon as possible."[12] Birnbaum located the constitutional basis of this right to treatment in the due process clause; "substantive due process of law does not allow a mentally ill person who has committed no crime to be deprived of his liberty by indefinitely institutionalizing him in a mental prison."[13] This article was widely acknowledged as "supplying much of the theoretical support for the subsequent development of the right-to-treatment litigation."[14]

Birnbaum is the creator of the term "sanism." It is not coincidental that the person who first raised this issue also crafted the idea of a right to treatment.[15] Birnbaum understood how a sanist society could thoughtlessly relegate persons with mental disabilities to institutions that provided no adequate treatment. His attempts to craft a legal cause of action to remedy that reality were implicit efforts to eradicate sanism in mental disability law policy.

The existence of a *statutory*[16] right to treatment was first judicially recognized by the District of Columbia Circuit Court of Appeals in the unlikely setting of a *habeas corpus* case brought by an insanity acquittee. In *Rouse v. Cameron,*[17] the court found that a District of Columbia hospitalization law established such a statutory right, reasoning that "the purpose of involuntary hospitalization is treatment, not punishment," quoting a statement by the act's sponsor that, when a person is deprived of liberty because of need of treatment and that

---

[9]Harry Solomon, *Presidential Address: The American Psychiatric Association in Relation to American Psychiatry,* 115 AM. J. PSYCHIATRY 1, 7 (1958).

[10]2 PERLIN, *supra* note 1, § 4.04 at 14–15, quoting CONSTITUTIONAL RIGHTS OF THE MENTALLY ILL, HEARING BEFORE THE SENATE SUBCOMM. ON CONSTITUTIONAL RIGHTS OF THE JUDICIARY, 87th Cong., 2d Sess., 40–42 (1961) (statement of Albert Deutsch).

[11]Morton Birnbaum, *The Right to Treatment,* 46 A.B.A. J. 499 (1960).

[12]*Id.* at 502.

[13]*Id.* at 502–03.

[14]2 PERLIN, *supra* note 1, § 3A-2.1, at 8–12 (2d. ed. 1999).

[15]*See* Morton Birnbaum, *The Right to Treatment: Some Comments on Its Development, in* MEDICAL, MORAL AND LEGAL ISSUES IN HEALTH CARE 97, 106–07 (Frank Ayd Jr. ed. 1974); Koe v. Califano, 573 F.2d 761, 764 n.12 (2d Cir. 1978). *See supra* . . .

[16]D.C. CODE §§ 21–562 (1966); *See generally* 2 PERLIN, *supra* note 1, § 3A-2.2, at 13–15 (2d. ed. 1999).

[17]373 F.2d 451 (D.C. Cir. 1966).

treatment is not supplied, such deprivation is "tantamount to a denial of due process."[18] The hospital thus needed to demonstrate that it had made a "bona fide effort" to "cure or improve" the patient, that inquiries into the patient's needs and conditions were renewed periodically, and that the program provided was suited to the patient's "particular needs."[19]

Rouse was the subject of considerable academic and scholarly commentary—mostly favorable[20]—but was nonetheless criticized sharply by the American Psychiatric Association for interfering with medical practice: "The definition of treatment and the appraisal of its adequacy are matters for medical determination."[21] This position, to be sure, was not unanimously held by the psychiatric establishment—Alan Stone, for instance, referred to it as a "monument to bureaucratic myopia"[22]—but it provides a context through which some of the incessant criticisms of the mental health advocacy movement can be reexamined. The trade association for the service providers most closely linked with inpatient mental health care took the position that the hands-off doctrine[23] required a policy of judicial nonintervention in the relationship between institutionalization and constitutional rights.

The most important case finding a *constitutional* right to treatment was, without doubt, *Wyatt v. Stickney. Wyatt* was clear: "The purposes of involuntary hospitalization for treatment purposes is *treatment* and not mere custodial care or punishment. This is the only justification from a constitutional standpoint, that allows civil commitment to [a state hospital]. . . . To deprive any citizen of his or her liberty upon the altruistic theory that the confinement is for humane therapeutic reasons and then fail to provide adequate treatment violates the very fundamentals of due process."[24] It subsequently found three "fundamental conditions for adequate and effective treatment": (a) a humane psychological and physical environment, (b) qualified staff in numbers sufficient to administer adequate treatment, and (c) individualized treatment plans.[25] Following a hearing (to which the court had invited a broad cross section of interested professional associations to participate), the court issued supplemental orders detailing the "medical and constitutional minimums . . . mandatory for a constitutionally acceptable minimum treatment program."[26] These standards covered the full range of hospital conditions, including environmental standards, civil rights, medical treatment criteria, staff qualifications, nutritional requirements, and need for compliance with Life Safety Code provisions.[27]

On what sources did *Wyatt* draw? An examination of the transcript, briefs, and court documents in *Wyatt* (and in *New York State Ass'n for Retarded Children v. Rockefeller,*[28] a parallel suit brought in federal court in New York on behalf of residents of the Willowbrook facility for individuals with mental retardation) reveals that therapeutic motivations drove each and every important aspect of the litigation in question.

---

[18]*Id.* at 455.

[19]*Id.*

[20]*See generally* 2 PERLIN, *supra* note 1, § 3A-2.3, at 15–19 (2d. ed. 1999).

[21]Council of the American Psychiatric Association, *Position Statement on the Question of the Adequacy of Treatment,* 123 AM. J. PSYCHIATRY 1458 (1967).

[22]Alan Stone, *The Right to Treatment and the Medical Establishment,* 2 BULL. AM. ACAD. PSYCHIATRY & L. 159, 161 (1974).

[23]*See, e.g.,* Banning v. Looney, 213 F.2d 771 (10th Cir. 1943), *cert. denied,* 348 U.S. 859 (1959).

[24]*Wyatt,* 325 F. Supp. at 784–85.

[25]*Id.,* 334 F. Supp. at 1343.

[26]*Id.,* 334 F. Supp. at 376.

[27]*Id.* at 379–86; *see generally* 2 PERLIN, *supra* note 1, § 3A-3.1, at 28–30 (2d. ed. 1999).

[28]357 F. Supp. 752 (E.D.N.Y. 1973) (*Willowbrook*).

The complaint in *Willowbrook,* for instance, specifically articulated therapeutic ends:

> 32. Care, treatment, education and training are all included within a broader concept referred to by mental retardation professionals as ''habilitation.'' The goal of habilitation is to assist each mentally retarded person to lead a life as close to normal as is possible.
>
> . . .
>
> 35. Defendants, however, have created, fostered, and condoned conditions, policies and practices at Willowbrook that are directly contrary to professionally accepted concepts of habilitation. As a consequence, Willowbrook is not a therapeutic institution. It more closely resembles a prison, and the residents confined therein have therefore been denied due process of law.
>
> . . .
>
> 37. A . . . prerequisite to an adequate habilitation program is a humane physical and psychological environment. The environment at Willowbrook is inhumane and psychologically destructive. Examples of the anti-therapeutic environment include . . .
>
> [listing examples]
>
> . . .
>
> 54. Because of the foregoing, the vast majority of residents at Willowbrook have actually regressed and deteriorated since their admission . . .
>
> 55. Because of the foregoing, residents have been deprived of the habilitation necessary to enable them to speak, read, communicate, mix and assemble with others . . .
>
> 56. Because of the foregoing, residents have been deprived of their rights to privacy and dignity protected by the Fourteenth Amendment.
>
> . . .
>
> 59. Because of the foregoing, residents have been denied due process and equal protection of the law, in violation of the Fourteenth Amendment.[29]

At trial, experts and even *defendants'* witnesses testified about the regression suffered by Willowbrook residents.[30] The consent order eventually entered in this case[31] was overtly premised on therapeutic ends: ''[The] conditions [at Willowbrook] are hazardous to the health, safety, and sanity of the residents. They do not conform with the standards published

---

[29]*Excerpts From Complaint in* New York State Association for Retarded Children v. Rockefeller, 1 LEGAL RIGHTS OF THE MENTALLY HANDICAPPED 591 (Bruce Ennis & Paul Friedman eds.1973) (LEGAL RIGHTS).

[30]*See, e.g., Excerpt From Plaintiffs' Post-Trial Memorandum in* New York State Association for Retarded Children v. Rockefeller, *in* 2 LEGAL RIGHTS, *supra* note 29, at 747 (1973) (defendant Grunberg testified that patient records revealed ''regression after institutionalization at Willowbrook''; expert witness Clements testified Willowbrook failed to provide even a ''minimal level of custodial care''; expert witness Roos testified that condition of Willowbrook residents was largely function of ''long exposure to noxious debilitating environmental conditions'), and *see id.* at 770 (''*It is obvious that there were many children who could possibly have walked if they had proper* [physical] *therapy from the beginning. It is questionable whether they could ever walk now. Their chances will definitely decrease as the time passes without proper developmental therapy*'') (emphasis in original) (quoting from posttrial memorandum, relying on case record).

[31]2 PERLIN, *supra* note 1, § 4.28, at 136 (reprinting New York State Ass'n for Retarded Citizens v. Carey, No. 72–C-356/357 (E.D.N.Y. 1975), *approved,* 393 F. Supp. 715 (E.D.N.Y. 1975)).

On recent developments in the law of consent judgments, see Catherine Patsos, *The Constitutionality and Implications of the Prison Litigation Reform Act,* 42 N.Y.L. SCH. L. REV. 205 (1998) (carefully and persuasively critiquing the Prison Litigation Reform Act (PLRA), *see* 18 U.S.C. § 3626; 28 U.S.C. § 1915; 42 U.S.C. § 1997(3)); *cf.* Ross Sandler & David Schoenbrod, *How to Put Lawmakers, Not Courts, Back in Charge,* CITY J. (Autumn 1996), at 61 (characterizing PRLA as a ''much-needed legislative gift'').

by the American Association of Mental Health Deficiency in 1964, or with the proposed standards published on May 5, 1973 by the United States Department of Health, Education and Welfare."[32] Under the court's analysis, residents were, *inter alia,* entitled to "protection from assaults by fellow inmates or by staff," to "correction of conditions which violate 'basic standards of human decency,'" to medical care, to exercise and outdoor recreation, to adequate heat during cold weather, and to the "necessary elements of basic hygiene."[33]

The conditions that faced the court in *Wyatt* were, to be charitable, abysmal. During the course of trial, the following uncontradicted facts were found: "a resident was scalded to death by hydrant water, . . . a resident was restrained in a strait jacket for nine years in order to prevent hand and finger sucking, . . . and a resident died from the insertion by another resident of a running water hose into his rectum."[34] In each instance, the court noted that the incidents could have been avoided "had adequate staff and facilities been available."[35]

In the pretrial aspects of *Wyatt,* an expert testified about the way that operation of the Partlow facility "foster[ed] dehumanization" and reflected a "long-term warehousing operation,"[36] and a "deprived environment,"[37] in which staff had "little understanding as to the nature of the residents' disabilities"[38] and exhibited a "self-defeatist attitude" that "generates deterioration in the residents,"[39] and conditions on wards reflected "massive evidence of deprivation—emotional, social, . . . physical."[40] Briefs filed with the court relied on behavioral and medical experts to support arguments that institutional settings such as were present in Alabama "encourage disability rather than overcom[e] it," that such hospitalization is inevitably a "regressive experience with far reaching destructive repercussions," that such hospitalization is "antitherapeutic" and "negative," and that continued exposure to such conditions "has severely debilitating effects on the social and psychological condition of patients."[41] Again, these briefs and depositions indicted a morally corrupt system, one whose corruption went uncriticized, at least in large part because of sanism's pervasive power.

The court's original orders in *Wyatt*[42] drew specifically on many of these sources in coming to the conclusion that conditions at Alabama facilities violated the due process

---

[32]*Willowbrook,* 357 F. Supp. at 755.

[33]*Id.* at 764–65.

[34]*Wyatt,* 344 F. Supp. at 394 n.13.

[35]*Id.* For an even more graphic description of the way that Alabama state residents were fed in the facilities that were the subject of the *Wyatt* suit, see James Folsom, *The Early Constructive Approach to* Wyatt *by the Department of Mental Health, in* WYATT V. STICKNEY: RETROSPECT AND PROSPECT 41 (L. Ralph Jones & Richard R. Parlour eds. 1981) (RETROSPECT AND PROSPECT) (describing process as "patients being slopped like hogs").

[36]*See* 2 PERLIN, *supra* note 1, § 4.18, at 75, 80–81 (reprinting deposition testimony of Philip Roos).

[37]*Id.* at 87.

[38]*Id.* at 89.

[39]*Id.* at 94.

[40]*Id.* at 95. *Cf.* Philip Roos, *Basic Facts About Mental Retardation, in* 1 LEGAL RIGHTS, *supra* note 29, at 17, 23 ("Retarded persons should be viewed developmentally, capable of growth or learning, regardless of level of retardation or age").

[41]*The Right to a Durational Limitation on Involuntary Commitment, in* 1 LEGAL RIGHTS, *supra* note 29, at 437, 442–43 (excerpt from posttrial memorandum in *Wyatt*).

[42]For an analysis of subsequent litigation, *see* 2 PERLIN, *supra* note 1, § 3A-3.2a, at 50, 331 (2d. ed. 1999). More recently, in a comprehensive opinion the federal district court reconsidered the extent to which defendants had complied with each of the *Wyatt* standards, granting partial release from certain provisions of the decree with which defendants had complied, but denying release from others. *See* Wyatt by and Through Rawlins v. Rogers, 985 F. Supp. 1356 (M.D. Ala. 1997). For even more recent opinions, see Wyatt by and Through Rawlins v. Rogers, 1998 WL 862920, at (M.D. Ala. 1998), and Wyatt v. Sawyer, 1999 WL 965477 (M.D. Ala. 1999).

clause.[43] Even that aspect of *Wyatt* that appears to be the most purely "legal"—its invocation of the least-restrictive-analysis doctrine for institutional decision making[44]—is premised on therapeutic ends.[45]

On appeal, *amici* supporting *Wyatt* plaintiffs stressed the precise link between therapeutic outcome and constitutional rights, calling the court's attention to the fact finding that follows:

> The dormitories are barn-like structures with no privacy for the patients. For most patients there is not even a spaced provided which he can think of as his own. The toilets in the restrooms seldom have partitions between them. There are dehumanizing factors which degenerate the patients' self-esteem. Also contributing to the poor psychological environment are the shoddy wearing apparel furnished the patients, the non-therapeutic work assigned to patients, and the degrading and humiliating admissions procedures which creates in the patient an impression of the hospital as a prison or as a crazy house.[46]

In the same brief, *amici* stressed findings made by *defendants'* experts: "[The hospital] impressed me as a depressing and dehumanizing environment, reminding me of graveyard lots where the patients are essentially living out their lives without the rights of privacy (or ownership)."[47] And quoting further testimony: "Residents with open wounds and inadequately treated skin diseases were in immediate danger of infection because of the unsanitary conditions existing in the wards, including urine and feces on the floor. . . . There was evidence of insect infestation, including cockroaches in the kitchens and dining rooms."[48] And: "Not only are inmates of Alabama's mental institutions deprived of treatment, they are deprived of even the most minimal stimulation and activity, with the result that their condition seriously deteriorates."[49]

---

[43]*See, e.g., Wyatt*, 344 F. Supp. at 376–86, and *see* 2 PERLIN, *supra* note 1, § 3A-3.1, at 29 (2d. ed. 1999). "The standards ranged in subject matter from the global (e.g., 'Patients have a right to privacy and dignity') to the specific (e.g., 'Thermostatically controlled hot water shall be maintained [at 180°] for mechanical dishwashing. . . . They covered the full range of hospital conditions, including environmental standards, civil rights, medical treatment criteria, staff qualifications, nutritional requirements, and need for compliance with Life Safety Code provisions')."

On the question of the therapeutic jurisprudence aspects of the privacy standards, see Joseph O'Reilly & Bruce Sales, *Setting Physical Standards for Mental Hospitals: To Whom Should the Courts Listen,* 8 INT'L J. L. & PSYCHIATRY 301 (1986), and Joseph O'Reilly & Bruce Sales, *Privacy for the Institutionalized Mentally Ill: Are Court-Ordered Standards Effective?* 11 LAW & HUM. BEHAV. 41 (1987) (studying patient and staff attitudes on the importance of the individual *Wyatt* standards, and finding that the standards were, in several critical ways, an inadequate means of protecting the privacy of *Wyatt* class residents).

[44]*Wyatt,* 344 F. Supp. at 379, 396.

[45]*See, e.g.,* David Chambers, *Right to the Least Restrictive Alternative Setting for Treatment, in* 2 LEGAL RIGHTS, *supra* note 29, at 991, 1011 (theoretical support for application of least restrictive alternative principle to mental disability litigation, focusing on harms that often befall patients in large mental institutions, including "physical deterioration (loss of speech, inertia, passivity, etc.), . . . psychological deterioration (loss of social skills, loss of self-esteem, loss of identity, withdrawal, extreme dependency), . . . loss of liberty and dignity (lack of privacy, lack of movement, exposure to violence, extreme regimentation)."

[46]Brief of Amicus Curiae on Appeal to the Fifth Circuit in Wyatt v. Stickney, *in* 1 LEGAL RIGHTS, *supra* note 29, at 333, 354.

[47]*Id.* at 367.

[48]*Id.* at 367–68.

[49]*Id.* at 377.

On appeal the Fifth Circuit substantially affirmed. The court noted that there was "no significant dispute" about the level of conditions in the Alabama facilities in question,[50] relying on its recent decision in *Donaldson v. O'Connor*:[51]

> In *Donaldson,* we held that civilly committed mental patients have a constitutional right to such individual treatment as will help each of them to be cured or to improve his or her mental condition. We reasoned that the only permissible justifications for civil commitment, and for the massive abridgments of constitutionally protected liberties it entails, were the danger posed by the individual committed to himself or others, or the individual's need for treatment and care. We held that where the justification for commitment was treatment, it offended the fundamentals of due process if treatment were not in fact provided; and we held that where the justification was the danger to self or to others, then treatment had to be provided as the *quid pro quo* society had to pay as the price of the extra safety it derived from the denial of individuals' liberty.[52]

Wyatt has been characterized as "the most significant case in the history of forensic psychiatry" and "the foundation of modern psychiatric jurisprudence."[53] Further, it crystallized the issue: The right to treatment was consciously intended to achieve therapeutic gains.[54] Post-*Wyatt* cases endorsed the link, both in "pure" right to treatment cases,[55] in institutional rights cases that focused on one or more aspect of *Wyatt*—for example, the right to be paid for institutional labor,[56] or the right to freedom in religious practice[57]—and in early deinstitutionalization cases.[58]

Wyatt was both antisanist and antipretextual. It looked carefully at what occurred on a daily basis in Alabama's mental institutions, it exposed the paucity of treatment, the brutality, the lack of concern and lack of humanity reflected in the actions and inactions of state officials and of some treatment staff. It rejected the long-standing doctrine that this was a population that was simply less worthy of judicial protection than other minorities or disenfranchised persons. It self-consciously faced constitutional issues, clinical issues, governmental issues, bureaucratic issues, and budgetary issues in a way that treated the persons subject to inpatient hospitalization with dignity and without pretext. In many ways,

---

[50]*Wyatt*, 503 F.2d at 1310.

[51]493 F.2d 507 (5th Cir. 1974), *vacated,* 422 U.S. 563 (1975). *See generally supra* Chapter 4.

[52]*Wyatt*, 503 F.2d at 1312.

[53]Milton Greenblatt, *Foreword, in* RETROSPECT AND PROSPECT, *supra* note 35, at ix, x.

[54]*See* David Wexler, *An Introduction to Therapeutic Jurisprudence, in* THERAPEUTIC JURISPRUDENCE: THE LAW AS A THERAPEUTIC AGENT 3, 9 (David Wexler ed. 1990), (citing Michael L. Perlin, *The Right to Participate in Voluntary, Therapeutic, Compensated Work Programs as Part of the Right to Treatment: A New Theory in the Aftermath of* Souder, 7 SETON HALL L. REV. 298 (1976).

[55]*E.g.,* Davis v. Watkins, 384 F. Supp. 1196 (N.D. Ohio 1974); Rone v. Fireman, 473 F. Supp. 92 (N.D. Ohio 1979).

[56]Schindenwolf v. Klein, L41293–75P.W. (N.J. Super Ct., Law Div. 1979), order reprinted at 2 PERLIN, *supra* note 1, § 6.23 at 509–19. For the complaint in *Schindenwolf* (setting out this link), see *id.,* § 6.22, at 495–509.

[57]Falter v. Veterans' Admin., No. 79–2284 (D.N.J. 1979) (complaint), *reprinted in id.,* § 6.05, at 446–66.

[58]Halderman v. Pennhurst State Sch. & Hosp., 446 F. Supp. 1295 (E.D. Pa. 1978), *modified,* 612 F.2d 84 (3d Cir. 1979), *rev'd,* 451 U.S. 1 (1981), *reinstated,* 673 F.2d 647 (3d Cir. 1982), *rev'd,* 465 U.S. 89 (1984) (*Pennhurst*), *discussed extensively in* MICHAEL PERLIN, LAW AND MENTAL DISABILITY § 2.48 (1994). *See, e.g., Excerpt From Original Plaintiff's Brief in* Halderman, *reprinted in* 2 LEGAL RIGHTS OF MENTALLY DISABLED PERSONS 715, 725 (Paul Friedman ed. 1979) (arguing that isolation and confinement "are counter-productive in the habilitation of the retarded").

Judge Frank Johnson's trial court opinions in the *Wyatt* case were mental disability law's finest hours.[59]

A Turn Toward Pretextuality

The scope of the right to treatment took a significant turn several years later in *Youngberg v. Romeo*.[60] The Supreme Court granted *certiorari* to review a Third Circuit decision that had held that the Fourteenth Amendment's due process clause[61] was the proper source for determining the constitutional basis for the rights asserted by the plaintiff, a severely mentally retarded, involuntary resident of a Pennsylvania state institution who had suffered a series of 63 significant injuries, both self-inflicted and inflicted by other facility residents.[62]

In applying this clause, the Third Circuit had found that involuntarily committed mentally disabled persons had "fundamental"[63] liberty interests in freedom of movement and in personal security that could be limited only by an "overriding, non-punitive" state interest,[64] as well as a "liberty interest in habilitation designed to 'treat' their mental retardation."[65] In assessing whether a resident's treatment rights had been violated, the circuit found that the defendants would be held liable only if the plaintiff's treatments were not "acceptable in the light of present medical or other scientific knowledge."[66]

The Supreme Court vacated and remanded,[67] holding that, in addition to the rights to "adequate food, shelter, clothing and medical care,"[68] the plaintiff had a constitutionally protected Fourteenth Amendment[69] liberty interest in "conditions of reasonable care and safety,"[70] "freedom from bodily restraint,"[71] and "such minimally adequate or reasonable training to ensure safety and freedom from undue restraint."[72] In determining whether an individual plaintiff's constitutional rights have been violated, these liberty interests must be balanced against relevant state interests.[73]

---

[59]*See* 2 PERLIN, *supra* note 1, § 3A-31, at 25-26 n.161 (2d. ed. 1999) citing, *inter alia,* Jonathan Brand, Pennhurst, Romeo, *and* Rogers: *The Burger Court and Mental Health Law Reform Litigation,* 4 J. LEGAL MED. 323, 325 (1983) (without Judge Johnson, "there would have been no substantial change" in Alabama's institutions), and Melvin J. Heller, *Extension of* Wyatt *to Ohio Forensic Patients, in* RETROSPECT AND PROSPECT, *supra* note 35, at 161, 1732 (Judge Johnson was a "phenomenon who . . . almost singlehandedly, as a *tour de force,* transfigured institutional care of the mentally ill").

[60]457 U.S. 307 (1982). This section is generally adapted from PERLIN, *supra* note 58, § 2.06.

[61]644 F.2d 147, 156 (3d Cir. 1981), *vacated,* 457 U.S. 307 (1982).

[62]*Youngberg,* 457 U.S at 310. His mother, as next friend, or one acting on behalf of an infant, filed a civil rights damages action alleging that the defendants, administrators of the facility where the plaintiff resided, knew or should have known that the plaintiff was suffering such injuries and that their failure to protect him appropriately and prevent injuries violated the Eighth and Fourteenth Amendments. *Id.*

[63]*Romeo,* 644 F.2d at 157–58.

[64]*Id.* at 158 (footnote omitted).

[65]*Youngberg,* 457 U.S. at 313. *See id.* at n.120 (court of appeals used "habilitation" and "treatment" synonymously).

[66]*Romeo,* 644 F.2d at 173. *Cf. id.* 173–81 (Seitz, J., concurring).

[67]*Youngberg,* 457 U.S. at 325.

[68]*Id.* at 315. The existence of these rights—characterized by the court as "substantive liberty interests under the Fourteenth Amendment," *id.*—were conceded by the defendants.

[69]At the Supreme Court level, the plaintiff no longer relied on the Eighth Amendment as a direct source of constitutional rights. *Youngberg,* 457 U.S. at 314 n.16.

[70]*Id.* at 324.

[71]*Id.* at 319.

[72]*Id.*

[73]*Id.* at 321.

The standard for making this determination is whether professional judgment has been exercised.[74] A decision made by a professional is "presumably valid":[75] "Liability may only be imposed when the decision by the professional is such a substantial departure from accepted professional judgment, practice or standards as to demonstrate that the person responsible actually did not base the decision on such a judgment."[76]

The Supreme Court also abandoned the Third Circuit's least-intrusive-means methodology,[77] and instead found that the plaintiff was entitled to "reasonably non-restrictive confinement conditions."[78] This phrase was neither defined nor elaborated on, yet it appears to be the Court's first acknowledgment that some calibration of restrictivity of treatment is essential in any case construing substantive treatment rights.[79]

Justice Blackmun—writing for himself, Justice Brennan, and Justice O'Connor—stated that he would grant the plaintiff an additional right beyond those articulated in the majority's opinion: the right to "such training as is reasonably necessary to prevent a person's pre-existing self-care skills from *deteriorating* because of his commitment.[80] In Justice Blackmun's view, an institutional resident's interest in not losing such skills "alleged a loss of liberty quite distinct from—and as serious as—the loss of safety and freedom from unreasonable restraints."[81] He went on to write, "For many mentally retarded people, the difference between the ability to do things for themselves within an institution and total dependence on the institution for all of their needs is as much liberty as they will ever know."[82] However, because Justice Blackmun agreed with the majority that, on the record before the Court, it was unclear whether plaintiff "[in fact] seeks any 'habilitation' or

---

[74]*Id.* at 322.

[75]*Id.* at 323. The term "professional" is defined at *id.* n.30:

By professional decisionmaker, we mean a person competent, whether by education, training or experience, to make the particular decision at issue. Long-term treatment decisions normally should be made by persons with degrees in medicine or nursing, or with appropriate training in areas such as psychology, physical therapy, or the care and training of the retarded. Of course, day-to-day decisions regarding care—including decisions that must be made without delay—necessarily will be made in many instances by employees without formal training but who are subject to the supervision of qualified persons.

For a comprehensive and critical reading of the *Youngberg* standard, see Susan Stefan, *Leaving Civil Rights to the "Experts": From Deference to Abdication Under the Professional Judgment Standard*, 102 YALE L.J. 639 (1992).

[76]*Youngberg*, 457 U.S. at 323. In an action for damages against a professional in his or her individual capacity, there will be no liability if the professional "was unable to satisfy his [or her] normal professional standards because of budgetary constraints; in such a situation, good-faith immunity would bar liability." *Id.*

[77]*Romeo*, 644 F.2d at 166. This argument had ultimately been abandoned at the U.S. Supreme Court level by plaintiff's counsel, who conceded that the issue was no longer present in the case. *Youngberg*, 457 U.S. at 313.

[78]*Id.* at 324. The Court never specifically reject the "least intrusive means" text; it simply ignored it.

[79]The Court, of course, had applied the similar concept of the "least drastic means" many times in entirely different fact contexts. *See, e.g.,* Aptheker v. Secretary of State, 378 U.S. 500 (1964); Sherbert v. Verner, 374 U.S. 398 (1963); Shelton v. Tucker, 364 U.S. 479 (1960). More recently, the Court returned to this latter standard in its analysis of the right of criminal defendants to resist the imposition of antipsychotic medication at trial. *See* Riggins v. Nevada, 504 U.S. 127 (1992); *see, e.g.,* Michael L. Perlin & Deborah A. Dorfman, *Sanism, Social Science, and the Development of Mental Disability Law Jurisprudence*, 11 BEHAV. SCI. & L. 47 (1993); Bruce Winick, *Psychotropic Medication in the Criminal Trial Process: The Constitutional and Therapeutic Implications of Riggins v. Nevada*, 10 N.Y.L. SCH. J. HUM. RTS. 637 (1993); *see infra* Chapter 6. On the relationship between *Riggins* and *Youngberg*, see Michael L. Perlin, *"Make Promises by the Hour": Sex, Drugs, the ADA, and Psychiatric Hospitalization*, 46 DEPAUL L. REV. 947, 972 (1997).

[80]*Youngberg*, 457 U.S. at 327 (emphasis in original).

[81]*Id. Cf.* Society for Good Will to Retarded Children, Inc. v. Cuomo, 737 F.2d 1239 (2d Cir. 1984).

[82]*Youngberg*, 457 U.S. at 327.

training unrelated to safety and freedom from bodily restraints,"[83] he "accept[ed] its decision not to address [plaintiff's] additional claim."[84]

Chief Justice Burger wrote a separate concurring opinion to articulate one theme: "I would hold flatly that [the plaintiff] has no constitutional right to training, or 'habilitation,' per se."[85] Although Burger agreed with the majority that "some amount of self-care instruction may be necessary to avoid unreasonable infringement of a mentally retarded person's interest in safety and freedom from restraint,"[86] it was also "clear" to the Chief Justice that the Constitution "does not otherwise place an affirmative duty on the State to provide any particular kind of training or habilitation—even such as might be encompassed under the essentially standardless rubric 'minimally adequate training' to which the Court refers."[87]

Youngberg is profoundly antitherapeutic. It is also sanist and pretextual. First, its adoption of a "substantial professional judgment" standard sharply limits the need to inquire into the adequacy of a patient's treatment.[88] The presumption of validity given to institutional decision making, in effect, signals lower courts to close their eyes to the landscape on which *Wyatt* was litigated as well as to the history of American public psychiatric institutions.[89] Further, it serves to chill civil rights lawyers seeking to vindicate claims of institutionalized patients in a wide variety of subject matter areas.[90]

Second, its abandonment of the least-restrictive-alternative construction (and its embrace of the reasonably-nonrestrictive-confinement conditions standard) is, at best, curious. This phrase appeared nowhere in the case law, nor was it ever discussed at oral argument. Although it might appear that the phrase is a shaggy dog—in the 17 years since *Youngberg* was decided, this phraseology has been used rarely by other courts, and its contours have never truly fleshed out[91]—its use as a *replacement* for the other standard again sends a crystal-clear message that the therapeutic values that underlay the application of the least-restrictive-alternative test to mental disability law cases have been abandoned.[92]

Finally, the Court's empirical rationale for limiting the right to habilitation is bizarre. In supporting this conclusion, the Court stated that professionals in mental retardation "disagree strongly on the question whether effective training of all severely or profoundly retarded individuals is even possible," citing to four articles from the journal *Analysis and*

---

[83]*Id.* at 327–28, and *see id.* at 328 n.3.

[84]He added, though, that if the plaintiff sought to maintain basic self-care skills "necessary to his personal autonomy within Pennhurst [the institution where plaintiff resided, *see id.* at 310]," the plaintiff should be free to assert such claims on remand. *Id.* at 328.

[85]*Id.* at 329 (Burger, C.J., concurring). *Cf.* O'Connor v. Donaldson, 422 U.S. 563, 578 (1975) (Burger, C.J., concurring).

[86]*Youngberg,* 457 U.S. at 330.

[87]*Id.*

[88]*See* Stefan, *supra* note 75.

[89]At least one earlier decision stressed that the presence of treatment can serve as a bulwark against the pretext of "arbitrary governmental action." *See* Morales v. Turman, 562 F.2d 993, 997 (5th Cir. 1977).

[90]*See, e.g.,* Michael L. Perlin, *Are Courts Competent to Decide Competency Questions? Stripping the Facade From* United States v. Charters, 38 U. KAN. L. REV. 957 (1990).

[91]*But see* Hicks v. Feeney, 596 F. Supp. 1504, 1513 (D. Del. 1984); *Petition of* Thompson, 394 Mass. 502, 476 N.E.2d 216, 219 (1985). In *In re* R.A., 146 Vt. 289, 501 A.2d 743, 744 (1985), the Vermont Supreme Court underscored that the state's statutory scheme, see VT. STAT. ANN. tit. 18, § 7617(e) (mandating treatment "adequate and appropriate to [the patient's] condition"), might require "something more" than the 'reasonably nonrestrictive confinement conditions' which the Fourteenth Amendment requires."

[92]On the impact of the Supreme Court's decisions in Olmstead v. L.C., 119 S. Ct. 2176 (1999), on this question in the context of the Americans with Disabilities Act, see *infra* Chapter 8, text accompanying notes 239–41.

Intervention in Disabilities.[93] However, a reading of the very articles cited by the court—articles never cited previously or subsequently by any other court in any reported opinion—shows that they considered only the "small fraction" of persons with mental retardation who were "permanently ambulatory" and "extremely debilitated,"[94] a grouping that is a tiny percentage of all institutionalized persons. The court's selection of social science data appears pretextual as well.

Conclusion

An analysis of the right to treatment litigation reveals some fairly clear results. *Wyatt v. Stickney* was a nonsanist and nonpretextual case, and, not coincidentally, was perhaps the most therapeutically focused case in the history of American mental disability law. Cases that adhered to the spirit of *Wyatt* similarly advanced therapeutic ends. *Youngberg v. Romeo,* on the other hand, was profoundly antitherapeutic, sanist, and pretextual, and cases that have followed it reflect similar values.[95]

Not all post-*Youngberg* cases embrace the narrow vision posited by that Court's majority or by Chief Justice Burger; some, in adhering to the broader read of Justice Blackmun in his concurrence, endorse therapeutic, nonsanist and nonpretextual values. Other post-*Youngberg* cases continue to endorse both the spirit and letter of *Wyatt.*[96]

Yet there can be no question that *Youngberg* served as a brake on expansion of the gestalt of the *Wyatt* litigation. Since that time, the nonsanist decision in institutional disability rights law is the exception, the nonpretextual case the curiosity.

---

[93]*Youngberg,* 457 U.S. at 316–17 n.20.

[94]*See* David Ferleger, *Anti-Institutionalization and the Supreme Court,* 14 RUTGERS L.J. 595, 628–29 (1983), *discussed in* 2 PERLIN, *supra* note 1, § 3A-9.2, at 92–93 n.726 (2d. ed. 1999).

[95]*See, e.g.,* Perlin, *supra* note 90 (discussing United States v. Charters, 829 F.2d 479 (4th Cir. 1987), *on reh'g,* 863 F.2d 302 (4th Cir. 1988) *(en banc), cert. denied,* 494 U.S. 1016 (1990)).

[96]*See, e.g.,* Dolihite v. Videon, 847 F. Supp. 918, 936 (M.D. Ala. 1994): "Most importantly . . . , the continuing deficiencies reflect a non-compliance with the *Wyatt* standards. In the case at bar, the failure to comply with the spirit and letter of *Wyatt* allegedly created an anti-therapeutic environment which was a proximate cause of [plaintiff's] injuries."

Chapter 6
THE RIGHT TO REFUSE TREATMENT

The question of the right to refuse antipsychotic medication remains the most important and volatile aspect of the legal regulation of mental health practice.[1] The issues that are raised—the autonomy of individuals institutionalized because of mental disability to refuse the imposition of treatment that is designed (at least in part) to ameliorate their symptomatology, the degree to which individuals subjected to such drugging are in danger of developing irreversible neurological side effects, the evanescence of terms such as *informed consent* or *competency,* the practical and administrative considerations of implementing such a right in an institutional setting, and the range of the philosophical questions raised[2]—mark the litigation that has led to the articulation of the right to refuse treatment as ''a turning point in institutional psychiatry''[3] and ''the most controversial issue in forensic psychiatry today.''[4] The right to refuse antipsychotic medication raises compelling issues: The potential infringement of individuals' constitutional rights, including the First Amendment rights to privacy and mentation, the Sixth Amendment right to a fair trial, the Eighth Amendment right to freedom from cruel and unusual punishment, and the Fourteenth Amendment's due process guarantee. Given the multiplicity and gravity of the issues involved in these cases, their significance frequently transcends the narrow focus of a mental disability law case.[5]

The conceptual, social, moral, legal, and medical difficulties inherent in the articulation of a coherent right-to-refuse-treatment doctrine have been made even more complicated by the U.S. Supreme Court's reluctance to confront most of the underlying issues in cases arising in civil settings.[6] As a result of the Court's decision in *Mills v. Rogers* to sidestep the core constitutional questions[7] and its concomitant articulation of the doctrine that a state is always free to grant more rights under *its* constitution than might be minimally mandated by the U.S. Supreme Court under the *federal* constitution,[8] two parallel sets of cases have emerged.

---

[1]*See generally* Alexander Brooks, *The Right to Refuse Antipsychotic Medications: Law and Policy,* 39 RUTGERS L. REV. 339 (1987); Sheldon Gelman, *Mental Hospital Drugging: Atomistic and Structural Remedies,* 32 CLEVELAND ST. L. REV. 221 (1983–84); Robert Plotkin, *Limiting the Therapeutic Orgy: Mental Patients' Right to Refuse Treatment,* 72 Nw. U. L. REV. 461 (1977).

[2]*See generally* 2 MICHAEL L. PERLIN, MENTAL DISABILITY LAW: CIVIL AND CRIMINAL Chapter 3B, at 153–385 (2d. ed. 1999).

[3]*See generally* Nancy Rhoden, *The Right to Refuse Psychotropic Drugs,* 15 HARV. C.R.-C.L. L. REV. 363, 365 (1980).

[4]*See generally* Jonathan Brant, Pennhurst, Romeo *and* Rogers: *The Burger Court and Mental Health Law Reform Litigation,* 4 J. LEGAL MED. 323, 345 (1983).

[5]For a general introduction to the right to refuse treatment, *see generally* MICHAEL L. PERLIN, LAW AND MENTAL DISABILITY § 2.08 (1994). For the most comprehensive available one-volume legal analysis, see BRUCE WINICK, THE RIGHT TO REFUSE MENTAL HEALTH TREATMENT (1997).

[6]Mills v. Rogers, 457 U.S. 291 (1982). *But cf.* Washington v. Harper, 494 U.S. 210 (1990), and Riggins v. Nevada, 504 U.S. 127 (1992), *discussed in* Michael L. Perlin & Deborah A. Dorfman, *Sanism, Social Science, and the Development of Mental Disability Law Jurisprudence,* 11 BEHAV. SCI. & L. 47 (1993).

[7]2 PERLIN, *supra* note 2, § 3B-5.7, at 237–40 (2d. ed. 1999); David Wexler, *Seclusion and Restraint: Lessons for Law, Psychiatry and Psychology,* 5 INT'L J.L. & PSYCHIATRY 285, 290 (1982).

[8]*Mills,* 457 U.S. at 300; *see generally* Michael L. Perlin, *State Constitutions and Statutes as Sources of Rights for the Mentally Disabled: The Last Frontier?* 20 LOY. L.A. L. REV. 1249 (1987).

In one, state courts have generally entered broad decrees in accordance with an "expanded due process" model, in which the right to refuse treatment has been read broadly and elaborately, generally interpreting procedural due process protections liberally on behalf of the complaining client. These cases have frequently mandated premedication judicial hearings and heavily relied on social science data focusing on the potential impact of drug side effects, especially tardive dyskinesia.[9] In the other, federal courts have generally entered more narrow decrees in accordance with a limited due process model. These provided narrower administrative review and rejected broad readings of the Fourteenth Amendment's substantive and procedural due process protections, relying less on social science data (which was frequently ignored or dismissed as part of an incomprehensible system allegedly beyond the courts' self-professed limited competency.[10] Generally (but not always), the state cases have involved civil patients; more frequently the federal cases have dealt with individuals originally institutionalized because of involvement in the criminal trial process.[11]

As this short overview should demonstrate, it is impossible to authoritatively articulate *one* doctrine to cover all right-to-refuse-treatment litigation. Doctrinal analysis was made even more difficult by the Supreme Court's decision in *Riggins v. Nevada*,[12] in which the Court followed the "expanded due process" model in finding that defendant's due process rights to a fair trial (at which he had raised the insanity defense) were violated by the involuntary imposition of antipsychotic drugs, and requiring "an overriding justification and a determination of medical appropriateness" prior to such forcible medication.[13] The majority's decision in *Riggins* is by no means an end to the debate surrounding the rights of persons with mental disabilities to refuse antipsychotic medication. On one hand, Justice Kennedy's concurring opinion would have banned the use of antipsychotic medication to make a defendant fit to stand trial "absent an *extraordinary* showing" on the state's part;[14] on the other, Justice Thomas's dissent appears to reject the notion that a defendant such as Riggins (who had originally asked for medical assistance as a jail inmate because he was "hearing voices") could ever raise a refusal-of-medication claim within the criminal trial context.[15]

To understand the scope and breadth of this right, it is necessary to try to decode it. We must try to separate its component parts, examine its constitutional roots, determine the "spin factors" that will likely drive future decisions in areas in which there have not yet been significant litigation,[16] and try to determine whether doctrinal coherence can ever be achieved in this area.

---

[9]*See, e.g.,* Rivers v. Katz, 67 N.Y.2d 485, 495 N.E.2d 337, 504 N.Y.S.2d 74 (1986); Riese v. St. Mary's Hosp. & Medical Ctr., 198 Cal. App. 3d 1388, 243 Cal. Rptr. 2431 (1987), *appeal dismissed,* 774 P.2d 698, 259 Cal. Rptr. 669 (1989); *see generally* Michael L. Perlin, *Reading the Supreme Court's Tea Leaves: Predicting Judicial Behavior in Civil and Criminal Right to Refuse Treatment Cases,* 12 AM. J. FORENS. PSYCHIATRY 39 (1991); *see also* Harold Bursztajn et al., *Micro-Effects of Language on Risk Perception on Drug Prescribing Behavior,* 20 BULL. AM. ACAD. PSYCHIATRY & L. 59 (1992).

[10]*See generally* United States v. Charters, 863 F.2d 302 (4th Cir. 1988) *(en banc) cert. denied,* 494 U.S. 1016 (1990); Michael L. Perlin, *Are Courts Competent to Decide Competency Questions? Stripping the Facade from* United States v. Charters, 38 U. KAN. L. REV. 957 (1990). On the significance of courts' refusal to seriously consider social science data in this context, see generally Perlin & Dorfman, *supra* note 6.

[11]*See generally* Perlin, *supra* note 9.

[12]504 U.S. 127 (1992). *See generally* 2 Perlin, *supra* note 2, § 3B-8.3, at 323–30 (2d. ed. 1999).

[13]*Riggins,* 504 U.S. at 135.

[14]*Id.* at 139 (Kennedy, J., concurring).

[15]*Id.* at 146–57 (Thomas, J., dissenting).

[16]*See generally* Perlin, *supra* note 9.

In this section, I will first review the roots of right-to-refuse-treatment law and explain the factors that led to a dual-track system of case law, consider the impact of this law in other settings and on other populations, attempt to decode this area of the law, look at the critical role of counsel in right-to-refuse-treatment cases, and explore the sanist and pretextual underpinnings of this area of the law.

State and Federal Systems

It is important to begin this inquiry in the context of the particular time in legal history that institutional right-to-refuse litigation began.[17] The timing of the emergence of this case law and public scrutiny in the late 1970s was no coincidence. The strategic impetus for this litigation flowed from decisions earlier in the decade on behalf of institutionalized individuals that had repudiated the hands-off doctrine[18] in a wide variety of cases broadening the applicability of both procedural and substantive due process protections to institutionalized individuals.[19] Although this litigation first arose in the state prison and jail settings,[20] lawyers representing persons with mental disabilities—a classically hidden and disenfranchised group[21]—began to turn to the federal courts in an effort to seek vindication of fundamental constitutional and civil rights,[22] at first primarily in cases involving the right to treatment.[23] In the first rush of cases—arising from fact settings involving shocking disclosures of patient brutality, mistreatment, and abuse[24]—federal judges openly embraced an activist model that "transfigured institutional care of the mentally ill in the nation."[25]

By the time that the litigation largely shifted focus from the right to treatment to the right to *refuse* treatment, some recession from this position was noticeable.[26] Refusal-of-treatment litigation challenged the autonomy and authority of state hospital doctors to provide what had been considered "standard" treatment: the administration of psychotropic

---

[17]The text *infra* accompanying notes 18–55 is largely adapted from Perlin, *supra* note 9.

[18]*See, e.g.,* Banning v. Looney, 213 F.2d 771 (10th Cir.), *cert. denied,* 348 U.S. 854 (1954); Siegel v. Ragan, 180 F.2d 785, 788 (7th Cir. 1950). *See generally* Note, *Beyond the Ken of the Courts: A Critique of Judicial Refusal to Review the Complaints of Convicts,* 72 YALE L.J. 506 (1963).

[19]*See generally* Perlin, *supra* note 8, at 1249–52; 1 PERLIN, *supra* note 2, § 1-2.1, at 7–9 (2d ed. 1998).

[20]*See generally* Elizabeth Alexander, *The New Prison Administrators and the Court: New Directions in Prison Law,* 56 TEX. L. REV. 963, 964–65 (1978).

[21]*See, e.g.,* City of Cleburne v. Cleburne Living Ctr., 473 U.S. 432, 461–62 (1985) (Marshall, J., concurring in part and dissenting in part) (mentally retarded individuals have been subject to "'lengthy and tragic' history of segregation and discrimination that can only be called grotesque"). *See generally* United States v. Carolene Prods. Co., 304 U.S. 144, 152 n.4 (1938).

[22]1 PERLIN, *supra* note 2, § 1-2.1, at 8 (2d ed. 1998). The seminal article explaining the court's role in such litigation remains Abram Chayes, *The Role of the Judge in Public Law Litigation,* 89 HARV. L. REV. 1281 (1976).

[23]*See generally* 2 PERLIN, *supra* note 2, chap. 4; *see supra* Chapter 5.

[24]*See, e.g.,* New York State Ass'n for Retarded Children, Inc. v. Rockefeller, 357 F. Supp. 752, 755–56 (E.D.N.Y. 1973); Wyatt v. Aderholt, 503 F.2d 1305, 1311 n.6 (5th Cir. 1974), and *see supra* Chapter 4, text accompanying notes 33–34, discussing the death of a state hospital patient after a garden hose had been inserted into his rectum for five minutes.

[25]Melvin Heller, *Extension of* Wyatt *to Ohio Forensic Patients, in* WYATT V. STICKNEY: RETROSPECT AND PROSPECT 161, 172 (L. R. Jones & R. Parlour eds. 1981) (RETROSPECT).

[26]This recession did not affect the earliest right-to-refuse cases that had involved the forcible administration of drugs for purely punitive purposes. *See, e.g.,* Knecht v. Gillman, 488 F.2d 1136, 1137-40 (8th Cir. 1973) (use of apomorphine as "aversive stimuli"); Mackey v. Procunier, 477 F.2d 877–78 (9th Cir. 1973) (use of succinylcholine as aversive conditioning).

medication to institutionalized, mentally ill patients.[27] On the surface this was a seeming far cry from the type of shock-the-conscience physical brutality present in the prototypic right-to-treatment case of *Wyatt v. Stickney.*[28] Thus even in *Rennie v. Klein,* one of the broadest, most scholarly, and most sensitive of the first generation of right-to-refuse treatment cases, Judge Stanley Brotman eloquently laid out the dilemma facing him: "A little knowledge can be dangerous, and this court is hesitant to diagnose mental illness and prescribe medication."[29] Later, when the Third Circuit first modified Judge Brotman's decision in *Rennie,* it limited the substantive and procedural sweep of its protections and recalibrated its reading of the least-restrictive-alternative construct.[30] The Circuit warned carefully about overintrusion by the courts into the daily operation of mental institutions: "This is not to say that the least intrusive means requires hourly or daily judicial oversight. Obviously that would be an unworkable standard. Rather, what is reviewable is whether the choice of a course of treatment strikes a proper balance between efficacy and intrusiveness."[31]

The Supreme Court gave little guidance. In 1982 in *Mills v. Rogers,*[32] a case that arose contemporaneously with *Rennie,*[33] it side-stepped the constitutional issues by remanding the case to the First Circuit for consideration of the impact of an intervening Massachusetts state court decision.[34] The Supreme Court then remanded *Rennie*[35] in light of its contemporaneous decision in *Youngberg v. Romeo*[36] that had, in establishing a minimal right to training for institutionalized mentally retarded individuals, announced as its benchmark for assessing

---

[27]On the interplay between the administration of such medication and the historic roots of deinstitutionalization, see Michael L. Perlin, *Competency, Deinstitutionalization, and Homelessness: A Story of Marginalization,* 29 HOUS. L. REV. 63, 102–04 (1991).

[28]325 F. Supp. 781 (M.D. Ala. 1971), *aff'd sub. nom.,* Wyatt v. Aderholt, 503 F.2d 1305 (5th Cir. 1974); *see also* Jack Drake, *The Development of* Wyatt *in the Courtroom,* in RETROSPECT, *supra* note 25, at 36 (characterizing "horror" of pre-*Wyatt* institutions in Alabama). As the right-to-refuse litigation developed, it became clear that this dichotomy was frequently illusory. *See, e.g., Rennie,* 476 F. Supp. at 1302 (hospital staff increased patient's medication as "reprisal" for his decision to contact an attorney).

[29]*Rennie,* 462 F. Supp. at 1140. The question in *Rennie,* Judge Brotman found, tracked the question asked rhetorically by Judge Bazelon: "How real is the promise of individual autonomy for a confused person set adrift in a hostile world?" *Id.* at 1146, quoting David Bazelon, *Institutionalization, Deinstitutionalization, and the Adversary Process,* 75 COLUM. L. REV. 897, 907 (1975).

[30]The *Rennie* trial court had extended the doctrine of the "least restrictive alternative"—regularly used previously in mental health litigation to questions of custodial settings, *see, e.g.,* Welsch v. Likins, 373 F. Supp. 487, 501 (D. Minn. 1974)—to medication choices. *See Rennie,* 462 F. Supp. at 1146, quoting Bruce Winick, *Psychotropic Medication and Competence to Stand Trial,* 1977 AM. B. FOUND. RES. J. 769, 813 (patient "may challenge the forced administration of drugs on the basis that alternative treatment methods should be tried before a more intrusive technique like psychotropic medication is used"). On subsequent developments, see *supra* Chapter 4, note 79 (discussing relationship between Youngberg v. Romeo, 457 U.S. 307 (1982), and Riggins v. Nevada, 504 U.S. 127 (1992). The Supreme Court returned to the question of "least restrictive alternative" in Olmstead v. L.C., 119 S. Ct. 2176-2181 (1999), finding a qualified right to community treatment for some institutionalized persons with mental disabilities under the Americans with Disabilities Act. *See infra,* Chapter 8.

[31]*Rennie,* 653 F.2d at 847. *See also, e.g., Rogers,* 634 F.2d at 656–57 (in accord).

[32]457 U.S. 291 (1982).

[33]At the trial level, the District Court had originally entered an even broader antidrugging injunction than had Judge Brotman in *Rennie. See* Rogers v. Okin, 478 F. Supp. 1342 (D. Mass. 1979), *modified,* 634 F.2d 650 (1st Cir. 1980), *vacated and remanded sub. nom.,* Mills v. Rogers, 457 U.S. 291 (1982), *on remand,* 738 F.2d 1 (1st Cir. 1984).

[34]*Mills,* 457 U.S. at 306, remanding in light of Richard Roe III, 383 Mass. 415, 421 N.E.2d 40, 51–52 (1981) (holding that a noninstitutionalized incompetent patient had a right to a prior judicial hearing at which he could assert the desire to refuse antipsychotic drug treatment). *See supra* text accompanying note 7.

[35]457 U.S. 1119 (1982).

[36]457 U.S. 307 (1982).

patients' rights claims the test of "substantial professional judgment."[37] On remand (in *Rennie II*), a sharply divided Third Circuit reiterated most of its earlier holding that involuntarily committed patients do have a qualified right to refuse the administration of psychotropics,[38] but, as part of its holding, relied on *Youngberg* in jettisoning the least-restrictive-alternative standard for drugging decisions.[39]

In the wake of *Youngberg*, *Rogers*, and *Rennie II*, the focus of litigation turned swiftly to state courts, and state constitutional law became an increasingly more important vehicle through which right-to-refuse claims were assessed.[40] In *Rivers v. Katz*,[41] a paradigm state constitutional law case, the New York Court of Appeals concluded that state constitutions afforded involuntary patients a fundamental right to refuse, holding that neither mental illness nor institutionalization per se could stand as a justification for overriding such a right on either police power or *parens patriae* grounds.[42] State cases such as *Rivers*[43] rejected arguments that involuntarily committed patients were "presumptively incompetent" because of their institutionalization.[44] Thus in the case of a competent patient, the right "to determine what shall be done with [one's] body" must be honored "even though the recommended treatment may be beneficial or even necessary to preserve the patient's life."[45]

Cases such as *Rivers* and the California state decision in *Riese v. St. Mary's Hospital and Medical Center*[46] made it appear that the federal forum was, simply, a venue of the past for the adjudication of right-to-refuse-treatment cases.[47] Moreover, it appeared that the jurisprudential inquiries engaged in by the federal courts were irrelevant to state court judges. The *Rivers* opinion, for instance, was silent on the jurisdictional split that followed the *Mills*

---

[37]*Id.* at 323 ("Liability may be imposed only when the decision by the professional is such a substantial departure from accepted professional judgment, practice, or standards as to demonstrate that the person responsible did not base the decision on such a judgment"). The Supreme Court's subsequent decision in Riggins v. Nevada, 504 U.S. 127 (1992), may be read to be questioning the continuing vitality of this doctrine in right-to-refuse contexts. *See* Michael L. Perlin, *"Make Promises by the Hour": Sex, Drugs, the ADA, and Psychiatric Hospitalization*, 46 DePaul L. Rev. 947, 972 (1997).

[38]*Rennie*, 720 F.2d at 269–70.

[39]*Id.* at 270.

[40]*See* Perlin, *supra* note 8.

[41]504 N.Y.S.2d 74 (1986).

[42]*See generally* 2 Perlin, *supra* note 2, at §§ 3B-7.2a to 3B-7.2b at 261-76 (2d. ed. 1999).

[43]Other similar cases are cited in *id.*, § 3B-7.2c, at 280-84 (2d. ed. 1999). For empirical considerations of the impact of *Rivers*, see, for example J. Richard Ciccone et al., *Medication Refusal and Judicial Activism: A Reexamination of the Effects of the* Rivers *Decision*, 44 Hosp. & Community Psychiatry 555 (1993); J. Richard Ciccone et al., *Right to Refuse Treatment: Impact of* Rivers v. Katz, 18 Bull. Am. Acad. Psychiatry & L. 203 (1990).

[44]The court reasoned that, without more, neither the fact of mental illness nor commitment "constitutes a sufficient basis to conclude that [such patients] lack the mental capacity to comprehend the consequences of their decision to refuse medication that poses a significant risk to their physical well-being." *Rivers*, 504 N.Y.S.2d at 78, 79. On the ways that courts frequently subvert this doctrine in the trials of involuntary civil commitment and incompetency-to-stand-trial cases, see Michael L. Perlin, *Pretexts and Mental Disability Law: The Case of Competency*, 46 U. Miami L. Rev. 625 (1993).

[45]*Id.* at 78. On the empirical impact of *Rivers*, see, for example Julie Zito et al., *One Year Under* Rivers: *Drug Refusal in a New York State Psychiatric Facility*, 12 Int'l J.L. & Psychiatry 295 (1989); Frances Cournos et al., *A Comparison of Clinical and Judicial Procedures for Reviewing Requests for Involuntary Medication in New York*, 39 Hosp. & Community Psychiatry 851 (1988).

[46]243 Cal. Rptr. 241 (App. 1987), *appeal dismissed*, 259 Cal. Rptr. 609 (1989).

[47]*See* Perlin, *supra* note 8, at 1265 ("the use of state constitutions and state statutes in state courts may be the last frontier for the mentally disabled").

remand.[48] It astonishingly did not even mention the opinion in *Project Release v. Prevost*,[49] in which the Second Circuit (the federal circuit that includes New York) had upheld the constitutionality (on *federal* constitutional grounds)[50] of the very regulation struck down on *state* constitutional grounds by the *Rivers* court.

Rivers ringingly endorsed a preadministration judicial hearing in right-to-refuse cases in which the patient was not a present danger. This stands in sharp contrast to the methodology implicitly endorsed by the U.S. Supreme Court that apparently seemed to accept a more informal, medically focused model to adequately satisfy the demands of the due process clause of the federal constitution,[51] that would employ the ''substantial professional judgment'' test as the benchmark for institutional treatment adequacy,[52] and that would not constitutionally compel adherence to the ''least restrictive alternative'' in institutional drugging cases.[53]

The subsequent decision by the Fourth Circuit in *United States v. Charters*, severely limiting the rights of pretrial detainees to refuse medication and requiring only the most minimalist compliance with the *Youngberg* professional judgment test, appeared to augur the demise of the federal court as a forum for right-to-refuse cases.[54] However, the Supreme Court's later decision in *Riggins v. Nevada* may have served to resuscitate federal courts as an alternative site for litigation in such cases.[55]

Other Settings and Different Populations

Although the great bulk of right-to-refuse-treatment litigation has involved institutionalized persons with mental illnesses, more recent cases have also dealt with the application of the right in other facilities (e.g., in jails, in the community, in state schools for retarded persons) and to cases involving special populations (e.g., persons found not guilty by reason of insanity).[56] Although these cases are still relatively numerically few,[57] they at least indicate that the scope of the problem extends beyond simple decision making involving civilly committed mental patients. Also, the fact that the Supreme Court did address the

---

[48]*See* 2 PERLIN, *supra* note 2, § 3B-7.2f, at 291-92 (2d. ed. 1999).

[49]722 F.2d 960 (2d Cir. 1983).

[50]*Id.* at 980–81. I discuss this anomaly in 2 PERLIN, *supra* note 2, § 3B-7.2b, at 271-72 (2d. ed. 1999).

[51]*See, e.g., Youngberg,* 457 U.S. at 322–23 (''There certainly is no reason to think judges or juries are better qualified than appropriate professionals in making such decisions [about internal operations of state mental institutions]''); Loren Roth, *The Right to Refuse Psychiatric Treatment: Law and Medicine at the Interface,* 35 EMORY L.J. 139, 157 (1986) (''while the 'right to refuse' is a fascinating issue for law and psychiatry, the problem remains clinical''). *Cf. Riggins, supra* notes 12-15 (discussed in this context in Perlin, *supra* note 37, at 972, and in Michael L. Perlin, *Therapeutic Jurisprudence: Understanding the Sanist and Pretextual bases of Mental Disability Law,* 20 N. ENG. J. ON CRIM. & CIV. CONFINEMENT 369, 381 n.86 (1994)).

[52]*See Youngberg,* 457 U.S. at 323.

[53]In its resurrection of the least-restrictive-alternative standard, *Rivers* made no mention of the *Youngberg* decision.

[54]*See* Perlin, *supra* note 10, discussing United States v. Charters, 863 F.2d 302 (4th Cir. 1988) *(en banc), cert. denied,* 494 U.S. 1016 (1990). *Compare* United States v. Brandon, 158 F. 3d. 947 (6th Cir. 1998) (Strict scrutiny standard applies to refusal of medication questions in this context).

[55]*See supra* notes 15–18; Perlin & Dorfman, *supra* note 6; PERLIN, *supra* note 2, § 3B-8.3, at 327-28 (2d. ed. 1999).

[56]*See, e.g.,* 2 PERLIN, *supra* note 2, §§ 5.60–5.65, and *id.,* §§ 3B-9 to 3B-9.6 (2d. ed. 1999).

[57]On the question of applying the right to individuals in private hospitals, see Riese v. St. Mary's Hosp. & Med. Ctr., 243 Cal. Rptr. 241 (App. 1987), *appeal dismissed,* 259 Cal. Rptr. 669 (1988), *discussed in* 2 PERLIN, *supra* note 2, at § 3B-9.3, at 337-39 (2d. ed. 1999). On the question of applying the right to voluntary patients, see Perlin, *supra* note 9, at 50.

question of the refusal of medication in the context of a fair trial question in *Riggins v. Nevada*[58] should likely lead to greater attention paid to this area in the future.

In this section, I will discuss only two of these subgroups—cases involving persons whose homelessness was allegedly the result of their invocation of the right to refuse treatment and cases involving persons whom the government has sought to medicate to make them competent to stand trial (focusing virtually exclusively on the litigation in the case of *United States v. Charters*).[59] In these areas, the relationship between sanism and pretextuality and the development of mental disability law jurisprudence is clearest.

The Relationship Between Deinstitutionalization and the Right to Refuse Treatment

One of the most charged issues in mental disability law is the question of whether there is an interrelationship between homelessness and the right to refuse treatment.[60] Although common wisdom seems to suggest that one of the key factors in the creation of deinstitutionalization policies was the mass marketing of psychiatric drugs,[61] there has been virtually no exploration of the impact of forced public hospital drugging on increased homelessness.[62]

It has been argued that side effects such as akinesia and akathesia have the inevitable effect of retarding social skill progress and of making expatients even less employable once they are deinstitutionalized.[63] Notwithstanding the drugs' apparent effectiveness in reducing the floridity of symptomatology and lessening the excesses of psychic pain,[64] the link

[58]504 U.S. 127 (1992).

[59]829 F.2d 479 (4th Cir. 1987) *(Charters I), on reh'g,* 863 F.2d 302 (4th Cir. 1988) *(en banc) (Charters II), cert. denied,* 494 U.S. 1016 (1990). *Compare* United States v. Brandon, 158 F. 3d 947 (6th Cir. 1998), discussed *supra* note 54.

[60]*See generally* 2 PERLIN, *supra* note 2, at §§ 7.23–7.27. *See generally* Perlin, *supra* note 27, at 104–06.

[61]*See, e.g.,* E. FULLER TORRES, *Nowhere to Go: The Tragic Odyssey of the Homeless Mentally Ill, in* THE HOMELESS MENTALLY ILL 75, 87–88 (H. Richard Lamb ed. 1984) (use of drugs in state hospital "a miracle"). *Cf. id.* at 158 (criticizing court decisions such as Rogers v. Okin, 478 F. Supp. 1342 (D. Mass. 1979), *modified,* 634 F.2d 650 (1st Cir. 1980), *vacated and remanded,* 457 U.S. 291 (1982), *on remand,* 738 F.2d 1 (1984), and Rennie v. Klein, 462 F. Supp. 1131 (D.N.J. 1978), suppl. 476 F. Supp. 1294 (D.N.J. 1979), *modified,* 653 F.2d 836 (3d Cir. 1981), *vacated and remanded,* 458 U.S. 1191 (1982), *on remand,* 720 F.2d 266 (3d Cir. 1983), for permitting mentally ill individuals "once released from a hospital, to remain free and psychotic in the community"), *to* Sheldon Gelman, *Mental Hospital Drugs, Professionalism, and the Constitution,* 72 GEO. L.J. 1725, 1727 n.23 (1984) ("Drugging of the mentally ill in the 'community' is all but universal"). For a comprehensive analysis of all related issues involved in right-to-refuse medication decision making in community settings, see Steven Schwartz & Cathy E. Costanzo, *Compelling Treatment in the Community: Distorted Doctrines and Violated Values,* 20 LOY. L.A. L. REV. 1329 (1987). For a fuller consideration of this issue, see Michael L. Perlin, Book Review of A.B. JOHNSON, OUT OF BEDLAM: THE TRUTH ABOUT DEINSTITUTIONALIZATION (1990), 8 N.Y. L. SCH. J. HUM. RTS. 557 (1991); Keri A. Gould, *"Madness in the Streets" Rides the Waves of Sanism* 9 N.Y. L. SCH. J. HUM. RTS. 567 (1992) (book review of R.J. ISAAC & V.C. ARMAT, MADNESS IN THE STREETS: HOW PSYCHIATRY AND THE LAW ABANDONED THE MENTALLY ILL (1990)).

[62]*Compare* Olmstead v. L.C., 119 S. Ct. 2176, 2191 (1999) (Kennedy, J., concurring) (expressing concern that failure to self-medication in community setting will lead to homelessness).

[63]*Cf. Rennie,* 462 F. Supp. at 1146 (likelihood of patient contracting tardive dyskinesia raises question of whether "the cure would be worse than the illness"); Leopold Bellack & Sonja Mueser, *A Comprehensive Treatment Program for Schizophrenia and Chronic Mental Illness,* 22 COMMUNITY MENT. HEALTH J. 175, 177 (1980) (as many as 50% of schizophrenics may not benefit from antipsychotic medication; such medications do not help patients "develop skills of daily living that enhance the quality of life").

[64]*See Rennie,* 462 F. Supp. at 1137: "Psychotropic drugs are effective in reducing thought disorders in a majority of schizophrenics. With first admission patients, success rates as high as 95% have been obtained. . . . Success rates are less impressive with chronic patients. . . . However, no other treatment modality has achieved equal success in the treatment of schizophrenia. . . ."

between these drug side effects, the failure of patients to be meaningfully reintegrated into society after their release, and homelessness has not yet been considered critically. The link may be especially pernicious in light of the parallel literature illuminating the ways in which institutional dependency progressively leads to losses of social and vocational competencies, precisely the sort of "competencies" that are essential if homeless individuals are to reintegrate themselves meaningfully into mainstream society.[65]

There is now some hard evidence that some deinstitutionalized homeless individuals remain on the streets to avoid regimens of compulsory drugging in hospitals.[66] Parenthetically, other researchers have learned that the homeless persons who have been deinstitutionalized *will* accept medication in social service settings.[67] It is unclear whether other evidence—that these individuals reject the alternative of mental hospitals[68] but frequently seek out medical care in *general hospitals*[69]—can fully explain this paradox. It is clear, though, that further attention must be paid to this inquiry.[70]

Perhaps deinstitutionalized homeless persons know, from searing personal experience, that the indictment of public mental hospitals leveled by then-president of the American Psychiatric Association Harry Solomon, more than 30 years ago—"bankrupt beyond remedy"[71]—is still frequently a valid critique,[72] and that drugging policies at such facilities

---

[65]CHARLES A. KEISLER & AMY A. SIBULKIN, MENTAL HOSPITALIZATION: MYTHS AND FACTS ABOUT A NATIONAL CRISIS 148 (1987), discussing C.A. McEwen, *Continuities in the Study of Total and Non-Total Institutions,* 6 AM. REV. SOC. 143 (1980), and Abraham S. Goldstein, *The Sociology of Mental Health and Illness,* 5 AM. REV. SOC. 381 (1979).

[66]*See* Pamela Fischer & William R. Breakey, *Homelessness and Mental Health: An Overview,* 14 INT'L J. MENT. HEALTH 6, 29 (1986), finding that a proportion of the mentally ill homeless have "opted out" of the mental health system, preferring the "life of the streets" to the alternative of institutional life, and have elected to "live with" the symptoms of mental illness rather than suffer from the unwanted side effects of antipsychotic medication. This result may be seen, depending on the reader's perspective, as good judgment or as evidence of the degree to which mental illness has impaired the individual's thought systems. *See id.* (of a series of 15 problem areas, mental illness was rated as 13th in importance by the homeless). *See also* Lillian Gelberg et al., *Mental Health, Alcohol and Drug Use, and Criminal History Among Homeless Adults,* 145 AM. J. PSYCHIATRY 191, 193 (1988) (deinstitutionalized patients the least likely of the homeless to sleep in emergency shelters).

[67]Anthony Arce, Marilyn Tadlock, Michael Vergare, & Stuart Shapiro, *A Psychiatric Profile of Street People Admitted to an Emergency Shelter,* 34 HOSP. & COMMUNITY PSYCHIATRY 812 (1983) (86% of the homeless mentally ill were willing to comply with psychotropic medications in community support service settings); *see* Judith Clark Turner & William J. TenHoor, *The NIMH Community Support Program: Pilot Approach to a Needed Social Reform,* 4 SCHIZOPHRENIA BULL. 319 (1978).

[68]*See* Farr, *A Mental Health Treatment Program for the Homeless Mentally Ill in the Los Angeles Skid Row Area, in* TREATING THE HOMELESS 64, 71 (Billy E. Jones ed. 1986) (the "vast majority" of population studied "would rather live in filth and be subjected to beatings and violence than to be institutionalized, even in our *finest* mental hospitals") (emphasis added).

[69]*See* Hedy M. Silver, *Voluntary Admission to New York City Hospitals: The Rights of the Mentally Ill Homeless,* 19 COLUM. HUMAN RTS. L. REV. 399, 400–01 n.3, 402–03 n.5 (1988) (substantial numbers of homeless mentally ill seek treatment in emergency rooms of city general hospitals).

[70]On the ways that clinicians fail to follow proper legal procedures in appointing surrogate decision makers, see C. Dennis Barton et al., *Clinicians' Judgment of Capacity of Nursing Home Patients to Give Informed Consent,* 47 PSYCHIATRIC SERV. 956 (1996).

[71]*See* Jonas Robitscher, *Implementing the Rights of the Mentally Disabled: Judicial, Legislative and Psychiatric Action, in* MEDICAL, MORAL AND LEGAL ISSUES IN HEALTH CARE 145, 146 (Frank Ayd Jr. ed. 1974) (commenting on inadequate staffing in state mental hospitals).

[72]*See, e.g.,* Thomas S. by Brooks v. Flaherty, 699 F. Supp. 1178, 1201–02 (W.D.N.C. 1988) (holding that conditions at a North Carolina public hospital violated the "reasonable professional judgment" standard of Youngberg v. Romeo, 457 U.S. 307 (1982)), *aff'd,* 902 F.2d 250 (4th Cir.), *cert. denied,* 498 U.S. 951 (1990); *cf. Beds for Mental Patients,* MIAMI HERALD, Feb. 7, 1990 ("For the lack of bed space, patients suffering from crises wait, restrained with leather ankle straps, in the emergency rooms at Broward General Medical Center or Memorial Hospital in Hollywood. . . . Shackling patients for several days in an emergency room is a scandal in 1990"). Litigation in the most important right-to-treatment case in history—Wyatt v. Stickney—continues to this day. *See supra* chapter 4, and *see, e.g.,* Wyatt by and Through Rawlins v. Rogers, 985 F. Supp. 1356 (M.D. Ala. 1997), in

still frequently violate constitutional norms.[73] Although there is episodic evidence of idiosyncratic improvement,[74] a reading of case law and literature suggests little reason for the wide-ranging optimism that implicitly buttresses the current critique of the American Psychiatric Association; If these folks were back in the hospital, they would be a lot safer.[75]

They might not necessarily be safer, but perhaps we would be relieved. Again, as I discussed in the chapter on involuntary civil commitment,[76] the issue is frequently one of social class and of racial and economic marginalization.[77] Deinstitutionalized homeless persons reflect the socioeconomic characteristics of those hospitalized in public facilities— a universe increasingly more populated by ethnic minorities, the poor, the young, and those with few social supports. Those who have been hospitalized and feel a profound sense of social isolation are subsequently cut adrift without social support.[78] No inquiry into the specific problems can begin to make sense if we fail to come to grips with the significance of this reality: It is the "once and future" marginalized that we target in our attacks on the homeless mentally ill persons who have been deinstitutionalized.[79] Again, the relationship

---

which the federal district court reconsidered the extent to which defendants had complied with each of the *Wyatt* standards, granting partial release from certain provisions of the decree with which defendants had complied but denying release from others. More recently in Wyatt v. Sawyer, 1999 WL 805285 (M.D. Ala. 1999); The court released the defendants from more standards.

[73]*See* PERLIN, *supra* note 2, §§ Chapter 3B (2d. ed. 1999) (discussing right-to- refuse-treatment developments of the 1990s).

[74]On the willingness of the judiciary to confront meaningfully the underlying issues, compare Arnold v. Department of Health Servs., 775 P.2d 521 (Ariz. 1989) (state and county under mandatory statutory duty to provide mental health care to indigent chronically mentally ill persons), with K. C. v. State, 771 P.2d 774 (Wyo. 1989) (no constitutional right to treatment in community residential facilities); *see also* Board of Supervisors v. Superior Court, 254 Cal. Rptr. 905, 909 (App. 1989) (reading state statute to set "absolute limit" on county's mental health obligations).

[75]*See, e.g.,* H. LAMB, *Deinstitutionalization and the Homeless Mentally Ill, in* THE HOMELESS MENTALLY ILL 75 (H. Lamb ed. 1984). Dr. Lamb limits the universe of those whom he sees to be in need of rehospitalization to "a small proportion of long-term, severely-disabled psychiatric patients [that] lack sufficient impulse control to handle living in an open setting such as a board-and-care home or with relatives." *Id.* He also criticizes the views of those who recommend massive rehospitalization as simplistic, exaggerative, and overly romantic (as to the role and capabilities of state hospitals). *See id.* at 67. Nevertheless, the APA Task Force report prepared under his direction is viewed in the public debate as an important argument in favor of exactly such massive reinstitutionalization. *See, e.g.,* P. S. Hyde, *Homelessness in America: Public Policy, Public Blame,* 8 PSYCH. SOC. REHAB. J. 21, 22 (1985) (APA report evaluated through the "give me an immediate solution" demands of the public).

[76]*See supra* Chapter 4.

[77]*See* Hendrick Wagenaar & Dan A. Lewis, *Ironies of Inclusion: Social Class and Deinstitutionalization,* 14 J. HEALTH POL., POL'Y & L. 503, 508 (1989) (pointing out that "the class dimension in mental hospitalization is largely ignored"). Lamb explicitly acknowledges the role of cultural bias on U.S. deinstitutionalization policy:

> An important issue related to goal setting is that the kinds of criteria that theorists, researchers, policymakers, and clinicians use to assess social integration have a distinct bias in favor of the values held by these professionals and by middle-class society generally. Thus holding a job, increasing one's socialization and relationships with other people, and living independently may be goals that are not shared by a large proportion of the long-term mentally ill. Likewise, what makes the patient happy may be unrelated to these goals. . . .

H. Richard Lamb, *Deinstitutionalization and the Homeless Mentally Ill,* 35 HOSP. & COMMUNITY PSYCHIATRY 899, 942 (1984).

[78]*See generally* W. WILSON, THE TRULY DISADVANTAGED: THE INNER CITY, THE UNDERCLASS, AND PUBLIC POLICY (1987) (graphically demonstrating the extent to which the "extremely poor" or "socially marginalized" are cut off from mainstream society); *see also* David Luban, *Difference Made Legal: The Court and Dr. King,* 87 MICH. L. REV. 2152, 2160 n.22 (citing the "wealth of horrendous detail concerning the emiseration of black Americans," and the "grim, even terrifying, summary of the emergency conditions under which we live").

[79]*See, e.g.,* Schumer, *Shutting the Doors on the Poor,* N.Y. TIMES, Mar. 9, 1988, at A31 (noting that the effect of the deinstitutionalization of many mentally ill patients in the 1960s and 1970s reinforced already existing stereotypes of homeless individuals).

between hospital drugging policies—and the sanism and pretextuality that frequently come into play in the case law that construes those policies—and our stand on deinstitutionalization and homelessness must be carefully considered.

In Criminal Law Settings: Defendants Awaiting Trial

Prior to 1987 medication cases involving defendants awaiting incompetency to stand trial (IST) determinations had "resulted in a series of apparently random decisions from which almost no doctrinal threads could be extracted," leading to "significant and genuine confusion" in this area.[80] Subsequently, though, two separate decisions in one case—with radically different opinions—appear to have since brought some measure of coherence to this area.[81]

In 1987 a panel of the Fourth Circuit Court of Appeals issued the first decision in *United States v. Charters.*[82] *(Charters I)* on the right of a federal pretrial detainee to refuse psychotropic medication. *Charters I* rejected the notion that the "exercise of professional judgment standard" articulated by the Supreme Court in *Youngberg v. Romeo* applied to antipsychotic medication cases, resurrected right-to-privacy and freedom-of-thought-process arguments that had been generally abandoned in the years since the Supreme Court's decision in *Mills v. Rogers,* established a right to be free from unwanted physical intrusion as an integral part of an individual's constitutional freedoms, and articulated a complex substituted judgment–best interests methodology to be used in right-to-refuse-treatment cases.[83]

On *en banc* rehearing, the full Fourth Circuit vacated the panel decision *(Charters II),* "suggesting that the panel was wrong about almost everything."[84] Although it agreed that the defendant possessed a constitutionally retained interest in freedom from bodily restraint that was implicated by the forced administration of psychotropic drugs and was protected "against arbitrary and capricious action by government officials,"[85] it found that informal institutional administrative procedures were adequate to protect the defendant's due process interests. It applied the substantial-professional-judgment test of *Youngberg,* and limited questioning of experts to one matter: "Was this decision reached by a process so completely out of bounds as to make it explicable only as an arbitrary, nonprofessional one?"[86] Although the court briefly acknowledged the possibility of side effects (a factor stressed heavily in *Charters I*), it quickly dismissed the magnitude of their potential harm by noting that they were simply "one element" to be weighed in a best-interests decision. The court conceded that it did not do an "exhaustive analysis" of the conflicting literature before it, demurring to that literature's importance: "It suffices to observe that, while there is universal agreement in the professional discipline that side-effects always exist as a risk, there is wide disagreement within those disciplines as to the degree of their severity."[87]

---

[80]Perlin, *supra* note 10, at 963; *cf., e.g.,* State v. Hayes, 389 A.2d 1379 (N.H. 1978), *to* Whitehead v. Wainwright, 447 F. Supp. 898 (M.D. Fla. 1978), *vacated and remanded on other grounds,* 609 F.2d 223 (5th Cir. 1980).

[81]*But cf.* Riggins v. Nevada, 504 U.S. 127 (1992), disscussed *infra* text accompanying notes 178-88.

[82]829 F.2d 479 (4th Cir. 1987) *(Charters I), on reh'g,* 863 F.2d 302 (4th Cir. 1988) *(en banc) (Charters II), cert. denied,* 494 U.S. 1016 (1990).

[83]*See generally* Perlin, *supra* note 10; 2 PERLIN, *supra* note 2, § 3B-8.1a (2d. ed. 1999).

[84]Perlin, *supra* note 10, at 965.

[85]*Charters,* 863 F.2d at 306.

[86]*Id.* at 313.

[87]*Id.* at 310–11.

The two views of the rights of pretrial detainees to refuse medication reflected in *Charters I* and *Charters II* could not be more diametrically opposed. Also, the ultimate *en banc* decision has led to some important strategic decision making. Although as a federal detainee Charters was forced to litigate in federal court, in cases in which litigants do have an option of availing themselves of a state forum, *Charters II* made it more likely they would choose that jurisdictional alternative. *Charters II* thus appeared to "signal the death knell for the litigation of right-to-refuse treatment issues in the federal forum" in cases in which litigants retain discretion as to where to sue.[88]

Decoding the Right to Refuse Treatment

The jurisprudence of the right to refuse treatment is complex. Separate bodies of doctrine have developed in parallel court systems and in cases involving civil and criminal litigants. The Supreme Court's decisions in *Youngberg v. Romeo* and *Mills v. Rogers* led to an exodus from federal courts, but its subsequent opinion in *Riggins v. Nevada* has somewhat augured a return to that forum. Some courts choose to read the social science literature on side effects carefully and others profess that they are unable to make meaningful distinctions among the data. In two years time[89], the Supreme Court did nearly a complete about face in its reading of the same evidence. There has been virtually no litigation in cases involving some of the most important "categories" of potential right-to-refuse litigants in other settings. The vast majority of litigation has involved antipsychotic drugs, although commentators and a handful of cases raise the question of the application of the doctrine to a full range of other treatments.

Is it possible to extract meaningful doctrinal coherence from these conflicting findings? My reading of nearly two decades of legal developments in this area suggests that sense can be made only if we first look at a question that is rarely asked in this context: *Why* has the law developed as it has in this volatile area? The seemingly incoherent splits in right-to-refuse decision making can best be explained by considering these jurisprudential constructs. Judges who use heuristic devices, make sanist assumptions, and employ pretextual thinking[90] decide cases that ignore social science data, privilege myths, and misstate established legal doctrine. Others, however, read social science data carefully, avoid sanist thought processes, and reject pretextual decision making.

The split between the panel and the *en banc* Fourth Circuit in *United States v. Charters*[91] or the differences between the majority and the dissent in *Riggins v. Nevada*[92] perfectly mirror this dichotomy. The *Charters I* court carefully analyzed the available social science

---

[88]Perlin, *supra* note 10, at 994. *But compare* United States v. Brandon, 158 F. 3d 947 (6th Cir. 1998), discussed *supra* note 54.

[89]*Compare* Washington v. Harper, 494 U.S. 210 (1990) to Riggins v. Nevada, 504 U.S. 127 (1992); *See generally,* 2 PERLIN, *supra* note 2, §§ 3B-8.2 to 3B-8.3 (2d. ed. 1999).

[90]For a more recent right-to-refuse case that perpetuates sanism, see *Matter of* R. S. C., 921 S.W.2d 506 (Tex. App. 1996) (trial court had no duty to make written findings regarding statutory factors in need-for-medication hearing); for more recent cases that are nonsanist, see, for example *In re* Israel, 664 N.E.2d 1032 (Ill. App. 1996) (patient's right to refuse upheld where patient provided rational reason for refusal); Enis v. Department of Health and Social Servs., 962 F. Supp. 1192 (W.D. Wis. 1996) (striking down statute governing administration of antipsychotic medication to insanity acquittees). *See* Susan Ruscher et al., *Psychiatric Patients' Attitudes About Medication and Factors Affecting Noncompliance,* 48 PSYCHIATRIC SERV. 82 (1997).

[91]829 F.2d 479 (4th Cir. 1987) *(Charters I), on reh'g,* 863 F.2d 302 (4th Cir. 1988) *(en banc) (Charters II),* cert. denied, 494 U.S. 1016 (1990); *see generally* Perlin, *supra* note 10.

[92]504 U.S. 127 (1992).

data as to the prevalence and severity of side effects.[93] The *Charters II* court, on the other hand, rejected as incredulous the possibility that a court could make a meaningful distinction between competency to stand trial and competency to engage in medication decision making: "[Such a distinction] must certainly be of such subtlety and complexity as to tax perception by the most skilled medical or psychiatric professionals. . . . To suppose that it is a distinction that can be fairly discerned and applied even by the most skilled judge on the basis of an adversarial fact-finding proceeding taxes credulity."[94]

The *Charters II* court was correct in its observation that "while there is universal agreement in the professional discipline that side-effects always exist as a risk, there is wide disagreement within those disciplines as to the degree of their severity."[95] Although this is certainly true, this does not excuse the court from refusing to critically analyze the scientific research in coming to its ultimate decision.[96]

The *Charters II* court revealed its "apprehensiveness about dealing with underlying social, psychodynamic and political issues that form the overt and hidden agendas in any right-to-refuse case."[97] The court's decision also incorporated a broad array of heuristic devices in a way that led to the trivialization and misuse of the social science data before it.[98] By using these devices, the court:

> abdicated its responsibilities to read, harmonize, distinguish, and analyze social science data on the issues before it. It not only inadequately addressed the issue of side effects, but it also failed to adequately address issues concerning competency determinations, the therapeutic value of decision making, the empirical results of an announcement of a right to refuse treatment, and the courts' role in such processes.[99]

The trivialization of social science serves additional instrumental ends. It allows courts to more comfortably seek refuge in expressing common-sense "morality," to employ heuristic devices in a wide variety of cases in uncomfortable areas of the law, and to use sanist behavior in deciding such cases.[100]

The Fourth Circuit *en banc* avoided dealing with serious legal issues by using cursory quotations from off-point precedent, evaded important underlying issues of social science and empiricism, and relied on heuristic reasoning devices and an unarticulated notion of "ordinary common sense" in reaching its decision. It thus revealed several hidden

---

[93]*Charters*, 829 F.2d at 489 n.2.

[94]*Charters*, 863 F.2d at 310. *Cf.* Mark Munetz & Gregory Peterson, *Documenting Informed Consent for Treatment With Neuroleptics: An Alternative to the Consent Form*, 47 PSYCHIATRIC SERV. 302 (1996), at 303 (critiquing view of many clinicians that a signed consent form "equate[s] . . . with informed consent").

[95]*Id.* at 311

[96]*See* Perlin, *supra* note 10, at 990–92; *cf.* John Monahan & Laurens Walker, *Judicial Use of Social Science Research*, 15 LAW & HUM. BEHAV. 571, 582–83 (1991) (setting out steps to be used by courts in analyzing social science evidence). As Monahan and Walker observed in a different context on the question of judicial self-professed scientific illiteracy, "Anyone who can comprehend the Federal Tort Claims Act can learn what standard deviation and statistical significance mean." John Monahan & Laurens Walker, *Social Authority: Obtaining, Evaluating, and Establishing Social Science in Law*, 134 U. PA. L. REV. 477, 511 n.119 (1986).

[97]Perlin, *supra* note 10, at 966.

[98]Perlin & Dorfman, *supra* note 6.

[99]Perlin, *supra* note 10, at 999.

[100]The *Charters II* opinion "reflects inappropriate heuristic thinking in a variety of contexts. It uses such distorting devices as availability, typification, the myth of particularistic proofs, and the 'vividness effect.'. . . The opinion's attempts to simplify one of the most complex problems facing decision makers, assessing mentally disabled individuals' capacity to retain some autonomous decision-making power, further reflects the pernicious effect of the heuristic of attribution theory." Perlin, *supra* note 10, at 986–87 (footnotes omitted).

agendas that must be illuminated if the psychodynamics of its reasoning are to be understood fully.

The court's reliance on *Youngberg* incorporates two significant errors of omission. The *en banc* court failed to confront the way that the *Charters I* court had carefully distinguished *Youngberg* based on some fundamental factual differences between the two cases. In a significant textual reference to *Youngberg*, the *Charters II* court characterized the plaintiff as an "institutionalized mental patient."[101] This reference is incorrect; the *Youngberg* plaintiff was a severely mentally retarded resident of a state school for persons with mental retardation.[102] Although the *Charters I* panel had noted the significance of this distinction by stating that *Youngberg* "did not consider the rights of a competent patient to determine the course of his medical treatment,"[103] the *en banc* court ignored this on rehearing.

Perhaps even more curious is the court's failure to refer to distinguish or even recognize the existence of its own then-recent decision in *Thomas S. v. Morrow*,[104] involving a young adult with mental disabilities who had been shuffled through 40 foster homes and institutions after having been given up for adoption at birth.[105] Substantially affirming a district court decision that the plaintiff had a right to treatment in a suitable community residence, the Fourth Circuit stressed that *Youngberg* "did not allow the professionals free rein."[106] Paradoxically, in *Thomas S.*, the treatment that the institutional defendants provided to the plaintiff conflicted with professional judgment; the district court pointed out that the plaintiff's treatment had been modified "to conform to the *available* treatment, rather than to the *appropriate* treatment, for plaintiff's condition."[107]

The *en banc* court in *Charters II* relied repeatedly on *Parham v. J. R.*[108] for the proposition that more relaxed due process procedures might be appropriate. That reliance is puzzling. *Parham* dealt with the civil commitment of juveniles, and the Court premised its holdings specifically on the assumption that parents make certain medical decisions for their children with their offsprings' best interests at heart. Former Chief Justice Burger thus wrote, "Our jurisprudence historically has reflected Western civilization concepts of the family as a unit with broad parental authority over minor children. . . . The law's concept of the family rests on a presumption that parents possess what a child lacks in maturity, experience, and capacity for judgment required for making life's difficult decisions. More important, historically, it has recognized that natural bonds of affection lead parents to act in the best interests of their children."[109] Aside from the universal criticism of these assumptions as lacking an empirical or scientific basis,[110] it strains credulity that the same paternalistic impulses motivate federal correctional institutional officials in their dealings with pretrial detainees. Similarly, the *Charters II* court's citation to *Parham*'s invocation of

---

[101]*Charters*, 863 F.2d at 308.

[102]Youngberg v. Romeo, 457 U.S. 307, 309 (1982) (plaintiff had mental capacity of 18-month-old child).

[103]*Charters*, 829 F.2d at 488. The "treatment" in *Youngberg* was soft arm restraints. *Youngberg*, 457 U.S. at 310-11.

[104]781 F.2d 367 (4th Cir.), *cert. denied*, 476 U.S. 1124, 479 U.S. 869 (1986); *Thomas S.* is discussed extensively in 2 PERLIN, *supra* note 2, § 3A-12, at 114-17 (2d. ed. 1999).

[105]601 F. Supp. 1055, 1056–57 (W.D.N.C. 1985), *aff'd in part and modified in part*, 781 F.2d 367 (4th Cir.), *cert. denied*, 476 U.S. 1124, 479 U.S. 869 (1986).

[106]*Id.* at 1957–60, 781 F.2d at 375, 379.

[107]*Thomas S.*, 601 F. Supp. at 1059 (emphasis in original).

[108]442 U.S. 584 (1979); *see generally supra* Chapter 4.

[109]*Id.* at 602 (citations omitted). For a careful analysis of the history of the political and governmental regulation of family life, see Robert Dingwall & John Eekelaar, *Families and the State: An Historical Perspective on the Public Regulation of Private Conduct*, 10 LAW & POL'Y 341 (1988).

[110]*See supra* Chapter 4.

"common human experience" that suggests that the "supposed protections of an adversary proceeding . . . may well be more illusory than real[111] simply ignores the entire body of post-*Parham* social science literature rebutting the Supreme Court's allegedly common-sense reading.[112]

In the years since the *Parham* Court concluded that there was no reason to expect that courts could add to the diagnostic work that mental health professionals have done in public hospitals, there has been ample development, both in the case law and in the social science literature, of the realities of drug management in such facilities. The trial records of cases such as *Rennie v. Klein*,[113] *Rogers v. Okin*,[114] and *Davis v. Hubbard*[115] are eloquent testimony to the sad reality that, unpoliced, a significant number of such hospitals have engaged in patterns and practices of serious misuse of psychotropic drugs on a regular basis.[116]

The *en banc Charters II* court's reference to the "cumbersomeness, expense, and delay incident to judicial proceedings"[117] tellingly is without citation. This bare conclusion has no basis in empirical fact. As noted in the vacated panel opinion, few patients actually avail themselves of the due process protections available.[118] The reference further ignores the burgeoning database of empirical studies that has begun to examine what actually happens when a right-to-refuse-treatment order is entered. These studies address such questions as "to what extent the hospital staff complies with court orders; how many patients actually wish to refuse antipsychotic medication; to what extent they are representative of all patients; [and] the impact the refusal has on treatment."[119] The studies virtually unanimously belie the fear of creating an expensive, time-consuming, counterproductive layer of due process hearings.[120]

---

[111]*Parham*, 442 U.S. at 310.

[112]*See, e.g.,* Gail S. Perry & Gary B. Melton, *Precedential Value of Judicial Notice of Social Facts:* Parham *as an Example,* 22 J. FAM. L. 633, 645 (1983–84):

> The *Parham* case is an example of the Supreme Court's taking advantage of the free rein on social facts to promulgate a dozen or so of its own by employing one tentacle of the judicial notice doctrine. The Court's opinion is filled with social facts of questionable veracity, accompanied by the authority to propel these facts into subsequent case law, and, therefore, a spiral of less than rational, legal policy making.

[113]476 F. Supp. 1294 (D.N.J. 1979).

[114]478 F. Supp. 1242 (D. Mass. 1979).

[115]506 F. Supp. 915 (N.D. Ohio 1980).

[116]*See, e.g., Rennie,* 476 F. Supp. at 1299–1302. The trial record indicated that psychotropic drugs were the "be all and end all" of state psychiatric hospitals, *id.* at 1299; the defendant state hospital medical director conceded that medication was used "as a form of control and as a substitute for treatment, *id.;* hospital doctors regularly failed to diagnose tardive dyskinesia and other neurological side effects present in 35 to 50% of all state hospital pedants, *id.* at 1300; and "unjustified polypharmacy" was common, *id.* The district court emphasized that the defendant state officials exhibited "conscious and deliberate indifference to breaches of patients' rights by hospital personnel," *id.* at 1309; *see also Davis,* 506 F. Supp. at 926 ("testimony at trial established that the prevalent use of drugs is countertherapeutic and can be justified only for reasons other than treatment—namely, for the convenience of staff and for punishment"); 2 PERLIN, *supra* note 2, § 3B-2, at 160-64, and 3B-5.1h, at 201-05 (2d. ed. 1999).

[117]*Charters,* 863 F.2d at 309.

[118]*Charters,* 829 F.2d at 499 n.28 (citing David B. Bushwood & Joseph L. Fink III, *Right to Refuse Treatment With Psychotropic Medication,* 42 AM. J. HOSP. PHARMACY 2709 (1985).

[119]2 PERLIN, *supra* note 2, § 3B-14, at 367 (2d. ed. 1999).

[120]*See* 2 PERLIN, *supra* note 2, § 3B-5.4, at 215-24 (2d. ed. 1999); *see also* Franklin J. Hickman, Phillip J. Resnick, & Kathyrn B. Olson, *Right to Refuse Psychotropic Medication. An Interdisciplinary Proposal,* 6 MENTAL DIS. L. REP. 122, 129–30 (1982) (Ohio state hospital's compliance with *Davis* decision created "no significant administrative burden"); Donald J. Kemna, *Current Status of Institutionalized Mental Health Patients' Right to Refuse Psychotropic Drugs,* 6 J. LEGAL MED. 107, 119 (1985) (implementing due process procedures has cost little and has resulted in unexpected savings). *But see* Joseph Bloom et al., *An Empirical View of Patients Exercising Their Right to Refuse Treatment,* 7 INT'L J.L. & PSYCHIATRY 315, 327 (1984) (because refusers were hospitalized longer than nonrefusers, hospital incurred "substantial expenditures" for these additional patient stays).

For example, Julie Zito and her associates' comprehensive study of the implementation of *Rivers v. Katz* at Rockland Psychiatric Center, a New York state psychiatric facility, revealed that (a) numerically the percentage of drug refusers whose cases went to court was tiny (1.3% of the involuntary patients, 0.6% of the total population); (b) requests to medicate objecting patients were granted in 13 of 15 cases, but drug refusers had shorter hospital stays (to a degree approaching statistical significance); and (c) remarkably, patients *never* cited their legal rights' as a reason for refusing.[121] Concluding that the meritorious refusals were probably an "unnecessary burden on the court," Dr. Zito and her colleagues apparently suggest that staff doctors' passive–aggressiveness[122] was partially to blame: "Clinical approaches which overcome these problems are typically found in everyday practice. If these cases reflect a simplistic interpretation of the court decisions or an inability to engage patients in treatment, then the judicially-mandated program could be subverted by a lack of understanding of when to use the courts and when to work with the patient until a mutually satisfactory solution emerges."[123]

Stephen Rachlin has suggested that prior to seeking a court-ordered refusal override the doctor should attempt "all other psychotherapeutic measures," including "a negotiation process with the patient."[124] Quoting Brooks's observation that the right-to-refuse litigation has had a "heuristic" value, he concluded, "If we have learned some principles of law that will help patients and if some improper prescribing practices have been altered, this is to the good."[125] The disaster scenario that the *Charters II* court predicted is simply unrealistic.

The opinion also ignores the advantages that may flow from due process protections. A modest body of literature suggests that involuntary civil commitment hearings have a therapeutic potential.[126] A study conducted by Francine Cournos and her associates at Manhattan Psychiatric Center, another New York public hospital under the *Rivers* order, concluded that the new procedures offered patients "considerably greater representation and participation" because it gave them "the opportunity to hear a detailed discussion of their physician's reasoning and to present their own views."[127] This perhaps enabled the

---

[121]Zito et al., *supra* note 45. To some extent these data conflict with some studies done by Paul Appelbaum & Steven Hoge, *The Right to Refuse Treatment: What the Research Reveals,* 4 BEHAV. SCI. & L. 279, 281 (1986) (refusers range from 1% to 15%, with a mean of 10%). Zito has suggested that this difference may simply reflect different populations, different definitions of refusal, and different settings in which the refusal process operates. Zito, *supra* note 45.

[122]*See* JAMES PAGE, PSYCHOPATHOLOGY 316–17 (1971) (passive–aggressive personalities exhibit "covert styles of expressing resentment and hostility"). For an example of such passive–aggressive behavior in the context of right-to-treatment litigation, see Phillip Leaf, Wyatt v. Stickney: *Assessing the Impact in Alabama,* 28 HOSP. & COMMUNITY PSYCHIATRY 351, 354 (1977) (discussing the "overreaction" of Alabama state hospital staff to the court's decision in that case).

[123]Zito et al., *supra* note 45, at 357 (on therapeutic benefits of right-to-refuse hearing).

[124]Steven Rachlin, *One Right Too Many?* 3 BULL. AM. ACAD. PSYCHIATRY & L. 99 (1975), at 221. For Rachlin's views on the appropriate scope of the right to refuse treatment, see Steven Rachlin, *Rethinking the Right to Refuse Treatment,* 19 PSYCHIATRIC ANN. 213 (1989) (arguing that the right to refuse is antithetical to the right to treatment, and that should be no right to refuse standard, well-accepted treatment).

[125]Rachlin, *supra* note 124, at 222.

[126]*See, e.g.,* John Ensminger & Thomas Liguori, *The Therapeutic Significance of the Civil Commitment Hearing: An Unexplored Potential,* 6 J. PSYCHIATRY & L. 5 (1978); *see also* Tom Tyler, *The Psychological Consequences of Judicial Procedures: Implications for Civil Commitment Hearings,* 46 SMU L. REV. 433 (1992); Jack Susman, *Resolving Hospital Conflicts: A Study on Therapeutic Jurisprudence,* 22 J. PSYCHIATRY & L. 107 (1994); Douglas Stransky, *Civil Commitment and the Right to Refuse Treatment: Resolving Disputes From a Due Process Perspective,* 50 U. MIAMI L. REV. 413 (1996).

[127]Cournos et al., *supra* note 45, at 855.

patients to "gain a better understanding of the need for treatment through a process that offers this degree of patient involvement."[128]

The *Charters II* court's fear of time-consuming "battles of the experts"[129] is similarly unfounded. It reflects a failure to evaluate studies of the impact of similar decisions elsewhere. Such studies include the developing database in *Rivers*, revealing quicker decisions in drug refusal cases, which "should benefit all concerned."[130] The Cournos study at Manhattan Psychiatric Center concluded that adopting more stringent legal procedures "did not delay or diminish requests for or approval of involuntary treatment."[131]

To buttress its argument on this point, the *Charters II* court engaged in selective docket reading, citing an unreported case to support its assertion that under the panel's due process formulation medication refusals will be routinely upheld.[132] Inexplicably, the court failed to note that the one reported post-*Charters I* case granted the government's motion to forcibly medicate under the terms of the *Charters I* opinion.[133]

The *Charters II* opinion also reflects inappropriate heuristic thinking in a variety of contexts.[134] It uses such distorting devices as availability, typification, the myth of particularistic proofs, and the "vividness effect"[135] in its broad-brush characterization of a psychiatrists "poignant testimony" about whether "any factual inquiry" into the competency of "schizophrenic patients" might ever be valid.[136] The opinion's attempts to simplify one of the most complex problems facing decision makers—assessing mentally disabled individuals' capacity to retain some autonomous decision-making power—further reflects the pernicious effect of the heuristic of attribution theory.

In its apparent inability to differentiate between competency to stand trial and competency to accept medication,[137] a distinction that the panel[138] and the other courts that stand "in uniform agreement that incompetency to stand trial is not defined in terms of mental illness"[139] had made, the *Charters II* court engaged in passive–aggressive behavior.[140] Scholars have patiently clarified the difference between these concepts and have warned of the serious consequences that may befall the adjudicator who falls prey to this "simplistic equation."[141] The courts have also underscored that incompetency to engage in medication decision making cannot be presumed from the fact of institutionalization (or even civil commitment).[142] In addition, empirical scientists have begun studying the

---

[128]*Id. See also* Appelbaum & Hoge, *supra* note 121, at 283 (studies suggest that "the more persistent refusers may retain a greater sense of control over their lives").

[129]*Charters,* 863 F.2d at 309 n.5.

[130]Zito et al., *supra* note 45.

[131]Cournos et al., *supra* note 45, at 855.

[132]*Charters,* 863 F.2d at 309 n.5.

[133]United States v. Waddell, 687 F. Supp. 208, 210 (M.D.N.C. 1988).

[134]*See generally supra* Chapter 1.

[135]*See e.g.,* Michael L. Perlin, "Make Promises by the Hour": Sex, Drugs, The ADA, and Psychiatric Hospitalization, 46 DE PAUL L. REV. 947, 980-81 (1997).

[136]*Charters,* 863 F.2d at 309 n.5.

[137]*Charters,* 863 F.2d at 310.

[138]*Id.,* 829 F.2d at 488.

[139]Martin v. Dugger, 686 F. Supp. 1523, 1572 (S.D. Fla. 1988); *see* 3 PERLIN, *supra* note 2, § 14.09 at 236.

[140]*See supra* note 122.

[141]Linda Fentiman, *Whose Right Is It Anyway?: Rethinking Competency to Stand Trial in Light of the Synthetically Sane Insanity Defendant,* 40 U. MIAMI L. REV. 1109, 1119 (1986).

[142]*Rennie,* 462 F. Supp. at 1145.

connections between acceptance of medication and criminal trial incompetency,[143] and the critics have assumed that any linkage between the two had "finally been abandoned by both the courts and the medical profession."[144] The *Charters II* court, however, resurrected this merger with neither doctrinal, empirical, nor scientific grounding.

This passive–aggressive style surfaces elsewhere in the opinion as well. By suggesting that because medical professionals will "now [be] aware of the [appropriate] standard," they "may be as willing to proceed without prior judicial approval as" other bureaucrats and civil servants in the federal prison system,[145] the court implies an acknowledging acceptance of passive–aggressive behavior by the very doctors whose professional judgments it seeks to insulate from scrutiny. This expectation of resistance was ably responded to a decade ago by Brooks:

> It is hypothesized that some treating physicians will be reluctant to participate in a "hearing" because of unwillingness to be challenged, fear of examination and cross-examination, unwillingness to prepare or spend the time, and the like. Treating psychiatrists may in a passive–aggressive manner concede and accede, perhaps against their better judgment, to the patient's asserted wishes in order to avoid participation in such procedures. But experience with thousands of civil commitment proceedings indicates that in the relatively few cases in which negotiation fails, psychiatrists have been willing to participate in legal proceedings that are more formal and time consuming than those now proposed in *Rennie*.[146]

Concerning the veiled suggestion that a contrary decision would have hastened the exodus from public facilities, Brooks noted further that this argument replicated others previously advanced every time due process protections were expanded and that, empirically, there was "no significant evidence . . . that this has happened or will happen."[147]

The *Charters II* court's reliance on these reasoning devices reflects the unconscious turmoil—and sanism—that cases involving mentally disabled criminal defendants cause. The court professes an institutional inability to sort out "opposing scientific assessments,"[148] notwithstanding the many recent scholarly and thoughtful contributions to this area on how courts can and should interpret and weigh social science data.[149]

The court's criticism of the panel for relying on "selected items in the legal and medical literature" is also baffling.[150] The panel had cited extensively to standard medical works as well as to survey articles summarizing the important scientific developments in this area over the past two decades.[151] A reading of the law review articles that the panel cited

---

[143]*See* Jean C. Beckham et al., *Don't Pass Go: Predicting Who Returns From Court as Remaining Incompetent for Trial*, 13 CRIM. JUST. & BEHAV. 99 (1986).

[144]Note, *State Mental Health Patients' Right to Refuse Forcible Administration of Medication Narrowly Construed*, 11 SETON HALL L. REV. 796, 807 (1981).

[145]*Charters*, 863 F.2d at 314.

[146]Alexander Brooks, *The Constitutional Right to Refuse Antipsychotic Medications*, 8 BULL. AM. ACAD. PSYCHIATRY & L. 179, 207 (1980).

[147]*Id.* at 211.

[148]*Charters*, 863 F.2d at 311 n.6.

[149]The most notable studies are by John Monahan and Laurens Walker. *See, e.g.,* John Monahan & Laurens Walker, *Social Authority: Obtaining, Evaluating, and Establishing Social Science in Law*, 134 U. PA. L. REV. 477 (1986).

[150]*Charters*, 863 F.2d at 307 n.3.

[151]*Id.*, 829 F.2d at 483 n.2.

illuminates these sources' general reliance for their data on standard medical journals and medical texts and on other law review articles by acknowledged medical experts.[152]

By characterizing judicial involvement in this area as "already perilous,"[153] the *Charters II* court revealed the depth of its apprehensions. This rhetoric is not accidental; it reflects the court's almost palpable discomfort in having to confront the questions before it. The court's pretextual refusal to even *weigh* the side effects evidence leaves the nonexpert reader in a quandary: Are there two equal bodies of studies that simply cancel each other out? Are there differences in the methodologies that somehow tip the scales in one way or another? Should all of the values under consideration be given equal weight? Are there new scientific breakthroughs that are just over the horizon?

The court's similar refusal to engage in scholarly discourse offers no clues to the answers to these questions and no insight into then-contemporaneous developments in "neuroleptic malignant syndrome"[154] and other topics of significance to serious researchers in this area.[155] For instance, the court quoted Ross Baldessarini,[156] but ignored more recent qualifications by the same author that (a) chronic patients respond least satisfactorily to any treatment (including psychopharmacology); (b) the optimal role of such drugs in long-term treatment "remains a matter of investigation;" (c) antipsychotic agents are of "uncertain benefit in some conditions" and their use "is compromised by common and characteristic forms of early and late-onset neurological side-effects;" and (d) "*all* of the antipsychotic agents" currently in use "exact some unwanted effects on the central nervous system."[157] Again, the reader has no sense of this, partly because the court abdicated its obligation to weigh, analyze, and apply the best available social science data to the case before it.

Other curiosities in the opinion also reflect the court's discomfort. For example, the court's incantation of *Parham v. J. R.'s*[158] language regarding the use of "accepted medical practices in diagnosis, treatment and prognosis"[159] assumes that such practices are actually used in public psychiatric institutions. This assumption is belied by two decades of litigation that flowed from a scandalous abdication of such professional responsibility in facilities across the nation.[160] The court's conclusion that Charters's failure to offer evidence that the initial drugging decision lay "completely beyond the bounds of tolerable professional judgment. . . . *undoubtedly* reflects the fact that no such evidence was available"[161] suggests a picture totally at odds with history. Without making any reference to the specific level of counsel available to Charters in this case, it can be said that counsel generally provided to

---

[152]*See, e.g.,* Fentiman, *supra* note 141, at 1110 n.2 (citing, among other sources, Thomas Gutheil & Paul Appelbaum, *"Mind Control," "Synthetic Sanity," "Artificial Competence," and Genuine Confusion: Legally Relevant Effects of Antipsychotic Medicine,* 12 HOFSTRA L. REV. 77 (1983)); *id.* at 1129 n.98 (citing Theodore Van Putten, *Why Do Schizophrenic Patients Refuse to Take Their Drugs?,* 31 ARCHIVES GEN. PSYCHIATRY 67 (1974)).

[153]*Charters,* 863 F.2d at 310.

[154]"Neuroleptic malignant syndrome is an uncommon but potentially fatal reaction to antipsychotic medication, characterized by muscular rigidity, fever, autonomic dysfunction, and altered consciousness." Levenson, *Neuroleptic Malignant Syndrome,* 142 AM. J. PSYCHIATRY 1137, 1137 (1985).

[155]*E.g.,* Ross Baldessarini et al., *Significance of Neuroleptic Dose and Plasma Levels in the Pharmacological Treatment of Psychoses,* 45 ARCH. GEN. PSYCHIATRY 79 (1988).

[156]*Charters,* 863 F.2d at 313 ("the use of available antipsychotic agents continues to be the cornerstone of management for those serious and disabling mental illnesses").

[157]Baldessarini et al., *supra* note 155 at 79.

[158]442 U.S. 584 (1979).

[159]*Charters,* 863 F.2d at 312, citing *Parham,* 442 U.S. at 607–08.

[160]*See* Sheldon Gelman, *Mental Hospital Drugs, Professionalism, and the Constitution,* 72 GEO. L.J. 1725, 1765 n.213 (1984), discussing *Rennie* litigation (New Jersey state doctors "at every level—including the Department of Mental Health directorate—ignored and subverted the rules").

[161]*Charters,* 863 F.2d at 313. (emphasis added)

involuntarily confined mental patients is grossly inadequate.[162] This inadequacy is magnified in cases involving right-to-refuse-treatment matters,[163] in cases involving mentally disabled criminal defendants,[164] and the situation is further exacerbated by the general lack of funds available to indigent criminal defendants to pay for expert witnesses in cases that do not fall strictly within the holding of *Ake v. Oklahoma*.[165] It is inconceivable to suggest that the Fourth Circuit majority was surely aware of this reality.

Finally, by applying the most minimalist perspective to *Youngberg v. Romeo* and *Parham v. J. R.* in the sterile context of the *Mathews v. Eldridge*[166] "balancing" calculus, the court created a standard that is virtually impregnable: a sole test of whether the decision-making process was "so completely out of professional bounds as to make it explicable only as an arbitrary, nonprofessional one."[167] How could this standard be violated? Some hypothetical examples of actions that might meet this test include (a) intentionally medicating a patient into a coma to amorously pursue the patient's spouse; (b) in a drunken stupor, injecting the wrong medicine into the patient's vein; (c) taking a bribe from a patient's business competitor to ensure the patient's long-term institutionalization; or (d) posing as a doctor.[168] For the type of drugging scenario typically found in public hospitals, however, the standard appears to be a nonstandard.

The acid test by which to assess the *Charters II* standard would be to apply it to the trial record in *Rennie*.[169] There the defendants' medical directors agreed that drugs were used for control and "as a substitute for treatment."[170] In addition, the medical director's "questionable judgment in failing to acknowledge" overt physical manifestations of tardive dyskinesia was because of "institutional self-interest."[171] It is not at all clear that a literal reading of the *Charters II* test would find a violation in this behavior.

It is also necessary to consider *Charters II* in the context of the two subsequent U.S. Supreme Court cases: *Washington v. Harper*[172] and *Riggins v. Nevada*.[173] The Supreme Court's 1990 decision in *Harper* sharply limited the right of convicted felons to refuse treatment under the federal constitution. Although the Court agreed that prisoners (like all other citizens) possessed a significant liberty interest in avoiding the unwanted administra-

---

[162]*See generally,* Michael L. Perlin, *Fatal Assumptions: A Critical Evaluation of the Role of Counsel in Mental Disability Cases,* 16 Law & Hum. Behav. 39 (1992).

[163]Michael L. Perlin & Deborah A. Dorfman, *Is It More Than "Dodging Lions and Wastin' Time"? Adequacy of Counsel, Questions of Competence, and the Judicial Process in Individual Right to Refuse Treatment Cases,* 2 PSYCHOL., PUB. POL'Y & L. 114 (1996).

[164]*See* President's Commission's Task Panel on Legal & Ethical Issues, *Mental Health and Human Rights: Report of the Task Panel on Legal and Ethical Issues,* 20 ARIZ. L. REV. 49, 55 (1978).

[165]470 U.S. 68, 83 (1985); *see generally* 1 PERLIN, *supra* note 2, § 2B-13 (2d ed. 1998); 3 *id.,* § 17.16.

[166]424 U.S. 319, 335 (1976). For an explanation of *Mathews, see* Carolyn Kubitschek, *A Re-Evaluation of* Mathews v. Eldridge *in Light of Administrative Shortcomings and Social Security Nonacquiesences,* 31 ARIZ. L. REV. 53 (1989).

[167]*Charters,* 863 F.2d at 313.

[168]These examples would all meet tests for medical malpractice and delicensure and may violate criminal statutes as well. *Cf., e.g.,* Stephen v. Drew, 359 F. Supp. 746, 748 (E.D. Va. 1973) (improper civil commitment tort claim stated where psychiatrist was allegedly involved in conspiracy to deprive plaintiff of his constitutional rights). For a discussion of the different grounds on which a tardive dyskinesia malpractice suit might be premised, see Robert Wettstein, *Tardive Dyskinesia and Malpractice,* I BEHAV. SCI. & L. 85, 88–89 (1983).

[169]476 F. Supp. 1274 (D.N.J. 1979).

[170]*Id.* at 1299.

[171]*Id.* at 1302.

[172]494 U.S. 210 (1990).

[173]504 U.S. 127 (1992).

tion of antipsychotic drugs,[174] it found that the need to balance this interest with prison safety and security considerations would lead it to uphold a prison rule regulating drug refusals as long as it was "reasonably related to legitimate penological interest," even where fundamental interests were otherwise implicated.[175] Thus a state policy—that provided for an administrative hearing (before a tribunal of mental health professionals and correctional officials) at which there was neither provision for the appointment of counsel nor regularized external review—was found to pass constitutional muster.[176]

In a sharply worded opinion, Justice Stevens dissented, arguing that the refusal of medication was "a fundamental liberty interest deserving the highest order of protection," especially where the imposition of such medications might create "a substantial risk of permanent injury and premature death."[177]

Then in 1992 mental disability law jurisprudence took a dramatic turn in *Riggins v. Nevada*.[178] *Riggins* held that the use of antipsychotic drugs violated the defendant's right to fair trial (at which he had raised the insanity defense), focusing on the drugs' potential side effects and construing its previous decision in *Washington v. Harper*[179]—limiting the rights of convicted prisoners to refuse medication—to require "an overriding justification and a determination of medical appropriateness" prior to forcibly administering antipsychotic medications to a prisoner.[180] The Court focused on what might be called the "litigational side effects" of antipsychotic drugs, and discussed the possibility that the drug use might have compromised the substance of the defendant's trial testimony, his interaction with counsel, and his comprehension of the trial.[181]

Although the court in *Riggins* did not set out a bright-line test for determining the state's burden in involuntarily medicating a pretrial detainee at trial, it did find that the burden would be met if the state proved that it was medically appropriate and either (a) considering less intrusive alternatives, "essential for the sake of Riggins' own safety or safety of others" or (b) there was a lack of less intrusive means by which to obtain an adjudication of the defendant's guilt or innocence.[182] *Riggins'* ultimate impact on the rights of civilly committed persons to refuse medication is still ambiguous.[183]

In a concurring opinion, Justice Kennedy (the author of *Harper*) took an even bolder position. He would not allow the use of antipsychotic medication to make a defendant competent to stand trial "absent an *extraordinary* showing" on the state's part, and noted further that he doubted this showing could be made "given our present understanding of the properties of these drugs."[184] Justice Thomas dissented, suggesting (a) the administration of the drug might have increased the defendant's cognitive ability;[185] (b) because Riggins had originally asked for medical assistance (while a jail inmate, he had "had trouble sleeping"

---

[174]*Harper,* 494 U.S. at 221, quoting Vitek v. Jones, 445 U.S. 480, 488–91 (1980).

[175]*Id.* at 223.

[176]*Id.* at 223–24.

[177]*Id.* at 241 (Stevens, J., concurring in part and dissenting in part).

[178]504 U.S. 127 (1992). *See generally* Perlin & Dorfman, *supra* note 163.

[179]Washington v. Harper, 494 U.S. 210 (1998). *See* PERLIN, *supra* note 1, § 3B-8.2, at 313-22 (2d. ed. 1999).

[180]*Riggins,* 504 U.S. at 135. *See generally* Marybeth Zietnek, Riggins v. Nevada: *Medicated Defendants and Courtroom Demeanor From the Jury's Perspective,* 30 AM. CRIM. L. REV. 215 (1992).

[181]*Riggins,* 504 U.S. at 142.

[182]*Id.* at 135–36.

[183]Cases construing *Riggins* are discussed in PERLIN, *supra* note 2, § 3B-8.3, at 328-29 nn. 1348-54 (2d. ed. 1999).

[184]*Riggins,* 504 U.S. at 139 (Kennedy, J., concurring) (emphasis added).

[185]*Id.* at 150 (Thomas, J., dissenting). Trial testimony had indicated that Riggins's daily drug regimen (800 mgs. of Mellaril) was enough to "tranquilize an elephant." *Id* at 143 (Kennedy, J., concurring), quoting trial record.

and was "hearing voices"), it could not be said that the state ever "ordered" him to take medication;[186] (c) if Riggins had been aggrieved, his proper remedy was a § 1983 civil rights action;[187] and (d) under the majority's language, a criminal conviction might be reversed in cases involving "penicillin or aspirin."[188]

Can these decisions be reconciled? And can they be reconciled with *Charters II* (a case that the Supreme Court declined to hear).[189] Indeed, *Harper* and *Riggins* seem virtually irreconcilable if they are both read as right-to-refuse-treatment cases. However, if *Harper* is seen as a prison security case and *Riggins* as a fair trial case, then the rationales for the differences become clearer. Because the Court, for a variety of normative and instrumental reasons, needed to reiterate strong prison security values, it decided *Harper* pretextually.[190] Because this issue was absent from *Riggins* (who had not yet been convicted at the time of the employment of forced medications), the majority did not need to resort to such pretexts in its decision.

Justice Thomas' *Riggins* dissent reflects both sanism and pretextuality. His opinion raises grave questions for defense counsel: Had his position prevailed, would defense lawyers have felt as if they were assuming a risk in ever seeking pretrial medical help for defendants awaiting trial?[191] His analogizing psychiatric drug side effects to penicillin or aspirin may be disingenuous or it may be cynical. What *is* clear is that nowhere in the lengthy *corpus* of right to refuse litigation is this analogy ever seriously investigated.[192]

Charters II is a case that is both sanist and pretextual. The *en banc* court's fear of dealing with the "underlying social, psychodynamic and political issues that form the overt and hidden agendas in any right-to-refuse case"[193] is textbook pretextuality. Its refusal to address the issue of side effects is sanist—trivializing, as it does, the impact of those side effects on the population at risk.[194] Its misstatement of the facts of *Youngberg*, confusing mental illness with mental retardation,[195] is a different kind of sanism—a sloppiness in drafting that reflects a dehumanization of the persons who are at the heart of such cases. Its adoption of trial testimony questioning whether "*any* factual inquiry" into the competency of "schizophrenic patients" might ever be valid[196] is both sanist and pretextual.[197]

It is not sufficient, however, to lay the blame for sanism and pretextuality at the feet of the judiciary; the blame can also realistically be placed on counsel as well. It is to this question that I wish to turn next.

---

[186]*Id.* at 152 (Thomas, J., dissenting).

[187]*Id.* at 153. At his trial, Riggins had been sentenced to death.

[188]*Id.* at 155.

[189]Charters v. United States, 494 U.S. 1016 (1990) (denying *certiorari*).

[190]*See* PERLIN, *supra* note 2, § 3B-8.2, at 318-20 (2d. ed. 1999), discussing Justice Stevens opinion, critiquing the majority's read of the factual record in *Harper*.

[191]*Riggins,* 504 U.S. at 151–51 (Thomas, J., dissenting), discussed in Perlin & Dorfman, *supra* note 163, at 40–41.

[192]*See* Perlin & Dorfman, *supra* note 163, at 41–42, and *see id.* at 42 n.117, discussing *Matter of* Salisbury, 524 N.Y.S.2d 352, 354 (Sup. Ct. 1988) (no right to refuse antibiotics), the only case in which a remotely similar issue is raised.

On prisoners' access to prescription medications, *cf.* Ledford v. Sullivan, 105 F.3d 354 (7th Cir. 1997) (no constitutional violation to confiscate such medication), *to* Steele v. Shah, 87 F.3d 1266 (11th Cir. 1996) (jury could find deliberate indifference where prison discontinued prisoner's antipsychotic medication).

[193]Perlin, *supra* note 10, at 966.

[194]*See* Perlin, *supra* note 37, at 972.

[195]*See supra* text accompanying notes 101-02.

[196]*Charters,* 863 F.2d at 309 n.5.

[197]*See* 2 PERLIN *supra* note 2, § 3B-14.5 at 373-75 (2d. ed. 1999). (Discussing the MacArthur Network's most recent research on this question).

Adequacy of Counsel

The assumption that individuals facing involuntary civil commitment are globally represented by adequate counsel is an assumption of a fact not in evidence.[198] The data suggest that, in many jurisdictions, such counsel is woefully inadequate—disinterested, uninformed, roleless, and often hostile.[199] A model of paternalism–best interests is substituted for a traditional legal advocacy position, and this substitution is rarely questioned.[200] Few courts have ever grappled with adequacy-of-counsel questions in this context; fewer yet have found assigned involuntary civil commitment to be inadequate.[201] The question of adequacy of counsel in this context has at least been subject to some scholarly attention.[202] There is scant literature that addresses the question of the availability and adequacy of counsel in right-to-refuse-medication hearings, however.[203] This near-total lack of attention is even more striking when juxtaposed with the extensive scholarship that has developed discussing the law reform–test case litigation that led directly to the judicial articulation of a right to refuse treatment.[204]

Lawyers representing individuals with mental disabilities must familiarize themselves with information about the right to refuse treatment, both as to the law and as to the pharmacology.[205] The track record of lawyers representing the mentally disabled, with some important exceptions, has ranged from indifferent to wretched;[206] in one famous survey, lawyers were so bad that patients had a better chance of being released at a commitment hearing if they appeared *pro se*.[207] Further, simply educating lawyers about psychiatric technique and psychological nomenclature does not materially improve lawyers' perform-

---

[198]Michael L. Perlin, *Fatal Assumption: A Critical Evaluation of The Role of Counsel in Mental Disability Cases*, 16 LAW & HUM. BEHAV. 39 (1992).

[199]*Id.* at 43. On the "rolelessness" of sanist lawyers, *see, e.g.,* Michael L. Perlin, *On "Sanism,"* 46 SMU L. REV. 373, 404 (1992).

[200]*Id.* at 43–44.

[201]*Id.* at 50–52; *see generally* 1 PERLIN, *supra* note 2, § 2B-11.3, at 267–71 (2d ed. 1998). In Strickland v. Washington, 466 U.S. 668 (1984), the Supreme Court established as the standard for evaluating adequacy-of-counsel claims in criminal cases as "whether counsel's conduct so undermined the proper function of the adversarial process that the trial court cannot be relied on as having produced a just result"); see Perlin, *supra,* note 198, at 53 (characterizing standard as "sterile and perfunctory").

[202]*See, e.g.,* Perlin, *supra* note 198, at 43–45 nn.21–34 (citing sources).

[203]*See* Melvin Shaw, *Professional Responsibility of Attorneys Representing Institutionalized Mental Patients in Relation to Psychotropic Medications,* 22 J. HEALTH & HOSP. L. 186 (1989) (characterizing lawyers' arguments seeking to vindicate a right to refuse medication as an "injustice").

[204]For recent literature, *see, e.g.,* 2 PERLIN, *supra* note 2, § 3B-1, at 155 n. 1 and § 3B-2, at 157 n. 2 (2d. ed. 1999) (citing sources).

[205]*See generally* Perlin & Dorfman, *supra* note 163, at 60–61.

[206]*See* Perlin, *supra* note 198, at 43–45; *see also, e.g.,* Steven J. Schwartz, *Damage Actions as a Strategy for Enhancing the Quality of Care of Persons With Mental Disabilities,* 17 N.Y.U. REV. L. & SOC. CHANGE 651, 662 (1989–90) (describing "wholesale lack of legal advocacy" available to patients in public mental institutions).

[207]Elliott Andalman & David L. Chambers, *Effective Counsel for Persons Facing Civil Commitment: A Survey, a Polemic, and a Proposal,* 45 MISS. L.J. 43, 72 (1974). One half of the lawyers assigned to represent individuals in civil commitment cases in Dallas were unaware of the existence of either of the two treatises written specifically about Texas's mental health law. Daniel W. Shuman & Richard Hawkins, *The Use of Alternatives to Institutionalization of the Mentally Ill,* 33 Sw. L.J. 1181, 1193–94 (1980) (attorneys received $25 per case); *accord,* Perlin, *supra* note 198, at 50 n.66 (Virginia attorneys received $25 per case as of 1984).

ance when underlying sanist attitudes are not changed.[208] If counsel is to become even minimally competent in this area, it is critical that the underlying issues be confronted.[209] This is underscored by judges' lack of basic knowledge about mental disability law; in one astonishing case, a Louisiana civil commitment order was reversed when the trial court did not even know of the existence of a state-mandated mental health advocacy service.[210] If lawyers continue to so abdicate their advocacy role, it is not surprising that many areas of application of the right to refuse treatment remain judicially unexplored.[211]

Like other legal rights, the right to refuse treatment is not self-executing.[212] A statement by a state supreme court or a federal court of appeals that a patient has a "qualified right to refuse treatment" does not, in and of itself, automatically translate into a coherent structure through which hearings are scheduled, counsel appointed, and hearing procedures established. Of the important right to refuse cases only *Rivers v. Katz* establishes any mechanism for appointing counsel in individual right-to-refuse cases;[213] *Rennie v. Klein,*[214] one of the first federal cases finding a substantive constitutional right to refuse, originally mandated the appointment of counsel[215] but later receded from this position and required only the presence of "patient advocates" (employees of the state Division of Mental Health and Hospitals) to serve as "informal counsel to patients who wish to refuse [antipsychotic medication]").[216]

A handful of statutes mandate the appointment of counsel in right-to-refuse-treatment hearings;[217] on the other hand, at least one court has held that failure to appoint counsel is not reversible error.[218] And only a few cases have spoken to the role or scope of counsel at

---

[208]Norman Poythress, *Psychiatric Expertise in Civil Commitment: Training Attorneys to Cope With Expert Testimony,* 2 LAW & HUM. BEHAV. 1, 15 (1978). There is similar evidence in other areas of the law that knowledge alone is an insufficient impetus for attitudinal change. *See, e.g.,* Robert M. Bohm et al., *Knowledge and Death Penalty Opinion: A Test of the Marshall Hypothesis,* 28 J. RES. CRIME & DELINQ. 360 (1991).

[209]For a rare judicial acknowledgment of the impact of lawyer incompetency in another area in which inadequate counsel leads to morally intolerable results, see Engberg v. Meyer, 820 P.2d 70, 104 (Wyo. 1991) (Urbigkit, C. J., dissenting in part and concurring in part) ("We . . . let 'chiropractors' with law degrees perform the equivalent of brain surgery in capital cases, and, predictably, the 'patient' often dies. This is intolerable.").

[210]*In re* C. P. K., 516 So.2d 1323, 1325 (La. App. 1987). See *supra* Chapter 2, text accompanying note 270.

[211]On patients' attitudes about forced medications, see Susan Ruscher et al., *Psychiatric Patients' Attitudes About Medication and Factors Affecting Noncompliance,* 48 PSYCHIATRIC SERV. 82 (1997) (desire to change medication regimen positively related to level of patient's education).

[212]*See, e.g.,* Bruce Winick, *Restructuring Competency to Stand Trial,* 32 UCLA L. REV. 921, 941 (1985); Perlin, *supra* note 198, at 47; *see also* Alan H. Macurdy, *The Americans With Disabilities Act: Time for Celebration, or Time for Caution?,* 1 PUBLIC INTEREST L.J. 21, 29 (1991); John Parry, *Rights Aplenty but not Enough Money: A Paradox in Federal Disability Policies,* 12 MENT. & PHYS. DIS. L. REP. 486 (1988) (pointing out that although there has been legislation to enhance the civil rights of persons with disabilities, the laws are not always fully implemented because of the lack of funding and other resources).

[213]*Rivers,* 504 N.Y.S.2d at 81. Representation in *Rivers* hearings is provided by the state-funded Mental Hygiene Legal Services (MHLS) office. *Application of* St. Luke's–Roosevelt Hosp. Ctr., 607 N.Y.S.2d 574, 580 n.11 (Supp. 1993).

[214]462 F. Supp. 1131 (D.N.J. 1978), suppl., 476 F. Supp. 1294 (D.N.J. 1979), *modified,* 653 F.2d 836 (3d Cir. 1981), *vacated and remanded,* 458 U.S. 119 (1982), *on remand,* 720 F.2d 266 (3d Cir. 1983); *see generally* 2 PERLIN, *supra* note 2, §§ 3B-5 to 3B-5.1j (2d. ed. 1999).

[215]*Rennie,* 462 F. Supp. at 1147.

[216]*Rennie,* 476 F. Supp. at 1311. *See also id.* at 1313 (patient advocates may be attorneys, psychologists, social workers, registered nurses, or paralegals, "or have equivalent experience"). This recession followed the Supreme Court's decision in Parham v. J. R., 442 U.S. 584 (1979), allowing for relaxed procedures in the cases of the involuntary civil commitment of juveniles.

[217]*See, e.g.,* OKLA. STAT. ANN. § 5-212(B)(1) (1985); WIS. STAT. ANN. § 880.33(1) (1989); N.M. STAT. ANN. §§ 43-1-4 (1977), 43-1-15 (1977); 405 ILL. COMP. STAT. ANN. 5/2-107.1 (1982).

[218]*In re* Steen, 437 N.W.2d 101, 105 (Minn. App. 1989). *Cf.* Cornett v. Donovan, 51 F.3d 894 (9th Cir. 1995) (right to legal assistance extended only through pleading stage of *habeas* or civil rights action).

medication hearings.[219] Although more courts are beginning to articulate the criteria to be considered at a medication refusal hearing,[220] this level of specificity is simply not present in the assessment of the role and responsibilities of counsel.[221]

Without such an articulation of specificity, the authentic meaning of a "right to refuse" remains murky. A right without a remedy[222] is no right at all; worse, a right without a remedy is meretricious and pretextual—it gives the illusion of a right without any legitimate expectation that the right will be honored.[223] This is especially significant in light of the research in procedural justice done by Tom Tyler that individuals subject to involuntary civil commitment hearings, like all other citizens, are affected by such process values as participation, dignity, and trust, and that experiencing arbitrariness in procedure leads to "social malaise and decreases people's willingness to be integrated into the polity, accepting its authorities, and following its rules."[224] And recent research by Steven Hoge and Thomas Feucht-Haviar provides further empirical support for Tyler's insights. Their study of long-term psychiatric patients found, in an informed-consent context, that "capable patient involvement is an important check on a physician's judgment."[225] Empirical surveys consistently demonstrate that the quality of counsel "remains the single most important factor in the disposition of involuntary civil commitment cases."[226] Certainly, the presence of adequate counsel is of critical importance in the disposition of right-to-refuse-treatment cases as well.

These findings take on even more importance when considered in the context of the findings by the MacArthur Research Network[227] that mental patients are not always incompetent to make rational decisions, and are not inherently more incompetent than nonmentally ill medical patients.[228] Contemporaneous constitutional case law and some statutory law generally reject the idea that mental illness and incompetency can be equated,

[219]See, e.g., Rennie, 476 F. Supp. at 1313 (patient advocates "must be given training in the effects of psychotropic medication and the principles of legal advocacy"); Matter of Jarvis, 433 N.W.2d 120, 123–24 (Minn. App. 1988) (criticizing failure to give counsel adequate time to explore basis for treating psychiatrist's choice of medications); Williams v. Wilzack, 573 A.2d 809, 821 reconsideration denied (Md. 1990) (criticizing failure to give counsel opportunity to present evidence or cross-examine witnesses).

[220]See, e.g., Virgil D. v. Rock County, 524 N.W.2d 894, 899–900 (Wis. 1994), reconsideration denied, 531 N.W.2d 331 (Wis. 1995), discussed infra text accompanying note 281.

[221]See Perlin, supra note 198, at 56 n.101 (as mental disability law becomes more complex, it is essential that counsel for patients understand differing right-to-refuse-treatment doctrines and their rationales).

[222]Donald Zeigler, Rights Require Remedies: A New Approach to the Enforcement of Rights in the Federal Courts, 38 HASTINGS L.J. 665, 678–79 (1987).

[223]This is not to suggest that the existence of a constitutional right is somehow illegitimate if it is not honored in each individual case seeking to vindicate it. Rather, "honored" refers to the presence of a legally legitimate hearing at which a decision about whether to honor the right is fairly assessed.

[224]Tom Tyler, The Psychological Consequences of Judicial Procedures: Implications for Civil Commitment Hearings, 46 SMU L. REV. 433, 443 (1992).

[225]Steven K. Hoge & Thomas C. Feucht-Haviar, Long-Term, Assenting Psychiatric Patients: Decisional Capacity and the Quality of Care, 23 BULL. AM. ACAD. PSYCHIATRY & L. 343, 349 (1995). And see id. ("our findings seem to undermine physicians' arguments that informed consent is an unnecessary intrusion into the doctor–patient relationship, which interferes with the provision of effective treatment"); see also Bruce Winick, Competency to Consent to Treatment: The Distinction Between Assent and Objection, 28 HOUS. L. REV. 15, 46–47 (1991); Zito et al., supra note 145.

[226]Perlin, supra note 198, at 49, citing 2 PERLIN, supra note 2, § 8.02, at 744 (now updated as 1 PERLIN, supra note 2, § 2B-2, at 192–94 (2d ed. 1998)).

[227]See supra Chapter 4.

[228]See generally Thomas Grisso & Paul S. Appelbaum, Abilities of Patients to Consent to Psychiatric and Medical Treatments, 19 LAW & HUM. BEHAV. 149 (1995).

and often specifically endorse a presumption of competency.[229] Yet what Bruce Winick refers to as "Nineteenth Century notions equating mental illness with incompetence," still, in practice, "continue to influence legal rules and practices in this area."[230] If judges uncritically conflate institutionalization with incompetency, lack of meaningful counsel— to structure statutory, case-law-based and empirical arguments—may be fatal to the patient's case.[231] The mere existence of counsel on behalf of institutionalized mental patients is often invisible to trial courts;[232] certainly, there is no reason for optimism about judicial knowledge or interest in this area of the law, absent aggressive, advocacy-focused counsel.

If ward psychiatrists demonstrate a propensity to make equivalent the phrases *incompetent* with *makes bad decisions* and to assume, in the face of statutory and case law, that incompetence in decision making can be presumed from the fact of institutionalization,[233] lack of counsel—to inquire into the bases of these views on cross-examination and to demonstrate to the court that they are dissonant with established case and statutory law— may similarly make the legal process an illusory safeguard.

In spite of the impressive body of case law outlined previously, the existence of a right to refuse treatment remains enigmatic—at best—for many clinicians.[234] Some are resistant, arguing—unsuccessfully in court but perhaps more successfully in clinical practice—that the existence of the right is destructive; certainly, the provocative titles of early articles written about the right to refuse treatment suggest a basic tension that may not be resolvable absent sensitive articulation of the underlying legal concepts.[235]

Individual Right-to-Refuse-Treatment Cases

It is impossible to truly grasp the meaning of the right of institutionalized persons with mental disabilities to refuse antipsychotic medications without considering the actual implementation of court decisions purportedly mandating this right. Implementation must be considered when analyzing the impact of such laws on mental health patients, particularly with regard to the way representation is provided. Merely because due process protections

---

[229]*See* Bruce Winick, *The MacArthur Treatment Competence Study: Legal and Therapeutic Implications,* 2 Psychol., Pub. Pol'y & L. 138, 152 n.87 (1996) (citing sources).

[230]*Id.* at 153 (for an explanation of these "Nineteenth Century notions," *see id.* at 151).

[231]On counsel's educative role, see 1 Perlin, *supra* note 2, § 2B-8.3d, at 241–42 (2d ed. 1998); Michael L. Perlin & Robert L. Sadoff, *Ethical Issues in the Representation of Individuals in the Commitment Process,* 45 Law & Contemp. Probs. 161, 168–73 (Summer 1982).

[232]*See, e.g., In re* C. P. K., 516 So.2d 1323, 1325 (La. Ct. App. 1987) (reversing commitment order where trial court failed to comply with statute expressing explicit preference for representation by state Mental Health Advocacy Service, rejecting as "untenable" argument that trial court should be excused "since it did not know . . . whether the Service really existed").

[233]*See, e.g.,* Brian Ladds et al., *The Disposition of Criminal Charges After Involuntary Medication to Restore Competency to Stand Trial,* 38 J. Forens. Sci. 1442 (1993) (Ladds I); Brian Ladds et al., *Involuntary Medication of Patients Who Are Incompetent to Stand Trial: A Descriptive Study of the New York Experience With Judicial Review,* 21 Bull. Am. Acad. Psychiatry & L. 529 (1993) (Ladds II).

[234]I have been presenting papers on this topic to mental health professionals for the better part of 25 years. Consistently, there are always questions from the audience expressing surprise that there *is* such a right and often expressing the view that such a right is clinically unwarranted.

[235]*See, e.g.,* Paul Appelbaum & Thomas Gutheil, *Rotting With Their Rights On: Constitutional Theory and Clinical Reality in Drug Refusal by Psychiatric Patients,* 7 Bull. Am. Acad. Psychiatry & L. 306 (1979); Rachlin, *supra* note 124; Darryl Treffert, *Dying With Their Rights On,* 130 Am. J. Psychiatry 1041 (1973). *But cf.* Hoge & Feucht-Haviar, *supra* note 225 at 349.

are statutorily or judicially required prior to imposing involuntarily medication in a nonemergency, there is no guarantee that these protections will actually be present in any individual case.[236] It is no surprise that jurisdictions are wildly inconsistent in implementing the right-to-refuse laws in general, especially with regard to the specific issue of the provision of counsel.

I will examine the differences regarding the implementation of right-to-refuse laws, focusing on the right to counsel or other representation in involuntary medication hearings. First I will analyze this difference within individual jurisdictions, specifically looking at how state laws actually anticipate and allow for inconsistency, examining the data in three states—California, Washington, and Utah—illustrating the disparities regarding the provision of counsel in right-to-refuse cases within jurisdictions.[237] Next, I will discuss the significance of these differences in relationship to the conclusions of the MacArthur Study and will conclude that it is impossible to even discuss meaningful reform in this area without reflecting on the impact of sanism and pretextuality.

The interstate inconsistency in implementing right-to-refuse-medication laws[238] is confounded further by intrastate disparities *within* individual jurisdictions. I will analyze such inconsistency in three jurisdictions, each representing a different due process model, then look at the involuntary medication laws of each of these jurisdictions and discuss how these laws actually anticipate and often allow for inconsistency in implementing these laws, and next consider some of the actual data that illustrates the differences in the right to counsel in right-to-refuse cases within each of the three discussed states.

California

Under California law, persons institutionalized by reason of mental disability are afforded expanded due process protections in right-to-refuse cases, known as "capacity hearings" or "*Riese* hearings."[239] Nonetheless, there is a significant difference in the manner in which these hearings are conducted in different California counties, including whether or not attorneys are provided by the state to represent mental health patients in the hearings.[240] The most obvious evidence of this inconsistency is language in the section of the California Welfare and Institutions Code codifying the *Riese* decision.[241] The statute allows for the capacity hearings to be conducted either by a superior court judge, a superior court commissioner or referee, or a court-appointed hearing officer.[242] In addition, although it mandates representation at such hearings, it allows for representation to be provided by the public defender, patients' rights advocate, or other representative, who may be a nonattorney.[243] Finally, the California statute requires that each county develop its own

---

[236]*See* Michael L. Perlin & Deborah A. Dorfman. *Is It More Than "Dodging Lions and Wastin 'Time' "? Adequecy of Counsel, Questions of Competence, and the Judicial Process in Individual Right to Refuse Treatment Cases*, 2 PSYCHOL. PUB POL'Y & L 114, 118 (1996).

[237]*See id.* at 122.

[238]See Perlin, *supra,* note 37 at 971-72 (discussing two models of right-to-refuse cases).

[239]*See* Riese v. St. Mary's Hosp. & Medical Ctr., 243 Cal. Rptr. 241, 254 (App. 1987), *appeal dismissed,* 774 P.2d 698 (1989); *see generally* 2 PERLIN, *supra* note 2, § 3B-7.2c, at 276-79 (2d. ed. 1999).

[240]*See California Office of Patients' Rights Report on Informed Consent/Capacity Hearing Services (Report)* (November 6, 1995) (on file with author).

[241]CAL. WELF. & INST. CODE §§ 5332–5334.

[242]*Id.* at § 5334(c).

[243]*Id.* at 5333(a). It should be noted that some of the patients' rights advocates in at least one county (Santa Clara) are also attorneys.

policies and procedures for implementing the hearings.[244] Thus the implementation of *Riese*—the test case decided by the California Supreme Court articulating a right to refuse treatment—varies from one county to the next on the important variable of the type of representation provided to the patient.

A study conducted by the California Office of Patients Rights[245] in 1994 on informed consent and capacity hearing services illustrates these variations. The study involved data reported from 29 out of a total of 37 counties in California with involuntary psychiatric facilities.[246] Of the 29 counties[247] reporting data, 13 counties reported using public defenders to represent patients in capacity hearings, 15 counties reported use patients' right advocates, and 2 counties reported using other individuals as representatives.[248]

The California study also examined the amount of time spent by counsel, advocates, and other representatives on the capacity hearings.[249] The data were broken down into three categories: time spent preparing for hearings, time spent conducting the hearings, and time spent in follow-up activities related to the hearings.[250] The data showed a substantial range. The average length of time spent preparing for the hearing on behalf of the patient was 43.83 minutes,[251] ranging from 5 minutes to 240 minutes.[252]

The average length of time spent conducting the hearings was 26 minutes[253] (ranging from 10 to 60 minutes).[254] The average length of time spent on follow-up activities related to the hearings was 11.67 minutes (ranging from 5 minutes to 60 minutes).[255]

The length of time spent on hearings is important from the point of view of actual effectiveness of the representation provided to the patient. Advocates and attorneys who spend only a short time preparing for and representing the patient in the hearing may compromise the quality of their representation.[256] To effectively prepare for a hearing, advocates or attorneys should meet with patients to advise them of their legal rights at the hearing, should conduct full interviews, and should review the patients' medical charts.[257] If

---

[244]*Id.* at § 5334.

[245]The California Patients' Rights Office is created and mandated pursuant to state statute. *See* CAL. WELF. & INST. CODE § 5510. Its purpose is to ensure ''that mental health laws, regulations and policies on the rights of recipients of mental health services are observed in State hospitals and in licensed health and community care facilities.'' *Id.*

[246]*Report, supra* note 240.

[247]The reporting counties include Alameda, Butte (includes Colusa), Contra Costa, El Dorado, Fresno, Glenn, Humbolt (includes Del Norte), Inyo, Kern, Los Angeles, Marin, Mendocino (including Lake), Merced, Napa, Orange, Placer, Riverside, Sacramento, San Bernardino, San Diego, San Francisco, San Luis Obispo, San Mateo, Santa Barbara, Santa Clara, Sonoma, Stanislaus, Ventura, and Yolo (includes Colusa Plumes). *Id.* at 4.

[248]*Report, supra* note 240, at 4.

[249]*Id.* at 6.

[250]*Id.*

[251]*Id.* at 3.

[252]*Id.*

[253]*Id.* The mean time for involuntary civil commitment hearings studied in the 1970s ranged from 3.8 to 9.2 minutes. *See* Parham v. J. R., 442 U.S. 584, 609 n.17 (1979). This finding has been the topic of astonishingly little academic commentary. *See,* however, Perlin, *supra* note 44, at 651 n.115; Robert Burt, *Withholding Nutrition and Mistrusting Nurturance: The Vocabulary of In re Conroy,* 2 ISSUES L. & MED. 317, 330 n.21 (1987).

[254]*Report, supra* note 240, at 3.

[255]*Id.*

[256]*See, e.g.,* Perlin, *supra* note 162 at 43-44; *see generally* Perlin & Sadoff, *supra,* note 231.

[257]*See, e.g.,* ABA Commission on the Mentally Disabled, *How to Prepare for an Involuntary Civil Commitment Hearing,* 37 PRAC. LAW. 39 (Jan. 1991) (attorneys should, *inter alia,* review all medication orders; check possible side effects of each medication; check any prehearing changes in medication or behavior; be prepared to introduce evidence as to medication's effects). *See generally Medication Capacity Hearings: Policies and Procedures From Los Angeles County* 6 (1994) (spelling out duties); Superior Court of Santa Clara, *Capacity Hearings: Policies and Procedures* 7–8 (July 1993).

an advocate or attorney only spends five minutes preparing for the hearing, it is unlikely that either the representative or the patient will be adequately prepared, and the effectiveness of representation is likely to be compromised.[258]

Also, the time spent in pretrial preparation is significant in terms of the impact it has on the patient's *perception* of its meaningfulness.[259] If attorneys and advocates do not spend a reasonable amount of time preparing for (and providing representation at) such hearings, the patient may potentially see the entire hearing as a sham.[260] It can also undermine the trust that patients have in their attorneys or advocates as the patients may—often, correctly—view this lack of zealous advocacy as reflecting either apathy or constructive complicity with the agency or facility seeking the involuntary imposition of medication. Again, given the MacArthur study's findings undermining the "ordinary common sense" notion that mentally ill persons are per se incompetent[261]—a notion that is reflected on a daily basis in individual right-to-refuse hearings nationwide[262]—the need for zealous counsel is especially critical.

Finally, this data suggests that, despite legislation that appears to provide expanded due process procedures, there is no guarantee that patients will in fact receive adequate representation at medication hearings.

Washington

Washington's right to refuse law reflects a hybrid of expanded and limited due process protections, a hybrid that has created disparity in implementing the right to refuse medication in Washington state. Prior to the Supreme Court's decision in the prison case of *Washington v. Harper,*[263] Washington state cases had required a judicial hearing consonant with the expanded due process model.[264] After *Harper,* however, the state legislature modified existing law so that the extent of the due process afforded a civilly committed mental health patient became dependent on the length of commitment.[265] In the case of a patient committed for 0 to 30 days who is to be involuntarily medicated in a nonemergent circumstance, the medication order must only be reviewed by another psychiatrist.[266] Patients committed for 30 to 180 days are afforded a review by the facility medical director or his or her designee of the order for involuntary medication.[267] However, patients committed for 180 days or longer are given expanded due process protections including a

[258]On the multiple roles of counsel in the representation of institutionalized mentally disabled persons in general, *see* 1 PERLIN, *supra* note 2, § 2B-8.1, at 229–37 (2d ed. 1998).

[259]*See* Perlin & Dorfman, *supra* note 6, at 113–16.

[260]*Id.* at 116–17. *See also* Tyler, *supra* note 224.

[261]*See generally* Winick, *supra* note 229.

[262]*See* text accompanying note 236.

[263]494 U.S. 210 (1990); *see supra* text accompanying notes 179–81.

[264]*See, e.g., In re* Schouler, 723 P.2d 1103 (Wash. 1986); *In re* Ingram, 689 P.2d 1363 (Wash. 1984); *In re* Colyer, 660 P.2d 738 (Wash. 1983).

[265]In Washington, mental health patients committed for involuntary mental health treatment are statutorily committed for different lengths of time, depending on treatment needs and restrictivity decisions. *See* REV. CODE WASH. §§ 71.05.150 (1984) *et seq.* Each patient begins the commitment process on a 72-hour hold, and is then subsequently placed on a 14-day hold, then a 30–180-day hold, and if further treatment is necessary, a 180-day hold that is subject both to review and renewal. *Id.*

[266]REV. CODE WASH. § 71.05.215 (1991); WASH. ADMIN. CODE § 275-55-241(1)(c)(ii) (1991). REV. CODE WASH. § 71.05.215(2) (1991) gives the Washington Department of Social and Health Services the authority to promulgate regulations and rules regarding the right of mental health patients to refuse antipsychotic medications.

[267]*See* REV. CODE WASH. § 71.05.215(2)(c) (1991); WASH. ADMIN. CODE § 275-55-241(c)(iii)(B) (1991).

court hearing, counsel, the right to present evidence and cross-examine witnesses, and appeal.[268] In other words, the amount of due process protection available to an institutionalized patient in Washington is directly related to her legal status. It is necessary to reflect on the pretextual implications of this conclusion. One of the central issues of right to refuse treatment law is the existence of (often irreversible) neurological side effects that may result from administering antipsychotic drug medication.[269] Indeed, much of the class action and test case litigation in this area has focused specifically on these side effects in structuring a constitutional remedy.[270] There is, intuitively, no inevitable difference in the level of neurological side effects to which a person committed under one section of the Washington state laws may be subjected to as opposed to a person committed pursuant to a different section of the same law.[271]

Yet the fact is that one set of patients (those committed pursuant to § 71.05.215(2)(c)) receives no counsel, and another set (those committed pursuant to § 71.05.370(7)) receives counsel. The first set receives a nonjudicial review; the second is statutorily entitled to a court hearing. Assuming that the lawyers assigned to represent the second set of patients actually do provide authentic independent advocacy services, and assuming that the study's recommendations are accepted by Washington state law makers, there will still be a gross disparity in the ways that individuals in the Washington state system—those whose clinical conditions may be alike but whose legal statuses differ—will be dealt with if they seek to assert their right to refuse treatment. This disparity makes neither clinical nor conceptual sense.

Utah

Utah follows a limited due process model in implementing medication hearings.[272] As in California and Washington, there is a great deal of inconsistency regarding the implementation of right-to-refuse laws in Utah. However, although California and Washington have elaborate involuntary medication statutes and regulations, Utah has neither. In 1994 the previous Utah involuntary medication statute—which had provided for medication hearings at which the treatment order would be reviewed by a committee of mental health professionals[273]—was repealed.[274] The intent of the Utah legislature in repealing the statute was to allow each mental health facility to establish its own policies and procedures to deal with the involuntary medication of mental health patients ''since this area of the law is a rapidly evolving area.''[275] This repeal followed the decision of *Woodland v. Angus*,[276] declaring the statute unconstitutional as violative of the due process clause.

---

[268]*See* REV. CODE WASH. § 71.05370(7) (1991); WASH. ADMIN. CODE § 275-55-241(c)(iii)(B) (1991).

[269]*See generally* PERLIN, *supra* note 5, § 2.08, at 214–18.

[270]*See, e.g.,* Rivers v. Katz, 504 N.Y.S.2d 74, 81 (1984); Riggins v. Nevada, 504 U.S. 129, 1816 (1992), and *see id.* at 138–43 (Kennedy, J., concurring).

[271]*Compare* 2 Perlin, *supra* note 2, § 3B-8.3 at 327 (2d. ed. 1999) (posing similar questions in context of Supreme Court's decision in *Riggins* and in Washington v. Harper 494 U.S. 210 (1990).

[272]After the research on this section was completed, the Tenth Circuit decided Jurasek v. Utah State Hosp., 158 F.3d 506 (10th Cir. 1998), rejecting a patient's arguments that the system in place in Utah hospitals violated his right to refuse treatment.

[273]UTAH CODE ANN. § 62A-12-234.1 (1992) *(repealed).* Committee members could not be directly involved in the individual patient's treatment. *Id.*

[274]*See* UTAH CODE ANN., Compiler's Notes, 62A-12-234.1, 62A-12-234.2 *(repealed)* (1994).

[275]*See id.*

[276]820 F. Supp. 1497 (D. Utah 1993).

As a result of this repealer, the extent of due process afforded mental health patients in Utah, including the right to counsel, differs by facility. For instance, the Utah State Hospital involuntary medication policies and procedures mirror the due process standards set out in *Harper*.[277] Patients having medication hearings at the Utah State Hospital are not provided counsel at the hearings, and are in fact prohibited from having an attorney represent them in the hearing, even if they pay for it.[278] Instead patients are provided only with a lay patient advocate who is an employee of the hospital.[279] However, at the Utah State Prison, prisoners are provided with attorneys to represent them at the medication hearings.[280]

Utah's "solution" to the providing of counsel problem is even more off-kilter. The only mentally ill institutionalized individuals with a right to assigned counsel are those in the Utah State Prison; those in the Utah State Hospital—even those who are independently wealthy and can afford to retain counsel—are prohibited from being represented.

Elsewhere, some nonsanist courts have begun to more carefully articulate criteria to be considered at a judicial right-to-refuse hearing. The Wisconsin Supreme Court, for example, in *Virgil D. v. Rock County*, set out five relevant factors:

(a) whether the patient is able to identify the type of recommended medication or treatment;

(b) whether the patient has previously received the type of medication or treatment at issue;

(c) if the patient has received similar treatment in the past, whether he or she can describe what happened as a result and how the effects were beneficial or harmful;

(d) if the patient has not been similarly treated in the past, whether he or she can identify the risks and benefits associated with the recommended medication or treatment; and

(e) whether the patient holds any patently false beliefs about the recommended medication or treatment which would prevent an understanding of legitimate risks and benefits.[281]

But it is almost a conceptual impossibility to conjure an image of a *pro se* patient— presumptively seen as incompetent by the court—convincing a fact finder in a Utah State Hospital case to conduct a probing and careful assessment of each of these factors in an individual case. From an analytic perspective, the Utah system fails miserably.

---

[277]*See Utah State Hospital Operational Policy and Procedure, Section 13: Involuntary Medication of Civilly Committed Patients* 3–6 (1994) (Utah Policy). *See generally* Washington v. Harper, 494 U.S. 210 (1992).

[278]*See* Utah Policy *supra* note 277 at 4. The specific language of the relevant part of the policy states, "The patient has the right to attend the hearing, present evidence, including witnesses; and cross-examine staff witnesses. Because the issue before the committee is purely a medical one, it is not necessary or advisable for attorneys to be present to represent either the patient or the physician. For that reason the patient is allowed representation only by a lay advisor who understands the psychiatric issues involved however, [*sic*] the lay advisor need not be provided at government expense. The patient and his treating physician are not allowed representation by an attorney."

[279]*Id.*

[280]*See State of Utah Department of Corrections Institutional Operations Division Manual, Vol. Facilities Operation: Medical/Mental/Dental Health, Chapt. FI 15 Involuntary Treatment* § 2.04, E2 (1991), at 15: "At the hearing an opportunity to be represented by counsel shall be afforded to every inmate/parolee." It should be noted that this only applies to inmates in custody of the Department of Corrections who are at the Utah State Prison. Those who are in the forensic unit of the Utah State Hospital are only afforded minimal due process protections.

[281]524 N.W.2d 894, 899–900 (Wis. 1994), *reconsideration denied,* 531 N.W.2d 331 (Wis. 1995).

Conclusion

Consider all of the right-to-refuse-treatment issues that are touched on by sanism and pretextuality:

- The attitudes of trial judges toward patients;
- The attitudes of counsel toward patients;
- The implication of courts' articulating expansive remedies in right-to-refuse class-action litigation, without providing counsel to represent patients in individual cases;
- The assignment of nonspecialized counsel and uneducated judges to represent patients in right to refuse cases;
- The failure of appellate courts to take seriously the *pro forma* quality and nature of hearings in many instances;
- The propensity of decision makers to make equivalent *incompetent* with *makes bad decisions* and to assume, in the face of statutory and case law, that incompetence in decision making can be presumed from the fact of institutionalization;[282]
- The perception of a positive relationship between implementing the right to refuse and failed deinstitutionalization policies; and
- The perception of drugs as the only "cure" for dangerousness.[283]

Each of these issues must be considered. If sanist trial judges assume that patients are incompetent (and thus discredit their testimony), the entire enterprise may be doomed to fail. Any hearings will become little more than empty shells. What difference will the MacArthur Network Study's recommendations make—as to the ability of these patients to engage in autonomous medication-choice decision making—if trial judges simply ignore patients' testimony? If sanist counsel similarly disparage their clients' stories—or, just as inappropriately, present them to the court with an overt or covert "wink" that asks the judge to share in a complicitous sham (suggesting that the lawyer is simply participating in what he or she sees as a charade)[284]—then again the potential impact of the study's findings is seriously compromised.[285]

If appellate courts enter broad orders in right-to-refuse cases without thinking about the operationalization of these orders in subsequent individual cases (or if only perfunctory assignment of disinterested counsel is made),[286] the initial order becomes little more than a pretext. And if other appellate courts close their eyes to the level of inadequacy of counsel, this willful blindness simply adds one extra layer of pretextuality to the process.

Finally, we need to consider some other underlying social issues. The common wisdom is clear. Drugs serve two major purposes of social control: They "cure" dangerousness, and they are the *only* assurance that deinstitutionalized patients can remain free in community

---

[282]*See, e.g.,* Ladds I, *supra* note 233; Ladds II *supra* note 233.

[283]*See* cases cited in 1 PERLIN, *supra* note 2, § 2C-5.2, at 409–13 nn.782–803 (2d ed. 1998).

[284]On the problems raised when a lawyer feels "foolish" or "awkward" in representing an individual at an involuntary civil commitment hearing, see Perlin & Sadoff, *supra* note 231, at 167.

[285]*See id.* at 166 (on how a lawyer's perceptions that his or her client is not credible can have a devastating impact on the presentation of the client's case). For a recent thoughtful and comprehensive therapeutic jurisprudence analysis of the role of lawyers in the representation of mentally disabled individuals, see Jan Costello, *"Why Would I Need a Lawyer?": Legal Counsel and Advocacy for Persons With Mental Disabilities, in* LAW, MENTAL HEALTH, AND MENTAL DISORDER 15 (Bruce Sales & Daniel Shuman eds. 1996).

[286]On a startling variation between jurisdictions, see 1 PERLIN, *supra* note 2, § 2B-9, at 245–46 (2d ed. 1998) (contrasting experiences in Minnesota and Virginia).

settings.[287] Both of these assumptions are reflected in the case law that has developed in individual involuntary civil commitment cases (in which a judge's perception of the likelihood that an individual will self-medicate becomes the critical variable in case dispositions);[288] they are also reflected in the public discourse that is heard in classrooms, hospital corridors, and courtrooms.[289]

Neither of these assumptions has any base in science or in law. Yet without counsel to serve as a brake—to ask questions, to challenge assumptions, to identify faux "ordinary common sense", to point out the dangerous pitfalls of heuristic thinking—these assumptions will continue to dominate and control the disposition of individual right-to-refuse-treatment cases, notwithstanding the MacArthur Network Study's recommendations.

Again, counsel's significance increases even more drastically in the context of the improper "presumption of incompetency" discussed earlier. Winick has suggested, "Unless a *parens patriae* commitment statute requires an individualized determination of incompetence to engage in hospital admission decisionmaking, it would seem deficient as a matter of substantive due process."[290] Without vigorous independent counsel, it is doubtful that such challenges would ever be launched. This is especially problematic in light of the fact that the equation of incompetency to mental illness *does* appear consonant with "ordinary common sense."[291] Counsel's role is especially important in areas of the law where OCS is so dissonant with empirical fact. If there is any expectation that the issues listed previously will be considered critically and thoughtfully in the context of individual right-to-refuse-treatment determinations, it is essential that the issue of presence and adequacy of counsel be moved to center stage.

---

[287]*See, e.g.,* Deborah A. Dorfman, *Through a Therapeutic Jurisprudence Filter: Fear and Pretextuality in Mental Disability Law,* 10 N.Y.L. SCH. J. HUM. RTS. 805 (1993); Perlin, *supra* note 5; Michael L. Perlin, *Competency, Deinstitutionalization, and Homelessness: A Story of Marginalization,* 28 HOUS. L. REV. 63 (1991); Frances Cournos, *Involuntary Medication and the Case of Joyce Brown,* 40 HOSP. & COMMUNITY PSYCHIATRY 736 (1989).

[288]*See supra* Chapter 4 text accompanying notes 134-40; *see also* 1 PERLIN, *supra* note 2, § 2C-5.2, at 409–13 (2d ed. 1998) (citing cases).

[289]The public discourse on the Internet can be included in this list as well. *See* Jon Mankowski, *Re:[PSYC-SOC] Accountability* (Sept. 16, 1997) (post on FORENSIC-PSYCH LISTSERV) ("Inpatient, it practically takes a court order to MAKE any patient take [antipsychotic medications]") (capitalization in original).

[290]Winick, *supra* note 212, at 145.

[291]*See also id.* at 145 ("While the assumption that all mentally ill people are incompetent may not be irrational, the MacArthur study strongly suggests its incorrectness").

Chapter 7
THE RIGHT TO SEXUAL INTERACTION

Institutionalization does not rob persons of their sexuality. Susan Stefan—perhaps the most perceptive critic of institutional sex policies—has stressed,

> Any discussion of this issue should start with three premises. First, people's needs for intimacy, romance, and physical and emotional connection do not vanish either when they are diagnosed or when they are institutionalized. These needs are intrinsic parts of our shared humanity. If anything, they are greater for people who are isolated from the community, locked where they don't want to be, confused, and in pain.[1]

This question of the right of persons institutionalized because of medical disability to voluntary sexual interaction is one of the most threatening for clinicians, line workers, administrators, advocates, attorneys, or family members ("a public policy question as controversial as they get").[2] Taboos and stigmas attached to sexual behavior are inevitably heightened when coupled and conflated with stereotypes of the meaning of mental disability.[3] The question of sexuality and sexual behavior in an institution challenges the traditional "liberal" position on questions of institutionalization and civil rights enforcement; it reflects the massive use of ego defenses (such as denial) in the way most of us think about hospitalization questions;[4] it serves ultimately as a "Rorschach test" for the degree to which we are willing to punish people via the restriction of their ability to exercise civil rights because they suffer from mental illness.

Sanism is the cause of this discomfort and the attitudes that motivate such restrictions. It is this irrational prejudice—based on stereotypes, myths, superstitions, and deindividualization in ways that reflect a community's dominant morality—that governs the treatment and regulates the sexuality of persons institutionalized because of mental disability. It is astonishingly underdiscussed[5] (and the fact of this underdiscussion has a

---

[1]Susan Stefan, *Sex in Institutional Settings: Institutional and Agency Policies in Massachusetts,* 42 ADVISOR: NOTES FROM THE MENTAL HEALTH LEGAL ADVISORS COMMITTEE 1 (Spring 1995).

[2]Rob Karwath, *Mental Center Sex Rule Studied,* CHICAGO TRIBUNE, April 9, 1989, at 1.

[3]For the most comprehensive and thoughtful study, see SANDER GILMAN, DIFFERENCE AND PATHOLOGY: STEREOTYPES OF SEXUALITY, RACE AND MADNESS (1985). *See also* David Shelton, *Client Sexual Behavior and Staff Attitudes: Shaping Masturbation in an Individual With a Profound Mental and Secondary Sensory Handicap,* 20 MENT. HANDICAP 81 (1992).

[4]*See, e.g.,* Deborah A. Dorfman, *Through a Therapeutic Jurisprudence Filter: Fear and Pretextuality in Mental Disability Law,* 10 N.Y.L. SCH. J. HUM. RTS. 805 (1993).

[5]With rare exceptions—*see, e.g.,* Susan Stefan, *Whose Egg Is It Anyway? Reproductive Rights of Incarcerated, Institutionalized, and Incompetent Women,* 13 NOVA L. REV. 405 (1989) [hereinafter Stefan, *Reproductive Rights*]; *see also* Susan Stefan, *Silencing the Different Voice: Feminist Theory and Competence,* 47 U. MIAMI L. REV. 763, 791–99 (1993) (discussing the applicability of statutory rape laws to women with mental disabilities) [hereinafter Stefan, *Silencing*]—the law reviews have been silent about this specific topic. On the related question of how persons with mental disabilities are deprived of their parental rights, see Robert L. Hayman, *Presumptions of Justice: Law, Politics, and the Mentally Retarded Parent,* 103 HARV. L. REV. 1201 (1990). On the rights of a mentally disabled person to resist state-sponsored sterilization, *see* Edward J. Larson & Leonard J. Nelson III, *Involuntary Sexual Sterilization of Incompetents in Alabama: Past, Present, and Future,* 43 ALA. L. REV. 399 (1992); Julie Marcus, *In re* Romero: *Sterilization and Competency,* 68 DENV. U. L. REV. 105 (1991); Elizabeth S. Scott, *Sterilization of Mentally Retarded Persons: Reproductive Rights and Family Privacy,* 1986 DUKE L.J. 806. However, the overall area is bereft of structured and organized analysis. This stands in stark contrast to other areas of patients' rights that have spawned cottage industries of commentary (such as the right to refuse the imposition of antipsychotic medication or the meaning of dangerousness at an involuntary civil commitment proceeding).

special significance in light of the fundamentality of sexuality as an expressive human experience).[6]

In this section I will discuss the importance of perspective and will attempt to address (or at least raise) the full range of ancillary questions that must be addressed in constructing a comprehensive response. Then I will discuss the development of the patients rights movement, and explain how the right to sexual interaction does or does not "fit" in this context, briefly consider the sparse litigation on this issue, and offer some thoughts about the potential impact of the Americans With Disabilities Act (ADA) on future developments.[7] I will consider attitudinal issues, and explore how sanism and pretextuality affect the way we feel about this area of the law. Then I will try to articulate some of the unanswered (and perhaps unanswerable) questions, many of which reflect what the law calls "incredible dilemmas" (the result of clashing contradictory rights or social values).

Perspectives on Patients and Sex

Before we can approach analytically the question posed, we must attempt at least some modest deconstruction. No doctrinal or theoretical formulation can be undertaken seriously until we articulate our perspective in examining the issues and until we unpack the different legal and clinical categories that are implicated in such analysis.

I do not believe that any useful answer to the question that I have raised can be even tentatively formulated unless we clarify our perspective: Are we looking for a legal answer, a clinical answer, a social answer, an administrative answer, or a behavioral answer (or, as we must, a combination of all of these)? We must consider each of these ancillary questions if we want to construct a meaningful multitextured and comprehensive response.

First, let us consider legal categories: To what statutorily or judicially defined civil rights are involuntarily committed mental patients generally entitled, and, in the articulation of such rights, have the courts or the legislatures specifically considered sexual autonomy or interaction rights?[8] Will the ADA[9] force public institutions to change how they treat patients in this context?[10] Is it necessary to initially inquire into an individual patient's competency to enter into sexual decision making—and if it is, how is this to be determined?[11] Do competent institutionalized patients have the same autonomy rights as all other persons, allowing them

---

[6]Although the Supreme Court has never expressly held that sexual intercourse among adults is a fundamental right, it has recognized a fundamental right to be free, "except in very limited circumstances, from unwanted governmental intrusions into one's privacy." Stanley v. Georgia, 394 U.S. 557, 564 (1969). For a list of all areas in which the court has recognized this right in areas of sexual privacy, see Whisenhunt v. Spradlin, 464 U.S. 965, 971 (1983) (Brennan, J., dissenting from denial of *certiorari*).

[7]The ADA will be discussed in full in the next chapter, where I will discuss the significance of the Supreme Court's 1999 decision in *Olmstead v. L.C.,* 119 S. Ct. 2176 (1999).

[8]This is the way that a standard doctrinal analysis of the problem would probably proceed, and is basically how I have previously addressed this (albeit briefly). *See* MICHAEL L. PERLIN, MENTAL DISABILITY LAW: CIVIL AND CRIMINAL § 3C-5.1 at 416-21 (2d. ed. 1999). On how this traditional doctrinal analysis runs the risk of intellectual sterility, *see infra* text accompanying notes 8 and 9.

[9]42 U.S.C. §§ 12101 *et seq.* (1990).

[10]The most important analysis of the ADA from an institutionalization focus is Timothy Cook, *The Americans With Disabilities Act: The Move to Integration,* 64 TEMP. L. REV. 393 (1991). I consider the interplay between ADA enforcement and sanist attitudes in Michael L. Perlin, *The ADA and Persons With Mental Disabilities: Can Sanist Attitudes Be Undone?* 8 J.L. & HEALTH 15 (1993–94); *see generally infra* section 3.

[11]*See infra* text accompanying notes 122–29.

to engage in the same level of sexual self-determination as any of the rest of us?[12] Putting aside inquiries into mental capacities, are all "patients" to be treated in the same way? Is there a difference between voluntary patients and involuntarily committed patients?[13]

Does involuntary commitment involve an implicit restriction on one's freedom to engage in sexual activity?[14] Are there additional restrictions that are necessary in the cases of patients who have been committed following their involvement in the criminal justice system? Among those in this group, is there a difference between patients awaiting trial, those permanently incompetent following a *Jackson v. Indiana* determination,[15] or those found not guilty by reason of insanity?[16] Between patients who have been found to be incompetent (for any reason) and those who have not?[17]

Next we need to turn our attention to clinical questions. Has the patient in question ever expressed or articulated any wish to either engage in sexual activity or to abstain from it? Is it clinically beneficial or antitherapeutic to allow institutionalized patients some (any) (much) autonomy in sexual decision making?[18] To what extent must we factor in research on the therapeutic value of touching and physical intimacy?[19] Does it matter if the patient is expected to be hospitalized briefly or for a longer period of time? What is the impact of sexual activity on different modalities of treatment? On the overall ward milieu? What responsibilities come with the assertion of rights? Is the potential relationship between sexual repression and neurotic behavior (articulated most vividly by Wilhelm Reich) worth considering?[20]

---

[12]On autonomy in this context generally, see Bruce Winick, *On Autonomy: Legal and Psychological Perspectives,* 37 VILL. L. REV. 1705 (1992). On the question of consent to sexual activity in institutions for the mentally disabled, see David Carson, *Legality of Responding to the Sexuality of a Client With Profound Learning Disabilities,* 20 MENT. HANDICAP 85 (1992).

[13]*See generally* Zinermon v. Burch, 494 U.S. 113, 130–37 (1990) (patient's "voluntary" status often illusory).

[14]On the rationales for involuntary commitment in general, see 1 PERLIN, *supra* note 8, at chapt. 2A (2d ed. 1998).

[15]406 U.S. 715 (1972). After *Jackson* a patient cannot be confined indefinitely in a maximum security forensic facility if it is not likely that he or she will regain competence to stand trial within the foreseeable future. *Id.* at 737–38.

[16]On postacquittal insanity defense commitments, see 3 PERLIN, *supra* note 8, §§ 15.20–15.22.

[17]On judges' self-described discomfort with their inability to make this discrimination, see Michael L. Perlin, *Are Courts Competent to Decide Competency Questions? Stripping the Facade From* United States v. Charters, 38 U. KAN. L. REV. 957, 991 (1990).

[18]The recent development of therapeutic jurisprudence as an academic discipline—*see infra* Chapter 12—should force us to consider the therapeutic outcomes of different "sex policies." In formulating our analysis, we need to be mindful of Wexler's and Winick's caveat that, in the articulation of policy choices, therapeutic outcome should not trump civil liberties values. See David Wexler & Bruce Winick, *Introduction, in* ESSAYS IN THERAPEUTIC JURISPRUDENCE ix, xi (D. Wexler & B. Winick eds. 1991). See *supra* Chapter 6.

[19]*See, e.g.,* ASHLEY MONTAGU, TOUCHING: THE HUMAN SIGNIFICANCE OF THE SKIN (1972); Harry F. Harlow et al., *From Thought to Therapy,* 1959 AM. SCIENTIST 538 (1971); *see generally* Bill Mossman, Therapeutic Benefits Correlated With Sexuality (1992) (unpublished manuscript, on file with author). For a historical review, see Henry L. Minton, *American Psychology on the Study of Human Sexuality,* 1 J. PSYCHOL. & HUM. SEXUALITY 17 (1988).

[20]*See, e.g.,* WILHELM REICH, SEX-POL 126–29 (A. Bostock Trans. 1972) [hereinafter REICH I]; WILHELM REICH, SELECTED WRITINGS: AN INTRODUCTION TO ORGONOMY 184–85 (1973); WILHELM REICH, CHARACTER ANALYSIS 130–33, 158–68 (T. Wolfe Trans., 3d ed. 1949); WILHELM REICH, THE INVASION OF COMPULSORY SEX-MORALITY 4–11 (W. Grossmann & D. Grossmann trans. 1971) (sexual activity inhibits neuroses; sexual repression transforms everyday psychic conflicts into neuroses). Although Reich was widely discredited at the time of his death, see Bertell Ollman, *Foreword, in* REICH I, *supra,* at v; his arguments are still worthy of consideration in this context. On Reich's role in the development of post-Freudian psychiatry, see JONAS ROBITSCHER, THE POWERS OF PSYCHIATRY 385–92 (1980).

Let us next consider the multiple textures of sexual relationships and the definitional reality that a psychiatric hospital is a closed institution. Under the best of circumstances, entering into a new sexual relationship can be stressful and confusing. Are these stresses inappropriately exacerbated when the universe in question is that of institutionalized mental patients? If persons with serious mental disability have more difficulty processing stress, need this clinical reality be factored into any policy ultimately adopted? Can preoccupation with sex add a systemic distortion to all matters involving ward behavior? Will excessive concern with sex blunt important consideration of other issues such as the quality of a full range of interpersonal relationships, self-esteem, and an ability to deal with intimacy issues? How does this focus affect questions of individual versus group needs?

A closed institution also implies limits on individuals' mobility and freedom of action. When people in the "free world" terminate a stormy love affair, they frequently can adjust their life so as not to have much contact with former lovers; what happens if the exlover is on the same floor of an inpatient hospital (especially if it is a locked ward hospital), and neither can leave without a court order? Conversely, what happens when a couple is split up by a court order transferring one patient to another ward or facility for either clinical or legal reasons?[21] Is it realistically possible to monitor sexual practices in a facility such as a psychiatric hospital, so as to best ensure that an individual patient's exercise of the right to sexual autonomy does not result in nonconsensual sex, in unwanted pregnancies, or in the spread of sexually transmitted diseases?

In any event, can patients be stopped from having sex?[22] Are there worthwhile analogies that can be made to rules that attempted to govern college dormitories in the 1960s and 1970s (when administrators vainly and with futility tried to suppress sexual activity among undergraduates)?[23]

This leads to considering this question from the perspective of hospital officials. Why are hospital administrators resistant to expanded sexual activity on the part of patients? Is it more than simple inconvenience, or even the fear of unwanted pregnancies? How much of a factor is fear of a potential hospital-wide AIDS epidemic, and how realistic is this fear? How will the well-documented fear on the part of many mental health professionals of being sued—what Stanley Brodsky and his colleagues have called "litigaphobia"[24]—affect the

---

[21]As to clinical considerations, see, for example, Johnson v. United States, 409 F. Supp. 1283, 1293 (M.D. Fla. 1976); Predoti v. Bergen Pines County Hosp., 463 A.2d 400 (N.J. App. Div. 1983) (patients may now be treated consonant with an open-door policy with fewer restrictions on mobility and actions). Legal considerations include, e.g., the possibility that a criminal detainer may be placed in a patient's file, thus necessitating his or her transfer to a locked ward in spite of contrary clinical considerations.

[22]See Stefan, supra note 1, at 1: "Both voluntary and involuntary sex happens in institutions and always has." And see id.: "Policies that prohibit sex do not necessarily eliminate sex."

[23]There are self-evidently major differences between a college dorm and a psychiatric hospital. On the other hand, there are remarkable similarities between the parens patriae theory that supports danger-to-self commitments, see 1 PERLIN, supra note 8, §§ 2A-4.6 to 2A-4.6c (2d ed. 1998), and the in loco parentis doctrine that governed campus life until the late 1960s. There are also similarities in the impossibility of enforcing such rules of behavior in either setting. See generally Natalie Russo & Katherine Bishop, Sexual Abuse Among People With Developmental Disabilities, QUALITY OF CARE (Jan.–Feb. 1994), at 6, 7 (sexual activity among persons with developmental disabilities occurs "frequently").

[24]See, e.g., Stanley Brodsky, Fear of Litigation in Mental Health Professionals, 15 CRIM. JUST. & BEHAV. 492 (1988). I discuss the impact of "litigaphobia" on therapist behavior in cases involving duties to protect third parties in Michael L. Perlin, Tarasoff and the Dilemma of the Dangerous Patient: New Directions for the 1990's, 16 LAW & PSYCHOL. REV. 29, 61-62 (1992). For more empirical research, see Ann Lawthers et al., Physicians' Perceptions of Being Sued, 17 J. HEALTH POL., POL'Y & L. 463, 468 (1992) (doctors significantly overestimate the risk of being sued). On the specific question of liability in cases of sexual activity in facilities for persons with mental disabilities, see David Carson, Legality of Responding to the Sexuality of a Client With Profound Learning Disabilities, 20 MENT. HANDICAP 85 (1992).

adoption of or compliance with any policy that appears to liberalize sexual interaction policies (for fear that litigation might quickly follow unwanted births or the spread of STDs)?[25] One commentator has suggested that the threat of litigation has led hospital administrators to "attempt to minimize the complexity of patient sexuality by focusing on the symbolic, simplistic reassurance of written procedures."[26] Is this conclusion an idiosyncratic one (based on the circumstances at the hospital about which he was writing), or is this practice more common?[27]

How does the whole question of sexual autonomy in a public institution fit with the resolution of other social–cultural–political issues such as AIDS reporting[28] or condom distribution?[29] What happens when individual line staff at a hospital (the individuals on whom the implementation of any social policy inevitably falls) simply refuse to cooperate with such a policy because their own sense of religious morality forbids it[30] (i.e., their religion teaches them that unmarried persons—of any mental capacity—should not have sex, and that married persons—of any mental capacity—should not have extramarital

---

[25]Robert L. Sadoff, one of the nation's preeminent forensic psychiatrists, points to expansion of provider liability in cases such as Schuster v. Altenburg, 424 N.W.2d 159 (Wis. 1988) (doctor might be liable for failing to warn of medication side effects if those side effects should have led him or her to caution a patient against driving where it was foreseeable that an accident could result) as the source of realistic concerns on the part of therapists that an ever-expanding range of clinical decisions may lead to ever-expanding personal liability. (Robert L. Sadoff, personal communication, Nov. 8, 1992).

[26]Terry Holbrook, *Policing Sexuality in a Modern State Hospital,* 40 HOSP. & COMMUNITY PSYCHIATRY 75, 79 (1989).

[27]Eighty-three percent of state facilities polled reported that they had some sort of policy addressing sexual activity by patients. *See* Peter Buckley & Jodi Hyde, *State Hospitals' Responses to the Sexual Behavior of Psychiatric Inpatients,* 48 PSYCHIATRIC SERV. 398 (1997). By contrast, a 1981 survey of 70 psychiatric units in Canada revealed that *none* had such a written policy. C. Keitner & P. Grof, *Sexual and Emotional Intimacy Between Psychiatric Inpatients: Formulating a Policy,* 32 HOSP. & COMMUNITY PSYCHIATRY 188 (1981). For recent policies, see, for example, *State of Florida, Dep't of H&RS, Operating Procedure No. 130–5* (March 7, 1995) (G. Pierce Wood Memorial Hospital, Arcadia, FL), and *Guidelines for Agency Policies Concerning Sexual Contact and Consent Issued by Office of Mental Retardation and Developmental Disabilities,* QUALITY OF CARE (Sept.–Oct. 1993), at 4.

[28]*See, e.g.,* N.J. STAT. ANN. § 26:4–15; IDAHO CODE § 39–602; N.Y. PUB. HEALTH LAW §§ 2101, 2306; *see generally* Julie Edwards, *Controlling the Epidemic: The Texas AIDS Reporting Statute,* 41 BAYLOR L. REV. 399 (1989); Donald Hermann & Rosalind Gagliono, *AIDS, Therapeutic Confidentiality, and Warning Third Parties,* 48 MD. L. REV. 55 (1989); Sharron Rennert, *AIDS/HIV and Confidentiality: Model Policy and Procedures,* 39 U. KAN. L. REV. 656 (1991).

[29]This is, of course, a controversial topic in noninstitutional settings. *See, e.g.,* Nick Chiles, *Judge OKs School Condom Program,* NEWSDAY, Apr. 24, 1992, (city ed.), at 8; Gail Collins, *The Board of Education Retreats in Condom Wars,* NEWSDAY, May 29, 1992, (city ed.), at 4; Edna Negron, *Condom Issue Revisited,* NEWSDAY, Sept. 16, 1992, (city ed.), at 83.

[30]*See* Russo & Bishop, *supra* note 23, at 7:

Finally, providers typically employ staff who hold personal values and beliefs about sexuality ranging from very liberal views to strongly conservative views. In order for providers to implement policies that are consistent with established regulations and guidelines, they need to make a concerted effort to train staff in their policies to avoid the likelihood that each person will be guided by differing personal views about sexuality. Oftentimes, direct care staff are in the difficult position of implementing interventions at the most basic level. Therefore, providers must be especially sensitive to their staff's dilemmas and provide them with the consistent support, oversight, training and resources necessary to implement their policy.

sex)?[31] Can (or should) there be separate rules in the cases of private facilities that are church affiliated or private nonsectarian facilities that retain units specially designated for practitioners of specific religions?[32]

Finally, we need to speculate on whether any of these answers depend on what we mean by "sex"? Do we need to consider each possible permutation of sexual behavior? Does it make a difference if we are discussing monogamous heterosexual sex, polygamous heterosexual sex, monogamous homosexual sex, polygamous homosexual sex, bisexual sex? Does "sex" mean intercourse? What about oral sex? Anal sex? Masturbation?[33] Voyeurism? Exhibitionism? Should pornography be made available? If so, what sorts? Mens' magazines that one can buy in a convenience store (such as *Penthouse* or *Hustler*) or "hard core" magazines? What about sexually explicit literature that might appear to involve (or condone or encourage) violence? Should sexually explicit videos or movies be available for patients to see? If so, should they view them communally or individually? What if a patient's prehospitalization behavior involved significant sexual acting out in what had been seen as inappropriate ways?[34] Can patients' decisions to engage in what is sometimes perceived as "deviant" sexual behavior subsequently be used as evidence of either their danger to self or others or of "grave disability"?[35]

This list of questions should underscore the point that this topic is, indeed, a complex one. Its complexity is further increased (and made more difficult) by society's generally irrational attitudes toward mentally disabled persons. Despite the passage of the ADA and two decades of litigation on behalf of institutionalized mentally disabled persons (substantially geared to inquire simply into whether mental patients are being treated "like human beings"),[36] society tends to either infantilize such persons (denying the reality that they may retain the same sort of sexual urges, desires, and needs the rest of us have and generally act

---

[31]On the ways that morality issues are especially difficult in mental disability law cases in a broad variety of fact settings, see, for example, Michael L. Perlin, *Morality and Pretextuality, Psychiatry and Law: Of "Ordinary Common Sense, Heuristic Reasoning, and Cognitive Dissonance,* 19 BULL. AM. ACAD. PSYCHIATRY & L. 131 (1991) [hereinafter Perlin, *Morality*]; Michael L. Perlin, *Pretexts and Mental Disability Law: The Case of Competency,* 47 U. MIAMI L. REV. [hereinafter Perlin, *Pretexts*]. On the way that morality issues were raised in the debate on the ADA, see Michael L. Perlin, *The ADA and Persons with Mental Disabilities: Can Sanist Attitudes Be Undone?* 8 J.L. & HEALTH 15, 27-28 (1994) [hereinafter Perlin, *Sanist Attitutdes*], (discussing Senator Helms' arguments that an employer's sense of "morality" might lead him or her to refuse to hire a manic-depressive person for a job).

[32]This latter practice, abandoned in most states, still continues *de facto* in some sections of California (personal communication, Deborah Dorfman, J.D., Nov. 12, 1992; Dorfman at the time was a patients' rights advocate with the Mental Health Advocacy Project of San Jose, CA).

[33]*See, e.g.,* Diane Civic, Grace Walsh, & Dennis McBride, *Staff Perspectives on Sexual Behavior of Patients in a State Psychiatric Hospital,* 44 HOSP. & COMMUNITY PSYCHIATRY 887, 887 (1993) (masturbation allowed on wards "if done in private").

[34]For a traditional reading on "sexual deviance" in this context, see, for example, JAMES PAGE, PSYCHOPATHOLOGY 367–79 (1971). On the ways that mental health professionals' attitudes toward sex are influenced by the nature of the sexual activity and the patients' sexual orientation, see Michael Commons et al., *Professionals' Attitudes Towards Sex Between Institutionalized Patients,* 46 AM. J. PSYCHOTHERAPY 571 (1992).

[35]*See, e.g.,* Virginia Aldigé Hiday & Lynn Smith, *Effects of the Dangerousness Standard in Civil Commitment,* 15 J. PSYCHIATRY & L. 433, 499 (1987).

[36]Falter v. Veterans Admin., 502 F. Supp. 1178, 1185 (D.N.J. 1980). On the impact of legal change on attitudinal change, see Sheri Johnson, *Black Innocence and the White Jury,* 83 MICH. L. REV. 1611, 1650 (1985) ("Where discrimination is not legally or socially approved, social scientists predict it will be practiced only where it is possible to do so covertly and indirectly"); Emily Campbell & Alan Tomkins, *Gender, Grades, and Law Review Membership as Factors in Law Firm Hiring Decisions: An Empirical Study,* 18 J. CONTEMP. L. 211, 250 n.122 (1992) (reporting on empirical evidence suggesting that, in the years since the passage of race-based civil rights legislation, "racial attitudes and stereotypes among white Americans have become more tolerant").

on)[37] or, paradoxically, to demonize them (expressing fear of their ''hypersexuality'' and the correlative need of protections and limitations to best stop them from acting on these ''primitive'' urges).[38]

Both these seemingly paradoxical and contrary feelings stem from sanist attitudes.[39] Justice Holmes' chilling epigram in *Buck v. Bell*—''three generations of imbeciles is enough''[40]—is a perfect *exemplar* of these attitudes,[41] and is particularly telling in light of the questions under discussion. The legal system's treatment of questions involving sexuality and mentally disabled persons reflects the pernicious power of sanism, and results in pretextual decisions arrived at through teleological reasoning.

Development of Patients' Rights

The history of the development of substantive constitutional rights of institutionalized mental patients[42] began with *Wyatt v. Stickney,*[43] where federal district court Judge Frank Johnson fleshed out the contours of a constitutional right to treatment by articulating a broad range of civil rights to which all patients were entitled.[44] These ''*Wyatt* standards'' became the inspiration and role model[45] for other litigation[46] and for legislation—generally labeled as ''patients' bills of rights''—that was enacted in virtually all the states[47] as well as by Congress.[48] Many of these statutes contain provisions that are also reflected in the robust case law: That an individual is institutionalized does not mean that the patient is necessarily or presumptively incompetent for all or any purposes.[49]

There appears to be a growing consensus among institutional health care providers, behaviorists, other mental health professionals, and legal advocates that the expansion of the

---

[37]*See* Michael L. Perlin, *On ''Sanism,''* 46 SMU L. REV. 373, 394 (1992) (discussing sanist myth that, ''At the best, the mentally disabled are simple and content, like children''). *See generally* Mary Romano, *Sex and Disability, in* DISABLED PERSONS AS SECOND-CLASS CITIZENS 64 (M. Eisenberg ed. 1982).

[38]*See* GILMAN, *supra* note 3, at 24–25, 142–48, 162 (on how U.S. society views certain racial and religious minority groups in the same way). *See* Perlin, *supra* note 37, at 394 (discussing sanist myth that, ''at the worst, [mentally disabled persons] are invariably more dangerous than non-mentally ill persons''); Holbrook, *supra* note 26, at 79 (''Mental hospitals today are often portrayed by the media as inhabited by sexual deviates, psychopaths and rapists whose uncontrolled sexual impulses and polymorphous sexual perversities require protracted treatment and confinement'').

[39]*See infra* text accompanying notes 90–107.

[40]274 U.S. 200, 207 (1927).

[41]*See, e.g.,* Stephen Jay Gould, *Carrie Buck's Daughter,* 2 CONST. COMMENTARY 331 (1985); Paul Lombardo, *Three Generations, No Imbeciles: New Light on* Buck v. Bell, 60 N.Y.U. L. REV. 30 (1985); Robert Cynkar, Buck v. Bell: *''Felt Necessities'' vs. Fundamental Values,* 81 COLUM. L. REV. 1418 (1981) (all demonstrating the utter lack of scientific basis for Holmes' *dicta*).

[42]This section is generally adapted from Andrew Payne et al., *Sexual Activity Among Psychiatric Inpatients: International Perspectives,* 4 J. FORENS. PSYCHIATRY 109 (1993) (author of book was coauthor of article). *See supra* Chapter 5.

[43]325 F. Supp. 781 (M.D. Ala. 1971), 344 F. Supp. 373 (M.D. Ala. 1972), *aff'd sub. nom.,* Wyatt v. Aderholt, 503 F.2d 1305 (5th Cir. 1974); *see* 2 PERLIN, *supra* note 8, §§ 3A-3.1 to 3A-3.2d, at 24–56 (2d. ed. 1999).

[44]*Wyatt,* 344 F. Supp. at 379–83; *see* 2 PERLIN, *supra* note 8, § 3A-3.1a, at 33–36 (2d. ed. 1999).

[45]*See id.,* § 3A-14.2, at 128–29 (2d. ed. 1999).

[46]*See id.,* § 3A-3.3, at 57–60 (2d. ed. 1999); *see, e.g.,* Davis v. Watkins, 384 F. Supp. 1196 (N.D. Ohio 1974).

[47]Martha Lyon et al., *Patients' Bills of Rights: A Survey of State Statutes,* 6 MENT. DIS. L. RPTR. 178, (1982) (Lyon).

[48]*See, e.g.,* the Mental Health Systems Act, 42 U.S.C. § 9511; the Protection and Advocacy for the Mentally Ill Act, 42 U.S.C. §§ 10802 *et seq.*

[49]*See, e.g., In re* LaBelle, 728 P.2d 138 (Wash. 1986); Rivers v. Katz, 504 N.Y.S.2d 74 (1986); for representative statutes, see, for example, N.J. STAT. ANN. § 30:4–24.2 (1998); N.D. CEN. CO. 625-01.2–03 (1997).

civil rights revolution to institutionalized mental patients is both good therapy and good law.[50] Although there is occasional litigation in idiosyncratic cases over the limits of these rights and over such questions as the extent of a patient's right to free expression[51] or right to receive payment for work,[52] the area has generally been free of the acrimony that has accompanied debates over the extent of the right to refuse treatment,[53] the relationship between deinstitutionalization and homelessness,[54] the extent of state power of an insanity acquittee,[55] or the ability of a state to medicate a defendant to make him or her competent to be tried[56] or to be executed.[57]

There has been, however, a stunning lack of attention paid to what would seem to be one of the most basic and fundamental of all civil and human rights: the right to sexual interaction.[58] Most of the *Wyatt* standards were simply adopted whole cloth by state legislatures in their subsequent patients' bills of rights enactments; however, only four of the states adopted that portion of the standards that guaranteed patients the right to "reasonable" interaction with members of the opposite sex.[59] There has also been no follow-up litigation based on any of the statutes that do provide for this right, and only a scattering of cases has been litigated anywhere that have sought to vindicate this right.[60] In addition, this

---

[50]*See, e.g.,* Michael L. Perlin, Keri K. Gould, & Deborah A. Dorfman, *Therapeutic Jurisprudence and the Civil Rights of Institutionalized Mentally Disabled Persons: Hopeless Oxymoron or Path to Redemption?* 1 PSYCHOL., PUB. POL'Y & L. 80 (1995).

[51]Compare Rennie v. Klein, 476 F. Supp. 1294 (D.N.J. 1979), *to* Doe v. Public Health Trust of Dade County, 696 F.2d 901 (11th Cir. 1983).

[52]Compare Schindenwolf v. Klein, No. L-41293–75 P.W. (N.J. Super. Ct., Law Div. 1979), *to* Bayh v. Sonnenburg, 573 N.E.2d 398 (Ind. 1991), *cert. denied,* 502 U.S. 1094 (1992).

[53]*See generally* 2 PERLIN, *supra* note 8, Chap. 3B (2d. ed. 1999). On an individual's capacity to refuse to consent to have sex, *see* State v. Frost, 686 A.2d 1172, 1177–78 (N.H. 1996), *discussed infra* text accompanying notes 100–03.

[54]Compare Michael L. Perlin, *Competency, Deinstitutionalization, and Homelessness: A Story of Marginalization,* 28 HOUS. L. REV. 63 (1991), and Douglas Mossman & Michael L. Perlin, *Psychiatry and the Homeless Mentally Ill: A Reply to Dr. Lamb,* 149 AM. J. PSYCHIATRY 951 (1992), *to* H. Richard Lamb, *Will We Save the Homeless Mentally Ill?* 147 AM. J. PSYCHIATRY 649 (1990).

[55]Compare Foucha v. Louisiana, 504 U.S. 71 (1992), *to id.* at 101–11 (Thomas, J., dissenting); this split is discussed in Michael L. Perlin & Deborah A. Dorfman, *Sanism, Social Science, and the Development of Mental Disability Law Jurisprudence,* 11 BEHAV. SCI. & L. 47, 60–62 (1993).

[56]Compare United States v. Charters, 829 F.2d 479 (4th Cir. 1987), *to id.,* 863 F.2d 302 (4th Cir. 1988) (*en banc*), *cert. denied,* 494 U.S. 1016 (1990). The contrasting *Charters* opinions are discussed generally in Perlin, *supra* note 17, at 963–68, and in Perlin, *Pretexts, supra* note 31, at 666–67; *see generally supra* Chapter 6.

[57]Compare State v. Perry, 543 So.2d 487 (La. 1989), *to* State v. Perry, 610 So.2d 746 (La. 1992).

[58]Although the U.S. Supreme Court has never found sexual interaction to be a specifically protected right, it has found a fundamental privacy right to exist in a broad array of cases involving reproductive choice, contraception, marriage, procreation, and family relationships. *Cf.* Stephen Schulhofer, *Taking Sexual Autonomy Seriously: Rape Law and Beyond,* 11 LAW & PHIL. 35, 35 (1992) (seeing sexual autonomy as "a distinctive constituent of personhood and freedom"); Note, *Constitutional Barriers to Civil and Criminal Restrictions on Pre- and Extramarital Sex,* 104 HARV. L. REV. 1660, 1660 (1991) (arguing that consensual, heterosexual sex is a constitutionally protected activity).

[59]*See* Lyon, *supra* note 47, at 185–200 (listing all state statutes). At the time that Lyon and her colleagues conducted this survey, Kansas, Montana, New Jersey, and Ohio had enacted such laws. Since that time, Kansas has repealed its statute, and similar laws have been signed in Colorado (on behalf of developmentally disabled persons) and Louisiana (on behalf of institutionalized minors).

[60]*See, e.g.,* Davis v. Watkins, 384 F. Supp. 1196, 1205 (N.D. Ohio 1974); Gary W. v. State of Louisiana, 437 F. Supp. 1209, 1228 (E.D. La. 1976) (both following *Wyatt*). *But cf. Davis,* 384 F. Supp. at 1208 ("Patients shall be provided counseling or other treatment for homosexuality").

Prior to the Supreme Court's decision in Youngberg v. Romeo, 457 U.S. 307 (1982) (sidestepping the question of the existence of a broad constitutional right to treatment), I argued that institutionalization could not "meet constitutional muster if it [did not] enhance [a patient's] likelihood of being released." Michael L. Perlin, *Ex-Patients in the Community: The Next Frontier?* 8 BULL. AM. ACAD. PSYCHIATRY & L. 33, 33 (1980). An argument

right is conspicuous by its absence from either piece of complementary federal civil rights legislation.

Although the Americans With Disabilities Act has been hailed as a "breathtaking promise for persons with . . . disabilities"[61] and as "the Emancipation Proclamation for those with disabilities,"[62] and promises to be a "national mandate to end discrimination against individuals with disabilities and to bring [them] into the . . . social mainstream of American life,"[63] it is not at all clear if this Act—whose aim is the eradication of discrimination against the mentally and physically disabled—will have a significant impact on the question of sexual expression.

I have found nothing in the voluminous literature and congressional history that has suggested that this issue was in the forefront of the drafters' minds. The irony, in fact, is that the efforts of ADA opponents were largely focused on eliminating individuals with certain gender identity and sexual behavior disorders—for example, transvestism, transsexualism, exhibitionism, voyeurism[64]—from the Act's coverage. When the floor debate touched on the ADA and sex, it was in the context of Senator Helms' fears that the bill would protect pedophiles, a group that Helms malignantly "twinned" with schizophrenics as individuals who should be excluded from the Act's coverage.[65] There has yet been no ADA litigation on this topic.[66]

The general lack of attention, litigation, and commentary may appear anomalous. Self-evidently, institutionalized persons do not lose their sexuality or sexual desires when they lose their liberty. On the other hand, there is, I expect, some added irony to be found in the fact that litigation over antipsychotic medication refusal—the most contentious aspect of institutional patients' rights law—centers on drug side effects, and loss of sexual desire is clearly one of those noted side effects.[67] We acknowledge that sexual desire is a sufficiently important personal trait so that its diminution is a factor that must be weighed into the formulation of an antipsychotic drug-refusal policy; yet we simultaneously deny the power and importance of sexual desire on hospital ward life.

Most states, nonetheless, do not recognize their patients' right to personal or interpersonal relationships. Often the right to sexual interaction depends on the whim of line-level staff or on whether such interaction is seen as an aspect of an individual patient's treatment plan.[68] It has even been suggested that "sexual activities between psychiatric inpatients should be strictly prohibited, and when it occurs patients should be isolated . . . and tranquilized if necessary."[69] One hospital's guidelines stated, "If you develop a relationship

---

could be made that one's ability to act in a "sexually appropriate" way in community settings is an indication of whether the expatient will subsequently require future reinstitutionalization.

[61]Bonnie Milstein, Leonard Rubenstein, & Renée Cyr, *The Americans With Disabilities Act: A Breathtaking Promise for Persons With Mental Disabilities*, 25 CLEARINGHOUSE REV. 1240 (1991).

[62]Bonnie Tucker, *The Americans With Disabilities Act of 1990: An Overview*, 22 N. MEX. L. REV. 13, 16 n.4 (1992).

[63]HOUSE COMMITTEE ON ENERGY AND COMMERCE, H.R. REP. NO. 484, 101st Cong., 2d Sess., pt. 4, at 25 (1990).

[64]*See* 42 U.S.C. § 12208 (1990). On the implications of the debate that led to these exclusions, see Perlin, *supra* note 10, at 26–29.

[65]*See* 135 CONG. REC. S10,765–01 (Sept. 7, 1989), 1989 WL 183216 (Cong. Rec.) *see* Perlin, *supra* note 10, at 28–29 (discussing significance of Helms' comments).

[66]*See generally* Michael L. Perlin, *"Make Promises by the Hour": Sex, Drugs, the ADA, and Psychiatric Hospitalization,* 46 DEPAUL L. REV. 947 (1997); *see generally infra* Chapter 8.

[67]*See* 2 PERLIN, *supra* note 8, § 3B-2, at 159-64 nn. 14-23 (2d. ed. 1999), quoting BARRY FURROW, MALPRACTICE IN PSYCHIATRY 61 (1980), *and see* 2 PERLIN, *supra* note 8, § 3B-2, at 159 (2d. ed. 1999), (citing sources); *see supra* Chapter 6.

[68]Stefan, *Reproductive Rights, supra* note 5, at 431, citing Renée Binder, *Sex Between Psychiatric Inpatients,* 57 PSYCHIATRY. Q. 121, 125 (1985).

[69]Binder, *supra* note 68, at 125.

with another patient, staff will get together with you to help decide whether this relationship is beneficial or detrimental to you.''[70] Hospital staff is often hostile to the idea that patients are sexually active in any way.[71]

Although more enlightened institutional mental health professionals and behaviorists now recognize that patients ''are and wish to be sexually active,''[72] and that sexual freedom often has therapeutic value,[73] and although others call attention to societal obligation to provide family planning assistance to women institutionalized in psychiatric hospitals,[74] these authors accurately recognize the lack of literature and policy statements generally available to guide hospital practices and the reluctance with which many hospitals are willing to promulgate such policies.[75] This gap is complemented by a similar gap in the case law and in the legal literature.[76]

Of the few litigated cases, probably the most interesting one is *Foy v. Greenblott.*[77] An institutionalized patient and her infant child (conceived and born while the mother was a patient in a locked psychiatric ward) sued the mother's treating doctor for his failure to either maintain proper supervision over her to prevent her from having sex or to provide her with contraceptive devices or sexual counseling.[78] The court rejected plaintiffs' claims of improper supervision, finding that institutionalized patients had a right to engage in voluntary sexual relations as an aspect of either the ''least restrictive environment'' or ''reasonably non-restrictive confinement conditions''[79] and that that right included suitable opportunities for the patient's interactions with members of the opposite sex.[80] On the other hand, it did characterize the defendant's failure to provide plaintiff with contraceptive devices and counseling as a deprivation of her right to reproductive choice.[81] It also rejected a claim for ''wrongful birth'' by the infant child, concluding, ''Our society has repudiated

---

[70]Gabor Keitner & Paul Grof, *Sexual and Emotional Intimacy Between Psychiatric Inpatients: Formulating a Policy,* 32 HOSP. & COMMUNITY PSYCHIATRY 188, 193 (1981).

[71]*Cf.* SUSAN SHEEHAN, IS THERE NO PLACE ON EARTH FOR ME? 93 (1982) (staff aides at Creedmoor Psychiatric Hospital refused to fill out ''incident reports'' on patient sexual activity because they found the subject matter ''so unsavory''); *see generally* Shelton, *supra,* note 3. On the negative impacts of overreporting sexual activity at a state psychiatric hospital, see Holbrook, *supra* note 26, at 78–79.

[72]Steven Welch et al., *Sexual Behavior of Hospitalized Chronic Psychiatric Patients,* 42 HOSP. & COMMUNITY PSYCHIATRY 855 (1991).

[73]Binder, *supra* note 68, at 125.

[74]*See, e.g.,* Virginia Abernethy et al., *Family Planning During Psychiatric Hospitalization,* 46 AM. J. ORTHOPSYCHIATRY 154 (1976).

[75]*See, e.g.,* Katherine Bishop, Responding to Sexual Activity Between Clients: Legal and Ethical Dilemmas (unpublished conference materials, 1992, on file with the author). *See also* Tracee Parker & Paul Abramson, *The Law Hath Not Been Dead: Protecting Adults With Mental Retardation From Sexual Abuse and Violation of Their Sexual Freedom,* 33 MENTAL RETARDATION 257, 257 (1995) (''the failure to provide relevant and tailored sex education for persons with mental retardation invariably denies them the right to privacy—and hence sexual expression—because they cannot satisfy the legal criteria for distinguishing consensual sexual acts from sexual abuse'').

[76]At least one early right-to-treatment case found that, to meet the constitutional predicate of a ''trained and qualified staff,'' a ''full range [of] both professional and nonprofessional . . . staff training'' was mandated. *See* Davis v. Hubbard, 506 F. Supp. 915, 921 (N.D. Ohio 1980), discussed in this context in 2 PERLIN, *supra* note 8, § 3A-5.2 at 69-71 (2d. ed. 1999). An argument could be made that training in patient sexuality issues would be explicitly required under this aspect of *Davis.*

[77]190 Cal. Rptr. 84 (App. 1983).

[78]*Id.* at 87.

[79]*See, e.g.,* State, DHRS v. Lee, 665 So.2d 304 (Fla. Dist. App. 1995), *approved & remanded,* 698 So.2d 1194, 1196 (Fla. 1997) (state not liable under theory of negligent supervision for pregnancy of severely retarded institutionalized woman; placement of woman in more restrictive setting would have been inconsistent with Department's legislatively mandated ''normalization'' policy).

[80]*Foy,* 190 Cal. Rptr. at 90 n.2.

[81]*Id.* at 90.

the proposition that mental patients will necessarily beget unhealthy, inferior or otherwise undesirable children if permitted to reproduce."[82]

Although *Foy* has been applauded as "a model exposition of the reproductive rights of institutionalized women,"[83] it is an isolated case. A reading of the case law reveals that this area simply does not exist as an active area of patients' rights litigation.[84]

This cannot be attributed to mere oversight or coincidence. One of the U.S. Supreme Court's most chilling decisions of the 20th century came in the infamous forced sterilization case of *Buck v. Bell*.[85] The handful of recent cases that *has* been litigated on questions of sexual rights of institutionalized persons convey a dominant set of messages: Judges—some of whom continue to endorse Justice Holmes's *dictum* in *Buck*[86]—are excruciatingly uncomfortable deciding these cases;[87] lawyers are often quick to abandon any allegiance to advocacy roles in litigating such cases,[88] and frequently these cases serve as a battlefield in which parents are pitted against their children over the question of the extent to which institutionalized persons with mental disabilities can enforce this right.[89] This is, in sum, an area in which virtually all participants in the judicial system join with a significant number of hospital staff employees in wishing the underlying problem would simply go away.

Sanism, Pretextuality, Teleology, and Sex

Sanist myths, based on stereotypes, are the result of rigid categorization and overgeneralization; they are created to "localize our anxiety, to prove to ourselves that what we fear does not lie within."[90] As I discuss elsewhere in this book, I believe this is the primal myth about persons with mental illness:

> Mentally ill individuals are 'different,' and, perhaps, less than human. They are erratic, deviant, morally weak, sexually uncontrollable, emotionally unstable, lazy, superstitious, ignorant, and demonstrate a primitive morality. They lack the capacity to show love or affection. They smell different from 'normal' individuals, and are somehow worth less.[91]

---

[82]*Id.* at 93.

[83]Stefan *Reproductive Rights, supra* note 5, at 432–33

[84]*See* 2 PERLIN, *supra* note 8, § 3A-14.5a at 144 (2d. ed. 1999), (characterizing Foy as "unique").

[85]274 U.S. 200, 207 (1921).

[86]K. Robertson, *Letter to the Editor*, 11 DEVS. IN MENT. HEALTH LAW 4 (Jan.–June 1991).

[87]*See, e.g., In re* the Guardianship of Mikulanec, 356 N.W.2d 683 (Minn. 1984).

[88]*See, e.g.,* Michael L. Perlin, *Fatal Assumption: A Critical Evaluation of the Role of Counsel in Mental Disability Cases*, 16 LAW & HUM. BEHAV. 39, 49–52 (1992). Lawyers are generally lackluster in representing mentally disabled individuals and often fail to provide vigorous advocacy services, preferring a "best-interests" model that capitulates to institutional power or preference. *See generally* Michael L. Perlin & Robert L. Sadoff, *Ethical Issues in the Representation of Individuals in the Commitment Process*, 45 LAW & CONTEMP. PROBS. 161 (Summer 1982); Perlin, *supra* note 37, at 405.

[89]Paul Stavis & Linda Tarantino, *Sexual Activity in the Mentally Disabled Population: Some Standards of the Criminal and Civil Law*, QUALITY OF CARE 2 (Oct.–Nov. 1986). The bulk of litigation has come from the applications of parents and guardians seeking to sterilize mentally disabled daughters whom they fear will become sexually active. *See, e.g., Matter of* Guardianship of Eberhardy, 307 N.W.2d 881, 882 (Wis. 1981) (parents feared their 22-year-old daughter had sexual contact with a male camper at a summer program for mentally retarded young adults); In Interest of M. K. R., 515 S.W.2d 467, 468 (Mo. 1974) (parents sought sterilization of their "overly friendly" 13-year-old institutionalized daughter). On the way that sterilization is seen as the "vindication" of the reproductive rights of institutionalized women, see Stefan, *Reproductive Rights, supra* note 5, at 454.

[90]GILMAN, *supra* note 3, at 240.

[91]Perlin, *supra* note 37, at 393–94, citing, *inter alia,* GORDON ALLPORT, THE NATURE OF PREJUDICE (1984), at 196–98; Peggy Davis, *Law as Microaggression*, 98 YALE L.J. 1559, 1561 (1989) (other footnotes omitted). *See supra* Chapter 2, text accompanying notes 181–85.

Our attitudes toward the sexuality of mentally disabled persons reflect and reify this myth. By focusing on alleged "differentness,"[92] we deny their basic humanity and their shared physical, emotional and spiritual needs. By asserting a primitive morality, we allow ourselves to censor their feelings and their actions.[93] By denying their ability to show love and affection, we justify this disparate and unequal treatment.

Paradoxes abound. Laws that are designed to protect persons with mental disabilities from sexual coercion can affect the "legitimacy of sexual expression." Lack of sex education, for instance, often precludes such persons from "demonstrating competency to give consent," especially the ability to convey an "understanding of the [sexual act], its nature and its possible consequences."[94]

Sanist myths lead to pretextual decision making. As Susan Stefan has perceptively noted, courts routinely find mentally disabled women *incompetent* to engage in sexual intercourse (i.e., to have sufficient competence to engage willingly, knowingly, and voluntarily in such behavior), but just as routinely find such individuals *competent* to consent to give their children up for adoption.[95] In one startling case, a court made both these findings simultaneously about the same woman.[96]

Other pretextual decision making is regularly present in cases involving criminal prosecutions of men charged with having sex with mentally disabled women. Again, Stefan's analysis of these cases suggests that courts regularly use a series of pretexts (as to the woman's capacity to consent) in cases in which, otherwise, a conviction might not be sustainable under rape law standards.[97] In other contexts, mentally disabled parents can lose custody of their children because of behavior—such as having a "bad attitude" or being sexually promiscuous—that would rarely (if ever) be invoked in cases of "normal" parents.[98] Expert testimony in parental rights termination cases that disabled persons "cannot show love and affection as well as can persons of normal intelligence" is relied on to support termination findings.[99]

Not all decisions are pretextual. In *State v. Frost,*[100] the New Hampshire Supreme Court reversed a defendant's conviction for "engaging in sexual penetration with a 'mentally

---

[92]*See generally* MARTHA MINOW, MAKING ALL THE DIFFERENCE: INCLUSION, EXCLUSION, AND AMERICAN LAW (1990).

[93]*See also* Paul Abramson, Tracee Parker, & Sheila Weisberg, *Sexual Expression of Mentally Retarded People: Educational and Legal Implications,* 93 AM. J. MENT. RETARDATION 328, 331 (1988) (discussing sexual stigmatization of persons with mental retardation).

[94]Abramson, Parker, & Weisberg, *supra* note 93, at 329, citing Gary Melton & Elizabeth Scott, *Evaluation of Mentally Retarded Persons for Sterilization: Contributions and Limits of Psychological Consultation,* 15 PROF. PSYCHOL.: RES. & PRAC. 34 (1984). *Compare* Russo & Bishop, *supra* note 23, at 6 ("First and foremost, [statistics as to sexual activity in facilities for persons with developmental disabilities] serve as reminders of the challenges faced by providers to balance the rights of individuals to sexual expression with their obligations to protect individuals from harm and provide appropriate supervision").

[95]Stefan, *Silencing, supra* note 5, at 775. *See also* Elizabeth Reed, *Criminal Law and the Capacity of Mentally Retarded Persons to Consent to Sexual Activity,* 83 VA. L. REV. 799 (1997).

[96]*See* Stefan, *Silencing,* supra note 5, at 775, discussing State v. Soura, 796 P.2d 109 (Idaho 1990). *See also id.* at 775 n.71, discussing *In re* Interest of Burbanks, 310 N.W.2d 138, 143–51 (Neb. 1981) (social service employees testified that parents did not have mental capability to be parents, but willingly assisted them in processing papers to authorize an abortion and subsequent sterilization of their daughter).

[97]Stefan, *Silencing, supra* note 5, at 798–802.

[98]Stefan, *Reproductive Rights, supra* note 5, at 448, discussing, *inter alia,* In Interest of J. L. P., 416 So.2d 1250, 1251–53 (Fla. App. 1982).

[99]Stefan, *Reproductive Rights, supra* note 5, at 449, discussing *In re* McDonald, 201 N.W.2d 447, 450 (Iowa 1972).

[100]686 A.2d 1172 (N.H. 1996).

defective' person'' (in that case, a mildly mentally retarded woman in her mid 20's). To be ''mentally defective'' under the statute, the court ruled, it was necessary that she:

> (1) suffers from a ''mental disease or defect'' and (2) is incapable of freely arriving at an independent choice whether or not to engage in sexual conduct. The second prong addresses a person's capacity to appraise in a meaningful way the physical nature and consequences of his or her sexual conduct, including its potential to cause pregnancy or disease. The emphasis is on the individual's capacity—capacity to learn about physical consequences and to make a decision based on whatever evaluative process the person chooses to employ, as long as the decision is legitimately the person's own. A complainant is not ''mentally defective'' merely because he or she does not in fact take any action to learn about consequences, or fails to consider alternatives prior to choosing a particular course of action.[101]

The state had argued that a person was ''mentally defective'' under this statute if she or he lacked ''the capacity to comprehend a 'wide array of possible consequences' of sexual conduct, including how the conduct 'will be regarded in the framework of the societal environment and taboos to which a person will be exposed.'''[102] In rejecting this argument, the state supreme court pointedly stressed,

> To impose a requirement that a complainant be capable of understanding and evaluating the potential emotional and moral consequences of sexual activity, including the ''societal environment and taboos,'' would require of ''mentally defective'' persons something that we do not require of others whom society permits to engage in sexual relations without criminalizing their partners' conduct. To impose such a requirement would result in a natural tendency for the jury, no matter how carefully instructed, to base its decision on its own moral judgment of the sexual conduct instead of on its determination of whether the complainant freely chose to engage in that conduct.[103]

Frost is an exception. The other decisions in this area are pretextual, and these pretextual decisions are, at base, teleological:[104] Again, in Stefan's words, courts judge competence ''quite blatantly in terms of the desirability of the outcome.''[105] As in many other areas of mental disability law,[106] the pretexts of trial testimony and judicial decision making—premised on sanist myths—pervades all judicial decision making in this area.[107]

---

[101]*Id.* at 1175–76.

[102]*Id.* at 1175.

[103]*Id.* at 1176.

[104]*See generally* Perlin & Dorfman, *supra* note 55 (criticizing teleological use of social science in development of mental disability law jurisprudence).

[105]Stefan, *Reproductive Rights, supra* note 5, at 774; *see also id.* at 798 (courts ''must'' find women incompetent in statutory rape prosecutions ''in order to circumvent the discontinuity between rape law and women's experiences of forced sex'').

[106]*See generally* Perlin, *Morality, supra* note 31; Perlin, *Pretexts, supra* note 31.

[107]On the way that dressing in what might be considered a sexually inappropriate way (e.g., ''pos[ing] provocatively in front of a mirror in a [hospital] day room in a tight-fitting leotard'') has been relied on as an indicia of dangerous-to-self behavior that supports a commitment finding, see People v. Stevens, 751 P.2d 768, 775 n.12 (Colo. 1988). On the way that a patient's sexual fantasies can serve as confirmatory evidence supporting his or her need for treatment under a state Sexual Offenders Act, see State v. Hass, 566 A.2d 1181 (N.J. Super. Ct. Law Div. 1988). On the way that a state prosecutor urged that an insanity acquittee's (apparently consensual) sexual contact (e.g., kissing and touching of nonerogenous zones) evidenced his potential risk to the community if he were to be released into a transitional services program, see State v. Murphy, 760 P.2d 280, 281 (Utah 1988).

Rights in Collision

Let us assume that we can—somehow—identify and eliminate these sanist myths, this pretextual decision making, and the use of teleological thinking in the disposition of these cases. Resolving issues that I am discussing will still be difficult to achieve because of the likelihood that many of the rights in question may be in collision with yet other rights. Putting aside those cases in which there appear to be fairly obvious clinical override issues (e.g., what happens when a patient with a delusion that she is pregnant with Elvis Presley's love child actually *becomes* pregnant, or when a patient who is convinced that his sperm contains radioactive poison that can annihilate the world becomes sexually active, or the less graphic but more likely example of a woman who was sexually abused as a child and whose mental illness may stem at least partially from those experiences), we are left in more than several occasions with what are called "incredible dilemmas"[108]: what can or should be done when multiple civil, constitutional, or statutory rights and policies clash, or where the assertion of one right may conflict with the assertion of another?

Say we assume that there *is* a baseline right to "meaningful sexual interaction" (no matter what content we give to that phrase). First, consider the standard tort law dilemma that confronts contemporaneous mental hospital administrators: how to reconcile the "open door"/"least restrictive alternative" policy with the correlative duty to protect?[109] Broken love affairs or bad sexual experiences do not improve the mental health of nonmentally disabled individuals: Do we (may we/can we/must we) risk scarring the presumably more fragile psyches of institutionalized patients (and is *this* assumption of mine simply reconstituted paternalism, infantilization, or sanism?)?

Next, consider the right to be left alone.[110] If we expand the right of patients to be sexually active, the universe of individuals with whom they can be active is fairly limited. Is there some sort of clash here? Note that this passes over the important, interesting, and unasked question about conjugal visitation.[111] Should (must) birth control devices be supplied to psychiatric patients who are given unescorted hospital leave?[112]

---

[108]*See generally* Peter Westen, *Incredible Dilemmas: Conditioning One Constitutional Right on the Forfeiture of Another,* 66 Iowa L. Rev. 741 (1985). On the application of this doctrine in another mental disability law setting, see 3 Perlin, *supra* note 8, § 16.07, at 438–47, discussing Smith v. Murray, 477 U.S. 527 (1986).

[109]*See* 3 Perlin, *supra* note 8, § 12.18 at 54. The argument has been made that courts should be involved in release decision making of *all* patients involuntarily committed pursuant to a dangerousness finding. *See* Perlin, *supra* note 54, at 127 n.380 (panel discussion on this topic— "Discharging 'Dangerous' Patients: Who Decides?" (Presented at the annual conference of the American Academy of Psychiatry and Law, San Diego, CA, Oct. 1990). *See also* Paul Stavis, *Harmonizing the Right to Sexual Expression and the Right to Protection From Harm for Persons With Mental Disability,* 9 Sexuality & Disability 131 (1991).

[110]*Cf.* Kent v. Johnson, 821 F.2d 1220, 1226 (6th Cir. 1987), *en banc reconsideration denied* (1987) (fundamental constitutional right to be free from forced exposure of one's self to strangers of opposite sex when not reasonably necessary for legitimate, overriding reason).

[111]There is neither case law, statutory law, nor commentary on the question of conjugal visits in psychiatric hospitals. On the issues involved in prison conjugal visit policies, see Bonnie Carlson & Neil Cervera, *Inmates and Their Families: Conjugal Visits, Family Contact, and Family Functioning,* 18 Crim. Just. & Behav. 318 (1991). *Cf.* Doe v. Coughlin, 523 N.Y.S.2d 782 (1987) (fact that prisoner had AIDS provided rational basis for excluding him from prison conjugal visit program).

[112]This has apparently been a *de facto* policy in at least one New York state psychiatric hospital (personal communication, Keri Gould, Nov. 11, 1992; Gould was previously a senior trial attorney with the New York Mental Hygiene Legal Services office).

What about AIDS? Do we segregate HIV-positive patients? Does this conflict with other policies?[113] Can we risk increasing the number of HIV-positive individuals in *any* aspect of society, much less in institutions?

What about birth control issues? Will the right to sexual autonomy lead to increased efforts to sterilize institutionalized individuals? How will groups opposed to sex education and the distribution of condoms in city schools react if condoms are distributed in psychiatric hospitals?

What about gender differences? In at least one New York City hospital, male patients leaving the facility on unsupervised community leave are given condoms on request; female patients, on the other hand, have their competency (informally) assessed before birth control pills can be prescribed.[114] Certainly this raises arguable equal protection claims.[115]

What about abortion rights? Does an institutionalized person have a right to an abortion?[116] How about a right to *resist* an abortion? There is at least one reported example of a damage suit being filed in response to an unauthorized abortion being performed on an institutionalized mentally disabled individual.[117] Further anecdotal evidence suggests that it is not rare for state hospital doctors at certain facilities to attempt to coerce patients into terminating pregnancies;[118] if there is subsequent litigation on this question, how will courts respond?[119]

Many drugs—including many antipsychotic medications—are contraindicated in cases of pregnancy;[120] do right-to-refuse antipsychotic medication rules and regulations have to be reconceptualized if more patients become sexually active and a higher pregnancy rate results?[121]

Next, at what point do inquiries about "competency" take center stage? On one hand, almost all courts adhere to the catechism that competency is *not* a unitary status and that an

---

[113]*See generally* in a prison context, Ayesha Khan, *The Application of Section 504 of the Rehabilitation Act to the Segregation of HIV-Positive Inmates,* 65 WASH. L. REV. 839 (1990). Compare Nolley v. County of Erie, 7776 F. Supp. 715 (W.D.N.Y. 1991) (policy unconstitutional), *to* Harris v. Thigpen, 945 F.2d 1495 (11th Cir. 1991) (blanket policy not violative of constitutional rights).

[114]I learned of this at a grand rounds presentation at a New York state psychiatric hospital. There is apparently no written memorandum or regulation memorializing this policy.

[115]On the random ways that condom distribution policies are often implemented, see Miranda Perry, *Kids and Condoms: Parental Involvement in School Condom-Distribution Programs,* 63 U. CHI. L. REV. 727 (1996).

[116]*See, e.g., In re* Doe, 533 A.2d 523, 526 (R.I. 1987) (court found that mentally retarded woman, if competent, would have exercised her right to terminate pregnancy; thus decision to perform abortion was reasonable).

[117]McCandless by McCandless v. State, 166 N.Y.S.2d 272 (Cl. 1956), *aff'd in part & rev'd in part,* 162 N.Y.S.2d 570 (App. Div. 1957), *aff'd,* 173 N.Y.S.2d 530 (1958).

[118]Personal communication, Keri Gould, Nov. 11, 1992.

[119]*Cf.* Doe v. Gen. Hosp. of D.C., 434 F.2d 427 (D.C. Cir. 1970) (hospital regulations, pre-*Roe v. Wade,* allowed for abortions only where necessary to protect pregnant woman's mental health where patient could establish a history of mental illness predating the pregnancy); People v. Barksdale, 503 P.2d 257 (Cal. 1972) (challenge to state's therapeutic abortion act allowing for abortions only where continued pregnancy would create a substantial risk of gravely impaired physical or mental health).

[120]*See, e.g.,* David Lourwood & June Riedlinger, *The Use and Safety of Drugs in Pregnancy: Trends and Issues in Pharmacy Practice,* 133 DRUG TOPICS (1989), at 60.

[121]For a rare example of related litigation, see In Interest of K. S. T., 578 N.E.2d 306 (Ill. App. 1991) (parental rights termination case involving patient who stopped taking Prolixin during her pregnancy).

individual may be competent for one status but not for another.[122] On the other hand, current research in progress shows that in real life clinicians tend to reject this line of thinking.[123] Other research suggests that clinicians are far more likely to find incompetency when a patient disagrees with the professional's conclusions as to what treatment would be in the patient's best interests.[124]

How will all of this play out in the context of the questions that we are addressing?[125] Is there one "sexual competency"? And what if one person in the relationship is "sexually competent" and the other is not?[126] It is black-letter, or informal, law that, in criminal prosecutions, a "mentally defective" person is deemed incapable of consenting to sexual intercourse.[127] Need there be a statutory override? One court has recently reversed a sexual assault charge that had been premised on the "victim's" mental incapacitation by nature of her institutionalization, finding that she retained the ability to consensually engage in sexual intercourse;[128] yet courts generally uphold statutes proscribing sexual intercourse with mentally ill individuals as not violative of either the equal protection or due process clauses.[129]

Should this version of "statutory rape" be consigned to the historical scrap heap? What are the downsides for community cases?[130] Is there a difference between prosecutors' attitudes toward sexual crimes in hospitals and toward those committed in the commu-

---

[122]For a recent illustrative example involving civil and criminal standards, see Koehler v. State, 830 S.W.2d 665 (Tex. App. 1992), *rev. denied* (1992) (determination that criminal defendant was incompetent to manage his own affairs was not *prima facie* showing of his incompetency to stand trial). *See infra* section 3 (discussing standards in competency to waive counsel and competency to plead guilty cases).

This, though, is not an entirely unanimous point of view; the *en banc* Fourth Circuit in United States v. Charters, 863 F. 2d 302, 310 (4th Cir. 1988) *(en banc), cert. denied,* 494 U.S. 1016 (1990), flatly *rejected* that notion (in that case in the context of the competency to stand trial and the competency to refuse antipsychotic medications) as a distinction "of such subtlety and complexity as to tax perception by the most skilled medical or psychiatric professionals." *See generally supra* Chapter 6.

[123]*See generally* Brian Ladds & Antonio Convit, *Involuntary Medication of Patients Who Are Incompetent to Stand Trial: A Review of Empirical Studies,* 22 BULL. AM. ACAD. PSYCHIATRY & L. 519 (1994); Brian Ladds et al., *Involuntary Medication of Patients Who Are Incompetent to Stand Trial: A Descriptive Study of the New York Experience With Judicial Review,* 21 BULL. AM. ACAD. PSYCHIATRY & L. 529 (1993); Brian Ladds et al., *The Disposition of Criminal Charges After Involuntary Medication to Restore Competency to Stand Trial,* 38 J. FOREN-SIC SCI. 1442 (1993).

[124]Stefan, *Silencing, supra* note 5, at 784, citing, *inter alia,* GEORGE ANNAS ET AL., AMERICAN HEALTH LAW 652 (1990); FAY ROZOVSKY, CONSENT TO TREATMENT: A PRACTICAL GUIDE 23 (2d ed. 1990).

[125]The weight of empirical research strongly suggests that persons with mental retardation, for example, appear "capable of stringent sexual self-control in both institution and community settings," are "sexually expressive and capable of sexual discretion." Abramson, Parker, & Weisberg, *supra* note 93, at 330.

[126]On capacity assessments in this context, see Russo & Bishop, *supra* note 23.

[127]*See, e.g.,* People v. Blunt, 212 N.E.2d 729 (Ill. App. 1965); People v. McMullen, 414 N.E.2d 214 (Ill. App. 1980); Hall v. State, 504 N.E.2d 298 (Ind. App. 1987). *See also* Reed, *supra* note 95; Stavis & Taratino, *supra* note 89; Clarence Sundrum & Paul Stavis, *Sexuality and Mental Retardation: Unmet Challenges,* 32 MENT. RETARDA-TION 255 (1994); Clarence Sundrum & Paul Stavis, *Sexual Behavior and Mental Retardation,* 17 MENT. & PHYS. DIS. L. REP. 448 (1993).

[128]State v. Green, 1990 WL 143777, at *2–3 (Tenn. Cr. App. 1990).

[129]*See, e.g.,* State v. Hill, 406 A.2d 1334 (N.J. App. Div. 1979); People v. McMullen, 414 N.E.2d 214 (Ill. App. 1980); Stafford v. State, 455 N.E.2d 402 (Ind. App. 1983), *trans. denied* (1984); Bozarth v. State, 520 N.E.2d 460 (Ind. App. 1988), *trans. denied* (1988).

[130]For a vivid example, see Karen Houppert, *Boystown: Glen Ridge Circles the Wagons,* VILLAGE VOICE, Nov. 10, 1992, at 11. *See generally* Hilary Brown & Vicky Turk, *Defining Sexual Abuse as It Affects Adults With Learning Disabilities,* 20 MEN. HANDICAP 44 (1992); Vicky Turk & Hilary Brown, *Sexual Abuse and Adults With Learning Disabilities: Preliminary Communication of Survey Results,* 20 MENT. HANDICAP 56 (1992).

nity?[131] Will awareness of the underlying issues bring about changes in state administrative policies on the investigation of criminal sexual assaults in psychiatric hospitals?[132] Will constitutional tort and state tort claims increase, and how will courts construe such cases?[133]

Is the competency to consent to sexual intercourse the same as the competency to choose a certain method of birth control (or to choose to not use birth control)? Or to have (or not have) an abortion? Is there a different competency for sexual intercourse and for sexual interaction that stops short of coitus?

And how do any of these competencies relate to more commonly confronted competency questions such as medication refusal or voluntary admission? In *Zinermon v. Burch,* for example, in the course of its holding that a patient could maintain a civil rights suit alleging that he had a right to a due process hearing prior to his "voluntary" admission to a mental health facility, the Supreme Court noted that the "very nature of mental illness" makes it "foreseeable" that such a person "*will* be unable to understand *any* preferred 'explanation and disclosure of the subject matters' of the forms that such a person is asked to sign, and *will* be unable to 'make a knowing and willful decision' whether to consent to admission."[134] What impact will this language from *Zinermon*—contrary to virtually all valid and reliable current social science research[135]—have on efforts to expand notions of patient autonomy and competency?[136]

Finally, how does the ADA affect all of this?[137] To what extent does the ADA's bar on discrimination against disabled persons[138] cause the reconceptualization of hospital policies prohibiting sexual interaction? If it appears that the ADA might be a tool to attack such policies, might that cause some former ADA supporters to rethink their position on the act?[139]

In coming to our ultimate conclusions, we not only have to decide which right "trumps" which other right,[140] but we must also decide how we set priorities in defining the underlying question. Do we look first at autonomy rights? At civil libertarian concerns? At due process requirements? At privacy interests? At competency criteria? At clinical needs?

---

[131]In Great Britain, for instance, out of 1000 cases per year of rape and sexual abuse of mentally disabled women, there are only 10 prosecutions (resulting in three convictions in 1992). Letter from David Carson to author, Dec. 7, 1992. *Cf.* Holbrook, *supra* note 26 (on the dangers of overreporting sexual abuse in cases involving institutionalized mentally disabled persons). On a recent state initiative in this area, see Linda Lynwander, *Sex Abuse and the Mentally Retarded,* N.Y. TIMES, Dec. 27, 1992, New Jersey weekly section, at 1.

Cf. State v. Frost, 686 A.2d 1172 (N.H. 1996), discussed *supra* text accompanying notes 100–03.

[132]*See Investigation Into Sexual Abuse of Mentally Disabled Woman Prompts Call for State Policy on Reporting Crimes,* QUALITY OF CARE 5 (Sept.–Oct. 1987); *In the Matter of* Lisa Cohen: *The Need for a Policy in the Developmental Disabilities System for Reporting Apparent Crimes to Law Enforcement Agencies* (report prepared by New York State Committee on Quality of Care for the Mentally Disabled, April 1987).

[133]*See, e.g.,* Martin v. City of Eastlake, 686 F.Supp. 620 (N.D. Ohio 1988) (constitutional tort claim); Gutierrez v. Thorme, 537 A.2d 527 (Conn. App. 1988) (state tort claim).

[134]494 U.S. 113, 133 (1990).

[135]*See, e.g.,* Paul Appelbaum & Loren Roth, *Clinical Issues in the Assessment of Competency,* 138 AM. J. PSYCHIATRY 1462, 1465 (1981); Loren Roth et al., *Tests of Competence to Consent to Treatment,* 134 AM. J. PSYCHIATRY 279, 279 (1977); *see generally,* 2 Perlin, *supra* note 8, § 3B-14.5, at 343-45 (2d. ed. 1999).

[136]On *Zinermon's* troubling failure to use available social science data in this context, see Perlin & Dorfman, *supra* note 55, at 55–56.

[137]*See generally* Perlin, *Sanist Attitudes, supra* note 31, at 30–36.

[138]*See, e.g.,* Cook, *supra* note 10, at 427; *see also* Stacy Seicshnaydre, *Community Mental Health Treatment for the Mentally Ill—When Does Less Restrictive Treatment Become a Right?* 66 TUL. L. REV. 1971 (1992).

[139]*See, e.g.,* Perlin, *Sanist Attitudes, supra* note 31, at 39 (questioning whether congressional support might evaporate if litigators attempt to implement Cook's theory that the ADA is the basis for ending segregated institutions for the mentally disabled). *See* Cook, *supra* note 10, at 429.

[140]*See* Perlin, *Sanist Attitudes, supra* note 31 at 39 (discussing meaning of "trump"—the supremacy of one right or duty over another right or duty—in the mental disability law context).

At therapeutic jurisprudential concerns? At legal status? At tort liability worries? At voluntariness constructs? At the immutable fact that "sexual interaction"—by its very description—assume the participation of more than one individual?[141] No resolution of the underlying issues can even be aspired to unless we sort out these approaches and carefully articulate their interrelationships, their potential conflicts, and their relative values as competing social choices. In short, this is a very difficult project.

Conclusion

Various sets of guidelines governing sexual behavior have recently been drafted, and some have already been adopted in institutional settings.[142] The mere promulgation and adoption of such policies will not be enough to lead to meaningful change, however. Above all, it is necessary to come to grips with the way that sanist and pretextual attitudes govern and overwhelm our treatment of the sexual lives of institutionalized persons with mental disabilities. Only then can it be hoped that there will be any meaningful change in this highly charged and emotional area of life.

---

[141]*But see* Shelton, *supra* note 3 (on the teaching of masturbation skills to a seriously mentally disabled institutionalized patient).

[142]*See, e.g.,* Guidelines for Agency Policies Concerning Sexual Contact and Consent Issued by Office of Mental Retardation and Developmental Disabilities, *Quality of Care* (Sept.–Oct. 1993), at 4; Douglas Mossman, Michael Perlin & Deborah Dorfman, *Sex on the Wards: Conundra for Clinicians,* 25 J. AM. ACAD. PSYCHIATRY & L. 441, 456–58 (1997) (setting out model policy).

Chapter 8
THE AMERICANS WITH DISABILITIES ACT

The Americans With Disabilities Act[1] has been hailed by advocates for persons with disabilities as "a breathtaking promise,"[2] "the most important civil rights act passed since 1964,"[3] and as the "Emancipation Proclamation for those with disabilities."[4] It is, without question, Congress's most innovative attempt to address the pervasive problems of discrimination against physically and mentally handicapped citizens[5] by providing, in the words of a congressional committee, "a clear and comprehensive national mandate to end discrimination against persons with disabilities."[6] The ADA provides basically the same bundle of protections for persons with disabilities as the Civil Rights Acts of the 1960s did for citizens of color[7] with clear, strong, and enforceable standards.[8]

The language that Congress chose to use in its introductory fact findings is of extraordinary importance.[9] Its specific finding that individuals with disabilities are a "discrete and insular minority . . . subjected to a history of purposeful unequal treatment, and relegated to a position of political powerlessness"[10] is not just precatory flag-and-apple-pie rhetoric.[11] This language—granted "the force of law"[12]—was carefully chosen; it comes

---

[1]*See generally* Michael L. Perlin, *The Americans With Disabilities Act and Mentally Disabled Persons: Can Sanist Attitudes Be Undone?* 8 J.L. & HEALTH 15 (1993–94). *See supra* Chapter 7, text accompanying notes 62–66.

[2]Bonnie Milstein, Leonard Rubenstein, & Renée Cyr, *The Americans With Disabilities Act: A Breathtaking Promise for Persons With Mental Disabilities,* 25 CLEARINGHOUSE REV. 1240 (1991).

[3]Kent Jenkins, Jr., *Spotlight Finds Hoyer,* WASHINGTON POST, May 28, 1990, at D1, col. 5, *as cited in* Kimberly Ackourey, *Insuring Americans With Disabilities: How Far Can Congress Go to Protect Traditional Practices?* 40 EMORY L.J. 1183, 1183 n.1 (1991).

[4]Americans With Disabilities Act of 1990: Summary and Analysis, Special Supplement (BNA), at S-5, *as cited in* Ackourey, *supra* note 3, at 1183 n.2 (statement by bill's sponsors). *See also, e.g.,* Sandra Law, *The Americans With Disabilities Act of 1990: Burden on Business or Dignity for the Disabled?* 30 DUQ. L. REV. 99 (1991) (ADA a "solid and positive step toward making this country a better nation").

[5]MICHAEL L. PERLIN, MENTAL DISABILITY LAW: CIVIL AND CRIMINAL (1989), § 6.44A, at 137 (1998 Cum. Supp.) (ADA stands as Congress' "most innovative attempt to address the pervasive problem of discrimination against mentally and physically handicapped citizens").

[6]HOUSE COMM. ON THE JUDICIARY, AMERICANS WITH DISABILITIES ACT OF 1990, H.R. REP. NO, 485 (III), 101st Cong., 2d. Sess., at 23 (1990).

[7]For a comprehensive overview, see Bonnie Tucker, *The Americans With Disabilities Act of 1990: An Overview,* 22 N.M. L. REV. 13 (1992).

[8]*See, e.g., id.* at 43-48, 63-64, 93-95, 101-02 (discussing enforcement provisions). *Cf.* Pamela Karlan & George Rutherglen, *Disabilities, Discrimination, and Reasonable Accommodation,* 46 DUKE L.J. 1 (1996) (reading ADA to provide more protections than do other civil rights acts).

[9]On the "shocking and eye-opening" nature of these findings, see Amy Lowndes, *The Americans With Disabilities Act of 1990: A Congressional Mandate for Heightened Judicial Protection of Disabled Persons,* 44 FLA. L. REV. 417, 446 (1992).

[10]42 U.S.C. § 12101(a)(7) (1990).

[11]*Cf.* Pennhurst State Sch. & Hosp. v. Halderman, 451 U.S. 1, 11 (1981) (rights language in Developmentally Disabled Assistance and Bill of Rights Act, see 42 U.S.C. §§ 6010 *et seq.* (1976), simply created a federal–state granting statute, and did not vest developmentally disabled individuals with a legally enforceable cause of action). This conclusion was criticized as "absurd" and "objectionable" in an article coauthored by the plaintiffs' lead counsel in the *Pennhurst* case. *See* David Ferleger & Edward Scott, *Rights and Dignity: Congress, the Supreme Court, and People With Disabilities After Pennhurst,* 5 W. NEW ENG. L. REV. 327, 350 (1983). For a survey of all commentary, see 2 PERLIN, *supra* note 5, § 7.13 at 617–23. On the question of whether key sections of the ADA will be seen as little more than hortatory language, see *infra* text accompanying notes 91–106.

[12]James Miller, *The Disabled, the ADA, and Strict Scrutiny,* 6 ST. THOMAS L. REV. 393, 413 (1994).

from the heralded footnote 4 of the *United States v. Carolene Products* case, which has served as the springboard for nearly a half century of challenges to state and municipal laws that have operated in discriminatory ways against other minorities,[13] and reflects a congressional commitment to provide protected-class categorization for persons with disabilities.[14] This in turn forces courts to use a compelling state interest or strict scrutiny test in considering statutory and regulatory challenges to allegedly discriminatory treatment.[15] The law's invocation of the "full sweep of congressional authority, including the power to enforce the Fourteenth Amendment"[16] simply means that any violation of the ADA must be read in the same light as a violation of the equal protection clause of the Constitution, guaranteeing—for the first time—that this core constitutional protection will finally be made available to persons with disabilities.[17]

---

[13]*See* United States v. Carolene Prods. Co., 304 U.S. 144, 152 n.4 (1938). I discuss the impact of this footnote on the development of mental disability law in Michael L. Perlin, *On "Sanism,"* 46 SMU L. REV. 373, 380–81 n.51 (1992), and in 1 PERLIN, *supra* note 5, § 1-2.1 at 7 (2d ed. 1998).

On the significance of the *Carolene Products* language to the ADA, see, for example, Leonard Rubenstein, *Ending Discrimination Against Mental Health Treatment in Publicly Financed Health Care*, 40 ST. LOUIS U. L.J. 315, 339 (1996) (ADA's invocation of *Carolene Products* footnote demonstrates justification for using "heightened judicial scrutiny" test); Susan Lee, Heller v. Doe: *Involuntary Civil Commitment and the "Objective" Language of Probability*, 20 AM. J.L. & MED. 457, 477 n.90 (1994) (language reflects congressional intent to identify disabled persons as group "deserving heightened scrutiny"); Lisa Montanaro, *The Americans With Disabilities Act: Will the Court Get the Hint? Congress' Attempt to Raise the Status of Persons With Disabilities in Equal Protection Cases*, 15 PACE L. REV. 621, 663 (1995) (by adopting the ADA, Congress attempted to use *Carolene Products* theory to imply that a "heightened level of scrutiny" should be used in ADA cases).

[14]*See, e.g.,* Montanaro, *supra* note 13, at 663–64 (Congress intended to transform disabled into suspect class for purposes of constitutional and statutory interpretation); Lowndes, *supra* note 9, at 446 ("Congress clearly intended to create a new protected class—the disabled"); Miller, *supra* note 12, at 412 (Congress applied "suspect class" test in ADA statutory language); Phyllis Coleman & Ronald Shellow, *Ask About Conduct, Not Mental Illness: A Proposal for Bar Examiners and Medical Boards to Comply With the Americans With Disabilities Act and the Constitution*, 20 J. LEGIS. 147, 177 n.23 (1994) ("the ADA treats disabled persons as a suspect class").

A suspect class is one "saddled with such disabilities, or subjected to such a history of purposeful unequal treatment, or relegated to such a position of policital powerlessness as to command extraordinary protection from the majoritarian political process." Massachusetts Board of Retirement v. Murgia, 427 U.S. 307, 313 (1976).

In a trilogy of employment cases, the Supreme Court has just narrowed the category of persons who are to be treated as "disabled" under the ADA. *See* Sutton v. United Air Lines, 119 S. Ct. 2139, 2145–49, (1999); Murphy v. United Parcel Serv., Inc., 119 S. Ct. 2133, 2137–39, (1999), and Albertsons, Inc v. Kirkinburg, 119 S. Ct. 2162, 2167–70, (1999) (sometimes "the *Sutton* trilogy"). Nothing in these decisions, however, goes to the question of how the Court would construe discrimination cases involving individuals found to be disabled within the ADA's meaning.

[15]On the relationship between this language and the heightened scrutiny requirement, see, for example, Crowder v. Kitagawa, 842 F. Supp. 1257, 1264 (D. Hawaii 1994) (assuming application of strict scrutiny level in ADA cases); William Christian, *Normalization as a Goal: The Americans With Disabilities Act and Individuals With Mental Retardation*, 73 TEX. L. REV. 409, 424 (1994) (laws treating persons with disabilities differently should be subject to heightened scrutiny).

In City of Cleburne v. Cleburne Living Ctr., 473 U.S. 432, 441–42 (1985), the Supreme Court had ruled that mental retardation was neither a suspect class nor a quasi–suspect class for purposes of equal protection analysis. In supporting its conclusion, it noted that a contrary decision would have made it difficult to distinguish other groups, such as groups of persons with mental illness "who have perhaps immutable disabilities setting them off from others, who cannot themselves mandate the desired legislative responses, and who can claim some degree of prejudice from at least part of the public at large." *Id.* at 445–46.

[16]42 U.S.C. § 12101(b)(4) (1990).

[17]*See, e.g.,* Timothy Cook, *The Americans With Disabilities Act: The Move to Integration*, 64 TEMP. L. REV. 393, 434 (1991): "[Congressional] findings indicate unambiguously that Congress considered disability classifications to be just as serious and just as impermissible as racial categorizations that are given 'strict' or 'heightened' scrutiny, sustainable by the courts only if they are tailored to serve a 'compelling' governmental interest."

Cook's article is cited approvingly in, *inter alia*, Heather K. by Anita K. v. City of Mallard, Iowa, 887 F. Supp.

This chapter will focus on a fairly narrow (but extraordinarily important) question of ADA law: its application to individuals in inpatient psychiatric hospitals and its potential use as a tool for creating of community-based treatment programs. This is a population that is classically voiceless, friendless, with few contacts in the free world. It is a population whose disenfranchisement starkly mirrors the sort of powerlessness and marginalization spoken to by the Supreme Court in the *Carolene Products* case and, of course, spoken to by Congress in the ADA's initial findings section.[18]

By its terms, the entire ADA applies to persons with mental disabilities, including persons with mental illness. Yet very little of the final statute, the legislative history, or floor debate focused on the "grotesque" history of discrimination and mistreatment suffered by such individuals,[19] the crushing economic, social, and psychological burdens borne by such persons in their day-to-day lives, the conditions faced by such persons when institutionalized in public facilities or when discharged from such facilities to lives of misery on our city streets without adequate transitional mental health, medical or social services, or the pernicious legal effects that flow from the badge of mental disability.

The phrase *mental impairment* or *mental disability* is mentioned only a handful of times in the final act. In the initial findings section, Congress noted that 43 million Americans "have one or more physical or *mental* disabilities";[20] *disability* is defined to include a "physical or *mental* impairment";[21] *discrimination* includes failure to make "reasonable accommodation" to an otherwise-qualified person's "known physical or *mental* limitations,"[22] and a section on paratransit and special transportation services requires that public entities provide such services to any individual who is unable, "as a result of a physical or *mental* impairment" to use other public transportation vehicles.[23] And that is all.

The legislative history is similarly skimpy, and speaks to only two relevant considerations. First, it reflects congressional awareness of the pernicious danger of stereotyping behavior. It makes this clear through its heavy reliance on the Supreme Court's language in *School Board of Nassau County v. Arline*[24] that "society's accumulated myths and fears about disability and diseases are as handicapping as are the physical limitations that follow from the actual impairment."[25] Congress stressed that its inclusion in the definition of

---

1249, 1263–64 (N.D. Iowa 1995); Valentine v. American Home Shield Corp., 939 F. Supp, 1276, 1388 (N.D. Iowa 1996); Fink v. Kitzman, 881 F. Supp. 1347, 1368 (N.D. Iowa 1995); Hutchinson v. United Parcel Service, Inc., 883 F. Supp. 379, 387 (N.D. Iowa 1995), and Muller v. Hotsy Corp., 917 F. Supp. 1389, 1402 (N.D. Iowa 1996).

[18]*See* Rubenstein, *supra* note 13, at 339, 350.

[19]City of Cleburne v. Cleburne Living Ctr., 473 U.S. 432, 454 (1985) (Stevens, J., concurring); *id.* at 461 (Marshall, J., concurring in part and dissenting in part); *see generally* Cook, *supra* note 17, at 399–407.

[20]42 U.S.C. § 12101(a)(1) (1990).

[21]*Id*, § 12102(2)(A) (emphasis added).

[22]42 U.S.C. § 12112(b)(5)(A) (1990) (emphasis added).

[23]*Id.* § 12143(c)(1)(A)(I) (emphasis added).

The only other section of the act that speaks specifically to mental disability is an exclusion section that states that the act is inapplicable, *inter alia*, to certain "sexual disorders" (e.g., transvestism, transsexualism, and other "gender identity disorders," *see id.* § 12211(B)(1)) and to compulsive gambling (*id.* § 12211(b)(2)).

[24]480 U.S. 273 (1987) (individual with tuberculosis a "handicapped individual" under 29 U.S.C. § 794 (§ 504 of the Rehabilitation Act of 1973)). On the relationship between the ADA and the Rehabilitation Act, see Michael L. Perlin, *The ADA and Persons with Mental Disabilities: Can Sanist Attitudes Be Undone?* 8 J.L. & HEALTH 15, 23 n.40 (1993–94), discussing Jill Adams, *Judicial and Regulatory Interpretation of the Employment Rights of Persons With Disabilties,* 22 J. APPLIED REHAB. COUNSELING 28 (1991); Note, *Civil Rights and the Disabled: A Comparison of the Rehabilitation Act of 1973 and the Americans With Disabilties Act of 1990 in the Employment Setting,* 54 ALB. L. REV. 123 (1989).

[25]*Arline,* 480 U.S. at 284.

disability an individual who is regarded as being impaired[26] acknowledges this teaching about the power of myths.[27]

Thus employment decisions cannot be based on "paternalistic views" of what is best for a person with a disability.[28] The employment title of the ADA was designed, in significant part, to prevent employers from relying "on presumptions, stereotypes, misconceptions and unfounded fears" in making employment decisions,[29] and as a means of breaking the chain of misperception that disabled individuals are a "permanently helpless and separate class, unable to work or otherwise contribute to society."[30]

Second, the history of the direct-threat section—again relying on the *Arline* case—specifies that, for persons with mental disabilities, the employer must identify "the specific behavior on the part of the individual that would pose the anticipated direct threat" and that the determination must be based on such behavior, "not merely on generalizations about the disability."[31] In such a case, there must be "objective evidence . . . that the person has a recent history of committing overt acts or making threats which caused . . . or which directly threatened harm."[32]

Although these two excerpts are praiseworthy and important, that's all there is. Nowhere else in any of the lengthy congressional reports are the specific biases and prejudices faced by persons with mental illness—the bias of sanism—discussed. Although there is recognition that much of the discrimination faced by disabled persons flows from "unfounded, outmoded stereotypes and perceptions and deeply imbedded prejudices,"[33]

---

[26]*See* 42 U.S.C. § 12102(2)(C) (1990).

[27]H.R. Rep. No. 485, 101st Cong., 2d Sess. (1990), 1990 U.S.C.C.A.N. 303, 1990 WL 125563, at 72–73; *see also id.* at 7–8, 55.

[28]*Id.* at 121.

[29]*Id.* at 21–22 (discrimination against disabled persons "often results from false presumptions, generalizations, misperceptions, patronizing attitudes, ignorance, irrational fears and pernicious mythologies").

[30]Elizabeth Morin, *Americans With Disabilities Act of 1990: Social Integration Through Employment,* 40 Cath. U. L. Rev. 189, 189, 212 (1990). On employers' myths in this context, see Peter Blanck, *Empirical Study of the Employment Provisions of the Americans With Disabilities Act: Methods, Preliminary Findings, and Implications,* 22 N.M. L. Rev. 119, 129 (1992) [hereinafter Blanck, Empirical], and *see generally* Peter Blanck, *The Emerging Work Force: Empirical Study of the Americans With Disabilities Act,* 16 J. Corp. L. 693 (1991) [hereinafter Blanck, *Work Force*]; on the significance of "misinformed stereotypes" generally, see W. Robert Gray, *The Essential-Function of the Civil Rights of People With Disabilities and John Rawls's Concept of Social Justice,* 22 N.M. L. Rev. 295, 317 (1992).

[31]H.R. Rep. No. 485(II), *supra* note 27, 1990 WL 125563. *See also,* Cheryl Fells, *Employee Benefit Plan Implications of the Americans With Disabilities Act,* 714 PLI/Corp 117 (1990), WESTLAW at *547: "The determination that an individual with a disability will pose a safety threat to others must be made on a case-by-case basis and must not be based on generalizations, misperceptions, ignorance, irrational fears, patronizing attitudes, or pernicious mythologies"); Renée Cyr, *The Americans With Disabilities Act: Implications for Job Reassignment and the Treatment of Hypersusceptible Employees,* 57 Brook. L. Rev. 1237, 1273 (1992) (generalized fear about risks from the employment environment "cannot be used by an employer to disqualify a person with a disability").

[32]H.R. Rep. No. 485(III), *supra* note 6, 1990 WL 121680. This language closely parallels that of the Fair Housing Act Amendments of 1988, under which an otherwise-qualified disabled person can be excluded from the definition of *handicap* only where a landlord can establish that the individual's tenancy would be a "direct threat" to others based on "a history of overt acts or current conduct." *See* 24 C.F.R. § 100.202(c) (1990). To trigger this section, the legislative history stressed that "there must be objective evidence from the person's prior behavior that the person committed overt acts which caused harm or which directly threatened harm." H.R. Rep. No., 711, 100th Cong., 2d Sess. 18, 29 *reprinted in* 1988 U.S.C.C.A.N. 2173, *as discussed in* Richard B. Simring, Note, *The Impact of Federal Antidiscrimination Laws on Housing for People With Mental Disabilities,* 59 Geo. Wash. L. Rev. 413, 441 (January 1991).

[33]H.R. Rep. No. 485(III), *supra* note 6, at 7–8.

the legislative history in no way illuminates the specific prejudices and biases faced by persons with mental disabilities, especially those who were formerly institutionalized.[34]

Although the entire ADA recognizes that much of the discrimination faced by persons with disabilities flows from "unfounded, outmoded stereotypes and perceptions and deeply imbedded prejudices,"[35] the legislative history in no way illuminates the specific prejudices and biases faced by mentally disabled persons, especially those who have been institutionalized because of mental illness.[36] It is a failure that screams out for attention.

The ADA is not the first federal statute that has purported to provide legal rights for persons with mental disabilities—section 504 of the Rehabilitation Act of 1973,[37] the Mental Health Systems Act,[38] the Protection and Advocacy for Mentally Ill Individuals Act (PAMI Act),[39] the Developmental Disabilities Assistance and Bill of Rights Act (DD Act)[40] all, on their faces, provide such individuals with a broad range of constitutional and civil rights. Yet each of these has been found wanting. Section 504 of the Rehabilitation Act by its own terms applies only to discrimination "under any program or activity receiving Federal financial assistance";[41] its shortcomings have been noted by both courts and commentators.[42] The title of the Mental Health Systems Act of 1980 that urged states to revise their laws to "ensure that mental health patients receive the protection and services they require"[43] was repealed less than a month after its enactment as part of the Omnibus Budget Reconciliation Act of 1981.[44] Although the protection and advocacy systems established under the PAMI Act have certainly resulted in the provision of much "needed rights enforcement services for certain institutionalized mentally disabled persons,"[45] the legislation is not a panacea nor a total palliative for the underlying problems facing institutionalized persons;[46] also, courts have generally held that the PAMI Act does not provide a private

---

[34]On the way that these negative stereotypes affect U.S. policies on homelessness, see Michael L. Perlin, *Competency, Deinstitutionalization, and Homelessness: A Story of Marginalization,* 28 HOUS. L. REV. 63 (1991); Pedro Greer, *Medical Problems of the Homeless: Consequences of Lack of Social Policy—A Local Approach,* 45 U. MIAMI L. REV. 407 (1990–91).

[35]H.R. REP. NO. 485(III), *supra* note 6, at 7–8.

[36]*Cf.* Valentine v. American Home Shield Corp., 939 F. Supp, 1276, 1388 (W.D. Iowa 1999). (citing congressional testimony that a New Jersey zoo keeper refused to allow children with Down's Syndrome to tour the zoo because he feared they would upset the chimpanzees). On the ADA's implications for persons with developmental disabilities in general, see, for example, Cook, *supra* note 17, at 442–48.

[37]29 U.S.C. § 794.

[38]42 U.S.C. § 9401 (1983), repealed Oct. 1, 1981; *see* Note, *Effective Date of Repeal,* to 42 U.S.C. § 9502 (1983) (repealed).

[39]42 U.S.C. § 10801

[40]42 U.S.C. § 6000

[41]29 U.S.C. § 794.

[42]*See, e.g.,* Heather K. by Anita K. v. City of Mallard, Iowa, 887 F. Supp. 1249, 1263 (N.D. Iowa 1995) ("Congress found that section 504 . . . simply was not working as a means of eradicating discrimination and segregation on the basis of disability in this country"); Helen L. v. DiDario, 46 F.3d 325, 331 (3d Cir. 1995), *cert. denied,* 516 U.S. 813 (1995) ("shortcomings and deficiencies" of § 504 "quickly became apparent"); Robert Burgdorf, *The Americans With Disabilities Act: Analysis and Implications of a Second–Generation Civil Rights Statute.* 26 HARV. C.R.-C.L. L. REV. 413, 431 (1991) (enumerating § 504's weaknesses and inadequacies).

[43]42 U.S.C. § 9501 (1983), since restated at 42 U.S.C. § 10841 (1986).

[44]*See* 2 PERLIN, *supra* note 5, § 8.15 at 797 (discussing repeal).

[45]David Harvey & Curtis Decker, *Protection and Advocacy for Persons With Mental Illness: A Resource for Rights Enforcement,* 14 LAW & PSYCHOL. REV. 211, 220 (1990).

[46]PERLIN, *supra* note 5, § 8.16 at 263 (1998 Cum. Supp.); *see generally* Michael L. Perlin, *Fatal Assumption: A Critical Evaluation of the Role of Counsel in Mental Disability Cases,* 16 LAW & HUM. BEHAV. 39 (1992).

cause of action to individual litigants.[47] And the Supreme Court has made it clear that the DD Act is to be construed merely as a voluntary "federal–state grant program"[48] conferring no rights on mentally disabled individuals enforceable by private civil litigation.[49]

In short, none of these federal laws has had an impact remotely approaching a transformative effect on the lives of persons institutionalized because of mental disability. And we still do not know whether the ADA will ultimately have such a transformative effect or whether it will be simply another "paper tiger" filled with promise but bereft of substance.

To consider the question of whether the ADA will have a transformative effect, it is also necessary to consider the question of timing. The euphoria of the 1970s—when litigators representing persons with mental disabilities eagerly awaited the latest federal court decision, knowing instinctively that there would be new rights created, new causes of actions found[50]—crashed over 15 years ago with the ascension of a new, conservative federal judiciary and a conservative Supreme Court.[51] Decisions such as *Youngberg v. Romeo* (establishing a pallid "substantial professional judgment" test in assessing liability in institutional cases),[52] *Pennhurst State School and Hospital v. Halderman II* (expanding the scope of the Eleventh Amendment's sovereign immunity theory far beyond any prior court decision),[53] and even *Mills v. Rogers* (sidestepping the issue of a federal constitutional basis of a right to refuse antipsychotic drug treatment)[54] all seemed to clarify that the federal courts were no longer going to be the forum of choice for litigants representing persons with mental disabilities.[55]

At the same time, the public—originally somewhat sympathetic to the cause of persons with mental disabilities—turned hostile.[56] The day has long passed when commitment abolitionists appeared to be amassing support for their efforts.[57] The familiar pendulum swing[58] has resulted in a call for *expanded* commitment powers in many jurisdictions;[59] the perceived linkages between involuntary civil commitment requirements and homelessness

---

[47]*See, e.g.,* Brooks v. Johnson & Johnson, Inc., 685 F. Supp. 107 (E.D. Pa, 1988), *aff'd o.b.,* 875 F.2d 309 (3d Cir.), *cert. denied,* 493 U.S. 940 (1989); Croft v. Harder, 730 F. Supp. 342 (D. Kan. 1989), *aff'd,* 927 F.2d 1163 (10th Cir. 1991); Monahan v. Dorcester Counseling Ctr., Inc., 961 F.2d 987 (1st Cir. 1992) (no private cause of action).

[48]Pennhurst State Sch. & Hosp. v. Halderman, 451 U.S. 1, 11 (1981).

[49]*Id.* at 12. *Cf.* Olmstead v. L.C., 119 S. Ct. 2176, 2178–79, (1999) (explaining how the ADA "stepped up" earlier aspirational and hortatory disability rights statutes). *Olmstead* is discussed extensively *infra* at text accompanying notes 195–243.

[50]*See generally* Michael L. Perlin, *Ten Years After: Evolving Mental Health Advocacy and Judicial Trends,* 15 FORDHAM URB. L.J. 335 (1986–87) (discussing this period of euphoria).

[51]*See, e.g.,* Michael L. Perlin, *The Voluntary Delivery of Mental Health Services in the Community, in* LAW, MENTAL HEALTH AND MENTAL DISORDER 150 (Bruce Sales & Daniel Shuman eds. 1996)

[52]457 U.S. 307 (1982); see *supra* Chapter 5.

[53]465 U.S. 84 (1984). Under the ADA, states may not raise Eleventh Amendment immunity arguments. *See* 42 U.S.C. § 12202.

[54]457 U.S. 291 (1982); *see supra* Chapter 6.

[55]*See* PERLIN, *supra* note 5, § 3B-8.2, at 321–22 (2d. ed. 1999).

[56]*See generally* Perlin, *supra* note 34.

[57]1 PERLIN, *supra* note 5, at § 2.24. In 1978 President Jimmy Carter's Commission on Mental Health's Task Force Panel on Legal and Ethical Issues recommended a "modified abolition" position. *See id.,* § 2.26, at 172–75.

[58]*See, e.g.,* Mary Durham & John LaFond, *Empirical Consequences and Policy Implications of Broadening the Statutory Criteria for Civil Commitment,* 3 YALE L. & POL'Y REV. 395, 398 (1985); Daniel W. Shuman, *Innovative Statutory Approaches to Civil Commitment: An Overview and Critique,* 13 LAW, MED. & HEALTH CARE 284, 286 (1985).

[59]*See, e.g.,* 1 PERLIN, *supra* note 5, § 2A–7.2, at 188–89 (2d ed. 1998).

make it likely that the time of the abolition movement has come and gone.[60] The public is indignant when it appears—in a few idiosyncratic yet widely publicized cases—that a "clearly crazy" person is to be released from a psychiatric hospital because of some purported technical deficiency in the court papers or because judges allegedly unthinkingly accept abstract civil libertarian arguments from young, naive lawyers.[61] It appeared, in short, as if the mental disability law movement was in danger of becoming the public interest law equivalent of pop music's one-hit wonders. As a result of these factors—coupled with budget shortfalls, increased cynicism about the role of the government in even ameliorating social conditions, a growing mean-spiritedness in public life[62]—it appeared that the time that persons institutionalized for reasons of mental disability could rely on federal courts to craft broad prophylactic remedies in institutional reform litigation was long past. The passage of the ADA, however, has made us rethink this conventional wisdom. If the ADA does what some commentators say it does and what Congress seems to have said it *should* do, then the time may be right for a counter-*counter*-revolution in this area of the law.

The first question to pose is this: What impact, if any, has the ADA had on these trends and on this population? A simple ALLFEDS computer search on WESTLAW of "AMERICANS WITH DISABILITIES ACT" & MENTAL + 2 (ILLNESS DISABILITY) reveals a universe of 525 decisions,[63] but a reading of those cases suggests that the vast majority of those with substantive holdings deal with two issues largely unrelated to the problems faced by inpatients: the impact of the ADA on professional-licensure decision making (both regarding special accommodations for examinations and the questions that may be asked in the application process as to past or present psychiatric treatment)[64] and the extent to which employers have made reasonable accommodations to persons with mental disabilities in job settings.[65] Only a handful of cases even touch on the issues that are of daily significance to individuals who reside in large, public psychiatric institutions.[66] Prior to its decision in *Olmstead v. L.C.*[67] the Supreme Court had acknowledged the potential connection only once—in the course of its opinion in *Heller v. Doe*[68] upholding a Kentucky statutory scheme that established a heightened standard of review for involuntary civil commitment based on mental illness but a lesser standard for commitment based on mental retardation[69]—but refused to consider the question on the merits, finding that applicability had not been

---

[60]H. Richard Lamb—organized psychiatry's most visible critic of deinstitutionalization, as discussed previously—has in fact called for a moratorium on future deinstitutionalization programs. *See* H. Richard Lamb, *Is It Time for a Moratorium on Deinstitutionalization?* 43 HOSP. & COMMUNITY PSYCHIATRY 669 (1992); *cf.* Douglas Mossman & Michael L. Perlin, *Psychiatry and the Homeless Mentally Ill: A Reply to Dr. Lamb*, 149 AM. J. PSYCHIATRY 951 (1992). The specter of inappropriate deinstitutionalization has been raised by Justice Kennedy in his concurrence in *Olmstead v. L. C.*, 119 S. Ct. 2176, 2191 (1999); *see infra* text accompanying notes 210–12.

[61]*See supra* Introduction, text accompanying note 60, quoting Michael L. Perlin, *Book Review*, 8 N.Y.L. SCH. J. HUM. RTS. 557, 559–60 (1991), (reviewing ANN BRADEN JOHNSON, OUT OF BEDLAM: THE TRUTH ABOUT DEINSTITUTIONALIZATION (1990)) (characterizing the public's take on this issue).

[62]*See generally* Perlin, *supra* note 34.

[63]As of November 14, 1999.

[64]*See* PERLIN, *supra* note 5, § 6.44A at 179–81 n.473.43d (1998 Cum. Supp.) (citing cases).

[65]*See id.* at 181–83 n.473.43d1 (citing cases). For important empirical considerations of the ADA and employment issues, *see*, for example, Peter Blanck, *Assessing Five Years of Employment Integration and Economic Opportunity Under the Americans With Disabilities Act*, 19 MENT. & PHYS. DIS. L. REP. 384 (1995); Peter Blanck, *Empirical Study of the Americans With Disabilities Act: Employment Issues From 1990 to 1994*, 14 BEHAV. SCI. & L. 5 (1996). It is still premature to consider the impact of the *Sutton* trilogy, *see supra* note 14, on future developments in this area of the law.

[66]*See, e.g.*, 2 PERLIN, *supra* note 5, § 6.44A at 183–903 nn.473.43.e–473.43z23 (citing cases).

[67]119 S. Ct. 2176 (1999).

[68]509 U.S. 312 (1993).

[69]*Id.* at 318–28.

properly presented.[70] Similarly, there has been an explosion of law review articles and articles in the trade press and legal newspapers on all aspects of the ADA (a simple "AMERICANS WITH DISABILITIES ACT" search on the LRI database of WESTLAW revealed 1576 separate listings).[71] Yet of all of these, only a few—most notably, the late Timothy Cook's brilliant *Move to Integration* piece[72]—are remotely relevant to questions involving inpatient hospitalization.

This section seeks to shed some light on these issues: If and when cases are brought seeking to apply the ADA to individuals institutionalized in psychiatric hospitals, will federal courts interpret the ADA as it was written (in light of Congress's clear statutory intent) or will the key language to which I have already alluded be seen as little more than hortatory shibboleths? Will courts say, "No, Congress really didn't mean what it said"? Will they say, "Well, Congress may have meant it, but only in an aspirational way, and there's really nothing for us here"?[73] Or will they say, "Yes, Congress said it, Congress *meant* it, and, damn it, we're gonna enforce it."

Persons with mental disabilities have faced the brunt of discrimination for years. Surveys show that mental disabilities are the most negatively perceived of all disabilities.[74] Individuals with mental disabilities have been denied jobs, refused access to apartments in public housing or entry to places in public accommodation, and turned down for participation in publicly funded programs because they appear "strange" or "different."[75] A series of behavioral myths has emerged suggesting that mentally disabled persons are deviant, worth less than "normal" individuals, disproportionately dangerous, and presumptively incompetent.[76] Yet putting aside the two exceptions discussed earlier, nothing in the ADA speaks directly to these myths or to the special problems faced by mentally disabled persons in attempting to combat them.[77] Ironically, the only time that mental disability issues were clearly the focal point of an ADA debate came when a group of conservative senators, led by Jessie Helms, sought to *exclude* specified mental disabilities—including schizophrenia and

---

[70]*Id.* at 319; *cf. id.* at 337 (Souter, J., dissenting) (addressing the applicability of the ADA to the case before the Court).

[71]As of November 14, 1999.

[72]*See* Cook, *supra* note 17.

[73]*See, e.g.,* Niece v. Fitzner, 941 F. Supp. 1497, 1508 (E.D. Mich. 1996) (refusing to follow Torcasio v. Murray, 57 F.3d 1340 (4th Cir. 1995) (declining to apply the ADA to state prison cases)). *Cf.* Pennsylvania Dep't of Corrections v. Yeskey, 118 S. Ct. 1952 (1998) (unanimously finding that the ADA applies to state prisons), discussed extensively *infra* text accompanying notes 148–159.

[74]Jane West, *The Social Policy Context of the Act, in* THE AMERICANS WITH DISABILITIES ACT: FROM POLICY TO PRACTICE 3, 9 (Jane West ed. 1991) citing A. J. ARANGIO, BEHIND THE STIGMA OF: EPILEPSY: AN INQUIRY INTO THE CENTURIES-OLD DISCRIMINATION AGAINST PERSONS WITH EPILEPSY (1979). *See also infra* text accompanying note 77 (comments of Senator Helms in floor debate on the ADA).

[75]Simring, *supra* note 32, at 422. *See also* Cook, *supra* note 17, at 399–414, 424. Particularly cruel examples are listed in Tucker, *supra* note 7, at 16–17.

[76]*See, e.g.,* Perlin, *supra* note 13, at 393–97, citing, *inter alia,* SANDER GILMAN, DIFFERENCE AND PATHOLOGY: STEREOTYPES OF SEXUALITY, RACE AND MADNESS (1985); Steven Schwartz, *Damage Actions as a Strategy for Enhancing the Quality of Care of Persons With Mental Disabilities,* 17 N.Y.U. REV. L. & SOC. CHANGE 651, 681 (1989–90); Michael L. Perlin, *Unpacking the Myths: The Symbolism Mythology of Insanity Defense Jurisprudence,* 40 CASE W. RES. L. REV. 599, 693–96 (1989–90); Linda Teplin, *The Criminality of the Mentally Ill: A Dangerous Misconception,* 142 AM. J. PSYCHIATRY 593, 597–98 (1982); Thomas Grisso & Paul Appelbaum, *Mentally Ill and Non–Mentally Ill Patients' Abilities to Understand Informed Consent Disclosures for Medication,* 15 LAW & HUM. BEHAV. 377, 385–86 (1991).

[77]On the way that public perceptions of mental illness and the accompanying stigma perpetuate inadequate treatment of the mentally ill, see generally Wayne Ramage, *The Pariah Patient: The Lack of Funding for Mental Health Care,* 45 VAND. L. REV. 951 (1992).

manic depression—from the ADA's coverage.[78] Robert Burgdorf described a portion of the debate this way:

> At one point, Senator Armstrong stood on the Senate floor and pointed to a long list of conditions in the *Diagnostic and Statistical Manual of Mental Disorders* of the American Psychiatric Association as an example of all the conditions included. His remarks raised the specter of a potential roll call on individual amendments to resolve each of these conditions.
>
> Attacks upon certain conditions provoked a strong response from other Senators. . . . Senator Domenici gave a spirited speech on behalf of individuals with manic-depression and schizophrenia, suggesting that Winston Churchill and Abraham Lincoln suffered from such disturbances. Other conditions did not have the advantage of such Senatorial advocacy.[79]

These amendments were ultimately defeated;[80] however, other amendments—which excluded from the act's coverage a wide range of gender-identity disorders (including transvestism, transsexualism, pedophilia, exhibitionism, and voyeurism), compulsive gambling, kleptomania and pyromania, and psychoactive drug use disorders—were successful.[81]

The debate is illuminating. As Burgdorf noted, several senators spoke eloquently about the role of the ADA in "breaking down those barriers of fear and prejudices" and in "eliminat[ing] the automatic stigma" attached to mental illness.[82] Others, though, reflected the depth and malignity of their bias. In his colloquy with Senator Harkin about hiring practices, Senator Helms asked, "How is an employer . . . supposed to find out whether a man is a *pedophile or a schizophrenic?*"[83] He also asked whether an "employer's own *moral* standards" enabled him to make hiring judgments about transvestites, kleptomaniacs, or manic depressives.[84] Revealingly, Senator Helms made it clear that his attack was not meant to cover physically disabled persons: "If this were a bill involving people in a wheelchair or those who had been injured in the war, that is one thing."[85]

This debate and its ultimate *denouement* may turn out to be a double-edged sword. On one hand, the exclusions appear to reflect little more than congressional members' "own negative reactions, fears and prejudices"[86] in a spirit wholly inconsistent with the ADA's overall spirit that encourages "individualized determinations of actual ability and not

---

[78]According to the National Institutes of Mental Health, 2% of the population sufferers from schizophrenia and .4% from manic depression. It has been estimated that 60 million American adults will experience some sort of mental disorder prior to their 65th birthday, and that 15 million of these will experience a severe mental illness. *See* Blanck, *Work Force, supra* note 30, n.48; Milt Freudenheim, *Law Will Protect Mentally Ill at Work,* N.Y. TIMES, Sept. 23, 1991, at 1A.

[79]Robert L. Burgdorf Jr., *The Americans With Disabilities Act: Analysis and Implications of a Second-Generation Civil Rights Statute,* 26 HARV. C.R.-C.L. L. REV. 413, 451–52 (footnotes omitted).

[80]*See* 135 CONG. REC. S10765-86 (Sept. 7, 1989).

[81]*See* 42 U.S.C. §§ 12208, 12211(B) (1990).

[82]*See* 135 CONG. REC. S10765-86 (Sept. 7, 1989), 1998 WL 183216 (comments of Senator Harkin), and at 110 (comments of Senator Domenici).

[83]*Id.* at 10 (comments of Senator Helms).

[84]*Id.* at 6–7.

[85]*Id.* at 24. *See also id* at 136 (comments of Senator Humphrey): "We are not simply talking here about the blind, the deaf, or persons confined to wheelchairs." *Cf.* Joyce v. Runyon, 1997 WL 104958, at *1 (S.D.N.Y. 1997) (characterizing plaintiff in this manner: "Plaintiff is a forty-four year old white male who, *by his own admission,* suffers from *no physical handicap*") (emphasis added).

[86]Burgdorf, *supra* note 78, at 519.

preconceived assumptions and stereotypes.''[87] On the other, the specific repudiation of Helms's attempt to gut the bill's coverage of individuals with some of the most serious mental disabilities—persons with schizophrenia or manic-depression—should put to rest any lingering question as to whether members of Congress actually knew what they were doing when they drafted this law.

This analysis is limited here to considering only one substantive rights issue: the application of the ADA to public psychiatric hospitals and its potential use as a force to compel the creation and expansion of community treatment programs.[88] This is a highly contentious issue, and is one of critical importance to the population in question, both in the context of the individuals' current status as inpatients and in the context of the likelihood that they can be reintegrated into the community once they are released from an inpatient hospital setting.[89] And I believe that the actual application of the ADA to this key area of patients' civil rights law might result in the total transformation of these areas of the law, and might do so in ways that combat sanism, expose pretextuality, and provide a building block of therapeutic jurisprudence.

Initially, I will look at both the meager ADA case law and the scant scholarly literature that has emerged in this area, with an eye toward determining the extent to which courts see the ADA as merely offering hortatory or aspirational words to this population and the extent to which courts have taken the act's findings, its incorporation of the equal protection clause, and its invocation of the *Carolene Products* language seriously. The answers to these questions lead us to the first overarching question that must be addressed: Under the ADA, is institutionalization enough of a rationale on which to premise rights deprivation? Put another way, can the state (through hospital authorities) demonstrate a compelling state interest to deprive plaintiffs of otherwise-guaranteed constitutional, civil, and statutory rights? Then I will consider the substantive question of community treatment, by looking both at the recent Supreme Court case of *Olmstead v. L. C.*[90] (which breathes life into the ADA as a tool to mandate some community-based treatment)[91] as well as the U.S. Supreme Court's 1998 decision of *Pennsylvania Department of Corrections v. Yeskey,*[92] which settles the question of the application of the ADA to public institutions. Finally, I will consider the meanings of sanism and pretextuality and will assess the impact that an ADA that is taken seriously and enforced seriously would have on these hidden variables in mental disability law jurisprudence.

---

[87]*Id.* at 452. *See also id.* at 520:

> For while the ADA represents a huge advance for people with disabilities, those of us who have worked on the bill will continue to cringe when a focus on provisions of the Act that exclude from protection those individuals having real and difficult psychological and psychiatric disorders such as compulsive gambling, kleptomania and pyromania. It detracts from the principle underlying the Act that such people were denied protection because of stereotypes, ignorance and prejudice toward them and that their exclusion was permitted primarily because they had no organized representation present during the negotiations and no congressional champion arose to their defense.

[88]*See* Michael L. Perlin, *''Make Promises by the Hour': Sex, Drugs, the ADA, and Psychiatric Hospitalization,* 46 DePaul L. Rev. 947 (1997); Michael L. Perlin, *''I Ain't Gonna Work on Maggie: Farm No More'': Institutional Segregation, Communal Treatment, the ADA, and the Promise of* Olmstead v. L.C., 17 T.M. Cooley L. Rev. _____ (2000) (in press).

[89]*See infra* notes 195–244 discussing the Supreme Court's decision in *Olmstead v. L.C.,* 119 S. Ct. 2176 (1999).

[90]119 S. Ct. 2176, (1999), *aff'g in part, rev'g in part and remanding in part,* 138 F.3d 893 (11th Cir. 1998).

[91]*See infra* text accompanying notes 195–244.

[92]118 S. Ct. 1952 (1998) and *see infra* text accompanying notes 148–59.

The ADA and Mental Disability

How, then, is the ADA to be construed in decisions involving institutionalized psychiatric patients? What does the case law teach us, what can we glean from the scholarly literature, and what sort of tests should courts apply in deciding question that arise under the act? Before addressing these questions though, it is necessary to consider a forerunner question that may give us insights into how these questions will be substantively resolved: What is the likelihood that the ADA will be seen as more than merely hortatory or aspirational in this context? It is to this question that I first turn.

Hortatory Language

Little attention has been paid to the ways that disability rights statutes may be read as simply aspirational or hortatory, but I think it is a key concern. For years, environmental law scholars have written critically about the dilemma caused by enactment of ''aspirational statutes''—laws with high-sounding, ambitious aims but passed without either meaningful appropriations or workable enforcement powers.[93] Put another way, aspirational laws are laws that ''express goals that we wish we could achieve, rather than what we can realistically achieve.''[94] One judge has characterized such statutes as ''a perfect device for evading the truly hard policy decisions.''[95]

Susan Rose-Ackerman has written more broadly in this area, focusing on federal courts' failure to require Congress to either authorize or appropriate funds when it passes prophylactic or remedial legislation (thus allowing Congress to eventually set appropriations at zero without actually repealing such a law).[96] Such a result ''encourage[s] members of Congress to include language in substantive statutes that appears to promise benefits that legislators have no intention of funding adequately.''[97]

Rose-Ackerman pointed directly to an important mental disability law case: *Pennhurst State School and Hospital v. Halderman I*.[98] There, the Supreme Court rejected the plaintiffs' argument that the federal Bill of Rights for the Developmentally Disabled (that including findings that persons with developmental disabilities ''have a right to appropriate, treatment and habilitation'' that should be provided in the setting ''that is least restrictive of the person's liberty'')[99] created substantive, privately enforceable rights. In the course of his opinion that characterized this language as nothing more than a ''federal–state grant program,''[100] Chief Justice Rehnquist quoted with approval this language from *Rosado v. Wyman:* ''Congress sometimes legislates by innuendo, making declarations of policy and indicating a preference while requiring measures that, though falling short of legislating its goal, serve as a nudge in the preferred direction.''[101]

---

[93] John Dwyer, *The Pathology of Symbolic Legislation,* 17 ECOLOGY L.Q. 233, 245–50 (1990); James Henderson & Richard Pearson, *The Limits of Aspirational Commands,* 78 COLUM. L. REV. 1429, 1451 (1978).

[94] Carolyn McNiven, *Using Severability Clauses to Solve the Attainment Deadline Dilemma in Environmental Statutes,* 80 CALIF. L. REV. 1255, 1295 (1992).

[95] John Fennelly, *Non-Delegation Doctrine and the Florida Supreme Court: What You See Is Not What You Get,* 7 ST. THOMAS L. REV. 247, 281 (1995).

[96] Susan Rose-Ackerman, *Judicial Review and the Power of the Purse,* 12 INT'L REV. L. & ECON. 191, 205 (1992).

[97] *Id.*

[98] 451 U.S. 1 (1981).

[99] 42 U.S.C. § 6010(1)–(2). (recodified as 42 U.S.C. § 6009(1), (2) (1999)).

[100] *Pennhurst,* 451 U.S. at 11.

[101] 397 U.S. 397, 419 (1970), *as quoted in Pennhurst,* 451 U.S. at 19.

Will the Supreme Court read the ADA in the same stingy way it read the DD Act Bill of Rights in *Pennhurst,* thus gutting it of most of its force? In an earlier article, I wondered in print whether full enforcement of the ADA—full enforcement that could potentially lead to profound ''sea changes'' in the ways that society treats persons with disabilities—might lead to a congressional repeal effort.[102]

There are certainly differences between the two acts (the ADA is silent on funding questions; the ADA's inclusion of the *Carolene Products* language and its citation to the Fourteenth Amendment are both absent from the DD Act), and on at least one more recent occasion the Supreme Court has—in the context of a case interpreting a mandatory federal Medicaid funding law—distinguished *Pennhurst* on the basis of differences in statutory language.[103] And the legislative history of the ADA certainly is unequivocal in its commitment to transforming the lives of persons with disabilities. But will the Supreme Court take it seriously?

I concluded an earlier law review article this way:

> Finally, once ''Rip Van Winkle'' is awakened, how will Congress respond? In speaking against the ADA, Senator Humphrey referred to it as ''one of the most radical pieces of legislation'' he had encountered in his eleven years in the U.S. Senate. I believe that he was right, but with entirely the wrong spin: if the ADA does force a change in our social attitudes, then it *will* have worked a fundamental change in our social fabric. It will have forced us to reevaluate centuries of discrimination, bigotry, and prejudice, and will have forced us to acknowledge that disabled persons—*mentally* disabled persons; mentally *ill* persons; formerly *institutionalized* mentally ill persons—are full citizens of this country, and that they, like all other citizens, deserve to be treated ''as human beings.'' That thought would be radical, indeed.[104]

On June 22, 1999, the Supreme Court decided four ADA cases: the institutional case of *Olmstead v. L.C.*[105] and three employment cases (the *Sutton* trilogy).[106] *Olmstead* was a qualified victory for persons with mental disabilities in state institutions; the employment cases (involving individuals with visual problems and hypertension) were outright defeats for persons with those disabilities (although the Court's opinions in the latter three cases was limited to a determination of whether the plaintiffs in question qualified for ADA coverage, and expressed no opinion on most of the questions raised in this chapter).[107] When read together, however, they provide some clues that the extent to which the Court does believe that persons with disabilities deserve to be treated ''as human beings.''[108]

---

[102]Perlin, *supra* note 1, at 43. To some extent, this question has been answered by The Court's decision in Olmstead v. L.C., 119 S. Ct. 2176 (1999); *see infra* text accompanying notes 195–244.

[103]Wilder v. Virginia Hosp. Ass'n, 496 U.S. 498, 511 (1990), discussed in this context in Visiting Nurse Ass'n of North Shore, Inc. v. Bullen, 93 F.3d 997, 1004–05 (1st Cir. 1996).

[104]Perlin, *supra* note 1, at 45.

[105]119 S. Ct 2176 (1999).

[106]Sutton v. United Air Lines, 119 S. Ct. 2139 (1999); Murphy v. United Parcel Service, Inc., 119 S. Ct. 2133 (1999), and Albertsons, Inc. v. Kirkinburg, 119 S. Ct. 2162 (1999).

[107]*See, e.g., Sutton,* 119 S. Ct. at 2149 (individuals with correctable vision not considered ''disabled'' under act).

[108]*See supra* text accompanying note 102. The language is from Falter v. Veterans Admin., 502 F. Supp. 1178, 1185 (D. N.J. 1980).

Early Case Law

The ADA title most important to persons institutionalized because of mental disabilities is Title II. Under Title II, "No qualified individual with a disability shall, by reason of such disability, be excluded from participation in or be denied the benefits of the services, programs, or activities of a public entity, or be subjected to discrimination by any such entity."[109] The legislative history stressed that discrimination continued in "such critical areas as institutionalization."[110] Although this title has not been the subject of much consideration in institutional cases, courts have held that "allegations of restraint, isolation and segregation could constitute discriminatory treatment" under the ADA,[111] and that the Act requires that a psychiatric patient "be placed in the most integrated setting which meets the need of his disability but which gives him the most freedom."[112]

Most of the ADA–mental disability case law has focused on questions of professional licensure and examinations and on the range of accommodations necessary in employment situations.[113] Several courts have enjoined bar committees from inquiries into applicants' history of having been treated for mental disorders, but others have declined to do so.[114] Yet other courts have considered the application of the ADA to conditions under which professional licensure exams are to be taken.[115] On whether accommodations are reasonable in the employment context, courts are split, and it appears that most decisions have been fact based, turning on the individual judge's perception about whether the plaintiff could perform the job tasks satisfactorily, even with the statutorily mandated "reasonable accommodation."[116]

There is a smattering of other mental disability cases that focus on issues somewhat closer to the ones that are at the heart of this section. For instance, a district court in Florida found an ADA violation when a town's budget cuts eliminated community recreational programs that were solely for persons with disabilities,[117] as did a district court in Massachusetts considering a state law that required state hospital residents to contribute to

---

[109]42 U.S.C. § 12132.

[110]HOUSE COMM. ON EDUC. & LABOR, H.R. REP. NO. 485, 101st Cong., 2d Sess., at 50 (1989).

[111]Roe v. Community Comm'n of Monongalia County, 926 F. Supp. 74, 76 (N.D.W. Va, 1996).

[112]Charles Q. v. Houstoun, Civ. A., No. 1, CV-95-280 (M.D. Pa., Apr. 22, 1996), *reported in Rights in Facilities,* 20 MENT. & PHYS. DIS. L. REP. 490, 490 (1996). *See also* Halderman v. Pennhurst State Sch. & Hosp., 784 F. Supp. 215, 224 (E.D. Pa. 1992), *aff'd,* 977 F.2d 568 (3d Cir. 1992) ("in enacting the Americans with Disabilities Act of 1990, Congress affirmed that § 504 prohibits unnecessary segregation").

[113]*See* PERLIN, *supra* note 5, § 6.44A, at 179–83 n.473.43d1 (1998 Cum. Supp.) (citing cases).

[114]*See, e.g.,* Clark v. Virginia Bd. of Bar Examiners, 880 F. Supp. 430 (E.D. Va. 1995); Ellen S. v. Florida Bd. of Bar Examiners, 859 F. Supp. 1489 (S.D. Fla. 1994) (enjoining inquiries), and Campbell v. Greisberger, 805 F. Supp. 115 (W.D.N.Y. 1994); McReady v. Illinois Bd. of Admissions to the Bar, 1995 WL 29609 (N.D. Ill. 1995) (allowing inquiries). Immediately after it handed down its decisions in the *Sutton* trilogy, *see supra* note 14, the Supreme Court vacated the Second Circuit's decision in another bar case. *See* Bartlett v. New York State Bd. of Bar Examiners, 156 F.3d 321 (2d Cir. 1998), *vacated,* 119 S. Ct. 2388, (1999). *See infra* note 143.

[115]*See, e.g.,* Application of Underwood, 1993 WL 649283 (Me. 1993); Argens v. New York State Bd. of Bar Examiners, 860 F. Supp. 84 (W.D.N.Y. 1994); Petition of Rubenstein, 637 A.2d 1131 (Del. 1994).

[116]*See, e.g.,* Susie v. Apple Tree Preschool & Child Care Center, 866 F. Supp. 390 (N.D. Iowa 1994); Kerno v. Sandoz Pharmaceuticals Corp., 1994 WL 511289 (N.D. Ill. 1994); Voytek v. University of Calif., 1994 WL 478805 (N.D. Cal. 1994).

See generally Susan Stefan, *"You'd Have to Be Crazy to Work Here": Worker Stress, the Abusive Workplace, and Title I of the ADA,* 31 LOY. L.A. L. REV. 795 (1998); SUSAN STEFAN, PSYCHIATRIC DISABILITY AND DISCRIMINATION LAW (in press); Susan Stefan, *Whose Egg Is It Anyway? Reproductive Rights of the Incarcerated, Institutionalized and Incompetent Women,* 13 NOVA L. REV. 405 (1989).

[117]Concerned Parents to Save Dreher Park Ctr. v. City of West Palm Beach, 846 F. Supp. 986 (S.D. Fla.), *supplemented,* 853 F. Supp. 424 (S.D. Fla. 1994).

the costs of assigned counsel.[118] On the other hand, a District of Columbia district court ruled that mentally disabled residents of a homeless shelter failed to state a claim in their allegations that restrictions on their freedom of expression were in violation of the same act.[119] The most important of these cases is *Helen L. v. DiDario*,[120] finding that a state welfare department regulation that forced certain patients to receive required care services in the segregated setting of a nursing home (rather than through a community-based attendant care program) violated the ADA.

Helen L. is significant for several reasons. First, the Third Circuit read the act's antidiscrimination language broadly and loudly. It cited congressional findings that "historically, society has tended to isolate and segregate individuals with disabilities, and . . . such forms of discrimination . . . continue to be a serious and pervasive social problem,"[121] and that "the Nation's proper goals regarding individuals with disabilities are to assure equality of opportunity, full participation, independent living, and economic self-sufficiency for such individuals."[122] Next it read the ADA as being intended to ensure that "qualified individuals receive services in a manner consistent with basic human dignity rather than a manner which shunts them aside, hides, and ignores them," and declared that it would not "eviscerate the ADA by conditioning its protections upon a finding of intentional or overt 'discrimination,'"[123] focusing specifically on Congress's finding that "discrimination against individuals with disabilities persists in such critical areas as . . . institutionalization."[124] And finally, it rejected the state's argument that it could not change the plaintiff's regimen of care because the two programs in question were funded on separate budgetary lines. In language that has potential impact on all cases assessing the potentially discriminatory basis of the provision of public hospital service benefits, the court was clear:

> The ADA applies to the General Assembly of Pennsylvania, and not just to DPW [the Department of Public Welfare]. DPW can not rely upon a funding mechanism of the General Assembly to justify administering its attendant care program in a manner that discriminates and then argue that it can not comply with the ADA without fundamentally altering its program.
>
> Because the Commonwealth, including all its branches, is bound by the decree, the argument of inability to comply rings hollow. Even if the executive branch defendants were physically or legally incapable of complying with the decree, those Commonwealth officials sitting in the General Assembly certainly are not incapable of insuring the Commonwealth's compliance. [citation omitted] The same applies here: since the Commonwealth has chosen to provide services to [plaintiff] under the ADA, it must do so in a manner which comports with the requirements of that statute.[125]

The Literature

By far the most important analytic piece discussing the ADA and its potential impact has been Timothy Cook's *Move to Integration* article in *Temple Law Review*.[126] Cook was

---

[118]T. P. v. DuBois, 843 F. Supp. 775 (D. Mass. 1993).

[119]Melton v. Community for Creative Non-Violence, 1993 WL 367113 (D.D.C. 1993).

[120]46 F.3d 325, 331 (3d Cir. 1995), *cert. denied*, 516 U.S. 813 (1995).

[121]*Id.* at 332, quoting 42 U.S.C. § 12101(a)(2).

[122]*Id.*, quoting 42 U.S.C. § 12101(a)(8).

[123]*Id.* at 335.

[124]*Id.* at 336, quoting 42 U.S.C. § 12101(3).

[125]*Id.* at 338–39.

[126]Cook, *supra* note 17.

explicit, arguing that the ADA meant an end to what he termed the segregation of institutions for the mentally disabled.[127] He read congressional intent through the legislative history to abolish, in Senator Weicker's words, "the monoliths of isolated care in institutions and segregated educational settings. . . . Separate is not equal. It was not for blacks; it is not for the disabled."[128] The House Judiciary report was equally explicit: "Integration is fundamental to the purposes of the ADA. Provisions of segregated accommodations and services relegate persons with disabilities to second-class citizen status."[129] Cook read the act to bar intentional and unintentional discrimination,[130] and quoted researchers who concluded that "institutions and other segregated settings are simply unacceptable."[131] He concluded that the act's invocation of the Fourteenth Amendment effectively overruled the "substantial professional judgment" standard of *Youngberg v. Romeo.*[132]

Can these same arguments be made about cases involving persons institutionalized because of mental illness? Are there clear differences? Do police power considerations inherent in the involuntary civil commitment process make a difference? Does the invocation of the Fourteenth Amendment and the use of "discrete and insular minority" language significantly alter the *Youngberg* standard?[133]

I wrote five years ago that "these are difficult questions for which there are no ready or apparent easy answers,"[134] and little has changed my mind since then. Cook's article has been cited in a number of trial court decisions in cases—all mostly decided by the same judge[135]—involving a range of ADA topics, ranging from a case brought by a child with a severe respiratory condition who sought to ban exceptions to a city's ban on open burning,[136] to employment discrimination cases brought by persons suffering from asthma,[137] shoulder injury,[138] carpal tunnel syndrome,[139] and spinal injury.[140] None of these cases, though, involve the sort of "big issue" that Cook's methodology might eventually reach. Yet it provides litigators with a blueprint for frontal attacks on *Youngberg*-based case law[141] that

---

[127]*Id.* at 429.

[128]*Id.* at 423.

[129]*Id.* at 424.

[130]*Id.* at 427.

[131]*Id.* at 413.

[132]*Id.* at 466, discussing *Youngberg,* 457 U.S. 407 (1982). On the professional judgment standard, see Susan Stefan, *Leaving Civil Rights to the Experts: From Deference to Abdication Under the Professional Judgment Standard,* 102 YALE L.J. 639 (1992); 2 PERLIN, *supra* note 5, § 3A-9.4 (2d. ed. 1999).

[133]*Cf.* Sutton v. United Air Lines, 119 S. Ct. 2139, 2152 (1999) (Ginsburg, J., concurring) ("Congress' use of the ['discrete and insular minority'] phrase . . . is a telling indication of its intent to restrict the ADA's coverage to a confined, and historically disadvantaged, class").

However, The Supreme Court's willingness to be deferential to institutional treating professionals, see *Olmstead v. L.C.,* 119 S. Ct. 2176, 2184 (1999), discussed *infra* text accompanying notes 162–244, suggests that this court would not be receptive to arguments urging that the *Youngberg* standard be overruled.

[134]Perlin, *supra* note 1, at 38.

[135]In addition to the cases cited *infra* notes 136–40, *see also Helen L.,* Helen L. v. Di Dario, 46 F.3d. 325, 331 (3d. Cir. 1995), and Easley v. Snider, 841 F. Supp. 668, 677 (E.D. Pa. 1993).

[136]Heather K. by Anita K. v. City of Mallard, Iowa, 887 F. Supp. 1249, 1263 (N.D. Iowa 1995).

[137]Valentine v. American Home Shield Corp., 939 F. Supp. 1276, 1388 (N.D. Iowa 1996).

[138]Hutchinson v. United Parcel Service, Inc., 883 F. Supp. 379, 387 (N.D. Iowa 1995).

[139]Fink v. Kitzman, 881 F. Supp. 1347, 1368 (N.D. Iowa 1995).

[140]Muller v. Hotsy Corp., 917 F. Supp. 1389, 1402 (N.D. Iowa 1996).

[141]PERLIN, *supra* note 5, § 3A-12.1 at 120–21 n. 965 (2d. ed. 1999) (citing cases). Another major potential persuasive scholarly force is Rubenstein, *supra* note 13 (urging litigators to focus on the ADA as source of rights in combating discrimination in health benefits for persons with psychiatric disabilities).

limits patients' civil and treatment rights. The unanswered question is whether institutional plaintiffs' litigators will take the challenge.[142]

Applying a Test

Let me now turn to the methodology that I believe should be applied to ADA cases. The first question must be this: do defendant's policies discriminate against plaintiffs?[143] And if they do, is there a compelling state interest to justify that discrimination? Early cases that struck down overbroad involuntary civil commitment statutes had used this test in challenges both to the procedural and substantive limitations of the commitment power,[144] and even a few have done so since the Supreme Court declined in the case of *City of Cleburne v. Cleburne Living Center*[145] in 1985 to apply a heightened-scrutiny test to a zoning case involving group homes for persons with mental retardation.[146] I am convinced, however, that the ADA—if properly construed—legislatively overrules this aspect of the *Cleburne* case, and now requires a compelling state-interest justification for discrimination.[147]

More Recent Developments

The Supreme Court has found that the ADA applies to state prisons. In *Pennsylvania Department of Corrections v. Yeskey*,[148] the Court unanimously—per Justice Scalia—affirmed a Third Circuit decision that had allowed the plaintiff to maintain his suit against the state department of corrections, alleging that he was denied placement in a motivational boot camp first-offender program because of his medical history of hypertension.[149]

The court found that the ADA's language "unmistakably includes State prisons and prisoners in its coverage," noting that the law contained no "exception that could cast the coverage of prisons into doubt."[150] In doing so, it rejected the state's argument, based on *Gregory v. Ashcroft*,[151] that federal courts should be loath, absent an "unmistakably clear" expression of intent, to "alter the usual constitutional balance between the States and the Federal Government."[152] Although control over state prisons may well be: a "traditional

---

[142]*See infra* text accompanying notes 161–244 (discussing L. C. by Zimring v. Olmstead, 138 F.3d 893 (11th Cir. 1998), *aff'd in part, rev'd in part, and remanded in part,* 119 S. Ct. 2176 (1999).

[143]The *Sutton* trilogy—*see supra* note 14—makes this inquiry more difficult, because these cases refocus attention away from this question, stressing instead the threshold issue of whether a person is, in fact, disabled under the terms of the ADA. Within days of the *Sutton* decisions, the Court vacated another ADA case for reconsideration in light of those cases. *See* New York State Bd. of Law Examiners v Bartlett, 119 S. Ct. 2388 (1999), *vacating,* 156 F.3d 321 (2d Cir. 1998).

[144]*E.g.,* Lessard v. Schmidt, 349 F. Supp. 1078, 1084 (E.D. Wis. 1972); Colyar v. Third Judicial Dist. Ct., 469 F. Supp. 424, 430 (D. Utah 1979); Doremus v. Farrell, 407 F. Supp. 509, 514 (D. Neb. 1975).

[145]473 U.S. 432 (1985).

[146]City of Cleburne v. Cleburne Living Ctr., 473 U.S. 432, 441–42 (1985); *see supra* note 15. Post-*Cleburne* cases that have used this methodology include Guardianship of K. N. K., 497 N.W.2d 281, 290–91 (Wis. App. 1987); Matter of Shirley J. C., 493 N.W.2d 382, 385–86 (Wis. App. 1992), and Matter of Seman, 1992 WL 135878 (N. Mariana Islands 1992).

[147]This issue was not reached in any of the 1999 ADA cases. The *Olmstead* court, for example, noted specifically that the case—as presented—raised "no constitutional question," thus confining the scope of its review to "solely . . . statutory grounds." 119 S. Ct. at 2181. And *see id.* (contrasting *Olmstead* to *Cleburne,* a pre-ADA case).

[148]118 S. Ct. 1952 (1998).

[149]*Id.* at 1953.

[150]*Id.*

[151]501 U.S. 452 (1991).

[152]*Id.* at 460–61.

and essential State function,''[153] the explicit language of the ADA defeated the state's *Gregory*-based argument.

The court also rejected arguments by the state that state prison programs were not "benefits" under the ADA,[154] that the phrase *qualified individual with a disability* was ambiguous as to state prisoners (on the theory that the statute's use of the words *eligibility* and *participation* implied a level of voluntariness that a prisoner could not meet),[155] and that, because the law's statement of findings did not specifically mention prisons, the ADA should not apply to such facilities.[156]

However, the Court noted that it was not addressing the difficult questions of whether application of the ADA to state prisons was a constitutional exercise of Congress's power under either the Commerce Clause[157] or section 5 of the Fourteenth Amendment,[158] because neither of those issues were raised before or considered by the court of appeals.[159]

Yeskey resolves an important split in the lower courts on the prison applicability question, and, just as important, it tells us, for the first time, that the Supreme Court will take the plain language of the ADA seriously. The ADA's ultimate impact on persons with mental disabilities may turn on whether much of its language is seen as mandatory or merely as hortatory.[160] The interpretation given to it by the unanimous court in *Yeskey* suggests that arguments urging a merely hortatory position will be rejected, a conclusion buttressed by the Court's more recent decision in *Olmstead v. L. C.*[161]

In *Olmstead*, the Court qualifiedly affirmed a decision by the Eleventh Circuit that had provided the first coherent answer to the question of the right of institutionalized persons with mental disabilities to community services under the ADA.[162] In *L. C.*, the Court had found that the ADA entitled plaintiffs—residents of Georgia State Hospital—to treatment in an "integrated community setting" as opposed to an "unnecessarily segregated"[163] state hospital.

Plaintiffs L. C. and E. W. had challenged their placement at Georgia State Hospital, arguing that Title II of the ADA entitled them to "the most integrated setting appropriate to [their] needs."[164] The district court granted summary judgment to plaintiffs, finding that the state's failure to place them in an "appropriate community-based program" so violated the

---

[153]*Yeskey,* 118 S. Ct. at 1953.

[154]*Id.* at 1955. Under the statute, a qualified individual with a disability is anyone "who, with or without reasonable modifications to rules, policies, or practices, the removal of architectural, communication, or transportation barriers, or the provision of auxiliary aids and services, meets the essential eligibility requirements for the receipt of services or the participation in programs or activities provided by a public entity." 42 U.S.C. § 12131(2).

[155]*Yeskey,* 118 S. Ct. at 1955

[156]*Id.,* at 1955–56.

[157]Compare Printz v. United States, 521 U.S. 898 (1997), *with* Garcia v. San Antonio Metro. Transit Auth., 469 U.S. 528 (1985). *See Yeskey,* 118 S. Ct. at 1956.

[158]*See* City of Boerne v. Flores, 117 S. Ct. 2157 (1997); *see also Yeskey,* 118 S. Ct. at 1956.

[159]*Yeskey,* 118 S. Ct. at 1956, quoting Adickes v. S. H. Kress & Co., 398 U.S. 144, 147 n.2 (1970).

On the question of whether Congress lacked authority to abrogate the states' Eleventh Amendment immunity for the ADA. *Compare* Alsbrook v. City of Maumelle, 184 F.3d 999 (8th Cir. 1999), petion for cert. filed (Sept. 8, 1999) (finding Congress liable authority), to Martin v. Kansas, 190 F.3d. 1120 (10th Cir. 1999) (ADA proper exercise of Congress' 14th Amendment powers).

[160]*See* Perlin, *supra* note 88.

[161]119 S. Ct. 2176, 2186–87 (1999); *see infra* text accompanying notes 162–244.

[162]138 F.3d 893 (11th Cir. 1998), *aff'd in part, rev'd in part, and vacated in part,* 119 S. Ct. 2176 (1999).

[163]*L. C.,* 138 F.3d at 897.

[164]*Id.* at 895. Although both plaintiffs were transferred to community settings prior to the court's decision, the court declined to find the case moot as such cases were "capable of repetition, yet evading review." *Id.* at 895 n.2., citing, *inter alia,* Honig v. Doe, 484 U.S. 305, 318–25 (1988).

ADA,[165] and the state appealed. On appeal, the Eleventh Circuit affirmed the judgment that the state had discriminated against the plaintiffs, but also remanded for further findings related to the state's defense that the relief sought by plaintiffs would "fundamentally alter the nature of the service, program, or activity."[166]

The court began its opinion by reviewing the pertinent statutory sections[167] and the relevant regulations promulgated by the U.S. Attorney General pursuant to statutory authority.[168] Under these regulations, a "public entity shall administer services, programs, and activities in the most integrated setting appropriate to the needs of qualified individuals with disabilities,"[169] and placement is required in a setting that "enables individuals with disabilities to interact with non-disabled persons to the fullest extent possible."[170] Placement in the community provides an integrated treatment setting, the court found, allowing disabled individuals to interact with nondisabled persons—"an opportunity permitted only in limited circumstances within the walls of segregated state institutions such as [the state hospital]."[171] It thus concluded that the express terms of the regulation, supported by the Attorney General's consistent interpretation, "plainly prohibit a state from treating individuals with disabilities in a segregated environment where a more integrated setting would be appropriate."[172]

It then looked at the congressional findings and legislative history that "make clear" Congress's aim: "to eliminate the segregation of individuals with disabilities":[173]

> In enacting the ADA, Congress determined that discrimination against individuals with disabilities persists in a wide variety of areas of social life, including "institutionalization," 42 U.S.C. § 12101(a)(3) (1995), and that "individuals with disabilities continually encounter various forms of discrimination, including outright intentional exclusion ... [and] segregation. ... " 42 U.S.C. § 12101(a)(5); *see also* 42 U.S.C. § 12101(a)(2) ("[H]istorically, society has tended to isolate and segregate individuals with disabilities, and . . . such forms of discrimination against individuals with disabilities continue to be a serious and pervasive social problem.").
>
> Indeed, the legislative history makes clear that Congress considered the provision of segregated services to individuals with disabilities a form of discrimination prohibited by the ADA. See S.Rep. No. 101-116 at 20 (1989) (noting "compelling need to provide a clear and comprehensive national mandate . . . for the integration of persons with disabilities into the economic and social mainstream of American life"); H.R.Rep. No. 101-485, pt. 2 at 29 (1990), reprinted in 1990 U.S.C.C.A.N. 267, 310 (listing "segregation" as a form of "[d]iscrimination against people with disabilities").[174]

On this point the court concluded, "Certainly, the denial of community placements to individuals with disabilities such as L.C. and E.W. is precisely the kind of segregation that Congress sought to eliminate."[175]

---

[165]*Id.* at 895.

[166]*Id.*, citing 28 C.F.R. § 35.130(b)(7) (1999).

[167]*Id.* at 896, citing 42 U.S.C. §§ 12134 and 12134(a).

[168]*Id.* at 896–98.

[169]28 C.F.R. § 35.130(d).

[170]28 C.F.R., pt. 35, App. A. at 478.

[171]*L. C.*, 138 F.3d at 897.

[172]*Id.*

[173]*Id.* at 898.

[174]*Id.*

[175]*Id.*

The court continued with its focus on the "basic goal" of the ADA: "The ADA does not only mandate that individuals with disabilities be treated the same as persons without such disabilities. Underlying the ADA's prohibitions is the notion that individuals with disabilities must be accorded reasonable accommodations not offered to other persons in order to ensure that individuals with disabilities enjoy 'equality of opportunity, full participation, independent living, and economic self-sufficiency. . . . '''[176]

It described the reasonable accommodation duty as requiring the state to "place individuals with disabilities in the most integrated setting appropriate to their needs,"[177] and relied on language from both the Third Circuit's decision in *Helen L. v. DiDario*[178] and Justice Marshall's separate opinion in *City of Cleburne v. Cleburne Living Center*[179] that "the ADA is intended to ensure that qualified individuals receive services in a manner consistent with basic human dignity rather than a manner that shunts them aside, hides, and ignores them."[180]

Malevolent intent is not required, the court found. The state's "indifference to L.C. and E.W.'s needs—manifested by their refusal to place them in the community while recognizing the propriety of such a placement—is exactly the kind of conduct that the ADA was designed to prevent."[181] Here it drew on Supreme Court language from a section 504 case, *Alexander v. Choate:*[182]

> Discrimination against the handicapped was perceived by Congress to be most often the product, not of invidious animus, but rather of thoughtlessness and indifference—of benign neglect. Thus, Representative Vanik . . . described the treatment of the handicapped as one the country's "most shameful oversights," which caused the handicapped to live among society "shunted aside, hidden, and ignored." . . . Federal agencies and commentators on the plight of the handicapped similarly have found that discrimination against the handicapped is primarily the result of apathetic attitudes rather than affirmative animus.[183]

The court rejected the state's argument that plaintiffs' claims must fail because the denial of community-based placements was based on lack of funds. "The plain language of the ADA's Title II regulations, as well as the ADA's legislative history, make clear that Congress wanted to permit a cost defense only in the most limited of circumstances, . . . [only] where those accommodations "would fundamentally alter the nature of the service, program, or activity."[184] It cited a House Judiciary report that explained, "The fact that it is more convenient, either administratively or fiscally, to provide services in a segregated manner, does not constitute a valid justification for separate or different services under Section 504 of the Rehabilitation Act, or under this title. . . . The existence of such programs

---

[176]*Id.* at 899, quoting 42 U.S.C. § 12101(a)(8), and citing Willis v. Conopco, Inc., 108 F.3d 282, 285 (11th Cir. 1997) (describing "the basic goal of the ADA" as "ensuring that those with disabilities can fully participate in all aspects of society").

[177]*Id.* at 899.

[178]46 F.3d 325 (3d Cir. 1995), *cert. denied,* 516 U.S. 813 (1995). *See supra* text accompanying notes 120–25.

[179]473 U.S. 432 (1985).

[180]*L. C.,* 138 F.3d at 899–900, quoting *Helen L.,* 46 F.3d at 335, and *City of Cleburne,* 473 U.S. at 432.

[181]*L. C.,* 138 F.3d at 901.

[182]469 U.S. 287 (1985).

[183]*L. C.,* 138 F.3d at 901, quoting *Alexander,* 469 U.S. at 295–96.

[184]*L. C.,* 138 F.3d at 902, quoting 28 C.F.R. § 35.130(b)(7).

can never be used as a basis to . . . refuse to provide an accommodation in a regular setting.''[185]

The court stressed that its holding did not ''mandate the deinstitutionalization of
individuals with disabilities.''[186] Instead, it clarified: ''We hold that where, as here, a
disabled individual's treating professionals find that a community-based placement is
appropriate for that individual, the ADA imposes a duty to provide treatment in a community
setting—the most integrated setting appropriate to that patient's needs. Where there is no
such finding, on the other hand, nothing in the ADA requires the deinstitutionalization of that
patient.''[187]

It pointed out that experts—including one of E. W.'s treating physicians—were
unanimous that E. W. could be treated in a community setting, provided she were given ''the
level of care and supervision she needed.''[188] Again, it underscored;

> We do not suggest that should a trial court find that a patient, for medical reasons, needs
> institutionalized care, it must nonetheless order placement in a community-based treatment
> program. We recognize that the determination whether a patient can be appropriately placed in
> a community-based treatment program is a fluid one, subject to change as the patient's medical
> condition improves or worsens. Over the course of litigation, there may be times that a patient
> can be treated in the community, and others where an institutional placement is necessary. But
> where, as here, the evidence is clear that all the experts agree that, at a given time, the patient
> could be treated in a more integrated setting, the ADA mandates that it do so at that time unless
> placing that individual would constitute a fundamental alteration in the state's provision of
> services. Nothing in the ADA, however, forbids a state from moving a patient back to an
> institutionalized treatment setting, as the patient's condition necessitates.[189]

The court then turned to the state's lack-of-funds argument. The duty to provide services
is not absolute, it noted, and the state need not provide the services in question, ''if to do so
would require a fundamental alteration in its programs.''[190] However, plaintiffs adequately
demonstrated to the court that the state could ''reasonably modify its provision of services''
by providing treatment to them in a community setting.[191] It continued by noting that ''the
ADA does not permit the State to justify its discriminatory treatment of individuals with
disabilities on the grounds that providing non-discriminatory treatment will require additional expenditures of state funds.''[192]

However, because the trial court did not consider the question of whether the additional
expenditures necessitated by community treatment would ''fundamentally alter the services
[the state] provides,'' the Eleventh Circuit remanded for the trial court to consider:

---

[185]*L. C.,* 138 F.3d at 902, quoting H.R. Rep. No. 485, pt. 3 at 50, *reprinted in* 1990 U.S.C.C.A.N. at 473.

The *L. C.* court distinguished cases such as S. H. v. Edwards, 886 F.2d 292 (11th Cir. 1989) (*see* PERLIN, *supra*
note 5, § 7.18, at 224 (1998 Cum. Supp.)) as those cases did not have occasion to consider the ''integration
regulation'' that was central to the methodology in deciding ADA cases. *L. C.,* 138 F.3d at 901–02.

[186]L.C., 138 F.3d at 901.

[187]*Id.* at 902.

[188]*Id.* at 903.

[189]*Id.* It stressed, ''Accordingly, because the State's own professionals agreed that E.W. could be placed in a
less segregated setting, the State has failed to demonstrate that there is a material issue of fact for trial. : . . '' *Id.*

[190]*Id.* at 904: ''Under Title II, '[a] public entity shall make reasonable modifications in policies, practices, or
procedures when the modifications are necessary to avoid discrimination on the basis of disability, unless the public
entity can demonstrate that making the modifications would fundamentally alter the nature of the service, program,
or activity.' 28 C.F.R. § 35.130(b)(7).'' *Id.*

[191]*Id.*

[192]*Id.* at 904–05, citing United States v. Board of Trustees for Univ. of Ala., 908 F.2d 740, 751 (11th Cir.
1990).

(1) whether the additional expenditures necessary to treat L.C. and E.W. in community-based care would be unreasonable given the demands of the State's mental health budget; (2) whether it would be unreasonable to require the State to use additional available Medicaid waiver slots, as well as its authority under Georgia law to transfer funds from institutionalized care to community-based care, to minimize any financial burden on the State; and (3) whether any difference in the cost of providing institutional or community-based care will lessen the State's financial burden.[193]

On appeal, the Supreme Court, in a split opinion per Justice Ginsburg,[194] qualifiedly affirmed.[195] After setting out the provisions of the ADA that focused on the institutional segregation and isolation of persons with disabilities, and the discrimination faced by persons with disabilities (including "exclusion . . . and segregation"),[196] the Court reviewed the key Department of Justice regulations, including the integration-mandate regulation,[197] pointing out that the case, as presented, did not challenge their legitimacy.[198] It then set out its holding:

> We affirm the Court of Appeals' decision in substantial part. Unjustified isolation, we hold, is properly regarded as discrimination based on disability. But we recognize, as well, the States' need to maintain a range of facilities for the care and treatment of persons with diverse mental disabilities, and the States' obligation to administer services with an even hand. Accordingly, we further hold that the Court of Appeals' remand instruction was unduly restrictive. In evaluating a State's fundamental-alteration defense, the District Court must consider, in view of the resources available to the State, not only the cost of providing community-based care to the litigants, but also the range of services the State provides others with mental disabilities, and the State's obligation to mete out those services equitably.[199]

The Court endorsed the Department of Justice's position that "undue institutionalization qualifies as discrimination 'by reason of . . . disability,' "[200] and then characterized the ADA as having "stepped up earlier measures to secure opportunities for people with developmental disabilities to enjoy the benefits of community living,"[201] stressing how much more comprehensive the ADA was than had been aspirational or hortatory laws such as the Developmentally Disabled Assistance and Bill of Rights Act.[202] It then focused on what it saw as congressional judgment supporting the finding that "unjustified institutional isolation of persons with disabilities is a form of discrimination":

---

[193]*L. C.,* 138 F.3d 893, 905 (11th Cir. 1998). In an accompanying footnote, the court added, "We note that this case is not a class action, but a challenge brought on behalf of two individual plaintiffs. Our holding is not meant to resolve the more difficult questions of fundamental alteration that might be present in a class action suit seeking deinstitutionalization of a state hospital." *Id.* at 905 n.10.

[194]Justices O'Connor, Breyer, Souter, and Stevens (the latter in a separate opinion) joined Justice Ginsburg in most of her opinion. Justice Stevens, who would have preferred to simply affirm the Eleventh Circuit's opinion, *see infra* text accompanying note 216, joined with these four justices in all of the opinion save that portion that outlined the state's obligations in such cases. Justice Kennedy filed a concurring opinion, joined in part by Justice Breyer, *see infra* text accompanying notes 217–29. Justice Thomas dissented for himself, the Chief Justice, and Justice Scalia, *see infra* text accompanying notes 230–234.

[195]119 S. Ct. 2176, (1999).

[196]*Id.* at 2181, quoting 42 U.S.C. §§ 12101 (a)(2), (3), (5).

[197]28 C.F.R. pt. 35, App. A, at 540 (1998).

[198]*Olmstead,* 119 S. Ct. at 2183.

[199]*Id.* at 2185.

[200]*Id.* at 2185–86

[201]*Id.* at 2186.

[202]*Id.,* at 2186–87, discussing 42 U.S.C. § 6010 (2), as construed in Pennhurst State Sch. & Hosp. v. Halderman, 451 U.S. 1, 24 (1984); *see supra* text accompanying notes 98–100.

First, institutional placement of persons who can handle and benefit from community settings perpetuates unwarranted assumptions that persons so isolated are incapable or unworthy of participating in community life. Cf. Allen v. Wright, 468 U.S. 737, 755, 104 S. Ct. 3315, 82 L.Ed.2d 556 (1984) ("There can be no doubt that [stigmatizing injury often caused by racial discrimination] is one of the most serious consequences of discriminatory government action."); Los Angeles Dept. of Water and Power v. Manhart, 435 U.S. 702, 707, n. 13, 98 S. Ct. 1370, 55 L.Ed.2d 657 (1978) (" 'In forbidding employers to discriminate against individuals because of their sex, Congress intended to strike at the entire spectrum of disparate treatment of men and women resulting from sex stereotypes.' ") (quoting Sprogis v. United Air Lines, Inc., 444 F.2d 1194, 1198 (C.A.7 1971)). Second, confinement in an institution severely diminishes the everyday life activities of individuals, including family relations, social contacts, work options, economic independence, educational advancement, and cultural enrichment. See Brief for American Psychiatric Association et al. as Amici Curiae 20-22. Dissimilar treatment correspondingly exists in this key respect: In order to receive needed medical services, persons with mental disabilities must, because of those disabilities, relinquish participation in community life they could enjoy given reasonable accommodations, while persons without mental disabilities can receive the medical services they need without similar sacrifice. See Brief for United States as Amicus Curiae 6-7, 17.[203]

The majority immediately clarified some qualifications in its opinion. It emphasized that the ADA did not "condone termination of institutional settings for persons unable to handle or benefit from community settings,"[204] that the states "generally may rely on the reasonable assessments of its own professionals" in determining whether an individual is eligible for community-based programs,[205] and that there was no requirement that "community-based treatment be imposed on patients who do not desire it."[206] None of these issues, however, were present in the case before it: Georgia's professionals determined that community-based treatment would be appropriate for the plaintiffs, both of whom desired such treatment.[207] The Court added one additional word of caution:

> We do not in this opinion hold that the ADA imposes on the States a "standard of care" for whatever medical services they render, or that the ADA requires States to "provide a certain level of benefits to individuals with disabilities." . . . We do hold, however, that States must adhere to the ADA's nondiscrimination requirement with regard to the services they in fact provide.[208]

The Court then turned to the questions of remedy and enforcement.[209] It rejected the Eleventh Circuit's construction of the "reasonable modification regulation" as "unacceptable" in that it would leave the state "virtually defenseless" if the plaintiff demonstrates she or he is qualified for the program or placement she or he seeks.[210] Rather, it concluded, "Sensibly construed, the fundamental-alteration component of the reasonable-modifications regulation would allow the State to show that, in the allocation of available resources,

---

[203]*Olmstead,* 119 S. Ct. at 2187.

[204]*Id.* at 2187.

[205]*Id.* at 2188.

[206]*Id.*

[207]*Id.*

[208]*Id.* at 2188 n.14.

[209]Although this section of the opinion was cosigned only by four justices (Ginsburg, Souter, Breyer, and O'Connor), a reading of it in tandem with Justice Kennedy's concurrence, *see infra* text accompanying notes 217–19, makes it likely that it will be treated by lower courts as having the weight of a majority opinion.

[210]*Id.* at 2188. *Cf. supra* text accompanying notes 190–192

immediate relief for the plaintiffs would be inequitable, given the responsibility the State has undertaken for the care and treatment of a large and diverse population of persons with mental disabilities."[211]

The ADA, it determined, "is not reasonably read to phase out institutions, placing patients in close care at risk," nor is the law's mission "to drive states to move institutionalized patients into an inappropriate setting, such as a homeless shelter."[212] For other patients, "no placement outside the institution may ever be appropriate."[213] These factors led Justice Ginsburg to conclude that the state must have more leeway than offered by the Eleventh Circuit's remedy:

> If, for example, the State were to demonstrate that it had a comprehensive, effectively working plan for placing qualified persons with mental disabilities in less restrictive settings, and a waiting list that moved at a reasonable pace not controlled by the State's endeavors to keep its institutions fully populated, the reasonable-modifications standard would be met.[214]

She summarized in this way:

> Under Title II of the ADA, States are required to provide community-based treatment for persons with mental disabilities when the State's treatment professionals determine that such placement is appropriate, the affected persons do not oppose such treatment, and the placement can be reasonably accommodated, taking into account the resources available to the State and the needs of others with mental disabilities.[215]

Justice Stevens concurred, stating that he would have preferred simply affirming the Eleventh Circuit's opinion, but that, because there were not five votes for that disposition, he joined in all of Justice Ginsburg's opinion, except for the remedy-enforcement portion.[216] Justice Kennedy concurred, urging "caution and circumspection" in the enforcement of the *Olmstead* case.[217] After stressing that persons with mental disabilities "have been subject to historic mistreatment, indifference, and hostility,"[218] Justice Kennedy traced what he saw as the history of deinstitutionalization: that although it has permitted "a substantial number of mentally disabled persons to receive needed treatment with greater freedom and dignity," it has "had its dark side" as well.[219] He quoted extensively from the writings of E. Fuller Torrey:

> For a substantial minority . . . deinstitutionalization has been a psychiatric Titanic. Their lives are virtually devoid of "dignity" or "integrity of body, mind, and spirit." "Self-determination" often means merely that the person has a choice of soup kitchens. The "least

---

[211]*Id.* at 2189.

[212]At one point, Georgia had proposed such a placement for one of the named plaintiffs, and then later retracted it. *Id.*

[213]*Id.* On this point, the opinion cited, *inter alia,* Justice Blackmun's concurrence in Youngberg v. Romeo, 457 U.S. 307, 327 (1982): "For many mentally retarded people, the difference between the capacity to do things for themselves within an institution and total dependence on the institution for all of their needs is as much liberty as they ever will know."

[214]*Id.*

[215]*Id.* at 2190.

[216]*Id.* at 2190.

[217]*Id.* at 2191.

[218]*Id.*

[219]*Id.*

restrictive setting" frequently turns out to be a cardboard box, a jail cell, or a terror-filled existence plagued by both real and imaginary enemies.[220]

It would be a "tragic event," Justice Kennedy warned, if states read the ADA—as construed in *Olmstead*—in such a way as to create an incentive to states, "for fear of litigation, to drive those in need of medical care and treatment out of appropriate care and into settings with too little assistance and supervision,"[221] and he thus emphasized that opinions of "a responsible treating physician" should be given the greatest of deference."[222] He underscored what he saw as a "common phenomenon": "It is a common phenomenon that a patient functions well with medication, yet, because of the mental illness itself, lacks the discipline or capacity to follow the regime the medication requires. This is illustrative of the factors a responsible physician will consider in recommending the appropriate setting or facility for treatment."[223]

Because of these concerns—and his fear that "States may be pressured into attempting compliance on the cheap, placing marginal patients into integrated settings devoid of the services and attention necessary for their condition"—Justice Kennedy again urged "caution and circumspection" and "great deference to the medical decisions of . . . responsible, treating physicians."[224]

He continued[225] by articulating what he saw as the necessary elements of a discrimination finding,[226] and then raised federalism concerns: "Grave constitutional concerns are raised when a federal court is given the authority to review the State's choices in basic matters such as establishing or declining to establish new programs. It is not reasonable to read the ADA to permit court intervention in these decisions."[227]

Finally, he parted company from Justice Ginsburg on the weight she gave to the congressional findings. The findings in question, he concluded, "do not show that segregation and institutionalization are always discriminatory or that segregation or institutionalization are, by their nature, forms of prohibited discrimination."[228] Instead, he reasoned, "they underscore Congress' concern that discrimination has been a frequent and pervasive problem in institutional settings and policies and its concern that segregating disabled persons from others can be discriminatory."[229]

Justice Thomas dissented, criticizing the majority opinion for its interpreting "discrimination" to encompass "disparate treatment" among members of the same protected class,[230] arguing that the congressional findings on which the majority premised its

---

[220]*Id.*, quoting E. FULLER TORREY, OUT OF THE SHADOWS 11 (1997).

[221]*Id.*

[222]*Id.*

[223]*Id.*

[224]*Id.* 2192.

[225]Justice Breyer joined in the prior portion of Justice Kennedy's concurrence, but not in the portion discussed *infra* text accompanying notes 226–29.

[226]If they could show that persons needing psychiatric or other medical services to treat a mental disability are subject to a more onerous condition than are persons eligible for other existing state medical services, and if removal of the condition would not be a fundamental alteration of a program or require the creation of a new one, then the beginnings of a discrimination case would be established. *Id.* at 2192.

[227]*Id.* at 2193.

[228]*Id.*

[229]*Id.*

[230]*Id.* at 2194.

conclusions were "vague" and written in "general hortatory terms,"[231] that its approach imposed "significant federalism costs,"[232] and warning that states "will now be forced to defend themselves in federal court every time resources prevent the immediate placement of a qualified individual."[233] He concluded, "Continued institutional treatment of persons who, though now deemed treatable in a community placement, must wait their turn for placement, does not establish that the denial of community placement occurred 'by reason of' their disability. Rather, it establishes no more than the fact that petitioners have limited resources."[234]

Olmstead is significant for several reasons. First, it is the first time that the Supreme Court has ruled on the applicability of the ADA to community-based treatment programs. Second, it breathes important life into the congressional findings on questions of institutional segregation, discrimination, and exclusion. Third, it specifically focuses on the way that "unjustified isolation . . . is properly regarded as discrimination based on disability."[235] Fourth, it comprehends how, in its own words, the ADA had stepped up prior congressional efforts in this area.[236] Fifth, it underscores how institutional isolation "perpetuates unwarranted assumptions that persons so isolated are incapable or unworthy of participating in community life,"[237] and how such isolation "severely diminishes the everyday life activities of institutionalized individuals."[238]

On the other hand, the Court's qualifiers are equally important. It sanctions reliance on state professionals in determining community-treatment eligibility, thus implicitly endorsing a perpetuation of *Youngberg v. Romeo's* "substantial professional judgment" standard.[239] It emphasizes that *Olmstead* cannot be read as an opinion designed to phase out institutions or to move patients to inappropriate community settings.[240] And its "reasonable modification" formula—by which a state must be able to "demonstrate that it had a comprehensive, effectively working plan for placing qualified persons with mental disabilities in less restrictive settings"[241]—provides an early partial blueprint for the resolution of similar future litigation.

Justice Kennedy's concurrence may turn out to be of critical importance for several reasons. First, he focuses squarely on the specter of inappropriate deinstitutionalization, relying on Fuller Torrey's powerful critique.[242] Second, he raises the concern that the fear of litigation may lead the state to prematurely and inappropriately release patients "with too little assistance and supervision."[243] Third, he links institutional release with patients'

---

[231]*Id.* at 2197.

[232]*Id.* at 2198.

[233]*Id.* at 2199.

[234]*Id.*

[235]*Id.* at 2185.

[236]*Id.* at 2186.

[237]*Id.* at 2187.

[238]*Id.*

[239]*See supra* text accompanying note 132.

[240]*Olmstead,* 119 S. Ct. at 2189.

[241]*Id.*

[242]In my mind, Fuller Torrey's critique is a terribly flawed one. *See* Perlin, *supra* note 34, at 87; *see generally* Michael L. Perlin, Keri K. Gould, & Deborah A. Dorfman, *Therapeutic Jurisprudence and the Civil Rights of Institutionalized Mentally Disabled Persons: Hopeless Oxymoron or Path to Redemption?* 1 PSYCHOL., PUB. POL'Y & L. 80, 84–118 (1995).

[243]*Olmstead,* 119 S. Ct. at 2191. On the impact of "litigaphobia" (fear of litigation) on mental disability law jurisprudence, *see,* for example, Michael L. Perlin, Tarasoff *and the Dilemma of the Dangerous Patient: New Directions for the 1990's,* 16 LAW & PSYCHOL. REV. 29, 61–62 (1992).

subsequent failure to self-medicate in community settings, an argument that resonates in the current debate over involuntary outpatient commitment laws that premise community treatment on medication compliance.[244] It can be expected that these arguments of Justice Kennedy's will be as much a factor in the subsequent debate on community treatment questions as will Justice Ginsburg's majority opinion.

In short, *Olmstead* has the capacity to be a truly transformative ADA case, and one that may serve as the template for future developments in this area.

Sanism and the ADA

Any analysis of ADA developments must be undertaken contextually in light of the role of sanism and pretextuality. The "direct threat" language in the ADA[245] is a potential laboratory for sanist and pretextual experimentation.[246] What sort of behavior will allegedly pose such a threat? If an employee starts to discuss obscure political conspiracies, is that a threat? If an individual taking psychotropic medication develops side effects that create an agitated or a "zombie-like" condition, is that a threat? If an employee appears to be fixated with, say, frogs or turtles, and talks to customers about their importance to the world, is that a threat? To what extent can we expect that employers will tolerate[247] "aberrant" behavior on the part of workers? Let one local news station pick up a story that a group of schoolchildren stopped going to a downtown luncheonette because an employee was "acting odd," and that anecdote will become the centerpiece of the next debate on amending the ADA.

If the plain language of the ADA conflicts with what trial judges think is best for mentally disabled persons, will judges enter pretextual decisions (and encourage pretextual testimony)? Michael Saks has reported on a trial judge's explanation as to why he has ordered civil commitment of individuals notwithstanding his overt acknowledgment that the state failed to meet its burden of proof; he did so because he felt compelled "to do what [he thought] was right."[248] Should we expect judges to be less pretextual in ADA decision making?[249]

In at least one section, the ADA drafters seem to acknowledge the dangers of pretexts. Although the act explicitly does not restrict the ability of insurance companies to limit mental illness disability benefits,[250] it specifies that this nonrestriction section may not be used as a subterfuge to evade the purposes of either the employment or public accommoda-

---

[244]*See supra* Chapter 4.

[245]*See supra* text accompanying notes 31–32.

[246]*See, e.g.,* EEOC v. Kinney Shoe Corp., 917 F. Supp. 419 (W.D. Va. 1996) (decision to fire employee due to timing of his epileptic seizures was not "unlawful discrimination" under the ADA).

[247]I use the word *tolerate* purposely; it is impossible to assess the ADA's ultimate impact without considering, at least in part, the value of *tolerance. See, e.g.,* Martha Minow, *Putting Up and Putting Down: Tolerance Reconsidered,* 28 Osgoode Hall L.J. 409 (1990); Steven D. Smith, *The Restoration of Tolerance,* 78 Calif. L. Rev. 305 (1990).

[248]Michael Saks, *Expert Witnesses, Nonexpert Witnesses, and Nonwitness Experts,* 14 Law & Hum. Behav. 291, 293 (1990), *discussed in* Michael L. Perlin & Deborah A. Dorfman, *Sanism, Social Science, and the Development of Mental Disability Law Jurisprudence,* 11 Behav. Sci. & L. 47 (1993).

[249]*See, e.g.,* Taylor v. Principal Financial Group, Inc., 93 F.3d 155, 165 (5th Cir. 1996), *reh'g denied,* (1996) (discussing disabilities that are not "open, obvious and apparent); *see also* Julie Odegard, *The Americans With Disabilities Act: Creating "Family Values" for Physically Disabled Parents,* 11 Law & Inequality 533 (1993).

[250]42 U.S.C. § 12201(c)(1) (1990). *Compare* Parker v. Met. Life Ins. Co., 121 F.3d 1006 (6th Cir. 1997), *cert. den.,* 118 S. Ct. 871 (1998) (ADA's prohibition against disability discrimination in public accommodations did not prohibit employer from providing long-term disability plan which contained longer benefits for employees who become disabled due to illness than for those who become disabled due to mental illness).

tions titles.[251] This expectation of pretextual behavior on the part of an industry subject to regulation under this act is both realistic and troubling, because it reflects the extent to which pretexts can color the way we treat persons with mental disability.

The potential superimposition of morality has already been raised explicitly in the floor debate by Senator Helms. His revealing comment—asking about the consequences if an employer's "moral standards" prevent him or her from hiring a manic depressive[252]—reflects the reality that sanist behavior may be seen as moral behavior.[253] Will this lead to a spate of literature suggesting that the ADA be subverted in the same way that psychiatrists have written articles suggesting that strict involuntary civil commitment laws be subverted?[254]

As I have said in numerous other instances in this book, I believe that one of the many reasons why society reacts in different ways toward persons with mental disabilities than it does when it discriminates against other minorities is that the distinguishing characteristics of the latter groups are frequently immutable.[255] With rare exceptions, few people change gender or change race; when individuals change religion, it is generally a voluntary act undertaken with some knowledge of the dimensions and consequences of the decision. On the other hand, each one of us can become mentally ill—and none of us chooses it volitionally. This combination of non-immutability and fear may help explain the level of virulence we often show toward persons with mental disabilities.[256]

---

[251]*Id.*, at § 12201(c); *see generally* Ramage, *supra* note 76; Christopher Jones, *Legislative "Subterfuge"?: Failing to Insure Persons With Mental Illness Under the Mental Health Parity Act and the Americans With Disabilities Act,* 50 VAND. L. REV. 753 (1997).

[252]*See supra* text accompanying note 75.

[253]*See, e.g.,* Adrienne Higel, *Sexual Exclusions: The Americans With Disabilities Act as a Moral Code,* 94 COLUM. L. REV. 1451 (1994); Deborah K. Dallmann, *The Lay View of What "Disability" Means Must Give Way to What Congress Says It Means: Infertility as a "Disability" Under the Americans With Disabilities Act,* 38 WM. & MARY L. REV. 371, 395(1996), discussing factual backdrop of Pacourek v. Inland Steel Co., 858 F. Supp. 1393 (N.D. Ill. 1994):

> Ms. Pacourek alleged that in 1992, an Inland manager, Thomas Wides, "verbally abused [her] concerning her pregnancy related condition by expressing doubt as to her ability to become pregnant and her ability to combine pregnancy and her career." She claimed that she was "treated like she had an infectious disease" and that one top-level manager told her, "I don't give a damn about the law. I only care about Inland Steel. If God had wanted you to have children, . . . he would have given them to you." (footnotes omitted).

[254]*See generally* Perlin, *supra* note 1, and 1 PERLIN, *supra* note 5, § 2A–7.1, at 186–88 (2d ed. 1998), citing and discussing, *inter alia,* Paul Chodoff, *The Case for Involuntary Hospitalization of the Mentally Ill,* 133 AM. J. PSYCHIATRY 496, 501 (1976); Paul Chodoff, *Involuntary Hospitalization of the Mentally Ill as a Moral Issue,* 141 AM. J. PSYCHIATRY 384, 388 (1984); William McCormick, *Involuntary Commitment in Ontario: Some Barriers to the Provision of Proper Care,* 124 CAN. MED. ASS'N J. 715, 717 (1981).

On efforts to limit the ADA's protections to the "truly disabled," see, for example, Overton v. Tar Heel Farm Credit, 942 F. Supp. 1066, 1068 (E.D.N.C. 1996), relying on the language of Forrisi v. Bowen, 794 F.2d 931, 934 (4th Cir. 1986), a pre-ADA case; *cf.* Robert Hammel, *Some Reflections on New York City's Disability Law,* 23 FORDHAM URB. L.J. 1195, 1216 (1996) (local human rights law should be limited to protect only the "seriously disabled"). Hammel is responded to carefully, thoughtfully, and persuasively in Janet Eriv, *Persistent Misconceptions: A Response to Robert Hammel,* 23 FORDHAM URB. L.J. 1219 (1996).

[255]*Cf.* United States v. Cohen, 733 F.2d 128, 134–35 (D.C. Cir. 1985) (Scalia, J.) (rejecting immutability argument in equal protection challenge to constitutionality of postinsanity acquittal commitment statute), discussed in James Wilson, *Constraints of Power: The Constitutional Opinions of Judges Scalia, Bork, Posner, Easterbrook and Winter,* 40 U. MIAMI L. REV. 1171, 1198–99 (1986).

[256]On the way that public fears about the purported link between mental illness and dangerousness "drive the formal laws and policies governing mental disability jurisprudence," see John Monahan, *Mental Disorder and Violent Behavior: Perceptions and Evidence,* 47 AM. PSYCHOLOGIST 511, 511 (1992). On the ways that stereotypes pervade our views of persons with disabilities, see Alan H. Macurdy, *The Americans With Disabilities Act: Time for Celebration, or Time for Caution?,* 1 PUB. INT'L L.J. 21, 32–34 (1991).

The ADA floor debate on this question of the nonimmutability of mental illness was illuminating. Senator Armstrong made this point graphically in his arguments on behalf of a narrowed law: "A person is or is not a man or a woman, A person is or is not a Catholic, a Jew, a Mormon, whatever. . . . That is something we can readily determine. A person either is or is not Irish, Italian and so on. This bill proceeds from an entirely different point of view. . . ."[257]

On the other hand, Senator Domenici, a cosponsor and ardent supporter, used the same information in an entirely different context: "It is very simple to say that it is only a matter of sex discrimination and perhaps race, and perhaps religion, as some have suggested. Those are easy ones. But they just scratch the surface in terms of the suffering that goes on in the lives of people who are assumed disabled because of some of the niches that they are put in, especially when it comes to serious mental illness. . . ."[258]

Our discomfort and lack of clarity as to who, exactly, *is* disabled and who is not is, at base, sanist. Just as we wish to be able to categorize individuals in the criminal law as sane or insane, competent or incompetent,[259] we wish for a real world without tinges and shades of gray, especially on the question of who is mentally disabled for purposes of an act such as the ADA.

The ADA, if enforced, makes us abandon sanist stereotypes in this area of the law.[260] It makes us reject presumptions of incompetence, broadly drawn nonindividualized pictures of mentally disabled persons, and policy rationales that are premised on prejudice and bias. The ADA, if enforced, gives institutional plaintiffs a litigational vehicle to bring some coherence to the state–federal morass in right-to-refuse-treatment law and to seek to force courts to confront issues about personal autonomy and sexuality that judges have been all too happy to avoid for years.

Olmstead provides some powerful antisanist ammunition. Its focuses on the ravages of isolation—and its linkage of that isolation to the perpetuation of stereotypes, stigma, and the diminution of everyday life—is the Supreme Court's strongest language yet in a majority opinion that implicitly acknowledges the corrosive impact of sanist behavior. On the other hand, there may be reason for concern in *Olmstead's* willingness to be deferent to institutional professionals.[261] The history of institutional treatment of persons with mental disabilities is, to be charitable, a checkered one.[262] By no means is it at all clear that the shock-the-conscience scenarios uncovered in cases ranging from *Wyatt v. Stickney*[263] to *Halderman v. Pennhurst State School and Hospital*[264] are all mere historical artifacts.[265] The

---

[257]135 CONG. REC. S10765–86 (Sept. 7, 1989), 1989 WL 183216 (remarks of Senator Armstrong).

[258]*Id.* at *112 (remarks of Senator Domenici).

[259]*See generally* Perlin, *supra* note 76. On the multiple meanings of competency, see generally, Bruce Winick, *Competency to Consent to Voluntary Hospitalization: A Therapeutic Jurisprudence Analysis of* Zinermon v. Burch, *in* ESSAYS IN THERAPEUTIC JURISPRUDENCE 83, 102–05 (David Wexler & Bruce Winick eds. 1991) (ESSAYS). For an illustrative case, see Koehler v. State. 830 S.W. 2d 665 (Tex. App. 1992), *rev. denied* (1992) (determination of incompetence to manage one's own affairs not a *prima facie* showing of incompetency to stand trial).

[260]*See, e.g.,* PETER BLANCK, THE AMERICANS WITH DISABILITIES ACT AND THE EMERGING WORKFORCE: EMPLOYMENT OF PEOPLE WITH MENTAL RETARDATION 59–60 (1998); Peter Blanck, *Civil Rights, Learning Disability, and Academic Standards,* 2 J. GENDER, RACE & JUST. 33, 53–54 (1998) (specifically linking sanism to ADA inquiries).

[261]It is not at all clear how it is to be determined if the judgment is reflective of "reasonable assessments of [the state's] own professionals" Olmstead v. L.C., 119 S. Ct. 2176 (1999).

[262]*See, e.g.,* 2 PERLIN, *supra* note 5, Chapter 3A (2d. ed. 1999).

[263]Wyatt v. Stickney, 325 F. Supp. 781 (M.D. Ala. 1971); *see generally* 2 PERLIN, *supra* note 5, §§ 3A-3.1 to 3A-3.2d (2d. ed. 1999).

[264]446 F. Supp. 1295 (E.D. Pa. 1977); *see generally* 2 PERLIN, *supra* note 5, §§ 7.10–7.12.

[265]*E.g.,* Wyatt by and through Rawlings v. Rogers, 985 F. Supp. 1356 (M.D. Ala. 1997); *see generally* 2 PERLIN, *supra* note 5, § 3A-3.1, at 29 n. 184 (2d. ed. 1999).

potential for pretexts is real and is worthy of careful scrutiny in the next inevitable generation of *Olmstead*-like cases.

At least three other concerns flow from the other *Olmstead* opinions. As I have already suggested, Justice Kennedy's endorsement of Fuller Torrey's florid description of deinstitutionalization as a "Titanic-like" disaster[266] may (perhaps unwittingly) serve to frame the continuing debate as to the success and failures of differing approaches to deinstitutionalization. The pages of journals such as *American Psychologist* or *Psychiatric Services* are regularly filled with reports of successful deinstitutionalization programs that have "worked";[267] Fuller Torrey's vivid heuristic should not serve to preempt the terms of this important debate.

Next, Kennedy's connection between deinstitutionalization and refusals to take medication is perplexing on two independent levels. Concurring in 1992 in *Riggins v. Nevada*,[268] Kennedy wrote eloquently about the dangers of drug side effects, dangers that so worried him that he concluded he would not allow the use of antipsychotic medications to make a defendant competent to stand trial absent an "extraordinary showing," a showing he doubted was possible to make "given our present understanding of the properties of these drugs."[269] None of these concerns is present in his *Olmstead* opinion. This is even more surprising given the attention paid by the Court to antipsychotic drug side effects in *Sutton v. United Air Lines*.[270] In *Sutton* (an opinion joined by Justice Kennedy), the Court discussed—*in dicta*—the fact that "antipsychotic drugs can cause a variety of adverse effects, including neuroleptic malignant syndrome, and painful seizures."[271] Again, there is no reference to this in Kennedy's *Olmstead* concurrence.

Finally, both Justice Kennedy and Justice Thomas speculate about the possibility of state-motivated improper release as a result of a fear of litigation. This assumes a major fact not in evidence: that competent, qualified counsel is widely available to represent institutionalized persons in such litigation.[272] This fear—certainly related to the critique that has scapegoated patients' rights lawyers as the villain in the deinstitutionalization movement[273]—is a potentially pernicious one, and must be rebutted carefully by responsible advocates who provide legal services to persons with mental disabilities.

---

[266]*Olmstead,* 119 S. Ct. at 2191.

[267]*See, e.g.,* 2 PERLIN, *supra* note 5, § 7.02, at 211 n.26 (1998 Cum. Supp.).

[268]504 U.S. 127 (1992); *see* 2 PERLIN, *supra* note 5, § 3B-8.3, at 323-39 (2d. ed. 1999).

[269]*Riggins,* 504 U.S. at 139; *see supra* Chapter 6.

[270]119 S. Ct. 2139, (1999).

[271]*Id.* at 2147.

[272]*See* Michael L. Perlin, *Fatal Assumption: A Critical Evaluation of the Role of Counsel in Mental Disability Cases,* 16 LAW & HUM. BEHAV. 39 (1992).

[273]Nurtured by radical psychiatrists (such as Thomas Szasz and R.D. Laing), spurred on by politically-activist organizations pushing egalitarian social agendas (such as the ACLU), a cadre of brilliant but diabolical patients' rights lawyers dazzled sympathetic and out-of-touch judges with their legal legerdemain—abetted by wooly-headed social theories, inapposite constitutional arguments, some oh-my-god worst-case anecdotes about institutional conditions, and a smattering of "heartwarming, successful [deinstitutionalization] cases"—as a result of which courts entered orders "emptying out the mental institutions" so that patients could "die with their rights on." When cynical bureaucrats read the judicial handwriting on the hospital walls, they then joined the stampede, and the hospitals were thus emptied. Ergo deinstitutionalization. Ergo homelessness. Endgame.
Michael L. Perlin, *Book Review,* 8 N.Y.L. SCH. J. HUM. RTS. 557, 559–60 (1991) (reviewing ANN JOHNSON, OUT OF BEDLAM: THE TRUTH ABOUT DEINSTITUTIONALIZATION (1990)).

Conclusion

Olmstead was limited to the question of community-based treatment. But the applicability of the ADA to other institutional issues is potentially far broader. The ADA's legislative history gives powerful ammunition to advocates who seek to confront the attitudinal biases at the roots of policies that govern such complicated and contentious issues as patients' rights to sexual interaction[274] and to refuse antipsychotic medication.[275] It gives advocates an opportunity to articulate the sanist bases of policies that presume that psychiatric patients—by reason of their institutionalization—cannot enter into autonomous decision making in the areas of sexual choice and medication refusal. The MacArthur Network data[276] tells us that psychiatric patients are not necessarily more incompetent than nonmentally ill persons to engage in independent medication decision making; there is no evidence that study of sexual decision making would yield statistically significant differing results. In short, the ADA may be a strong tool to combat sanism and pretextuality in these areas of mental disability law as well. The coming months—and years—will tell us whether its potential promise will be fulfilled.

---

[274]*See* Douglas Mossman, Michael L. Perlin, & Deborah A. Dorfman, *Sex on the Wards: Conundra for Clinicians,* 25 J. AM. ACAD. PSYCHIATRY & L. 441, 455–58, app. A (1997) (setting out model policy). *See supra* Chapter 7.

[275]*See supra* Chapter 6.

[276]*See supra* 2 PERLIN, *supra* note 5, § 3B-14.5, at 373-75 (2d. ed. 1999).

Chapter 9
THE COMPETENCE TO PLEAD GUILTY AND THE COMPETENCE TO WAIVE COUNSEL

The public and the media rarely show interest in Supreme Court decisions in mental disability law cases. Both are intensely interested in cases involving famous litigants or victims in which mental disability is an issue (John Hinckley being the most celebrated case) or in which an individual mentally disabled person's case is seen as somehow emblematic of a flawed social policy (the sagas of Larry Hogue, and before that, Billie Boggs, known also as Joyce Brown, on the Upper West Side of New York City being two provocative examples).[1] If the Supreme Court were to decide, for instance, that involuntary civil commitment was unconstitutional (which is highly unlikely) or that the use of the insanity defense was unconstitutional (which is impossible), such stories might conceivably be the lead articles on the front page of the *New York Times* or the *Washington Post*. But other cases generally pass with little attention, unless—as in the zoning cases of *City of Cleburne v. Cleburne Living Center*[2] or the subsequent *City of Edmonds v. Oxford House*—[3] there are wide implications beyond the narrower world of mental disability law.

And so it was when the Supreme Court decided *Godinez v. Moran* in the spring of 1993.[4] By that time, the Supreme Court had, for more than a decade, been fascinated with the interplay between mental disability and the criminal trial process.[5] It had issued a lengthy series of decisions dealing with such issues as the privilege against self-incrimination, the interplay between competency and the death penalty, the right of an at-trial insanity defendant to refuse the imposition of antipsychotic medications, the application of the right to refuse treatment to convicted prisoners, the constitutionality of state laws allowing for the continued retention of insanity acquittees who are no longer mentally ill, the constitutionality of state laws allowing for the retention of insanity acquittees for longer periods of time than the maximum to which they could have been sentenced had they been convicted of the underlying charges, the allocation of the burden of proof at an incompetency-to-stand-trial proceeding, and more.[6] Few drew much attention (except perhaps for those involving insanity acquittees, and there the attention was primarily collateral to the facts of the Hinckley case). And *Godinez* was another in this series.

---

[1]*See, e.g., In re* Boggs, 522 N.Y.S.2d 407 (Supp.), *rev'd*, 523 N.Y.S.2d 71 (App. Div. 1987); Seltzer v. Hogue, 594 N.Y.S.2d 781 (App. Div. 1993). The *Boggs* case is discussed in Sherry Colb, *The Three Faces of Evil*, 86 GEO. L. J. 677, 717–718 (1998) (book review of ELYN SAKS WITH STEPHEN BEHNKE, JEKYLL ON TRIAL: MULTIPLE PERSONALITY DISORDER & CRIMINAL LAW (1997)). The *Hogue* case is discussed in Anthony Klapper, *Finding a Right in State Constitutions for Community Treatment of the Mentally Ill*, 142 U. PA. L. REV. 739, 741 (1993).

[2]473 U.S. 432 (1985) (striking down restrictive zoning ordinance).

[3]514 U.S. 725 (1995) (municipal zoning code's definition of a ''family'' not a maximum-occupancy restriction exempt from Federal Fair Housing Act Amendments banning discrimination against disabled persons).

[4]509 U.S. 389 (1993).

[5]*See generally* Michael L. Perlin, *The Supreme Court, the Mentally Disabled Criminal Defendant, and Symbolic Values: Random Decisions, Hidden Rationales, or Doctrinal Abyss?* 29 ARIZ. L. REV. 1 (1987).

[6]*See, e.g.,* Estelle v. Smith, 451 U.S. 454 (1981); Ford v. Wainwright, 477 U.S. 399 (1986); Penry v. Lynaugh, 492 U.S. 302 (1989); Riggins v. Nevada, 504 U.S. 127 (1992); Washington v. Harper, 494 U.S. 210 (1990); Foucha v. Louisiana, 504 U.S. 71 (1992); Jones v. United States, 463 U.S. 354 (1983); Medina v. California, 505 U.S. 437 (1992); *see generally* MICHAEL L. PERLIN, LAW AND MENTAL DISABILITY chap. 4 (1994).

In *Godinez,* the Supreme Court, per Justice Thomas and over an impassioned dissent by Justice Blackmun, held that the standard for determining a defendant's competency to plead guilty or to waive counsel was the same as the standard used to determine his or her competency to stand trial.[7] The decision reversed a Ninth Circuit finding that the former inquiries were to be more searching and that they obligated the trial judge to determine whether the defendant had the capacity for "reasoned choice" among the alternatives offered to him or her, a capacity that would require "a higher level of mental functioning than that required to stand trial."[8] A unitary competency finding in criminal cases was all that was constitutionally required, the Supreme Court ruled, concluding that there was "no basis for demanding a higher level of competence" for defendants who chose to plead guilty or waive counsel.[9]

At the time, *Godinez* was seen as yet another Supreme Court criminal procedure victory for prosecutors and as a means of ensuring both more convictions and fewer appellate reversals of convictions. If all that was required was a finding that the defendant could meet the incompetency-to-stand-trial test of *Dusky v. United States* (that the defendant had a "rational understanding of the proceedings"),[10] then it would be likely that more mentally ill but legally competent defendants would plead guilty and would waive counsel. In both instances, more convictions—convictions now nearly impervious (on these grounds, at least) on appeal—would flow.

Godinez has inspired surprisingly little critical commentary. A few student notes critiqued it (though others praised it); a piece by forensic psychiatrist Alan Felthous carefully analyzed it and found it wanting.[11] Yet compared to the outpouring of commentary that followed the decisions in *Riggins v. Nevada* (on the right of the insanity pleader to refuse medication at trial)[12] or *Foucha v. Louisiana* (on the constitutionality of statutes allowing the continued retention of no longer mentally ill insanity acquittees),[13] the decision virtually passed without notice.[14]

This, in retrospect, should probably not have been surprising. The public's obsession with the use of the insanity defense is matched by its profound disinterest in the role of incompetency in the criminal trial process.[15] There are reasons for this: Although incompetency is raised in far more cases than is the insanity defense, courts rarely find defendants to

---

[7]*Godinez,* 509 U.S. at 397–98. *See generally* MICHAEL L. PERLIN, MENTAL DISABILITY LAW: CIVIL AND CRIMINAL (1989), §§ 14.20A–14.21 (1998 Cum. Supp.).

[8]Moran v. Godinez, 972 F.2d 263, 266–67 (9th Cir. 1992), rev'd, 509 U.S. 389 (1993).

[9]*Godinez,* 509 U.S. at 397–98.

[10]362 U.S. 402, 402 (1960), quoted in *Godinez,* 509 U.S. at 398.

[11]*See, e.g.,* Luke Vadas, Note, Godinez v. Moran: *An Insane Rule for Competency?* 39 LOY. L. REV. 903 (1994) (*Godinez* leaves "unprotected the basic due process rights of mentally ill criminal defendants"); Brian Boch, Note, *Fourteenth Amendment—The Standard of Mental Competency to Waive Constitutional Rights Versus the Competency Standard to Stand Trial,* 84 J. CRIM. L. & CRIMINOLOGY 883, 883 (1994) (*Godinez* "correct[]" decision); Alan Felthous, *The Right to Represent Oneself Incompetently: Competency to Waive Counsel and Conduct One's Own Defense Before and After* Godinez, 18 MENT. & PHYS. DIS. L. REP. 105, 110 (1994) (in *Godinez* Supreme Court "missed an opportunity to promote reason, logic, and justice in American jurisprudence"); *see also* Sheila Taub, *Competency Standard Clarified,* NAT'L L. J., Oct. 18, 1993, at 25 (majority decision in *Godinez* "appears to be contrary to much professional opinion, both legal and medical, and to prevailing trends in the law").

[12]504 U.S. 127 (1992). See articles cited in 2 PERLIN, *supra* note 7, § 3B-8.3 at 329 n.1354 (2d. ed. 1999).

[13]504 U.S. 71 (1992). *See* 2 PERLIN, *supra* note 7, § 15.25A, at 537–39 n.479.46 (1998 Cum. Supp.).

[14]A search of the NEXIS/CURNWS database in LEXIS revealed not a single contemporaneous newspaper editorial commenting on the decision. The only contemporary law review commentary has been the articles cited *supra* note 11.

[15]*See generally* MICHAEL L. PERLIN, THE JURISPRUDENCE OF THE INSANITY DEFENSE 3–4 (1994); *see also* 3 PERLIN, *supra* note 7, § 14.02, at 206–07 n.1.

be incompetent.[16] When they do, prosecution is usually simply deferred (with the defendant in pretrial custody) until the defendant regains his or her competency to stand trial;[17] if it is unlikely that the defendant will regain such competency in the "foreseeable future" (a category reserved for the most seriously mentally impaired), it is most likely that he or she will be committed to a secure forensic hospital for a lengthy stay (in many cases, a lifetime commitment).[18] In such cases, defendants may very well simply fade away from public consciousness. Defendants in this category rarely are the type of defendants who commit the highly publicized acts that have generated controversy over the insanity debate.[19] In short, the public has never been terribly interested in this area of the law, an apathy usually shared by the press and other media.

The arrest and trial of Colin Ferguson, however, focused national attention on this question. Even without the issues that are central to this chapter, Ferguson's case had all the high cards of a media circus: a mass murder on a New York City commuter train by an African American defendant who sought out White victims as his targets.[20] When the level of Ferguson's mental illness became clear, the picture was complete. And public attention was intensified when Ferguson—relying (implicitly, at least) on *Godinez*—chose to represent himself at his trial and chose specifically to disavow an insanity defense (based on a purported "Black rage" theory) proposed by his lawyers, the high-profile William Kunstler and an associate.[21] The spectacle of a highly intelligent but seriously mentally ill defendant opening to the jury, doing direct and cross-examination of witnesses and victims, and entering evidentiary objections struck onlookers as yet another argument for the widely held view (endorsed by many) that the American judicial system was flawed beyond repair.[22]

And yet public attitudes toward the Ferguson trial were dramatically different from those toward other mentally ill defendants. In other cases, insanity pleaders were seen as shamming, malingering, pulling the wool over the courts' eyes, and so on.[23] The fact that Ferguson was allowed to represent himself—and his failure to enter an insanity plea—was seen as a charade, a travesty of justice, or a sham.[24] In other such cases, lawyers are regularly pilloried for their "sleazy" tactics in promoting mental state defenses (and once in a lifetime cases such as the alleged use of the "twinkie" defense in the Dan White case are discussed as if the use of such a plea is common;[25] the lack of counsel in *Ferguson*—even a counsel so regularly vilified by the public as Kunstler—was seen as, for want of a better phrase, utterly crazy.[26] In short, Ferguson's use of Justice Thomas's majority opinion in *Godinez* (in one of the many ironies of this case, Ferguson has likened himself to Thomas, as another victim of a

---

[16]Bruce Winick, *Restructuring Competency to Stand Trial*, 32 UCLA L. REV. 921, 922 n.3, 925 (1985).

[17]*See generally id.* at 921–31.

[18]*See* Jackson v. Indiana, 406 U.S. 715 (1972).

[19]*But see* Henry Steadman et al., *Maintenance of an Insanity Defense Under Montana's "Abolition" of the Insanity Defense*, 146 AM. J. PSYCHIATRY 357 (1989) (after Montana abolished its insanity defense, the ultimate effect was that courts found more defendants who would likely been previously found not guilty by reason of insanity (NGRI) to be incompetent to stand trial, and committed them to the same forensic maximum security facilities to which NGRI acquittees were previously sent).

[20]DeWayne Wickham, *Line Between Justice, Revenge*, GANNET NEWS SERVICE, Feb. 2, 1995.

[21]David Van Bieman, *A Fool for a Client*, TIME, Feb. 6, 1995, at 66.

[22]Larry McShane, *Ferguson's Defense of Himself May Be Grounds for Appeal*, AMERICAN-STATESMAN, Feb. 19, 1995, (Austin, TX), at A9.

[23]PERLIN, *supra* note 15, at 111–12.

[24]McShane, *supra* note 22.

[25]PERLIN, *supra* note 15.

[26]McShane, *supra* note 22.

"high-tech lynching")[27] caused the public to reverse—almost completely—many of the sanist attitudes that are regularly invoked in infamous cases involving mentally disabled criminal defendants.[28]

Why is this? And what are the implications for the development of mental disability law, for the criminal trial process in general, for the ways that competence is assessed, and for the way we generally construct mental disability? Does Ferguson's case truly hoist Thomas by his own petard? And what can we make of the public's astonishing about-face (relating to its attitudes toward mental status defenses and the role of counsel in the criminal trial process) in this case?

First I will discuss the *Godinez* case and place it in the context of earlier incompetency-to-stand-trial case law. Then I will discuss the Ferguson case in the context of *Godinez* and consider how some of the hidden factors in *Godinez* may be illuminated by the outcome of the Ferguson trial. After that I will consider the public attitudes toward the Ferguson trial and try to read those attitudes in the contexts of what we know about both sanism and pretextuality. I conclude that the conduct of the Ferguson trial was inevitable after the *Godinez* decision, and that, in the end, the criminal trial process was seriously robbed of its needed dignity.

The *Godinez* Case

The Trial

James Ellis and Ruth Luckasson have appropriately characterized the issue of assessing the competence of guilty pleas entered by mentally disabled defendants as presenting "one of the most difficult doctrinal and practical problems faced by the criminal justice system," a difficulty reflected in the "sharply divided" case law that has developed in this area.[29] Before *Godinez*,[30] courts traditionally had recognized that the standard for competence to plead guilty is generally higher than for other sorts of consent or waiver.[31] However, courts had split on the significant question of whether the standard to plead guilty is the same as, higher than, or otherwise different from the traditional standard for assessing competence to stand trial—for example, whether the defendant has "sufficient present ability to consult with his lawyer with a reasonable degree of understanding—and whether he has a rational as well as factual understanding of the proceedings against him."[32]

The majority view had held that there is no substantial difference, and that the same test applies in assessing the validity of a guilty plea.[33] Most of these decisions were merely

---

[27]Maureen Fan, *Ferguson Speaks: In Interview, Reiterates His Innocence,* Newsday (Nassau- Suffolk Ed.), Mar. 17, 1995, at A6.

[28]*See generally* Michael L. Perlin, *The ADA and Persons With Mental Disabilities: Can Sanist Attitudes Be Undone?* 8 J.L. & HEALTH 15 (1993–94).

[29]James Ellis & Ruth Luckasson, *Mentally Retarded Criminal Defendants,* 53 GEO. WASH. L. REV. 414, 460 (1985); *see generally* 3 PERLIN, *supra* note 7, § 14.20, at 265–69.

[30]This section is generally adapted from Michael L. Perlin, *A Major Step Backwards: Deciphering* Godinez v. Moran, 2 CRIM. PRAC. L. REP. 89 (1994); PERLIN, *supra* note 6, § 4.13; PERLIN, *supra* note 7, §§ 14.20A–14.21 (1998 Cum. Supp.).

[31]Ellis & Luckasson, *supra* note 29 § 461.

[32]*Dusky v. United States,* 362 U.S. 402, 402 (1960); *see generally* PERLIN, *supra* note 7, § 14.20, at 459–60 n.317.1 (1998 Cum. Supp.) (listing recent cases).

[33]*See, e.g.,* Malinauskas v. United States, 505 F.2d 649 (5th Cir. 1974); Stinson v. Wainwright, 710 F.2d 743 (11th Cir.), *cert. denied,* 464 U.S. 984 (1983); United States *ex rel.* McGough v. Hewitt, 528 F.2d 339 (3d Cir. 1975); Williams v. Bordenkircher, 696 F.2d 464 (6th Cir.), *cert. denied,* 461 U.S. 916 (1983); People v. Turner, 443 N.E.2d 1167 (Ill. App. 1982); State *ex rel.* Kessick v. Bordenkircher, 294 S.E.2d 134 (W. Va. 1982).

conclusionary and bereft of any sort of doctrinal analysis. Only in *People v. Heral* did a court offer substantive justifications for the unitary standard: that a finding of competency to stand trial necessarily involved a finding that a defendant was capable of waiving his or her constitutional rights and a dual standard might create "a class of semi-competent defendants who are not protected from prosecution because they have been found competent to stand trial, but who are denied the leniency of the plea bargaining process because they are not competent to plead guilty."[34]

This position was challenged, however, by a series of cases involving both mentally ill[35] and mentally retarded[36] defendants. These cases suggested a separate test: "A defendant is not competent to plead guilty if a mental [disability] has substantially impaired his ability to make a reasoned choice among the alternatives presented to him and to understand the consequences of his plea."[37] Such a test has been used by those courts that find it necessary for judges to "assess a defendant's competency *with specific reference to the gravity of the decisions* with which the defendant is faced,"[38] a decision applauded by Ellis and Luckasson.[39] The rationale for this more stringent standard was that a simple finding of trial competency was not a sufficient basis for finding that the defendant was able to "make [other] decisions of very serious import."[40]

On the question of waiver of counsel, a significant amount of case law had also developed over the question of the level of competency required for a defendant to waive representation by counsel. Since the U.S. Supreme Court's ruling in *Faretta v. California,*[41] holding that defendants have a federal constitutional right to represent themselves if they voluntarily elect to do so, courts have focused on the question of whether defendants have "the *mental capacity to waive the right to counsel* with a realization of the probable risks and consequences of [their] action."[42]

To meet such a standard, it is not necessary that defendants be technically competent to represent themselves but only that they be "free of mental disorder which would so impair his free will that his decision to waive counsel would not be voluntary."[43] To this end, neither bizarre statements and actions,[44] mere eccentric behavior,[45] nor a finding that the defendant had been diagnosed as a paranoid schizophrenic[46] have been found in specific cases to be enough to establish lack of capacity to represent one's self.

On the other hand, waiver of counsel should be "carefully scrutinized,"[47] and the record must reflect that "the accused was offered counsel and knowingly and intelligently

---

[34]342 N.E.2d 34, 37 (Ill. 1976), citing Comment, *Competence to Plead Guilty: A New Standard,* 1974 DUKE L. J. 149, 170.

[35]Seiling v. Eyman, 478 F.2d 211 (9th Cir. 1973); Steinsvik v. Vinzant, 640 F.2d 949 (9th Cir. 1981); State v. Walton, 228 N.W.2d 21 (Iowa 1975).

[36]*See* United States v. Masthers, 539 F.2d 721 (D.C. Cir. 1976).

[37]*Seiling,* 478 F.2d at 215; *see also* Schoeller v. Dunbar, 423 F.2d 1183, 1194 (9th Cir. 1970).

[38]*Seiling,* 478 F.2d at 215.

[39]Ellis & Luckasson, *supra* note 29, at 462–63.

[40]*Seiling,* 478 F.2d at 214–15.

[41]422 U.S. 806, 835 (1975).

[42]People v. Clark, 213 Cal. Rptr. 837, 840 (Cal. App. 1985) (emphasis in original); *see generally* 3 PERLIN, *supra* note 7, § 14.21, at 269–74. *But see In re* Irwin, 529 N.W.2d 366, 371 (Minn. 1995) (patient in psychopathic personality commitment case had no right to self-representation).

[43]Curry v. Superior Court of Fresno County , 141 Cal. Rptr. 884, 888 (Cal. App. 1977).

[44]People v. Miller, 167 Cal. Rptr. 816, 818 (Cal. App. 1980).

[45]*Curry,* 141 Cal. Rptr. at 888.

[46]State v. Evans, 610 P.2d 35 (Ariz. 1980).

[47]People v. Kessler, 447 N.E.2d 495, 499 (Ill. App. 1983), citing People v. Heral, 342 N.E.2d 34, 37–38 (Ill. App. 1982).

refused the offer."[48] The court is required to conduct "more than a routine inquiry when making that determination."[49] At least several courts have found that the standard for self-representation is a higher one than the standard for competency to stand trial,[50] because "literacy and a basic understanding over and above the competence to stand trial may be required."[51]

A New Jersey intermediate appellate court has thus recently considered the full range of pertinent issues:

> Without the guiding hand of counsel, a defendant may lose his freedom because he does not know how to establish his innocence. . . . Trained counsel is also necessary to vindicate fundamental rights that receive protection from rules of procedure and exclusionary principles. . . . Where the doctrine supporting these rights "has any complexities the untrained defendant is in no position to defend himself." . . .

> These considerations militate strongly in favor of exercising great caution in determining whether a proposed waiver of counsel satisfies constitutional standards. Within the context of the potential pitfalls of self-representation, it has been said "the court must make certain by direct inquiry on the record that defendant is aware of 'the nature of the charges, the statutory offenses included with them, the range of allowable punishments there under, possible defenses to the charges and circumstances in mitigation thereof, and all other facts essential to a broad understanding of the whole matter.'"[52]

Deconstructing Godinez

The Supreme Court ended both of these controversies in *Godinez,* holding that the standards for pleading guilty and for waiving counsel were no higher than for standing trial: Did the defendant have "sufficient present ability to consult with his lawyer with a reasonable degree of understanding" and a "rational as well as factual understanding of the proceedings against him."[53]

The facts of the *Godinez* case are straightforward. The defendant Moran shot a bartender and a patron and subsequently stole the bar's cash register. Nine days later he went to his former wife's apartment and shot her five times. He then shot himself in the abdomen and attempted (unsuccessfully) to slit his own wrists. All three of his victims died; he confessed to police from his hospital bed two days after shooting his wife.[54] He initially pled not guilty, and was evaluated by a pair of psychiatrists who found him competent to stand trial. Some two and a half months after these evaluations, Moran appeared before the court, seeking to discharge his attorneys and plead guilty, explaining that he wanted to prevent the presentation of mitigating evidence at his sentencing.[55] The court accepted his guilty plea and his waiver of counsel, finding that he could "intelligently and knowingly" waive his right to

---

[48]*Id.*

[49]*Id.* citing People v. Feliciano, 417 N.E. 824 (Ill. App. 1981).

[50]*See, e.g.,* United States *ex rel.* Konigsberg v. Vincent, 526 F.2d 131 (2d Cir. 1975); State v. Kolocotronis, 436 P.2d 774 (Wash. 1968); Pickens v. State, 292 N.W.2d 601 (Wis. 1980); State v. Harding, 670 P.2d 383, 391 (Ariz. 1983),

[51]*Pickens,* 292 N.W.2d at 611, citing Faretta v. California, 422 U.S. 806, 835 (1975).

[52]State v. Slattery, 571 A.2d 1314, 1320–21 (N.J. App. Div. 1990) (citations omitted) (defendant functioned at low-average range of intelligence).

[53]Godinez v. Moran, 509 U.S. 389, 396 (1983), quoting Dusky v. United States, 362 U.S. 402 (1960).

[54]*Godinez,* 509 U.S. at 391.

[55]*Id.* at 392.

assistance of counsel and that his guilty pleas had been "freely and voluntarily" given. He was subsequently sentenced to death by a three-judge court on each of the three murders.[56]

Subsequently, the Nevada Supreme Court affirmed the defendant's sentence for the tavern murders but reversed the sentence for his wife's murder, and remanded for imposition of a life sentence without possibility of parole.[57] Next, Moran filed a petition for postconviction relief in state court, at which the court rejected his claim that he was "mentally incompetent to represent himself."[58] His appeal was dismissed by the state supreme court, and the U.S. Supreme Court denied *certiorari*.[59]

He then filed a federal *habeas* petition that was denied by the district court, but that denial was reversed by the Ninth Circuit Court of Appeals, which concluded that the trial record should have led the trial court to "entertain a good faith doubt about [Moran's] competency to make a voluntary, knowing, and intelligent waiver" and that waiver of constitutional rights required a "higher level of mental functioning than that required to stand trial," a level it characterized as "the capacity for 'reasoned choice.'"[60] In coming to its decision, the court stressed the defendant's suicide attempt, his desire to prevent the presentation of mitigating evidence to the court at his sentencing hearing, his monosyllabic responses to the trial court's questions, and the fact that he was on four different prescription drugs at the time he sought to change his plea and discharge counsel.[61]

The Supreme Court reversed, per Justice Thomas, rejecting the notion that competence to plead guilty or waive counsel must be measured by a higher (or even different) standard from that used in incompetency-to-stand-trial cases.[62] It reasoned that defendants who were found competent to stand trial would have to make a variety of decisions requiring choices: whether to testify, whether to seek a jury trial, whether to cross-examine their accusers, and, in some cases, whether to raise an affirmative defense. Although the decision to plead guilty is a "profound one . . . it is no more complicated than the sum total of decisions that a defendant may be called upon to make during the course of a trial."[63] Finally, the court reaffirmed that any waiver of constitutional rights must be "knowing and voluntary."[64]

It concluded on this point: " Requiring that a criminal defendant be competent has a modest aim: It seeks to ensure that he has the capacity to understand the proceedings and to assist counsel. While psychiatrists and scholars may find it useful to classify the various kinds and degrees of competence, and while States are free to adopt competency standards that are more elaborate than the *Dusky* formulation, the Due Process Clause does not impose these additional requirements."[65]

---

[56]*Id.* at 393.

[57]Moran v. State, 734 P.2d 712 (Nev. 1987).

[58]*Godinez,* 509 U.S. at 392.

[59]Moran v. Warden, 810 P.2d 335 (Nev. 1989), *cert. denied,* 493 U.S. 874 (1989).

[60]Moran v. Godinez, 972 F.2d 263, 265–67 (9th Cir. 1992).

[61]*Id.* at 265, 268.

[62]*Godinez,* 509 U.S. at 398.

On remand, the Ninth Circuit held that although a reasonable judge should have entertained good-faith doubt about the defendant's competence during the change-of-plea hearing, so that failure to hold a competency hearing was violation of due process, that due process violation was cured by a retrospective competency hearing, and the record established that the defendant's waiver of counsel and entry of guilty pleas were voluntary and intelligent. Moran v. Godinez, 57 F.3d 690 (9th Cir. 1995), *cert. denied,* 516 U.S. 976 (1995), *stay denied sub. nom.,* Moran v. McDaniel, 80 F.3d 1261 (9th Cir. 1994).

[63]*Godinez,* 509 U.S. at 398.

[64]*Id.* at 400, quoting Parke v. Raley, 506 U.S. 20, 29 (1992).

[65]*Godinez,* 509 U.S. at 403, citing, in a *cf.* reference, Medina v. California, 505 U.S. 437 (1992) (not unconstitutional to place burden of proof on defendant at competency-to-stand-trial proceeding).

Justices Kennedy and Scalia concurred, noting their concern with those aspects of the opinion that compared the decisions made by a defendant who pleads guilty with those made by one who goes to trial, and expressing their "serious doubts" that there would be a heightened competency standard under the due process clause if these decisions were not equivalent.[66]

Justice Blackmun dissented (for himself and Justice Stevens), focusing squarely on what he argued was the likely potential that Moran's decision to plead guilty was the product of "medication and mental illness."[67] He reviewed the expert testimony about the defendant's state of depression, a colloquy between the defendant and the trial judge in which the court was informed that the defendant was being given medication, the trial judge's failure to inquire further and discover the psychoactive properties of the drugs in question, the defendant's subsequent testimony about the "numbing" state of the drugs, and the "mechanical character" and "ambiguity" of the defendant's answers to the court's questions at the plea stage.[68]

On the question of the multiple meanings of competency, Justice Blackmun added, "The majority cannot isolate the term 'competent' and apply it in a vacuum, divorced from its specific context. A person who is 'competent' to play basketball is not thereby 'competent' to play the violin. The majority's monolithic approach to competency is true to neither life or the law. Competency for one purpose does not necessarily translate to competency for another purpose."[69] He concluded, "To try, convict and punish one so helpless to defend himself contravenes fundamental principles of fairness and impugns the integrity of our criminal justice system. I cannot condone the decision to accept, without further inquiry, the self-destructive 'choice' of a person who was so deeply medicated and who might well have been severely mentally ill."[70]

Justice Blackmun's dissent in *Godinez* is a powerful document that speaks simultaneously to the empirical realities of the criminal trial process, the impact of mental illness and medication on a defendant's capacity for reasoned choice, and perhaps most important, the role of pretextuality in the incompetency-to-stand-trial process.[71] He rejects the formulistic approach of Justice Thomas's majority opinion, weighs the pertinent social science evidence, and demonstrates how the trial record reflects the ambiguity of the controlling colloquy between counsel and the trial judge.

The underlying tensions of the case are exacerbated even further because the defendant had been sentenced to death. The Supreme Court has considered the relationship between

---

[66]*Godinez,* 509 U.S. at 403.

[67]*Id.* at 410.

[68]*Id.; see also id.* at 416 ("'such drugs often possess side effects that may 'compromise the right of a medicated criminal defendant to receive a fair trial . . . by rendering him unable or unwilling to assist counsel,'" quoting Riggins v. Nevada, 504 U.S. 127, 142 (1992) (Kennedy, J., concurring)); *see* 2 PERLIN, *supra* note 7, § 3B-8.3 (2d. ed. 1999); Michael L. Perlin, *Forced Drugging and Fair Trial Rights: Understanding* Riggins v. Nevada, 1 CRIM. PRAC. L. REP. 37 (1993); Michael L. Perlin & Deborah A. Dorfman, *Sanism, Social Science, and the Development of Mental Disability Law Jurisprudence,* 11 BEHAV. SCI. & L. 47 (1993).

The drugs given Moran were primarily antiseizure medications, see *Godinez,* 509 U.S. at 393 n.2; Riggins had been receiving Mellaril, an antipsychotic drug. The fact that different types of drug were involved in the two cases was explored nowhere in any of the *Godinez* opinions.

[69]*Godinez,* 509 U.S. at 413, citing Richard Bonnie, *The Competence of Criminal Defendants: A Theoretical Reformulation,* 10 BEHAV. SCI. & L. 291, 299 (1992); RONALD ROESCH & STEPHEN GOLDING, COMPETENCY TO STAND TRIAL 10–13 (1980).

[70]*Godinez,* 509 U.S. at 414.

[71]*See, e.g.,* Michael L. Perlin, *Pretexts and Mental Disability Law: The Case of Competency,* 47 U. MIAMI L. REV. 625 (1993) (Perlin, *Pretexts*).

mental illness and the competency to be executed,[72] the relationship between mental retardation and the competency to be executed,[73] and has declined to consider on the merits the constitutionality of medicating a defendant to make him competent to be executed.[74] The decision in *Godinez*—virtually guaranteeing less searching inquiries in cases involving defendants of questionable competency—will likely complicate even further this area of mental disability law jurisprudence.[75]

The Court's decision is particularly troubling and perplexing, given its opinion the prior year in *Riggins* in which it had found that involuntary drugging of an insanity-pleading defendant at trial potentially violated that defendant's fair trial rights.[76] In *Riggins*, the Court concluded that because involuntary medication could impair a defendant's ability to "follow the proceedings," "the substance of his communication," and "the content of his testimony,"[77] such drugging would be proscribed unless the state could demonstrate medical appropriateness and that, considering less intrusive alternatives or means, that it was "essential for the sake of [defendant's] own safety or the safety of others" or to obtain an adjudication of the defendant's guilt or innocence.[78]

Moran was receiving such drugs and, as Justice Blackmun underscored in his dissent, the court's perfunctory questions "only augment[ed] the manifold causes for concern by suggesting that his waivers and his assent to the charges against him were not rendered in a truly voluntary and intelligent fashion."[79] Inexplicably, the majority in *Godinez* does not even cite *Riggins*.

Riggins is even more important because of its chronology in the court's refusal-of-medication jurisprudence. It came soon after the court had decided in *Washington v. Harper*[80] that an informal administrative procedure was sufficient to satisfy the refusal of medication rights of a convicted prisoner.[81] The difference between *Harper* and *Riggins* appeared to reflect the different status of the litigants: Harper, a convicted prisoner, and Riggins, a nonconvicted defendant at trial. The decision in *Harper* appeared to reflect an important strand of the court's institutional jurisprudence: that "prison security interests

---

[72]*See* Ford v. Wainwright, 477 U.S. 399 (1986); *see generally* 3 PERLIN, *supra* note 7, § 17.05, at 498–512; *cf.* Douglas Mossman, *The Psychiatrist and Execution Competency: Fording Murky Waters*, 43 CASE W. RES. L. REV. 1 (1992).

[73]*See* Penry v. Lynaugh, 492 U.S. 302 (1989); *see generally* PERLIN, *supra* note 7, § 17.06A (1998 Cum. Supp.).

[74]*See* Perry v. Louisiana, 498 U.S. 38 (1990); *see generally* 3 PERLIN, *supra* note 7, § 17.06B (1998 Cum. Supp.); *cf.* Douglas Mossman, *Denouement of an Execution Case: Is* Perry *Pyrrhic?* 23 BULL. AM. ACAD. PSYCHIATRY & L. 269 (1995).

[75]*See, e.g.*, United States v. Day, 998 F.2d 662 (8th Cir. 1993) (rejecting defendant's claim that the court should have conducted a competency hearing prior to allowing him to proceed pro se); *cf.* State v. Pollard, 657 A.2d 185, 189–90 (Vt. 1995) (construing *Godinez* to reverse trial court order allowing waiver of counsel in case of defendant who did not have "rational" understanding of proceedings): Miles v. Stainer, 108 F.3d. 1109 (9th Cir. 1997) (court's failure to ask defendant whether he has been taking psychotrophic medication prior to entering guilty plea raised reasonable doubt about defendant's competence).

For more recent cases, compare, for example, Government of Virgin Islands v. Charles, 72 F.3d 401 (3d Cir. 1995) (waiver of counsel voluntary), *to* Wilkins v. Bowersox, 933 F. Supp. 1496 (W.D. Mo. 1996) (finding that the petitioner did not knowingly, intelligently, and voluntarily waive his right to counsel); People v. Lego, 660 N.E.2d 971 (Ill. 1995) (same); *Charles*, 72 F.3d at 411 (Lewis, J., concurring).

[76]*Riggins v. Nevada*, 504 U.S. 127, 133–37 (1992). See *supra* Chapter 6.

[77]*Id.* at 137.

[78]*Id.* at 135.

[79]Godinez v. Moran, 509 U.S. 389, 417 (1983).

[80]494 U.S. 210 (1990).

[81]*See generally* 2 PERLIN, *supra* note 7, § 3B-8.2, at 315–16 (2d. ed. 1999).

will, virtually without exception, trump individual autonomy interests.''[82] Yet the potential side effects and other impacts of antipsychotic medications are ignored in *Godinez*, notwithstanding the reality that Moran (like Riggins and unlike Harper) had not yet been convicted at the moment that he entered his plea and discharged his counsel. The *Godinez* opinion is utterly bereft of any analysis of this issue.

In its other major holding, the *Godinez* Court found that there was ''no reason'' to believe that the decision to waive counsel requires an ''appreciably higher level of mental functioning than the decision to waive other constitutional rights.''[83] It rejected the defendant's arguments that a self-representing defendant must have ''greater powers of comprehension, judgment and reason, [*sic*] than would be necessary to stand trial with the aid of an attorney,'' concluding that this rested on a ''flawed premise; the competence that is required of a defendant seeking to waive his right to counsel is the competence to *waive the right,* not the competence to represent himself.''[84] Relying on its decision in *Faretta*,[85] the Court found that a defendant's ability to represent him- or herself ''has no bearing upon his competence to choose self-representation.''[86]

Justice Blackmun's dissented on this point as well, concluding, ''A finding that a defendant is competent to stand trial establishes only that he is capable of aiding his attorney in making the critical decisions required at trial or in plea negotiations. The reliability or even relevance of such a finding vanishes when its basic premise—that counsel will be present—ceases to exist. The question is no longer whether the defendant can proceed with an attorney but whether he can proceed alone and uncounselled.''[87]

The *Ferguson* Case

The Crime and Trial

On December 7, 1993, Colin Ferguson, a 37-year-old native of Jamaica, killed six people and wounded 19 others on a Long Island Rail Road (LIRR) commuter train from New York City as it arrived in Garden City, Long Island.[88] When arrested, Ferguson was found with 150 rounds of ammunition and notes in his pockets suggesting a hatred of Whites and persons of Asian ancestry.[89] Ferguson was originally represented by William Kunstler, a well-known lawyer often associated with unpopular or controversial causes. He fired Kunstler, however, when Kunstler announced that he planned to pursue an insanity defense based on a ''Black rage'' theory: Ferguson, a highly intelligent but mentally disturbed individual who had been raised as ''a child of privilege in his native Jamaica''[90] had been

---

[82]*See id.* at 320; *see generally* Perlin & Dorfman, *supra* note 68.

[83]*Godinez,* 509 U.S. at 398.

[84]*Id.* at 399 (emphasis in original).

[85]Faretta v. California, 422 U.S. 806 (1975); *see supra* text accompanying note 41.

[86]*Godinez,* 509 U.S. at 399.

[87]*Id.* at 411–12.

[88]John T. McQuiston, *In the Bizarre L. I. R. R. Trial, Equally Bizarre Confrontation,* N.Y. TIMES (L.I. edition), Feb. 5, 1995, 13LI at 1.

[89]Bruce Frankel, *Justice ''At Its Worst''/NY Defendant Acts as Lawyer,* USA TODAY, Jan. 27, 1995, at 40.

[90]Sheryl McCarthy, *Ferguson: Madness or Just Manipulation?* NEWSDAY (city edition), Feb. 22, 1995, at 6.

"pushed over the edge into murder by endemic American racism."[91] Ferguson stated he would represent himself and prove—in spite of a staggering number of eyewitnesses[92]—that a White perpetrator stole his gun and commited the shootings in question.[93]

At a pretrial hearing in December 1994, psychologists John D'Alessandro and Allen Reidman testified that Ferguson, although suffering from paranoid personality disorder, was rational and free from delusions.[94] Based on these reports and on his own questioning of the witness, Nassau County Court Judge Donald E. Belfi thus found Ferguson competent to stand trial.[95] This decision appeared totally consistent both with the teachings of *Godinez* and with both pre- and post-*Godinez* New York state decisions[96] that an "articulate, intelligent and rational" defendant such as Ferguson had a constitutional right to represent himself.[97]

At trial, Ferguson opened by telling the jury:

> 93 counts, only because it matches the year 1993. Had it been 1925, it would have been 25 counts. This is a case of stereotype victimization of a Black man and subsequent conspiracy to destroy him.[98]

His conduct of his defense was described aptly by a *Boston Globe* commentator as providing "uniquely creepy television," and, quoting Court TV president Steven Brill, the ultimate triumph of "form over substance."[99]

Ferguson's defense strategies in this case were not always successful: He announced, for example, that he would call as a witness a parapsychologist and exorcist who would testify that government agents had planted a microchip in Ferguson's head and that he had been "lasered out by a remote-control device."[100] During his cross-examination of the

---

[91]Van Bieman, *supra* note 21. *See, e.g.,* Claire Finkelstein, *Duress: A Philosophical Account of the Defense in Law,* 37 ARIZ. L. REV. 251, 280 (1995); J. Thomas Sullivan, *Psychiatric Defenses in Arkansas Criminal Trials,* 48 ARK. L. REV. 439, 454 (1995). The defense was rejected in State v. Lamar, 698 P.2d 735, 741 (Ariz. App. 1984). For a recent discussion of "syndromic defenses" in general, see Stephen Morse, *The "New Syndrome Excuse Syndrome,"* CRIM. JUST. ETHICS (Winter/Spring 1995), at 3.

[92]John T. McQuiston, *Adviser Says L. I. R. R. Suspect Prefers Conviction to Insanity Finding,* N.Y. TIMES, Feb. 10, 1995, at B5.

[93]Wickham, *supra* note 20.

[94]Robin Topping, *Weighing Competence vs. Sanity,* NEWSDAY (Nassau & Suffolk ed.), Feb. 5, 1995, at A6.

[95]*Id.*

[96]*See, e.g.,* People v. Reason, 372 N.Y.S.2d 614, 618 (1975) (determination that defendant was competent to stand trial, coupled with trial judge's "searching inquiry" about whether decision was made "knowingly and intelligently with full awareness of risks and consequences," sufficient to support waiver); People v. Schoolfield, 608 N.Y.S.2d 413, 416–17 (App. Div. 1994) ("A criminal defendant is entitled to be master of his own fate and 'respect for individual autonomy requires that he be allowed to go to jail under his own banner if he so desires and if he makes the choice "with eyes open,"' quoting, in part, from People v. Vivenzio, 477 N.Y.S.2d 318, 319 (App. Div. 1984) (*Godinez* not cited); People v. Meurer, 621 N.Y.S.2d 422, 423–24 (App. Div. 1994) (affirming conviction where, after defendant was found competent to stand trial, trial court found decision to waive was made "knowingly, intelligently and voluntarily with full awareness of the risks and consequences") (*Godinez* not cited).

[97]Topping, *supra* note 94.

[98]Weekend Edition (National Public Radio, Feb. 5, 1995, Transcript #1109-5).

[99]Frederic Biddle, *In Ferguson, TV Gets New Spectacle,* BOSTON GLOBE, Feb. 16, 1995, at 1.

[100]John T. McQuiston, *Commuter Killing Trial Goes to Jury: Ferguson Gives Incoherent Summation,* HOUSTON CHRONICLE (Feb. 17, 1995), at A2. The trial judge refused to allow Ferguson to present this evidence to the jury. For a flavor of other defense tactics, see, for example; Andrew Blum, *LIRR Gunman Goes Pro Se With Perplexing* Voir Dire, NAT'L L. J., Feb. 6, 1995, at A11; John T. McQuiston, *Abrupt End to Defense in Rail Case,* N.Y. TIMES, Feb. 16, 1995, at B1.

The delusion that a microchip has been planted in one's head may be symptomatic of paranoid schizophrenia, raising the question of whether another incompetency to stand trial inquiry should have been made at this point in the proceedings. *See* Drope v. Missouri, 420 U.S. 162 (1971).

ballistics expert, Ferguson asked whether the bullet fragments had been tested for "alcohol or substance abuse."[101]

In his summation—characterized uniformly as "rambling and sometimes incoherent"—he argued that the 19 shooting survivors had conspired with police authorities to convict him.[102] Finally, in his allocution statement at sentencing, he told the court: "Jeffrey Dahmer's death in prison was not coincidence. It was timed just moments before I was given *pro se* status in anticipation of my trial beginning in a matter where it was setting the precedent for my murder in an upstate prison."[103]

Ferguson was convicted on six counts of murder and 22 counts of attempted murder, weapons possession, and reckless endangerment (he was also acquitted on 25 counts of civil rights violations)[104] and was subsequently sentenced to more than 300 years in prison.[105] The observation that Ferguson's courtroom behavior ranged from the "bizarre to the surreal"[106] was never contradicted.

Ferguson *and* Godinez

How, then, does the *Ferguson* trial fit with the Supreme Court's *Godinez* decision? First, it demonstrates precisely how difficult the trial judge's task is in honoring *Godinez's* dictates. As Robin Topping—one of a small handful of trial observer–reporters who understood the link between *Godinez* and the Ferguson trial—pointed out in *Newsday*:

> It's not a simple situation for the judge. [Judge] Belfi has to perform a delicate balancing act. He is legally obligated to take extra precautions to make sure that Ferguson is given a fair trial—especially because he is not a lawyer. He must be careful that Ferguson doesn't disrupt the trial but he has to be equally careful in revoking his right to represent himself lest he, Belfi, be reversed by a higher court.[107]

Ferguson is yet another in a lengthy series of pre- and post-*Godinez* cases concluding that bizarre behavior is not necessarily evidence of incompetency.[108]

Godinez purports to balance fair trial and autonomy issues, concluding that "a criminal defendant's ability to represent himself has no bearing on his competence to choose self-representation."[109] On the other hand, it warns that the waiver of counsel must be "intelligent and voluntary" before it can be accepted.[110]

---

[101]*Court TV,* Tape FER5610104 (Feb. 2, 1995), Log time code 12:50.

[102]John T. McQuiston, *Murder Trial in L. I. R. R. Case Goes to the Jury for Deliberation,* N.Y. TIMES, Feb. 17, 1995, at B1.

[103]*Court TV,* Tape FER5610204 (Feb. 6, 1995), Log time code 11:18.

[104]Diana Rojas, *LIRR Massacre Gunman Convicted of Murder; The Verdict, Guilty; N.J. Family Says Ordeal Not Over,* BERGEN RECORD (NJ), Feb. 18, 1995, at A1.

[105]Maureen Fan, *315 2/3 Years for Ferguson; Protesting to the End, LIRR Killer Sentenced,* NEWSDAY (Nassau & Suffolk ed.), Mar. 23, 1995, at A4.

[106]*Railroad Shooter Telephones Lawyers: Kunstler Willing to Handle Ferguson Process of Appeals,* SPRINGFIELD STATE JOURNAL-REGISTER, Feb. 19, 1995, at 3.

[107]Robin Topping, *Crime and Courts; Law and Order; "The Pitfalls of Self-Representation,"* NEWSDAY (Nassau & Suffolk ed.), Feb. 1, 1995, at A29. Pre-*Godinez* case law on the right of criminal defendants to represent themselves is discussed *supra* note 96.

[108]*E.g.,* State v. Ploof, 649 A.2d 774, 778 (Vt. 1994); Boag v. Raines, 769 F.2d 1341, 1343 (9th Cir. 1985), *cert. denied,* 474 U.S. 1086 (1986); People v. Holma, 450 N.E.2d 432, 435 (Ill. 1983); *see generally* 3 PERLIN, *supra* note 7, § 14.04 at 218–19.

[109]*Godinez,* 509 U.S. at 402.

[110]*Id.*

To what extent was this standard complied with in the *Ferguson* trial? *Godinez* speaks only to questions of *decisional* competency: If the defendant has the capacity to *decide* to waive counsel, then the standard for determining his or her competence to stand trial will suffice. It ignores—fatally, in my view—the other question that is needed to give life to an otherwise sterile and formalistic legal doctrine: Does the defendant have the functional ability to represent him- or herself?[111] This is the question addressed by Justice Blackmun in his dissent, and studiously ignored by Justice Thomas in the majority. It is here that *Godinez* fails and the reason for the *Ferguson* charade becomes apparent: The key question—did Colin Ferguson, truly, have the capacity to conduct his own defense in a meaningful way, to conduct it with dignity—remains unasked.[112]

Godinez is an example of the Supreme Court's willful blindness at its worst. The Court is aware—it must be aware—of the pretextual way that incompetency-to-stand-trial proceedings are frequently conducted.[113] The Court is aware—it must be aware—of the way that incompetent defendants are shuttled back and forth between jail and mental hospital, reflecting frequent changes in their trial-competency status.[114] The Court is aware—it has stated that it is aware—of the potential impact of drug side effects on mentally disabled criminal defendants and the integrity of the trial process.[115] And yet in *Godinez* it blithely brushed all these empirical realities aside and endorsed a minimalistic test that is sure to further sap the integrity of the criminal trial process.

Was Colin Ferguson functionally competent to conduct his own defense?[116] Some guidance may be found in *McKaskle v. Wiggins*.[117] The Supreme Court listed there some of the tasks a *pro se* defendant must be allowed to perform without interference from "standby counsel": to control the organization and content of his own defense, to make motions, to argue points of law, to participate in *voir dire*, to question witnesses, and to address the court

---

[111]Felthous, *supra* note 11, at 105; Taub, *supra* note 11, at 28, 29.

[112]Topping, *supra* note 107. Courts and commentators have regularly discussed "dignity" in a fair trial context both in cases involving mentally disabled criminal defendants and in other settings. *See, e.g.,* Marquez v. Collins, 11 F.3d 1241. 1243 (5th Cir. 1994) ("Solemnity . . . and respect for individuals are components of a fair trial"); Heffernan v. Norris, 48 F.3d 331, 336 (8th Cir. 1995) (Bright, J., dissenting) ("the forced ingestion of mind-altering drugs not only jeopardizes an accused's rights to a fair trial, it also tears away another layer of individual dignity. . . ."); Faretta v. California, 422 U.S. 806, 834 n.46 (1975) ("The rights of self-representation is not a license to abuse the dignity of the courtroom.") Keith Nicholson, *Would You Like Some More Salt in That Wound? Post-Sentence Victim Allocution in Texas,* 26 ST. MARY'S L. J. 1103, 1128 (1995) (for trial to be fair, "it must be conducted in an atmosphere of respect, order, decorum and dignity befitting its importance both to the prosecution and the defense"); Felthous, *supra* note 11, quoting Bruce Ennis & Christopher Hansen, *Memorandum of Law: Competency to Stand Trial,* 4 J. PSYCHIATRY & L. 491, 512 (1976) (one of the four purposes of incompetency to stand trial determination is to "preserve the dignity and integrity of legal processes"); *see also* Tom R. Tyler, *The Psychological Consequences of Judicial Procedures: Implications for Civil Commitment Hearings,* 46 SMU L. REV. 433, 444 (1992) (significance of dignity values in involuntary civil commitment hearings); Deborah A. Dorfman, *Effectively Implementing Title I of the Americans With Disabilities Act for Mentally Disabled Persons: A Therapeutic Jurisprudence Analysis,* 8 J.L. & HEALTH 105, 121 (1993–94) (same).

[113]*See generally* Perlin, *Pretexts, supra* note 71.

[114]*See, e.g.,* Winick, *supra* note 16, at 936 n.57, *cited in* Commonwealth v. DelVerde, 496 N.E.2d 1357, 1360 (Mass. 1986); State v. Wilkins, 736 S.W.2d 409, 415 (Mo. 1987).

[115]*See, e.g.,* Riggins v. Nevada, 504 U.S. 127 (1992), discussed *supra* notes 76–78; *see also* Heller v. Doe, 509 U.S. 312, 324 (1993) (institutionalized mentally ill persons are subjected to "invasive" treatments such as the use of psychotropic drugs).

[116]For an important recent debate on this issue, compare Richard Bonnie, *The Competence of Criminal Defendants: Beyond Dusky and Drope,* 47 U. MIAMI L. REV. 539 (1993), to Bruce Winick, *Reforming Incompetency to Stand Trial and Plead Guilty: A Proposal and Response to Professor Bonnie,* 85 J. CRIM. L. & CRIMINOL. 571 (1995).

[117]465 U.S. 168 (1984).

where appropriate.[118] It defies credulity to suggest that Colin Ferguson was able to perform these tasks in a way that would ensure a trial that reflected the type of solemnity and dignity that are integral to a trial's fairness.

Sanism, Pretexts, the Public, and Colin Ferguson

Was the *Ferguson* trial pretextual? Was it a "sham, a charade" or was it the vindication of a defendant's Fourteenth Amendment right to self-representation? In one of the most unscriptable ironies of the entire affair, Ferguson likened himself to Clarence Thomas, claiming they had both been victims of "high tech legal lynchings."[119] The Court's holding in *Godinez* reflected the Court's profound disinterest in (and perhaps, cynicism about) the integrity of the criminal trial process. Its opinion must be read against the background of both its decision in *Strickland v. Washington*[120] and the reality that counsel generally made available to mentally disabled persons is substandard (and especially substandard in the case of mentally disabled criminal defendants).[121]

Was the *Ferguson* trial sanist? This is an exceedingly difficult question to answer. At first glance it appears that *Godinez* was the rarest of all creatures: a nonsanist opinion that captured the votes of Justices Scalia, Rehnquist, and Thomas, the core of the court that has consistently taken the most sanist positions in their opinions.[122] *Godinez*—specifically— appears to grant significant autonomy to mentally disabled criminal defendants, to treat them more like other defendants, to neither infantilize nor demonize them,[123] and to decline to focus solely on their mental disability in construing their criminal process trial rights.

That this, however, may be little more than a *trompe l'oeil* begins to become apparent as one contextualizes the public reaction to the *Ferguson* trial. First, Ferguson's initial set of lawyers fell over themselves in an effort to make Ferguson appear as mentally disabled as possible: "A delusional psychotic," declared Ronald Kuby, Kunstler's associate;[124] a "raving maniac," chimed in Kunstler;[125] a "deranged man with a crazy defense," again from Kuby.[126] Colin Moore, a Black activist attorney who had represented Ferguson on

---

[118]*Id.* at 176–79. These aspects of *McKaskle* are carefully discussed in Felthous, *supra* note 11, at 107.

[119]Fan, *supra* note 27. Ironically, Thomas and Ferguson are "twinned" in an opinion piece written shortly after O. J. Simpson was apprehended: "A black person says, 'The same spot in my heart that was bruised over *Clarence Thomas,* Mike Tyson, Michael Jackson, Tupac Shakur, and *Colin Ferguson,* the same spot that gets bruised by the nightly local news parade of black hands in handcuffs has been rebruised.'" Alison Taylor, *"Girl, There's Another Black Man Gone,"* Palm Beach Post (June 26, 1994), at 1F (emphasis added).

[120]466 U.S. 668, 687 (1984) (establishing a pallid, almost impossible to violate "reasonably effective assistance" standard in criminal cases). In *Strickland,* the Supreme Court established as the standard for evaluating adequacy of counsel claims in criminal cases as "whether counsel's conduct so undermined the proper function of the adversarial process that the trial court cannot be relied on as having produced a just result," *id.; see generally* Michael L. Perlin, *Fatal Assumption: A Critical Evaluation of the Role of Counsel in Mental Disability Cases,* 16 LAW & HUM. BEHAV. 37, 53 (1992) (characterizing standard as "sterile and perfunctory").

[121]*See generally* Perlin, *supra* note 120.

[122]*See generally* Perlin, *supra* note 5; Perlin & Dorfman, *supra* note 68; Michael L. Perlin, *Psychodynamics and the Insanity Defense: "Ordinary Common Sense" and Heuristic Reasoning,* 69 NEB. L. REV. 3, 61–69 (1990).

[123]Michael L. Perlin, *On "Sanism,"* 46 SMU L. REV. 373, 400–04 (1992).

[124]*Nightline,* ABC News (Feb. 10, 1995), Transcript #3580.

[125]Associated Press, *LIRR Shooting Suspect Rejects Insanity Defense; Contends That Court Wants to Cover up the Facts,* BERGEN RECORD, (NJ), Aug. 20, 1994, at A4.

[126]Bruce Frankel, *NY Rail Suspect Will Represent Self in Court,* USA TODAY, Jan. 17, 1995, at 2A.

another matter, called the trial a "ritualistic sacrifice."[127] And a prominent columnist characterized Ferguson as "nutty as peanut brittle."[128]

The irony was noted by a *Washington Post* commentator: "The Ferguson trial has the lawyer-hating masses clamoring for—you guessed it—a real lawyer. Suddenly, lawyers are agents of rationality and justice."[129]

Other lawyers raised the question of fundamental fairness in different ways. Said Jack Litman, "As horrific as the crimes are, when people see someone battling for himself and he doesn't know how to do it, they feel this isn't fair."[130] Leon Friedman focused on what he saw as Judge Belfi's failure to inquire into Ferguson's ability to *knowingly* and *intelligently* waive counsel.[131] Burt Neuborne speculated about the community's need for an "imprimatur of guilt": "It was important for everyone to say 'You did something terrible,' and they want to be sure Ferguson never gets out of jail. It served an important social purpose. But that is not the purpose of a trial."[132]

And although the trial had its "moments of catharsis for survivors," it left a "nasty, hollow feeling in its wake."[133] Jan Hoffman's analysis for the *New York Times* rings the most true: "Judge Belfi's ruling addressed a broader social need as well. Since 1981, when John Hinckley shot President Reagan, the public has grown weary and fearful of both the insanity defense and a defendant's being found continually unfit to stand trial. People are concerned that such defendants will somehow unjustly elude conviction and punishment, and that terrible crimes will never be brought to closure."[134]

By the time the trial was over, some observers shifted their original perspective on Ferguson. Said the widow of one victim who originally assumed Ferguson was insane ("because I couldn't believe any human being could actually do this"), "There is no doubt now that he is sane; . . . a very calculating, manipulating person."[135]

The *Ferguson* trial, in summary, concluded with the same sort of stereotypical constructions of mentally disabled criminal defendants as have most of the other important cases to draw media attention since the trial of John W. Hinckley.

Conclusion

As mentioned earlier, it is difficult to discuss the *Ferguson* trial—"one of the most bizarre cases in court history"[136]—without invoking *Hamlet*: Is Justice Thomas hoisted by his own petard? *Godinez* rejected the argument that an assessment of competence for counsel-waiver purposes need be more searching or detailed than one for ability-to-stand-trial purposes. This rejection resulted, ultimately, in affirming the defendant Moran's conviction in that case, a victory for the state of Nevada (where Moran's crimes were

---

[127]Alyson Alert, *United States: Lawyer/Killer Tests Rules for Mental Competence,* INTERPRESS SERVICE, Nov. 22, 1994.

[128]Otis Pike, *Insane Policy,* NEW ORLEANS TIMES-PICAYUNE, Feb. 23, 1995, at B7.

[129]*Letter From a Different Trial: Raising the Images of Lawyers by Proceeding Without Them,* WASHINGTON POST, Feb. 3, 1995, at A2.

[130]Jan Hoffman, *Lingering Emptiness,* N.Y. TIMES, Feb. 18. 1995, at 26.

[131]Marilyn Goldstein, *LIRR Case a "Catch-22" in Reverse,* NEWSDAY (Nassau & Suffolk ed.), Feb. 3, 1995, at A8 (characterizing Belfi's decision as "a mistake").

[132]Hoffman, *supra* note 130 at 26.

[133]*Id.*

[134]*Id.*

[135]John T. McQuiston, *Reporter's Notebook: Views Shift on Insanity in Killings on L.I.R.R.,* N.Y. TIMES, Feb. 12, 1995, at 42.

[136]McQuiston, *supra* note 88.

committed) and the U.S. Department of Justice (that shared argument on the Supreme Court level with the state).[137] It is beyond argument that one of the hoped-for results of a prosecutorial victory would be an increase in the number of convictions (and a concomitant decrease in the number of appellate reversals) in cases involving defendants of questionable competence.[138] And the outcome of Colin Ferguson's case was precisely such a result.

Richard Moran's original guilty plea attracted no national attention. The Supreme Court's decision in *Godinez* attracted little. The Ferguson case was a media circus. The heuristic of the vivid case[139] quickly educated the media and the American public about the broad outlines of the *Godinez* rationale (although few of the thousands of press stories about Ferguson made the explicit link between that case and the *Godinez* decision). For better or worse, just as the Hinckley case drove the insanity ''reform'' debate of the early 1980s,[140] so will the Colin Ferguson case drive whatever debate develops over competence questions in the late 1990s and beyond.[141]

Godinez is a cynical and meretricious decision. It is cynical because of its sole focus on the cognitive aspects of the capacity determination and its profound disinterest in the functional aspects. It is meretricious because it appears to simplify and unify a complex area of the law; in reality, it simply makes it more likely—*far* more likely—that more seriously mentally disabled criminal defendants will be convicted and subsequently imprisoned.[142] It is also meretricious because, though it appears to privilege autonomy in an almost libertarian way, it in fact exposes the majority's deep contempt for mentally disabled criminal defendants and its utter disinterest in the logical and likely results of the decision.[143] And this contempt extends to the victims of crimes such as those committed by Ferguson.[144]

---

[137]*See* 1993 WL 751849, at *13 (transcript of oral argument in Godinez v. Moran, 509 U.S. 389 (1993)).

[138]In 1992 the Supreme Court had ruled in Medina v. California, 505 U.S. 437, that it was not unconstitutional to place the burden of proof at an incompetency-to-stand-trial hearing on the defendant. Thus if the scales are equally balanced between competence and incompetency, cases may proceed to trial.

[139]*See, e.g.,* Michael L. Perlin, *Are Courts Competent to Decide Competency Questions? Stripping the Facade From* United States v. Charters, 38 U. KAN. L. REV. 957, 991 (1990); Michael L. Perlin, *Unpacking the Myths: The Symbolism Mythology of Insanity Defense Jurisprudence,* 40 CASE W. RES. L. REV. 599, 618–30 (1989–90).

[140]PERLIN, *supra* note 15.

[141]*Godinez* and the *Ferguson* trial raise an inquiry into an irony that, to the best of my knowledge, has never been considered in the literature: the parallels between the post-*Hinckley* insanity defense ''reform'' debate (on whether the affective–behavioral prong of the insanity defense should be jettisoned, leaving only a cognitive prong, *see id.* at 17–27) and the inquiry posed here (as to whether a cognitive inquiry is sufficient in a competence-waiver case or whether a functional standard must be met as well).

[142]*See id.* at 428–29 (offering similar argument against abolition of the insanity defense).

[143]Profound therapeutic jurisprudence questions are also raised by both the *Godinez* decision and the *Ferguson* trial. *See generally* PERLIN, *supra* note 6; Michael L. Perlin, *What Is Therapeutic Jurisprudence?* 10 N.Y.L. SCH. J. HUM. RTS. 623 (1993); David Wexler, *Putting Mental Health Into Mental Health Law,* 16 LAW & HUM. BEHAV. 27 (1992); David Wexler, *Therapeutic Jurisprudence and Changing Concepts of Legal Scholarship,* 11 BEHAV. SCI. & L. 12 (1993). *See generally infra* section 3.

There is an important—and unresolved—question in *Godinez* about the extent to which blame factors into the Court's decision. *See Godinez,* 509 U.S. at 400 n.2, referring to the plea colloquy between the defendant and the trial judge: ''During the course of this lengthy exchange, the trial court asked respondent whether he was under the influence of drugs or alcohol, and respondent answered as follows: 'Just what they give me in, you know, medications.' . . . The court made no further inquiry. The 'medications' to which respondent referred had been prescribed to control his seizures, *which were a byproduct of his cocaine use. . . .*'' (Emphasis added.)

[144]*See* Christopher Johns, *Kafkaesque Nightmare of a Trial,* ARIZ. REPUBLIC, Mar. 5, 1975, at F3: ''The justice system also fails victims. In the *Ferguson* case, the trial must have been a Kafkaesque nightmare. There is no justice when an accused roams the courtroom incapable of defending himself or taking responsibility for his actions. It was a spectacle, not a trial. It undermined the court's integrity and fostered the belief that the criminal justice system is not fair.''

Reaction to the *Ferguson* trial exposes the pretextuality that provides the underpinning of the *Godinez* decision. Although public and media response did not appear to be as overtly sanist as, say, typical responses to mitigating mental disability evidence in death penalty cases[145] or federal judges' construction of such evidence in their application of the federal sentencing guidelines,[146] the trial spectacle remained profoundly sanist.[147] The appearance of justice is a component of a fair trial;[148] that appearance was sadly lacking in Ferguson's trial.

Godinez, to be blunt, is a bad decision.[149] It is also a cruel decision. Few onlookers can quarrel with the ultimate verdict in the *Ferguson* case, but the steps along the way did nothing more than strain justice and mock the Constitutional guarantees of a fair trial. Sanism and pretextuality, in the end, robbed the judicial process of its needed dignity.

---

[145]Michael L. Perlin, *The Sanist Lives of Jurors in Death Penalty Cases: The Puzzling Role of "Mitigating" Mental Disability Evidence,* 8 NOTRE DAME J.L., ETHICS & PUB. POL'Y 239 (1994).

[146]Michael L. Perlin & Keri K. Gould, *Rashomon and the Criminal Law: Mental Disability and the Federal Sentencing Guidelines,* 22 AM. J. CRIM. L. 431 (1995).

[147]*See* Johns, *supra* note 144 ("Regrettably, Thomas' opinion does not fit reality or serve justice. It's a backward step in the face of a mushrooming population of mentally ill, developmentally disabled, and mentally retarded people ensnared in the criminal justice system").

[148]*E.g., In re* Murchison, 349 U.S. 133, 136 (1955); Walker v. Lockhart, 726 F.2d 1238, 1244 (8th Cir. 1984); City of Cleveland v. Cleveland Electric Illuminating Co., 503 F. Supp. 368, 381 (M.D. Ohio 1980).

[149]*Cf.* Government of Virgin Islands v. Charles, 72 F.3d 401, 411 (3d Cir. 1995) (Lewis, J., concurring) ("This difficult case presents us with a window through which to view the real-world effects of the Supreme Court's decision in *Godinez*—and it is not a pretty sight").

Chapter 10
THE INSANITY DEFENSE

The American insanity defense jurisprudence is incoherent. It reflects the public's episodic outrage at apparently inexplicable exculpations of "obviously" guilty acts, the legislatures' pandering, prereflective responses to constituency cries, and the judiciary's desperate ambivalence about having to decide hard cases involving mentally disabled criminal defendants.[1] Although paradoxically we are beginning to come to grips with some of the scientific, biological, neurological, and psychological reasons that play a role in the commission of some otherwise-inexplicable crimes, we simultaneously narrow and limit the substance of the insanity defense and the procedures used in such cases (and in postacquittal commitment hearings).[2] We do this narrowing ostensibly both to lessen the possibility of a "moral mistake" (i.e., the entry of an insanity acquittal where we cannot be sure of the defendant's nonresponsibility),[3] and to make the choice of an insanity defense—never a high card in any criminal defense lawyer's hand—an even less attractive option.

The jurisprudence's incoherence is important because of the full scope of its social impact. First, through a series of legislative "reform" measures, it sanctions the criminal punishment of a significant number of individuals who—by any substantive standard—are not responsible for their criminal acts. In addition to the evident punitive and damaging impact on these defendants from this "reform" the outcome are prisons that are more chaotic and dangerous places for other inmates and for correctional staff.

Second, it allows us—perhaps *forces* us—to deplete our intellectual and emotional resources and our creative energies by debating endlessly issues that are fundamentally irrelevant to the real-life impact of the defense (e.g., whether there should be a volitional as well as a cognitive standard used) and that lead to, at best, illusory change. At the same time, it allows us—perhaps, *encourages* us—to ignore empirical evidence, scientific study, and moral reasoning that seek to shed light on the underlying issues.

Third, it leads us to spend federal and state money in counterproductive ways. Recent reforms will lead to more individuals being institutionalized for longer periods of time in more punitive facilities, at precisely the same time that community resources are becoming scarcer. If the insanity defense is successful only in a fraction of 1% of all cases, why do we devote such time and capital to this question, and why do we dramatically and egregiously exaggerate the impact that these cases have on the operation of our criminal justice system?

Fourth, it leads us to avoid considering the single most important issue in mental disability law (one that is magnified many times in insanity defense analysis): Why do we feel the way we do about "these people," and how do these feelings control our legislative,

---

[1]Jodie English, *The Light Between Twilight and Dusk: Federal Criminal Law and the Volitional Insanity Defense,* 40 HASTINGS L.J. 1, 46 (1988) (criticizing the Insanity Defense Reform Act of 1988, 18 U.S.C. § 20 (1988), enacted in the wake of the *Hinckley* acquittal); Michael L. Perlin, On *"Sanism,"* 46 SMU L. REV. (1992) [hereinafter Perlin, *Sanism*]; Michael L. Perlin, *Pretexts and Mental Disability Law: The Case of Competency,* 47 U. MIAMI L. REV. (1993) [hereinafter Perlin, *Pretexts*].

[2]Lisa A. Callahan, Connie Mayer, & Henry J. Steadman, *Insanity Defense in the United States-Post-*Hinckley, 11 MENT. & PHYS. DIS. L. REP. 54 (1987) (Table 2).

[3]*See, e.g.,* Richard J. Bonnie, *The Moral Basis of the Insanity Defense,* 69 A.B.A. J. 194 (1993); Richard J. Bonnie, *Morality, Equality and Expertise: Renegotiating the Relationship Between Psychiatry and Law,* 12 BULL. AM. ACAD. PSYCHIATRY & L. 5 (1984) [hereinafter Bonnie, *Equality*].

judicial, and administrative policies? I believe that it is the answer to this question that is the wild card, and it is essential that we see its role in the incoherence of the policies I am discussing.

No aspect of the criminal justice system is more controversial than is the insanity defense. Nowhere else does the successful use of a defense regularly bring about cries for its abolition; no other aspect of the criminal law inspires position papers from trade associations spanning the full range of professions and political entities. When the defense is successful in a high-level publicity case (especially when it involves a defendant whose "factual guilt" is clear), the acquittal triggers public outrage and serves vividly as a screen on which each relevant interest group can project its fears and concerns. It symbolizes "the most profound issues in social and criminal justice."[4]

Although on one hand the defense is a reflection of the "fundamental moral principles of our criminal law,"[5] and serves as a bulwark of the law's "moorings of condemnation for moral failure,"[6] we as a society remain fixated on it as a symbol of all that is wrong with the criminal justice system and as a source of social and political anger. The defense is thus attacked by a U.S. Attorney General as a major stumbling block in the restoration of the "effectiveness of Federal law enforcement" and as tilting the balance "between the forces of law and the forces of lawlessness."[7]

Our fixation on the insanity defense has evolved into a familiar story. The insanity defense, so conventional wisdom goes, encourages the factually (and morally) guilty to seek refuge in an excuse premised on pseudoscience, shaky rehabilitation theory, and faintly duplicitous legal *légèrdemain*. The defense, allegedly, is used frequently (mostly in abusive ways), is generally successful, and often results in brief slap-on-the-wrist periods of confinements in loosely supervised settings; because it is basically a no-risk maneuver, the mythology goes, even when it fails the defendant will suffer no harm. Purportedly, the defense is used disproportionately in death penalty cases (often involving garish multiple homicides) and inevitably results in trials in which high-priced experts do battle in front of befuddled jurors who are inevitably unable to make sense of contradictory, highly abstract, and speculative testimony. Finally the defense is seen as being subject to the worst sort of malingering or feigning, and it is assumed that, through this gambit, clever defendants can "con" gullible, "soft" experts into accepting a fraudulent defense.

The largely unseen counterworlds of empirical reality, behavioral advance, scientific discovery, and philosophical inquiry paint quite a different picture. Empirically the insanity defense is rarely used, is less frequently successful, and generally results in lengthy stays in maximum security facilities (often far more restrictive than many prisons or reformatories) for far longer periods of time than the defendants would have been subject to had they been sentenced criminally.[8]

It is also a risky plea; where it fails, penal terms are generally significantly longer than in like cases where the defense was not raised. The defense is most frequently pled in cases not involving a victim's death, and is often raised in cases involving minor property crimes. The vast majority of cases are so-called walk-throughs (that is, where both state and defense experts agree both about the severity of the defendant's mental illness and his or her lack of

---

[4]Ingo Keilitz, *Researching and Reforming the Insanity Defense,* 39 RUTGERS L. REV. 289, 322 (1987).
[5]United States v. Lyons, 739 F.2d 994 (5th Cir. 1984) (Rubin, J., dissenting).
[6]Joseph M. Livermore & Paul E. Meehl, *The Virtues of* M'Naghten, 51 MINN. L. REV. 789, 797 (1967).
[7]*Insanity Defense Hearings Before the Senate Comm. on the Judiciary,* 97th Cong., 2d Sess., at 27 (1982).
[8]Michael L. Perlin, *Unpacking the Myths: The Symbolism Mythology of Insanity Defense Jurisprudence,* 40 CASE W. L. REV. 599 (1989–90).

responsibility). Feigned insanity is rare; successfully feigned insanity even rarer. It is far more likely for a jury to convict in a case in which the defendant meets the relevant substantive insanity criteria than to acquit where he or she does not.[9]

As a result of these myths, we demand legislative "reform." This reform leads to a variety of changes in insanity defense statutes—in substantive standards, in burdens of proof, in standards of proof, in the creation of hybrid verdicts such as "guilty but mentally ill," even, in a few instances, in supposed abolition of the defense itself. No matter what their final outcome, these reforms stem from one primary source: "the public's overwhelming fear of the future acts of [released insanity] acquittees."[10]

Behaviorally, researchers are beginning to develop sophisticated assessment tools that can translate insanity concepts into quantifiable variables that appear to easily meet the traditional legal standard of reasonable scientific certainty.[11] Scientifically, the development of hard science diagnostic tools (such as computerized tomograph scanning or magnetic resonance imaging) has helped determine the presence and severity of certain neurological diseases that may be causally related to some forms of criminal behavior.[12] Finally, moral philosophers are increasingly trying—with some measure of success—to clarify difficult underlying issues as to the contextual meaning of terms such as *causation, responsibility,* and *rationality.*[13]

Yet these discoveries and developments have had virtually no impact on the basic debate. They are ignored, trivialized, denied, and distinguished. And the gap between myth and reality is a vast one that widens exponentially with the passage of time. Although the gap is acknowledged by virtually every empirical researcher who has studied any of these issues,[14] it continues to grow. We continue to honor and reify the myths through legislative action and judicial decisions. In public forums the public continues to endorse a substantive standard for insanity that approximates the "wild beast" test of 1724,[15] and legislators look to the potential abolition of the insanity defense as a palliative for rampant crime problems in spite of incontrovertible statistics that show that the defense is raised in a fraction of 1% of felony prosecutions (and is successful only about one quarter of the time).[16] Our response to the most celebrated insanity acquittal of the twentieth century—that of John W. Hinckley— was to shrink the insanity defense in federal jurisdictions to a more narrow and restrictive version of an 1843 test that was seen as biologically, scientifically, and morally outdated even at the time of its creation.[17]

---

[9]Perlin, *supra* note 8, at 713–718.

[10]HENRY STEADMAN ET AL., REFORMING THE INSANITY DEFENSE: AN EVALUATION OF PRE- AND POST-HINCKLEY REFORMS 69 (1994).

[11]Joseph H. Rodriguez, Laura M. LeWinn, & Michael L. Perlin, *The Insanity Defense Under Siege: Legislative Assaults and Legal Rejoinders,* 14 RUTGERS L.J. 397, 401–02 (1983).

[12]*See, e.g.,* H. Jordan Garber, *Use of Magnetic Resonance Imaging in Psychiatry,* 145 AM. J. PSYCHIATRY 164 (1988); Jennifer Kulynych, *Brain, Mind, and Criminal Behavior: Neuroimages as Scientific Evidence,* 36 JURIMETRICS J. 235 (1996); Paul Nestor & Joel Haycock, *Not Guilty by Reason of Insanity of Murder: Clinical and Neuropsychological Characteristics,* 25 J. AM. ACAD. PSYCHIATRY & L. 161 (1997).

[13]*See, e.g.,* MICHAEL S. MOORE, LAW AND PSYCHIATRY: RETHINKING THE RELATIONSHIP (1984).

[14]*See, e.g.,* Lisa A. Callahan et al., *The Volume and Characteristics of Insanity Defense Pleas: An Eight-State Study,* 19 BULL. AM. ACAD. PSYCHIATRY & L. 331, 332–36 (1991); STEADMAN ET AL., *supra* note 10.

[15]Caton F. Roberts, Stephen L. Golding, & Frank D. Fincham, *Implicit Theories of Criminal Responsibility Decision Making and the Insanity Defense,* 11 LAW & HUM. BEHAV. 207 (1987), discussing Rex v. Arnold, 16 HOW. ST. TR. 695 (1724).

[16]Callahan et ai., *supra* note 14, at 334–36.

[17]3 MICHAEL L. PERLIN, MENTAL DISABILITY LAW: CIVIL AND CRIMINAL (1989), § 15.04, at 292–94.

Why? What is there about the insanity defense that allows for (perhaps encourages) such a discontinuity between firmly held belief and statistical reality? Why is our insanity defense jurisprudence so irrational? Why do we continue to obsess about questions that are fundamentally irrelevant to the core jurisprudential inquiry of who should be exculpated because of lack of mental responsibility? Why do we allow ourselves to be immobilized by an irresoluble debate? Why does our willful blindness allow us (lead us?) to ignore scientific and empirical developments and, instead, force us to waste time, energy, and passion on a series of fruitless inquiries that will have negligible impact on any of the underlying social problems? Again, and most important why do we continue to ignore the most fundamental and core question: Why do we feel the way we do about "these people" and why, when we engage in our endless debates and incessant retinkering with insanity defense doctrine, do we not seriously consider the answer to this question?

I believe that our insanity defense jurisprudence is a prisoner of a combination of empirical myths and related social metamyths. Born of a medievalist and fundamentalist religious vision of the roots of mental illness and the relationships between mental illness, crime, and punishment, the myths continue to dominate the landscape in spite of (in fact utterly independently of) the impressive scientific and behavioral evidence to the contrary.[18]

The legal system is a prisoner of these myths and of the concomitant powerful symbols that permeate any criminal trial (especially any highly visible criminal trial) at which a nonresponsibility defense is raised. It rejects psychodynamic explanations of human motivation and behavior, and remains intensely suspicious of concepts of mental health and disability, of mental health professionals, and of the ability of such professionals to assess or ameliorate mental disability.[19] As a result, it remains most comfortable with all-or-nothing tests of mental illness[20] and demands that nonresponsible defendants match visual images of "deranged madmen" who indisputably "look crazy."[21] Again, it does this in utter disregard of the past 150 years of scientific and behavioral learning.

I believe that sanism and pretextuality are—in great measure—responsible for the state of our insanity defense jurisprudence. And I believe further that sanism and pretextuality are at their most insidious in this area of the law, where so much decision making appears to be done out of consciousness. Throughout this book I have argued that sanism and pretextuality corrode our mental disability law jurisprudence. This corrosion is, I believe, its most pernicious in cases and laws involving the insanity defense. I believe that our efforts to understand the insanity defense and insanity-pleading defendants are doomed to eternal intellectual, political, and moral gridlock unless we are willing to acknowledge the way that prejudice, bias, and stereotyping have contaminated our jurisprudence and our decision making. Only in this manner can we attempt to articulate the sort of coherent and integrated perspective that is necessary if we are to truly unpack the myths from the defense's facade and reconstruct a meaningful insanity defense jurisprudence.

---

[18]Richard Rogers, William Seaman, & Charles R. Clark, *Assessment of Criminal Responsibility: Initial Validation of the* R-CRAS *with the M'Naghten and* GBMI *Standards,* 9 INT'L J.L. & PSYCHIATRY 67 (1986).

[19]Michael L. Perlin, *The Supreme Court, the Mentally Disabled Criminal Defendant, and Symbolic Values: Random Decisions, Hidden Rationales, or "Doctrinal Abyss?"* 29 ARIZ. L. REV. 1 (1987); Perlin, *Sanism, supra* note 1; Perlin, *Pretexts, supra* note 1; Michael L. Perlin & Deborah A. Dorfman, *Sanism, Social Science, and the Development of Mental Disability Law Jurisprudence,* 11 BEHAV. SCI. & L. 47, 60–61 (1993).

[20]Johnson v. State, 439 A.2d 542, 552 (Md., 1982): "For the purposes of guilt determination, an offender is either wholly sane or wholly insane."

[21]Battolino v. People, 199 P.2d 897, 901 (Colo., 1948) (finding no evidence of defendant exhibiting "paleness, wild eyes and trembling").

The Role of Externalities

One underlying theme throughout the centuries of insanity defense test formulation has been the question of the extent that externalities—empirical research, scientific advances, political confrontations, and teachings of moral philosophers—have had a significant impact on the actual structuring of the substantive legal formula for responsibility.

I believe that it is futile to be terribly concerned with the question of which school of moral philosophy wins or which set of scientific data is soundest or which database of empirical evidence is most persuasive. The empiricist, the scientist, and the moral philosopher all base their arguments on one important but unarticulated premise: That fact finders are ready, willing, and able to be rational, fair, and free of bias in their assessment of insanity defense cases, and it is only the absence of a missing link—the additional, irrefutable data as to NGRI demographics, the newest discovery in brain biology, the exact calibration of moral agency in the allocation of responsibility—that stands in the way of a coherent and well-functioning system. Yet there is virtually no evidence that the addition of any (or all) of these factors would make any difference.

Let us instead ask a different question: If we now understand so much more about science, human behavior, and empiricism than we did at the time of, say, the *M'Naghten* verdict, why have we shrunk our insanity defense to the point where it now approximates but is even more restrictive than what was scientifically, empirically, and morally out of date 145 years ago?[22] Do the positions of moral philosophers (or of contemporaneous scholars advocating the positions of such philosophers) really matter? Does the fact that virtually every belief held dear by the public (and by its elected representatives) as to who pleads the insanity defense, how it is abused, what happens to such defendants following an NGRI verdict, where such individuals are institutionalized (and for how long) is a myth—that ordinary common sense is, to be blunt, dead wrong—actually matter? Does the fact that scientists appear to understand more about brain chemistry, physiology, neurology, and the effect of physical and psychological trauma on criminally irresponsible behavior matter?[23]

If these facts do not matter, perhaps this is because the powerful symbolic values that surround and, in some important ways, strangle the development of an insanity defense jurisprudence have little, if anything, to do with empiricism, with science, or with philosophy. On the contrary, these symbolic values reflect and illuminate the importance of psychodynamic factors—unconscious decision making, political personality styles, authoritarianism—in the creation of an insanity defense doctrine that, paradoxically, overtly rejects psychodynamic factors when offered as an explanation for what would otherwise be criminal behavior. It is these psychodynamic factors that are at the root of our discomfort with the insanity defense—a discomfort that is a function of our psychodynamic outrage, of our authoritarian personality styles, and of our rejection of "psychological man."[24] The insanity defense is, to a significant majority of the American public, counterintuitive. We are generally uncomfortable with the entire notion of "excuse" defenses (putting aside self-defense); the use of the others (duress, choice of evils, etc.), however, does not appear to imperil the operation of the criminal justice system as the insanity defense appears to.

---

[22]*See* English, *supra* note 1, at 8.

[23]*See* David Wexler, *Redefining the Insanity Problem,* 53 GEO. WASH. L. REV. 528, 540 (1985).

[24]For an extended analysis of this concept, see Joel Friedlander, *Corporation and Kulturkampf: The Culture as Illegal Fiction,* 29 CONN. L. REV. 31, 103–06 (1996); On the role of authoritaranism in the journalization of the insanity defense policies, *see* Michael L. Perlin, *"The Borderline Which Separated You From Me": The Insanity Defence, The Authoritarian Spirit, The Fear of Faking, and the Culture of Punishment,* 82 IOWA L. REV. 1375 (1997).

Insanity Defense Myths

What is there about the insanity defense that inspires such massive societal irrationality? Why do we adhere to myths, ignore the reams of rational data that patiently rebut them, and willfully blind ourselves to the behavioral and empirical realities that are well-known to all serious researchers in this area? It is to these questions that I now turn.

Our insanity defense jurisprudence is premised on a series of empirical and behavioral myths, myths that empirical research has revealed to be ''unequivocally disproven by the facts.''[25] There are several separate empirical myths to be addressed briefly.

Myth #1: *The insanity defense is overused.* All empirical analyses have been consistent: the public at large and the legal profession (especially legislators) ''dramatically'' and ''grossly'' overestimate both the frequency and the success rate of the insanity plea, an error ''undoubtedly . . . abetted'' by media distortions. The most recent research reveals, for instance, that the insanity defense is used in only about 1% of all felony cases, and is successful just about one quarter of the time.[26]

Myth #2: *Use of the insanity defense is limited to murder cases.*[27] In one jurisdiction where the data has been closely studied, slightly fewer than one third of the successful insanity pleas entered over an eight-year period were reached in cases involving a victim's death.[28] Further, individuals who plead insanity in murder cases are no more successful in being found NGRI than persons charged with other crimes.[29]

Myth #3: *There is no risk to the defendant who pleads insanity.* Defendants who asserted an insanity defense at trial and who were ultimately found guilty of their charges served significantly longer sentences than defendants tried on similar charges who did not assert the insanity defense. The same ratio is found when only homicide cases are considered.[30]

Myth #4: *NGRI acquittees are quickly released from custody.* A comprehensive study of California practice showed that only 1% of insanity acquittees were released following

---

[25]Michael L. Perlin, *Whose Plea Is It Anyway? Insanity Defense Myths and Realities,* 79 PHILADELPHIA MED. 5, 6 (1983). On juror knowledge of the insanity defense, on juror attitudes toward the defense, and the impact of juror personality on insanity defense decision making, see Lynn McCutcheon & Lauren McCutcheon, *Not Guilty by Reason of Insanity: Getting It Right or Perpetuating the Myths?* 74 PSYCHOL. REP. 764 (1994); Norman Finkel & Christopher Slobogin, *Insanity, Justification, and Culpability: Toward a Unifying Schema,* 19 LAW & HUM. BEHAV. 447 (1995); James Claghorn et al., *Juror Personality Characteristics and the Insanity Defense,* 4 FORENS. REP. 61 (1991).

[26]*See* Rodriguez et al., *supra* note 11, at 401 (footnotes omitted); *see also* Callahan et al., *supra* note 14; Jeffrey Janofsky, *Insanity Defense Pleas in Baltimore City: An Analysis of Outcome,* 153 AM. J. PSYCHIATRY 1464 (1996) (insanity plea successful in 8 of 190 cases; in all eight cases, state agreed that defendant was insane). *See generally* Hava Villaverde, *Racism in the Insanity Defense,* 50 U. MIAMI L. REV. 209 (1995) (discussing statistical findings).

For a recent case, *see Ex parte* Trawick, 1997 WL 83703, at *5 (Ala. 1997), (*voir dire* exchange): [Juror W.C.]: No, I mean I just feel it is greatly overused. I feel there is a lot of cases in which maybe people for instance should have gotten the death penalty and might not really have a problem.

. . .

I mean, I just feel it is something that is greatly overused.

[27]*See* Richard Lowell Nygaard, *On Responsibility: Or, The Insanity of Mental Defenses and Punishment,* 41 VILL. L. REV. 95, 982 (1996) (''I note that the test for insanity and responsibility is most often employed, in a most crucial sense, where it is probably least germane—in trials on a charge of homicide;'' author is a judge on the Third Circuit Court of Appeals).

[28]Rodriguez et al., *supra* note 11, at 402.

[29]Henry Steadman et al., *Factors Associated With a Successful Insanity Plea,* 140 AM. J. PSYCHIATRY 401, 402–03 (1983).

[30]Rodriguez et al., *supra* note 11, at 401–02.

their NGRI verdict and that another 4% were placed on conditional release, the remaining 95% being hospitalized.[31]

Myth #5: *NGRI acquittees spend much less time in custody than do defendants convicted of the same offenses.* On the contrary, NGRI acquittees have been found to spend almost double the amount of time that defendants convicted of similar charges spend in prison settings, and often face a lifetime of postrelease judicial oversight. In California, those found NGRI of nonviolent crimes were confined for periods of more than nine times as long.[32]

Myth #6: *Criminal defendants who plead insanity are usually faking.* This is perhaps the oldest of the insanity defense myths, and is one that has bedeviled American jurisprudence since the mid-19th century. Of the 141 individuals found NGRI in one jurisdiction over an eight-year period, there was no dispute that 115 were schizophrenic (including 38 of the 46 cases involving a victim's death), and in only three cases was the diagnostician unwilling or unable to specify the nature of the patient's mental illness.[33]

Myth #7: *Most insanity defense trials feature "battles of the experts."* The public's false perception of the circus-like battle of the experts is one of the most telling reasons for the rejection of psychodynamic principles by the legal system. A dramatic case such as the *Hinckley* trial, of course, reinforced these perceptions. The empirical reality is quite different. On the average, there is examiner agreement in 88% of all insanity cases.[34]

Myth #8: *Criminal defense attorneys—perhaps inappropriately—use the insanity defense plea solely to "beat the rap."* Attorneys representing mentally disabled defendants have been routinely criticized for seeking refuge in the insanity defense as a means of technically avoiding a deserved conviction.[35] In reality, the facts are quite different. First, the level of representation afforded to mentally disabled defendants is frequently substandard.[36] Second, the few studies that have been done paint an entirely different picture; lawyers also enter an insanity plea to obtain immediate mental health treatment for their clients, as a plea-bargaining device to ensure that their clients ultimately receive mandatory mental health

---

[31]H. STEADMAN ET AL., *supra* note 10, at 58–61. It is this myth—the fear of the swiftly released acquittee—that probably has led to the most sanist and pretextual decision making in this area. *See, e.g.,* Abraham Halpern, *Misuses of Post-Acquittal Hospitalization for Punitive Purposes,* 22 PSYCHIATRIC ANN. 561 (1992). Although researchers have begun to publish an impressive array of data about value of conditionally releasing insanity acquittees (and the economic and social costs of policies that demand extensive hospitalization of this population), the myth retains its power. *See, e.g.,* Donald Linhorst & Ann Dirks-Linhorst, *The Impact of Insanity Acquittees on Missouri's Public Mental Health System,* 21 LAW & HUM. BEHAV. 327 (1997); Mark Widederlanders & Paul Chaote, *Beyond Recidivism: Measuring Community Adjustments of Conditionally Released Insanity Acquittees,* 6 PSYCHOLOG. ASSESSMENT 61 (1994); Patricia Griffin, Henry Steadman, & Kirk Heilbrun, *Designing Conditional Release Systems for Insanity Acquittees,* 18 J. MENT. HEALTH ADMIN. 231 (1991); Stuart Silver & Christiane Tellefsen, *Administrative Issues in the Follow-Up Treatment of Insanity Acquittees,* 18 J. MENT. HEALTH ADMIN. 242 (1991).

[32]Rodriguez et al., *supra* note 11, at 403–04; *see also* Mark Pogrebin et al., *Not Guilty by Reason of Insanity: A Research Note,* 8 INT'L J.L. & PSYCHIATRY 237, 240 (1986) (insanity acquittees do not spend fewer days in confinement via an NGRI plea than had they been convicted and sentenced); H. STEADMAN ET AL., *supra* note 10, at 58–61.

[33]Rodriguez et al., *supra* note 11, at 404; *See* Michael R. Hawkins & Richard Pasewark, *Characteristics of Persons Utilizing the Insanity Plea,* 53 PSYCHOL. REP. 191, 194 (1983) (citing studies).

[34]Richard Rogers et al., *Insanity Defense: Contested or Conceded?* 141 AM. J. PSYCHIATRY 885, 885 (1984); Kenneth Fukunaga et al., *Insanity Plea: Interexaminer Agreement in Concordance of Psychiatric Opinion and Court Verdict,* 5 LAW & HUM. BEHAV. 325, 326 (1981).

[35]MICHAEL KAVANAGH, THE CRIMINAL AND HIS ALLIES 90 (1928).

[36]Michael L. Perlin, *Fatal Assumption: A Critical Evaluation of the Role of Counsel in Mental Disability Cases,* 16 LAW & HUM. BEHAV. 39 (1992).

care, and to avoid malpractice litigation.[37] Third, the best available research suggests that jury biases exist relatively independent of lawyer functioning and are generally "not induced by attorneys."[38]

The Depths of the Mythology

We have long known of the depths of insanity defense mythology. Over the past 15 years, researchers and other scholars have been patiently rebutting these myths. The publication by Henry Steadman and his colleagues of their extended multijurisdiction study of virtually every empirical facet of insanity-defense pleading proves that the basic tenets are mythic.[39] The extent to which the dissemination of this data alters the terms of the insanity defense debate will reveal whether these myths, in fact, can be reinterpreted by lawmakers and the general public.[40]

I turn my attention now to a very different sort of inquiry: *Why* do we feel the way we do? What is it about our personality, our national spirit, our character, that leads us to the positions we take on this most insoluble issue of mental disability law?[41] And to what extent is this the reason for the sanism and pretextuality that plagues this area of U.S. jurisprudence?

The Roots of the Myths

To answer these questions it is necessary to look at the myths' roots. An examination of the literature and the case law reveals at least four reasons for the myths' persistence:

1. The irrational fear that defendants will "beat the rap" through fakery, a millennium-old fear that has in its roots a general disbelief in mental illness and a deep-seeded distrust of manipulative criminal defense lawyers invested with the ability to con jurors into accepting spurious expert testimony.[42]
2. The sense among the legal community and the general public that there is "something different" about mental illness and organic illness, so that although certain physiological disabilities may be seen as legitimately exculpatory, "mere" emotional handicaps are not.
3. The demand that a defendant conform to popular images of extreme "craziness" to be legitimately insane, a demand with which Chief Justice Rehnquist and other members of the current Supreme Court appear entirely comfortable.
4. A fear that the "soft," exculpatory sciences of psychiatry and psychology, claiming expertise in almost all areas of behavior, will somehow overwhelm the criminal justice system by thwarting the system's crime control component.

---

[37]Richard A. Pasewark & Paul L. Craig, *Insanity Pleas: Defense Attorneys' Views*, 8 J. PSYCHIATRY & L. 413 (1980).

[38]Alexander J. Tanford & Sarah Tanford, *Better Trials Through Science: A Defense of Psychologist–Lawyer Collaboration*, 66 N.C. L. REV. 741, 748–49 (1988).

[39]STEADMAN ET AL., *supra* note 10.

[40]Michael L. Perlin, *"The Borderline Which Separated You From Me": The Insanity Defense, the Authoritarian Spirit, the Fear of Faking, and the Culture of Punishment*, 82 IOWA L. REV. 1375, 1425–26 (1997).

[41]On the extent of these distortions, see generally Eric Silver et al., *Demythologizing Inaccurate Perceptions of the Insanity Defense*, 18 LAW & HUM. BEHAV. 63, 68–69 (1994).

[42]*See* Philip Resnick, *Perceptions of Psychiatric Testimony: A Historical Perspective on the Hysterical Invective*, 14 BULL. AM. ACAD. PSYCHIATRY & L. 203, 206 (1986) (concern dates to the tenth century).

I will here address solely the issue of "fear of faking."[43]

Fear of Faking

It has been believed that insanity was too easily feigned,[44] that psychiatrists were easily deceived by such simulation, and that the use of the defense has thus been "an easy way to escape punishment."[45] Because it could not be demonstrated conclusively that insanity had some "observable 'material' existence," charges of counterfeiting insanity quickly arose.[46] When Judge Darling characterized insanity in 1911 as "the last refuge of a hopeless defence,"[47] the factual basis of his assertion went unchallenged. As recently as 1986 Justice Lavorato of the Iowa Supreme Court, dissenting from a decision upholding the constitutionality of placing the burden of proof on the defendant in an insanity case, pointed out, "Placing proof of insanity with the defense originated over a hundred years ago with judicial concerns that *cunning defendants might pull one over sniffling jurors.*"[48]

This fear of successful deception, which has "permeated the American legal system for over a century,"[49] was seen as significantly weakening the deterrent effect of the criminal law.[50] The fear is one that has held some of this century's most respected jurists in its thrall.[51] The public's fear of feigned insanity defenses meshes with its fears of released insanity acquittees. If a defendant can successfully feign insanity, it is feared, he or she will likely be quickly released from confinement, thus both escaping "justly deserved punishment" and endangering other potential victims in the community.[52] Thus even lawyers for insanity

---

[43]The other myths are discussed extensively in MICHAEL L. PERLIN, THE JURISPRUDENCE OF THE INSANITY DEFENSE 247–62 (1994).

[44]This section is generally adapted from *id.* at 236–47.

[45]Diane Bartley, State v. Field: *Wisconsin Focuses on Public Protection by Reviving Automatic Commitment Following a Successful Insanity Defense,* 1986 WIS. L. REV. 781, 784. For what is probably the first recorded example of feigned insanity, see H. H. Cohn, *Some Psychiatric Phenomena in Ancient Law, in* PSYCHIATRY, LAW AND ETHICS 59, 61 (Ammon Carmi et al. eds. 1986) (David's decision to feign mental disorder to escape from King Saul; *see* 1 *Samuel* 21:13–16); *see also* Robert B. Brittain, *The History of Legal Medicine: The Assizes of Jerusalem,* 34 MEDICO–LEGAL J. 72 (1966) (feigned illness to avoid trial in 1100).

For a more recent example, see Boggs v. State, 667 So.2d 765 (Fla. 1996) (judge's statement to press that he believed defendant was "faking mental illness to avoid execution").

[46]Joel Eigen, *Historical Developments in Psychiatric Forensic Evidence: The British Experience,* 6 INT'L J.L. & PSYCHIATRY 423, 427 (1984). Thus in 1681 Sir Robert Holbrun wrote, "[A] man may counterfeit himself to be mad, he may do it so cunningly as it cannot be discerned whether he be mad or no." *Id.* at 427–28, quoting G. D. COLLINSON, A TREATISE ON THE LAW CONCERNING IDIOTS, LUNATICS, AND OTHER PERSONS "NON COMPOTES MENTIS" (1812).

[47]Rex v. Thomas, 7 Cr. App. R. 36 (1911), *discussed in* Homer D. Crotty, *The History of Insanity as a Defence to Crime in English Criminal Law,* 12 CALIF. L. REV. 105, 119 n.87 (1924).

[48]State v. James, 393 N.W.2d 465, 470 (Iowa 1986) (Lavorato, J., dissenting) (emphasis added).

[49]Perlin, *supra* note 19, at 98. *Cf.* Winiarz v. State, 752 P.2d 761, 763 (Nev. 1988) (reversible error for psychiatric expert to testify defendant was "feigning" in homicide cased where defendant pled mistake and misadventure as defenses). The alleged ease with which insanity can be feigned is also cited as a rationale for the tort law doctrine imposing tort liability on the "insane." *See, e.g.,* Williams by Williams v. Kearbey by and through Kearbey, 13 Kan. App. 2d 564, 775 P.2d 670, 672 (1989), citing RESTATEMENT (SECOND) OF TORTS § 895J, cmt. a (1977). For a more recent historical analysis, see Jeffrey Geller et al., *Feigned Insanity in Nineteenth Century America: Experts, Explanations and Exculpations,* 20 ANGLO-AM. L. REV. 443 (1991).

[50]Julian Eule, *The Presumption of Sanity: Bursting the Bubble,* 25 UCLA L. REV. 637, 649 (1978).

[51]*See, e.g.,* Lynch v. Overholser, 369 U.S. 705, 715 (1962) (Harlan, J.); United States v. Brown, 478 F.2d 606, 611 (D.C. Cir. 1973) (Leventhal, J.) (quoting *Lynch*).

[52]Gerald Neuman, *Territorial Discrimination, Equal Protection, and Self-Determination,* 135 U. PA. L. REV. 261, 361 (1987); Elyce Zenoff, *Controlling the Dangers of Dangerousness: The ABA Standards and Beyond,* 53 GEO. WASH. L. REV. 562, 569 (1985); ABA CRIMINAL JUSTICE MENTAL HEALTH STANDARDS, *Commentary to Standard* 7-7.3, at 409–10 (1989).

acquittees repeat these myths. In a press interview following a bench trial acquitting his client, defense counsel Jerome Ballarotto stated, ''Everybody who knew [the defendant] knew something wasn't right about this. . . . Prosecutors generally scoff at this type of defense, but *in this case, it was true.*''[53]

Yet this fear is unfounded.[54] There is virtually no evidence that feigned insanity has ever been a remotely significant problem of criminal procedure, even after more liberal substantive insanity tests were adopted. A survey of the case law reveals no more than a handful of cases in which a defendant free of mental disorder ''bamboozled''[55] a court or jury into a spurious insanity acquittal.[56]

Carefully crafted empirical studies have clearly demonstrated that malingering among insanity defendants is, and traditionally has been, statistically low.[57] Even where it is attempted, it is fairly easy to discover (if sophisticated diagnostic tools are used).[58] Clinicians correctly classify 92 to 95% of all individuals as either faking or not faking,[59] especially in cases in which defendants are faking severe forms of mental illness.[60] Some of

---

[53]Booth, *Trenton Firefighter Acquitted; Temporary Insanity Cited in 1991 Attack,* THE TIMES (Trenton, N.J.), March 17, 1993, at A19. The defendant, a firefighter, had suffered organic brain damage after having been struck on the head by a rock eight months prior to the incident that gave rise to the criminal charges. *Id.*

[54]Elizabeth Goldstein, *Asking the Impossible: The Negligence Liability of the Mentally Ill,* 12 J. CONTEMP. HEALTH L. & POL'Y 67, 75 (1995).

[55]United States v. Carter, 415 F. Supp. 15, 16 (D.D.C. 1975). *See* Mickenberg, supra *infra* note 112, at 981 (footnote omitted): ''Even the most vociferous opponents of the insanity defense are usually unable to cite actual cases of defendants who escaped justice by pretending to be mentally ill. United States Attorney Guiliani, when pressed on this point, cited the novel *Anatomy of a Murder* as a 'perfect example of how you can manipulate and use the insanity defense.' Needless to say, while *Anatomy of a Murder* is an excellent novel, it is still only fiction.''

[56]*See* People v. Lockett, 468 N.Y.S.2d 802 (Sup. Ct. 1983) (granting state's motion to vacate defendant's NGRI plea on ground defendant defrauded court); Sollars v. State, 316 P.2d 917 (Nev. 1957); People v. Schmidt, 110 N.E.2d 945 (N.Y. 1915). The defendant was *unsuccessful* in his effort in State v. Simonson, 669 P.2d 1092 (N.M. 1983).

Other anecdotal instances of feigned insanity are discussed in Sauer v. United States, 241 F.2d 640, 648 n.21 (9th Cir. 1957) (case of Martin Leven, *discussed in* FREDERICK WERTHAM, THE SHOW OF VIOLENCE (1949)), and in Rudolph Gerber, *The Insanity Defense Revisited,* 1984 ARIZ. ST. L.J. 83, 117–18 (speculating that President Nixon's charges that the insanity defense had been subject to ''unconscionable abuse by defendants stemmed from his reading press accounts of the case of United States v. Trapnell, 495 F.2d 22 (2d Cir. 1974), *cert. denied,* 419 U.S. 851 (1974), where the court admitted evidence that Trapnell, while a patient at a hospital, had counseled a fellow patient, Padilla, about how to feign insanity. Padilla subsequently had charges against him dropped and attributed his success to Trapnell's teachings on the art of acting insane. *Id.* at 24. For the complete story of Trapnell, see ELLIOT ASINOF, THE FOX IS CRAZY TOO: THE TRUE STORY OF GARRETT TRAPNELL, ADVENTURER, SKYJACKER, BANK ROBBER, CON MAN, LOVER (1976).

[57]Dewey Cornell & Gary Hawk, *Clinical Presentation of Malingerers Diagnosed by Experienced Forensic Psychologists,* 13 LAW & HUM. BEHAV. 375, 381–83 (1989); Linda Grossman & Orest Wasyliw, *A Psychiatric Study of Stereotypes: Assessment of Malingering in a Criminal Forensic Group,* 52 J. PERSONALITY ASSESSMENT 549 (1988).

For a rare case reflecting this reality, see United States v. Denny-Shaffer, 2 F.3d 999, 1009 (10th Cir. 1993).

[58]*See, e.g.,* Robert Wettstein & Edward Mulvey, *Disposition of Insanity Acquittees in Illinois,* 16 BULL. AM. ACAD. PSYCHIATRY & L. 11, 15 (1988) (one of 137 insanity acquittees seen as malingering).

For recent efforts to validate assessment tools designed to screen malingering, see Richard Rogers et al., *Improvements in the M Test as a Screening Measure for Malingering,* 20 BULL. AM. ACAD. PSYCHIATRY & L. 101 (1992); Richard Rogers et al., *Standardized Assessment of Malingering: Validation of the Structured Interview of Reported Symptoms,* 3 PSYCHOLOG. ASSESSMENT: J. CONSULTING & CLIN. PSYCHOL. 89 (1991); Richard Rogers, *Development of a New Classificatory Model of Malingering,* 18 BULL. AM. ACAD. PSYCHIATRY & L. 323 (1990).

[59]David Schretlen & Hal Arkowitz, *A Psychological Test Battery to Detect Prison Inmates Who Fake Insanity or Mental Retardation,* 8 BEHAV. SCI. & L. 75 (1990).

[60]Recent evidence suggests that tests that are accurate at detecting malingering of severe forms of psychosis may be less accurate in detecting malingering of posttraumatic stress disorder (PTSD). *See, e.g.,* Paul Lees-Haley, *Malingering Post Traumatic Stress Disorder on the MMPI,* 2 FORENSIC REP. 89 (1989). On juror suspicion in PTSD cases in general, see Judd Sneirson, *Black Rage and the Criminal Law: A Principled Approach to a Polarized Debate,* 143 U. PA. L. REV. 2251, 2280 (1995).

these cases involve defendants who, although feigning, are nonetheless severely mentally ill.[61] To some the mere act of pleading, say, multiple personality disorder syndrome is seen as malingering *in se*.[62]

Reported cases also reveal that attempted feigning is a risky gambit, and defendants have very few incentives to malinger.[63] Feigned attempts result in abandoned insanity defenses and convictions.[64] This, of course, should not be a surprise. Almost two centuries ago it was observed that feigning attempts would be "doomed to failure" because to "sustain the character of a paroxysm of active insanity would require a continuity of exertion beyond the power of the sane person."[65]

The empirical evidence is quite to the contrary: It is much more likely that seriously mentally disabled criminal defendants will feign *sanity* in an effort to not be seen as mentally ill, even where such evidence might serve as powerful mitigating evidence in death penalty cases.[66] Thus juveniles imprisoned on death row were quick to tell Dorothy Lewis and her associates, "I'm not crazy," or "I'm not a retard."[67]

---

[61]*See, e.g.*, Barton Gellman, *Acting Skills Gain Defendant an Extended Run in Prison: Mental Illness "Charade" Doesn't Fool Court*, WASHINGTON POST, July 6, 1989, at C1 (case of Tyrone Robinson) (data was consistent "both with psychosis and with desperate malingering"); People v. Kurbegovic, 188 Cal. Rptr. 268 (App. 1983) ("alphabet bomber case").

Other individuals suffer from Munchausen's syndrome, a mental disorder in which individuals voluntarily produce or simulate illness for no apparent purpose other than to assume a sick role. *See* Cohen v. Albert Einstein Med. Ctr., 592 A.2d 720, 724 (Pa. Super. 1991).

[62]Sarah Fields, *Multiple Personality Disorder and the Legal System*, 46 WASH. U. J. URB. & CONTEMP. L. 261, 284 (1994).

[63]*Id.* at 287–88.

[64]*See, e.g.*, People v. Bey, 562 N.Y.S.2d 896 (A.D. 1990) (defendant convicted; conviction affirmed); People v. Swan, 557 N.Y.S.2d 791 (A.D. 1990) (same); Ross v. Kemp, 393 S.E.2d 244 (Ga. 1990) (defendant convicted; conviction reversed on other grounds); Daniel v. Thigpen, 742 F. Supp. 1535, 1544–46 (M.D. Ala. 1990) (insanity defense abandoned; writ of *habeas corpus* granted on other grounds); *cf.* State v. Ondek, 584 So.2d 282, 291 (La. App. 1991), *rev. denied* (1991) (determination that defendant was malingering consistent with testimony that defendant was reading psychiatric diagnostic manual during forensic observation). For more recent cases affirming convictions, see, for example, State v. Smith, 872 P.2d 966 (Ore. 1994); State v. Medina, 636 A.2d 351 (Ct. 1994); State v. Thompson, 665 So.2d 643 (La. App. 1995), *writ denied* (1995); Love v. State, 909 S.W.2d 930 (Tex. App. 1995), *petition for discretion review refused* (1996); United States v. Duran, 891 F. Supp. 629 (D.D.C. 1995); Moranza v. State, 913 S.W.2d 718 (Tex. App. 1995); Cate v. State, 644 N.E.2d 546 (Ind. 1994).

For rare reversals in such cases, see, for example, Boggs v. State, 667 So.2d 765 (Fla. 1996); State v. Sparks, 891 S.W.2d 607 (Tenn. 1995); State v. Jackson, 890 S.W.2d 436 (Tenn. 1994).

[65]*See* Eigen, *supra* note 46, at 428, discussing JOHN HASLAM, JURISPRUDENCE AS IT RELATES TO INSANITY ACCORDING TO THE LAWS OF ENGLAND 60 (1817). *See also* People v. Schmidt, 216 N.Y. 324, 110 N.E. 945, 950 (1915) (emphasis added): "Cases will doubtless arise where criminals will take shelter behind a professed belief that their crime was ordained by God just as this defendant attempted to shelter himself behind that belief. *We can safely leave such fabrications to the common sense of juries.*"

But see Park Dietz, *Why the Experts Disagree: Variations in the Psychiatric Evaluation of Criminal Insanity*, 477 ANNALS 80, 82 (1985) ("To ask a murder defendant claiming hallucinations whether the voices encouraged the killing is to invite self-serving fabrication").

[66]*See, e.g.*, People v. McCleary, 567 N.E.2d 434, 437 (Ill. App. 1990) (defendant "malingered sanity"); Linda S. Grossman & James L. Cavanaugh Jr., *Do Sex Offenders Minimize Psychiatric Symptoms?* 34 J. FORENSIC SCI. 881 (1989) (answering question affirmatively); Grossman & Wasyliw, *supra* note 57 (22 to 39% of all insanity defendants studied showed evidence of minimizing their psychopathology).

[67]*See, e.g.*, Dorothy Lewis et al., *Neuropsychiatric, Psychoeducational, and Family Characteristics of 14 Juveniles Condemned to Death in the United States*, 145 AM. J. PSYCHIATRY 584, 588 (1988) (juveniles on death row "almost uniformly tried to hide evidence of cognitive deficits and psychotic symptoms"); Dorothy Otnow Lewis et al., *Psychiatric and Psychoeducational Characteristics of 15 Death Row Inmates in the United States*, 143 AM. J. PSYCHIATRY 838, 841 (1986) (all but one of sample of death row inmates studies attempted to *minimize* rather than exaggerate their degree of psychiatric disorders); P. J. Taylor, *Motives for Offending Among Violent and Psychotic Men*, 147 BRIT. J. PSYCHIATRY 491, 496–97 (1985) (in sample of 211 prisoners studied, nonpsychotic men never claimed psychotic justification for their offenses but half the psychotic men claimed ordinary, nonpsychotic motives).

In spite of this track record, the public remains highly skeptical of the abilities of forensic psychiatrists to determine legal insanity,[68] and continues to insist that "people are getting away with murder and [that the insanity defense] is an easy defense to fake."[69] Prosecutors have offered, as evidence of sanity, expert testimony that a defendant was "intelligent enough to feign sanity."[70] Anti-insanity defense prosecutors suggest that only "a defendant who is faking insanity" can reasonably fear disclosure of his response to postarrest *Miranda* warnings.[71] Prosecutors characterize the defense as a "fake" and the ensuing convictions are affirmed.[72]

Indeed, it may not even matter to some segment of the public whether an insanity defense is feigned or authentic; in either case it is equally rejected.[73] Even insanity defense supporters such as Richard Bonnie have recommended that "an exculpatory doctrine of insanity should be framed in a way that minimizes the risk of fabrication, abuse, and moral mistake."[74] Isaac Ray, known by many as the father of American forensic psychiatry, discussed the impact of these misperceptions more than a century ago: "The supposed insurmountable difficulty of distinguishing between feigned and real insanity has conduced, probably more than all other causes together, to bind the legal profession to the most rigid construction and application of the common law relative to this disease, and is always put forward in objection to the more humane doctrines."[75]

Courts are extraordinarily casual in their admission of both lay and expert testimony about feigning. Thus an expert's testimony that a defendant might have been feigning "because he could be released from an institution in only a few months" if he were found NGRI was considered an improper (albeit harmless) error only because there was no evidence in the case that the defendant had knowledge about the possibility of his potential release following such an insanity acquittal.[76] Nowhere in the court's brief opinion is there any indication about how such testimony fits within psychiatric expertise as to mental states.

---

[68]*See, e.g.,* Dan Slater & Valerie Hans, *Public Opinion of Forensic Psychiatry Following the Hinckley Verdict,* 141 AM. J. PSYCHIATRY 175, 177 (1984) (40% of those polled had "no confidence" in expert testimony in *Hinckley* trial; another 20% had only "slight" confidence); *see generally* Robert Homant & Daniel Kennedy, *Judgment of Legal Insanity as a Function of Attitude Toward the Insanity Defense,* 8 INT'L J.L. & PSYCHIATRY 67, 79–80 (1986).

[69]Amy Westfeldt, *Insanity Defense Rare, Very Hard to Prove,* ROCKY MTN. NEWS, Feb. 11, 1996, at 42A.

[70]Fulgham v. Ford, 850 F.2d 1529, 1534 (11th Cir. 1988). *Cf.* Francois v. Henderson, 850 F.2d 231, 235 (5th Cir. 1988), a case involving an insanity acquittee's *habeas corpus* application for release, in which the state alleged that the defendant was "faking sanity." Expert testimony was unanimous that sanity could be feigned for only a few hours, "No schizophrenic can feign sanity for years on end." *Id.*

[71]Richard Daley & Inge Fryklund, *The Insanity Defense and the "Testimony by Proxy" Problem,* 21 VAL. U. L. REV. 497, 521 (1987) (authors are Illinois state attorneys).

[72]*See* United States *ex rel* Ford v. O'Leary, 1990 WL 106498, at *2 (N.D. Ill. 1990) (denying writ of *habeas corpus*).

[73]*See* Gilbert Geis & Robert F. Meier, *Abolition of the Insanity Plea in Idaho: A Case Study,* 477 ANNALS 72, 73 (1985); (Idaho residents hold view that persons should not be allowed to avoid punitive consequences of criminal acts by relying on "either a real or a faked plea of insanity"); State v. Perry, 610 So.2d 746, 780 (La. 1992) (Cole, J., dissenting) ("Society has the right to protect itself from those who would commit murder and seek to avoid their legitimate punishment by a subsequently contracted, or feigned, insanity").

[74]Bonnie, *Equality, supra* note 3, at 15.

[75]ISAAC RAY, MEDICAL JURISPRUDENCE OF INSANITY § 247, at 243 (1962 ed.); *see generally* Richard Rogers, *Feigned Mental Illness,* 26 PROF. PSYCHOL. 312, 313 (1989) (labeling current model of malingering as "puritanical" and concluding it is "scientifically indefensible").

The issue of how jurors respond to fabricated defenses in general is discussed in State v. Eaton, 633 P.2d 921, 925 (Wash. App. 1981) (defendant claimed alcohol-induced blackout). *See also* Richard Singer, *On Classism and Dissonance in the Criminal Law: A Reply to Professor Meir Dan-Cohen,* 77 J. CRIM. L. & CRIMINOL. 69, 76 (1986) (discussing courts' fears of fabrication in cases involving prison inmates claiming duress in escape cases).

[76]People v. Christopher, 566 N.Y.S.2d 167, 168 (A.D. 1991).

Elsewhere, a conviction is affirmed based on expert testimony that "there is no blanket disturbance of reality just because a person is psychotic."[77]

In another case, testimony by a psychiatrist that an institutional chaplain had told him that he (the chaplain) felt the defendant "had tendencies to be a manipulative type of person" was admissible because that issue was "clearly relevant to . . . whether . . . [the defendant] was a malingerer."[78] Again, there is no discussion of why this is "clearly relevant" nor of the relationship that this testimony bears to the witness's expertise. This is especially telling in light of James Ogloff's conclusion that "unstructured interviews and projective tests are the least effective ways to identify malingerers."[79]

Courts are pretextual and teleological in the way they construe malingering testimony.[80] Where a defendant who committed a brutal murder gave himself up to police authorities, confessed, and showed no remorse for the killing, the court found that this evidence "wholly refute[d]" expert testimony about the defendant's insanity, leading to the initial conclusion that the defendant concocted evidence of delusions,[81] and to the broader holding that expert opinions are "especially entitled to little or no weight" when based on a "feigned state of mind."[82] Elsewhere, a court supported a finding that the defendant had "feigned incoherence" on evidence that his previous institutionalizations had made him "aware" of how to act during a psychological evaluation.[83] In neither of these instances is there any social science basis offered by the court to support its conclusions.

Lurking beneath the surface of this myth is another truism: The "'insanity dodge' has come into existence by popular concept as a symbol of sharp practice by unscrupulous attorneys and none too honest medical men."[84] Thus a comprehensive survey in the District of Columbia—the true laboratory for most major insanity defense developments in the past four decades—showed that court distrust of psychiatrists was "fully matched by distrust of defense counsel who appeared unorthodox in their approach to the insanity defense."[85] The parallels to the perception of the role of lawyers in death penalty cases[86] and in challenges to involuntary civil commitment standards[87] are remarkable.

---

[77]Abbott v. Cunningham, 959 F.2d 1, 2 (1st Cir. 1992).

[78]Sanders v. Commonwealth, 801 S.W.2d 665, 678 (Ky. 1990), rev. denied (1991).

[79]James Ogloff, *The Admissibility of Expert Testimony Regarding Malingering and Deception*, 8 BEHAV. SCI. & L. 27, 35 (1990).

[80]*See* Michael Perlin, *Morality and Pretextuality, Psychiatry and Law: Of "Ordinary Common Sense," Heuristic Reasoning, and Cognitive Dissonance*, 19 BULL. AM. ACAD. PSYCHIATRY & L. 131, 134 (1991).

[81]Commonwealth v. Patskin, 100 A.2d 472, 473 (Pa. 1953).

[82]*Id.* at 475.

[83]State v. Carr, 435 N.W.2d 194, 196–97 (Neb. 1989).

[84]WILLIAM A. WHITE, INSANITY AND THE CRIMINAL LAW 3 (1923); HENRY WEIHOFEN, MENTAL DISORDER AS A CRIMINAL DEFENSE 8 (1954); *see generally* Comment, *The Use of Illegally Obtained Evidence to Rebut the Insanity Defense: A New Exception to the Exclusionary Rule?* 74 J. CRIM. L. & CRIMINOL. 391, 402 (1983).

[85]Richard Arens & Jackwell Susman, *Judges, Jury Charges, and Insanity*, 12 How. L.J. 1, 5 (1966). Of 27 defense lawyers interviewed, all but one expressed the view that D.C. District Court judges "viewed the insanity defense with suspicion and at times hostility." *Id.* at 6; *see also* Keilitz, *supra* note 4, at 315 ("the promise of treatment" may draw defense counsel to the guilty-but-mentally-ill (GBMI) plea in cases where the insanity defense is unlikely to succeed).

[86]*See* Robert Burt, *Disorder in the Court: The Death Penalty and the Constitution*, 85 MICH. L. REV. 1741, 1793 (1987), characterizing Justice Rehnquist's dissent from *certiorari* in Coleman v. Balkcom, 451 U.S. 949, 958 (1981) (criticizing extensive judicial inquiry into capital punishment as a "mockery of our criminal justice system") as reflective of the fear that "shyster lawyers [have been] so successful in tricking gullible federal and state judges."

[87]*See* Michael L. Perlin, *Book Review of* ANN B. JOHNSON, OUT OF BEDLAM: THE TRUTH ABOUT DEINSTITUTIONALIZATION (1990), 8 N.Y.L. SCH. J. HUM. RTS. 557, 558–60 (1991) (refuting arguments blaming post-deinstitutionalization social problems on patients' rights' lawyers); *see generally* Perlin, *supra* note 36.

Forensic psychiatrists testifying in criminal cases were similarly viewed "as attempting to cloud our moral standards and to ignore the limits of community tolerance."[88] From their first involvement in court proceedings, "'alienists' . . . have been perceived as a threat to public security and a fancy means for 'getting criminals off.'"[89] Yet as long as 73 years ago, William A. White responded to these charges: "In my personal experience I have *never* known a criminal to escape conviction on the plea of 'insanity' where the evidence did not warrant such a verdict [except in jury nullification cases]."[90] Although the story was greeted initially with some amusement, the fact that the New Mexico legislature passed legislation in 1996 (subsequently vetoed by the state's governor) that would have required a mental health professional testifying during competency hearings to "wear a cone-shaped hat that is not less than two feet tall [,whose] surface . . . shall be imprinted with stars and lightning bolts"[91] suggests that little has changed over the past century.

More recently experts have been viewed as unnecessary to the process because the subject of their testimony appears to be within the lay individual's realm of "ordinary common sense." The Seventh Circuit recently noted that although psychologists and psychiatrists may sometimes demonstrate a "genuine expertise," their testimony is often "nothing more than fancy phrases for common sense."[92] In a recent commentary in a state bar journal, a Pennsylvania attorney put it this way:

> An "expert witness" is generally defined as one possessing, with reference to a particular subject, knowledge not acquired by ordinary persons. But what facet of human behavior is foreign to the average judge or jury? Who hasn't felt rage, anger, loss, despair, self-pity, fear, and depression? Haven't we all been in the vise-like grip of an irresistible impulse only to be surprised when a little self-restraint caused it to loosen its grip?[93]

In short, the fear of feigned insanity and the distrust of expert witnesses' ability to identify malingering behavior continues to dominate insanity defense jurisprudence.[94] The empirical data suggesting that this problem is minimal continues to be trivialized, and judges, legislators, and jurors continue to adhere to this most powerful of all myths.

---

[88]William Weitzel, *Public Skepticism: Forensic Psychiatry's Albatross,* 5 BULL. AM. ACAD. PSYCHIATRY & L. 456, 459 (1977).

[89]Andrew Watson, *On the Preparation and Use of Psychiatric Expert Testimony: Some Suggestions in an Ongoing Controversy,* 6 BULL. AM. ACAD. PSYCHIATRY & L. 226, 226 (1978). *Cf.* Alan Stone, *The Ethical Boundaries of Forensic Psychiatry: A View From the Ivory Tower,* 12 BULL. AM. ACAD. PSYCHIATRY & L. 209, 214 (1984):

> Indeed it seems there is a very comfortable ideological fit between being a forensic psychiatrist and being against capital punishment; being therapeutic rather than punitive; being against the prosecution and what was seen as the harsh status quo in criminal law. This ideological fit has begun to come apart in recent history, but during the days when David Bazelon and American psychiatry had their love affair, the fit was real. Those were the halcyon days when the concept of treatment and the concept of social justice were virtually indistinguishable.

[90]WHITE, *supra* note 84, at 3.

[91]*Psychological Limits,* CLEVELAND PLAIN DEALER, Feb. 8, 1996, at 10E.

[92]United States v. Hall, 93 F.3d 1337, 1343 (7th Cir. 1996). *But cf.,* People v. Strader, 663 N.E.2d 511, 515 (Ill. App. 1996) ("this court is not prepared to say that the entire field of psychology is a matter of knowledge common to all").

[93]Gerald McOscar, *Just the Facts, Please; Opinions by Mental Health Experts at Trial Are Useless or Worse,* PA. L.J. (Mar. 7, 1994), at 2.

[94]Such decisions continue unbated. *See e.g.,* People v. Robinson, 84 Cal. Rptr. 2d 832 (App. 1999); State v. Marshall, 1999 WL 126138 (Ohio App. 1999).

Sanism and the Insanity Defense

Insanity defense decision making is often irrational. It rejects empiricism, science, psychology, and philosophy, and substitutes myth, stereotype, bias, and distortion. It resists educational correction, demands punishment regardless of responsibility, and reifies medievalist concepts based on fixed and absolute notions of good and evil and of right and wrong. In short, our insanity defense jurisprudence is the jurisprudence of sanism.[95]

This irrationality is on occasion recognized by courts and by litigants.[96] In reversing a conviction in a case in which the trial judge refused to ask prospective jurors if they could fairly judge an insanity case, the Illinois Supreme Court specifically found, "Although the insanity defense upon which the defendant relied is a well-recognized legal defense, it remains a subject of intense controversy [, and one] 'which is known to be subject to bias or prejudice.'"[97] Also, a California appellate court has retroactively applied an earlier judicial decision that a defendant must be advised that his or her postinsanity acquittal may exceed the maximum possible term of imprisonment for the underlying crime.[98] On the other hand, the New Jersey Supreme Court affirmed a trial judge's rejection of a defendant's application for a nonjury trial on a murder charge where his insanity defense was based on "abnormal homosexual fantasies."[99] In its decision the court stressed "the importance of maintaining the public's confidence in our criminal justice system" and described the jury system as "the best vehicle for attaining justice."[100]

Other relatively recent cases reflect sanism in insanity defense trials. A Louisiana jury rejected the defense in the case of a defendant who had been diagnosed as paranoid-

---

[95]Media errors compound the problem. A *USA Today* article about the Jeffrey Dahmer case stated inaccurately that the American Law Institute test, *see* AMER. LAW INSTITUTE MODEL PENAL CODE § 64.01, was operative in all federal courts. *See* John Howlett, *The Dahmer Debate / Sanity Trial Raises Social-Legal Questions,* USA Today, Feb. 10, 1992, at 3A (full text available on NEXIS). Of course, that test was legislatively repealed nearly a decade ago in the Insanity Defense Reform Act of 1984, *see* 18 U.S.C. § 20, legislatively overruling United States v. Brawner, 471 F.2d 969 (D.C. Cir. 1972); *see generally* 3 PERLIN, *supra* note 17, § 15.39, at 397–402. At the time of the *Hinckley* trial, the *New York Times* incorrectly stated that the then-operative insanity defense was the *Durham* test. Stephen Roberts, *High U.S. Officials Express Outrage, Asking for New Law and Insanity Plea,* N.Y. TIMES, June 23, 1982, at B6, col. 3 (full text available on NEXIS). That test had been judicially overruled a decade prior to the publication of the article. *See Brawner,* 471 F.2d at 981, *overruling* Durham v. United States, 214 F.2d 862 (D.C. Cir. 1954); *see generally* 3 PERLIN, *supra* note 17, § 15.07, at 300–03.

[96]The role of sanism in insanity defense jurisprudence was raised specifically—albeit unsuccessfully—to the court in Matter of Francis S., 640 N.Y.S.2d 840 (1995) (fact that insanity acquittee's condition was stabilized during hospitalization did not preclude finding of current dangerousness as result of mental illness). *See* Appellant's Brief, at 73 n.28 (discussing impact of sanism on insanity defense fact finding). *Cf.* State v. Wilson, 700 A.2d 633, 649–50 (Conn. 1997) (Katz, J., concurring):

> No aspect of the criminal justice system is more controversial than is the insanity defense. Nowhere else does the successful employment of a defense regularly bring about cries for its abolition; no other aspect of the criminal law inspires position papers from trade associations spanning the full range of professional and political entities. When the defense is successful in a high-level publicity case (especially when it involves a defendant whose "factual guilt" is clear), the acquittal triggers public outrage and serves vividly as a screen upon which each relevant interest group can project its fears and concerns. M. Perlin, *The Jurisprudence of the Insanity Defense* (1994) p. 3.

[97]People v. Stack, 493 N.E.2d 339, 344 (Ill. 1986), quoting in part, People v. Bowel, 111 488 N.E.2d 995 (Ill. 1986).

[98]People v. Minor, 277 Cal. Rptr. 615, 616 (App. 1991).

[99]State v. Dunne, 590 A.2d 1144 (N.J. 1991). The trial judge had ruled that "this is the kind of case that it is appropriate to have the community decide," adding that proposed *voir dire* questions could sufficiently screen out prejudiced venire members. *Id.* at 1146.

[100]*Id.* at 1152. It concluded on this point: "We surrender to no clamor when we protect trial by jury; we simply accept the wisdom of the ages and benefit from the experience of thousands of judges over hundreds of years who continue to marvel at the consistent soundness of jury verdicts." *Id.*

schizophrenic more than 20 years prior to the crime (in which he beheaded a minister, whom he thought to be "the anti-Christ," in full view of several police officers) that took place three days after he was released from his eighth commitment to a mental institution.[101] Although the state supreme court reversed the conviction,[102] Justice Kimball nevertheless dissented, arguing that "a rational trier of the fact . . . could have concluded defendant failed to prove [insanity] by a preponderance of the evidence."[103] In other cases, juries rejected insanity defenses in spite of "overwhelming and *uncontradicted*" evidence of insanity,[104] and where such rejection "was so against the great weight and preponderance of evidence as to be manifestly unjust."[105]

Certainly not all insanity opinions are sanist.[106] But a reading of any sample of reported opinions leads to the ineluctable conclusion that our insanity defense jurisprudence is the jurisprudence of sanism.

Pretexts and the Insanity Defense

Pretextuality riddles the entire insanity defense decision making process; it pervades decisions by forensic hospital administrators, police officers, expert witnesses, and judges.[107] Hospital decision making is a good example. A National Institute of Mental Health (NIMH) task force convened in the wake of the *Hinckley* acquittal underscored this in its final report: "From the perspective of the Hospital, *in controversial cases such as Hinckley,* the U.S. Attorney's Office can be counted upon to oppose *any* conditional release recommendation."[108] As John Parry has explained, "Hospitals have been pressured by public outrage to bend over backwards to make sure that no insanity acquittee is released too soon, *even* if such pressure is contrary to the intent and spirit of being found not guilty by reason of insanity."[109]

There are legislative pretexts as well. For example, the House Report accompanying the House version of the Insanity Defense Reform Act explicitly acknowledged:

---

[101]State v. Armstrong, 671 So.2d 307 (La. 1996).

[102]*Id.* at 312–13:

> Thus, the defense's case on insanity consisted of the twenty-five year history of mental illness with delusions, auditory hallucinations, religious obsessions and occasional psychotic episodes, particularly when defendant was subjected to stress or failed to take his medication; the testimony of three psychiatrists and one psychologist who opined that defendant could not distinguish right from wrong at the time of the killing; evidence of defendant's dispute with his bank causing him stress, a precursor of psychotic episodes, and of his involuntary commitment to a mental institution shortly before the killing and his violent behavior there; and extensive evidence of bizarre behavior, before and after the killing, which was consistent with conduct that has led to his numerous hospitalizations.

[103]*Id.* at 313.

[104]Dixon v. State, 668 So.2d 65,71 (Ala. Crim. 1994), *reh'g denied* (1995) (emphasis added).

[105]Jackson v. State, 941 S.W.2d 351, 352 (Tex. App. 1997).

[106]*See, e.g.,* Janezic v. State, 1996 WL 637376, at *11 (Ala. Cr. App. 1996) (Patterson, J., dissenting); Taylor v. State, 640 So.2d 1127 (Fla. Dist. App. 1994), *reh'g denied* (1994); State v. Sheppard, 679 So.2d 899 (La. 1996).

[107]*See* Villaverde, *supra* note 25, at 214 (on the insanity defense system's need "to maintain the perception that [it is] free from bias"), and *id.* at 236–37 (on pretexts in insanity defense system).

[108]*Final Report of the National Institute of Mental Health (NIMH) Ad Hoc Forensic Advisory Panel,* 12 MENT. & PHYS. DIS. L. REP. 77, 96 (1988) (emphasis added). Hinckley's recent application for conditional release has been rejected. *See* United States v. Hinckley, 967 F. Supp. 557 (D.D.C. 1997), *aff'd* by Hinckley v. United States, 140 F.3d 277 (D.C. Cir. 1998); *see, e.g.,* Alex Chadwick, *Hinckley Petitions for Monthly Day Away From Custody* (NPR, Sept. 27, 1996), Transcript #1965-11 ("overwhelming majority view of public is that Hinckley should never be released).

[109]John Parry, *The Civil–Criminal Dichotomy in Insanity Commitment and Release Proceedings:* Hinckley *and Other Matters,* 11 MENT. & PHYS. DIS. L. REP. 218, 223 (1987) (emphasis added).

> Although abuses of the insanity defense are few and have an insignificant direct impact upon the criminal justice system, the Committee nonetheless concluded that the present defense and the procedures surrounding its use are in need of reform ... The insanity defense has an impact on the criminal justice system that goes beyond the actual cases involved. The use of the defense in highly publicized cases, and the *myths surrounding its use,* have undermined public faith in the criminal justice system.[110]

It is this concession—that Congress must act to assuage erroneous public sentiments (based on what all acknowledge to be myths)—that is especially astounding, and to which serious attention must be paid.

Expert witnesses are similarly pretextual. In one case, a testifying doctor conceded that he may have "hedged" in earlier testimony (as to whether an insanity acquittee could be released) "because he did not want to be criticized should [the defendant] be released and then commit a criminal act."[111] Law enforcement officials frequently act in similar ways. Thus at the same time that Attorney General William French Smith told Congress that the insanity defense "allows *so many persons* to commit crimes of violence," one of his top aides candidly told a federal judicial conference that the number of insanity defense cases was, statistically, "probably insignificant."[112] In addition, police officers act pretextually in cases involving potential insanity defendants. In analyzing police decisions about which defendants should be arrested and which should be hospitalized, researchers found that police often "invoked a form of insanity defense," governed by their perceptions of the actor's "degree of intentionality" and responsibility.[113]

Most important, all aspects of the judicial decision-making process embody pretextuality. To a significant extent this is caused by the fear that defendants will "fake" the insanity defense to escape punishment continues to paralyze the legal system in spite of an impressive array of empirical evidence that reveals (a) the minuscule number of such cases, (b) the ease with which trained clinicians are usually able to "catch" malingering in such cases,[114] (c) the inverse greater likelihood that defendants—even at grave peril to their life—will more likely try to convince examiners that they're "not crazy," (d) the high risk in pleading the insanity defense (leading to statistically significant greater prison terms meted out to unsuccessful insanity pleaders), and (e) the far greater length in stay that most successful insanity pleaders (a minute universe to begin with) remain in maximum security facilities than they would have served had they been convicted on the underlying criminal indictment.[115]

---

[110]H.R.REP. NO. 577, 98th Cong., 1st Sess., 9–10 (1983) (emphasis added).

[111]Francois v. Henderson, 850 F.2d 231, 234 (5th Cir. 1988).

[112]Perlin, *Pretexts, supra* note 1, at 637 n.50, quoting, *inter alia,* Ira Mickenberg, *A Pleasant Surprise: The Guilty but Mentally Ill Verdict Has Succeeded on Its Own Right and Successfully Preserved the Traditional Role of the Insanity Defense,* 55 U. CIN. L. REV. 943, 980 (1987), and *Proceedings of the Forty-Sixth Judicial Conference of the District of Columbia Circuit,* 111 F.R.D. 91, 225 (1985).

[113]Richard Rogers, *Policing Mental Disorder: Controversies, Myths, and Realities,* 24 SOC. POL. & ADMIN. 226, 231 (1990); *see also* Robert Menzies, *Psychiatrists in Blue: Police Apprehension of Mental Disorder and Dangerousness,* 25 CRIMINOLOGY 429 (1987); Linda Teplin & Nancy Pruett, *Police as Streetcorner Psychiatrists: Managing the Mentally Ill,* 15 INT'L J.L. & PSYCHIATRY 139, 154–55 (1992).

[114]*See, e.g.,* Alley v. State, 958 S.W.2d 138, 141 (Tenn. Crim. App. 1997) (testimony by lay mental health program specialist that defendant with multiple personality disorder often acted "normally"). For research identifying behavioral characteristics commonly found in malingerers, see Carl Gacono et al., *A Clinical Investigation of Malingering and Psychopathy in Hospitalized Insanity Acquittees,* 23 BULL. AM. ACAD. PSYCHIA-TRY & L. 387 (1995).

[115]*See* Perlin, *supra* note 39, at 1423. *See supra* text accompanying notes 25–38.

Thus some judges simply ignore appellate decisions that they perceive might make it more likely for defendants to be found NGRI.[116] Elsewhere, decision after decision—in obscure cases and famous ones—reveals appellate affirmances of conviction in insanity defense cases (or affirmances of trial court decisions to not charge jurors on the insanity defense) despite overwhelming expert testimony about defendants' profound mental disability and lack of responsibility,[117] or despite profound legal errors in jury charge.[118] In one case a jury conviction was affirmed where the state's insanity rebuttal was based on evidence that the defendant "could have gained knowledge of psychological testing" while a college student, and thus consequently "could lie and might have been faking."[119] In *Jones v. United States* the Supreme Court justified its upholding of a postinsanity acquittal commitment scheme on the grounds that the commission of an attempted misdemeanor (shoplifting) provided "concrete evidence" of the individual's continuing dangerousness.[120] Justice Thomas' dissent in *Foucha v. Louisiana*[121] is animated by pretextual reasoning at its most corrosive.[122]

---

[116]James Ogloff et al., *Empirical Research Regarding the Insanity Defense: How Much Do We Really Know?* in LAW AND PSYCHOLOGY: BROADENING THE DISCIPLINE 171, 187–88 (J. Ogloff ed. 1992) (following the *Durham* decision [*see* 3 PERLIN, *supra* note 17, § 15. 06, at 296–99] District of Columbia trial judges continued to substantially charge juries in language of *M'Naghten* decision).

[117]*See, e.g.,* Commonwealth v. Hildreth, 572 N.E.2d 18 (Mass. App. 1991) (evidence insufficient to support insanity instruction) (defendant had contemporaneously made multiple suicide attempts, was diagnosed with bipolar disorder, and had bragged about imaginary communications with individuals such as Donald Trump); State v. Jarrett, 591 A.2d 1225, 1228–29 (Conn. 1991) (conviction affirmed; uncontradicted expert testimony introduced that defendant suffered from delusional beliefs about "astroplaning," reincarnation, and life on other planets); Ellis v. State, 570 So.2d 744 (Ala. Crim. App.. 1990), *reh'g denied* (1990), *cert. denied* (1990) (conviction affirmed; uncontradicted expert testimony that defendant was not responsible; state produced no contrary expert testimony); People v. Beehn, 563 N.E.2d 1207 (Ill. App. 1990) (same); DePasquale v. State, 803 P.2d 218 (Nev. 1990), *reh'g denied,* 1991) (conviction affirmed despite defendant's psychiatric history that included pulling his own eye from its socket); State v. Stacy, 601 S.W.2d 696, 700 (Tenn. 1980) (Henry, J., dissenting) (conviction affirmed; dissenters charge that majority opinion operationally returns state to "wild beast" test, *see supra* text accompanying note 15; expert testimony gave "thundering support" to defendant's insanity plea)

[118]*See* State v. Chavez, 693 P.2d 936 (Ariz. App. 1984) (omission of first prong of *M'Naghten* test from judge's charge deemed harmless error).

[119]State v. Mercer, 625 P.2d 44, 50 (Mont. 1981).

[120]463 U.S. 354, 364–65 (1983). *See* Patrick Appel, *The Constitutionality of Automatic Commitment Procedures Applied to Persons Found Not Guilty by Reason of Insanity:* Jones v. United States, 21 HOUS. L. REV. 421, 440 (1984) (*Jones* decision based on "subterfuge of a statutory presumption). For a prototype post-*Jones* case, see, for example, State v. Randall, 532 N.W.2d 94 (Wis. 1995) (Wisconsin's statutory scheme for commitment of insanity acquittees based solely on dangerousness does not violate due process clause).

[121]504 U.S. 71 (1992) (insanity acquittee could not be retained in forensic mental hospital if he were no longer mentally ill, see PERLIN, *supra* note 17, § 15.25A, at 536–37 (1998 Cum. Supp.).

[122]Justice Thomas based his conclusion that Foucha's continued retention in a forensic psychiatric hospital (notwithstanding a finding that he was not mentally ill) was permissible on a variety of sources, including the 1962 commentary to the Model Penal Code, a 1933 text by Henry Weihofen, and a 1956 Supreme Court case that had stressed psychiatry's "uncertainty of diagnosis." *Foucha,* 504 U.S. at 110–12, 118. He focused at some length on the possibility of "calculated abuse of the insanity defense" by defendants who might feign the plea, and speculated about how the public might react to the specter of a "serial killer . . . returned to the streets immediately after trial." *Id.* at 111.

Justice Thomas' opinion is especially remarkable for several reasons. First, he relies on legal scholarship that precedes (by 10 to 40 years) the Court's application of the due process clause to cases involving the institutionalization of mentally disabled criminal defendants. *See* Jackson v. Indiana, 406 U.S. 715 (1972). Second, he relies on a mid-1950s characterization of psychiatric precision in diagnosis to suggest that psychiatry is so inexact that the

In the rare cases in which a court believes that a defendant is not faking, there is inevitably a physiological explanation available. Thus in *People v. Curry,* the court noted that the defendant could not be faking schizophrenia, relying on uncontradicted expert testimony that "a normal person would lapse into a coma under the massive doses of anti-schizophrenia drugs defendant was taking."[123]

On some occasions, judges recognize when their brethren are being pretextual. In *Geschwendt v. Ryan,* where the defendant's sole defense was insanity, the Third Circuit, sitting *en banc,* upheld a *habeas corpus* denial in a Pennsylvania multiple murder case in which the trial judge had not charged the jury that they could specifically find the defendant NGRI. In an especially tortured opinion for a seven-judge majority, Judge Morton Greenberg reasoned that, although the jurors were not informed of the insanity option, they had been told that they could find the defendant guilty of third-degree murder if they found that the defendant had a diminished mental capacity.[124] Because the defendant was convicted of first-degree murder, Judge Greenberg concluded, "We think that it would be irrational to believe, if the jury would have found Geschwendt [NGRI] if given that explicit choice, the same jury would reject a third degree murder verdict."[125]

In an impassioned opinion (on behalf of himself and three others), Judge Ruggero Aldisert dissented. After noting that the Pennsylvania Supreme Court had explicitly rejected the argument that a third-degree murder instruction was "fundamentally similar" to an insanity instruction,[126] Aldisert turned to the pretextual nature of the majority's decision:

> I had always thought there was a difference between being found guilty and being acquitted. I thought that this was a basic principle taught in junior high school civics classes. I am, therefore, somewhat distressed that the majority are not willing to extend the same right to be found not guilty by reason of insanity that the U.S. District Court for the District of Columbia accorded John Hinckley, Jr., who, after attempting to assassinate then President Ronald Reagan in 1981, successfully interposed this defense.
>
> The right to be committed to a mental institution, rather than imprisoned in a penitentiary, also was the critical issue in the plea entered this year in the internationally publicized case of Jeffrey L. Dahmer, who admitted strangling and dismembering 17 young males. He was permitted under Wisconsin law to plead not guilty of murder by reason of mental disease or defect, which constitutes an admission as to the elements of the substantive offense, except for the mental state, and raises a defense of insanity. Dahmer thus was entitled to a fair determination of his mental capacity, notwithstanding the extreme brutality of his crimes.

Court should discount expert testimony, saying that an individual once acquitted on grounds of insanity is not mentally ill; yet he finds that psychiatric predictions of dangerousness are sufficiently reliable to require the acquittee's future institutionalization (although the experts hedged on even this prediction).

Third, his twin foci on the sanist judges' worst fears about insanity acquittees—that they "faked" the insanity defense in the first place and that the improper use of the defense will allow for the speedy release of serial killers—profoundly demonstrates how judges can distort social science evidence. The empirical data is clear that the insanity defense is rarely feigned, that such attempts are invariably seen through by fact finders, and that successful acquittees are generally institutionalized in maximum security facilities for far longer periods of time than they would have been incarcerated in penal facilities had they been convicted of the predicate crimes. *See supra* text accompanying notes 30–32. His reference to "serial killers" is even more perplexing, given the fact that Foucha's underlying charges were burglary and firearms offenses.

[123]588 N.E.2d 423, 426 (Ill. App. 1992). *Cf.* Riggins v. Nevada, 504 U.S. 127, 143 (1992) (dosage of Mellaril prescribed for defendant sufficient to "tranquilize an elephant").

[124]967 F.2d 877, 885–87 (3d Cir. 1992), *cert. denied,* 506 U.S. 977 (1992).

[125]*Id.* at 887.

[126]*Id.* at 894–95, discussing Commonwealth v. Reilly, 549 A.2d 503, 510–11 (Pa. 1988).

I am melancholy that this court, long recognized as a shining acropolis of constitutional law protection, now stands in the shade. In the shade of a federal district court in our nation's capital and a state trial court in Wisconsin.

There is a fundamental difference between being found guilty of an offense and being acquitted, albeit by reason of insanity. Every member of this court knows this. And irrespective of the reprehensible acts committed in this case, we are a reviewing court of judges; we are not an ingathering or collection of the laity, untrained in the law. As judges we must rise above the passions of the streets, above superstition or popularity or opprobrium. In the words of Justice Felix Frankfurter, we are committed to the "institutionalized medium of reason, [and] that's all we have standing between us and the tyranny of mere will and the cruelty of unbridled, unprincipled, undisciplined feeling."[127]

Sometimes mental disability pretexts become intertwined with other pretexts. Thus it has been held that the defendant's decision to raise the insanity defense opened the door to prosecutorial cross-examination about his membership in the Black Muslim religion and his attitudes toward police authority.[128] On the other hand, a conviction was reversed where the court found that the prosecutor's sanist attitudes (striking a *venire* member employed in the mental health field because he allegedly believed that "someone who works in mental health would be more liberal than conservative") were a pretext for an impermissible racially based challenge.[129]

Yet another layer of pretext involves the quality of counsel provided to mentally disabled criminal defendants at insanity-defense proceedings. Counsel has traditionally been found to be grossly inadequate on behalf of all mentally disabled individuals, and especially substandard in cases involving mentally disabled criminal defendants.[130] This inadequacy is especially troubling because of the false assumption that adequate counsel is generally available for such persons.[131] For example, a conviction was reversed on the grounds of counsel's failure to have a competency evaluation done on his client prior to trial; when the defendant had asked for an adjournment to "get some help," counsel had opposed the request with this reasoning: "This is a lady who has never faced stress. She always tries to run from it. I don't think it's going to—this may sound harsh—I think making her stand trial might be good for her. It's going to be very difficult because I know she will interrupt, and everyone knows she's going to have trouble. But if she stands trial and gets through it, I think it will benefit her. . . ."[132]

This inadequacy has been further heightened in the aftermath of the Supreme Court's "sterile and perfunctory" adequacy standard established in *Strickland v. Washington*.[133] Most courts adhere to a minimalist reading of *Strickland,* and the Supreme Court has

---

[127]*Id.* at 869–87 (footnotes omitted).

[128]People v. Aliwoli, 606 N.E.2d 347, 354 (Ill. App. 1992) (expert was asked whether he was aware that, in the 1960s, the Black Muslim newspaper *Muhammad Speaks* referred to police officers as "pigs").

[129]House v. State, 1993 WL 48244, at *1 (Fla. Dist. App. 1993).

[130]Perlin, *supra* note 36, at 43. *See generally* Rodney Uphoff, *The Role of the Criminal Defense Lawyer in Representing the Mentally Impaired Criminal Defendant: Zealous Advocate or Officer of the Court?* 1988 WIS. L. REV. 65.

[131]*See generally* Perlin, *supra* note 36; *cf.* Louis Seidman, Brown and Miranda, 80 CALIF. L. REV. 673 (1992) (decisions such as *Brown* and *Miranda* provide "false sense of closure and resolution" about contradictions in democratic society).

[132]People v. Harris, 450 N.W.2d 239, 241–42 (Mich. App. 1990).

[133]Perlin, *supra* note 36, at 53. In *Strickland,* 466 U.S. 668, 687–88 (1984), the court found there to be no constitutional violation if counsel provided "reasonably effective assistance" to be measured objectively by "prevailing professional norms."

countenanced this reading, even in death penalty cases.[134] Although occasionally a conviction is reversed based on inadequacy of counsel in failing to raise an insanity defense,[135] refusal of courts to acknowledge the frequent substandard job done by counsel in this most the demanding area of the law is simply pretextual. In reporting on the way that trial judges basically ignored the dictates of the *Durham* decision in charging juries in the District of Columbia after 1954, James Ogloff and his colleagues thus noted, "It is troubling that the defendants' lawyers apparently did not understand the differences between *M'Naghten* and *Durham* sufficiently to appeal their clients' cases based on the incorrect instructions the judges had given the juries."[136]

William Crowley, a professor of law at Montana Law School and one of the architects of the bill abolishing the insanity defense in that state, has simply said, in response to arguments based on empirical data, that he had "a deep and basic mistrust of statistics."[137]

In short, pretextuality dominates insanity defense decision making. Again, Judge Aldisert's dissent in *Geschwendt* eloquently explains the roots of pretextuality:

> In a case such as this, where it is difficult to muster any sympathy for the petitioner, the task of determining whether the state trial court protected his constitutional rights taxes the accountability, if not the very integrity, of the federal judicial system in its obligation to implement the Great Writ. . . .
>
> As we measure the contours of the Constitution, federal judges are keenly aware that we do not engage in a popularity contest. We must disregard public opinion on a given issue or in a given case. As ultimate guardians of the Constitution, our role is to insure that society, when prosecuting those who breach its rules of conduct, does not breach its own rules of procedure. Our task in federal collateral review of state convictions, therefore, is not to inquire whether the habeas petitioner has violated rules of social conduct, but only whether society, in this case the Commonwealth of Pennsylvania, has respected the rules it has established to guarantee fair trials.[138]

The inability of judges to do just this—disregard public opinion and inquire into whether defendants have had fair trials—is both the root and the cause of pretextuality in insanity-defense jurisprudence.

Conclusion

I believe that much of the incoherence of insanity-defense jurisprudence can be explained by the phenomena I have discussed in this section. Stereotyped thinking leads to sanist behavior. And sanist decisions are rationalized by pretextuality on the part of judges, legislators, and lawyers. This combination of sanism and pretextuality fits with traditional ways of thinking about (and acting toward) persons with mental disabilities; it reifies centuries of myths and superstitions and is consonant with both the way we use heuristic cognitive devices and our own faux, nonreflective "ordinary common sense."

---

[134]*See, e.g.,* 1 PERLIN, *supra* note 17, § 2B-11.3, at 267–71 (2d ed. 1998) (discussing cases); Alvord v. Wainwright, 469 U.S. 956 (1984) (Marshall, J., dissenting from denial of grant of *certiorari*).

[135]*See, e.g.,* People v. Jones, MICH. LAWYERS WEEKLY (Aug. 31, 1992) (full text available on NEXIS).

[136]Ogloff et al., *supra* note 116, at 188.

[137]Rita Buitendorp, *A Statutory Lesson From "Big Sky Country" on Abolishing the Insanity Defense,* 30 VAL. U. L. REV. 965, 1021 n.169 (1996).

[138]*Geschwendt,* 967 F.2d at 892 (Aldisert, J., dissenting).

Despite the development of dynamic psychology and psychiatry, we regularly have rejected psychodynamic explanations for behavior because such explanations were cognitively dissonant with our need to punish: We choose to reinterpret information and experience that conflicts with our internally accepted beliefs to avoid the unpleasant state that such inconsistency produces.[139]

The development of the insanity defense has tracked the tension between psychodynamics and punishment and reflects our most profound ambivalence about both. On one hand, we are especially punitive toward the mentally disabled, "the most despised and feared group in society";[140] on the other, we recognize that in some narrow and carefully circumscribed circumstances, exculpation is—and historically has been—proper and necessary. This ambivalence infects a host of criminal justice policy issues that involve mentally disabled criminal defendants beyond insanity defense decision making: on issues of expert testimony, mental disability as a mitigating (or aggravating) factor at sentencing and in death penalty cases, and the creation of a "compromise" GBMI verdict.

So we accept an insanity defense system that is sanist, pretextual, and teleological, a system that rests in the shaky underpinnings of heuristic reasoning and a false "ordinary common sense". And this acceptance may ultimately doom to failure any attempt to reconstitute insanity defense policy, even when examined through the lens of therapeutic jurisprudence.[141]

Why is this? I believe that our refusal to care about or think about the objective realities that I have been discussing and our dogged, banal reliance on sanist myths and pretextual reasoning is made far easier by both phenomena that I discussed earlier: by our authoritarian spirit and our culture of punishment. These phenomena allow us—*encourage* us—to wilfully blind ourselves to behavioral, scientific, cultural, and empirical realities.

These dissonances, tensions, and ambivalences—again rooted in medieval thought—continue to control the public's psyche. They reflect the extent of the gap between academic discourse and social values and the "deeply rooted moral and religious tension" that surrounds responsibility decision making.[142] Ours is a culture of punishment. Only when we acknowledge that psychic and physical reality can we expect to make sense of the underlying jurisprudence. And our insanity defense jurisprudence thus continues to operate as it always has—out of consciousness.[143]

---

[139]*See generally* PERLIN, *supra* note 43.

[140]*See* Deborah C. Scott et al., *Monitoring Insanity Acquittees: Connecticut's Psychiatric Security Review Board,* 41 HOSP. & COMMUNITY PSYCHIATRY 980, 982 (1990). I believe that, at this point in time, convicted sexual predators have replaced insanity acquittees in the public's mind. *See* Michael L. Perlin, *"There's No Success Like Failure/and Failure's No Success at All": Exposing the Pretextuality of* Kansas v. Hendricks, 92 Nw. U. L. REV. 1247 (1998).

[141]*See infra* Chapter 13.

[142]Stephen L. Golding, *Mental Health Professionals and the Courts: The Ethics of Expertise,* 13 INT'L J.L. & PSYCHIATRY 281, 287 (1990).

[143]*See, e.g.,* Michael L. Perlin, *"Where the Winds Hit Heavy on the Borderline": Mental Disability Law, Theory, and Practice, "Us" and "Them",* 31 LOY. L. A. L. REV. 775, 777 (1998). The Freudian roots of the phrase are explained in a related context in Christopher Slobogin, *Psychiatric Evidence in Criminal Trials: To Junk or Not to Junk?* 46 WM. & MARY L. REV. 1, 7 n.25 (1998).

Chapter 11
THE FEDERAL SENTENCING GUIDELINES

The federal sentencing guidelines were written to eliminate (or at least to lessen) arbitrariness and caprice in sentencing and to establish objective, normative standards against which convicted defendants' behavior could be assessed.[1] The guidelines—promulgated in response to criticisms of indeterminate sentences and seemingly inexplicable disparities in sentences for like crimes—were meant to both advise judges and to educate the public about the factors that could either enhance or diminish sentences.[2]

One such factor is mental disability. A federal judge can depart from the prescribed guideline ranges when "the defendant committed a nonviolent offense while suffering from significantly reduced mental capacity not resulting from voluntary use of drugs or other intoxicants."[3] In such cases, a lower sentence may be warranted to reflect the extent to which the reduced mental capacity contributed to the commission of the offense, as long as the defendant's criminal history "does not indicate a need for incarceration to protect the public."[4] Further, a policy statement by the Sentencing Commission underscores that mental and emotional conditions are not "ordinarily relevant" in determining whether a sentence should be outside the guideline ranges.[5]

---

[1]*See* 18 U.S.C. §§ 3551-3742 and 28 U.S.C. §§ 991–998 (1988). The constitutionality of these guidelines was upheld in Mistretta v. United States, 488 U.S. 361 (1989). *See generally* Keri A. Gould, *Turning Rat and Doing Time for Uncharged, Dismissed or Acquitted Crimes: Do the Federal Sentencing Guidelines Promote Respect for the Law?* 10 N.Y.L. SCH. J. HUM. RTS. 835, 852–53 (1993).

[2]*See generally* Ilene Nagel, *Structuring Sentencing Discretion: The New Federal Sentencing Guidelines*, 80 J. CRIM. L. & CRIMINOLOGY 883 (1990); Julia Black, Note, *The Constitutionality of Federal Sentences Imposed Under the Sentencing Reform Act of 1984 After* Mistretta v. United States, 75 IOWA L. REV. 767 (1990). On the specific question of downward departures, see Kirk Houser, *Downward Departures: The Lower Envelope of the Federal Sentencing Guidelines,* 31 DUQ. L. REV. 361 (1993).

[3]UNITED STATES SENTENCING COMMISSION GUIDELINES MANUAL § 5k2.13 *(Manual).*

[4]*Id.* Deviation from the putative sentence because of factors bearing on mental capacity appear three times in the guidelines. *See, e.g.,* 28 U.S.C. § 944(d):

> (d) The Commission in establishing categories of defendants for use in the guidelines and policy statements governing the imposition of sentences of probation, a fine, or imprisonment, governing the imposition of other authorized sanctions, governing the size of a fine or the length of a term of probation, imprisonment, or supervised release, and governing the conditions of probation, supervised release, or imprisonment, shall consider whether the following matters, among others with respect to a defendant, have any relevance to the nature extent, place of service, or other incident of inappropriate sentence, and shall take them into account only to the extent that they do have relevance-
> (4) mental and emotional condition to the extent that such condition mitigates the defendant's culpability or to the extent that such condition is otherwise plainly relevant. . . .

[5]*See* Sentencing Commission's Policy Statement Regarding Mental and Emotional Conditions, USSG, 65H1.3, 18 U.S.C., Guideline 5H1.3 ("Mental and emotional conditions are not ordinarily relevant in determining whether a sentence should be outside the guidelines, except as provided in the general provisions of Chapter 5"). The legislative history of the commission's policy statement on the influence of mental disability is spotty at best. The binding nature of the policy statements was upheld in Williams v. United States, 503 U.S. 193, 201 (1992). The Court held that policy statements are an authoritative guide to determining the meaning of the applicable guideline. The brevity of the policy statement seems to be a result of Congress' failure to provide a coherent explanation of the weight due individual offender characteristics and a failure of the commission to conduct or refer to any empirical studies or evidence on the effect of mental disability on sentencing patterns. Although this omission was initially recognized by the commission, it was later deleted without any additional explanation.

Great discretion is vested in the trial courts in determining when a sentence reduction is appropriate under the guidelines, and decisions by courts *not* to depart from the guidelines are generally not appealable.[6] Only where it appears that the district court misunderstood its authority to reduce the defendant's sentence will appellate courts be willing to disturb sentencing determinations.[7] The cases so far reported reflect no coherent reading of the guidelines (if such a coherent reading is ever possible given their internal ambivalence and contradictions) and no real understanding of the role of mental disability (short of an exculpating insanity defense) in criminal behavior.[8] Federal judges are utterly inconsistent in their reading of mental disability.[9] The case law suggests that federal judges have not seriously considered the way mental disability should be assessed in sentencing decisions and that random decisions generally reflect a judge's (false) "ordinary common sensical" read of whether an individual defendant "really could have overcome" his or her disability.[10]

I contend that this is caused by several factors:

- A lack of understanding by federal judges and by defense counsel of the meaning of mental disability and its potential interrelationship with criminal behavior;[11]
- An attitude by federal prosecutors that such mitigating evidence is a mere play for sympathy and an inappropriate factor to consider the sentencing phase (an attitude given strong support by Justice Scalia's dissent in *Penry v. Lynaugh,* arguing that the presentation of testimony to a death penalty jury about a defendant's mental retardation and childhood sexual and physical abuse leads to an inappropriate "outpouring . . . [of] unfocused sympathy");[12]
- The way that the insanity defense is structured as an all-or-nothing alternative, causing many to believe that lesser evidence of mental disorder is simply an inappropriate factor to consider in sentencing decisions;[13] and

---

[6]*See, e.g.,* United States v. Yellow Earrings, 891 F.2d 650, 654–55 (8th Cir. 1989). *See also,* United States v. Ghannam, 899 F.2d 327 (4th Cir. 1990); United States v. Follett, 905 F.2d 195 (8th Cir. 1990), *cert. denied,* 501 U.S. 1204 (1991); *compare id.* at 197 (Heaney, S.C.J., dissenting); United States v. Patterson, 15 F.3d 169 (11th Cir. 1994); United States v. Schechter, 13 F.3d 1117 (7th Cir. 1994); United States v. Turner, 7 F.3d 228 (4th Cir. 1993).

[7]*See, e.g.,* United States v. Ruklick, 919 F.2d 95 (8th Cir. 1990) (reversing trial court's refusal to depart from guidelines in case in which defendant had mental capacity of 12 year old); On the need for specific findings in guideline decision making, see, for example, United States v. Perkins, 963 F.2d 1523 (D.C. Cir. 1992); United States v. Zackson, 6 F.3d 911 (2d Cir. 1993).

[8]*See generally* MICHAEL L. PERLIN, MENTAL DISABILITY LAW: CIVIL AND CRIMINAL (1989), § 16.18A (1998 Cum. Supp.) (discussing cases).

[9]*See generally* Michael L. Perlin, *The Supreme Court, the Mentally Disabled Criminal Defendant, and Symbolic Values: Random Decisions, Hidden Rationales, or "Doctrinal Abyss"?* 29 ARIZ. L. REV. 1 (1987) [herinafter Perlin, *Symbolic Values*]; Michael L. Perlin, *"No Direction Home": The Law and Criminal Defendants With Mental Disabilities,* 20 MENT. & PHYS. DIS. L. REP. 605 (1996) [hereinafter Perlin, *"No Direction"*].

[10]On the way that similar behavior drives insanity defense jurisprudence, see MICHAEL L. PERLIN, THE JURISPRUDENCE OF THE INSANITY DEFENSE, chap. 9 (1994); *see generally* Michael L. Perlin, *On "Sanism,"* 46 SMU L. REV. 373 (1992); *see generally supra* Chapter 10.

[11]*See generally* Michael L. Perlin, *Pretexts and Mental Disability Law: The Case of Competency,* 47 U. MIAMI L. REV. 625 (1993); Keri A. Gould, *A Therapeutic Jurisprudence Analysis of Competency Evaluation Requests: The Defense Attorney's Dilemma,* 18 INT'L J.L. & PSYCHIATRY 83 (1995).

[12]492 U.S. 302, 359–60 (1989) (Scalia, J., concurring in part and dissenting in part), *discussed in* PERLIN, *supra* note 8, § 17.09, at 626–27 (1998 Cum. Supp.), and in Michael L. Perlin, *The Sanist Lives of Jurors in Death Penalty Cases: The Puzzling Role of "Mitigating" Mental Disability Evidence,* 8 NOTRE DAME J.L., ETHICS & PUB. POL'Y 239 (1994).

[13]*Ruklick,* 919 F.2d at 97–98. *Cf.* United States v. Gentry, 925 F.2d 186, 188–89 (7th Cir.), *reh'g denied* (1991) (sentencing court must assess whether defendant possesses "*significantly* reduced mental incapacity" in justifying downward departure from guidelines) (emphasis in original).

- The way that our ambivalence about mental disability as an exculpatory excuse results frequently in putatively mitigating testimony serving an aggravating function (most notably in death penalty cases).[14]

At the roots of these misassumptions are another set of unconscious factors that drive judicial behavior in this area. Most important among these are (a) the ways that our punitive urges drive the criminal justice system in spite of occasional statutory or case law to the contrary,[15] (b) the role of sanist behavior in the criminal justice system,[16] and (c) the pretextual behavior of courts and other fact finders in that system.[17] Although there is a robust literature developing about almost all other aspects of the federal sentencing guidelines,[18] these questions (and the implications of the answers that I suggest) have been generally ignored.[19]

I will first present a brief history of the sentencing guidelines. Next, I will show how the language about mental disability in the guidelines was chosen. Then I will discuss how the reported cases have construed mental disability evidence. After that I will demonstrate how the courts' decisions reflect unconscious feelings about mentally disabled defendants, feelings that stem from the urge to punish and that are reflected in the sanist and pretextual court system.

The Guidelines

In response to criticisms of indeterminate sentencing,[20] Congress passed the 1984 Sentencing Reform Act[21] in an attempt to bring about a measure of regularity and uniformity in federal sentencing procedures and provide for a more efficient and just sentencing sys-

---

[14]For example, notwithstanding the Supreme Court mandate that sentencing authorities consider any relevant mitigating evidence that a defendant offers as a basis for a sentence less than death, see Lockett v. Ohio, 438 U.S. 586, 604 (1978); Eddings v. Oklahoma, 455 U.S. 104, 114 (1982), discussed in 3 PERLIN, *supra* note 8, § 17.09 at 521–23, mental disability is seen as a mitigating factor at the penalty phase in death penalty cases only where the crime is seen as not "planful" and the defendant previously sought help for his or her condition), *see, e.g.,* Perlin, *supra* note 12, at 245–49, discussing, *inter alia,* Lawrence White, *The Mental Illness Defense in the Capital Penalty Hearing,* 5 BEHAV. SCI. & L. 411, 414–19 (1987); *see generally* Michael L. Perlin, *"The Executioner's Face Is Always Well-Hidden": The Role of Counsel and the Courts in Determining Who Dies,* 41 N.Y.L. SCH. L. REV. 201 (1996).

[15]*See* PERLIN, *supra* note 10.

[16]*See* Perlin, *supra* note 10; Michael L. Perlin & Deborah A. Dorfman, *Sanism, Social Science Evidence, and the Development of Mental Disability Law Jurisprudence,* 11 BEHAV. SCI. & L. 47 (1993).

[17]Perlin, *supra* note 11.

[18]An August 15, 1999, simple search ("FEDERAL SENTENCING GUIDELINES") of the WESTLAW/ LRI index revealed 313 documents. For recent representative articles, see, for example, Kate Stith & Steve Koh, *The Politics of Sentencing Reform: The Legislative History of the Federal Sentencing Guidelines,* 28 WAKE FOREST L. REV. 223 (1993); Eric Berlin, *The Federal Sentencing Guidelines' Failure to Eliminate Sentencing Disparity: Governmental Manipulations Before Arrest,* 1993 WIS. L. REV. 187; Emmett Miller, *Federal Sentencing Guidelines for Organizational Defendants,* 46 VAND. L. REV. 197 (1993); Houser, *supra* note 2.

[19]*But see* Robert Weinstock et al., *Psychiatry and the Federal Sentencing Guidelines,* 15 AM. J. FORENSIC PSYCHIATRY 67 (1994) (arguing that psychiatry can potentially play a "significant role" in the outcome of the sentencing process but that this potential "has often been overlooked").

On the therapeutic jurisprudential implications of those guidelines that encourage defendants to testify against ("turn rat on") their codefendants. *See* Gould, *supra* note 1.

[20]*See* Mistretta v. United States, 488 U.S. 361 (1989) (discussing sentencing disparities).

[21]*See* 18 U.S.C. §§ 3551-3742 and 28 U.S.C. §§ 991–998 (1988). *See generally* Stephen Schulhofer, *Assessing the Federal Sentencing Process: The Problem Is Uniformity, Not Disparity,* 29 AM. CRIM. L. REV. 833 (1992).

tem.[22] Under this law, a Sentencing Commission was created[23] and was mandated to promulgate sentencing guidelines[24] in accordance with the act.[25] The constitutionality of these guidelines—a binding set of rules that courts must use in imposing sentences[26]—was subsequently upheld by the Supreme Court in *Mistretta v. United States.*[27]

The sentencing structure set up under the guidelines uses a mathematical calculation to arrive at the presumptive sentence.[28] Within the permissible sentencing range, the judge must determine an appropriate sentence, consistent with the concerns and purposes of the act, including the nature and circumstances of the offense, the history and characteristics of the defendant, the need to achieve the recognized purposes of sentencing, the kinds of sentences available, if the sentence is established in the guidelines, pertinent policy statements, the need to avoid unwarranted disparities among similarly situated defendants, and the need to provide restitution to any victims of the offense.[29] The enabling statute specifically mandates that the sentencing judge consider the history and characteristics of the defendant and the nature and circumstances of the offense.[30] In practice, the phrase *relevant information,* as used within the guidelines, has a "particular, rigid meaning and application," and judges are generally not free to use such information to fashion a sentence outside the boundaries set by the mathematical sentencing equation.[31]

It is generally accepted that there are four major purposes of sentencing: retribution, deterrence, incapacitation, and rehabilitation. Throughout history, one or the other of these

---

[22]Some states similarly adopted determinate sentencing laws. *See, e.g.,* State v. Allert, 117 Wash. 2d 156, 815 P.2d 752, *reconsideration denied* (1991) (combination of depression, personality disorder, and alcoholism did not justify exceptional sentence). For a careful opinion considering the appropriate scope of discretion in such cases, see People v. Watters, 231 Ill. App. 3d 370, 595 N.E.2d 1369 (1992), *appeal denied,* 146 Ill. 2d 649, 602 N.E.2d 473 (1992).

The state case law is scant. *See, e.g,* Lorenzo v. State, 483 So.2d 790 (Fla. Dist. App. 1986), *reh'g denied* (1986); Sweat v. State, 454 So.2d 749 (Fla. Dist. App. 1984) (judicial determination that convicted sex offender is mentally disordered is sufficient reason to depart from the sentencing guidelines, so that guidelines statute must yield to the mentally disordered sex offender (MDSO) statute to follow the judge's recommendation). However, a downward deviation from the guidelines sentence was not justified because there was no possibility of receiving MDSO treatment during incarceration. State v. Alexander, 591 So.2d 1029 (Fla. Dist. App. 1991), *rev. denied,* 599 So.2d 654 (Fla. 1992). Elsewhere, in Commonwealth v. Larkin, 542 A.2d 1324 (Pa. 1988), the fact that defendant was found guilty but mentally ill did not permit a reduction in the mandatory minimum sentence. And in Barrett v. State, 772 P.2d 559 (Alaska App. 1989), the court held that a finding that mental illness was the cause of the defendant's criminal behavior (escape) did not automatically require an adjustment of the presumptive sentence.

[23]*See* 28 U.S.C. § 991.

[24]*See generally* PERLIN, *supra* note 10, chap. 4.

[25]*See* 28 U.S.C. § 994(a)(1).

[26]*See id.* Under the act, a series of permissible sentencing ranges is created for each federal criminal offense. *See* 28 U.S.C. § 994(b)(2).

[27]488 U.S. 361 (1989); *see generally* Nagel, *supra* note 2; Black, *supra* note 2; Myrna Raeder, *Gender and Sentencing: Single Moms, Battered Women, and Other Sex-Based Anomalies in the Gender-Free World of the Federal Sentencing Guidelines,* 20 PEPP. L. REV. 905 (1993); Christina Montgomery, *Social and Schematic Injustice: The Treatment of Offender Personal Characteristics Under the Federal Sentencing Guidelines,* 20 N. ENG. J. CRIM. & CIV. CONFINEMENT 27 (1993); Deborah Young, *Fact-Finding at Federal Sentencing: Why the Guidelines Should Meet the Rules,* 79 CORNELL L. REV. 299 (1994).

[28]This section is largely informed by Gould, *supra* note 1, at 853–54.

[29]18 U.S.C. §§ 3553(a)(1)–(7) (1988).

[30]*See* 18 U.S.C. § 3553(a). *See also* United States v. Duarte, 901 F.2d 1498 (9th Cir. 1990); Marc Miller & Daniel J. Freed, *Offender Characteristics & Victim Vulnerability: The Differences Between Policy Statements and Guidelines,* 3 FED. SENT. R. 3 (1990).

[31]Gould, *supra* note 1, at 852–53; *see* 18 U.S.C. app. 4, § 1B1.3.

purposes has dominated sentencing theory and practice.[32] At the heart of each new sentencing philosophy is a series of goals that embraces the current favored purpose. At different times, the legislature,[33] the sentencing judge,[34] or various other administrative groups[35] have been entrusted with the primary responsibility of fulfilling sentencing goals.

The Sentencing Commission began its work at a time when enthusiasm for rehabilitation theory was waning.[36] Several studies had been conducted indicating that criminal rehabilitation was a dead-end goal.[37] Public outcry about increased violence and crime increased the pressure on law makers to move away from indeterminate sentencing,[38] which was believed to produce disparate sentences, and toward a "just desserts" sentencing rationale.[39] The just-desserts sentencing theory imputes a ranking of criminal behaviors by severity and applies a similarly ranked order of punishments. Thus, in theory, the just-desserts system of sentencing advocates a system that punishes those who violate the rights of others in accordance with their individual level of blameworthiness[40] and satisfies the

---

[32]Nagel, *supra* note 2, at 887. In her article, Nagel compiled an excellent review of sentencing theory from the time of Moses to the present.

[33]Congress has met this responsibility by creating the Federal Sentencing Commission and by passing legislation that delineates mandatory minimum sentences for certain crimes.

[34]Federal district judges were the prime arbiters of divining sentences under the indeterminate sentencing system in effect prior to the implementation of the federal sentencing guidelines. Sentences, as long as they were within the broad ranges set down by statute, were essentially unreviewable by the appellate courts. United States v. Schneider, 502 F.2d 8973 (1974), United States v. Barbara, 683 F.2d 164 (6th Cir. 1982), United States v. Bright, 710 F.2d 1404 (9th Cir. 1982) (limited appellate review to determine if district court properly exercised discretion).

[35]Under the present indeterminate sentencing system, the commission and perhaps the U.S. Attorney fulfill this role. Under an indeterminate sentencing system, the parole boards function in this way by determining when an inmate is rehabilitated and ready to be released from the correctional institution.

[36]Theresa Karle & Thomas Sager, *Are the Federal Sentencing Guidelines Meeting Congressional Goals?: An Empirical and Case Law Analysis,* 40 EMORY L.J. 393 (1991); Karen Bornstein, *5K2.0 Departures for 5H Individual Characteristics: A Backdoor Out of the Federal Sentencing Guidelines,* 24 COLUM. HUM. RTS. L. REV. 135 (1992–93); Nagel, *supra* note 2, at 884, 895–97.

[37]Douglas S. Lipton, Robert Martinson, & Judith Wilks, THE EFFECTIVENESS OF CORRECTIONAL TREATMENT: A SURVEY OF TREATMENT EVALUATION STUDIES (1975) (promoting the "nothing works" theory). Later Martinson renounced his views by first affirming the virtues of probation as a rehabilitative method, Robert Martinson & Judith Wilks, *Save Parole Supervision,* 41 FED. PROBATION 23 (1977), and later in finding "startling examples" of rehabilitative treatment programs. Robert Martinson, *New Findings, New Views: A Note of Caution Regarding Sentencing Reform,* 7 HOFSTRA L. REV. 242, 255 (1979).

Although the dominant congressional and public perception was that all social scientists had condemned rehabilitation as an idea that could not work, more sophisticated correctional rehabilitative research continued with some positive results. *See generally* Paul Gendreau & Robert R. Ross, *Revivification of Rehabilitation: Evidence From the 1980's,* 4 JUST. Q. 349 (1987) (extensive review of offender rehabilitation programs and theories).

[38]In indeterminate sentencing, an offender is sentenced to a "flexible sentence"—that is, where the length of actual incarceration is handed down by the sentencing judge in terms of a minimum–maximum range. The actual amount of time served is determined by both conditional good-time early releases (approved by the correctional facility administration) and periodic evaluations of the prisoner's overall rehabilitation (as determined by the parole board). Mark Miller, *Purposes at Sentencing,* 66 S. CAL. L. REV. 413, 435 n.94 (1992).

In other words, for an indeterminate sentence of two to four years, the inmate must serve at least two years, but, depending on his or her behavior within the facility and on parole hearing determinations, he or she may serve anywhere from two to a total of four years in the facility. Parole boards also determine if a prisoner may be transferred to a less restrictive correctional program. Under this model, it is believed that wardens and parole boards are in the best position to determine when the prisoner is rehabilitated and is able to resume living outside of the correctional facility.

[39]Stephen Breyer, *The Federal Sentencing Guidelines and the Key Compromises Upon Which They Rest,* 17 HOFSTRA L. REV. 1, 15 (1988).

[40]Nagel, *supra* note 2, at 898.

public hunger for the expression of communal blame on the culpable.[41] In this way, the criminal conduct is punished without regard to individual characteristics or circumstances.

After the passage of the Sentencing Reform Act, the Federal Sentencing Commission promulgated guidelines to aid the sentencing judge in adhering to the same goals of criminal punishment established by the enabling legislation.[42]

The Choice of Mental Disability Language

The use of the modifier *significantly* suggests that Congress sought to limit application of the guidelines to only the most mentally impaired defendants.[43] This tracks public sentiment that continues to endorse the 18th-century "wild beast" test[44] as the appropriate means of assessing criminal responsibility, as well as Congress's decision to enact a more restrictive version of the discredited 1843 *M'Naghten* rules in the Insanity Defense Reform Act of 1984 following public outrage over the Hinckley acquittal.[45]

Courts regularly find that to qualify for a downward departure a defendant's condition must be extraordinary or atypical. Thus in *United States v. Vela,*[46] the Fifth Circuit reversed a downward departure in the case of a defendant subjected to childhood incestuous sex abuse that was admittedly "shocking and repulsive," because that factor—although egregious—was insufficiently extraordinary to support such a departure.[47] And in *United States v. Lara,*[48] in which the Second Circuit affirmed a downward departure in the case of a "delicate looking" bisexual young man, Judge Metzner dissented, arguing that susceptibility to physical and sexual attack in prison is not sufficiently unusual so as to rise to the level of atypicality required by the guidelines.[49]

The guidelines' exclusion of mental disability stemming from voluntary alcohol or drug use suggests that Congress specifically sought to limit application to those who could not be

---

[41]Jennifer Moore, *Corporate Culpability Under the Federal Sentencing Guidelines,* 34 ARIZ. L. REV. 743, 748 (1992).

[42]Gould, *supra* note 1, at 849.

[43]See *supra* text accompanying note 3.

Offender characteristics are split between guidelines and policy statements. The criminal history provisions are contained within the guidelines whereas the noncriminal personal history including consideration of 5K21.3 (mental and emotional history) are relegated to policy statements. According to the *DOJ Prosecutorial Handbook on Sentencing Guidelines* (Nov. 1, 1987), this means that they are only advisory and nonbinding. See Miller & Freed, *supra* note 30, at 3.

The commission published no evidence to document or substantiate the "not ordinarily relevant" language added to the policy statement. The commission did not conduct a study of federal or state judicial practice on the influence of mental condition on sentencing. The commission offered no reasons pursuant to 28 U.S.C. § 994(p) to support its offender characteristics policy statement when the initial guidelines were submitted in May 1987. *Id.* at 4. In its *Supplemental Report to Initial Federal Sentencing Guidelines and Policy Statements of June 18, 1987,* the commission described many aspects of research and philosophy concerning the guidelines manual but said virtually nothing about offender characteristics polices. *Id.*

[44]See Caton Roberts et al., *Implicit Theories of Criminal Responsibility Decision Making and the Insanity Defense,* 11 LAW & HUM. BEHAV. 207 (1987).

[45]PERLIN, *supra* note 10, at 138–43.

[46]927 F.2d 197 (5th Cir. 1991).

[47]*Id.* at 198–99. *See generally* Jean Shuttleworth, *Childhood Abuse as a Mitigating Factor in Federal Sentencing: The Ninth Circuit Versus the United States Sentencing Commission,* 46 VAND. L. REV. 1333 (1993). On atypicality, see United States v. Studley, 907 F.2d 254, 258 (1st Cir. 1990).

[48]905 F.2d 599 (2d Cir. 1990).

[49]*Id.* at 608.

deemed "responsible" for their mental state.[50] Indeed, appellate courts have regularly ruled that downward departures are precluded even in cases in which defendants successfully complete postarrest drug rehabilitation.[51]

These limitations parallel legislative attitudes toward the insanity defense[52] as well as attitudes of jurors who refuse to treat mental illness as a mitigating factor in death penalty determinations.[53] In short, the guidelines present an extraordinarily cramped reading of "mental disability" as a mitigator, a reading that is totally consonant with public and legislative attitudes toward an exculpatory nonresponsibility defense (as well as toward mental disability as a mitigator in death penalty sentencing).

The Case Law

Stephen Schulhofer, a consultant to the U.S. Sentencing Commission, has noted, "In many courts, at the Department of Justice and at the Commission itself there has been a pervasive assumption that departures represent a threat to the Guidelines system or that they should be used sparingly and only as a last resort."[54] Appellate decisions have thus "sent a message to lower courts and contributed to an atmosphere in which departure is considered out of the question under virtually any circumstances."[55] This message is even more pronounced in cases involving mentally disabled criminal defendants.

Mental disability-based departures from the guidelines have been few and, more often than not, have come in cases in which a defendant's mental state more closely approximates that of a potentially successful insanity pleader.[56] In *United States v. Speight,* for instance, the court found that a defendant (convicted of drug and firearm offenses) who suffered from schizophrenia and other emotional disturbances met all the criteria of the guidelines and that a sentence reduction was thus warranted.[57] In *United States v. Ruklick*[58] the court emphasized that, under the guidelines it was not necessary to find that the defendant's

---

[50]*See, e.g.,* United States v. Tolliver, 992 F.2d 1218 (6th Cir. 1993) (rejecting downward departure because of defendant's "voluntary" decision to use drugs); *cf.* United States v. Dutchie, 91 F.3d 160 (10th Cir. 1996) (not error to refuse to make downward departure in case of defendant with fetal alcohol syndrome).

[51]United States v. Martin, 938 F.2d 162 (9th Cir. 1991); United States v. Harrington, 947 F.2d 956 (D.C. Cir. 1991).

[52]*See* PERLIN, *supra* note 10, chaps. 3, 9; *see, e.g.,* State v. Duckworth, 496 So.2d 624, 635 (La. App. 1986) (juror who felt defendant would be responsible for actions as long as he "wanted to do them" not excused for cause) (no error); J. R. Balkin, *The Rhetoric of Responsibility,* 76 Va. L. Rev. 197, 238 (1990) (Hinckley prosecutor suggested to jurors "if Hinckley had emotional problems, they were largely his own fault").

[53]*See generally* Perlin, *supra* note 12.

[54]Schulhofer, *supra* note 21, at 863.

[55]*Id.* at 864.

[56]*See also* United States v. Lara, 905 F.2d 599 (2d Cir. 1990) (upholding departure from guidelines based on defendant's likely "extreme vulnerability" in a correctional facility); United States v. Cotto, 793 F. Supp. 64 (E.D.N.Y. 1992) (defendant's near retardation, vulnerability, efforts at rehabilitation, and incompetence warranted downward departure).

There are limits to the use of mental disability as a reductive element. *See Sentencing Commission's Policy Statement Regarding Mental and Emotional Conditions,* Guideline 5H1.3 ("Mental and emotional conditions are not ordinarily relevant in determining whether a sentence should be outside the guidelines, except as provided in the general provisions of Chapter 5").

[57]726 F. Supp. 861, 867–68 (D.D.C. 1989). *See also* United States v. Adonis, 744 F. Supp. 336 (D.D.C. 1990); United States v. Glick, 946 F.2d 335 (4th Cir. 1991). *Cf.* United States v. Doering, 909 F.2d 392 (9th Cir. 1990) (prohibiting upward departure where evidence reflected need for psychiatric care).

[58]919 F.2d 95 (8th Cir. 1990).

reduced mental capacity amounted to "but-for causation"[59] to reduce a sentence, as long as his or her diminished mental capacity "comprised a contributing factor in the commission of the offense."[60]

Not all of the remainder of the reported cases are sanist. Several reflect the work of thoughtful judges who have carefully weighed mental disability testimony and applied this evidence sensitively to the cases before them. The Ninth Court of Appeals, for instance, in *United States v. Cantu*[61] reversed a trial court's refusal to grant a downward departure application in the case of a defendant diagnosed as suffering from posttraumatic stress disorder. *Cantu* carefully construed the pertinent guideline to include emotional disorders as well as organic syndromes and focused on what it saw as the purpose of the guidelines: to enable federal judges to show "lenity toward defendants whose ability to make reasoned decisions is impaired."[62] As defendant's posttraumatic stress disorder had the capacity to "distort or suppress the formation of reasoned decisions" or "impair the formation of reasoned judgments," this disorder would thus qualify for a downward departure.[63] And more recently, the Sixth Circuit vacated an upward departure, finding that the more adequate mechanism for protecting the public was a commitment proceeding rather than an enhanced sentence.[64] In rejecting the government's arguments, the court noted the existence of an extended commitment statute[65] "designed to forestall such danger through continued commitment after completion of the sentence"; otherwise, the court reasoned, "virtually every criminal defendant who, at the time of sentencing, met the dangerousness criteria of [the commitment statute] would also be subject to an upward departure."[66]

These, however, are the exceptions. Generally, applications for downward departures are summarily rejected. In some of these, uncontroverted evidence of major depression,[67] manic depression,[68] severe emotional stress,[69] or a long-term history of psychosis[70] is rejected as a grounds for departure. In others, evidence of failed insanity defense is used

---

[59]"But-for causation" is explained in Ann Woolhandler & Michael Collins, *Judicial Federation and the Administrative Stats,* 87 CALIFORNIA L. REV. 613, 699 n.346 (1999).

[60]*Id.* at 97–98. *Cf.* United States v. Gentry, 925 F.2d 186, 188–89 (7th Cir.), *reh'g denied* (1991) (sentencing court must assess whether defendant possesses "*significantly* reduced mental incapacity" in justifying downward departure from guidelines) (emphasis in original); United States v. Bissell, 954 F. Supp. 841 (D.N.J. 1996), *aff'd,* 142 F.3d 429 (3d Cir. 1998) (defendant not entitled to downward departure where he alleged a relationship between his diminished mental capacity and duress).

[61]12 F.3d 1506 (9th Cir. 1993).

[62]*Id.* at 1512.

[63]*Id.* at 1512–13.

Other courts have also carefully considered defendants' clinical conditions in assessing the propriety of a downward departure. *See, e.g.,* United States v. Garza-Juarez, 992 F.2d 896 (9th Cir. 1993); United States v. Lewinson, 988 F.2d 1005 (9th Cir. 1993); United States v. McMurray, 833 F. Supp. 1454 (D. Neb. 1993); United States v. Chatman, 986 F.2d 1446 (D.C. Cir. 1993); United States v. Cotto, 793 F. Supp. 64 (E.D.N.Y. 1992); United States v. McCarthy, 840 F. Supp. 1404 (D. Colo. 1993); United States v. Gigante, 1997 WL 781918 (E.D.N.Y. 1997), *supplemented,* 989 F. Supp. 436 (E.D.N.Y. 1998); *see also* Commonwealth v. Sheridan, 348 Pa. Super. 574, 502 A.2d 694 (1985).

[64]United States v. Moses, 106 F.3d 1273 (9th Cir. 1997).

[65]18 U.S.C. § 4246.

[66]*Moses,* 106 F.3d at 1280.

[67]*See, e.g.,* United States v. Eagan, 965 F.2d 887 (10th Cir. 1992); United States v. Frazier, 979 F.2d 1227 (7th Cir. 1992); United States v. Gudal, 980 F.2d 739 (9th Cir. 1992); United States v. Kimball, 995 F.2d 234 (9th Cir. 1993).

[68]*E.g.,* State v. Walker, 393 N.W.2d 204 (Minn. App. 1986).

[69]*E.g.,* State v. Rogers, 112 Wash. 2d 180, 770 P.2d 180 (1989).

[70]*E.g.,* United States v. Regan, 989 F.2d 44 (1st Cir. 1993).

either as a basis for an upward departure[71] or as a justification for a refusal to enter a downward departure.[72] In *United States v. Spedalieri*,[73] the entry of the insanity plea was seen as evidence of a failure to demonstrate contrition (presumably because the plea entry denied legal responsibility for the offense) and that lack of contrition was seen as a failure to accept responsibility, thus bringing the defendant out of the ambit of another guideline (3E1.1) that provided for a downward departure if the defendant "clearly demonstrates a recognition and affirmative acceptance of personal responsibility for his criminal conduct."[74] The defendant's entry of an insanity plea—containing in it the admission that he committed the underlying act (an armed robbery)—did not rise to the level of "contrition necessary . . . for acceptance of responsibility."[75] In yet another case, the Seventh Circuit affirmed a District Court denial of a sentence reduction in a failed insanity case in which the defendant stated he was "very ashamed because [he] could not control [his] illness and [was] sorry [he] not continue the [psychiatric] treatment that was necessary to bring him back to reality."[76]

In other cases, evidence of past insanity acquittals was seen as an aggravating circumstance worthy of an upward departure,[77] and even where conviction was followed by commitment to a federal medical center for psychiatric care and treatment,[78] that level of mental illness was not seen as sufficient to warrant a downward departure.[79]

In general, decisions by trial courts to reject downward departures are merely summarily affirmed, especially where the underlying crime was violent and where the defendant's violent criminal record raised the possibility that he or she would be a threat to public safety,[80] where the court simply found the defendant's disability too insignificant as to warrant such a reduction,[81] where the court did not find defendant's "extraordinary postarrest efforts" at drug rehabilitation sufficient to warrant such a reduction,[82] or where

---

[71]*E.g.,* United States v. Medved, 905 F.2d 935 (6th Cir. 1990).

[72]*E.g.,* United States v. Spedalieri, 910 F.2d 707 (10th Cir. 1990).

[73]*Id.*

[74]*Id.* at 712 (discussing guidelines).

[75]*Id.*

[76]United States v. Reno, 992 F.2d 739, 744 (7th Cir. 1993).

[77]United States v. McKenley, 895 F.2d 184 (4th Cir. 1990). *Cf.* United States v. Barnes, 46 F.3d 33 (8th Cir 1995) (allowing for downward departure in spite of failed insanity defense).

[78]*See* 18 U.S.C. § 4244.

[79]United States v. Hunter, 985 F.2d 1003 (9th Cir. 1993), *vacated and dismissed as moot on other grounds,* 1 F.3d 843 (9th Cir. 1993).

[80]United States v. Wilson, 891 F.2d 293 (6th Cir. 1989) (tabl.) (full text available on WESTLAW), *cert. denied,* 494 U.S. 1038 (1990); United States v. Hamilton, 949 F.2d 190 (6th Cir. 1991); United States v. Lauzon, 938 F.2d 326 (1st Cir. 1991), *cert. denied,* 502 U.S. 972 (1991); United States v. Fairman, 947 F.2d 1479 (11th Cir. 1991); United States v. Poff, 926 F.2d 588 (7th Cir. 1991), *cert. denied,* 502 U.S. 827 (1992); United States v. Coates, 996 F.2d 939 (8th Cir. 1993); United States v. Braxton, 19 F.3d 1385 (11th Cir. 1994); United States v. Lombardi, 5 F.3d 568 (1st Cir. 1993); United States v. Marquez, 827 F. Supp. 205 (S.D.N.Y. 1993).

[81]United States v. Regan, 989 F.2d 44 (1st Cir. 1993); United States v. Tucker, 986 F.2d 278 (8th Cir. 1993), *cert. denied,* 510 U.S. 820 (1993); United States v. Benson, 7 F.3d 226 (4th Cir. 1993).

One case has also explored the relationship between the sentencing guidelines and other federal statutes governing the provision of mental health care to prisoners during their period of sentence and the care of competent persons suffering from mental disease prior to sentencing. United States v. Roberts, 915 F.2d 889, 891–92 (4th Cir. 1990), *cert. denied,* 498 U.S. 1122 (1991) (no error for trial judge to sentence defendant provisionally pursuant to 18 U.S.C. § 4244(c) rather than in accordance with sentencing guidelines). Another has explored the relationship between diminished mental capacity and subsequent revocation of probation. United States v. Sylvester, 1994 WL 92035 (D. Or. 1994) (reconsidering revocation in case of defendant originally given downward departure because of "mental/emotional dysfunctions").

[82]United States v. Zeigler, 1 F.3d 1044 (10th Cir. 1993).

the court felt that the defendant did not take sufficient responsibility for his role in the criminal offenses in question.[83] In at least one case, it has been held that a defendant's "dangerous mental state" would make an upward departure appropriate.[84]

The question of the application of the guidelines to a defendant who alleged that his crimes were due to a compulsive gambling disorder is illuminating. In *United States v. Katzenstein,* the court concluded a departure would not be warranted unless a defendant could either demonstrate that total rehabilitation had been achieved or introduce evidence showing a lack of correlation between compulsive gambling disorder and increased propensity for criminal activity.[85] In *State v. O'Brien,*[86] the court rejected defendant's application for a downward departure in large part because of the "sophistication and planning" of his criminal activity (theft by swindle, through which defendant defrauded others into entering into car leasing joint ventures with him).[87] And in *United States v. Rosen,*[88] in the case of another compulsive gambler, the trial court found that because the crime was committed to pay off a home equity loan (a loan taken out to pay off the defendant's gambling debts) rather than to support gambling directly, the crime consequently resulted from personal financial and economic difficulties, grounds determined by the Sentencing Commission to be irrelevant to the sentencing process.[89]

Another important theme runs through each of the reported cases. In each one—without exception—the U.S. Attorney's office opposed the use of mental disability as a mitigating factor.[90] In at least one case, it apparently took the position that a defendant's need for psychiatric treatment justified an upward departure.[91] This is especially important given the way that the role of prosecutors has been greatly enhanced in the entire federal sentencing

---

[83]United States v. Haddad, 10 F.3d 1252 (7th Cir. 1993).

[84]United States v. Hines, 26 F.3d 1469 (9th Cir. 1994), *appeal after remand,* 68 F.3d 481 (9th Cir. 1995) (remanding for further explanation by the trial court). *Cf.* United States v. Moses, 106 F.3d 1273 (9th Cir. 1997), discussed *supra* text accompanying note 68.

[85]1991 WL 24386 (S.D.N.Y. 1991). *See also, e.g.,* United States v. Rosen, 896 F.2d 789 (3d Cir.), *reh'g and en banc denied* (1990) (defendant's compulsive gambling did not warrant downward departure); Lawrence Lustberg, *Sentencing the Sick: Compulsive Gambling as the Basis for a Downward Departure Under the Federal Sentencing Guidelines,* 2 SETON HALL J. SPORT L. 51 (1992).

In April 1998, the Guidelines were amended to read:

> A sentence below the applicable guideline range may be warranted if the defendant committed the offense while suffering from a significantly reduced mental capacity. However, the court may not depart below the applicable guideline range if (1) the significantly reduced mental capacity was caused by the voluntary use of drugs or other intoxicants; (2) the facts and circumstances of the defendant's offense indicate a need to protect the public because the offense involved actual violence or a serious threat of violence, or (3) the defendant's criminal history indicates a need to incarcerate the defendant or protect the public. If a departure is warranted, the extent of the departure should reflect the extent to which the reduced mental capacity contributed to the commission of the offense.

United States Sentencing Guidelines § 5K2.13 (amended 1998).

Relying on this new language, the Third Circuit found that its earlier decision in *Rosen* was thus superceded. United States v. Askari, 159 F.3d 774 (3d. Cir. 1998).

[86]429 N.W.2d 293 (Minn. 1988).

[87]*Id.* at 296.

[88]896 F.2d 789 (3d Cir. 1990).

[89]*Id.* at 790 n.2.

[90]There may be some methodological problems in this analysis. It is certainly possible that prosecutors have agreed to downward departures in unpublished cases. The universe of published cases, however, reveals these findings.

[91]United States v. Doering, 909 F.2d 392, 295 (9th Cir. 1990).

process.[92] This decision by the Justice Department mocks the spirit of the guidelines and exposes federal prosecutors as inflexible gatekeepers, interested solely in ensuring maximum prison time for all defendants convicted on federal charges, no matter how serious their mental disability.[93]

Mental Disability and the Guidelines

Cases decided under the federal sentencing guidelines reflect a lack of understanding by federal judges of the meaning of mental disability and its role as a potential sentencing mitigator. In attitudes that strikingly mirror attitudes of jurors in assessing mental disability in death penalty determinations,[94] judges conceptualize mental disability as an "all or nothing" absolute construct,[95] demand a showing of mental disability that approximates that needed for an exculpatory insanity defense,[96] continue to not "get" distinctions between mental illness, insanity, and incompetency; repeat sanist myths about mentally disabled criminal defendants and engage in pretextual decision making.

The ominous spirit of Justice Scalia's partial dissent in *Penry v. Lynaugh*—castigating the majority for allowing an "outpouring . . . of unfocused sympathy"[97]—looms over many of these cases. Finally, most of the few cases in which mental disability is seen as a mitigator eerily track the fact pattern of the few situations in which jurors grudgingly sanction the use of the insanity defense: where a defendant—especially one who has previously sought counseling—commits a nonplanful crime.[98]

The attitudes expressed in these cases are frequently sanist. In rejecting the defendant's "suicidal tendencies" as a possible basis for a downward departure in an embezzlement case, the Sixth Circuit held that departure would *never* be permissible on this basis, because any consideration of this argument would lead to "boilerplate claims" and force courts to "separate the wheat of valid claims from the chaff of disingenuous ones," a "path before which we give serious pause."[99] This argument tracks—nearly verbatim—the reasoning of the Fourth Circuit, refusing to depart downward in the case of a defendant who had suffered severe childhood sexual abuse, referring to the "innumerable defendants" who could plead "unstable upbringing" as a potential departure grounds.[100]

Just as evidence of organic disorder appears more "real" to judges in insanity cases (than does evidence of psychological disability)[101] so does such evidence appear more real in

---

[92]Jack McCall, *The Emperor's New Clothes: Due Process Considerations Under the Federal Sentencing Guidelines,* 60 Tenn. L. Rev. 467, 496 (1993).

[93]For a particularly troubling account, see Eva Rodriguez, *Blind Spot in U.S. Sentencing System: No Allowance Made for Mentally Retarded Defendants,* 132 N.J. L.J. 11 (Nov. 2, 1992). Press accounts of such behavior are legion. *See, e.g.,* Deborah Pines, *Heroism Wins Defendant Reduction in Sentencing,* N.Y. L.J. 1, 7 (Mar. 1, 1994) (reporting on United States v. Acosta, 93 Cr. 386 (S.D.N.Y. 1994)) ("Judge Lasker rejected arguments by federal prosecutors that [the defendant's mental] handicap [is a] permissible grounds for a sentencing reduction").

[94]*See generally* Perlin, *supra* note 12.

[95]*See* Perlin, *supra* note 10, at 77.

[96]An analogy may be drawn to the way that GBMI statutes in some jurisdictions basically track the language of the more "liberal" ALI-Model Penal Code insanity test, whereas the more rigid *M'Naghten* standard is used for insanity evaluations. *See* 3 Perlin, *supra* note 8, § 15.09; Perlin, *supra* note 10, at 91–95; *see also* Michael L. Perlin, Law and Mental Disability § 4.41 (1994).

[97]492 U.S. 302, 359–60 (1989) (Scalia, J., concurring in part and dissenting in part).

[98]Perlin, *supra* note 12, at 245–49, discussing, *inter alia,* research reported in White, *supra* note 14.

[99]United States v. Harpst, 949 F.2d 860, 871 (6th Cir. 1991), discussed in Schulhofer, *supra* note 21, at 866.

[100]United States v. Daly, 883 F. 313, 319 (4th Cir. 1989).

[101]Perlin, *supra* note 10, at 252–58.

guidelines cases. In *United States v. Hamilton,* the Sixth Circuit affirmed a trial court's refusal to enter a downward departure in the case of a defendant (a doctor of osteopathy) suffering a "major depressive episode" on the theory that the Sentencing Commission was "talking about things such as a borderline mental *intelligence* capacity," concluding that, because the defendant was "able to absorb information in the usual way and to exercise the power of reason," he did not suffer from a "significantly reduced mental capacity."[102]

The District of Columbia Circuit has explicitly rejected admitting expert testimony on an individual defendant's potential for successful rehabilitation on two grounds: that another defendant without access to such expert testimony might be able to make a similar case for leniency and that reliance on "scientific" predictions could transform sentencing hearings into an inappropriate "battle of experts."[103] As Schulhofer noted in his critique of this case, a district court always has the capacity to appoint expert witnesses to aid a defendant at sentencing, an option made explicitly constitutional in a different context in *Ake v. Oklahoma.*[104]

Beyond this, the court's professed inability to sort out potentially conflicting expert testimony reveals pretextuality at its worst: This type of judicial decision making is certainly not beyond the capabilities of federal judges (who, indeed, must weigh regularly conflicting expert testimony on a variety of scientific and technical subjects). This approach mirrors perfectly the behavior of judges in other mental disability law cases and tracks the methodology of the *en banc* Fourth Circuit in *United States v. Charters,* a case sharply curtailing the right of incompetent-to-stand-trial detainees to refuse antipsychotic medication,[105] by "abdicat[ing] its responsibility to read, harmonize, distinguish and analyze social science data on the issues before it."[106] This trivialization of social science simultaneously allows courts to more comfortably seek refuge in allegedly common sense "morality,"[107] use heuristic devices in a wide variety of cases in uncomfortable areas of the law, and use sanist behavior in deciding such cases.[108]

Underlying many of the guidelines cases is a powerful current of *blame:* The defendant succumbed to temptation (by not resisting drugs or alcohol, by not overcoming childhood abuse). This sense of blame mirrors courts' sanist impatience with mentally disabled criminal defendants in general, attributing their problems in the legal process to "weak character or poor resolve."[109] Thus we should not be surprised to learn that a trial judge, responding to a National Center for State Courts survey, indicated that incompetent-to-stand-trial defendants *could* have understood and communicated with their counsel and the

---

[102]949 F.2d 190, 193 (6th Cir. 1991) (emphasis added).

[103]United States v. Harrington, 947 F.2d 956, 960 (D.C. Cir. 1991). *Cf.* United States v. Cropp, 127 F.3d 354 (4th Cir. 1997), *cert. denied,* 118 S. Ct. 898 (1998) (no abuse of discretion to deny psychiatric examination prior to sentence), and United States v. Roman, 121 F.3d 136 (3d Cir. 1997), *cert. denied,* 118 S. Ct. 722 (1998) (funds not available under federal Criminal Justice Act for presentence psychiatric evaluation). On the pervasiveness of the insanity defense myth of the alleged "battle of the experts," see *supra* Chapter 10, text accompanying note 34.

[104]470 U.S. 68 (1985), discussed in Schulhofer, *supra* note 21, at 869.

[105]863 F.2d 302 (4th Cir. 1988), *cert. denied,* 494 U.S. 1016 (1990).

[106]Michael L. Perlin, *Are Courts Competent to Decide Competency Questions? Stripping the Facade From United States v. Charters,* 38 U. KAN. L. REV. 957, 999 (1990). *See supra* Chapter 6.

[107]*See supra* Chapter 3.

[108]Perlin, *supra* note 11, at 669.

[109]*Id.* at 670–71. *See generally* Bernard Weiner, *On Sin Versus Sickness: A Theory of Perceived Responsibility and Social Motivation,* 48 AM. PSYCHOLOGIST 957 (1993).

court "if they [had] only wanted."[110] Again, one of the leading texts on white-collar crimes sentencing stressed, "Judges considered two major concepts pertinent to individual attributes of the offender: blameworthiness and consequence. . . . Certain characteristics of offenders relate to the culpability of or degree of blameworthiness of the particular defendant. Illustrations include mental competency. . . ."[111]

Sentencing decisions are also often pretextual. In the case of a chronically depressed compulsive gambler under threats of violence to pay off his debts (apparently from organized crime figures), the Sixth Circuit justified its rejection of a downward departure on the grounds that the defendant could have "just said no." Moralized the court: "He had the option of reporting the threats he received to the authorities, of course, but he chose instead to engage in serious violations of the law."[112]

Just as judges don't "get" the differences between the differing legal standards in insanity and incompetency to stand trial cases,[113] they similarly don't get the difference between either of these statutes and the degree of mental capacity needed to justify a downward departure under the guidelines. Relying on the prosecutor's argument (a fact that makes the scenario even more troubling), a trial court thus concluded that the fact that the defendant (learning disabled, physically disabled, and of borderline intelligence) was found competent to stand trial and responsible for his act (the distribution of LSD) required him to deny the downward departure application.[114] This decision was affirmed by the First Circuit in an opinion "agree[ing with] and applaud[ing]" the trial judge's "thoughtful consideration" of the underlying issues.[115]

Conclusion

Misunderstandings such as these are likely to be exacerbated even further by the Supreme Court's decision in *Godinez v. Moran*,[116] finding that the standard for competency to plead guilty or to waive counsel was no greater than to stand trial. At least one trial court decision (approving a downward departure in the case of a *pro se* defendant with "serious mental health problems") suggests implicitly that *Godinez* may be a source of greater future confusion.[117] *Godinez* has the capacity to make far more likely the possibility of pretextual decision making under the guidelines.

Robert Weinstock and his colleagues have argued that psychiatric evidence should be more extensively and creatively developed in federal sentencing cases to "temper judicial rigidity" under the guidelines.[118] To the best of my knowledge, this is the only example in the legal or behavioral literature calling for such expanded use of mental disability evidence at the sentencing stage in guidelines cases. Given this level of academic apathy, it should not surprise us that the relevant cases sadly and predictably track the sanist and pretextual ways

---

[110]Perlin, *supra* note 11, at 671, quoting Keri A. Gould et al., *Criminal Defendants With Trial Disabilities: The Theory and Practice of Competency Assistance* 90 (manuscript in progress). *See also* Perlin, *supra* note 11, at 671 nn.230–31 (citing sources).

[111]STANTON WHEELER ET AL., SITTING IN JUDGMENT: THE SENTENCING OF WHITE COLLAR CRIMINALS 20–21 (1988).

[112]United States v. Hamilton, 949 F.2d 190, 193 (6th Cir. 1991).

[113]*See* Perlin, *supra* note 11, at 679; 3 PERLIN, *supra* note 8, § 14.02, at 208 n.7 (citing sources).

[114]United States v. Lauzon, 938 F.2d 326, 332 (1st Cir. 1991).

[115]*Id.*

[116]509 U.S. 389 (1993). *See generally* Perlin, *supra* note 12, at 274–76; PERLIN *supra* note 8, §§ 14.20A, 14.21 (1998 Cum. Supp.); PERLIN, *supra* note 96, § 4.13; *see supra* Chapter 9.

[117]*See* United States v. Stevens, 1993 WL 539125, at *1 (E.D. Pa. 1993).

[118]Weinstock et al., *supra* note 19, at 72.

that fact finders generally process mental disability evidence in the criminal trial process, leading to the now-familiar "doctrinal abyss."[119] Judges continue to narrowly construe such evidence, to attribute blame to mentally disabled offenders, to demand near-total incapacitation prior to invocation of the downward departure policy, and to misunderstand the relationship between mental disability and criminal behavior.

---

[119]*See generally* Perlin, *Symbolic Values, supra* note 9; Perlin, *"No Direction," supra* note 9; PERLIN, *supra* note 10.

PART III:

THERAPEUTIC JURISPRUDENCE: EXPOSING SANISM AND PRETEXTUALITY

Chapter 12
EXPOSING THE PREJUDICE

The most important and exciting new jurisprudential insights into mental disability law jurisprudence of the past two decades have come from the development—primarily by David Wexler and Bruce Winick—of the construct of therapeutic jurisprudence. Therapeutic jurisprudence (sometimes TJ) presents a new model by which we can assess the ultimate general, individual impacts of case law and legislation that affects persons with mental disabilities. It studies the role of the law as a therapeutic agent, recognizing that substantive rules, legal procedures, and lawyers' roles may have either therapeutic or antitherapeutic consequences, and questioning whether such rules, procedures, and roles can or should be reshaped to enhance their therapeutic potential, while not subordinating due process principles.[1]

Therapeutic jurisprudence stems from a variety of sources. First, recent changes in the judicial temperament have made it appear that the seemingly endless expansion of civil rights decisions in cases involving the constitutional and civil rights of mentally disabled persons has come to a halt,[2] and that federal courts can no longer be looked to as the last bastion of patients' rights.[3] Second, changes in the political and social climate (the residue of the Reagan years) eliminated any sort of political consensus that might have once supported the proposition that amelioration of the lives of mentally disabled individuals was a positive social goal.[4]

Next, the development of more sophisticated behavioral and empirical research began to shed some important light on the roots of mental disability and the reasons for some previously not understood behavior of mentally disabled persons.[5] Finally, the development of other sophisticated schools of jurisprudence (e.g., law and economics; feminist jurisprudence; critical legal studies; critical race studies) has begun to examine the entire legal system through a series of new lenses and filters.

Therapeutic jurisprudence looks at a variety of mental disability law issues in an effort to both shed light on past developments and to offer insights for future developments. Recent

---

[1]*See, e.g.,* THERAPEUTIC JURISPRUDENCE: THE LAW AS A THERAPEUTIC AGENT (David Wexler ed. 1990) [hereinafter TJ]; ESSAYS IN THERAPEUTIC JURISPRUDENCE (David Wexler & Bruce Winick eds. 1991) [hereinafter ESSAYS]; LAW IN A THERAPEUTIC KEY: RECENT DEVELOPMENTS IN THERAPEUTIC JURISPRUDENCE (David Wexler & Bruce Winick eds. 1996) [hereinafter KEY]; THERAPEUTIC JURISPRUDENCE APPLIED: ESSAYS ON MENTAL HEALTH LAW (Bruce Winick ed. 1998); David Wexler, *Putting Mental Health Into Mental Health Law: Therapeutic Jurisprudence,* 16 LAW & HUM. BEHAV. 27 (1992) [hereinafter Wexler I]; David Wexler, *Applying the Law Therapeutically,* 5 APP'L & PREVEN. PSYCHOL. 179 (1996); David Wexler, *Reflections on the Scope of Therapeutic Jurisprudence,* 1 PSYCHOL., PUB. POL'Y & L. 220 (1995); 1 MICHAEL L. PERLIN, MENTAL DISABILITY LAW: CIVIL AND CRIMINAL § 2D-3, at 534–41 (2d ed. 1998); *Bibliography of Therapeutic Jurisprudence,* 10 N.Y.L. SCH. J. HUM. RTS. 915 (1993); *see also,* Michael L. Perlin, *A Law of Healing,*—U. CIN. L. REV.—(2000) (in press).

[2]Michael L. Perlin, *State Constitutions and Statutes as Sources of Rights for the Mentally Disabled: The Last Frontier?* 20 LOY. L.A. L. REV. 1249 (1987).

[3]Wexler I, *supra* note 1, at 29–31; John Petrila, *Redefining Mental Health Law: Thoughts on a New Agenda,* 16 LAW & HUM. BEHAV. 89, 89–92 (1992).

[4]*See, e.g.,* Michael L. Perlin, *Competency, Deinstitutionalization, and Homelessness: A Story of Marginalization,* 28 HOUS. L. REV. 63 (1991).

[5]*See, e.g.,* Michael L. Perlin, *Unpacking the Myths: The Symbolism Mythology of Insanity Defense Jurisprudence,* 40 CASE W. RES. L. REV. 599 (1989–90); MICHAEL L. PERLIN, THE JURISPRUDENCE OF THE INSANITY DEFENSE (1994).

articles and essays have considered such matters as the insanity-acquittee conditional release hearing, health care of mentally disabled prisoners, the psychotherapist–patient privilege, incompetency labeling, competency decision making, juror decision making in malpractice and negligent-release litigation, competency to consent to treatment, competency to seek voluntary treatment, standards of psychotherapeutic tort liability, the effect of guilty pleas in sex offender cases, correctional law, health care delivery, "repressed memory" litigation, the impact of scientific discovery on substantive criminal law doctrine, and the competency to be executed.[6] Other scholars are beginning to use therapeutic jurisprudence insights in exploring other aspects of the legal system, including the processing of domestic violence cases, labor arbitration, family law, the law of advanced medical directives, elder law, preventive law, veterans' benefits, social security disability law, workers' compensation, probate law, and policies regarding sexual orientation in the military.[7]

This list should suggest the broad scope of substantive and procedural mental disability law topics to which therapeutic jurisprudence can be applied, but should also trigger thoughts about other areas of potential scholarly study as well. Although these are fresh, stimulating, and provocative ideas, at least two caveats need to be added to any therapeutic jurisprudence analysis.

First and most important, it is clear that an inquiry into therapeutic outcomes does *not* mean that therapeutic concerns trump civil rights and civil liberties. David Wexler under-scored this in a recent manuscript: The law's use of "mental health information to improve therapeutic functioning [cannot] impinge upon justice concerns."[8] Therapeutic jurisprudence does not, cannot, and must not mean, in Nicholas Kittrie's famous phrase, "a return to the therapeutic state."[9] Consideration of therapeutic jurisprudence issues cannot be used as an excuse to return to the days of the 1950s when courts were comfortable with a hands-off policy toward mental hospitals and their residents.[10]

Recent papers have given us new insights into therapeutic jurisprudence. They demonstrate that therapeutic jurisprudence is not and cannot be simply an elaborate academic justification for a return to the therapeutic state.[11] Therapeutic jurisprudence has not developed as a means by which mental health professionals can avoid legal accountabil-ity or by which civil libertarian principles can be subverted. In a paper on the TJ implications of right-to-refuse decision making, for example, Deborah Dorfman emphasized that a TJ inquiry will force clinicians to step back from our treatment choices and "assess. . . . why we are making this choice" in an effort to determine if society is really being driven by purported therapeutic outcomes or as a means of "reliev[ing . . . the] anxieties that the mentally ill instill within us."[12] In the same vein, an article by Bruce Winick demonstrates

---

[6]*See, e.g.,* articles cited in 1 PERLIN, *supra* note 1, § 2D-3, at 535–40 nn.83–132 (2d ed. 1998).

[7]*See id.,* § 2D-3, at 540 nn.133–43.

[8]David Wexler, *Therapeutic Jurisprudence and Changing Concepts of Legal Scholarship,* 11 BEHAV. SCI. & L. 17 (1993) [hereinafter Wexler, *Changing Concepts*]; David Wexler, *New Directions in Therapeutic Jurispru-dence: Law/Mental Health Scholarship Outside the Conventional Context of Mental Health Law,* 10 N.Y.L. SCH. J. HUM. RTS. 759 (1993) [hereinafter Wexler, *New Directions*].

[9]*See generally* NICHOLAS KITTRIE: THE RIGHT TO BE DIFFERENT: DEVIANCE AND ENFORCED THERAPY (1971).

[10]*See generally* 1 PERLIN, *supra* note 1, § 1-2.1, at 7; Perlin, *supra* note 2. For standard articulations of the doctrine, see for example, Banning v. Looney, 213 F.2d 771 (10th Cir. 1954), *cert. denied,* 348 U.S. 854 (1954); Siegel v. Ragan, 180 F.2d 785, 788 (7th Cir. 1950). Justice Thomas' dissent in Helling v. McKinney, 509 U.S. 25 (1993) (questioning constitutional underpinnings of doctrine articulated in Estelle v. Gamble, 429 U.S. 97 (1976) (right of incarcerated prisoners to medical care)) appears to long for a return to this jurisprudence.

[11]*See* Kittrie *supra* note 9.

[12]Deborah Dorfman, *Through a Therapeutic Jurisprudential Filter: Fear and Pretextuality in Mental Disability Law,* 10 N.Y.L. SCH. J. HUM. RTS. 805, 819 (1993).

how decisions expanding the right to refuse treatment (such as *Riggins v. Nevada*)[13]—by implicitly focusing on the nature of choice in the construction of a treatment calculus—will set up "expectancies of positive outcomes that predictably will increase patient motivation and treatment compliance, enhancing the chances that treatment will be successful."[14]

Second, familiarity with therapeutic jurisprudence cannot be limited to the worlds of the small circle of law professors and academic psychologists writing in this area.[15] If therapeutic jurisprudence is to be meaningful, there must be a concentrated outreach to members of the practicing bar, frequent forensic witnesses, and to clinicians.

Third, John Petrila has pointed out a potentially serious gap in the therapeutic jurisprudence methodology: its failure to explicitly incorporate the perspective of both the voluntary and involuntary consumer of mental health services in crafting a therapeutic jurisprudence perspective.[16] In this way, those who are involved in (or are the subjects of) the litigation that deals with individuals with mental disabilities can share their insights into how the therapeutic, antitherapeutic, or atherapeutic aspects of the justice system actually play out. Those of us who write in this field can and must learn from them. In another recent paper, Joel Haycock spoke to this directly: "The success of therapeutic jurisprudence will depend in part on the degree to which it *empowers* the objects of therapeutic and judicial attention."[17] This is a challenge that TJ must meet.

One example should do. Over 20 years ago, John Ensminger and Thomas Liguori (then colleagues of mine in the New Jersey Division of Mental Health Advocacy) wrote a piece on the therapeutic aspects of the civil commitment process, an essay reprinted in Wexler's first collection of therapeutic jurisprudence essays.[18] Not until the present time has another author significantly built on their insights about how the commitment process actually works, what effect it has on the individuals subject to commitment, and how state hospital employees respond to the litigational process.[19] Additional involvement of both legal and mental health practitioners in the therapeutic jurisprudence enterprise would help ensure that there are meaningful real-world results from any academic efforts in this field.

It is essential that therapeutic jurisprudence incorporate the viewpoints and perspectives of the eventual consumers[20] of mental health services—those who involuntarily and

---

[13]504 U.S. 127 (1992); *see supra* Chapter 6.

[14]Bruce Winick, *New Directions in the Right to Refuse Mental Health Treatment: The Implications of* Riggins v. Nevada, 2 WM. & MARY BILL RTS. J. 205, 234 (1993).

[15]For the most recent important collection of TJ writings, *see* KEY, *supra* note 1.

[16]John Petrila, *Paternalism and the Unrealized Promise of Essays in Therapeutic Jurisprudence,* 10 N.Y.L. SCH. J. HUM. RTS. 877 (1993) (review of ESSAYS, *supra* note 1).

[17]Joel Haycock, *Speaking Truth to Power: Rights, Therapeutic Jurisprudence, and Massachusetts Mental Health Law,* 20 N. ENG. J. CIV. & CRIM. CONFINEMENT 301, 317 (1993) ("the success of therapeutic jurisprudence will depend in part on the degree to which it empowers the objects of therapeutic and judicial attention").

[18]John J. Ensminger & Thomas Liguori, *The Therapeutic Significance of the Civil Commitment Hearing,* 6 J. PSYCHIATRY & L. 5 (1978), *reprinted in* TJ, *supra* note 1, at 245.

[19]*See* Bruce Winick, *Therapeutic Jurisprudence and the Civil Commitment Hearing,* 10 J. CONTEMP. ISSUES 37 (1999). For two other important perspectives on the question, compare Paul Appelbaum, *Civil Commitment From a Systems Perspective,* 16 LAW & HUM. BEHAV. 61 (1992) (suggesting new functionally independent system to assume all civil commitment responsibilities now shared by mental health and judicial systems), and Joel Haycock et al., *Thinking About Alternatives to the Current Practice of Civil Commitment,* 20 N. ENG. J. CIV. & CRIM. CONFINEMENT 265 (1994) (suggesting mediation as an alternative means of resolving involuntary civil commitment cases).

[20]*See, e.g.,* James Dudley et al., *A Consumer Satisfaction Survey of People With Mental Retardation and Mental Illness,* 48 PSYCHIATRIC SERV. 1075 (1997); David Rochefort, *Mental Health Reform and Inclusion of the Mentally Ill: Dilemmas of U.S. Policy-Making,* 19 INT'L J.L. & PSYCHIATRY 223 (1996).

voluntarily[21] enter the mental health system. There is now a vibrant and growing body of literature[22] by former recipients of mental health services. For years, the mental health system and the judiciary have ignored this perspective,[23] a willful blindness that is even more perplexing in light of the findings of Tom Tyler that perceptions of systemic fairness are driven, in large part, by "the degree to which people judge that they are treated with dignity and respect."[24] The next generation of TJ scholarship must incorporate these perspectives.[25]

Fourth, the recent literature shows how therapeutic jurisprudence can be used as a servant of law reform, by illuminating the therapeutic and antitherapeutic affects of rules that drive behavior in other institutional and litigational systems. Daniel Shuman, for instance, has looked at the tort system[26] and concluded that there is a "common agenda" shared by tort law and therapeutic jurisprudence,[27] raising provocative questions that tort scholars need to consider in the continued development of tort–compensation jurisprudence.[28] In and of itself, the consistent showing of an association of a reduction of postaccident pathology with "a shorter time between accident and settlement, a longer time after the settlement of the lawsuit, and having less severe symptomatology after the accident"[29] suggests the importance of therapeutic jurisprudence to tort law.

Fifth, recent developments demonstrate how therapeutic jurisprudence can be a powerful interpretive tool to make vivid the "stories" of individuals in other areas of the law. Keri Gould's examination of that aspect of the federal sentencing guidelines that

---

[21]*See, e.g.,* Zinermon v. Burch, 494 U.S. 113 (1990) (voluntary patient could proceed with § 1983 damages action against state hospital officials for allowing him to sign voluntary admissions forms at a time when they should have known he was incompetent to do so).

[22]*See generally* 1 PERLIN, *supra* note 1, § 1-2.1, at 10–11 n.43; Symposium, *Challenging the Therapeutic State: Critical Perspectives of Psychiatry and the Mental Health System,* 11 J. MIND & BEHAV. 1–318 (1990).

[23]*See, e.g.,* Michael L. Perlin, *On "Sanism,"* 46 SMU L. REV. 373 (1992) [hereinafter Perlin, *Sanism*]; Michael L. Perlin, *Pretexts and Mental Disability Law: The Case of Competency,* 47 U. MIAMI L. REV. 625 (1993) [hereinafter Perlin, *Pretexts*]; Eric Turkheimer & Charles Parry, *Why the Gap? Practice and Policy in Civil Commitment Hearings,* 47 AM. PSYCHOLOGIST 646 (1992); Charles Parry et al., *A Comparison of Commitment and Recommitment Hearings: Legal and Policy Implications,* 15 INT'L J.L. & PSYCHIATRY 25 (1992). For a rare judicial exception, see Rennie v. Klein, 476 F. Supp. 1294, 1306 (D.N.J. 1979) (other citations omitted), citing Theodore Van Putten & Phillip Ray, *Subjective Response as a Predictor of Outcome in Pharmacotherapy,* 35 ARCHIVES GEN. PSYCHIATRY 477, 480 (1978) ("'Schizophrenics have been asked every question except, How does the medication agree with you?' Their response is worth listening to.").

[24]Tom Tyler, *The Psychological Consequences of Judicial Procedures: Implications for Civil Commitment Hearings,* 46 SMU L. REV. 433, 442 (1992), and *see id.* at 444 (noting that these findings "have especially important implications for the study of commitment hearings"). For other important related readings on procedural justice in this context, see for example, Norman Poythress, *Procedural Preferences, Perceptions of Fairness, and Compliance With Outcomes,* 18 LAW & HUM. BEHAV. 361 (1994); P. Christopher Earley & E. Allan Lind, *Procedural Justice and Participation in Task Selection: The Role of Control in Mediating Justice Judgments,* 52 J. PERSONAL. & SOC. PSYCHOL. 1148 (1987); Tom Tyler, Kenneth Rasinski & Nancy Spodick, *Influence of Voice on Satisfaction With Leaders: Exploring the Meaning of Process Control,* 48 J. PERSONALITY & SOC. PSYCHOL. 72 (1985); Raymond Paternoster et al., *Do Fair Procedures Matter? The Effect of Procedural Justice on Spouse Assault,* 31 LAW & SOC'Y REV. 163 (1997). *Cf.* James Liu & Gerald Shure, *Due Process Orientation Does Not Always Mean Political Liberalism,* 17 LAW & HUM. BEHAV. 343 (1993).

[25]*See* Petrila, *supra* note 16, at 903–04; Haycock, *supra* note 17, at 317.

[26]*See* Michael L. Perlin, Tarasoff *and the Dilemma of the Dangerous Patient: New Directions for the 1990's,* 16 LAW & PSYCHOL. REV. 29 (1992).

[27]Daniel Shuman, *Making the World a Better Place Through Tort Law?: Through The Therapeutic Looking Glass,* 10 N.Y.L. SCH. J. HUM. RTS. 739, 758 (1993).

[28]*Id.* at 755–57.

[29]*Id.* at 757, quoting Renée Binder et al., *Is Money a Cure? A Follow-Up of Litigants in England,* 19 BULL. AM. ACAD. PSYCHIATRY & L. 151, 152 (1991).

permits departure from presumptive sentencing terms when the defendant "turns rat" (that is, informs on others)[30] takes TJ into new and totally unchartered waters. The questions that Gould asks provide an important research agenda for sophisticated criminal law scholars and empiricists.[31] Similarly, Murray Levine's empirical analysis of the impact of mandatory child abuse reporting by therapists demonstrates the complexity and ambiguity of the underlying issues and shows how a law written with an ostensibly therapeutic purpose[32] can result in feelings of anger and betrayal on the part of therapists and have significantly antitherapeutic outcomes.[33]

Sixth, other important papers contextualize these developments in two very different but complimentary ways: within the world of forensic mental health law practice and within the larger legal process. David Wexler has provided another enticing menu of alternative legal and behavioral areas that cry out for therapeutic jurisprudence analysis. He explicitly has called for an "expan[sion] of the reach of therapeutic jurisprudence beyond the conventional contours of mental disability law" to serve as "an eventual instrument of law reform."[34] Robert Sadoff has considered the entire school of TJ from the important perspective of the practicing forensic psychiatrists (although his insights are equally applicable to the other mental health professions as well) and demonstrated how therapeutic jurisprudence inquiries must extend far beyond the mental disability law borders.[35] This perspective forces us to consider a reality that is too often glossed over in all legal scholarship: That therapeutic jurisprudence will also restructure the contours of forensic testimony and of the relationship between fact finders and expert witnesses, a relationship already shaped to a large extent by constitutional dictates and statutory limitations as well as by self-imposed professional restrictions on expertise.[36]

Seventh, consideration of therapeutic jurisprudential values should end new inquiries into the behavior of the mental disability law system. Although the therapeutic jurisprudence construct is an enormously useful one and an excellent organizing tool, it does not answer all the questions before us. To understand the motivations of the responses of judges, lawyers, and litigators to the mental disability law system, it is also necessary to look at the influence of sanism and pretextuality.

There has not yet been a systematic investigation into the reasons why some courts decide cases therapeutically and others antitherapeutically. I believe that the answer can

---

[30]*See U.S. Sentencing Guidelines* § 5K1.1, and 18 U.S.C. § 3553(e). On the relationship between the guidelines and a defendant's mental disability, see PERLIN, *supra* note 1, § 16.18A, at 590–98 (1998 Cum. Supp.).

[31]Keri K. Gould, *Turning Rat and Doing Time for Uncharged, Dismissed, or Acquitted Crimes: Do the Federal Sentencing Guidelines Promote Respect for the Law?* 10 N.Y.L. SCH. J. HUM. RTS. 835, 869–70 (1993) ("Do accused and/or convicted federal offenders perceive the Federal Sentencing Guideline provisions as unjust? . . . [A]re federal defendants and inmates sophisticated enough to differentiate between their overall feelings of disempowerment within the system and their specific response to treatment under Guideline provisions? . . . [C]an an empirical instrument be designed to test such an inquiry?").

[32]*See, e.g.,* N.Y. SOC. SERVS. LAW § 413.1; *see generally* Margaret Meriwether, *Child Abuse Reporting Laws: Time for a Change,* 20 FAM. L.Q. 141 (1986).

[33]Murray Levine et al., *A Therapeutic Jurisprudence Analysis of Mandated Reporting of Child Maltreatment by Psychotherapists,* 10 N.Y.L. SCH. J. HUM. RTS. 711, 726–33 (1993).

[34]Wexler, *New Directions, supra* note 8, at 16.

[35]Robert L. Sadoff, *Therapeutic Jurisprudence: A View From a Forensic Psychiatrist,* 10 N.Y.L. SCH. J. HUM. RTS. 825, 825–26 (1993).

[36]*See, e.g.,* Michael L. Perlin, *Power Imbalances in Therapeutic and Forensic Relationships,* 9 BEHAV. SCI. & L. 111 (1992); *Specialty Guidelines for Forensic Psychologists,* 15 LAW & HUM. BEHAV. 655 (1991). On applying therapeutic jurisprudence in clinical practice, see David Wexler, *Therapeutic Jurisprudence in Clinical Practice,* 153 AM. J. PSYCHIATRY 453 (1996) (editorial) (discussing Paul Appelbaum & Rose Zoltek-Jick, *Psychotherapists' Duties to Third Parties: Ramona and Beyond,* 153 AM. J. PSYCHIATRY 457 (1996)).

be found, in significant part, in sanism. Sanism is such a dominant psychological force that it (a) distorts rational decision making, (b) encourages (albeit on at least a partially unconscious level) pretextuality and teleology, and (c) prevents decision makers from intelligently and coherently focusing on questions that are meaningful to therapeutic jurisprudential inquiries.[37]

The types of sanist decisions that I have discussed elsewhere in this volume operate in an ostensibly atherapeutic world; although some decisions may be, in fact, therapeutic and others may be antitherapeutic,[38] these outcomes seem to arise almost in spite of themselves.[39] In short, we cannot make any lasting progress in "putting mental health into mental health law"[40] until we confront the system's sanist biases and the ways that these biases blunt our ability to intelligently weigh and assess social science data in the creation of a mental disability law jurisprudence.

These constructs need to be considered in the context of any therapeutic jurisprudence inquiry because, unless we determine why the law has developed as it has, it will make little difference if we determine whether it is developing in a "therapeutically correct" way. In short, even if the legal system were to come to grips with all therapeutic jurisprudence issues in all aspects of mental disability law, these additional inquiries will still be required. Although I am thus convinced that therapeutic jurisprudence is an absolutely essential tool to be used in the reconstruction of mental disability law, if it is to truly illuminate the underlying system we must not fail to place it in the social–political context of why and how mental disability law has developed and what conscious and unconscious motivations have contributed to the law's development.

It is necessary to explicitly consider the relationship between TJ, sanism, and pretextuality. I believe that it is only through these perspectives that the "doctrinal abyss" that appears to define mental disability law jurisprudence can be understood.[41] Therapeutic jurisprudence—by forcing us to focus consciously on the therapeutic and antitherapeutic outcomes of court decisions, statutes, rules, and roles—illuminates the way that

---

[37]*See* Michael L. Perlin, "Law as a Therapeutic and Antitherapeutic Agent," Paper presented at the Massachusetts Department of Mental Health's Division of Forensic Mental Health's annual conference, Auburn, MA, May 1992) (suggesting that influence of sanism must be considered in therapeutic jurisprudence investigations); Michael L. Perlin, *Therapeutic Jurisprudence: Understanding the Sanist and Pretextual Bases of Mental Disability Law,* 20 N. ENG. J. CRIM. & CIV. CONFINEMENT 369 (1994) (same).

[38]For example, I believe that the decision in State v. Krol, 344 A.2d 289 (N.J. 1975) (expanding procedural due process protection rights at the postinsanity acquittal commitment hearing) is therapeutic and the decision in Jones v. United States, 463 U.S. 354 (1983) (restricting such rights) is antitherapeutic. *See* PERLIN, *supra* note 5, chap. (IV)(E)(2)(d).

[39]*See, e.g.,* discussions in David Wexler & Bruce Winick, *Therapeutic Jurisprudence as a New Approach to Mental Health Law Policy Analysis and Research,* 45 U. MIAMI L. REV. 979, 990–92 (1991); *id.* at 992–97 (treatment of incompetent death row inmates) and at 997–1001 (treatment of incompetency to stand trial) [hereinafter Wexler & Winick, *New Approach*]; David Wexler & Bruce Winick, *Therapeutic Jurisprudence and Criminal Justice Mental Health Issues,* 16 MENT. & PHYSICAL DIS. L. REP. 225, 229–30 (1992) [hereinafter Wexler & Winick, *Criminal Justice*] (sex offender guilty pleas); Bruce Winick, *Sex Offender Law in the 1990s: A Therapeutic Jurisprudence Analysis,* 4 PSYCHOL. PUB. POL'Y & L. 505 (1998) (same); *see also* Michael L. Perlin, Tarasoff *and the Dilemma of the Dangerous Patient: New Directions for the 1990's,* 16 LAW & PSYCHOL. REV. 29, 54–62 (1992) [hereinafter Perlin, *Tarasoff*] (duty to protect in tort law); Michael L. Perlin, *Reading the Supreme Court's Tea Leaves: Predicting Judicial Behavior in Civil and Criminal Right to Refuse Treatment Cases,* 12 AM. J. FORENS. PSYCHIATRY 37, 54 (1991) [hereinafter Perlin, *Tea Leaves*] (right to refuse treatment); Michael L. Perlin, *Hospitalized Patients and the Right to Sexual Interaction: Beyond the Last Frontier?* 20 NYU REV. L. & SOC. CHANGE 517 (1993–94) (right of institutionalized patients to sexual autonomy).

[40]*See* Wexler I, *supra* note 1.

[41]*See, e.g.,* Michael L. Perlin, *The Supreme Court, the Mentally Disabled Criminal Defendant, and Symbolic Values: Random Decisions, Hidden Rationales, or "Doctrinal Abyss"?* 29 ARIZ. L. REV. 1 (1987).

pretextuality and sanism drive the mental disability law system.[42] Recent literature advances this ongoing enterprise by reminding us that scholars and researchers in this area partially fulfill the role of systemic archaeologists who continue to unearth new discoveries that explain how and why the mental disability law system operates as it does.[43]

Let me look at this through the filter of a series of papers that were published several years ago in a TJ symposium in the *New England Journal on Criminal and Civil Confinement*.[44] I believe that an examination of these papers from a sanism–pretextuality perspective helps demonstrate my point.

Each of the papers in this symposium reflects these realities about both therapeutic jurisprudence and the mental disability law system. Richard Barnum and Thomas Grisso's article, by way of example, revealed that the application of incompetency to stand trial procedures to juvenile cases is often pretextual, that court-ordered evaluations often are sought for reasons that have little to do with the actual competency inquiry.[45] Joel Haycock's piece concluded that a seemingly innocuous financial recoupment law has ominous therapeutic (as well as humanitarian) implications and reflected on the sanist behavior of the Massachusetts legislature in passing the law in question.[46] Joel Haycock, David Finkelman, and Helene Presskreischer's article stripped the facade from the pretextual level of representation often afforded to persons facing the involuntary civil commitment process.[47] Ira Packer's essay showed the pretextual nature of one of the strongest arguments in support of ''widening the net''[48] in civil commitment (the argument that stricter, behavior-based criteria should lead to the ''criminalization of the mentally ill.'')[49] And finally, both David Wexler's general introduction to the concept of therapeutic jurisprudence and Thomas Grisso and David Finkelman's introduction to these papers demonstrated how each of these individual inquiries must be reconsidered in light of both the entire mental disability law system[50] and the legal system as a whole.[51]

An examination of each lead paper is instructive. Barnum and Grisso carefully analyzed the discontinuities between two sections of in the Massachusetts Juvenile Justice Act[52] in an

---

[42]For an especially rich example of the integration of therapeutic jurisprudence and pretextuality theory, see Dorfman, *supra* note 12.

[43]Judges are turning to therapeutic jurisprudence as a new means of exploring traditonally vexing legal problems. *See, e.g.,* Peggy Hora et al., *Therapeutic Jurisprudence and the Drug Treatment Movement: Revolutionizing the Criminal Justice System's Response to Drug Abuse and Crime in America,* 74 NOTRE DAME L. REV. 439 (1999). And scholars are beginning to integrate TJ with alternative applications such as preventive law. *See, e.g.,* Dennis P. Stolle et al., *Integrating Preventive Law and Therapeutic Jurisprudence: A Law and Psychology Based Approach to Lawyering,* 34 CAL. W. L. REV. 15 (1997); Dennis Stolle & David Wexler, *Therapeutic Jurisprudence and Preventive Law: A Combined Concentration to Invigorate the Everyday Practice of Law,* 39 ARIZ. L. REV. 25 (1997).

[44]*Symposium on Therapeutic Jurisprudence: Bridging the Gap From Theory to Practice,* 20 N. ENG. J. ON CRIM. & CIV. ON CONFINEMENT (Summer 1994).

[45]Richard Barnum & Thomas Grisso, *Competency to Stand Trial in Juvenile Courts in Massachusetts: Issues in Therapeutic Jurisprudence,* 20 N. ENG. J. ON CIV. & CRIM. CONFINEMENT 301 (1994)

[46]*See* Haycock, *supra* note 17.

[47]Joel Haycock et al., *Mediating the Gap: Thinking About Alternatives to the Current Practice of Civil Commitment,* 20 N. ENG. J. ON CIV. & CRIM. CONFINEMENT 265 (1994).

[48]The phrase comes from *In re* S. L., 462 A.2d 1252, 1257 (N.J. 1983).

[49]Ira Packer, *The Court Clinic System in Massachusetts: A Therapeutic Approach vs. a Rights- Oriented Approach,* 20 N. ENG. J. ON CIV. & CRIM. CONFINEMENT 291 (1994).

[50]Thomas Grisso & David Finkelman, *Therapeutic Jurisprudence: From Idea to Application,* 20 N. ENG. J. ON CIV. & CRIM. CONFINEMENT 243 (1994).

[51]David Wexler, *An Orientation to Therapeutic Jurisprudence,* 20 N. ENG. J. ON CIV. & CRIM. CONFINEMENT 259 (1994).

[52]MASS. GEN. L. ANN., ch. 123, § 15(a), (f).

attempt to decipher the legislature's ambiguities and to try to offer a coherent explanation of an incoherent statute.[53] Their analysis is careful and convincing, in stark juxtaposition to the sloppily drafted law they analyze. It also serves to highlight the lack of care and attention legislatures generally devote to mental disability law questions, yet another reflection of the sanist way that mentally disabled persons (and their legal problems) are marginalized.[54] Their careful review of commitment of juveniles being evaluated on the question of their incompetency to stand trial[55] can easily support an argument that the screening law is pretextual at base: that it gives the court an apparent "objective" and disinterested basis (the testimony of mental health professionals) to support the outcome it wished to reach.[56] Their focus on courts' *confusion*[57] demonstrates again the devaluation of these questions in the legal process.

This suggests another meta-issue lurking that could benefit from an ongoing therapeutic jurisprudence analysis: a consideration of the general level of sloppiness that permeates mental health legislation and court opinions. Statutes define mental illness and dangerousness using circular reasoning, and, in describing mental disability, use terminology that is literally centuries out of date.[58] Judicial decisions conflate inapposite legal constructs and remain similarly wedded to arcane and dated terminology.[59]

This sloppiness in drafting statutes stands in stark contrast to other substantive areas of the law, where *Restatements* and the American Law Institute drafts provide careful codifications.[60] I doubt that this is coincidental. Mental disability law has always been a poor stepchild of the law: No law school sees it as part of the core curriculum. Mental disability law cases are never favored assignments for trial judges. The civil commitment process is

---

[53]Barnum & Grisso, *supra* note 45, at 324–39.

[54]This is especially ironic in light of the fact that the entire juvenile court system was premised on a therapeutic basis, a premise that has failed miserably in the ensuing decades. *See, e.g.,* Barry C. Feld, *The Transformation of the Juvenile Court,* 75 MINN. L. REV. 691 (1991); Barry C. Feld, *The Juvenile Court Meets the Principle of Offense: Punishment, Treatment, and the Difference Treatment Makes,* 68 B.U. L. REV. 821 (1988); Charles Springer, *Rehabilitating the Juvenile Court,* 5 NOTRE DAME J.L., ETH. & PUB POL'Y 397 (1991). *See generally In re* Gault, 387 U.S. 1, 14–16 (1967) (historical roots of juvenile court jurisdiction).

[55]Barnum & Grisso, *supra* note 45, at 339–42. The underlying issues will become even more confounded in the future following the Supreme Court's decision in Godinez v. Moran, 509 U.S. 389 (1993), holding that the standard for assessing competency to enter guilty pleas or waive counsel is no higher than to stand trial. *See supra* Chapter 9; *see generally* Michael L. Perlin, *"Dignity Was the First to Leave":* Godinez v. Moran, Colin Ferguson, *and the Trial of Mentally Disabled Criminal Defendants,* 14 BEHAV. SCI. & L. 61 (1996).

[56]*See* Michael L. Perlin, *Morality and Pretextuality, Psychiatry and Law: Of "Ordinary Common Sense," Heuristic Reasoning, and Cognitive Dissonance,* 19 BULL. AM. ACAD. PSYCHIATRY & LAW 131, 137 (1991) (discussing the pretextual nature of this exact behavior). On the ways that expert witnesses may shape their testimony to comport with a judge's preexisting position on a case, see Perlin, *Pretexts, supra* note 23, at 664–69.

[57]Barnum & Grisso, *supra* note 45, at 333–34.

[58]*See* Jackson v. Indiana, 406 U.S. 715 , 721 (1972) (state statutes referred to institutions for the "feeble-minded"); *see also, e.g.,* Addkinson v. State, 608 So.2d 304, 308 (Miss. 1992) (psychiatrist characterized defendant as "high-end imbecile").

[59]*See* Perlin, *Pretexts, supra* note 23, at 679–80 (discussing courts' continued conflation and misunderstanding of different tests for incompetency to stand trial and insanity).

[60]The two exceptions are § 4.01 of the Model Penal Code (insanity defense formulation) and RESTATEMENT (SECOND) OF TORTS § 315 (duty of psychotherapists to protect potential victims of acts by mentally disabled persons). These are the only two areas of mental disability law in which lawyers are regularly available to litigate the issues in question. On the generally substandard job done by counsel representing persons with mental disabilities, see Michael L. Perlin, *Fatal Assumption: A Critical Evaluation of the Role of Counsel in Mental Disability Cases,* 16 LAW & HUM. BEHAV. 39 (1992).

subject to deformalization in a variety of ways;[61] much of the empirical literature that has developed around the question of the procedures needed to implement the constitutional right to refuse treatment focus on ways in which this stage can be delegalized.[62]

The apathy toward and disinterest in precision and accuracy in terminology reflects the sanist ways that both legislators and judges subordinate mental disability law issues (a reflection and extension of their subordination of mentally disabled persons). And given the frequency with which this sort of subordination occurs, it is difficult to conceive how therapeutic ends could ever be met in such a system.

The sanist and pretextual undercurrents are reflected in the other essays as well. Haycock, Finkelman, and Presskreischer, for example, began by informing readers of the historical fact—well-known to all who are familiar with this field but utterly and remarkably ignored by courts and legislatures—that "reports on failure to abide by procedural and substantive standards, and regular criticism of that failure, have not appreciably advanced the practice of civil commitment"[63] and by reminding us of the shoddy job traditionally done by lawyers assigned to represent patients in such hearings.[64] They quoted Paul Appelbaum's rueful conclusion that "at best . . . we have a justice system that is *marginally interested*" in the civil commitment process"[65] and point out with painful poignancy the sadness of such hearings when courts mechanically allow patients to make extemporaneous speeches protesting their commitments.[66] Their essay questions assumptions about the role of lawyers in the involuntary civil commitment process, considers the therapeutic jurisprudence implications of both an adversarial model and a best-interests model, and offers a third option—a mediation model—as a potential alternative.[67]

---

[61]*See, e.g.,* 1 PERLIN, *supra* note 1, § 2C-4.3, at 318–21 (discussing the question of whether a judicial officer must conduct the involuntary civil commitment hearing); for an important criticism of the use of nonjudicial hearing officers on the basis discussed, see Serena Stier & Kurt Stoebe, *Continuing Studies Project: Involuntary Hospitalization of the Mentally Ill in Iowa: The Failure of the 1975 Legislation,* 64 IOWA L. REV. 1284 (1979). On the ways that more formalized civil commitment hearings might be therapeutic, see generally Ensminger & Liguori, *supra* note 18, *reprinted in* TJ, *supra* note 1, at 245.

[62]*See generally* Michael L. Perlin, *Decoding Right to Refuse Treatment Law,* 16 INT'L J.L. & PSYCHIATRY 151, 157 n.50 (1993) For typical analyses following the decision of Rivers v. Katz, 504 N.Y.S.2d 74 (1986) (finding broad right to refuse antipsychotic drug treatment), *see generally* Francine Cournos et al., *A Comparison of Clinical and Judicial Procedures for Reviewing Requests for Involuntary Medication in New York,* 39 HOSP. & COMMUNITY PSYCHIATRY 851 (1988) (*Rivers* procedures neither delayed nor diminished the use of involuntary medication in large state hospital); J. Richard Ciccone et al., *Right to Refuse Treatment: Impact of* Rivers v. Katz, 18 BULL. AM. ACAD. PSYCHIATRY & L. 203, 214 (1990) (*Rivers* "diminished responsiveness, increased expense, and decreased the number of patients who had formal reviews of their refusal; in the process, the quality of care for some patients was significantly reduced"); Karen McKinnon et al., Rivers *in practice: Clinicians' Assessments of Patients' Decision-Making Capacity,* 40 HOSP. & COMMUNITY PSYCHIATRY 1159 (1989) (even though doctors may find capacity assessments "irrelevant," procedure may still be useful as it "encourages clinicians to discuss the proposed treatment with patients and to present information more effectively in court"); Francine Cournos et al., *Outcome of Involuntary Medication in a State Hospital System,* 148 AM. J. PSYCHIATRY 489 (1991) (involuntary medications did not appear to enhance insight or cooperation in cases of chronically severely ill patients).

[63]Haycock et al., *supra* note 47, at 265–66.

[64]*Id.* at 273; *see generally* Perlin, *supra* note 60.

[65]Haycock et al., *supra* note 47, at 274, quoting Paul Appelbaum, *Civil Commitment From a Systems Perspective,* 16 LAW & HUMAN. BEHAV. 61, 66 (1992) (emphasis added).

[66]Haycock et al., *supra* note 47 at 277–78.

[67]*Id.* at 279–88; *see also* Janet Abisch, *Mediational Lawyering in the Civil Commitment Context: A Therapeutic Jurisprudence Solution to the Counsel Role Dilemma,* 1 PSYCHOL., PUB. POL'Y & L. 120 (1995); Winick, *supra* note 19; Sharon Flower, *Resolving Voluntary Mental Health Treatment Disputes in the Community Setting: Benefits of and Barriers to Effective Mediation,* 14 OHIO ST. J. ON DISP. RESOL. 881 (1999).

Although I ultimately disagree with the mediation alternative—my sense (as one who has provided representation to individuals in this process and has supervised an office charged with the representation of thousands of such individuals)[68] is that the criticisms that the authors raised[69] are far more persuasive than the points they cited in its support—that in no way diminishes the paper's value to me as a means of using therapeutic jurisprudence to expose the pretextual nature of the civil commitment system.[70]

Kathy Yates' paper exposed sanism and pretextuality in the mental disability law system in a different context.[71] She examined constitutional decisions that now shape the contours of the relationship between forensic evaluations, confidentiality, and the *Miranda* doctrine and related them to other Supreme Court decisions on competency to stand trial[72] and competency to be executed.[73] Her analysis leads her to a series of thoughtful recommendations on how both forensic testimony and the forensic evaluative process can best be improved.[74]

In the course of this analysis—one within the very core of therapeutic jurisprudence envisioned by Wexler in his first collection[75]—Yates showed how legal pretexts lead to antitherapeutic law. Although the competency-to-stand-trial process appears to be grounded in constitutional doctrine,[76] the research demonstrates that judges regularly and uncritically accept conclusions of forensic experts,[77] despite confusion as to the meaning of the standard required prior to an acceptance of opinion testimony[78] and as to the actual substantive terminology used in competency determinations.[79] This confusion becomes even more troubling in light of evidence that professionals' attitudes, orientations, and political opinions have an impact on their forensic evaluations[80] and that the likelihood of subjective

---

[68]For eight years I was director of the New Jersey Division of Mental Health Advocacy, a state- level subcabinet office vested with the authority to provide representation in, *inter alia,* involuntary civil commitment cases. *See* Michael L. Perlin, *Mental Patient Advocacy by a Public Advocate,* 54 PSYCHIATRIC Q. 169 (1982).

[69]For example, that lack of potentially adversarial counsel would "further imbalance an already- imbalanced relationship"; that the disparity of bargaining positions would put patients at an "even greater disadvantage that they are now." Haycock et al., *supra* note 47, at 283. On the ways that hospital staff can routinely manipulate such disparity in bargaining to coerce patients into accepting voluntary commitment status (thus avoiding court hearings), see Susan Reed & Dan Lewis, *The Negotiation of Voluntary Admission in Chicago's State Mental Hospitals,* 18 J. PSYCHIATRY & L. 137 (1990).

[70]*See, e.g.,* Haycock et al., *supra* note 47, at 278: "[The patient's lawyers], with the collusion of the care-givers, disempower him or her, and thereby thwart the establishment of a voluntary treatment compact between patient and mental health professionals."

[71]*See, e.g.,* Estelle v. Smith, 451 U.S. 454 (1981); Powell v. Texas, 492 U.S. 380 (1989); Buchanan v. Kentucky, 483 U.S. 402 (1987).

[72]*See, e.g.,* Dusky v. United States, 362 U.S. 402 (1960); Jackson v. Indiana, 406 U.S. 715 (1972).

[73]*See, e.g.,* Ford v. Wainwright, 477 U.S. 399 (1986); Penry v. Lynaugh, 492 U.S. 302 (1989).

[74]*See* Kathy Faulkner Yates, *Issues Associated With Confidential and Informed Consent in Forensic Evaluations,* 20 N. ENG. J. ON CIV. & CRIM. CONFINEMENT 345, 362–68 (1994).

[75]TJ, *supra* note 1, at 5–6.

[76]*E.g., see Dusky,* 414 U.S. at 402; *Jackson,* 406 U.S. at 715.

[77]*See* Yates, *supra* note 74, at 349, *discussing research reported in* Stephen Golding, *Mental Health Professionals and the Courts: The Ethics of Expertise,* 13 INT'L J.L. & PSYCHIATRY 281 (1990), and *in* RONALD ROESCH AND STEPHEN GOLDING, COMPETENCY TO STAND TRIAL (1980).

[78]*See, e.g.,* Richard Rogers, *Ethical Dilemmas in Forensic Evaluations,* 5 BEHAV. SCI. & L. 149 (1987).

[79]*See, e.g.,* THOMAS GRISSO, EVALUATING COMPETENCIES: FORENSIC ASSESSMENTS AND INSTRUMENTS (1986); Perlin, *Pretexts, supra* note 23.

[80]*See, e.g.,* Charles Ewing, *Psychologists and Psychiatrists in Capital Sentencing: Experts or Executioners?* 8 SOC. ACTION & L. 67 (1982); Perlin, *Pretexts, supra* note 23.

bias is enhanced when clinical factors ''are not clear-cut and critical legal definitions are not precise.''[81]

The failure of professional associations to craft coherent and practical ethical guide-lines[82] adds yet another layer of pretextuality, an omission that becomes more troubling in cases of witnesses such as that of James Grigson, who testify in defiance of all existing professional ethical guidelines.[83] The problems are further exacerbated by evidence that courts misuse competency evaluations (using them to inappropriately address issues of guilt and punishment) and erroneously conflate concepts of competency and responsibility.[84]

Yates' paper thus used therapeutic jurisprudence as a diagnostic tool to identify the malignant way that pretexts poison forensic–judicial relationships and offers a series of prescriptive measures to attempt to best eliminate bias in the forensic process.

Packer's paper used therapeutic jurisprudence tools to assess the way that the Western Massachusetts Court Clinic evaluated criminal defendants in pretrial incompetency to stand trial and NGRI assessments and in presentencing examinations and studied whether this system has led to increased ''back door'' admissions to forensic psychiatric facilities.[85] He concluded that the data reject the popular criminalization hypothesis—that is, that restrictions on commitment have led and will lead to more mentally ill persons being arrested on a variety of nuisance charges[86]—and demonstrates how the court clinic has actually resulted in a decrease in the psychiatric hospitalization of mentally ill criminal defendants.[87]

Haycock's paper provided the ultimate unmasking of the pretextual charade that is mental disability law. He discussed a Massachusetts statute—enacted in response to ''hoary anecdotes'' about the occasional patient who receives large Veterans' Administration

---

[81]Yates, *supra* note 74, at 351.

[82]*See id.* at 353–54.

[83]*See* 3 PERLIN, *supra* note 1, § 17.13, at 529 n.270 (discussing testimony of James Grigson), and *id.* (citing sources criticizing Grigson's testimony); *see generally* RONALD ROSENBAUM, TRAVELS WITH ''DR. DEATH'' (1991). Grigson has testified for the prosecution in nearly one third of the Texas cases involving death row inmates. *See* JAMES W. MARQUART ET AL., THE ROPE, THE CHAIR, AND THE NEEDLE: CAPITAL PUNISHMENT IN TEXAS, 1923–1990, at 176 (1994); *see also* Charles P. Ewing, *''Dr. Death'' and the Case for an Ethical Ban on Psychiatric and Psychological Predictions of Future Dangerousness in Capital Sentencing Proceedings,* 8 AM. J.L. & MED. 407, 410 (1983); Stephen Garvey, *''As The Gentle Rain From Heaven'': Mercy in Capital Sentencing,* 81 CORNELL L. REV. 989, 1031–32 (1996), and *id.* nn.1067–71.

[84]Yates, *supra* note 74, at 357, reporting on research in Howard Owens et al., *The Judge's View of Competency Evaluations,* 13 BULL. AM. ACAD. PSYCHIATRY & L. 389 (1985); *see generally* Perlin, *Pretexts, supra* note 23.

[85]*See* Packer, *supra* note 49, at 293.

[86]*See, e.g.,* E. FULLER TORREY, NOWHERE TO GO: THE TRAGIC ODYSSEY OF THE HOMELESS MENTALLY ILL 13–14 (1988).

[87]*See* Packer, *supra* note 49, at 294–95. *Accord,* Thomas Arvanites, *The Impact of State Mental Hospital Deinstitutionalization on Commitments for Incompetency to Stand Trial,* 26 CRIMINOLOGY 307, 318 (1988); *see generally* PERLIN, *supra* note 1, § 7.24 at 243–451 n.632 (citing sources) (1998 Cum. Supp.).

Packer's article also raised intriguing therapeutic jurisprudence questions about the use (and the avoidance) of the insanity defense in pretrial plea bargaining (*see* Packer, *supra* note 49, at 296–98, discussing the entry of guilty pleas to minor charges as a way of avoiding the sometimes-draconian impact of a successful insanity defense). This lawyering gambit is an important (and perhaps troubling) one that reintroduces questions about the role of pretextuality in the trial of insanity defense cases, *see* PERLIN, *supra* note 23, chap. 9, and is worthy of significant further attention.

checks[88]—mandating that psychiatric patients with funds held in trust "shall contribute toward the cost of any counsel appointed" for that patient in an involuntary-commitment or medication-refusal hearing.[89] Haycock exposed the cruelty and cynicism underlying the statutory enactment and demonstrated the malignancy of a law that would "penalize those psychiatric patients who exercise their constitutional rights, while rewarding those compliant or simply needy individuals who decide to forgo legal representation."[90]

Haycock disavowed the characterization of this analysis as one that derives from therapeutic jurisprudence, and noted—correctly, I am sure—that a recitation of the law's antitherapeutic consequences "did not carry much weight with those who passed it" and that a rights-led attack was needed to challenge it successfully.[91] Yet I think that by saying this Haycock sold his own analysis short: What Haycock argued—persuasively and eloquently—is that in this case (and indeed, in the vast majority of cases that have heretofore been considered through this means of analysis), a rights-based critique *is,* ultimately, a therapeutic means of empowerment. His analysis of this shoddy and petty law shows me that the use of therapeutic jurisprudence may be the best means to erode the law's sanist and pretextual bases.

Conclusion

I will now turn to some of the specific mental disability law topics that I have previously discussed to reconsider them through a therapeutic jurisprudence filter.

---

[88]Haycock, *supra* note 17, at 307–08. He noted with absolute accuracy that this is the mental disability equivalent of stories, "so beloved by politicians about the welfare mother picking up her check in a Cadillac." *Id.* I believe that this analogy is an enormously important one, and that this sort of "vividness" heuristic drives the mental disability law system in a variety of important meretricious ways. *See* David Rosenhan, *Psychological Realities and Judicial Policies,* 10 STAN. LAW 10, 13–14 (1984); Marilyn Ford, *The Role of Extralegal Factors in Jury Verdicts,* 1 JUST. SYS. J. 16, 23 (1984); Perlin, *supra* note 56.

[89]MASS. GEN. L. ANN. ch. 123, § 18A.

[90]Haycock, *supra* note 17, at 308.

[91]*Id.* at 309.

Chapter 13
UNPACKING MENTAL DISABILITY LAW

A therapeutic jurisprudence analysis helps illuminate the impact of sanism and pretextuality on all areas of mental disability law. In this chapter I will limit my discussion to several aspects of mental health law. First, I will look at three of the most important institutional rights cases that set the stage for the major developments in civil commitment[1] and right to treatment law:[2] *Lessard v. Schmidt*,[3] *O'Connor v. Donaldson*,[4] and *Youngberg v. Romeo*.[5] Next, I will explore in some greater depth the right to refuse treatment. Then, I will consider issues centered about the application of the Americans With Disabilities Act to an institutional population. After this I will turn briefly to questions involving the federal sentencing guidelines. Finally, I will look at length to the application of therapeutic jurisprudence principles in cases involving the insanity defense.

Involuntary Civil Commitment and the Right to Treatment

Therapeutic jurisprudence proposes that we be sensitive to the consequences of governmental action and that we ask whether the law's antitherapeutic consequences can be reduced and its therapeutic consequences enhanced without subordinating due process and justice values.[6] In civil commitment case law, there is rarely any reference to the patient's perceived therapeutic response to the legal procedures or terms and conditions of the commitment.[7]

By the mid-1970s, it was universally accepted that some finding of mental illness was a prerequisite to involuntary commitment, following the Supreme Court's decision in *Jackson v. Indiana*[8] that "at the least, due process requires that the nature and duration of commitment must bear some reasonable relationship to the purpose for which the individual is committed."[9] *Jackson*'s principles were first given important life in an involuntary civil commitment context in *Lessard v. Schmidt*.[10] *Lessard* struck down Wisconsin's involuntary

---

[1]*See supra* Chapter 4.

[2]*See supra* Chapter 5.

[3]349 F. Supp. 1078 (E.D. Wis. 1972).

[4]422 U.S. 563 (1975).

[5]457 U.S. 307 (1982).

[6]David Wexler, *New Directions in Therapeutic Jurisprudence: Law & Mental Health Scholarship Outside the Conventional Context of Mental Health Law*, 10 N.Y.L. SCH. J. HUM. RTS. 759, 762 (1993).

[7]*See generally, e.g.*, cases discussed in 1 MICHAEL L. PERLIN, MENTAL DISABILITY LAW: CIVIL AND CRIMINAL § 2D-3, at chaps. 2A & 2C (2d ed. 1998) [hereinafter PERLIN, MDL], and in MICHAEL L. PERLIN, LAW AND MENTAL DISABILITY (1994) [hereinafter PERLIN, LMD] chap. 1.

[8]406 U.S. 715 (1972).

[9]*Id.* at 738. *See generally* PERLIN, CMD, *supra* note 7, § 1.03(d), at 24–25; 1 PERLIN, MDL *supra* note 7, § 2A-4.4, at 121–25 (2d. ed. 1998).

[10]349 F. Supp. 1078 (E.D. Wis. 1972), *vacated and remanded*, 414 U.S. 473, *on remand*, 379 F. Supp. 1376 (E.D. Wis. 1974), *vacated and remanded*, 421 U.S. 957 (1975), *reinstated*, 413 F. Supp. 1318 (E.D. Wis. 1976). Text accompanying footnotes 11–21 is generally adapted from PERLIN, LMD, *supra* note 7, § 1.04 at 25–28.

civil commitment scheme and established guidelines about the meaning of "dangerousness" that served as the model for the first generation of such challenges.[11]

Lessard v. Schmidt

Lessard was a class action brought on behalf of all adults then being held involuntarily
pursuant to any emergency, temporary, or permanent provision of Wisconsin's involuntary
civil commitment statutes.[12] It challenged a state statute that allowed for commitment if the
hearing court was "satisfied that he is mentally ill or infirm or deficient and that he is a proper
subject for custody and treatment."[13] According to plaintiff, the law failed to "describe the
standard for commitment so that persons may be able to ascertain the standard of conduct
under which they may be detained with reasonable certainty."[14]

In approaching the case, the court looked carefully at the common-law and historical
roots of the state involuntary civil commitment power.[15] In involuntary civil commitment
proceedings, it found that the same "fundamental liberties" are at stake as are in criminal
cases;[16] the police power must similarly be "tempered with stringent procedural safeguards
designed to protect the rights of one" subject to such power.[17] However, its review of the
pertinent history suggested that, traditionally, involuntary civil commitment procedures
have not "assured the due process safeguards against unjustified deprivation of liberty that
are accorded those accused of crime."[18]

The court then examined the state's statutory definition of *mental illness*[19] in light of the
U.S. Supreme Court's decision in *Humphrey v. Cady*,[20] which, in *dicta*, had interpreted the
section in question to require that a person's "potential for doing harm, to himself or to
others, is great enough to justify such a massive curtailment of liberty."[21] The *Lessard* court
construed this statement to mean that "the statute itself requires a finding of 'dangerousness'
to self or others in order to deprive an individual of his or her freedom."[22]

The use by the *Humphrey* court of the phrase "great enough" and its description of
commitment as such a "massive curtailment" of liberty implied "a balancing test in which

---

[11]Dix is clear: "Judicial activism began in 1972 . . . in *Lessard v. Schmidt*." George Dix, *Major Current
Issues Concerning Civil Commitment Criteria*, 45 LAW & CONTEMP. PROBS. 137 (Summer 1982). *Cf.* Fhagen v.
Miller, 29 N.Y.2d 348, 278 N.E.2d 615, 328 N.Y.S.2d 393, 397 (1972), *cert. denied*, 409 U.S. 845 (1972) (rejecting
similar challenge to New York state law) (decided nine months before *Lessard*).

[12]*Lessard*, 349 F. Supp. at 1082.

[13]WIS. STAT. ANN. § 51.02(5)(c) (1957).

[14]*Lessard*, 349 F. Supp. at 1082.

[15]The court began with the principle that the state's power to deprive a person of "the fundamental liberty to
go unimpeded about his or her affairs" must be based on a compelling state interest in such a deprivation, *Lessard*,
349 F. Supp. at 1084, citing J. S. MILL, ON LIBERTY 18 (Gateway, Inc. ed. 1962); *cf.* Jonas Robitscher, *Legal
Standards and Their Implications Regarding Civil Commitment Procedures*, *in* DANGEROUS BEHAVIOR: A PROBLEM
IN LAW AND MENTAL HEALTH 61, 69–70 (C. J. Frederick ed. 1974) (C. J. Frederick) (criticizing this citation to Mill as
a "bludgeon of reason" and an incomplete statement of Mill's philosophy).

[16]*Lessard*, 349 F. Supp. at 1084.

[17]*Id.*

[18]*Id.*

[19]*Mental illness* was defined as "mental disease to such extent that a person so afflicted requires care and
treatment for his own welfare, or the welfare of others, or of the community." WIS. STAT. ANN. § 51.75, art. II(f)
(1971).

[20]405 U.S. 504 (1972).

[21]*Lessard*, 349 F. Supp. at 1093, quoting *Humphrey*, 405 U.S. at 509.

[22]*Id.*

the state must bear the burden of proving that there is an extreme likelihood that if the person is not confined he will do immediate harm to himself or others."[23] Although predictions of future conduct are "always difficult" and confinement based on such predictions "must always be viewed with suspicion,"[24] civil confinement could be justified if the "proper" burden of proof were to be satisfied, and "dangerousness [were to be] based upon a finding of a recent overt act, attempt or threat to do substantial harm to oneself or another."[25]

Lessard was the forerunner of a generation of involuntary civil commitment cases,[26] all making some sort of finding that there must be a "real and present danger of doing significant harm" to show dangerousness sufficient to support such a commitment.[27] The cases were not unanimous—for example, as to the need for an actual overt act.[28] Yet they nevertheless reflected a clear "[break] with a century-old tradition that 'civil' commitment of the mentally ill, whether for their own good or that of society, demands fewer procedural protections than does incarceration for punishment."[29] More than 25 years after the case was decided, *Lessard* remains the "high-water mark in 'dangerousness' law."[30]

I believe that much of the *Lessard* court's opinion was based on a therapeutic jurisprudence perspective. In evaluating Wisconsin's commitment statutes, the court chose to look at the effects of civil commitment on those committed.[31] The court considered evidence that lengthy hospitalization, particularly involuntary hospitalization, may greatly increase the symptoms of mental illness and make adjustment to society more difficult.[32]

In addition, the court considered the substantial loss of substantive civil rights suffered by persons adjudicated mentally ill and unable to care for themselves or in need of

---

[23]*Id.*

[24]*Id.*

[25]*Id.* In addition, the court added that even an overt attempt to harm one's self substantially cannot be the proper foundation for a commitment unless the person in question is found to be (a) mentally ill, and (b) an immediate danger at the time of the hearing of doing further harm to him- or herself, *id.* at 1093 n.24, noting that the considerations that permit society to detain those likely to harm others because of mental illness "do not necessarily apply to potential harm to oneself," *id.*

[26]*See* Comment, *Progress in Involuntary Commitment,* 49 WASH. L. REV. 617, 618 (1974) (*Lessard* was "the most sweeping judicial change to date"), and *id.* at n.4 (*Lessard* opinion seems destined to be a classic"); John Myers, *Involuntary Civil Commitment of the Mentally Ill: A System in Need of a Change,* 29 VILL. L. REV. 367, 378–79 (1983–84) (*Lessard* was "landmark case" that articulated standards that have been "widely followed by courts and legislatures throughout the country"); Thomas Zander, *Civil Commitment in Wisconsin: The Impact of Lessard v. Schmidt,* 1976 WIS. L. REV. 503, 559 ("The *Lessard* decision will find its place in history not merely as the first comprehensive federal court decision on the constitutionality of civil commitment but also as one of the first major judicial recognitions of civil commitment as more than a court authorized medical decision").

[27]*See, e.g.,* Doremus v. Farrell, 407 F. Supp. 509, 514–15 (D. Neb. 1975) (commitment standards must be "(a) that the person is mentally ill and poses a serious threat of substantial harm to himself or to others; and (b) that this threat of harm has been evidenced by a recent overt act or threat").

[28]*See generally* PERLIN, LMD, *supra* note 7, § 1.05 at 36–38 (citing cases).

[29]Robitscher, *supra* note 15, at 69.

[30]Alexander Brooks, *Notes on Defining the "Dangerousness" of the Mentally Ill, in* C. J. Frederick, *supra* note 15, at 49. For an analysis of case law rejecting *Lessard*'s expansive construction of both substantive and procedural due process protections in the involuntary civil commitment context, see, for example, 1 PERLIN, CIVIL, *supra* note 7, § 2A-4.5 at 152–57 (2d ed. 1998) (discussing cases rejecting "overt act" requirement), §§ 2C-3.4 at 304–09, and 2C-4.1b at 312–15 (2d ed. 1998) (discussing cases rejecting *Lessard*'s mandate of an immediate preliminary hearing and its strict reading of time limitations between hospitalization and final commitment hearings).

[31]*Lessard,* 349 F. Supp. at 1084.

[32]*Id.* at 1087.

hospitalization.[33] On the other hand, the court gave little credence to the state's contention that notice and an evidentiary hearing within the first few days of confinement may be psychologically harmful to the patient.[34] In fact, the *Lessard* court contains at least one explanatory passage that seems to qualify as one of the true judicial forerunners of therapeutic jurisprudence:

> [The] conclusion [that due process is mandated at involuntary civil commitment hearings] is fortified by medical evidence that indicates that patients respond more favorably to treatment when they feel they are being treated fairly and are treated as intelligent, aware, human beings. In [plaintiff's] case, for example, Dr. Kennedy testified that her improvement had occurred "following a period of involvement with not only hospital individuals and hospital staff influence, but an involvement with other environmental influences that have included a number of judicial involvements, legal involvements."[35]

In using a therapeutic jurisprudence perspective, the court was able to fashion a workable standard that took into account the concerns of the state to protect society,[36] provide appropriate care and treatment to its mentally ill citizens,[37] and protect the dignity and civil rights of persons thought to be in need of involuntary civil commitment.

O'Connor v. Donaldson

When the Supreme Court next turned to mental disability law in 1975 in *O'Connor v. Donaldson*,[38] it considered the liberty interests of an involuntarily committed psychiatric patient. It reasoned, as had the *Lessard* court, that because involuntary commitment is a "massive curtailment of liberty,"[39] "a state cannot constitutionally confine, without more, a nondangerous individual who is capable of surviving safely in freedom by himself or with the help of willing and responsible family members or friends."[40] Although the case had begun as a right-to-treatment claim (and the jury had awarded the plaintiff damages for violation of that right),[41] that claim was abandoned at the Supreme Court level by Donaldson's counsel.[42] Chief Justice Burger concurred, writing that he could "discern no

---

[33]*Id.* at 1090–91.

[34]*Id.* at 1091: "Those who argue that notice and a hearing at this time may be harmful to the patient ignores the fact that there has been no finding that the person is in need of hospitalization."

[35]*Id.* at 1101–02.

[36]Through its acknowledgement of the state's police powers. *Id.* at 1084–85.

[37]Through its acknowledgement of the states *parens patriae* powers. *Id.*

[38]422 U.S. 563 (1975).

[39]*Humphrey v. Cady,* 405 U.S. 504 (1972).

[40]*O'Connor,* 422 U.S. at 575. Kenneth Donaldson was civilly committed to a psychiatric institution in Florida. He was kept in confinement against his will for almost 15 years. During that time, he made many requests for release and treatment within the facility. All his requests were denied. Donaldson filed a § 1983 federal civil rights action alleging violations in his constitutional right to liberty. At the trial level a verdict was returned assessing compensatory and punitive damages against the director of the hospital and a codefendant. The Court of Appeals for the Fifth Circuit affirmed the judgement, finding that there is no justification for involuntary commitment of a nondangerous person unless he or she is receiving such treatment as will give a realistic opportunity to be cured or to improve the mental condition. Donaldson v. O'Connor, 493 F.2d 507, 520 (5th Cir. 1974), *vacated on other grounds,* 422 U.S. 563 (1975).

[41]*Donaldson,* 493 F.2d at 530–31.

[42]As a tactical matter, the case was argued at the Supreme Court level as a narrow liberty interest issue, bypassing the broader question of a right to treatment. *See* George M. Grant, Donaldson, *Dangerousness, and the Right to Treatment,* 3 HASTINGS CONST. L.Q. 599, 608 n.41 (1976); *see generally* 1 PERLIN MDL, *supra* note 7, § 2A–4.4d at 145 n.601 (discussing this tactic).

basis for equating an involuntarily committed mental patient's unquestioned right *not* to be confined without due process of law with a constitutional right to treatment.''[43]

A therapeutic jurisprudence analysis underscores the difference between the majority and concurring opinions and highlights the discord between the two. The majority opinion positioned the court as legitimately involved in what was previously considered solely the domain of the state's mental health professionals. Wrote Justice Stewart, ''A finding of 'mental illness' alone cannot justify a State's locking a person up against his will and keeping him indefinitely in simple custodial confinement. . . . there is still no constitutional basis for confining such persons involuntarily if they are dangerous to no one and can live safely in freedom.''[44] It also flatly rejected the state's argument that the questions before the court were not justiciable: ''Where 'treatment' is the sole asserted ground for depriving a person of liberty, it is *plainly unacceptable* to suggest that the courts are powerless to determine whether the asserted ground is present.''[45]

The opinion went on to recognize the importance of the committed person's view of what may be most therapeutic, by acknowledging that the ''mere presence of mental illness does not disqualify a person from preferring his home to the comforts of an institution.''[46] The opinion then balanced the individual's rights with the public's interest in being free from living with mentally disabled persons in its midst: ''Mere public intolerance or animosity cannot constitutionally justify the deprivation of a person's physical liberty.''[47]

Justice Burger's concurrence, on the other hand, is, at its core, antitherapeutic. First, he appears to retreat from the majority's acceptance of the court's role in deciding issues involving psychiatric testimony: ''It is not for us to say in the baffling field of psychiatry that 'milieu' therapy is always a pretense.''[48] This observation rings hollow in light of the record that showed that ''milieu therapy'' in this case was nothing more than ''a euphemism for confinement in the 'milieu' of the mental hospital.''[49] Further, Justice Burger insisted that there was no evidence that Donaldson had been mistreated while hospitalized;[50] yet a defendant's testimony revealed that, although the hospital had neither sufficient staff, an individualized treatment program, nor treatment goals for the patient, he would have retained Donaldson in the hospital for the remainder of his life.[51]

Subsequently, Justice Burger's statement—on an issue no longer before the court— that he could discern ''no basis to support a patient's right to treatment[52]—presaged the Chief Justice's later position in *Youngberg v. Romeo* that he would hold ''flatly'' that there is no such constitutional right.[53] Justice Burger's legalistic objections to the right to treatment sowed the seeds of an antitherapeutic jurisprudence.

---

[43]*O'Connor*, 422 U.S. at 587–88.

[44]*Id.* at 575.

[45]*Id.* at 574 n.10 (emphasis added).

[46]*Id.* at 575.

[47]*Id.*

[48]*Id.* at 579 n.2. *See* 1 PERLIN, MDL, *supra* note 7, § 2A-4.4d, at 144 n. 596 (2d. ed. 1999).

[49]*O'Connor*, 422 U.S. at 569.

[50]*Id.* at 588 n.9.

[51]BRUCE J. ENNIS, PRISONERS OF PSYCHIATRY: MENTAL PATIENTS, PSYCHIATRISTS AND THE LAW 96 (1972) (Ennis was Donaldson's appellate counsel) (quoting from depositions). *See* 1 PERLIN, MDL, *supra* note 7, § 2A-4.4d, at 144 n. 596 (2d. ed. 1998).

[52]*See supra* text accompanying note 10.

[53]457 U.S. 307, 329 (1982) (Burger, C.J., concurring).

Youngberg v. Romeo

Youngberg[54] is profoundly antitherapeutic for the same reasons that I earlier argued that it was sanist and pretextual.[55] Its adoption of a substantial-professional-judgment standard sharply limits the need to inquire into the adequacy of a patient's treatment.[56] The presumption of validity given to institutional decision making in effect signals lower courts to close their eyes to the landscape on which *Wyatt v. Stickney*[57] was litigated as well as to the history of American public psychiatric institutions. Further, it serves to chill civil rights lawyers seeking to vindicate claims of institutionalized patients in a wide variety of subject matter areas.[58]

In addition, its abandonment of the least-restrictive-alternative construction (and its embrace of the reasonably nonrestrictive-confinement-conditions standard) is, at best, curious. This latter phrase appeared nowhere in the case law, nor was it ever discussed at oral argument. Although it might appear that the phrase is a shaggy dog—in the 17 years since *Youngberg* was decided, this phraseology has been used rarely by other courts, and its contours have never truly fleshed out[59]—its use as a replacement for the other standard again sends a crystal-clear message that the therapeutic values that underlay the application of the least-restrictive-alternative test to mental disability law cases have been abandoned.

Finally, the court's empirical rationale for limiting the right to habilitation is bizarre. In supporting this conclusion, it stated that professionals in the field of mental retardation "disagree strongly on the question whether effective training of all severely or profoundly retarded individuals is even possible," citing to four articles from the journal *Analysis and Intervention in Disabilities*.[60] However, a reading of the very articles cited by the court—articles never cited previously or subsequently by any other court in any reported opinion—shows that they considered only the "small fraction" of persons with mental retardation who were "permanently ambulatory" and "extremely debilitated," a grouping that represents but a tiny percentage of all institutionalized persons. The court's selection of social science data appears pretextual as well.[61]

---

[54]*See supra* Chapter 5.

[55]*See id.* text accompanying note 94.

[56]*See* Susan Stefan, *Leaving Civil Rights to the 'Experts': From Deference to Abdication Under the Professional Judgment Standard,* 102 YALE L.J. 639 (1992).

[57]325 F. Supp. 1341 (M.D. Ala 1971); *see supra* Chapter 5.

[58]*See, e.g.,* Michael L. Perlin, *Are Courts Competent to Decide Competency Questions? Stripping the Facade From* United States v. Charters, 38 U. KAN. L. REV. 957 (1990).

[59]*But see* Hicks v. Feeney, 596 F. Supp. 1504, 1513 (D. Del. 1984); Petition of Thompson, 476 N.E.2d 216, 219 (Mass. 1985). In *In re* R. A., 501 A.2d 743, 744 (Vt. 1985), the Vermont Supreme Court underscored that the state's statutory scheme, *see* VT. STAT. ANN. tit. 18, § 7617(e) (mandating treatment "adequate and appropriate to [the patient's] condition"), might require "something more" than the " 'reasonably nonrestrictive confinement conditions' which the Fourteenth Amendment requires." The Supreme Court's recent decision in Olmstead v. L.C., 119 S. Ct. 2176 (1999), reading the Americans with Disabilities Act to mandate a qualified right to community services, promises to reinvigorate this debate; *see supra* Chapter 8.

[60]*Youngberg,* 457 U.S. at 316–17 n.20.

[61]*See* David Ferleger, *Anti-Institutionalization and the Supreme Court,* 14 RUTGERS L.J. 595, 628–29 (1983), *discussed in* 2 PERLIN, MDL, *supra* note 7, § 3A-9.2 at 92–93 n. 726. On the reading of social science data in mental disability law, in general, *see e.g.,* Michael L. Perlin & Deborah A. Dorfman, *Sanism, Social Science, and the Development of Mental Disability Law Jurisprudence,* 11 BEHAV. SCI. & L. 47 (1993); Michael L. Perlin, *Pretexts and Mental Disability Law: The Case of Competency,* 47 U. MIAMI L. REV. 625 (1993) [hereinafter Perlin, *Pretexts*]; Michael L. Perlin, *Morality and Pretextuality, Psychiatry and Law: Of "Ordinary Common Sense," Heuristic Reasoning, and Cognitive Dissonance,* 19 BULL. AM. ACAD. PSYCHIATRY & LAW 131, 137 (1991) [hereinafter Perlin, *Morality.*]

Right to Refuse Treatment

The right to refuse treatment has a strong therapeutic jurisprudence component. Although public attention has been focused primarily on what is often seen as the antitherapeutic aspects of this right,[62] I believe that there are significant benefits as well: due process rights for the mentally disabled, better checks on doctors and clinical staff to ensure that medication and other treatment is not being administered as a means of punishment or convenience, and improved protection from administration of inappropriate medications or medications causing severe side effects, among others.

In this section, I will examine both the therapeutic and antitherapeutic jurisprudence values of right-to-refuse-treatment doctrine. I will first examine empirical research done on the effects of right to refuse treatment on mental health consumers and the enforcement of this right, and then I will look at real-world implementation of right-to-refuse-treatment laws.

Empirical Research

Much of the empirical research in the area of the right to refuse treatment for mentally disabled persons has focused on such areas as numbers, characteristics, and treatment outcomes of medication refusers and comparisons of clinical and judicial review regarding petitions for involuntary medication.[63] The results of these studies shed a great deal of light on the therapeutic jurisprudence value of the right to refuse mental health treatment and the current implementation of this law. In this section, I will examine the empirical research on the right to refuse treatment and how well this right is being enforced.

The Therapeutic Jurisprudence Effect of the Right to Refuse Treatment

Empirical research shows that the right to refuse medication[64] often has therapeutic value.[65] One therapeutic benefit of the right to refuse medication is that it expands the due process rights of mentally disabled individuals by providing them a judicial or administrative hearing on the issue of their capacity to refuse treatment.

This expansion of rights is therapeutic on several levels. Studies comparing clinical and judicial review of involuntary mental health treatment show that there are therapeutic jurisprudence benefits of judicial review in that it affords mentally disabled persons the

---

[62]*See, e.g.,* Stephen Rachlin, *One Right Too Many,* 3 BULL. AM. ACAD. PSYCHIATRY & L. 99 (1975); Darryl Treffert, *Dying With Their Rights On,* 130 AM. J. PSYCHIATRY 1041 (1973); Thomas Gutheil, *The Boston State Hospital Case: "Involuntary Mind Control," the Constitution, and the "Right to Rot,"* 137 AM. J. PSYCHIATRY 720 (1980).

[63]A seriously underdiscussed issue is that of the economic status of state hospital patients, especially chronic patients. On the impoverished economic status of such persons in general, see Hendrik Wagenaar & Dan Lewis, *Ironies of Inclusion: Social Class and Deinstitutionalization,* 14 J. HEALTH POL., POL'Y & L. 503 (1989).

[64]For an excellent and comprehensive overview of these issues, see Bruce Winick, *The Right to Refuse Treatment: A Therapeutic Jurisprudence Analysis,* 17 INT'L J.L. & PSYCHIATRY 99 (1994).

[65]*See generally id.* at 100–11 (on the relationship between therapeutic jurisprudence and the psychology of choice in the right to refuse treatment context); *id.* at 111–16 (effective implementation of the right to refuse treatment enhances the therapeutic relationship, making it into "a tool that is both more humane and more effective"; implementation of the right to refuse treatment best ensures that therapeutic relationship will be "characterized by voluntariness rather than coercion").

opportunity to present their cases in a more formal legal setting.[66] A study by John Ensminger and Thomas Liguori, for example, found that more formal court proceedings may have therapeutic value. Ensminger and Liguori explained the therapeutic value of formal hearings in the civil commitment process, arguing that such hearings are therapeutic because they force individuals to ''face reality'' and also give them an opportunity to present and hear evidence in a meaningful court procedure.[67] These same benefits can be attributed to medication hearings, particularly as—in some jurisdictions—these hearings are often more formal than commitment hearings.[68]

Another benefit of due process is that it provides the *appearance* of fairness. The perception of receiving a fair hearing is therapeutic because it contributes to the individual's sense of dignity and makes him or her feel as though he or she is being taken seriously.[69] Other studies show that medication judicial–administrative proceedings can be therapeutic because they allow patients the opportunity to better discuss the medications and their benefits and risks with their doctors.[70] By holding a medication hearing, the doctor must again discuss the medications, their purpose, and potential side effects.[71] At the same time, patients have the opportunity to explain the reasons why they do not want the medication and ask questions about the drugs.[72] This may be therapeutic because the patient's medication concerns can be better considered in making medication determinations, thus enhancing the efficacy of medication decisions.[73] This benefit is particularly important at large public hospitals where doctors, because of large case loads, often have less time to spend with their patients on a day-to-day basis. Also, when doctors know that patients do not have to agree with their prescribed regimen, it can be expected (or at least hoped) that doctors will better explain to patients why they believe a certain medication is appropriate, thus further enhancing the therapeutic relationship.[74]

---

[66]*See* Francine Cournos et al., *Outcome of Involuntary Medication in a State Hospital System,* 148 AM. J. PSYCHIATRY 489 (1991); at 854; *see also* Paul Sauvayre, *The Relationship Between the Court and the Doctor on the Issue of an Inpatient's Refusal of Psychotropic Medication,* 36 J. FORENS. SCI. 219, 221 (1991), citing Irwin Hasenfeld & Barbara Grumet, *A Study of the Right to Refuse Treatment,* 12 BULL. AM. ACAD. PSYCHIATRY & L. 65 (1984) (patients who initially refuse treatment and complete a judicial hearing about their capacity to refuse treatment did better after discharge than those who complied with treatment.)

[67]John J. Ensminger & Thomas Liguori, *The Therapeutic Significance of the Civil Commitment Hearing,* 6 J. PSYCHIATRY & L. (1978), *reprinted in* THERAPEUTIC JURISPRUDENCE: THE LAW AS A THERAPEUTIC AGENT, 243 (David Wexler, ed. 1990). (TJ)

[68]In California, for example, the burden of proof to show a doctor that a mental health patient lacks capacity to refuse medication is higher than to civilly commit that same patient. In an administrative capacity hearing, the burden of proof is clear and convincing evidence; in an administrative civil commitment hearing for a ''14-day hold,'' the burden of proof is only probable cause. CALIFORNIA WELFARE & INSTITUTIONS CODE § 5256.6. *Cf.* Heller v. Doe, 509 U.S. 312 (1993) (two-tier commitment system allowing for commitment of mentally retarded persons on a lesser standard of proof (clear and convincing evidence) than for mentally ill persons (beyond a reasonable doubt) is not violative of the equal protection clause).

[69]*See* Note, *The Role of Counsel in the Civil Commitment Process; A Theoretical Framework, in* TJ *supra* note 67, at 309, 323 n.83; *see also* Tom Tyler, *The Psychological Consequences of Judicial Procedures: Implications for Civil Commitment Hearings,* 46 SMU L. REV. 433, 444 (1992) (discussing therapeutic value of judicial civil commitment hearings and stressing that individuals benefit from hearings in which they can take part, are treated with dignity, and are ''fair'').

[70]Cournos et al., *supra* note 66, at 854; *see also* Julie Zito et al., *Drug Treatment Refusal, Diagnosis, and Length of Hospitalization in Involuntary Psychiatric Patents,* 4 BEHAV. SCI. & L. 327, 336 (1986).

[71]Cournos et al., *supra* note 66, at 854.

[72]*Id.*

[73]Zito et al., *supra* note 70, at 336.

[74]*See* Winick, *supra* note 64.

The research also shows that the right to refuse treatment and the legal procedures surrounding these rights also help to prevent the inappropriate use of psychiatric medication, such as using it as a means of punishment or convenience.[75] Misuses of psychotropic medication has been recognized as a significant concern justifying the need for checks on doctors and staff by both courts and social scientists.[76]

Similarly, medication hearings serve as a check to ensure that doctors are not prescribing the wrong medications, the wrong dosages, or ignoring patients' concerns regarding side effects.[77] A 1986 study comparing medical and judicial perceptions of the problem of side effects of psychiatric medication indicated that although both groups valued such treatment, judges were concerned more about the risk of side effects than were the doctors.[78] This check is important because psychiatric medication can be antitherapeutic—even where administered in good faith—if there is a misdiagnosis, a failure to monitor the patient after the drugs are given, or the beneficial effects of the medications are outweighed by the side effects.[79]

Despite the therapeutic components of the right to refuse treatment, there are arguments that this right has antitherapeutic aspects. For example, some argue that allowing mental health patients the right to refuse treatment will cause them to remain involuntarily committed for a longer period of time. Some researchers argue that treatment refusers stay hospitalized up to twice as long as those who consent to treatment.[80] However, other studies have shown that it is not necessarily the case that refusers are hospitalized longer than those who consent.[81]

A 1986 study by Julie Zito and her colleagues found no significant difference between refusers and consenters as to length of hospital stay.[82] Rather, the study found that the

---

[75]Davis v. Hubbard, 506 F. Supp. 915, 926–27 (N.D.Ohio 1980); *see also* Mary C. McCarron, *The Right to Refuse Antipsychotic Drugs: Safeguarding the Mentally Incompetent Patient's Right to Procedural Due Process,* 73 MARQUETTE L. REV. 477, 484 (1990).

[76]*See, e.g.,* Washington v. Harper, 494 U.S. 210, 242–43 (1990) (Stevens, J., dissenting); Riggins v. Nevada, 504 U.S. 127, 138 (1992) (Kennedy, J., concurring); Heller v. Doe, 509 U.S. 312, 335 (1993) (Souter, J., dissenting). In *Harper,* Justice Stevens expressed his concerns that the failure to require that medication decisions be made by an independent party could lead to the improper use of medication for control purposes rather than for treatment. *Id.* at 245–46; *see also, e.g.,* Rennie v. Klein, 476 F. Supp. 1294, 1299 (D.N.J. 1979) (evidence at trial indicated that psychiatric medications were being used routinely as a means of patient control and as a substitute for treatment).

[77]*Rennie,* 476 F. Supp. at 1305–06.

[78]Harold Bursztajn et al., *Medical and Judicial Perceptions of the Risks Associated With the Use of Antipsychotic Medication,* 19 BULL. AM. ACAD. PSYCHIATRY & L. 271, 273–74 (1991).

[79]Deborah Dorfman, *Through a Therapeutic Jurisprudential Filter: Fear and Pretextuality in Mental Disability Law,* 10 N.Y.L. SCH. J. HUM. RTS. 805, 816–19 (1993), citing McCarron, *supra* note 75, at 481–82; Delila M. J. Ledwith, Jones v. Gerhardstein: *The Involuntarily Committed Mental Patient's Right to Refuse Treatment With Antipsychotic Drugs,* 1990 WIS. L. REV. 1367, 1373 (1990).

The Supreme Court has held—on more than one occasion—that the possibility of side effects (especially irreversible neurological side effects such as tardive dyskinesia) is a factor to be considered in determining whether the Fourteenth Amendment has been violated in an individual case. *See e.g.,* Riggins v. Nevada, 504 U.S. 127, 133–35 (1992); Washington v. Harper, 494 U.S. 210, 229–30 (1990).

[80]*See* Steven K. Hoge et al., *A Prospective, Multicenter Study of Patient's Refusal of Antipsychotic Medication,* 47 ARCHIVES GEN. PSYCHIATRY 949 (1990); Shelly Levin et al., *A Controlled Comparison of Involuntarily Hospitalized Medication Refusers and Acceptors,* 19 BULL. AM. ACAD. PSYCHIATRY & L. 161, 169 (1991).

[81]On the competency of patients with schizophrenia to engage in such decision making, see, for example, Barry Rosenfeld et al., *Decision Making in a Schizophrenic Population,* 16 LAW & HUM. BEHAV. 651, 660 (1992) (after differences in verbal functioning controlled for, no differences remained between abilities of schizophrenics and nonpatients to consistently weigh risks, benefits, and probabilities).

[82]Zito et al., *supra* note 70, at 328.

difference in length of stay related to the diagnosis of the patient. Specifically, they found that individuals with schizophrenia tended to consent more often than those suffering from bipolar and schizoaffective disorder. Yet because of their diagnosis, schizophrenics were hospitalized for longer periods of time, notwithstanding the fact that they tended to consent to medications.[83]

Another concern regarding the therapeutic value of the right to refuse treatment for mental health patients is that patients will become less compliant with medications overall.[84] Researchers such as Zito and her colleagues, however, found, in a study comparing patients refusing drugs, mental health diagnosis, and length of hospital stay, that the rate of medication noncompliance was no different before due process requirements were established than afterward.[85]

Antitherapeutic Results of the Current Means of Implementing the Right to Refuse Treatment

Although empirical evidence indicates that the right to refuse treatment does have therapeutic jurisprudence value, research shows that the manner in which this right is enforced is not always as therapeutic. For example, research indicates that although the purpose of judicial review for patients wishing to refuse psychiatric treatment is meant to ensure that mental health patients are afforded due process protections, this is not always the case. Judges regularly defer to experts,[86] almost always approving involuntary medication applications.[87] Although such deference may be appropriate in instances in which the physician has met the burden of proving that the patient lacks capacity to refuse antipsychotic medication deference, automatic deference without a careful assessment of the evidence presented can render the right to refuse treatment meaningless and antitherapeutic.

Another problem is the general lack of interest of judges, lawyers, and society in mental disability law, a lack of interest often exacerbated in cases seeking to vindicate the civil rights of institutionalized mentally disabled persons.[88] Such disinterest conveys the message that patients' rights, including the right to refuse treatment, is not important.

The prevalence of ineffective assistance of counsel in mental disability cases, including medication hearings, further hampers the adequate implementation of the right to refuse

---

[83]*Id.*

[84]*Id.* at 334.

[85]*Id.*

[86]Cournos et al., *supra* note 66; *see also* Michael G. Farnsworth, *The Impact of Judicial Review of Patients' Refusal to Accept Antipsychotic Medications at the Minnesota Security Hospital,* 19 BULL. AM. ACAD. PSYCHIATRY & L. 33, 40 (1991); Perlin, Morality *supra* note 61; *see also* Stefan, *supra* note 56 (discussing the inappropriate reliance on the professional judgment standard by courts in "negative rights" claims such as the right to refuse treatment and the problems of excessive deference to experts).

[87]Sauvayre, *supra* note 66, at 221 (citing studies indicating that most medication hearings are decided in favor of the physician). These studies include one by Cournos et al., *supra* note 66 (petition for involuntary medication granted in 95% contested cases) and another by Jorge Veliz and William James, *Medicine Court:* Rogers *In Practice,* 14 AM. J. PSYCHIATRY 62 (1987) (in 100% of the cases of involuntary medication studied, the court ruled in favor of medicating the patient).

[88]Michael L. Perlin & Deborah A. Dorfman, *Is It More Than "Dodging Lions and Wastin' Time"? Adequacy of Counsel, Questions of Competence, and the Judicial Process in Individual Right to Refuse Treatment Cases,* 2 PSYCHOL., PUB. POL'Y & L. 114, 133–34 (1996); *see generally* Joel Haycock et al., *Mediating the Gap: Thinking About Alternatives to the Current Practice of Civil Commitment,* 20 N. ENG. J. ON CIV. & CRIM. CONFINEMENT 265, 272 (1994), quoting Perlin & Dorfman, *supra* note 61: "Mental disability law generally regulates powerless individuals represented by passive counsel in invisible court proceedings conducted by bored or irritated judges."

treatment.[89] For those with mental disabilities, there is a dearth of competent counsel.[90] This problem results from a variety of factors including mere ignorance of the law,[91] attorneys' fear of their own clients,[92] and a feeling of responsibility or blameworthiness for the acts of their clients.[93] As a result of these issues, advocates and attorneys run the risk of compromising their client's civil rights by not zealously representing their client's expressed interest but rather by representing what they feel is in the client's or society's best interest. In the context of the right to refuse treatment, this lack of zealous advocacy can lead to unnecessary forced medication as well as an increased perception (and potential reality) by doctors, courts, and patients that the right to refuse treatment is illusory.

With the difficulties in implementing the right to refuse treatment, many patients have grown to doubt the value of their own civil rights. Many patients view the right to refuse and the hearings as a sham.[94] They are leery of the entire process and thus often deterred from exercising their rights. When patients feel that it is useless or meaningless to bother trying to exercise their right to refuse treatment, not only do they get unwanted treatment but they also do not get the therapeutic benefits of having the right to refuse.

Finally, a significant problem with implementing judicial review is that of frequent delays.[95] Such delay causes unnecessarily long involuntary commitment, which compromises the liberty interests of patients to be free from involuntary confinement.

Much of the research done on implementing due process procedures for mental health patients wishing to refuse medications indicates that there is no significant difference in results between pre- and post–right-to-refuse laws.[96] This evidence and the other implementation problems suggested by research results indicates a need to review the means of enforcing the right to refuse treatment.

From a Broader Perspective

All aspects of right-to-refuse-treatment law raise therapeutic jurisprudence concerns. If sanist trial judges assume that patients are incompetent (and thus discredit their testimony), the entire enterprise may be doomed to failure. And all hearings will become little more than empty shells. The MacArthur Network has made a series of important and thoughtful recommendations about the ability of patients to engage in autonomous medication-choice

---

[89]See Michael L. Perlin, *Fatal Assumption: A Critical Evaluation of the Role of Counsel in Mental Disability Cases,* 16 LAW & HUM. BEHAV. 39 (1992) (on inadequate role of counsel in involuntary civil commitment cases).

[90]*Id.* at 42.

[91]Dorfman, *supra* note 79, at 815, citing Matter of Brazleton, 237 Ill. App. 3d 269, 604 N.E.2d 376, 376–77 (1992) In *Brazleton* counsel—who had been appointed to appeal an involuntary commitment order—sought leave to withdraw, based on the conclusion that counsel made that the appeal lacked merit and would be frivolous. The appellate court denied the motion as the attorney failed to present any issues that could be raised to support his client or any potential arguments that could be made. Also, the appointed counsel incorrectly believed that the burden on the state was preponderance of the evidence; in 1979, some 13 years before, the U.S. Supreme Court had ruled in Addington v. Texas, 441 U.S. 418 (1979), that the burden was at least clear and convincing evidence.

[92]Perlin, *supra* note 89, at 42.

[93]Eric Turkheimer & Charles D. H. Parry, *Why the Gap? Practice and Policy in Civil Commitment Hearings,* 47 AM. PSYCHOLOGIST 646, 650 (1992).

[94]Lisa A. Callahan, *Challenging Mental Health Law: Butting Heads With A Billygoat,* 4 BEHAV. SCI. & L. 305, 313 (1986) (patient interviews regarding the value of due process procedures used to determine whether a patient could be involuntarily medicated indicated that many were dissatisfied with the process and found it to be a sham).

[95]Farnsworth, *supra* note 86, at 40.

[96]See Paul S. Appelbaum and Steven K. Hoge, *The Right to Refuse Treatment: What the Research Reveals,* 4 BEHAV. SCI. & L. 279 (1986).

decision making,[97] but if trial judges simply ignore patients' testimony, then the recommendations will be hollow. If sanist counsel similarly disparage their clients' stories—or just as inappropriately, present them to the court with an overt or covert "wink" that asks the judge to share in a complicitous sham (suggesting that the lawyer is simply participating in what he or she sees as a charade)[98]—then again the potential impact of the study's findings is seriously compromised.[99]

If appellate courts enter broad orders in right-to-refuse cases without thinking about the operationalization of these orders in subsequent individual cases (or if only perfunctory assignment of disinterested counsel is made to represent patients in subsequent right to refuse hearings),[100] the initial order becomes little more than a pretext. And if other appellate courts close their eyes to the level of inadequacy of counsel, this "willful blindness" simply adds one extra layer of pretextuality to the process.

Finally, other underlying social issues need to be addressed. The common wisdom is clear. Drugs serve two major purposes of social control: They "cure" dangerousness and they are the only assurance that deinstitutionalized patients can remain free in community settings.[101] Both of these assumptions are reflected in the case law that has developed in individual involuntary civil commitment cases (in which a judge's perception of the likelihood that an individual will self-medicate becomes the critical variable in case dispositions);[102] they are also reflected in the public discourse that is heard in classrooms, the media, hospital corridors, and courtrooms.

Neither of these assumptions has any base in science or in law. Yet without counsel to serve as a brake—to ask questions, to challenge assumptions, to identify *faux* ordinary common sense, to point out the dangerous pitfalls of heuristic thinking—these assumptions will continue to dominate and control the disposition of individual right to refuse treatment cases, notwithstanding the study's recommendations.

Again, counsel's significance increases even more drastically in the context of the improper presumption of incompetency discussed earlier. Professor Bruce Winick suggests: "Unless a *parens patriae* commitment statute requires an individualized determination of incompetence to engage in hospital admission decisionmaking, it would seem deficient as a matter of substantive due process."[103] Without vigorous, independent counsel, it is doubtful that such challenges would ever be launched. This is especially problematic in light of the fact that the equation of incompetency to mental illness *does* appear consonant with

---

[97]*See* Elyn Saks & Stephen Behnke, *Competency to Decide on Treatment and Research: MacArthur and Beyond,* 10 J. CONTEMP. LEG. ISSUES 103 (1999).

[98]On the problems raised when a lawyer feels "foolish" or "awkward" in the representation of an individual at an involuntary civil commitment hearing, see Michael L. Perlin & Robert L. Sadoff, *Ethical Issues in the Representation of Individuals in the Commitment Process,* 45 LAW & CONTEMP. PROBS. 161, 167 (Summer 1982).

[99]*See id.* at 166 (on how a lawyer's perceptions that his or her client is not credible can have a "devastating" impact on the presentation of the client's case). For a thoughtful and comprehensive therapeutic jurisprudence analysis of the role of lawyers in the representation of mentally disabled individuals, see Jan Costello, *"Why Would I Need a Lawyer?": Legal Counsel and Advocacy for Persons With Mental Disabilities, in* LAW, MENTAL HEALTH, AND MENTAL DISORDER 15 (Bruce Sales & Daniel Shuman eds. 1996).

[100]On a startling variation between jurisdictions, see 1 PERLIN, MDL, *supra* note 7, § 2B-9, at 245–46 (contrasting experiences in Minnesota and Virginia).

[101]*See, e.g.,* Michael L. Perlin, *Competency, Deinstitutionalization, and Homelessness: A Story of Marginalization,* 28 HOUS. L. REV. 63 (1991); Frances Cournos, *Involuntary Medication and the Case of Joyce Brown,* 40 HOSP. & COMMUNITY PSYCHIATRY 736 (1989). On the relationship between deinstitutionalization and forced drugging, *see supra* Chapter 4.

[102]*See supra* note 101; *see also* 1 PERLIN, MDL, *supra* note 7, § 2C-5.2, at 409–16 (citing cases).

[103]Bruce Winick, *The MacArthur Treatment Competence Study: Legal and Therapeutic Implications,* 2 PSYCHOL., PUB. POL'Y & L. 137, 145 (1996).

"ordinary common sense".[104] Counsel's role is especially important in areas of the law in which ordinary common sense is so dissonant with empirical fact.[105]

Conclusion

The empirical research done regarding the right to refuse treatment for mental health patients coupled with a survey of the practical implementation of this right indicates that patients' rights advocates and attorneys, in enforcing the right to refuse treatment, could benefit from using therapeutic jurisprudence. Therapeutic jurisprudence provides a tool to allow counsel representing mentally disabled persons to identify antitherapeutic problems and to attempt to resolve these issues to enhance patients' civil rights in a therapeutic manner. Finally, therapeutic jurisprudence is a potential means for attorneys and advocates representing medication refusers to attempt to see how they can improve the quality of their advocacy to ensure that the expressed interest of their clients is represented.

The Americans With Disabilities Act[106]

Consider the Americans With Disabilities Act (ADA). If the ADA is taken at face value, it would appear to be both a potentially powerful weapon for litigators seeking to advance the cause of individuals with mental disabilities in community settings. It would also appear to be a significantly therapeutic law. On the other hand, any predictions about its ultimate impact may be nothing more than speculation. The history of all civil rights law enforcement is a rocky one; the passage of civil rights laws meant to empower Blacks and women has not eradicated discrimination against such persons[107] and it would be folly to expect a significantly different outcome with regard to persons with disabilities. On the other hand, Stephan Haimowitz has stressed the incalculable symbolic significance of the ADA in this context: "While the [ADA] is no more likely to completely eliminate the myths, fears, and discrimination faced by person with disabilities than earlier civil rights law eliminated discrimination based on race, the new legislation will nonetheless contribute to the enormous educational effort needed to combat widespread misinformation and stereotypes about disabilities."[108]

Authors have begun to look at ADA sections through the TJ lens (e.g., the reasonable accommodations provision of Title III;[109] the confidentiality provision)[110] and have begun to

---

[104]*See* Winick, *supra* note 103 at 145 ("While the assumption that all mentally ill people are incompetent may not be irrational, the MacArthur study strongly suggests its incorrectness").

[105]*See, e.g.,* Michael L. Perlin, *Psychodynamics and the Insanity Defense: "Ordinary Common Sense" and Heuristic Reasoning,* 69 NEB. L. REV. 3 (1990).

[106]*See supra* Chapter 8.

[107]*See, e.g.,* Michael A. Rebell, *Structural Discrimination and the Rights of the Disabled,* 74 GEO. L.J. 1435 (1986).

[108]Stephan Haimowitz, *Americans With Disabilities Act of 1990: Its Significance for Persons With Mental Illness,* 42 HOSP. & COMMUNITY PSYCHIATRY 23 (1991).

[109]David Wexler, *Therapeutic Jurisprudence and the Criminal Courts,* 35 WM. & MARY L. REV. 279, 299 n.9 (1993); Wexler, *supra* note 6, at 772.

[110]Rose A. Daly-Rooney, *Designing Reasonable Accommodations Through Co-Worker Participation: Therapeutic Jurisprudence and the Confidentiality Provision of the Americans With Disabilities Act,* 8 J.L. & HEALTH 89, 96–104 (1993–94) (discussing ADA's prohibition of preemployment medical inquiries about whether applicant is disabled, see 42 U.S.C. § 12112(d)(2)(A), § 12112(d)(4)(A) (1998). *See* David Wexler, *Reflections on the Scope of Therapeutic Jurisprudence,* 1 PSYCHOL., PUB. POL'Y & L. 220, 236 (1995) (characterizing Daly-Rooney's approach as "powerful").

consider how the ADA might apply to a range of cutting-edge legal issues (e.g., the military's "don't ask; don't tell" policy on disclosure of sexual orientation;[111] courtroom accessibility for persons with disabilities,[112] and conditions of confinement involving persons in jails and prisons).[113]

And Deborah Dorfman—a public interest lawyer who represents persons with disabilities—has written thoughtfully about how implementation of Title I of the ADA would be therapeutic for persons with disabilities:[114]

> For those with mental disabilities, the stakes are high when it comes to effective implementation of Title I of the ADA. If Title I is carried out as it was intended, the mentally disabled have a great deal to gain beyond just employment. They have the opportunity to become substantially more integrated and accepted into society, the ability to support themselves financially, and thus become better equipped to live independently and enhance the quality of their lives.

> If, however, Title I is not adequately enforced, mentally disabled individuals risk losing one of the most significant opportunities to overcome traditional barriers to employment and social integration. With so much riding on Title I for persons with mental disabilities, it is imperative that lawyers, advocates, disabled persons, and employers examine the different implementation and enforcement mechanisms of litigation and ADR. In doing so, it is useful to assess the options through a therapeutic jurisprudence filter to determine which means is the most beneficial in carrying out the provisions of Title I.[115]

I agree with Dorfman that the ADA is a therapeutic law. It gives persons with disabilities autonomy, allows them to engage in individual decision making in areas of life that we all hold dear, forces others to get beyond the label of "psychiatric patient," and—optimally—serves as the best tool in the arsenal to combat the sanism and pretextuality that dominate mental disability law jurisprudence.[116]

The Supreme Court's recent decision in *Olmstead v. L.C.*[117]—finding a qualified right to community services for some individuals institutionalized in psychiatric hospitals[118]—forces us to totally rethink the relationship between TJ and the ADA. The Court's language raises as many questions as it answers:

---

[111]Kay Kavanagh, *Don't Ask, Don't Tell: Deception Required, Disclosure Denied,* 1 PSYCHOL., PUB. POL'Y & L. 142, 160 n.64 (1995) (drawing on insights in Daly-Rooney, *supra* note 110). *See* David Wexler, *Applying the Law Therapeutically, in* LAW IN A THERAPEUTIC KEY: RECENT DEVELOPMENTS IN THERAPEUTIC JURISPRUDENCE 831, 832 (David Wexler & Bruce Winick eds. 1996) at 831, 832 (discussing relationship between Kavanagh's arguments and the ADA's confidentiality requirements).

[112]Keri Gould, *And Equal Protection for All . . . Americans With Disabilities Act in the Courtroom,* 8 J.L. & HEALTH 123 (1993–94).

[113]T. Howard Stone, *Therapeutic Implications of Incarceration for Persons With Severe Mental Disorders: Searching for Rational Health Care Policy,* 24 AM. J. CRIM. L. 283 (1997). The Supreme Court has held that the ADA applies to state prisons. *See* Pennsylvania Dept of Corrections v. Yeskey, 118 S. Ct. 1952 (1998), discussed in PERLIN, MDL, *supra* note 7, § 6.44A, at 190–91 (1998 Cum. Supp.).

[114]Deborah Dorfman, *Effectively Implementing Title I of the Americans With Disabilities Act for Mentally Disabled Persons: A Therapeutic Jurisprudence Analysis,* 8 J.L. & HEALTH 105 (1993) (when Dorfman wrote this article, she was co-coordinator of the Protection and Advocacy for Individuals with Mental Illness (PAIMI) Program at the Legal Center for People With Disabilities in Salt Lake City, Utah; she is currently a staff attorney at the Washington Protection and Advocacy Service in Seattle, Washington).

[115]*Id.* at 120–21.

[116]*See, e.g.,* Michael L. Perlin, *Therapeutic Jurisprudence: Understanding the Sanist and Pretextual Bases of Mental Disability Law,* 20 N. ENG. J. CRIM. & CIV. CONFINEMENT 369 (1994).

[117]119 S. Ct. 2176 (1999); *see supra* Chapter 8.

[118]*Id.* at 2185.

Unjustified isolation, we hold, is properly regarded as discrimination based on disability. But we recognize, as well, the States' need to maintain a range of facilities for the care and treatment of persons with diverse mental disabilities, and the States' obligation to administer services with an even hand. [On remand], the District Court must consider, in view of the resources available to the State, not only the cost of providing community-based care to the litigants, but also the range of services the State provides others with mental disabilities, and the State's obligation to mete out those services equitably.[119]

When might institutional isolation be ''justified''? How much of a ''range of facilities'' must a state maintain? How is the ''range of services'' to be provided to others with mental disabilities to be assessed, and what is the relationship among the existence and the quality of these services and the continued institutionalization of persons with mental disabilities? How carefully will courts examine the availability of resources and the administrative decision making that leads to the allocation of resources as between facilities or as between facilities and community programs?

This is an area that demands close and serious attention from a therapeutic jurisprudence perspective. Notwithstanding the ambiguities of the opinion, *Olmstead* clearly opens a door for a careful TJ examination of this entire area of the law.

Federal Sentencing Guidelines Cases

What is the ''fit'' between the federal sentencing guidelines[120] and therapeutic jurisprudence? The rationale of the downward departure aspect of the guidelines is clear: To some extent, some level of mental disability can serve as a mitigator of sentence in some cases. But on what theoretical basis is this rationale premised? That a mentally disabled person is less worthy of being punished? That the retributive basis of punishment is less applicable to such a person? That it offends proportionality theory to punish a person with mental disabilities as severely as a nonmentally disabled person? That a more severe punishment might be counterproductive in the case of a mentally disabled criminal defendant?

Congress' failure to provide any coherent explanation or clarification about the relative weight that the Federal Sentencing Commission was to give to individual offender characteristics and its failure to prioritize the philosophical purposes of sentencing combined to provide the Commission with very little in the way of a structured blueprint in the creation of its policy statements.[121] The Commission compounded this error by failing to include in the relevant policy statements any reference to empirical studies or evidence on the effect of mental disability on sentencing patterns.

It appears from these failures that neither the Sentencing Commission nor Congress was terribly interested in therapeutic issues or in the therapeutic effect of sentences, a disinterest certainly consistent with the guidelines' focus on retribution as the primary philosophical rationale of federal sentencing policies.[122]

---

[119]*Id.*

[120]*See supra* Chapter 11.

[121]Kate Stith & Steve Y. Koh, *The Politics of Sentencing Reform: The Legislative History of the Federal Sentencing Guidelines,* 28 WAKE FOREST L. REV. 223, 286 (1993).

[122]Karin Bornstein, *5K2.0 Departures for 5H Individual Characteristics: A Backdoor out of the Federal Sentencing Guidelines,* 24 COLUM. HUM. RTS. L. REV. 135, 142 (1992–93).

Also, we do know something about the way prisoners with mental disabilities are treated.[123] We know that mentally ill prisoners have always been relegated to low status in prison settings,[124] that they are often institutionalized in facilities bereft of even minimal mental health services, and are often treated more harshly than other inmates.[125] Any change in the law—be it restrictions on the use of the insanity defense,[126] diminution of inquiries into defendant's capacity to plead guilty or waive counsel,[127] or restrictive interpretations of the federal sentencing guidelines—that results in more persons with mental disabilities being incarcerated in prisons or in longer prison sentences for seriously mentally ill individuals will be antitherapeutic.[128]

What impact will this subordination of mental disability as a reductive factor have on the lives of mentally disabled criminal offenders (and on their keepers and their cellmates)? It is likely that only the most disabled (perhaps the group the least likely to show substantial improvement in a penal setting) will qualify for downward departures. Many seriously disabled defendants will be subject to lengthy terms of imprisonment. These terms will likely often have detrimental effects: Symptomatology will be exacerbated, and prison facilities will become even more dangerous. Also, it is likely that some defense counsel will discourage clients from making showings of mental disability (for fear of *upward* departures), thus diminishing the likelihood that such a defendant will receive any meaningful treatment once incarcerated; when such untreated inmates are eventually released into community settings, we can expect that recidivism rates will increase, having the effect of starting this vicious cycle once again. Again, these impacts are profoundly antitherapeutic.

Insanity Defense

Application of therapeutic jurisprudence principles to the insanity defense reveals many pressure points that bear on any jurisprudential reconstruction. To make our insanity defense system coherent, we need to weigh the therapeutic potential of the different policy choices that are presented at each of these points. If we do this, we may uncover a strategy that will enable us to combat the sanism and pretextuality that currently drives the insanity defense system. At the same time, this strategy should serve as an effective counterweight to the teleological ways that courts have traditionally weighed social science evidence in insanity defense cases.[129]

---

[123]*See, e.g.,* Fred Cohen & Joel A. Dvoskin, *Therapeutic Jurisprudence and Corrections: A Glimpse,* 10 N.Y.L. SCH. J. HUM. RTS. 777 (1993); Fred Cohen & Joel A. Dvoskin, *Inmates With Mental Disorders: A Guide to Law and Practice,* 16 MENT. & PHYS. DIS. L. RPTR. 339 (1992), & 16 MENT. & DIS. L. RPTR. 462 (1992).

[124]*See, e.g.,* Seymour Halleck, *The Criminal's Problem With Psychiatry, in* READINGS IN LAW AND PSYCHIATRY 51 (R. Allen et al. eds. 1975).

[125]Michael L. Perlin, THE JURISPRUDENCE OF THE INSANITY DEFENSE 428 n.55 (1994); *see, e.g.,* Deborah Baskin et al., *Assessing the Impact of Psychiatric Impairment on Prison Violence,* 19 J. CRIM. JUST. 271, 272 (1991).

[126]*See generally* PERLIN, *supra* note 125, at 427–29.

[127]*See* Michael L. Perlin, *"Dignity Was the First to Leave": Godinez v. Moran, Colin Ferguson, and the Trial of Mentally Disabled Criminal Defendants,* 14 BEHAV. SCI. & L. 61 (1996); PERLIN, LMD, *supra* note 7, § 4.13, at 528–34.

[128]PERLIN, *supra* note 125, at 428.

[129]*See* David Wexler, *Insanity Issues After* Hinckley: *Time for a Change,* 35 CONTEMP. PSYCHOL. 1068, 1069 (1990) (explicitly calling for therapeutic jurisprudence inquiries into insanity defense cases). On technology in insanity defense decision making, *see* Michael L. Perlin, "Half-Wracked Prejudice Leaped Forth": Sanism, Pretextuality, and Why and How Mental Disability Law Developed As It Did, 10 J. CONTEMP. LEGAL ISSUES 3, 30 (1999), *quoting* PERLIN, *supra* note 125, at 440–44.

Is a Nonresponsibility Verdict Therapeutic?

Given the "rivers of ink, mountains of printers' lead [and] forests of paper" that have been spilled over every aspect of the insanity defense,[130] it is astonishing that this question has been so rarely asked (and even more rarely answered). Insanity defense adherents often couch their support with reference to society's traditional disapproval of punishment without responsibility.[131] Opponents (mostly) raise fraudulent arguments about the ways that the insanity defense contributes to crime waves and allows "factually guilty" persons to evade punishment; other opponents construct principled arguments that look to other aspects of the criminal justice system to mediate against the punishment of mentally disabled criminal defendants.[132] Rarely are therapeutic jurisprudence issues raised anywhere in the debate.

There are, though, some exceptions. One undercurrent of the abolition movement is an insinuation of volition on the part of insanity defense pleaders: that certain defendants "indulge" in certain behaviors to "make themselves" not responsible. Thus, a popular sanist myth is as follows: "Mentally disabled individuals simply don't try hard enough. They give in too easily to their basest instincts, and do not exercise appropriate self-restraint."[133] These arguments, of course, are never buttressed by empirical support. Prosecutors or jurors make assertions as if they were givens, and rebuttals are rarely offered. Sanism underlies these allegations, and, as currently formulated, they can be dismissed out of hand in any therapeutic jurisprudence analysis.[134]

There are other approaches, however, that might illuminate the underlying issues. Labeling theory, for example, might appear to lend support to a finding that the insanity defense is antitherapeutic.[135] Labeling theory is the study of the process by which a label is, correctly or incorrectly, placed on a particular individual, as well as society's perception of and reaction to that label (and to the labeled person), and the labeled person's eventual

---

[130]*See* Norval Morris, *Psychiatry and the Dangerous Criminal,* 41 S. CAL. L. REV. 514, 516 (1968).

[131]*See, e.g.,* United States v. Lyons, 739 F.2d 994, 995 (5th Cir. 1984) (Rubin, J., dissenting) (insanity defense reflects "fundamental moral principles of our criminal law" and rests on "assumptions that are older than our Republic"); Richard J. Bonnie & Christopher Slobogin, *The Role of Mental Health Professionals in the Criminal Process: The Case for Informed Speculation,* 66 VA. L. REV. 427, 448 (1980) (insanity defense rests on "beliefs about human rationality, deterrability and free will"); Joseph M. Livermore & Paul E. Meehl, *The Virtues of* M'Naghten, 51 MINN. L. REV. 789, 797 (1967) (insanity defense is bulwark of law's "moorings of condemnation for moral failure").

[132]Compare, for example, *The Insanity Defense Hearings Before the Senate Comm. on the Judiciary,* 97th Cong., 2d Sess. 27 (1982) (comments of then-Attorney General William French Smith) (insanity defense is major stumbling block in the restoration of the "effectiveness of Federal law enforcement," and tilts the balance between the forces of law and the forces of lawlessness"), *to* PERLIN, *supra* note 125, at 315–19 (discussing work of Dr. Abraham Halpern, an abolitionist with a "sense of humanity").

[133]Michael L. Perlin, *On "Sanism,"* 46 SMU L. REV. 373 (1992); at 396. *See, e.g.,* State v. Duckworth, 496 So.2d 624, 635 (La. App. 1986) (juror who felt defendant would be responsible for actions as long as he "wanted to do them" not excused for cause) (no error); J. M. Balkin, *The Rhetoric of Responsibility,* 76 VA. L. REV. 197, 238 (1990) (Hinckley prosecutor suggested to jurors "if Hinckley had emotional problems, they were largely his own fault").

[134]If empirical support were to be offered in support of any of these propositions, it would, of course, be appropriate to reevaluate them in that context.

[135]*But cf.* Robert Weisberg, *Criminal Law, Criminology, and the Small World of Legal Scholarship,* 63 U. COLO. L. REV. 521, 527 (1992) ("The history of American sociological criminology has yielded largely a plethora of schemes—from deviance theory to strain theory to control theory to labeling theory to subcultural differential association to reintegrative shaming theories—that almost all criminal law scholars ignore out of a predisposed disdain for the intellectual power of sociology").

fulfillment of society's expectations concerning that label.[136] Labels are more readily accepted by the community if a highly respected person does the initial characterization.[137]

Labeling theorists believe that the potential negative consequences of stigmatizing offenders outweigh any benefits. Specifically, they argue that by labeling an offender "deviant," the state may produce "secondary deviance" or other antisocial acts that are a result of the labeling.[138] On the other hand, critics of labeling theory have responded that no empirical data prove that secondary deviance is, in fact, a result of the labeling.[139] These critics also see positive outcomes as flowing from labeling, such as isolation, incapacitation, and general deterrence, and, perhaps, "channeling [the labeled individual] toward appropriate rehabilitative services (specific deterrence and rehabilitation)."[140]

Labels accompany stereotypes. These labels stigmatize, assign negative associations to an outsider, "complicate[] any effort to resist the designation implied by difference,"[141] and allow the labeler to fail to imagine the perspective of the outsider.[142] Labels are especially pernicious, for they frequently lead labeled individuals to internalize negative expectations and social practices that majoritarian society identifies as characteristically endemic to the labeled group.[143] From these labels, "categorizations assume a life of their own."[144] In turn, any act that fails to follow standards set by a dominant group becomes a deviation.[145]

Labeling must be considered through the special filter of mental disability. There is, for example, a growing body of psychological research that the stigma attached to the label of mental illness can affect a person's self-perception and interpersonal relations, as well as the

---

[136]Karim Lynn, *Unconstitutional Inhibitions: "Political Propaganda" and the Foreign Agents Registration Act,* 33 N.Y.L. SCH. L. REV. 345, 368 n.153 (1988), citing, *inter alia,* FRANCIS CULLEN & JOHN CULLEN, TOWARD A PARADIGM OF LABELLING THEORY 30 (1978).

[137]Lynn, *supra* note 136, at 368, citing EARL RUBINGTON & MARTIN WEINBERG, DEVIANCE, THE INTERACTIONIST PERSPECTIVE 6 (4th ed. 1981).

[138]Toni M. Massaro, *Shame, Culture, and American Criminal Law,* 89 MICH. L. REV. 1880, 1919 (1991), discussing, *inter alia,* ROBERT C. TROJANOWICZ & MERRY MORASH, JUVENILE DELINQUENCY: CONCEPTS AND CONTROL 59–61 (4th ed. 1987); Walter R. Gove, *The Labelling Perspective: An Overview, in* THE LABELING OF DEVIANCE 9 (W. Gove ed., 2d ed. 1980).

[139]Massaro, *supra* note 138, at 1920, citing, *inter alia,* Gove, *supra* note 138, at 13–15 (collecting empirical work).

[140]Massaro, *supra* note 138 at 1920, citing Gove, *supra* note 138, at 18.

[141]Martha Minow, *1984 Forward: Justice Engendered,* 101 HARV. L. REV. 10, 38 (1987); STEPHAN GILMAN, DIFFERENCE AND PATHOLOGY: STEREOTYPES OF SEXUALITY, RACE AND MADNESS 12, 18–35 (1985).

[142]Minow, *supra* note 141, at 51 n.201; see generally NEW YORK STATE OFFICE OF MENTAL HEALTH, FINAL REPORT: TASK FORCE ON STIGMA AND DISCRIMINATION (Mar. 6, 199) at 1–2.

[143]Note, *Teaching Inequality: The Problem of Public School Tracking,* 102 HARV. L. REV. 1318, 1333 (1989); Mark Glassner, LABELING THEORY, IN THE SOCIOLOGY OF DEVIANCE 71 (1982); LAMAR TEMPEY, AMERICAN DELINQUENCY: ITS MEANING AND CONSTRUCTION 341–68 (1978); *see generally* Lois A. Weithorn, *Mental Hospitalization of Troublesome Youth: An Analysis of Skyrocketing Admission Rates,* 40 STAN. L. REV. 773, 805–07, 820–26 (1988); Robert W. Sweet, *Deinstitutionalization of Status Offenders: In Perspective,* 18 PEPP. L. REV. 389 (1991).

[144]Richard Delgado et al., *Fairness and Formality: Minimizing the Role of Prejudice in Alternative Dispute Resolution,* 1985 WIS. L. REV. 1359, 1381: "What enables people to reject members of other races is the supportive (unconscious and automatic) bias elicited by categorization," quoting Knud S. Larsen, *Social Categorization and Attitude Change,* 111 J. SOC. PSYCHOL. 113, 114 (1980).

[145]Walter Chester, *Perceived Relative Deprivation as a Cause of Property Crime,* 22 CRIME & DELINQ. 17, 22 (1976), *as quoted in* Christine L. Wilson, *Urban Homesteading: A Compromise Between Squatters and the Law,* 35 N.Y.L. SCH. L. REV. 709, 714–15 n.38 (1990).

response of society in general.[146] Society's attitudes toward persons with mental disabilities have a demonstrable effect on how patients see themselves and how adequately they adjust, and the public is more tolerant of deviance when it is not described by a mental disability label.[147]

What impact should this have on the insanity defense? The phrase *insanity acquittee* is clearly a pejorative label. Does that labeling affect the individual's self-perception?[148] If the individual were, instead, labeled "criminal," would that be a better or worse alternative? What other negative attributions does society make about such a person? Would society still make these attributions if there were no insanity defense? Do insanity acquittees act in certain ways to conform their behavior to public perceptions?

Several scholars have discussed the question of whether defendants could be denied the use of the insanity defense if they were found to have been "culpable" in causing the conditions that led to the use of the defense.[149] On the other hand, as David Wexler has pointed out, patients with schizophrenia who fail to take antipsychotic medication may not be culpable if their impaired mental state led to that refusal.[150] In such an instance, Finkel argued, "When we recognize . . . that we are in danger of coming apart at the psychic seams, so to speak . . . then we should get ourselves help; . . . the alternative course, to do nothing, is unacceptable and inexcusable. . . ."[151]

Taking a slightly different tack, Robert Fein has claimed that the insanity defense encourages NGRI acquittees to absolve themselves of responsibility for their actions and

---

[146]Stephanie L. Splane, *Tort Liability of the Mentally Ill in Negligence Actions,* 93 YALE L.J. 153, 167 n.75 (1983), citing, *inter alia,* Amerigo Farina et al., *Mental Illness and the Impact of Believing Others Know About It,* 77 J. ABNORMAL PSYCHOL. 1 (1971) (believing others to be aware of their status as mentally ill caused persons to feel less appreciated, appear more tense, and to find performance tasks more difficult); Amerigo Farina, et al., *Role of Stigma and Set in Interpersonal Interaction,* 71 J. ABNORMAL PSYCHOL. 421 (1966) (mentally ill persons described as less desirable as friends and neighbors than criminals).

[147]Walter J. Johannsen, *Attitudes Toward Mental Patients: A Review of Empirical Research,* 53 MENTAL HYGIENE 218, 222–23 (1969); Amal Sarbin & Anthony Mancuso, *Failure of a Moral Enterprise: Attitudes of the Public Toward Mental Illness,* 35 J. CONSULTING & CLINICAL PSYCHOL. 159, 159 (1970).

[148]On the impact of sex offender labeling, see Anthony Walsh, *Twice Labeled: The Effect of Psychiatric Labels on the Sentencing of Sex Offenders,* 37 SOC. PROBS. 375, 385–86 (1990) (both probation officers and judges "are consistently and powerfully influenced" by labels).

[149]*See, e.g.,* David Wexler, *Inducing Therapeutic Compliance Through the Criminal Law,* in ESSAYS IN THERAPEUTIC JURISPRUDENCE 187, 196 (David Wexler & Bruce Winick eds. 1991) [hereinafter ESSAYS] quoting, *inter alia,* Paul H. Robinson, *Causing the Conditions of One's Own Defense: A Study of the Limits of Theory in Criminal Law Doctrine,* 71 VA. L. REV. 1, 23–25 (1985); *see, e.g.,* WASH. REV. CODE ANN. § 10.77.010 (7) (1990) ("No condition of the mind proximately induced by the voluntary act of a person charged with crime shall constitute 'insanity'"); *see also, e.g.,* Michael D. Slodov, *Criminal Responsibility and the Noncompliant Psychiatric Offender: Risking Madness,* 40 CASE W. RES. L. REV. 271 (1989); Laurence P. Tiffany, *The Drunk, the Insane, and the Criminal Courts: Deciding What to Make of Self-Induced Insanity,* 69 WASH. U. L.Q. 221 (1991).

[150]Wexler, *supra* note 149, at 195; *see generally* Slodov, *supra* note 149. This issue is addressed, albeit elliptically, in People v. Smith, 465 N.E.2d 101, 103 (Ill. App. 1984) (antipsychotic medication had been prescribed for defendant which he took only one time; "One week later, the defendant fatally stabbed the victim in the instant case").

Other questions are raised if an individual asserts a constitutional right to refuse medication, see Michael L. Perlin, *Reading the Supreme Court's Tea Leaves: Predicting Judicial Behavior in Civil and Criminal Right to Refuse Treatment Cases,* 12 AM. J. FORENS. PSYCHIATRY 37, 54 (1991), and then commits a criminal act, or if he or she commits a criminal act while under the influence of a prescribed antipsychotic drug, see People v. Caulley, 494 N.W.2d 853 (Mich. App. 1992) (reversing conviction; defendant could establish viable insanity defense if he could demonstrate that the "involuntary use," via medical prescription, of drugs created a state of mind equivalent to insanity).

[151]NORMAN J. FINKEL, INSANITY ON TRIAL 288 (1988). This argument assumes a fact not necessarily in evidence: that such "help" is available to all individuals who might seek it.

retards their treatment progress.[152] His thesis is this: For the NGRI verdict to work, insanity acquittees must "accept emotional responsibility for actions committed during periods of gross mental disorder"; operationally, the fact of acquittal serves to retard the acceptance of this responsibility.[153]

He gives several examples to illustrate his thesis (drawn from his experiences at Bridgewater State Hospital in Massachusetts). In one case, a patient to whom he refers as H. B. stated, "The judge said I was not guilty; I shouldn't be here. I am no longer sick." The same patient complained further that it was "unfair" that he was institutionalized because he had not committed a crime. In addition, the patient refused to participate in psychotherapy and "was granted his wish to stop taking his medicine."[154] A second insanity acquittee (A. L.), when asked by the judge at his recommitment hearing to describe how he felt about having injured his victims, replied, "The judge said I was not guilty. I'm sorry I did it but I think I've done enough time. . . . I haven't gotten in any fights here."[155]

According to Fein, the fact that the insanity defense implies "that violent behavior is caused by 'illness' and is not committed by persons with thoughts and feelings . . . appears to decrease the possibility that mentally disordered persons will be able to utilize treatment services," and that the NGRI verdict thus "may work against the needs of the defendants labeled by the courts as 'sick.'"[156] The verdict, Fein concluded, "provides a convenient way for the offender to avoid thinking about his violent behavior and its meaning."[157]

Fein's arguments are provocative, but to my mind fail to prove his point.[158] First, H. B.'s perception of the verdict is simply wrong; a finding of NGRI does not mean that a defendant is "no longer sick" or that he "shouldn't be in the hospital." On the other hand, this misunderstanding may be an indication of the degree of severity of his illness; he may be *so* seriously mentally disabled that he cannot frame the type of thought process that would lead him to understand the limits of his responsibility. Second, his refusal to participate in psychotherapy and his decision to exercise his right to refuse the involuntary imposition of medication may raise therapeutic jurisprudence questions about the right to refuse treatment[159] but not about the underlying substantive insanity verdict.[160]

---

[152]Robert Fein, *How the Insanity Acquittal Retards Treatment,* in TJ, *supra* note 67, at 49.

[153]*Id.* at 52.

[154]*Id.* at 53.

[155]*Id.* at 54.

[156]*Id.* at 58.

[157]*Id.* at 55.

[158]First, both of his NGRI examples are exceptional cases. H. B. was a former police officer and marine whose victim was a bar bouncer who had attacked the defendant a year prior to the murder that led to his insanity acquittal. *Id.* at 52–53. As I have discussed, such verdicts are disproportionately entered in cases in which law enforcement officials are defendants; the additional fact that the victim was a nonstranger–former aggressor might make the verdict even more understandable. *See* PERLIN, *supra* note 125, at 182–86. A. L., a quiet, withdrawn person who attacked several strangers (leaving one permanently disfigured), was visited daily in the forensic hospital by members of his family, who referred to the series of attacks as "A. L.'s accident." Fein, *supra* note 152, at 54. Certainly, this constant exculpatory "support" by his family could have served as a powerful incentive leading him to deny responsibility for his actions.

[159]*See, e.g.,* Perlin, *supra* note 150; Bruce Winick, *Competency to Consent to Treatment: The Distinction Between Assent and Objection, in* ESSAYS *supra* note 149 at 41. On the right of insanity acquittees to refuse medication, *see* 2 PERLIN, MDL, *supra* note 7, § 3B-9.6, at 341–42 (2d. ed. 1999).

[160]There has also been virtually no litigation on the question of a "right to refuse psychotherapy," and what little has been attempted has been unsuccessful. *See* 2 PERLIN, MDL *supra* note 7, § 3B-10.2, at 347–48 (2d. ed. 1999) (discussing United States v. Stine, 675 F.2d 69, 71–72 (3d Cir. 1982)). *Cf.* Griffin v. Coughlin, 649 N.Y.S.2d 903 (1996), *cert. denied,* 519 U.S. 1054 (1997) (conditioning prisoner's eligibility for family reunion program on his participation in Alcoholic's Anonymous's 12-step treatment program impermissible; program's practices constituted endorsement of religion).

On the other hand, H. B.'s complaint that it was "unfair" to not know when he would be discharged may raise a serious issue but not necessarily one that supports Fein's central thesis. This uncertainty *may* be antitherapeutic. However, if it is, it would seem to call into question postcommitment retention schemes such as the one upheld by the Supreme Court in *Jones v. United States*[161] under which a defendant can be held in a forensic hospital beyond the maximum term to which he or she could have been sentenced had the individual been convicted of the underlying crime. This does not challenge the therapeutic potential of the insanity defense but of a commitment system that ensures lengthier stays in hospitals for insanity acquittees.

What about Fein's conclusions? Does failure to assign responsibility lessen an insanity acquittee's initiative to get better? Does this question imply some quantum of blame; that the patient could get better "if he really wanted to"?[162] Is there any responsibility on institutional staff? Should they be held accountable to try to deal with the type of behavior exhibited in the H. B. and A. L. cases?

What about Fein's conclusion that the verdict implies that violent behavior is "caused" by mental illness? This use of causation sounds like the *Durham* product test, a formulation that was abandoned in the District of Columbia in 1972.[163] Neither the *M'Naghten* nor the American Law Institute tests are couched in causal language; to make this link is to set up an ultimate straw man.

Also, the implication that the insanity verdict suggests that the behavior in question is not that of individuals with "thoughts and feelings" falls wide of the mark. The insanity defense is usually pled only by people with the most disordered thoughts; when the verdict is successful, it is often the reflection of jurors' conclusions that the underlying crime was a response to the power of those strong thoughts.

In short, although I find Fein's piece thoughtful, I do not believe that it makes the case that the insanity defense is antitherapeutic. It appears that no one in the facility in which H.B. and A.L. resided ever explained to the two acquittees the actual meaning of the jury's verdict nor, apparently, did anyone ever counsel A. L.'s family that their reinforcement of his denial was most likely antitherapeutic.[164] Fein provides no evidence that his criticism would be valid if such explanations had been offered. It is not the *fact* of the nonresponsibility verdict that is antitherapeutic but the way that the verdict is processed by the defendant after the insanity acquittal. It would seem that some measure of cognitive restructuring as to the defense's meaning and its likely consequences for the defendant would eliminate almost all of Fein's criticisms.

What about the other side? May a nonresponsibility defense be "therapeutic"? I believe that it may be. The standard explanation as to why the defense is therapeutic is articulated best by Judge Bazelon: "By declaring a small number not responsible, we emphasize the responsibility of all others who commit crimes."[165] In other words, the existence of the insanity defense gives coherence to the entire fabric of criminal sentencing. We punish responsible defendants for a variety of reasons: to incapacitate them, to deter others, to educate others, (perhaps) to rehabilitate them.[166] By punishing nonresponsible defendants,

---

[161] 463 U.S. 354 (1983).

[162] *See* PERLIN, *supra* note 125, at 385 n. 43, discussing State v. Duckworth, 496 So.2d 624, 635 (La. App. 1986).

[163] *See* PERLIN, *supra* note 125, at 85–89. *Durham* was overruled by United States v. Brawner, 471 F. 2d. 969, 973 (D.C. Cir. 1973); see *generally,* PERLIN, *supra* note 125, at 87–88.

[164] Of course, if the individuals' mental states were so impaired that they could not understand the meaning of the insanity acquittal, it is unlikely that *any* explanation would have been therapeutic or antitherapeutic.

[165] DAVID L. BAZELON, QUESTIONING AUTHORITY: JUSTICE AND CRIMINAL LAW 2 (1988).

[166] *See* PERLIN, *supra* note 158, at 49–70.

we diminish all the rationales for punishment of the others whom we believe to be responsible for their crimes.

However, this argument may simply be a retrospective rationalization and not a therapeutic justification. It may be that we allow the insanity defense to survive precisely because so few criminal defendants come within its scope.[167] This allows us to isolate those few without endangering the overall administration of the criminal justice system.[168] This may also explain why Judge Bazelon's consideration of "rotten social background" as potentially providing a basis for an insanity defense (on the theory that it significantly impaired the defendant's ability to exercise free choice)[169] never attracted more positive public support.[170] Recognition or acceptance of this position would imperil the legal system's "tensile strength"[171] by calling into question literally thousands of criminal convictions entered each year. In other words, this argument in support of the insanity defense is an important instrumental one, but may not normatively provide a therapeutic basis for the defense.

On the other hand, the insanity defense system recognizes that certain individuals— because of mental disability—are to be diverted from the criminal justice system.[172] If such defendants receive constitutionally meaningful treatment in psychiatric hospitals, then this diversion will be therapeutic.[173] More important, if these defendants are spared prison— where mentally disabled prisoners are often institutionalized in facilities bereft of even minimal mental health services and are often treated more harshly than other inmates[174]—

---

[167]See id. at 108–14.

[168]This may actually be a *sanist* justification for the insanity defense, because it enables us to say that these few defendants are so sufficiently not "like us" that we can treat them safely as an outgroup. Not coincidentally, such individuals are often treated in facilities in areas at a significant distance from major population centers.

[169]United States v. Alexander, 471 F.2d 923, 957–65 (D.C. Cir. 1972) (Bazelon, J., concurring in part and dissenting in part).

[170]For a sampling of the academic debate, see, for example, David L. Bazelon, *The Morality of the Criminal Law,* 49 S. Cal. L. Rev. 385 (1976); Stephen J. Morse, *The Twilight of Welfare Criminology: A Reply to Judge Bazelon,* 49 S. Cal. L. Rev. 1247 (1976); Richard Delgado, *"Rotten Social Background": Should the Criminal Law Recognize a Defense of Severe Environmental Deprivation?* 3 Law & Inequality 9 (1985).

[171]See Perlin, *supra* note 158, at 377–83.

[172]Cf. Abraham Halpern, *The Insanity Defense in the 21st Century,* 35 Int'l J. Offender Therapy & Comp. Criminology 188, 188 (1991) (arguing that insanity defense draws resources of forensic hospitals "while individuals with clear-cut psychiatric illnesses . . . are left to deteriorate in prison without a modicum of therapy"). On the recent increase in the number of mentally ill pretrial jail detainees, see George B. Palermo et al., *Mental Illness and Criminal Behavior Revisited,* 36 Int'l J. Offender Therapy & Comp. Criminology 53 (1992).

[173]In the pecking order of prisoners, those with mental illness have always been plagued by an exceptionally low status. *See* Halleck, *supra* note 124.

[174]See, e.g., Tillery v. Owens, 907 F.2d 418, 424–25 (3d Cir. 1990) (mentally ill inmates often double-celled with inmates in administrative custody, a practice characterized by an expert witness as "putting the chickens in the fox's lair"); Baskin et al., *supra* note 125, at 272 (psychiatrically impaired inmates more likely to be victimized by other prisoners due to displays of bizarre or inappropriate behavior). On the multiple roots of homicide defendants' postdetention psychotic reactions, see Julio Arboleda-Florez, *Post-Homicide Psychotic Reaction,* 25 Int'l J. Offender Therapy & Comp. Criminology 47 (1981). On the relationship between prison violence and mental illness, *see* Baskin et al., *supra* note 125.

Proponents of abolishing involuntary civil commitment have conceded that this might result in more mentally disabled persons being imprisoned. *See* Carol Warren, The Court of Last Resort: Mental Illness and the Law 100–01 (1982) (section written by Stephen J. Morse). Responds Andrew Scull: "While Morse may not balk at the prospect of sending the mentally ill to prison, a . . . system of justice built around the concept of criminal responsibility almost certainly will." Andrew Scull, *The Theory and Practice of Civil Commitment,* 82 Mich. L. Rev. 793, 803 (1984).

then there may be an additional therapeutic impact.[175] If, in a prison context, we are likely to cognitively resolve the "logical dissonance of classifying mad/bad persons as bad persons,"[176] then the separation of severely mentally disabled individuals from prison population will have yet an extra therapeutic outcome.[177]

I suggest that this analysis is a starting point for a more comprehensive investigation of the question posed. As I will argue in my concluding section, unless scholars and insanity-defense decision makers confront the importance of this inquiry, our endless tinkering with the procedural and substantive contours of the defense will have little ultimate meaning.

Does the Substantive Standard Matter?

The much ballyhooed Insanity Defense Reform Act eliminated the volitional prong from the insanity defense in federal courts because of the fear that this was not "measurable" (as cognition presumably was),[178] and that this reduction would eliminate verdicts that had been termed "moral mistakes."[179] Yet the best available empirical studies suggest that volition may be accurately measurable, in some instances perhaps even more accurately than cognition.[180]

This same evidence offers an important therapeutic jurisprudence insight. The very individuals who meet the volitional standard (but not the cognitive test) may be exactly those individuals who would be the most problematic prison inmates and whose mental disabilities might be most treatable in a controlled forensic hospital setting.[181] It appears that

---

[175]On the way that progressive conditional release of NGRI acquittees is therapeutically beneficial, see Margaret A. McGreevey et al., *New York State's System of Managing Insanity Acquittees in the Community,* 42 HOSP. & COMMUNITY PSYCHIATRY 512 (1991). On the other side of this coin, if severely mentally disabled persons are diverted from prisons, it may serve to make those facilities safer for nonmentally disabled prisoners as well.

[176]Robert L. Hayman, *Beyond Penry: The Remedial Use of the Mentally Retarded Label in Death Penalty Sentencing,* 59 UMKC L. REV. 17, 47 n.161 (1990) (quoting HANS TOCH & KENNETH ADAMS, THE DISTURBED VIOLENT OFFENDER 18–19 (1989)),

[177]*See generally* HANS TOCH & KENNETH ADAMS, COPING: MALADAPTATION IN PRISONS (1989); HANS TOCH, MOSAIC OF DESPAIR: HUMAN BREAKDOWN IN PRISON (rev. ed. 1992). On the other hand, if adequate treatment is not offered in forensic mental health facilities, the ensuing institutionalization in such environments may also be antitherapeutic.

[178]For the purposes of this section I will assume that the choice of standard has at least a symbolic value. *See, e.g.,* Robert J. Homant & Daniel B. Kennedy, *Subjective Factors in Clinicians' Judgments of Insanity: Comparison of a Hypothetical Case and an Actual Case,* 18 PROF. PSYCHOL.: RES. & PRAC. 439, 455 (1987): "Insanity defense trials . . . will continue to play an important symbolic role. They will underline the fact that reasons for criminal behavior are indeed important, and that a principled and effective response to offenders must follow from an understanding of the individuals." At the least, the choice of standard conveys a paramessage, *see* PERLIN, *supra* note 125, at 304, to jurors about the legislature's feelings about the role of the insanity defense in a criminal justice system. This is an area that has seen significant empirical inquiry. *See id.* at 303–30, discussing, *inter alia,* the work of Norman Finkel and his colleagues.

[179]*See* PERLIN, *supra* note 125, at 242.

[180]*See* Stuart Silver & Michael Spodak, *Dissection of the Prongs of ALI: Retrospective Assessment of Criminal Responsibility by the Psychiatric Staff of the Clifton T. Perkins Hospital Center,* 11 BULL. AM. ACAD. PSYCHIATRY & L. 383, 390 (1983) (contemporaneous empirical research has shown some evidence that the elimination of this prong from the insanity defense "may systematically exclude . . . that class of psychotic patients [patients with manic disorders] whose illness is clearest in symptomatology, must likely biologic in origin, most eminently treatable, and potentially most disruptive in penal detention"); *see also* Richard Rogers et al., *Assessment of Criminal Responsibility: Empirical Advances and Unanswered Questions,* 15 J. PSYCHIATRY & L. 73, 78 (1987) (arguments that volitional nonresponsibility cannot be measured are "an intellectual charade played for the benefit of an uninformed public"). *See* PERLIN, *supra* note 125, at 314–15 n.239.

[181]*See* Silver & Spodak, *supra* note 180.

our political cant and rhetoric has blunted any efforts to inform ourselves of the therapeutic potential of substantive insanity formulations less restrictive than the *M'Naghten* test.

Do Procedural Rules Matter?

As I have discussed elsewhere at length, the allocation of proof to the state or the defendant may be a critical decision in formulating an insanity defense standard.[182] Placing the burden on the defendant (especially where it involves a clear and convincing quantum of evidence) will make it more likely that insanity defenses offered by severely mentally disabled criminal defendants will be rejected.[183] This in turn may increase the number of imprisoned seriously mentally disabled prisoners, an outcome that is self-evidently antitherapeutic for the unsuccessful insanity pleaders and may also be potentially hazardous for prison staff and other prisoners.[184]

Other procedural issues call out for further study as well. The Supreme Court decision in *Shannon v. United States*—holding that, as a matter of federal criminal procedure, the defendant had no right to have the jury informed about the possible consequences of an NGRI verdict[185]—will only increase the amount of pretextuality in decisionmaking in this area of the law. If we learn that jurors are misinformed about the ultimate outcome of a successful insanity plea[186] and that jurors may overconvict "legitimate" insanity defendants (because of a false fear that they will be quickly released from all custodial restraints, a fear often exacerbated by inflammatory prosecutorial summations),[187] then decisions that deprive them of this empirical information (and allow for the dissemination of inaccurate information) are antitherapeutic.[188]

In *Ake v. Oklahoma*, the Supreme Court ruled if a criminal defendant were to make an "ex parte threshold showing . . . that his sanity was likely to be a significant factor in his defense," the state must assure the defendant access to a "competent psychiatrist . . . [to] assist in the evaluation, preparation, and presentation of the defense."[189] Most post-*Ake* decisions have read that holding tepidly,[190] and defendants are frequently deprived of

---

[182]*See* PERLIN, *supra* note 125, at 96–100.

[183]For a pointed case example, see State v. Zmich, 770 P.2d 776 (Ariz. 1989), discussed *id.* at 99 n.126.

[184]By saying this I am *not* suggesting that mentally disabled criminal defendants are, as a class, more dangerous than other criminal defendants. I am arguing rather that the placement of such individuals into a general prison population (supervised by a prison staff who may have no training or experience in the identification or treatment of such disabilities) may create hazardous and harmful conditions for all involved.

[185]512 U.S. 573 (1994). For recent cases, see 3 PERLIN, MDL, *supra* note 7, § 15.16A, at 510–11 n.372.42 (1998 Cum. Supp.).

[186]*See, e.g.,* Price v. State, 412 N.E.2d 783, 788 (Ind. 1980) (De Bruler, J., concurring in result) (explaining that, as a result of his "success," the insanity acquittee "is placed on a separate track towards confinement under the auspices of attendants and doctors rather than on a track toward confinement under the auspices of guards and wardens").

[187]*See* PERLIN, *supra* note 158, at 107–14.

[188]For perhaps the most incomprehensible decision dealing with judicial instructions, see Geschwendt v. Ryan, 967 F.2d 877 (3d Cir. 1992) *(en banc),* and *id.* at 891 (Aldisert, J., dissenting). See *supra* Chapter 10.

[189]470 U.S. 68, 82–83 (1985).

[190]*See* 3 PERLIN, MDL *supra* note 7, § 17.17, at 549–53, and *id.* at 647–49 n.404.1 (1998 Cum. Supp.) (listing cases).

adequate expert assistance.[191] Again, in those few cases in which insanity is contested, this may lead to some legitimately nonresponsible defendants being improperly convicted.

In *Barefoot v. Estelle,* the Supreme Court approved of expert testimony on future dangerousness, even where the expert testimony had not examined the defendant in question.[192] This uniformly criticized decision[193] ''flies in the face of . . . relevant scientific literature, . . . is inconsistent with the development of evidence law doctrine, and . . . makes a mockery of earlier Supreme Court decisions cautioning that *extra* reliability is needed in capital cases.''[194] Again, it heightens the likelihood of inappropriate convictions in insanity cases—an antitherapeutic outcome.

This leads to another set of inquiries. What impact do examiners' preexisting political attitudes have on insanity case dispositions? A body of research literature has developed that demonstrates that various sorts of political biases affect mental health professionals' judgments of insanity in particular cases,[195] and that the primary predictor of an expert witness' view on a particular case is his or her preexisting feelings about the defense.[196] Other research shows that most expert witnesses do not know the actual substantive insanity standard used in their jurisdiction.[197] If improper or inaccurate verdicts in insanity cases are entered because of these biases or lack of knowledge, this would clearly also affect any therapeutic effect that the defense might have.

Should Postacquittal Commitment Procedures Track the Traditional Involuntary Civil Commitment Model?

Few contrasts in insanity defense jurisprudence are more stark than the difference between postacquittal commitments in states that follow the model of the New Jersey Supreme Court in *State v. Krol*[198] and those that adhere to the system found to be constitutional by the U.S. Supreme Court in *Jones v. United States.*[199] *Krol* finds the distinction between criminal and civil commitment a meaningless one; *Jones,* on the other hand, sees the prior commission of a criminal act (even a *de minimis* one) as a sufficient predicate for an entirely different set of procedural and substantive rules.

---

[191]*See, e.g.,* Brown v. State, 743 P.2d 133 (Okla. Crim. App. 1987); State v. Bearthes, 329 N.C. 149, 405 S.E.2d 170 (1991); Henderson v. Dugger, 925 F.2d 1309 (9th Cir. 1991). *But see* De Freece v. State, 848 S.W.2d 150 (Tex. Cr. App. 1993), *cert. denied,* 510 U.S. 195 (1993) (*Ake* requires more than a disinterested witness; expert must be able to assist in developing favorable testimony, supply bases on which to cross-examine state's expert and, if necessary, testify on behalf of the defendant).

[192]463 U.S. 880 (1983); *see* PERLIN, *supra* note 158, at 210–12.

[193]*See* 3 PERLIN, MDL *supra* note 7, § 17.14, at 536–40; *see, e.g.,* D. Michael Risinger et al., *Exorcism of Ignorance as a Proxy for Rational Knowledge: The Lessons of Handwriting Identification "Expertise,"* 137 U. PA. L. REV. 731, 780–81 n.215 (1989) (''We have yet to find a single word of praise for, or in defense of, *Barefoot* in the literature of either science or law'').

[194]Michael L. Perlin, *The Supreme Court, the Mentally Disabled Criminal Defendant, Psychiatric Testimony in Death Penalty Cases, and the Power of Symbolism: Dulling the* Ake *in* Barefoot's *Achilles Heel,* 3 N.Y.L. SCH. HUM. RTS. ANN. 91, 111 (1985) (emphasis in original).

[195]*See, e.g.,* Robert J. Homant et al., *Ideology as a Determinant of Views on the Insanity Defense,* 14 J. CRIM. JUST. 37, 57 (1986).

[196]Robert J. Homant & Daniel B. Kennedy, *Judgment of Legal Insanity as a Function of Attitude Toward the Insanity Defense,* 8 INT'L J.L. & PSYCHIATRY 67 (1986).

[197]Richard Rogers & R. Edward Turner, *Understanding of Insanity: A National Survey of Forensic Psychologists and Psychiatrists,* 7 HEALTH L. CAN. 71 (1987).

[198]344 A.2d 289 (N.J. 1975); *see* PERLIN, *supra* note 158, at 198–99.

[199]463 U.S. 354 (1983); *see* PERLIN, *supra* note 158, at 199–201.

Self-evidently, the *Krol* system should lead to fewer defendants being institutionalized and shorter terms of confinement; the *Jones* scheme would do just the opposite. Is it therapeutic for defendants to be released from custody more quickly, or is it more therapeutic for insanity pleaders to be institutionalized for longer periods of time (longer, perhaps, than had they been sentenced to the maximum for the underlying crime)?[200]

In addition, the *Krol/Jones* split has a symbolic value that may also mask therapeutic content. If we say (as did the *Krol* court) that there is no difference between criminal and civil commitment, then we are minimizing the criminal component of the insanity defense finding and maximizing the mental disability component. On the other hand, if we say that a defendant's original criminal act (no matter how minor) colors all subsequent aspects of the criminal process, then we are saying that *any* involvement in that process serves as a trump over any other individual facet of the case. The resolution of this symbolic split is likely to be longer terms of postacquittal hospitalization in *Jones* jurisdictions and shorter in *Krol* jurisdictions. Again, therapeutic jurisprudence questions are raised by this inquiry.

In a careful analysis of the collateral issue of how the release hearing should be structured, Wexler has examined the work of Donald Meichenbaum and Dennis Turk[201] that was written to help medical professionals increase patient treatment adherence.[202] Meichenbaum and Turk's research led them to conclude that such adherence is likely to be increased when a patient is given choice and participation in the selection of treatment alternatives and goals.[203]

Placing this work in the context of the release hearing, Wexler looked for ways that courts might use these compliance principles to increase a patient's adherence behavior once released.[204] Such strategies as the use of behavioral contracts, the creation of procedures that track plea bargain approval hearings,[205] and the involvement of the acquittee in the hearing itself ("to test the patient's understanding of the regimen and to insure that the patient agrees with it and had input into its design")[206] would ensure a greater level of patient compliance. Under this model, "the court is itself an HCP [health care professional]," and Wexler has recommended behaviors to the judge to enhance patient adherence.[207]

Wexler has acknowledged that courts may resist these behaviors for many of the same reasons that health care professionals may resist, the procedures are too complicated, enhancement strategies are a "frill," the strategies will not work with the population in

---

[200]Michael Jones, the appellant in the Supreme Court case, had been arrested and charged with attempted petit larceny in 1975, was still institutionalized at the time of the Supreme Court decision in 1983, and remains institutionalized today.

[201]DONALD MEICHENBAUM & DENNIS C. TURK, FACILITATING TREATMENT ADHERENCE: A PRACTITIONER'S GUIDEBOOK (1987) (FACILITATING).

[202]David Wexler, *Health Care Compliance Principles and the Insanity Acquittee Conditional Release Process,* in ESSAYS, *supra* note 149, at 199.

[203]Bruce Winick, *Harnessing the Power of the Bet: Wagering With the Government as a Mechanism for Social and Individual Change,* in ESSAYS, *supra* note 149, at 245 n.93, citing FACILITATING, *supra* note 201, at 157, 159, 175.

[204]Wexler, *supra* note 202, at 209.

[205]*See* FED. R. CRIM. PROC. 11 (1999).

[206]Wexler, *supra* note 202, at 210.

[207]*Id.* at 212.

For instance, the judge can make sure to introduce himself or herself to the patient, can be attentive, can avoid using legal or medical jargon, can allow the patient to tell his or her story without undue interruption, can make sure the patient understands the precise treatment regimen, and can even sit at the same level and at the same conference table as the patient—perhaps in a mental health facility conference room rather than in a courtroom.

question.[208] Notwithstanding these potential (and likely) complaints, Wexler concluded that this approach is one that deserves experimental implementation. "Like it or not [it is probable that] the behavior of courts play a critical role in the adherence behavior of conditionally released insanity acquittees."[209] The simple recognition by courts that their decisions and actions have a therapeutic or antitherapeutic consequence should be a critical factoring in this sort of decision making.[210]

Wexler's arguments are compelling and offer a blueprint for scholars and other insanity-defense decision makers. As the face of mental disability law scholarship changes,[211] we can hope that researchers turn their attention to this important question.

Once Institutionalized, How Are Insanity Acquittees to Be Treated?

Little academic attention has been paid to the question of the institutional treatment rights of insanity acquittees. Although a smattering of case law finds that both the right to treatment and the right to refuse treatment apply,[212] there has been little systemic consideration of this question since Anne Singer and June German's ground-breaking analysis in 1976.[213]

As to a right to refuse treatment, several questions are raised from a therapeutic jurisprudence perspective. If refusal of treatment serves autonomy values (by allowing institutionalized patients to make individual health care decisions that they could freely make in the community), is it therapeutic to expand this right for this population? On the other hand, if refusal of medication leads to more florid symptomatology (and an exacerbation of delusions and hallucinations), is that antitherapeutic *in se*? If drugs merely mask symptoms and result in damaging neurological side effects will that be factored into TJ analysis? Will Justice Kennedy's bold and expansive prorefusal position in his autonomy-privileging concurrence in *Riggins v. Nevada*[214] lead to further attention to this issue? Until rigorous therapeutic jurisprudence analyses are applied, arguments about whether insanity acquittees should have the same rights, fewer rights, or more rights than civil patients in these areas will likely remain unresolved.

---

[208]*Id.* at 217.

[209]*Id.* at 218.

[210]*Id.* at 218 n.147, citing David Wexler & Robert Schopp, *Therapeutic Jurisprudence: A New Approach to Mental Health Law, in* HANDBOOK OF PSYCHOLOGY AND LAW (D. K. Kagehiro & W. S. Laufer eds., 1992).

[211]*See* David Wexler, *Therapeutic Jurisprudence and Changing Conceptions of Legal Scholarship,* 11 BEHAV. SCI. & L. 17 (1993).

[212]*See* Perlin, *Tea Leaves, supra* note 150.

[213]June R. German & Anne C. Singer, *Punishing the Not Guilty: Hospitalization of Persons Found Not Guilty by Reason of Insanity,* 29 RUTGERS L. REV. 1011, 1017–35 (1976). At least one case has expanded the right of access to a law library and to legal research materials—previously held to apply to prisoners, pretrial detainees, and persons committed following a finding of incompetency to stand trial—to patients institutionalized after an NGRI verdict. *See* Hatch v. Yamauchi, 809 F. Supp. 59 (E.D. Ark. 1992).

[214]504 U.S. 127, 138–45 (1992); *see supra* Chapter 6. Justice Kennedy's concurrence is considered in this context in, *inter alia,* People v. Tally, 1999 WL 249129, *3 (Colo. App. 1999), and United States v. Brandon, 158 F. 3d. 947, 954 (6th Cir. 1998).

How Should Insanity Acquittees Be Monitored in Community Settings?

The paradox should be self-evident. Insanity acquittees have been seen as the most despised group of individuals in society.[215] Most commentators agree that one of the reasons the U.S. insanity defense jurisprudence is so repressive is to make it as difficult as possible for insanity acquittees to ever reenter society; the thought that such individuals are ever to be released fills much of the public with dread or consternation.[216] On the other hand, most research studies show that individuals who are subject to gradual lessening of restraints are better reintegrated into the community on release.[217] Some sort of monitoring appears to be appropriate, but little attention has been paid in the legal literature to this question from a therapeutic jurisprudence perspective.[218]

Other Therapeutic Jurisprudence Issues

In addition to these questions, there remain a whole menu of other issues that need to be considered from a therapeutic jurisprudence perspective: the procedural due process requirements needed at the recommitment process,[219] the right of defendants to refuse to enter an insanity plea,[220] the impact of a failed insanity plea on a subsequent sentence,[221] the impact of a successful plea on other legal statuses,[222] the systemic ways that counsel is

---

[215]It is likely that they have now been supplanted by sexually violent predators. *See* Michael L. Perlin, *"There's No Success Like Failure/And Failures No Success At All:" Exposing the Pretextuality of* Kansas v. Hendricks, 92 Nw. U. L. Rev. 1247, 1248 (1998).

[216]*See* PERLIN, *supra* note 158, at 198–207. *See, e.g.,* James W. Ellis, *The Consequences of the Insanity Defense: Proposals to Reform Post-Acquittal Commitment Laws,* 35 CATH. U. L. REV. 961, 962 (1986) ("the public's concern is less with whether blame properly can be assigned to a particular defendant than with determining when he will get out").

[217]*See, e.g.,* McGreevey, *supra* note 175; Wexler, *supra* note 202, at 213–14.

[218]For a parallel inquiry, see Renaud, R. v. Fuller: *Time to Brush Aside the Rule Prohibiting Therapeutic Remands?* 35 CRIM. L.Q. 91 (1992) (Part I), and *id.,* 35 CRIM. L.Q. 156 (1993) (Part II).

On the social and economic costs of policies that mandate lengthy periods of hospitalization for insanity acquittees, see Donald Linhorst & P. Ann Dirks-Linhorst, *The Impact of Insanity Acquittees on Missouri's Public Mental Health System,* 21 LAW & HUM. BEHAV. 327 (1997).

[219]On the procedural due process protections required in civil cases following a conditional release, *see* 1 PERLIN, MDL *supra* note 7, § 2C-6.1 to 2C-6.1b, at 434–44 (2d ed. 1998). The case law that has developed around conditional release generally calls for procedural due process protections much like those at initial involuntary civil commitment hearings. As of yet, there has been virtually no case law dealing with this specific question as it applies to the population of insanity acquittees.

Some questions that must be addressed include the following: Is a hearing with full procedural due process protections therapeutically valuable for individuals facing recommitment? Or is the possibility that such protections might result in fewer recommitments antitherapeutic? Does the Supreme Court's decision in Foucha v. Louisiana, 504 U.S. 71 (1992) (declaring unconstitutional a state law that provided for the continued insanity commitment of an NGRI acquittee who was no longer mentally ill) apply in this context?

[220]*See generally* 3 PERLIN, MDL *supra* note 7, § 15.34, at 384–88.

[221]Statistics seem to indicate that defendants who are unsuccessful in their NGRI pleas are frequently given lengthier sentences than like defendants who do not raise a nonresponsibility defense. *See supra* Chapter 10. If we assume that a significant percentage of these defendants are mentally ill, this finding suggests that the plea is even a riskier gambit than has generally been thought.

[222]*See, e.g.,* Catherine A. Salton, *Mental Capacity and Liability Insurance Clauses: The Effect of Insanity Upon Intent,* 78 CALIF. L. REV. 1027 (1990). When a defendant is found NGRI, there are potential effects on other legal interactions. Can an NGRI defendant be prosecuted for "criminal" acts that take place in forensic hospitals or other mental institutions? Can he or she be disciplined for violating institutional rules? Can he or she be civilly liable for tortious acts?

Cf. Koehler v. State, 830 S.W.2d 665 (Tex. App. 1992), *rev. denied* (1992) (determination of incompetence to manage one's own affairs not a *prima facie* showing of incompetency to stand trial).

assigned to potential insanity pleaders[223] are all questions that can and should be considered in therapeutic jurisprudence analyses.

Conclusion

TJ must not be used as a rationale to support a return to the days of the hands-off policy in which courts unthinkingly and inevitably deferred to the expertise of institutional keepers[224] and in which treatment questions were seen as nonjusticiable.[225] Perhaps not coincidentally this is the position with which Justice Thomas—the member of the court with the fewest insights into therapeutic issues and mental health concepts—seems the most comfortable with.[226] On the other hand, if TJ *is* used in the ways that it has been employed in recent papers—as a tool for exposing pretextuality,[227] as a means of integrating concepts born in mental disability law into other areas of jurisprudence,[228] as a means of revealing the unexpected "litigational side-effects"[229] of a seemingly benign antichild abuse law,[230] as a means of insuring that therapeutic jurisprudence inquiries retain their constitutional moorings,[231] and as a means of attacking and uprooting "the we/they distinction that has traditionally plagued and stigmatized the mentally disabled"[232]—then that result *will be* therapeutic: for the legal system, for the development of mental disability law jurisprudence, and ultimately for all of us.

One of the major forces behind the development of therapeutic jurisprudence was the sense that the federal courts were no longer interested in theoretical or constitutional arguments made on behalf of mentally disabled persons, nor were they sympathetic to (nor could they empathize with) the plight of such persons, especially in an institutional context.[233] Therapeutic jurisprudence was seen as an antidote to that judicial antipathy and as a

---

[223]Counsel made available to mentally disabled criminal defendants is often substandard. *See* Perlin, *supra* note 89. Lawyers representing such persons often ignore potential mental status defenses, or, in some cases, contradictorily, seek to have the insanity defense imposed on their client over his or her objection. Such lawyers often succumb to sanist stereotypes and are compliant coconspirators in pretextual court decisions. *See* Perlin, *supra* note 133, at 404–06.

[224]*See supra* Chapter 12.

[225]*Cf.* O'Connor v. Donaldson, 422 U.S. 563, 574 n.10 (1975) ("Where 'treatment' is the sole asserted ground for depriving a person of liberty, it is *plainly unacceptable* to suggest that the courts are powerless to determine whether the asserted ground is present") (emphasis added).

[226]*See, e.g.,* Perlin & Dorfman, *supra* note 61, at 58–61; Michael L. Perlin, *Decoding Right to Refuse Treatment Law*, 16 INT'L J.L. & PSYCHIATRY 151, 174 (1993) (discussing the sanist and pretextual nature of Thomas' dissents in *Riggins* and *Foucha*); PERLIN, MDL *supra* note 7, § 14.20A at 461–65 (1998 Cum. Supp.) (discussing Thomas' majority opinion in *Godinez*).

[227]*See* Dorfman, *supra* note 79.

[228]*See, e.g.,* Keri K. Gould, *Turning Rat and Doing Time for Uncharged, Dismissed, or Acquitted Crime: Do the Federal Sentencing Guidelines Promote Respect for the Law?* 10 N.Y.L. SCH. J. HUM. RTS. 835 (1993); Daniel Shuman, *Making The World a Better Place Through Tort Law & Through the Therapeutic Looking Glass,* 10 N.Y.L. SCH. J. HUM. RTS. 739 (1993).

[229]*See* Perlin, *Decoding, supra* note 226, at 166 (discussing this concept in the context of *Riggins*).

[230]Murray Levine et al., *A Therapeutic Jurisprudence Analysis of Mandated Reporting of Child Maltreatment by Psychotherapists,* 10 N.Y.L. SCH. J. HUM. RTS. 711, 726–33 (1993).

[231]*See* Winick, *supra* note 64.

[232]*See* Wexler, *New Directions, supra* note 6, at 17.

[233]*See, e.g.,* Wexler, *supra* note 211; David Wexler, *Putting Mental Health Into Mental Health Law: Therapeutic Jurisprudence,* 16 LAW & HUM. BEHAV. 27 (1992) [hereinafter Wexler I]; Wexler, *supra* note 6.

palliative for the "sterility" of mental disability law jurisprudence[234] and as a response to the lack of any "social echo" in the current development of that law.[235]

Although an impressive body of literature has been produced,[236] there has not yet been a systematic investigation into the reasons why some courts decide cases therapeutically and others antitherapeutically. My preliminary conclusion is that sanism is such a dominant psychological force that it (a) distorts "rational" decision making, (b) encourages (albeit on at least a partially unconscious level) pretextuality *and* teleology, and (c) prevents decision makers from intelligently and coherently focusing on questions that are meaningful to therapeutic jurisprudential inquiries.

The papers in the *New England Journal on Criminal and Civil Confinement* symposium that I discussed earlier[237] advance the cause of therapeutic jurisprudence and demonstrate its value in analyzing the forensic mental health law system in one state. But they do more than that. They illuminate two separate points. First, they show how the sanist and pretextual ways that mental disability law has developed in Massachusetts reflect the sanist and pretextual bases of much of the entire mental disability system. Second, they make clear that any effort to explain that system solely on the bases of legal doctrine is doomed to fail. And in doing so, they force us to consider the issues of empowerment and disempowerment[238] that are at the basis of the mental disability system, the mental disability law system, and the mental disability lawyering system.

We cannot make any lasting progress in "putting mental health into mental health law"[239] until we confront the system's sanist biases and the ways that these sanist biases blunt our ability to intelligently weigh and assess social science data in the creation of a mental disability law jurisprudence.

I contend that therapeutic jurisprudence is our best strategy for confronting those biases. A practice based on the tenets of therapeutic jurisprudence forces such lawyers to adopt a multidisciplinary investigation and evaluation of the therapeutic effects of the lawyering process and a case's ultimate disposition. In therapeutic jurisprudence, the client's perspective should determine the therapeutic worth or impact of a particular course of events. As a scholarly matter, it is helpful to use therapeutic jurisprudence as a framework within which to investigate and reformulate areas of law reform aimed at resolving difficult societal

---

[234]Wexler, *Putting Mental Health Into Mental Health Law, supra* note 233 at 29–31; John Petrila, *Redefining Mental Health Law: Thoughts on a New Agenda,* 16 LAW & HUM. BEHAV. 89, 89–92 (1992). I generally concur with this pessimistic analysis of the way that the once "seeming-endless expansion of civil rights decisions involving. the constitutional and civil rights of mentally disabled persons has come to a stuttering halt." *See* Michael L. Perlin, *What Is Therapeutic Jurisprudence?* 10 N.Y.L. SCH. J. HUM. RTS. 623, 624 (1993) [hereinafter Perlin, Therapeutic]; *see generally* Michael L. Perlin, *State Constitutions and Statutes as Sources of Rights for the Mentally Disabled: The Last Frontier?* 20 LOY. L.A. L. REV. 1249 (1987) [hereinafter Perlin, Last Frontier]. Yet I believe that this may overstate the case a bit. *See e.g., supra* Chapter 8, discussing the Supreme Court's recent decision in Olmstead v. L.C., 119 S. Ct. 2176 (1999).

[235]*See* Joel Haycock, *Speaking Truth to Power: Rights, Therapeutic Jurisprudence, and Massachusetts Mental Health Law,* 20 N. ENG. J. CIV. & CRIM. CONFINEMENT 301, 317 (1993).

[236]*See* David Wexler & Bruce Winick, *Therapeutic Jurisprudence as a New Approach to Mental Health Law Policy Analysis and Research,* 45 U. MIAMI L. REV. 979, 981 n.9 (1992).

[237]*See supra,* Chapter 12.

[238]*See* Haycock, *supra* note 235, at 304; Haycock et al., *supra* note 88, at 289.

[239]*See* Wexler I *supra* note 111; *see also, e.g.,* discussions in Wexler & Winick, *New Approach, supra* note 236, at 990–92 (right to refuse treatment), 992–97 (treatment of incompetent death row inmates), and 997–1001 (treatment of incompetency to stand trial); David Wexler & Bruce Winick, Therapeutic Jurisprudence and Criminal Justice Mental Health Issues, 16 MENT. & PHYSICAL DIS. L. REP 225, 229–30 (1992) (sex offender guilty pleas); *see also* Michael L. Perlin, Tarasoff *and the Dilemma of the Dangerous Patient: New Directions for the 1990's,* 16 LAW & PSYCHOL. REV. 29, 54–62 (duty to protect in tort law); Perlin, *supra* note 150, at 54 (right to refuse treatment).

dilemmas.[240] As a practical legal tool, I believe that therapeutic jurisprudence has the far-reaching potential to allow us—finally—to come to grips with the pernicious power of sanism and pretextuality and to offer us an opportunity to make coherent what has been incoherent—and to expose what has been hidden—for far too long.

---

[240]Gould, *supra* note 228. Keri A. Gould, *Therapeutic Jurisprudence and the Arraignment Process; The Defense Attorney's Dilemma: Whether to Request a Competency Evaluation? in* MENTAL HEALTH LAW AND PRACTICE THROUGH THE LIFE CYCLE 67 (S. Verdun-Jones & M. Layton eds. 1994); Ensminger & Liguori, *supra* note 67, at 245.

Chapter 14
CONCLUSION

I suggested in the introductory chapter that mental disability law was, in large part, a *trompe l'oeil*: On one hand, the U.S. Supreme Court seems fascinated with all cutting-edge issues in mental disability law; on the other, "it is a topic dealt with on a daily basis by trial courts across the country in a series of unknown cases involving unknown litigants, where justice is often administered in assembly-line fashions."[1] In the vast majority of these cases, decisions by the U.S. Supreme Court regarding, say, the scope of a constitutional right to liberty,[2] the impact of antipsychotic medication side effects on the construction of the due process clause,[3] and the application of due process protections to the voluntary commitment process[4] are honored—if at all—only in the breach. I also suggested that mental disability law suffers from both overattention and underattention; that the famous, vivid case (usually involving a notorious criminal defendant) is subject to intense analysis and scrutiny, whereas the unknown case is "litigated"[5] in the dark.

One of the most venerable underpinnings of American jurisprudence is the theory of "neutral principles," most closely associated with the writings of Herbert Wechsler.[6] According to Wechsler, legal reasoning had to be "genuinely principled, resting with respect to every step that is involved in reaching judgment on analysis and reasons quite transcending the immediate result that is achieved."[7] Judges, this theory suggested, "could impersonally decide cases through the process of 'reasoned elaboration,' i.e., the elaboration of 'principles and policies [that yielded] a reasoned, if not analytically determined result in particular cases.'"[8]

This approach, of course, assumes a fact not in evidence: that judges and fact finders *are able* to approach cases analytically with the sort of reasoned elaboration and neutrality urged by Wechsler and his adherents. An examination of the development of mental disability law jurisprudence suggests that "neutral principles" are simply not a factor in the case law in this area, and that, rather, the twin themes of sanism and pretextuality dominate the mental disability law landscape. My review of public mental disability law sadly confirms both the *trompe l'oeil* image and the disjunction of over- and underattention. It also puts the lie—at least from the perspective of mental disability law—to Wechsler's theory of neutral principles.

Mental disability law is neither rational, neutral, nor objective. Rather, it is irrational and incoherent, and this irrationality and incoherence disables and corrupts civil commit-

---

[1]*See supra*, Chapter 1, at text following note 37.

[2]O'Connor v. Donaldson, 422 U.S. 563 (1975). *See supra* Chapter 4.

[3]Washington v. Harper, 494 U.S. 210 (1990); *see supra* Chapter 5.

[4]Zinermon v. Burch, 494 U.S. 113 (1990); *see* 1 MICHAEL L. PERLIN, MENTAL DISABILITY LAW: CIVIL AND CRIMINAL, § 2C-7.2a, at 488–91 (2d ed. 1998).

[5]My use of quotation marks is to suggest the paucity of litigation that actually goes on in such cases. *See supra* Chapter 1, text accompanying note 38.

[6]*Toward Neutral Principles of Constitutional Law,* 73 HARV. L. REV. 1 (1959).

[7]*Id.* at 15. For a helpful explanation, see Anthony Sebok, *Misunderstanding Positivism,* 93 MICH. L. REV. 2054, 2114–15 (1995).

[8]John Hasnas, *Back to the Future: From Critical Legal Studies Forward to Legal Realism, or How Not to Miss the Point of the Indeterminacy Argument,* 45 DUKE L.J. 84, 93 (1995).

ment law, institutional treatment law, civil rights law, and criminal procedure law. There are important exceptions—to be found in selected opinions by both U.S. Supreme Court justices and by other appellate and trial court judges in both the state and federal systems.[9] But they are rare.

Rather, mental disability law is premised on stereotype and prejudice, on typification, and on fear. It distorts and it marginalizes, relying vividly on the heuristic of the statistically exceptional but graphically compelling case of the person with major mental disorder who is randomly violent,[10] and then using false ordinary common sense to justify this intellectual reductionism. These sanist distortions are sanitized by pretextual decision making that encourages (or at the least, condones) testimonial untruthfulness (often offered under the guise or rubric of a greater "morality")[11] and that teleologically "cherry picks" social science evidence to justify such decisions.[12] And this happens in ways that are hidden from public view.

I divided up the majority of this book by subject area, but there is little difference in the ways that courts—and the general public—treat the various substantive topics. Sanist involuntary civil commitment decision making implicates pretextual right-to-refuse-treatment decision making.[13] Sanist assumptions about the relationship between deinstitutionalization and homelessness reflect the demand for pretextual recommitment testimony.[14] Sanist attitudes toward patient sexuality may lead to pretextual constructions of the Americans With Disabilities Act.[15] And sanism in each and every aspect of the criminal trial process leads to pretextuality at all stages of such litigation.[16]

I am convinced that what I have written about is only the tip of a very large and ominous iceberg. Decisions about whom to apprehend for commitment purposes, whom to arrest, whom to turn down for community placement are largely invisible.[17] Untrammeled discretion vested in police officers leads to inexplicable disjunctions in mental disability law

---

[9]*See supra* Chapter 4.

[10]Recall that at least 90% of persons with mental disabilities never exhibit any risk of violence. *See* Jeffrey Swanson et al., *Violence and Psychiatric Disorder in the Community: Evidence from the Epidemiologic Catchment Area,* 41 HOSP. & COMMUNITY PSYCHIATRY 761 (1990); John Monahan, The Scientific State of Research on Clinical and Actuarial Predictions of Violence, in MODERN SCIENTIFIC EVIDENCE, THE LAW AND SCIENCE OF EXPERT TESTIMONY §§ 7-2.0 to 7-2.4 (David Faigman et al eds. 1997). *see generally* Chapter 4.

[11]*See, e.g.,* Paul Chodoff, *Involuntary Hospitalization of the Mentally Ill as a Moral Issue,* 141 AM. J. PSYCHIATRY 384, 388 (1984), discussed *supra* chapter 3, text accompanying notes 59–61.

[12]The Supreme Court's choice of sources in Youngberg v. Romeo, 457 U.S. 307, 316–17 (1982) (limiting the scope of a constitutional right to treatment) is a glaring example of this phenomenon. *See supra* Chapter 5.

[13]*See* Michael L. Perlin & Deborah A. Dorfman, *Sanism, Social Science, and the Development of Mental Disability Law Jurisprudence,* 11 BEHAV. SCI. & L. 47, 49 (1993).

[14]*See* Michael L. Perlin, *Competency, Deinstitutionalization, and Homelessness: A Story of Marginalization,* 28 HOUS. L. REV. 63 (1991).

[15]*See* Michael L. Perlin, *"Make Promises by the Hour": Sex, Drugs, the ADA, and Psychiatric Hospitalization,* 46 DEPAUL L. REV. 947 (1997).

[16]*See* Michael L. Perlin, *"No Direction Home": The Law and Criminal Defendants With Mental Disabilities,* 20 MENT. & PHYS. DIS. L. REP. 605 (1996).

[17]*See, e.g.,* Linda Teplin, *The Criminality of the Mentally Ill: A Dangerous Misconception,* 142 AM. J. PSYCHIATRY 676 (1985) (mentally disabled persons more likely to be arrested than nonmentally disabled persons for similar behavior).

developments.[18] And the general unavailability of competent, trained counsel makes it likely that this invisibility will continue unabated.

Several years ago, I concluded my book on the insanity defense with a series of recommendations. I argued that, first, "we must discuss the underlying issues openly,"[19] at which time "system decisionmakers must regularly engage in a series of 'sanism checks' to insure—to the greatest extent possible—a continuing conscious and self-reflective evaluation of their decisions to best avoid sanism's power."[20] At the same time, "judges must acknowledge the pretextual basis of much of the case law in this area and consciously seek to eliminate it from future decisionmaking."[21]

Next, the issues considered must be "added to the research agendas of social scientists, behaviorists and legal scholars" to "help illuminate the ultimate impact of sanism on this area of the law, aid lawmakers and other policymakers in understanding the ways that social science data is manipulated to serve sanist ends."[22] We must also find ways to "attitudinally educate counsel . . . so that representation becomes more than the hollow shell it all too frequently is."[23] Further, "we need to consider carefully the burden of heuristic thinking,"[24] especially the ways that judges use such devices in deciding important cases. Finally, we must rigorously apply therapeutic jurisprudence principles to all aspects of mental disability law, to "take what we learn from therapeutic jurisprudence to strip away sanist behavior, pretextual reasoning and teleological decisionmaking [so as to] enable us to confront the pretextual use of social science data in an open and meaningful way."[25]

To what extent are these prescriptions and proscriptions equally applicable to all mental disability law? It is essential that sanism and pretextuality be exposed—that they be articulated, discussed, debated, and weighed. Participants in the mental disability law system must acknowledge these concepts and must use the bully pulpits of the courtroom, the legislative chamber, the public forum, the bar association, the psychology or psychiatry conference, and the academic journals to identify and deconstruct sanist and pretextual behaviors whenever and wherever they occur. Courts have largely been silent in the face of institutionalized sanism and pretextuality in mental disability law cases, and lawyers have been lax in pressing courts on these questions.

That is not to say that courts have been entirely blind. A concurrence in a Connecticut state Supreme Court insanity defense decision identifies the vividness effect as a factor in developments in that area of the law.[26] Our willful blindness toward new advances in

---

[18]Cf., e.g., the fact settings in Addington v. Texas, 441 U.S. 418 (1979), and Jones v. United States, 463 U.S. 354 (1983). Addington—whose case ultimately settled the question of the constitutional burden of proof quantum in *civil* cases—had originally been apprehended following an alleged "assault by threat" on his mother. *Addington,* 441 U.S. at 420. Jones—whose case ultimately gave constitutional sanction to providing insanity acquittees with fewer procedural due process protections in a retention hearing—had originally been apprehended after he allegedly attempted to shoplift a jacket in a downtown Washington, D.C., department store. *Jones,* 463 U.S. at 359. Addington's acts appear more serious (and more "dangerous") than did Jones's; yet, for undisclosed and unarticulated extrajudicial reasons, Addington was brought into the mental health system and Jones was arrested and thus brought into the criminal justice system.

[19]MICHAEL L. PERLIN, THE JURISPRUDENCE OF THE INSANITY DEFENSE 440 (1994).

[20]*Id.*

[21]*Id.*

[22]*Id.* at 440–41.

[23]*Id.* at 441.

[24]*Id.* at 443.

[25]*Id.*

[26]State v. Wilson, 700 A.2d 633, 649 (Conn. 1997) (Katz, J., concurring).

medicine and psychology has been identified as a major culprit in jurisprudential incoherence in a Tenth Circuit case involving a defendant with multiple personality disorder, and the same case identified the sanist myth as to the alleged short stays that insanity acquittees serve following institutionalization.[27] In a case involving a tort committed by a mentally disabled person, the Minnesota Supreme Court noted our degree of skepticism about mental illness when a person "doesn't look sick."[28] And an Eleventh Circuit judge partially dissenting from an affirmance in a death penalty case has pointed out that defendants' unsuccessful attempts to raise insanity defenses positively correlate with death penalty verdicts.[29] But these cases are the exception; generally, sanism and pretextuality are as invisible in the courtroom as they are to the public at large.

Heuristics and ordinary common sense are the *lingua franca* of mental disability law. They set the stage for a system in which sanism and pretextuality can fester. System participants must listen with a keen ear for the uses of these distortive devices and must anticipate their use in appellate arguments, in legislative hearings, and in public forums.

It is equally essential that researchers begin to study the questions I have raised in an effort to develop instruments and tools that can effectively measure sanism and root out pretextuality. And it is essential that lawyers—both occasional counsel and regularly-appointed counsel—begin to confront sanism and attack pretextuality as part of their advocacy role.[30] It is also essential that state-of-the-art research currently being published by the MacArthur Network be read carefully from this perspective to incorporate these insights into a new jurisprudence.[31] And it is just as essential that scholars locating themselves in the school of therapeutic jurisprudence integrate sanism and pretextuality analyses into their work.

Mental disability is no longer an obscure subspecialty of legal practice and study—if it *ever* was obscure. Each of its multiple strands forces us to make hard social policy choices about troubling social issues—psychiatry and social control, the use of institutions, informed consent, personal autonomy, the relationship between public perception and social reality, the many levels of competency, the role of free will in the criminal law system, the limits of confidentiality, the protection duty of mental health professionals, the role of power in forensic evaluations. These are all difficult and complex questions that are not susceptible to easy, formulistic answers. When sanist thinking distorts the judicial process, the resulting doctrinal incoherence should not be a surprise.[32]

The same forces motivate decision making in all of mental disability law that motivate such decision making in insanity defense law. And the hard policy choices that must be made in every aspect of this area of law cannot be made rationally and coherently if our thinking is to blunted by sanism and pretextuality.

I was putting the finishing touches on the first draft of this chapter when I caught sight of a headline in the *Philadelphia Inquirer* that promised a discussion of recent plans to close Haverford State Hospital and move some of its psychiatric patients to nearby Norristown

---

[27]United States v. Denny-Shaffer, 2 F.3d 999, 1009 (10th Cir. 1993), and *id.* at 1021 n.30.

[28]State Farm Fire & Cas. Co. v. Wicka, 474 N.W.2d. 324, 327 (Minn. 1991).

[29]Waters v. Thomas, 46 F.3d 1506, 1535 (11th Cir. 1995) (Clark, J., concurring in part and dissenting in part).

[30]*See* Michael L. Perlin, *Fatal Assumption: A Critical Evaluation of the Role of Counsel in Mental Disability Cases,* 16 LAW & HUM. BEHAV. 39 (1992).

[31]*See, e.g.,* VIOLENCE AND MENTAL DISORDER: DEVELOPMENTS IN RISK ASSESSMENT (John Monahan & Henry Steadman eds. 1994).

[32]PERLIN, *supra* note 19, at 443–44.

State Hospital.[33] The spin of the story was this: Norristown is ''employment-starved'' and the transfer of patients would create about 270 mental health jobs in an economically beleaguered town. Yet, ''no one here,'' according to the story, ''wants this to happen.'' Said the (Norristown) borough Planning Commission chair: ''They defecate in the alleys. They're shadow boxing . . . talking to themselves and fighting with that [imaginary person]. . . . If they're not taking their medication, they can be quite violent.''[34] She continued, ''I'm for NIMBYism this time (using the acronym for Not In My Back Yard). It's terrible. I just want them to go right back to where they came from.''[35] And a local businesswoman added, ''Sixty percent of my customers are whacked . . . and are either on some kind of medication or not taking it.''[36] I cringed when I read the story, but wasn't particularly surprised.

Of course, had an interviewee used a common derogatory epithet to describe Blacks or women or gays or Jews or lesbians, a conscientious copy editor would have caught it and replaced it with some version of ''[expletive deleted].'' But ''whacked'' was alright, because to speak of mental patients this way was not seen as offensive or troubling to the copy editor. And there was no question as to the authority of the Planning Commission chair to correlate failure (or refusal) to take medication with violence. It was simply accepted as a given, and the story continued in its predictable way. I have little doubt that a significant percentage of the members of the bar and the bench in the same town would endorse each of these assertions and attitudes. And that is what this book has been about.

The following day I read a story in the *Ft. Lauderdale Sun-Sentinel,*[37] headlined ''Mentally Ill Fall Through Cracks in Law.''[38] The article dealt with the frustration that Florida county judges felt because of their inability to order that certain mental ill defendants charged with misdemeanors receive mental health treatment. In one case the trial judge sentenced a defendant (arrested for being disorderly) to the county jail for a 179-day contempt term (the maximum allowed before the defendant's right to a jury trial would apply) as a means of seeking to ensure that the defendant receive some mental health treatment. According to the article, ''[The trial judge] said the law left him no avenue to [order the defendant to a mental hospital for treatment] and [he thus] had no choice but to try to get [the defendant] treatment 'through the back door,' the jail's psychiatric unit.''[39] The contempt sentence was clearly pretextual; the defendant had cursed at the judge in court, but the story makes it clear that *that* fact simply gave the judge a ''trigger'' to impose a relatively lengthy misdemeanor sentence solely as a means of mandating mental health treatment. No one interviewed in the story questioned the propriety of manipulating the criminal law in this way.

The sanism and pretextuality that drives mental disability law is rooted in prejudice. It is a prejudice that is invisible and hidden, is rarely recognized, and is largely socially acceptable. And this prejudice has corrupted all of us who are players in the system: lawyers, mental health professionals, judges, and forensic witnesses. And it is persons with mental disabilities who have suffered—and who continue to suffer.

---

[33]Scott Cech, *In Norristown, Lamenting the Plan for More State Patients,* PHILADELPHIA INQUIRER, Sept. 8, 1997, (North ed.), at B1.

[34]*Id.*

[35]*Id.*

[36]*Id.*

[37]For this, I am eternally grateful to my mother, Sophie Perlin, who has always been on the lookout for relevant articles in her local press.

[38]*The Sun Sentinel,* Sept. 14, 1997, at 1B.

[39]*Id.* at 4B.

Sanist attitudes trump all efforts at the creation of a rational, coherent, structured jurisprudence. And pretextual decisions trump the application of constitutional principles and constitutionally inspired (or constitutionally compelled) legislation. Sanist diatribes that are based on stereotypes, on prejudices, and on typification permeate mental disability law; Justice Thomas' pretextual dissent in *Riggins v. Nevada*[40] and his majority opinion in *Godinez v. Moran*[41] are but two glaring examples.

There are hundreds—thousands—of reported decisions each year in mental disability law.[42] The public press is crowded with stories about vivid examples of violent behavior by persons with mental disabilities,[43] and the Supreme Court, like a moth to the flame,[44] is fleetingly fascinated with all aspects of mental disability law. In the end, however, as applied on a daily basis—in commitment courts, in institutional settings, and in criminal trial calendars—mental disability law remains dominated by mostly invisible prejudice and pretexts.

"Down in the basement" has for years been a metaphor used by clinical legal scholars to describe the way that "traditional" academics perceive clinical courses, clinical professors, clinical students, and clinical cases: marginalized and distanced from the "real" law school.[45] And so it has been—and, to a great extent, still is—with mental disability law. I believe that one of the main reasons for this is the insidious and invisible way that sanism and pretextuality have corroded our jurisprudence. Perhaps a new, hard, and careful investigation of mental health law can begin to rescue this law—and, more importantly, the persons whose lives it regulates—from the prejudices that continue to drive and shape it. Perhaps then, we will finally approach this area from a perspective of strength, consciousness, and coherence.

---

[40]504 U.S. 127, 146 (1992); *see supra* Chapter 6.

[41]509 U.S. 389 (1993); *see supra* Chapter 9; *see generally* Michael L. Perlin, *"Dignity Was the First to Leave": Godinez v. Moran, Colin Ferguson, and the Trial of Mentally Disabled Criminal Defendants,* 14 BEHAV. SCI. & L. 61 (1996).

[42]Compare PERLIN, *supra* note 4, to *id.* (1997 Cum. Supp.). to *id.* (1998 Cum. Supp.).

[43]*See, e.g.,* Michael L. Perlin, *Myths, Realities, and the Political World: The Anthropology of Insanity Defense Attitudes,* 24 BULL. AM. ACAD. PSYCHIATRY & L. 5, 14–15 (1996) (reporting on searches of NEXIS NEWS databases).

[44]*See* Perlin, *supra* note 16, at 605.

[45]*See* Keri K. Gould & Michael L. Perlin, *"Johnny's in the Basement/Mixing Up His Medicine": Therapeutic Jurisprudence and Clinical Teaching"* (manuscript submitted for a publication), manuscript at 6, discussing Marjorie McDiarmid, *What's Going On Down There in the Basement: In-house Clinics Expand Their Beachhead,* 35 N.Y.L. SCH. L. REV. 239 (1990).

TABLE OF AUTHORITY

Cases

INDEX

ABOUT THE AUTHOR

Michael L. Perlin, JD, is a professor of law at New York Law School and an adjunct professor of psychiatry and law at both the New York University Medical School and the New York College of Medicine. He graduated magna cum laude from Rutgers University and from Columbia University Law School, where he was a Harlan Fiske Stone Scholar. He has held several positions, including the Director of the Division of Mental Health Advocacy in the NJ Department of the Public Advocate and Deputy Public Defender in charge of the Mercer County (Trenton), NJ Office of the Public Defender. He now serves on the National Advisory Board of the Institute of Mental Disability and Law of the National Center for State Courts and on the Board of Directors of the International Academy of Law and Mental Health. In 1988, he received the Amicus Award from the American Academy of Psychiatry and Law. His three-volume treatise, *Mental Disability Law: Civil and Criminal,* won the 1990 Walter Jeffords Writing Prize. His book, *The Jurisprudence of the Insanity Defense,* received the Manfred Guttmacher Award from the American Psychiatric Association and the American Academy of Psychiatry and Law as the best book of the year in law and forensic psychiatry in 1994-95. He has also written a one-volume treatise, *Law and Mental Disability,* and a casebook, *Mental Disability Law: Cases and Materials.* In his spare time, he plays the clarinet in the Lawrence Township Community Band, and is an avid freshwater fisherman, a novice guitarist, and a retired youth soccer coach. He is currently writing an article on the jurisprudence of Bob Dylan.

8/01 ① 6/01
9/02 ⑤ 7/02
5/05 6 10/03
12/07 ⑦ 4/06
12/11 ⑦ 4/06